DIALOGUE AND TRADITION

Dialogue
and
Tradition

The Challenges of Contemporary Judeo-Christian Thought

by Jacob Bernard Agus

Abelard-Schuman
London   New York   Toronto

LONDON	NEW YORK	TORONTO
Abelard-Schuman	Abelard-Schuman	Abelard-Schuman
Limited	Limited	Canada Limited
8 King St. WC2	257 Park Ave. So.	228 Yorkland Blvd.

An Intext Publisher

Printed in the United States of America

PREFACE

We are now entering the Age of the Dialogue. People in all faiths and cultures are beginning to appreciate that they are sharing in the formation of one universal society. In part, this emergent society is being fashioned by economic and social forces; in part, it is likely to be molded by the diverse cultures and faiths of the past. No faith and no culture can now claim the right or even entertain the hope of imposing itself upon all of mankind, and by the same token, every faith is challenged to contribute its insights to the common treasury of ideas and values.

In our open society, the dialogue takes place along several levels. There is the struggle between the secular ideologies of our day and religious humanism, taken as a whole. There is the tension within religious humanism between faith and the various domains of secular study. Among the several religions of the Judeo-Christian tradition, the dialogue has largely replaced the missionary kerygmata and the defensive apologetics of the past. And within each faith, a restructuring of ideas is a prior condition as well as an inevitable consequence of the dialogue.

In this collection of essays and addresses, Part One is devoted to essays on the Jewish-Christian dialogue; Part Two, to the dialogue with historians—Toynbee and other interpreters of Jewish history; Part Three, to the meaning of God in the post-Auschwitz age; Part Four, to the challenge of the ideologies and the secular world; Part Five, to the tension and dialectic within Judaism.

These essays were written in the course of the past two decades. Nearly all were previously published in magazines and books. However, two articles were written especially for this volume to document and expound the main theme, namely, the realm of religious humanism as the common universe of discourse of Judaism and Christianity.

v

ACKNOWLEDGMENTS

I wish to thank the editors, publishers, and sponsoring organizations of the following publications for permission to include certain articles and addresses in this book.

> Judaism, A Quarterly Journal of Jewish Life and Thought
> The National Jewish Monthly
> The Minnesota Review
> Midstream, A Monthly Jewish Review
> Conservative Judaism
> Hebrew Union College Annual
> Torah and Gospel
> Dialogue with Israel
> Dictionary of Christian Ethics
> The American Jewish Congress
> The Theodor Herzl Foundation
> The American Jewish Committee
> The A.D.L. — B'nai B'rith
> The International Conference on Jewish-Christian Relations of 1966 at Cambridge University
> Helicon Press
> Sheed and Ward
> Westminster Press
> Cornell University

I am happy to acknowledge my indebtedness to my colleagues at the Rabbinical Assembly, the Board of Editors of *Judaism*, the Religion Department of Temple University, the Faculty of the Reconstructionist Rabbinical College, and the Faculty of the Jewish Theological Seminary. I am grateful to the Protestant,

Catholic, and humanist friends whom I met at various interfaith conferences.

I am particularly grateful to Prof. Mordecai M. Kaplan for teaching me by precept and example the unity of the love of truth and the truth of love in Judaism. My first printed essay was a review of his monumental work, *Judaism as a Civilization*.

To Rabbi Marc H. Tanenbaum, Director of the Interreligious Affairs Department of the American Jewish Committee, I owe special thanks. His inspired leadership in the area of Jewish-Christian relations has provided the occasions for my writing of several of the essays herein included.

I am thankful to the officers and members of Beth El Congregation, Baltimore, whose encouragement has made possible my literary and scholarly efforts in the past twenty years.

Above all, I am grateful to my wife, Miriam, and children, Zalman and Sandra, Edna and Larry, Robert and Deborah, for their love and understanding; to my parents of blessed memory, Judah Leib and Bela Devorah; to my brothers, Irving, Hayim, and Paul, and my sisters, Jenny Bruch and Esther Stein.

INTRODUCTION

The central theme of this collection of essays is the tension between tradition and dialogue. When a tradition is alive and relevant, it is engaged in dialogue with other traditions and contemporary movements. The dialogue between Jews and Christians in our day is but one manifestation of a many-sided quest. Indeed, no one can truly engage in the Jewish-Christian dialogue who does not experience within his own mind the tension and turmoil of several dialogues—those between faith and reason, between ethnocentrism and universalism, between the humanist perspective and that of a parochial tradition, between our diverse and apparently contradictory visions of God—for in our own personal life, we can feel His Presence either as peace, or as truth, or as the redeemer.

In nearly every human situation requiring an act of decision, a polarity of principles applies. A generation ago, existentialists stressed the need and right of bringing contending claims to the point of crisis and then making a whole-souled decision. Wise as that insight is, the quest for truth amidst the changing contours of our existence involves the continual questioning of every decision and the ceaseless restructuring of the values by which we live. All the decisions that we make out of the depths of our being involve some reference to a philosophy of life, a grasp of the ultimate, a glimpse of the absolute. But we can never possess the absolute. So, as we are carried forward on the stream of life, we are called upon constantly to reopen the decisions of yesterday.

Does it mean that we exclude the possibility of absolute truth? No, absolute truth exists and perpetually challenges our complacency. But it does mean that we exclude the possibility of our present possession of absolute truth.

If like the Cyclops of Greek legend, we were to look at the world with one huge eye, we would see only a two-dimensional world of lights and shadows. Possessing two eyes, we are able to superimpose two images upon each other and to experience the dimension of depth. This is also true in the realm of spirit. I know of no insight in history so true and penetrating that it did not at the same time involve a measure of blindness to some aspects of reality.

Doubtless, the most powerful idea that was ever projected into human affairs was the concept of the one God. It provided an immense thrust to the life of Israel, later to the Christian world, and still later to the community of Islam. It had the effect of integrating the human personality, as the image of the one Divine Being, and it set into motion waves upon waves of social energy. But, in each of its historic expressions, monotheism was a restrictive, fanatical, and paralyzing force as well as a liberating and inspiring philosophy of life. It is only through the juxtaposition of several different points of view that any healing glimpse of truth may come to us. Like the glow of an electric arc, light reaches us only in the momentary sparks that fly between two poles.

This basic insight is at the heart of all my studies, from the analysis of the philosophies of Hermann Cohen and Martin Buber, Franz Rosenzweig and Mordecai M. Kaplan, in *Modern Philosophies of Judaism* to my recent work, *The Vision and the Way: An Interpretation of Jewish Ethics.*

In Judaism, thought and life are so intimately commingled that any discussion of Jewish philosophy must perforce contain a philosophy of Jewish history. Our last three thousand years of tragedy and glory is a running commentary on the ideas of the tradition. Thus, *The Evolution of Jewish Thought* was followed by *The Meaning of Jewish History.*

But when the canvas is large and the picture is richly detailed, the central ideas are at times overlooked.

In this volume, various facets of Jewish life and thought are examined within the limited compass of the essay. In every case, ancient decisions are reopened and the effort is made to recognize the tension between opposing truths.

By the dialogue as a truth-seeking effort, I mean the attempt to understand and to appropriate the truths of others as well as to exhibit the truth of one's own heritage. It will be apparent that I do not conceive of truth in the realm of human values as a collection of statements, polished, packaged, and stamped with the seal of authority, but as an ongoing quest, which results at any one time in partial, relative truths. "How good is a word in its time," the biblical author exclaims, but time moves on, and in human affairs its advance is steadily accelerated, and there is always the need for a new word. This is particularly true in the case of Judaism, which has undergone a radical transformation in this century.

Above all, we as a people face today a crisis of identity. In the nineteenth century, a similar crisis was faced by the individual who had to decide whether he would stay within the community or resign from it. Today, the question is addressed to the entire Jewish community with all its uneven and uncertain boundaries: Shall it maintain the isolation of "a people that dwells alone" or shall it assume a humanist orientation and re-energize the universal elements in its own tradition?

From the very beginning of their appearance upon the stage of history, the Jewish people thought of themselves as being "different"—not merely different from others in the way all historical groups differ from one another, but different from *all* others, in a unique and cosmic way. This awareness was nourished historically by the feeling of upholding the one true faith amidst the erring nations. It was reinforced by the imposed isolation of the Jew in the Christian world. The frustrations of an incomplete emancipation in the nineteenth century rubbed Jewish nerves raw. Even today liberal Jews and secularists frequently subscribe to the quasi-metaphysical notion of transcendental uniqueness—as if the Lord had created two species of humanity, Jews and Gentiles.

This feeling of being "radically different"—the "meta-myth," as I call it—is especially in need of close scrutiny now, when it has become possible at last to end our ancient and involuted insularity, a situation which made us appear dark and sinister in the eyes of the world.

In the heart of the Jew, the scales are still trembling uncertainly between the old isolationist uniqueness and the new faith in the fellowship of humanity. The decision is still to be made, both in Israel and in the Diaspora. Humanists wonder whether the state of Israel will be modeled after Pakistan or India. Will Israel strive to be an outpost of world Jewry, or will it become a secular state with only tenuous and sentimental ties to the Jewish Diaspora? In the countries of the West, a similar question awaits decision: Will Jews cling to an exceptionalist self-image, or will they cease to be "strangers within the gate"?

The Hellenizers in the days of Judah Maccabee sought to make a "covenant" with the nations and to lose their identity in the process. In contrast, Jewish people today affirm their heritage by their labors for a modern state, and in America, Jews are affirming the central prophetic impetus in their tradition when they restructure their life along strictly religious and humanist lines. The choice is not between survival and extinction, but between two orientations: the one looking to hold on to a unique past, at once tragic and glorious; the other, to build a new future. In both cases, the ancient notion of "radical difference" can only serve as a prisoner's ball and chain, preventing escape from the dark dungeons of history.

Unfortunately, the feeling of being set apart as an exception to humanity has been reinforced in our generation by a number of factors. Hitler's distinction between Aryans and non-Aryans, with only Jews being put in the latter category, has by its terrible consequences obtained a macabre grip on the minds of many thoughtful people. In the era of resurgence and national renaissance that followed the Nazi debacle, the concept of Jewish uniqueness served as a protective shield against the challenges of the day. The time for self-questioning is past—we are "different."

To overcome the impetus of this metaphysical myth, we need to launch a careful scrutiny of our being along several lines—in the realms of theology, of ethics, and of history.

At this point, the two chapters in this book dealing with Toynbee's interpretation of Jewish history are particularly relevant. Toynbee's earlier views of the Jewish people were largely reflections of the conventional notions of European historiography, including the views of many Jewish writers, as is demonstrated in my essay, "Toward a Philosophy of Jewish History." Toynbee's basic approach, however, is a modern erudite version of biblical prophecy, which esteems very highly the worth of the Jewish faith while it denigrates the passion and posture of self-centered nationalism. In *Reconsiderations,* the twelfth volume of his *Study of History,* Toynbee presents this revised version of his understanding of Jewish history. While he credits the revision of his views to his correspondence and association with me, we are by no means in full agreement. In that volume, some of my letters are printed in the Appendix and others are quoted in his notes. None of these letters is reprinted in this volume. The essay, "Toynbee and Judaism," was published before our association was begun. Toynbee and I agree, first, that Jewish history must be viewed within the perspective of universal history and judged by universal categories; second, that Jewish people have to revise their impassioned insularity, on many fronts.

The articles on the Jewish-Christian Dialogue take account of the sinister, fanatical components in both traditions, which appear in new combinations in some modern ideologies. If freedom can only flourish within the soil of theistic humanism derived from both faiths, many diseases of social life are also likely to emerge from the darker elements in the religious heritage of the Western world. Judaism and Christianity are ideally suited to correct each other's tendencies toward exclusiveness.

We point out that religion includes the whole of personality—hence, also the intellectual, ethical, and esthetic aspects of life. Therefore, there is a common realm of discourse for people of different faiths, especially within the Judeo-Christian religious community. We do not affirm the notion that "all religions are the same" or that "their message to society lies solely in the common core of ethical-religious ideas." The "common core" is itself interpreted and applied in different ways, and this diversity of interpretation can be most fruitful for the society of the future. In the examination of religious thought, our argument calls for openness and a diversity of approaches; in our critique of Jewish life and history, we call for the attainment of a healthy self-image, free from the distortions of exceptionalism.

The essays in this volume carry forward the ideas presented in *Guideposts in Modern Judaism,* especially insofar as the idea of God and the nature of Conservative Judaism are concerned. While the views expressed in my earlier essays may differ in some details from those I now hold, they still move within the same course of development from a self-enclosed stream of tradition to the open sea of universal thought.

CONTENTS

Part One
The Jewish-Christian Dialogue

THE CASE
FOR THE
DIALOGUE

Now that voices of caution and even antagonism have been raised against the so-called dialogue movement, it is time to place the entire question in context. We need to ask how the issue arose, what dimensions and forms it is likely to assume, which concerns, if any, it is designed to meet, what dangers, if any, it is liable to present.

First, then, a glance backward. In one sense, the dialogue is as old as America itself. The emergence of an open society in the modern world implied that members of all faiths would come together for a variety of public functions and, it might have been expected, that they would not lock their faiths in strongboxes before leaving their homes. So, at municipal and cultural gatherings, it became customary to include religious leaders in the program. No public function was complete without the participation of a minister, a priest, and a rabbi. While the task of "invoking" or "benedicting" could be burdensome and even irksome to a busy clergyman, no one could question that this practice was a public action-symbol of tolerance. If in all phases of religion it is true that the deed is prior to the creed, there is no reason to feel that this rule does not apply to the sentiments of fraternity.

As Jews we are heirs of a tradition that has always contained this insight: *naase venishma* ("we shall do and we shall understand"); *mitoch shelo lishmo, bo lishmo* ("ceremonies performed, not for the sake of faith itself, eventually lead to genuine faith").

That the American pattern of interreligious cooperation has served to restrain and repress the passions of prejudice may be regarded as a truism. Anti-Semitism flourishes chiefly in the rural and small-town areas, where rabbis are scarce, and in the massed ethnic ghettoes of big cities, where deracinated and atomized men and women, for lack of roots in the higher culture of the land, tend to hang on to the familiar landmarks of prejudice. In any case, there is a long tradition of inter-religious meetings in the vigorous substructure of American democracy.

Without entering into a detailed analysis of the varied factors in the "goodwill movement," we recognize that it has now entered a new phase. A sense of urgency was given to this movement as the enormity of the Nazi crime began to sink into the public mind. It took time for the magnitude of the moral failure of the West to be experienced emotionally as well as intellectually. The Nürnberg trials, the trials of Nazi criminals by German courts, the Eichmann trial, the staging of *The Diary of Anne Frank* and of *The Deputy,* and the impact of William L. Shirer's *The Rise and Fall of the Third Reich*—all these events had a cumulative effect.

Then, too, the massive upsurge of education could not but place religion itself on trial. Young clergymen were compelled to ask themselves whether religious teachers had failed to act as the ethical mentors of their followers. The movement to involve religious leaders in the social problems of the day gathered momentum from year to year. The old image of prominent clergymen fighting sin and corruption was supplemented by that of priests and rabbis in picket lines, nuns in racial demonstrations, and ministers "witnessing" to the rightness of "negotiation" rather than "escalation." This moral upsurge generated also an intellectual curiosity about all religions— almost an "agonizing reappraisal." The academic campus be- came the Athenian Forum of the open society, which is steadily becoming more open. Courses in comparative religion or in the "living religions of America" were instituted in many univer-

4

sities in response to the growing demands of students.

At that time, a powerful and fresh impetus was given to the interfaith movement by the truly revolutionary developments in the Catholic Church. Those of us who were in contact with liberal Catholic scholars knew that behind the façade of a seeming monolith, mighty forces of regeneration were at work. But it took the gentle guidance of a great pope to bring to light the movement of *aggiornamento*, and ecumenism is one of the central motifs of this "spiritual awakening."

Strictly speaking, ecumenism is defined as "the pursuit of Christian unity." As such, the ecumenical movement does not refer to Jews at all. But the resurgent tide of self-renewing faith contains also a spiritual dimension, an endeavor to return to the first principles of religion, the quest for Divine truth and human brotherhood. The great leaders of this religious awakening are eager to bring the Church into the open society in heart and soul, and in keeping with this reassertion of humanism, they are eager to prevent the abuse of Catholic doctrine through the sowing of the seeds of anti-Semitism.

It is difficult to present the teachings of any historical faith without building up "negative images" of those who do not so believe. Even within Judaism itself, the preachers of Orthodoxy or Conservatism or Reform have to be on guard lest they convey a pejorative nuance to their descriptions of those who differ from them. But, in the case of Judaism, Christians find that the normal difficulties are multiplied many times over. Hence, the call for dialogues and fraternal discussions in the Schema on the Jews adopted by the Vatican Council.

Every religious renaissance involves a re-examination of the sources of the faith. So, too, the Catholic *aggiornamento* was preceded by a change of attitude toward the critical study of the Scriptures. On a superficial reading, many New Testament passages appear to drip with anti-Semitic venom. Indeed, in a recent essay on this theme, a Jesuit author produced a comprehensive examination of "Anti-Semitism in the New Testament."[1]

5

Does it follow that it is idle to attempt the removal of anti-Semitism from the Christian religions? By no means. In the life of faith it is the living interpretation of the sacred documents that counts, and Catholicism has always stressed the role of the living tradition. More than eight hundred years ago, Maimonides pointed out that "the gates of interpretation are not closed to us." Certain it is that in the medieval era the prevailing interpretation of the New Testament was anti-Semitic in character. Even then, however, the Jews were declared to be in a unique position, unlike all other heretics. A special "mystery" of a benevolent Providence required their protection and preservation to the "End of Days." Were it not for this theological doctrine, only Oriental Jewry would have survived into the modern world. Jewish survival in a state of spiritual somnolence would hardly have been "half a consolation." That we are here, bloodied but unbowed, fully abreast of the civilized world, is due to the European branch of world Jewry, which survived by the grace of the Catholic interpretation of the New Testament, distorted though it was by the "teaching of contempt."

Now, given the goodwill of Catholic authorities, the residual elements of contempt can be completely rooted out of the interpretation of the New Testament. (Let not this goal be light in our eyes. A recent study by the Anti-Defamation League showed that the "religious" roots of anti-Semitism are still potent.) Two complementary procedures for this purpose are available, the one embodying the objective quest for truth, the other reflecting the genuine logic of religious feeling.

In the search for historic truth, we recognize that the Divine light in Scripture is necessarily clouded by the contingent passions and limitations of the human agents of revelation. To understand the meaning of the Living Word, we have to filter out the crude impurities of human passion and prejudice. In the gradual separation of Judaism and Christianity, the feelings and myths of hate were generated on both sides. Christian anathemas had their counterpart in the *birchat haminim,* which,

6

as we know from the publications of the Genizah, specifically condemned the Christians. In the course of time, the wall of hatred between Jews and Christians grew apace, with a murderous climax being reached in Palestine in the time of the Byzantine emperor Heraclius and the Jewish leader Benjamin of Tiberias.

On this basis, a critical study of history is required in order to tell what the faith is not. On the higher levels of scholarship, historians are called upon to reconstruct the intellectual context of the early centuries of our era. For historians it is clear that the pre-modern versions of Christian origins were childish. The rabbis did not represent a "degenerate" form of Judaism. They were heirs of the prophets, in the sense of being concerned with the translation of principles into practice. And the early Christians absorbed Essenic as well as Rabbinic ideas, continuing the stream of prophetic-apocalyptic speculations, so much of which has been revealed in the recently uncovered Dead Sea Scrolls and in the Gnostic literature of Chonoboskion.

For historians, too, it is clear that no generation stands outside the flux of historic change. The Jews of today are not fossilized remnants of the pre-Christian era, and the Christians of today are not obligated to nurture the embers of ancient hates. Both groups identify themselves with the respective positions of their predecessors, but not in an absolute, totalitarian way, which excludes all detachment. Both share in the objective values of historic scholarship. For this reason, the study of the New Testament-Rabbinic age can be a liberating factor. In the words of Lord Acton, "if the Past has been an obstacle and a burden, knowledge of the Past is the safest and surest emancipation."

If the historical approach appears to contradict the basic axiom of an orthodox faith—the possession of absolute truth—we must remember the distinction between the possession of truth and its personal appropriation. Any fool can repeat Einstein's formula, but he cannot possibly appropriate it; certainly, the majority of mankind is unable ever to grasp it fully, even with the most sustained training. How much more is this true in the case of Divine truth, where the process of appropriation is all too human, partial and contingent upon the particular intellectual climate of an epoch!

These considerations lead us to the second procedure whereby the impact of the anti-Jewish passages is neutralized, namely, the consideration of them as preachments in the style of the Hebrew prophets. The writers of the New Testament address themselves as Jews to Jews. They refer to instances of Gentile fidelity in the same way as the classical prophets did. They excoriate their people, because in the light of the infinite dimension of piety no man or group is perfect. Wherever "Jews" are mentioned by John, for instance, humanity is intended, and not merely human beings as such but those who esteem themselves with apparent justice to be "good" and "saved" already. The Pharisees of that day represent the religious establishment of every day, for the life of faith consists of the paradoxical unity of possession and privation, at one and the same time. The pride of being "near" unto God must be constantly balanced by the humble confession that He escapes the meshes of our thoughts and sentiments. The passage of Matthew 27:25, which speaks of the guilt of the Crucifixion falling upon "all the people" and their children, has already been interpreted by the Council of Trent to mean that all human beings become guilty in the sight of God insofar as they reject the implication of Divine love. In other words, the Jews of the New Testament as of the Old Testament are to be regarded as the representatives of humanity as a whole.

On several occasions, I advocated that, in many instances, the word "Jews" in the Gospels should be rendered in the light of the context to mean "the crowd," or "the opponents," or "some people," or "those present"—locutions reflecting the actual situation and devoid of references to the mythical image of the Jewish people as a whole. There is ground to believe that some such renderings will be employed in the passages of the Gospels which are included in the liturgy.

8

At the conference on "Ecumenism in Catholic Education" at St. Meinrad's, which I attended, the Catholic representatives suggested a number of guidelines for the implementation of the "ecumenical spirit" insofar as Jews are concerned. Representing the power structure of the American Catholic Church, the National Bishops' Conference set to work to translate the vague abstractions of the Vatican documents into concrete and meaningful educational guidelines for seminaries, colleges, Newman clubs, and high schools. All the quibbling about words and phrases in the much discussed Schema was reduced to insignificance in the face of this firm decision of the authorities not to permit the declaration to remain merely a historical curiosity.

Of all the guidelines for Catholic educators, two recommendations are particularly relevant to our theme. First, a permanent office will be established, to which suggestions concerning unfair statements in textbooks will be referred for discussion and emendation. Anyone familiar with the vast accumulation of anti-Jewish material, dating from the medieval and modern periods as well as the ancient world, will realize the immense significance of this decision.

Second, all seminaries and colleges will be urged to appoint Jewish scholars to their faculties for the purpose of teaching Rabbinic Judaism and its development to the present day. The so-called dialogue, or better, the trialogue, involving Protestants as well as Catholics and Jews, it can now be seen, promises to go far beyond "the interfaith smile" of previous decades; it is a deeply earnest and sustained endeavor to overcome the shadows of malice that heretofore appeared inseparable from the massive structures of organized religions.

What then are the dangers that this new epoch might entail?

First in importance is the danger of vulgarization, to which Professor Heschel pointed in his excellent essay "Religion Is Not an Island." Every ideal turns into a mockery when it falls into the hands of the shallow and the ignorant. What is to prevent the trialogue from degenerating into another gimmick of pro-

9

gram chairmen? Ours is a most undisciplined community, with no holds barred in the rat race for public attention. Do we have any basis for believing that the exponents of Judaism in all the trialogues of the country and on all the levels of discussion will be equal to their task? I can sympathize with those who fear *hillul hashem.*

Yet, I feel that our duty to future generations of Jewish people requires that we exert every effort to meet this challenge. If we now have the opportunity to prevent the buildup of future catastrophes, dare we weakly surrender to fear? We may not be worthy spokesmen for the martyrs of the past, as some writers maintain, but we cannot escape the responsibility to do our level best for our descendants and the future.

It would be desirable to have only high-ranking scholars engage in interfaith discussions, but then one learns soon enough that much of the enmity in Christian circles is generated by the actions of our present secular agencies—their absolutization of the distinction between religion and politics, their crusading against governmental support for church-related colleges, their exhibitionist drives to secure the limelight for themselves and their regnant figureheads. The strange fact is that many of our public relations agencies live in a world of their own, bounded by the First and Tenth Amendments and completely isolated from the religious realities in the non-Jewish world. I feel therefore that on balance there is more to be gained in *kiddush hashem,* if the dialogue is extended to laymen and to service organizations, than is to be lost in *hillul hashem,* through the possible misuse of this undertaking. Did not Moses make a similar choice when he rejected the offer to restrict the Torah to his descendants and accepted the risks involved in giving it to erstwhile worshipers of the Golden Calf? It is quite possible that the upsurge of the dialogue movement will have a most beneficial effect, promoting a renewed interest in Jewish learning on all levels. We are challenged to train new scholars for seminaries, new professors for colleges, new philosophically sophisticated rabbis for our communities, and laymen capable of holding their own in interfaith discussions. Having met so many challenges before, shall we fail to meet this one?

One objection in principle has been raised to the dialogue movement. Religion, it is said, is a subjective phenomenon. It is subjective in a personal sense—"what the individual does with his isolation"—and it is also subjective in a communal sense. Only the second meaning is relevant to this discussion. A dialogue requires a common realm of discourse if it is not to degenerate into a meaningless talk-fest, where people talk at, instead of to, one another. But every historic religion, so it is argued, generates its own pattern of rhetoric, values, and symbols. The same words possess different nuances of meaning in different traditions. To use a mathematical analogy, we face here the problem of incommensurability between two series of numbers.

This insight is true and precious, but one-sided. It is important to bear it in mind whenever the attempt is made to assay the "psychological equivalence" of religious rites and institutions in different traditions. The inner dimension of faith can only be experienced; it can neither be weighed nor measured. But, then, the truth of this observation by no means shuts the door against meaningful dialogues. For religion does possess an objective or universal phase, which is essential to its nature as a meaningful philosophy of life. At this point, we shift attention from religion in general to Judaism and the faiths deriving from it. While some religions were so completely nonrational or even irrational as to merge with myth and magic, Judaism has always undertaken to appeal to the intellect as well as to the private promptings of the soul.

The Jewish religion arose as a protest against the pagan cults, condemning them as mythology and sorcery. Its very character as a faith derived from its emphasis on reason and ethics; hence, its condemnation of magic and its repudiation of the comforting myths that appealed so powerfully to man's feelings and phantasies.

We are so impressed today by the standardized distinctions

11

between Hellenism and Hebraism, or between "Atticism" and "Abrahamism," as Luzzato put it, that we tend to forget that Judaism performed the historic role of demolishing paganism, shattering the idols that reflected the private and shadowy side of human nature. On the other hand, in respect to Greek philosophy, Jewish thinkers, from Aristobulus and Philo to Maimonides and Mendelssohn, found themselves largely in agreement with its major trends. Actually, both Judaism and Hellenism repudiated the fancies of mythology and produced the ideal of the individual standing alone and passing judgment on the collective tradition. In Judaism, the prophet and the sage exercised this function, but chiefly the prophet, speaking in the name of "the still, small voice" in his heart. In Hellenism, the philosopher played the same role, speaking in the name of the intellect. And the great philosophers, Socrates, Plato, Aristotle, conceived of reason as including the values of ethics, even as the prophets aimed at an informed and rational morality, scorning mere feminine sentiment, as in the famous phrase, "those who eat men and kiss calves."[2]

So Judaism contained a philosophy of life, more or less reasoned, though it did not succumb as readily as Christianity to the decayed and broken fragments of Greek rhetoric, which were the stock-in-trade of the schools in the first centuries of our era. As one reads the medieval works of Jewish philosophy, one can easily translate the same arguments into their equivalent formulations in Christian or in Moslem thought. The incommensurability is in the practice of the faith and in the complexity of some central concepts, not in the philosophy of life, which is addressed to the individual and to the community.

It is said that philosophy may be discussed, but not theology. What then is Jewish theology? Is it the priestly component of the tradition as distinct from the prophetic and philosophical ones? If the peculiar reasoning of Halachah is intended, then this attitude is understandable, though not defensible. The extent of condemnation of "Talmudism" in Christian circles is amazing. Even Mother Hargrove, who devoted a lifetime to the improvement of Jewish-Christian relations, refers in her last

12

book, *The Star and the Cross*, to the "genuine fears of the ill teachings of the Talmud."[3] I cannot agree that Christians studying the Talmud under the guidance of a Jewish scholar would misunderstand it more than if they were to study it on their own or read about it in a secondary source.

Anyone who has been part of the dialogue movement knows that we are still very far from the time when Talmud and Midrash could be studied jointly or even discussed in the setting of a living room. But if that time should come, I can see nothing but good resulting from such an undertaking.

If Talmud and Midrash are not to be barred on principle, what then is "Jewish theology"? Is it the Hebrew Bible or the commentaries upon it? Who does not know that Rashi's commentaries had been used already by Nicholas de Lyra and, through his mediation, by Martin Luther? Bible studies have been common ground for scholars for more than a century.

Personally, I consider that "Jewish Theology" consists of the various *taamai hamizvot* ("the reasons for the Commandments"). For it is in this area that general philosophy and the historical faith converge. Should a rabbi, then, refrain from discussing the various reasons for, let us say, the dietary laws? I see no reason why he should leave those reasons to the imagination of Christians. He must take care, however, to represent accurately the various schools of Jewish thought, in the past as in the present. But this injunction applies to every subject of discussion, not merely to "the reasons of the Commandments."

As a question of Halachah, I assume that all Orthodox rabbis would concur in the judgment that the Christians of today are not in the category of the "worshipers of stars," mentioned in the Talmud, whom it was not permitted to instruct in the precepts of Torah.[4] Though there were hesitation and uncertainty on this score during the Middle Ages, there should be none today.[5] It is time to recall the gentle words of Rabbi Meir, whose teaching is incorporated in the Mishnah:

" 'You shall keep My laws and My norms, by the pursuit of which man shall live: I am the Lord.'

The verse does not say, 'Priests, Levites or Israelites,' but, man, to teach us that even a Gentile becomes equal to the High Priest when he is engaged in the study of Torah."[6]

The attempt has also been made to delimit the area of dialogues by drawing the line of demarcation between social problems and concerns, on the one hand, and principles of belief, on the other hand. But the purpose of dialogue is to achieve a larger measure of mutual understanding. To understand one another we have to refer to first principles, which are matters of faith; furthermore, there is a history to every problem, and historic attitudes to live down as well as historic affirmations to live up to. Hence, there is the need of revealing criteria, whereby the essential is separated from the accidental, and the genuine message of religion is distinguished from the accumulated encrustations of history. As a matter of fact, differences in regard to contemporary issues constitute the greatest source of interreligious friction today. It is therefore impossible to set arbitrary limits to the scope of the dialogue, nor is it necessary, since the discussants generally choose their topics by unanimous consent.

The basic objection to Jewish-Catholic colloquies, as distinct from the older liberal confabs, is the continued dedication of the Church to the conversion of Jews and Protestants as well as pagans. How can a discussion be oriented to the quest for truth when one of the parties firmly believes that he, and only he, is in possession of the absolute truth? Does the Church promote the dialogue movement as an instrument of conversion?

Here we enter delicate ground. No one is in a position to speak dogmatically concerning the ulterior motives of others. We are obligated to judge our colleagues "in the scale of merit." In common courtesy we accept the assurance of the Church authorities that the planned colloquies, dialogues, and trialogues are not undertaken as agencies for the conversion of Jews. In the ground rules, worked out by Robert McAfee Brown, a conversionist goal is disavowed. The dialogue is "offered up to God"; that is, we seek to further mutual understanding, cut out the weeds of hate and suspicion from the hearts of our people,

14

and learn from one another. As to the final consequence of our labors—we leave this up to God. For ourselves, it is sufficient that truth, fraternity, and charity are good in their own right.

Again, some basic distinctions are needed in order that this attitude may be rightly understood. First, on the human level, we distinguish between wanting to do something and undertaking a series of acts that are designed to result in a desired goal. Clearly, then, the Church does desire the conversion of Jews and the return of the "separated brethren." They stand committed to this purpose as an ultimate consummation. But the dialogue movement is a good in itself, valid within the human context, regardless of the ways that Providence employs to fulfill its ends.

Conversion is an act of God in Christian as well as in Jewish thought. All that men can do is preliminary and preparatory. So, Paul asserts that "no man can say Jesus is the Lord, but in the Holy Spirit."[7] Similarly, Maimonides calls Obadiah the proselyte a "son of God," in contrast to Jews who are "sons of Abraham," on the supposition that he was led by God to "enter under the wings of the Shechinah." In Qabbalah it was asserted that the new soul of the convert was generated in heaven through the meeting of the spirits of Abraham and Sarah.

In any case, two motifs and one dogma are conjoined in the ambition to convert others: the desire to open oneself and one's faith to others, and the attempt to force the hand of God, as it were. The dogma is that at the End of Days all men will acknowledge the one true faith. This belief is found in Judaism, too, not merely in the prophets but also in the Code of Maimonides. But to force the hand of God was always regarded in Judaism as a sin, for God draws us to Himself in a thousand different ways and at His own pace. However, the first motif, to open oneself up to all who are interested that they might not sin by misjudging or mistreating us, is a *mizvah*, for it is in the nature of removing a stumbling block from the path of a nearsighted neighbor. For this reason, I feel that we should

15

open well-staffed libraries and information centers in the great cities of the world, though I do not favor our undertaking missionary endeavors.

Can one who believes he possesses the absolute and perfect truth still engage in dialogue for the purpose of being enlightened and in order to enlighten others? This question is relevant, for a genuine dialogue must be conceived as a two-way channel of communication and instruction.

The answer is *yes,* because of the distinction already mentioned between having a truth and appropriating it. We all "have" the Torah, but we are warned, "it is broader than the sea and longer than the earth." After a lifetime of preaching, I still find familiar verses of the Bible and Prayer Book light up suddenly with new meaning. We come to understand more deeply the truths of our heritage, as with sympathetic understanding we apprehend the insights of men of other faiths. Religious truth is infinite in depth. The more religious truth is grasped, the more the mystery we face is deepened. As the Besht put it: when we think we face Him, we are far from Him; when we know we are far, we approach him.[8] Whatever we say of God, of ourselves, and of our relation to God is in the nature of a pointing to a transcendent reality. Maimonides ascribed only negative meaning to all Divine attributes and yet he centered the whole of life around the love of God and the steady growth in the knowledge of His Being. To small minds the piety of Maimonides was self-contradictory. Not so to those who, however feebly and haltingly, have followed in his pathway.

The basic quality of the modern mind is a certain attitude toward the flow of time in all its three tenses—the past, the present, and the future. The past was not the Golden Age of Perfection; in the present, we are caught within the flux of history; in the future, advance toward perfection is not inevitable, but possible. This fundamental posture of the modern mind provides the context for the dialogue movement.

The past was not perfection. Even if the Divine act of

revelation occurred in the past, it was not then understood, for the human recipients of the Divine Word were children of their primitive and unenlightened age. Hence, the blind momentum of tradition is restrained and subjected to rational criticism. The synagogues and the churches, after their diverse kinds, may cheerfully acknowledge ancient shortcomings and errors.

In the present, we know that the weeds of bias and hate may be taking root among us, as they did in previous ages. The past, with its satanic drives, is not dead; it is alive within us. But if history molded our being, it can be transcended in part as we subject it to criticism and observe it from different angles. The six million died, not on account of anything they did, but because of the clouds of hate and bias that were generated at various times. And let it be said, in passing, that Christianity in general and the Catholic Church in particular were not the only sources of anti-Semitism either in the ancient, or in the medieval, or in the modern world—not by a long shot.

As to the future, there are some among us who fear any "innovation" lest it change our character. But did we ever claim to be so perfect as to be capable of changing only for the worse? Should we not endeavor to dissipate as much of the evil momentum of the past as we can? Should we not in the present shun that insularity which permitted the walls of misunderstanding and malice to rise from generation to generation? Should we not prepare the way for a better future?

THE DIALOGUE MOVEMENT:
Retrospect and Prospect*

We recognize three stages in the evolution of the Jewish-Christian dialogue. These may be symbolized respectively by the fire engine, the fire department, and the city-planning commission. The first approach deals with the existing emergencies; the second aims to restrict the use of inflammables but leaves the existing buildings intact, though they may well be potential firetraps; the third projects the vision of a city so well structured that it reduces the hazards of fire and other catastrophes to a minimum, paying attention as well to the promotion of those positive values that a good society should offer to its members.

The dialogue movement is for the most part still in its first and second stages. Following the Nazi holocaust, the noblest spirits of the Protestant and Catholic worlds realized that some sort of public endeavor was needed in order to combat the fires of hate. And this endeavor is peculiarly the responsibility of religious leaders, firstly, because it is their task to build the spirit of mutual appreciation and respect in society, and, secondly, because the momentum of their historic teachings provided the inflammable material for the conflagration of the "Final Solution." Clearly, modern anti-Semitism generally and Nazism in particular were not direct developments of Christian teaching. In fact, Nazism at least was essentially and truly the essence of anti-Christianity. Nevertheless, the satanic drive of the Nazis made use of the ongoing Christian disputation against the Jews in three ways: first, the isolation of the Jew from the

*Address at the International Conference on Jewish-Christian Relations of 1966 at Cambridge University, England.

18

Christian world, as if he were separated not merely by explicit beliefs but by an abyss that was ultimate and metaphysical; second, the casting of the Jew in the role of the mysterious antagonist who is doomed by his frustration to witness to the truth of that which he denies; third, by discrediting the authority of reason and universal moral principles and extolling the virtue of dark instinctive affirmations that prevailed in ancient and medieval times.

Now, some Christian and Jewish leaders are content to remain at the first level of the dialogue—the fire engine approach. They are willing to deal with the various areas of friction, if, as, and when they arise. They would favor occasional conferences for the purpose of easing contemporary strains or disproving some specific charges or dispelling mutual suspicions in one or another domain of public life, but they would shun any attempt to examine the theological sources of the various myths that have bedeviled Christian-Jewish relations.

To the great credit of the authors of the Vatican Schema on the Jews and the earlier Protestant declaration it must be said that they inaugurated the second stage of the dialogue, that of a fire department, which regulates and restricts the uses of inflammable material to minimize the incidence of fires. So, the endorsement of joint Christian-Jewish discussion in the study of the Scriptures, in the interpretation of history, and in the analysis of contemporary issues and ideologies is a great step forward. It means that we are determined to combat the danger of mass-hatred at its source and not to wait until after the fires of malice have taken hold. A series of interfaith conferences is anticipated, and it is believed that such meetings will prevent the distortion of theological dogmas and the sprouting of the dragon-seeds of hate from the soil of religions. The historical city will be retained with all its "medieval charm," its tortuous roads, its twisted alleys, its gloomy homes, but guards will be posted to caution against fires and other hazards.

The second stage of the dialogue movement is a great advance over the first, but I submit that a third stage, that of

19

the city planners, is needed. In the fire department stage, the old buildings and the inflammable material are left intact, though rules governing their use are laid down, and inspectors are appointed to make their rounds. However, we live in a rapidly changing world, and we are called upon to guide the process of urban renewal so that it shall make possible the good society of the future. To this end, we need to lay down the broad outlines of the ideal society. Within this larger perspective, the old buildings will be reset and restructured. The arteries of communication will then be given first consideration. Dialogues will no longer be merely showpieces designed for ornamentation; on the contrary, interfaith education and mutual appreciation will form part of the equipment of all cultured men and women.

Before we can seriously discuss the eventual shape of the dialogue movement, we have to take account of the obstacles that have appeared in its way down to the present moment, for the future will have to grow out of the present. I propose to describe the objections that have been raised in Jewish circles and to indicate to what extent, if any, they are valid. Once these barriers are removed, the way to the full realization of interfaith amity will be clear.

I shall not debate with those of our faith who prefer to rebuild the ancient barriers of medieval times. In their view, walls of misunderstanding and even mild hatred are a blessing, for the threat of increasing intermarriage is a greater menace than the threat of intensifying anti-Semitism. Fortunately, they are small in number. We need to remind them of the bitter lessons of Jewish history as well as of the central teachings of our tradition—The Name of God is Peace, His seal is Truth, and His work in history is Justice.

The first objection that we have to consider is the challenge to the very idea of a dialogue. It runs as follows: Why encourage men of different faiths to discuss their diverse beliefs or to talk about their several interpretations of Scriptures? They will not come to agree, and they might irritate one another. Is it not better for each group to reduce its contacts with those of another group to the absolute minimum so as to avoid abrasive situations? Don't "good fences make good neighbors"?

In general, my answer, as a student of Jewish history, to the question, Why dialogues? is that the alternative to the dialogue is not an indifferent neutrality, but an impassioned disputation. With the New Testament as its basic text, Christianity is committed to an ongoing debate with Judaism, a debate which, left to itself, inevitably degenerates into a denunciation. Through the momentum of its tradition, Christianity cannot but project the image of the Jew as the polar counterpart of all that is distinctively Christian. This tendency must be balanced by opposing factors deriving from humanist studies and from contact with Jewish life. Similarly, the Jew, living in a Christian world, cannot blind himself to the realities of Christian life and thought. So it is that Jews and Christians could esteem one another in love, or condemn one another with unearthly passion; they could even condemn and esteem, hate and love at the same time, but one thing they could not do—they could not be blithely indifferent to each other. The Christians in ancient times devised a special anathema for the Jews, and the Jews recited a special curse for those of their numbers who turned Christian.

We tend to regard Christian-Jewish disputations as a peculiarly medieval phenomenon, but as a matter of fact there were disputations in the ancient world as well. The dialogue of Justin Martyr may have been a literary device, but it certainly reflected a familiar phenomenon. We know that in the third century some rabbis attended those disputations, while others avoided them. In the Middle Ages, the disputations were formal, structured and patterned in accord with the prevailing principles of logic.

But in a deeper, less formal sense, these disputations never ceased. Jewish and Christian writers continued the ancient argument in their own way, even when they seemed to break with their own religious traditions. So basic was the metaphysical and meta-historical contrast between Jews and Christians in their basic texts that, as movement followed movement in the modern world, this fundamental abyss continued to be assumed as an ineluctable axiom. A few examples will illustrate this phenomenon. Voltaire directed the arrows of his bitter satire against the Christian churches, but he carried over from the old faith an inveterate scorn for the people of the Old Testament, who, as he thought, loved only money and children. There was no nobler spirit in the Age of Enlightenment than Immanuel Kant. Yet, he took the Jewish faith to be the typical example of the slavish mentality succumbing to the yoke of a *heteronomous* law, while in his interpretation, Jesus became the spokesman of the principle of autonomy. It is interesting that the Jewish followers of Kant—and no modern philosopher was taken so closely to heart by Jewish thinkers as Kant—made the opposite identification; namely, Judaism was the religion of autonomy, while Christianity, by reason of its scheme of salvation, substituted the chains of dogma for the law of freedom. Who was right? It is obvious that the sentiments of loyalty to one's own heritage determined which faith was to be extolled as the beacon of light; the moment this identification was fixed, the other faith, by the impetus of disputation logic, had to play the role of the satanic counterpart.

This inverse relationship was maintained not only by individual thinkers but by entire movements. The rationalists of the French Revolution brought the gift of emancipation to Jews as individuals, but they bridled at any residual manifestations of Jewish collective existence. It is well to recall Clermont-Tonnerre's declaration: "To the Jews as individuals, everything; to the Jews as a nation, nothing." The liberals in all European countries resisted the onslaught of anti-Semitism, but they persistently questioned the efforts of Jewish people to fortify their communal structure. In their view, the Jews strove too officiously to survive, and Jewish survival was somehow an offense to the bright new world of their vision. The historian Mommsen, courageous fighter against anti-Semitism that he was, nevertheless called upon the liberal Jews of his day to accept the Christian faith and, at the very least, to reduce the structures of communal life to an inconspicuous minimum. If liberalism was the latter-day version of Christianity, the Jewish people was symbolic of the dark medieval past. (Ernst Renan, it will be recalled, has given felicitous expression to this mood in his popular tract, *The Life of Jesus.*

The romantic movement was far more pervasive and many-sided than the liberal current. It gathered to itself the nationalistic protest against cosmopolitanism, the agrarian protest against the urban explosion, the protest of master-artisans against the new mass-industries, the protest of a limited and simple economy against the "boom and bust" industrial economy of the modern world—in brief, every manner of reaction against the emergent complexities of our time. It sought its roots in the dark underworld of instinct, intuition, and the racial unconscious, attacking the superficialities of reason, which was calculating, mean, and unbelieving. The romanticists, too, identified their philosophy as the essence of Christian faith, taking the Jew to be the symbol of the hardheaded rationalist who asks for a sign and coldly assays and measures all things. We have the image of the Jew and the Frenchman in Fichte—people who are enslaved to *Verstand* and incapable of the intuitive penetration of *Vernunft.* And in Schleiermacher, the Englishman becomes the companion of the Jew, who is blind to the true glories of religious feeling. But Englishmen and Frenchmen come and go in romantic literature, in keeping with the vagaries of contemporary politics, while the Jew continues to be the enduring symbol of calculating reason, with Sombart and others maintaining that the soul of the modern commercial economy was essentially Jewish. The romantics were far from being traditional believers. They were actually neo-Christian, but they retained the old myth of the Jew as the satanic antagonist, a dark and mysterious figure, whose error is funda-

23

mental and metaphysical. He does not merely entertain erroneous opinion. He *is* wrong.

The utopian socialists of France and Belgium carried on the medieval disputation on the plane of economics. They too regarded themselves as the interpreters of the Gospel, bringing the good tidings of love to the poor and the meek. To Fourier, Toussenel, Leraux, the Jew was the embodiment of money-culture and of all the false values of the bourgeoisie. God designed His world to be good and simple, but along came the Jew, "who would not so believe," and the beautiful economy of love and cooperation was transformed into the ruthless, soulless monster that it is today. Populism in America built up a similar mythology, the "Agrarian Myth."

Scientific socialism, the movement derived from Marx and Engels, wavered for several decades. Eventually, it opted in favor of reason and morality, stigmatizing anti-Semitism as the "Socialism of fools." But then the opposition to socialism sought to tap the dark springs of nationalistic feeling and the underworld of mythology that thrives below the surface world of religion.

Hence, there is the proliferation of "Christian" anti-Marxist parties, suggesting by their very name that the Jew belonged to the opposition. And he was so aligned not by accident and not by choice, but through the inexorable necessity of history. In the popular mind, the Jew was a socialist from the very beginning, since his Messiah belonged to this world and his vision of the world to come was this-worldly, conceived in the concrete terms of earthly well-being and prosperity. Often enough, the Jew continued to serve as the symbol of the capitalists, for the utopians and Populists, even as he became the symbol of the Bolshevik. How could he embrace this contradiction within himself? The answer again is that for the pseudo-religious, disputatious mentality the Jew was a mystery, like Satan, and like God, at once chosen and accursed. The mysterious is always ambivalent.

To replace disputations with dialogue is to move from the

field of battle to the halls of learning. The cosmic contrast between the absolute good and the metaphysical evil is replaced by the variations between several forms of light. It is no longer a question of the Divine versus the demonic, but of patterns drawn along the dimension of the holy, where an infinite variety of gradations and shades are possible. Furthermore, the dialogue takes place within a realm, where the secular and the objective worlds coalesce along with the diverse religious traditions. As Tillich pointed out, religion today is experienced "on the boundary," between intersecting traditions. It is no longer an island, complete unto itself.

This analysis brings us to the second objection to the dialogue, which has been raised in Jewish circles, namely, that a genuine dialogue is impossible because the same words have different meanings within the several religions. Often enough those meanings are incommensurate with one another, it is contended, so that the very attempt to communicate may confuse much more than it can clarify. This is particularly true in the case of Judaism and Christianity, where the same traditional terms of Scripture are freighted with different shades and nuances. This observation on the semantics of the dialogue is a most pertinent warning. It is true that terms like the Messiah, salvation, belief, redemption, and sin are not like simple geometric figures cast on a Euclidean plane; they are many-storied structures projected into the paradoxical universe of non-Euclidean space. Those who engage in dialogue must guard against this danger, for every faith is a universe of discourse, unique and incomparable.

But after allowing due weight to this argument, we have to recognize that the Judeo-Christian religions are objective as well as subjective. We are the heirs of Amos and Socrates as well as of priests and saints. Amos insisted on the element of moral objectivity within the tradition, so that he could dare to criticize the authority of both the high priest and the king. Socrates elaborated the element of rational objectivity within the culture of his day. For us today, Amos and Socrates speak

25

clearly out of the tumult of the marketplace and the forums of universities. Their voices are every bit as religious as those of Jewish legalists or of Christian mystics.

To be sure, the Jewish, the Catholic, and the Protestant faiths are fields of tension between two poles—the moral-rational, objective realm of values and facts, on the one hand, and the private, subjective realm of sentiments, beliefs, and traditional rhetoric, on the other hand. Those in each faith who reject completely the validity of objective reason and ethical judgment in the domain of faith cannot really partici-pate in the dialogue. The line of division between dialogue and disputation cuts across each group; above that line, where objective insights and values are welcomed, Amos and Socrates hold court, and their modern counterparts discourse.

The third and fourth objections to the dialogue may be dis-cussed together. They refer to the claim of being "the one true faith" and to the missionary commitment of nearly all Christian groups. How can we engage in the give and take of free discussion, when one party to the dialogue lays down in advance the dogma that it and it alone disposes of the keys to heaven? In that event, some of our men ask, is not the dialogue simply a device for the conversion of Jews and heretics?

Our answer to these two objections is an assertion of faith in the wisdom and goodwill of our neighbors. We recognize that the missionary ambition itself is compounded of two motives—a genuinely idealistic desire to share one's deepest treasures in love and fellowship, and a narrow, simplistic belief that the infinite God could think of only one way of com-municating with his children. We acknowledge, too, that in all religions there is a private kind of rhetoric, which has become, through historical forces, an approved way of speaking for the members of that group. But, along with these structured locutions, there flows the mighty current of prophetic religion, which is the common heritage of Jews and Christians. The men of the churches and the synagogues are jointly committed to the task of building justice and love in the all-embracing society of mankind. All the faiths of the Judeo-Christian tradition are God-centered, believing that man as an individual and society as a whole find fulfillment through faith in God; they are also man-centered, believing that secular culture and humanist values constitute an integral portion of Divine revelation. It is on this common ground of religious humanism that we meet in dialogue. As to how the contemporary insights of religious humanism are to be reconciled with the traditional panoply of rituals and dogmas, we need not be concerned. This is the task of theologians within each of the three major faiths. It is sufficient for us as Jews to know that our colleagues across the table are humanists as well as Christians.

This does not mean that we as Jews are completely indifferent to those elements of the private rhetoric of Christians, which directly and specifically degrades either our faith or our historical character or our collective destiny. I read in a review of Cardinal Bea's last book, *The Church and the Jews,* that, in his view, we as Jews must still be regarded as being collectively "perverse" and "of evil heart." These and similar terms are imbedded in the traditional rhetoric of the Church. If the Church had only this to say to us, we and all religious humanists, Catholic as well as Protestant, would have no basis for a continuing conversation. But the Church has principles as well as rhetoric, spiritual depth as well as sanctified speech. The desiccated epithets flung at us from the medieval past are as much an offense against human reason and conscience as they are unjust to us. We affirm our faith in the hearts and minds of our Christian colleagues, as they do in ours, and we want nothing from them that a critical intelligence and a keen conscience do not dictate. We believe that coming together as religious humanists, we shall gradually discover how the truths of our respective traditions may be harmonized with that universal, growing truth in which all of us share. The dialogue then is not for us a ceremonial way of blessing an accomplished fact; it is rather a beginning, a determination to walk

27

up "the mountain of the Lord," advance through different pathways to the same blessed summit. Judaism teaches that religious enlightenment grows out of religious deeds—*naase venishma* ("we shall do and we shall understand"). Even so, out of our mutual confrontation, there will emerge an illumination that will bless the lives of all of us.

The other day, I heard a renowned Bible scholar talk about the prophet Micah. He referred to verses 1 and 2 of Chapter 4, in which Micah quotes Isaiah's prophecy about the End of Days, when all the nations will flow to the "mountain of the Lord" and agree to walk "in His paths." Micah, you will recall, then adds in verse 5, "For all the peoples walk every one in the name of his god, and we will walk in the name of the Lord our God for ever and ever." Said this scholar, Micah did not understand what Isaiah was saying, for Isaiah predicted that all the nations will accept the Jewish faith. Micah quotes the words of Isaiah, but he distorts their meaning when he says that every people will continue to walk in the name of its own god. When two prophets are engaged in an argument, who am I to intervene? But, as a counsel of wisdom, not of prophecy, I have no doubt that Micah improved upon the message of Isaiah, for his way is the one consistent with human freedom and with the pluralistic way in which God calls people to Himself. Pluralism in human progress is the testimony of all history. Even the gift of speech, the first revelation of the Image of God in the heart of man, according to Genesis 2:19, was given to different groups in different ways.

In sum, our answer to the objection raised against the dialogue within the Jewish community is threefold: first, that it is inescapable, the only alternative being the one-sided disputation of previous years; second, that within each of the great faiths in the Judeo-Christian tradition, there operates a moral and rational component, as well as a private, subjective realm of rites and dogmas; third, that while the subjective rhetoric of some faiths may appear to make any true dialogue illusory, we meet on the common ground of religious humanism, the implications of which will be of the greatest service to mankind.

To pick up the analogy I suggested earlier, we still have to move from the fire department stage to that of city planning. What does this task imply?

Its first implication is an expansion of perspective. We have to see the Judeo-Christian debate against the background of the whole of humanity advancing toward God. The spiritual unity of mankind is no longer a distant vision, but an immediate task. The differences among us are reduced to size when they are viewed against the spiritual history of mankind as a whole. The image of the Jew as antagonist, so basic to Western history, is recognized as a ludicrous anachronism the moment the canvass is extended to the entire globe, for then we see the emergence from the worldwide sea of paganism of a small people laboring to bring forth the vision of ethical monotheism. For more than a thousand years it stands alone, beating back the tides of paganism. Then, from among this people there emerges "a sect or a way," call it what you will, which succeeds in winning large numbers of the human family to this faith. Later, out of both Judaism and Christianity, still another group emerges and wins many millions to the same faith. Yet, even so, all together comprise but a minority of the human race. And within the lands, officially Jewish, or Catholic, or Protestant, or Moslem, the actual faith of many millions is but a latter-day version of paganism. "The little god of the world is always of the same stripe," said Goethe. The essence of paganism is the fragmentation of human values and therefore the loss of the feeling of man's transcendence and his dignity. Paganism shatters the unity of personality by attributing different instincts and ideals to different sources. Since man seeks to achieve wholeness of spirit, pseudo-religions arise to re-establish unity by the idolatrous worship of one force or one ideal. Thus, paganism, nihilism, and pseudo-religion are the principalities and powers against which we continue to struggle. By now, it is virtually a truism to point out that Bolshevism and Nazism were essentially pseudo-religions. This, then, is our first task, to reveal the true perspective of human history so that the image of the Jew in the Christian world can be seen as that of an ally, not of an antagonist.

This change of image involves a deeper understanding of many passages in the New Testament that were previously interpreted naïvely and literally. Viewed in the context of general history, the thrust of the teaching of Jesus was not to show that Judaism was evil, but that even the best teachers and the noblest faith were still human, fallible, and corruptible. Similarly, throughout the range of Christian and Jewish teaching, from ancient times to the present day, the differences are of nuance, arrangement, and emphasis, not those of antagonistic philosophies of life. The usual contrasts between Jewish law and Christian love, between creed and deed, between sinfulness as a state of the soul and sinfulness as the deposit of transgressions, between love as self-sacrifice and love as community-building, between a philosophy of life that makes history secondary and illustrative and between an event of history that makes all philosophy secondary and apologetic, all these contrasts, real as they may be within limited contexts, fall into place as matters of emphasis in the perspective of religious humanism.

The second implication of religious humanism is that it is a dialectical dynamic quest, rather than a set of so many principles. In 1946 the common principles of Judaism and Christianity were formulated by an interfaith conference, but every such endeavor must be regarded as proximate and relative to the issues of the day. Religious humanism is not a religion in itself: it comes to life at the crossroads of several religions and at the boundary between them and secular culture. It is dynamic, revealing new implications as the contemporary context changes, and dialectical, confronting the religious traditions and secular culture with a *yes* and a *no*.

It says *yes* to the values of humanism, insofar as they help to uplift the stature of man, but also *no*, insofar as these values are affirmed to be absolute and self-sufficient. We maintain that "the measure of all things" is not man in himself, but *man facing God*. In his quest for truth and value, a human being is open-ended, reaching out toward the Infinite and the Unknowable.

At the same time, religious humanism says *no* as well as *yes* to the several bodies of religious tradition—*yes*, to the values and concerns fostered by them, *no*, to their claims of exclusiveness and simplistic absolutism.

In a very real sense, the modern humanist is more religious than ancient or medieval man, for the essence of the modern spirit is historicistic—the feeling of living within the flux of history. This awareness corresponds to the Einsteinian revolution in our vision of the universe. Our humility is genuine because it corresponds to the human situation. For the same reason, we cannot allow that any of our predecessors were lifted above the contingencies of history. Thus we are kept from imagining that we possess the Absolute because we believe in Him. At the same time, the humanist is not likely to be deflected from the heart of faith, the love of God and man, by any illusion that the ethical and the rational have somehow been suspended. Religion is the cutting edge of man's spirit in its quest for reality. It can never fall below the norms of spirit and yet be true to itself.

Humanism and religious traditionalism are the two poles of the field of tension that is the human spirit, for the creative moments in our life are the fleeting encounters between our finite souls and the Infinite Spirit. Inescapably, such encounters are tangential, as the contact between a finite circle and an infinite line. Therefore, they leave us with the paradoxical feeling of *privation* as well as *possession*. We feel that we have been included in the Divine harmony, yet we remain but a tiny fragment and cannot lay hold of Him, in whom we live and move and have our being. The entire body of Holy Writ preaches this intimacy of God as well as His elusiveness. But paradoxes are difficult to live with; hence, the tendency to break the tension by opting for the one or the other pole of spirit: humanism tends to turn secular, ignoring all intimations of the Divine; and religious traditionalism tends to ignore that we can know of the Supreme Being only *that* He is, not *what* He is. It is in their mutual and ongoing confrontation that humanism and traditionalism create the field of tension for the life of spirit.

As a dialectical dynamic, religious humanism is the heir of Socrates and Amos, as I mentioned earlier. Both men criticized the faiths of their contemporaries in the name of faith itself, and they maintained the sanctity of the quest itself. Socrates asserted that "the unexamined life is not worth living," and Amos declared, "Seek Me and live." The Talmud asserts that this verse is the sum and substance of monotheism—without God, life is not worth living.

Since it is in the tension of dialectic that religious humanism comes to light, it becomes necessary for us to regard inter-religious conferences as direct incarnations of the life of faith, not merely as occasional activities of a fire-preventive character. I therefore propose the establishment of interreligious institutes for the purpose of studying their interrelationships in the past, the common tasks in the present day, and the horizons of the future.

We have to urge the validity of the new insight of our times, namely, that interreligious studies and interfaith social action are direct expressions of the life of faith itself. But in view of the difficulties that I described, it is obvious that such endeavors will be helpful only if they are undertaken on a high intellectual plane, at least in the beginning. The concepts and attitudes that have grown up in the hothouse atmosphere of the previous era need to be revised and adjusted to the open air and fresh breezes of our time. We need to guard against new vulgarisms, even as we battle against old forms of fanaticism. So formidable are the obstacles in the way of inter-religious activity that some of our leaders may prefer not to venture out of the ancient, rutted grooves of religious institutions. Such a fainthearted response to the contemporary challenge, however, would be catastrophic to the life of faith and to the destiny of mankind.

It is on the plane of the questing intellect that a genuine dialogue can take place; so, it is in the academic world that our labors must begin. But, from the very beginning, the academic enterprise must be life-centered, oriented toward the winning of the churches and the synagogues to the new approach. For this reason, I propose that we center attention on the building up of institutes of interreligious studies, the structure of which is described in the appended *Plan*.

If the spiritual life of man is to keep pace with his exploding technical progress, we have to provide a permanent setting for the continuous confrontation of the several faiths in a common quest for truth, for love, and for peace. How this goal may be attained in different countries is up to the local leaders of this work to determine. But I submit that the time has come for us to attempt the third stage of interfaith activity —that of planning the ideal city here on earth, a city that would reflect "Jerusalem that is above" on this muddy and bloody planet of ours.

Plan for a Graduate Institute of Interreligious Studies

I. *Purpose*: To promote the understanding in love of the faiths of one's neighbors, as well as his own.

II. *Structure*: A graduate institute, associated with a great university, but financed and operated independently. The staff would consist of professors of the various faiths—Catholicism, Protestantism, Judaism. Hopefully, other faiths would be added later. In addition, guest professors would be invited. *Committed* teachers of each faith would be chosen.

III. *Operation*: The staff members and the holders of fellowships would give regular undergraduate and graduate courses.

33

A certain number of fellowships would be awarded every year to clergymen in various parts of the world, for a year's study on their sabbatical leave.

A certain number of four-day institutes would be run during the year.

IV. *Fields*: The fields of study would comprise:

a) *Textual* studies of one faith in the context of the other faiths, such as, The New Testament and Rabbinic Literature, The Ethics of the Fathers, and Patristic Literature, etc.

b) The *historical* interplay of the faiths.

c) *Philosophical* themes, the meaning of the faith beyond the faiths. Dialogues with men of other disciplines.

d) Ethical and Social Issues.

e) Educational Problem. How to teach the ideals of faith and about religions.

f) Publications in all these areas.

MUTUALLY CHALLENGING,
NOT
MUTUALLY CONTRADICTORY

The differences between Judaism and Christianity were seen as polar opposites not only in the dark centuries of medieval fanaticism but even in the enlightened decades of the modern period. Both Jewish and Christian scholars seemed to feel that in order to establish the validity of one faith they had to denigrate the other. In the modern world, people became more concerned with the ethical philosophies of the various faiths than with their dogmatic theologies. But even the progressive secularization of Western society did not automatically dissipate this *odium theologicum*. On the contrary, every "defender of the faith" was tempted to identify his modernist version of the good life with the natural development of his own religion. Christian scholars felt that they had to prove the "superiority" of their faith to Judaism; otherwise, Christianity would not be the final essence of man's quest for absolute truth. Similarly, Jewish scholars felt that they were called upon to prove the absolute superiority of their historic heritage; otherwise, why bother to carry the Jewish "burden"?

This preoccupation with public relations made it difficult to produce a fair and balanced presentation. Those whose pre-eminent concern was to generate ardor for "Jewish survival" tended to see the contrast between Judaism and Christianity in terms of black and white. One scholar put it, "Judaism is Judaism because it is not Christianity, and Christianity is Christianity because it is not Judaism," as if we were still in the first century, debating whether or not the messianic verses were all "fulfilled" in the career of Jesus. But if we really represent contradictory and irreconcilable philosophies of life, then we should in all honesty withdraw from the public affairs of such countries as England and America, where we constitute a small percentage of the population. Nor should we take it amiss, on this isolationist premise, if the Christian majority organizes to protect the integrity of its "culture."

On the other hand, those who were primarily concerned with the integration of the Jewish group into the general community wrote as if Judaism and Christianity differed only in their respective terminologies. The rhetoric is diverse, but the substance is the same. As usual, the truth lies between the two extremes. Neither Judaism nor Christianity is monochromatic, and their relationship is one of mutuality and challenge, not of antagonism and contradiction. Both "stain the white radiance of eternity"; the resulting spectra of colors and shades are different, but also mutually supplementary.

Every historic tradition, like a mighty river draining many hills and valleys, contains muddy trends as well as clear waters. As Jews and Christians, we do not begin our quest for truth and holiness *de novo*, but as navigators upon the historic streams. Our task is twofold—to promote the flow of the stream and to enhance the purity of its waters. We cannot stop the world in order to get off. We have to accept the fact of diversity among the several streams of faith just as we acknowledge the differences within each faith. If it is through history that God brings us closer to Himself, then we cannot doubt that He employs many and diverse pathways. Nothing is more characteristic of His glory, either in physical nature or in the history of humanity, than the rich diversity of its manifestations.

Once we admit that many ways may lead to God, we no longer feel called upon to prove that only our faith, whatever it be, is true. Then, we begin to discern the different approaches within each historic tradition, and in this process discover instructive parallels in other faiths. We are not antagonists, but neither are we carbon copies of one another. Our differences are not "scandals," as the ancients thought, but sources of enrichment. In fact, the one certain way of stultifying the human spirit is to impose a prefabricated monolith upon it.

In the following analysis of some basic contrasts between the Jewish and Christian tradition, I intend to show that the differences between them are dialectical, rather than contradictory. In a dialectical situation, different positions constitute various combinations of the same elements within the same universe of discourse. There is no one position that excludes any of the elements. Furthermore, this variety of syntheses is essential to progress. The consequence of the interplay of these varied combinations is the creation of a dynamic tension within each group and among the different groups, a tension that generates an ongoing quest. As we stated earlier, our task is to deal with different spectra of light, not with the contrast between light and darkness.

The impression of absolute opposition between Judaism and Christianity is conveyed by a superficial reading of the New Testament and reinforced by the historical "anathemas" that each faith hurled at the other. These mutual denunciations hopefully belong to the past. We know from one of the Genizah fragments that the old form of one of the eighteen benedictions, the *birchat haminim,* did include a condemnation of Christians. But in today's prayer books, there is no trace of such a curse. At the New Delhi Conference of 1961, the World Council of Churches (Protestant) undertook to remove any pejorative references to Jews and Judaism from their literature and to combat anti-Semitism. At the Vatican Council II, the Catholics adopted with great solemnity a similar resolution.

However, an ambiguity persists. Many scholars, chiefly Catholic, maintain that while Jewish people are free from guilt, Judaism continues to be condemned. This unfortunate and pernicious interpretation seems to flow from the pages of the New Testament itself. Indeed, a Jesuit author recently arrived at the conclusion that the New Testament dripped with anti-Semitism.[1] So, too, Cardinal Bea accounts for the ugly epithets directed at the Jews in the Gospel of John as being due to the mutual hostility between Jews and Christians at the time that that Gospel was composed.

As modern people, we are history-conscious; we realize that every age is limited in its understanding of truth by the prevailing cultural context. The Talmudic rabbis declared that "the Torah spoke in the language of men," that is, of the men of that generation. Theological debates in the past were notorious for their acrimony. Who today would want to teach children the words that Luther used in condemning the pope and the Catholics? The study of history makes it possible for us to appropriate from the past that which is good, true, and holy, discarding the profane, the ugly, and the hateful. The penalty for not studying history, it has been said, is to be condemned to repeat it. But, as we see the events of history in their own context, we can separate the eternal seeds of Divine truth from the temporary chaff that belongs to the dead past.

The New Testament is a sacred text for Christians as well as a collection of historical documents. Insofar as it is a text, it is more the locus of instruction than its source, with the vitality of the faith being expressed in the ongoing process of interpretation. It is up to Christians to interpret their fixed texts in keeping with their basic teaching concerning the love of God and the love of man. The function of a religious text is to serve as a telescope, so that the worshipers may look through it and see the heavens of God. In a religious text, the ancient references to people and events are always contemporary, but only in a symbolic sense. It is important therefore for Christians to realize that the hostile references to Jews in the New Testament refer only to *some Jews,* indeed to *some persons,* the denotation being limited in every instance by the context. After all, the apostles and nearly all the authors of the New Testament books were Jews by birth and by conscious conviction. Nearly the entire impetus of anti-Semitism in the Gospels would disappear if the translators of liturgical readings were to substitute the real meaning in every instance for the generic term "Jews," using such terms as the crowd, the enemies, the opponents, the people present, and so on.

The unfortunate impression that Jesus set out to condemn and even to curse the Jewish religion, as it was understood then or since, is not sustained at all by an objective reading of the New Testament in the light of the Apocryphal and Rabbinic writings. This impression is due to the rancorous disputations in patristic literature and in medieval writings. The Gospel of John consists of a narrative section and a theological tract, conceived in the acrid "smog" of ancient polemics. Jewish scholars, since the days of Abraham Geiger, had no difficulty in placing the New Testament within the context of first-century Judaism, which included in addition to the Jerusalem Pharisees, the folk-Pharisees and the adherents of the "Fourth Philosophy," the Sadducees, the Essenes, the Apocalyptic circles, and the Hellenists. Today, with the discovery of the sectarian writings of the Qumran sect, the picture is much clearer.

From the historical viewpoint, two conclusions emerge with great clarity. First, the message of Jesus was stated within the context of Jewish thought at that time. His ethics and his faith were within the prophetic tradition; the only point at issue was whether or not he was the expected Messiah, or "Son of Man." Second, neither the Jews of today nor the Christians of today can identify themselves completely with the positions of their predecessors in the first century. To know that we live within the stream of history is to know that we can no more go home again than a chick can return to the egg from which it came.

The truth of the first proposition becomes clear only through a prolonged study of Rabbinic and New Testament literature. This is why I feel that Christian ministers and Jewish rabbis should become thoroughly familiar with each other's basic literature. If the bitterness of the Jewish-Christian dispute is ever to be allayed, the scholars of both groups must become conversant with the inner depths of the two branches of the same "tree of life."

The truth of the second proposition becomes equally clear to the historian. Outside the fringe group of the ultra-Orthodox, Jews today do not expect to restore the Holy Temple and to bring animal sacrifices upon the altar. Though the ancient prayers are retained in the Orthodox Prayer Book, they convey different shades of meaning. That each worshiper is to regard his heart and mind as a Holy Temple, endeavoring to make it a fit "dwelling place for the *Shechinah*," is a central theme of Philo and the Midrash.[2] Similarly, it has become clear to Christian scholars that the "interim-ethik" of Jesus reflected his conviction of the imminent end of the world and the speedy advent of the World to Come.

No dogma is so passionately affirmed in Judaism as that of the unity of God. Jewish martyrs would breathe their last with the word *ehad* on their lips. On the other hand, the Trinitarian formula is equally basic to Christians—belief in the Father, the Son, and the Holy Ghost. Theologically, the difference is irreconcilable. But as seen from the human viewpoint, the component elements of the doctrine appear in both traditions.

The affirmation of Divine unity in Judaism was not a simplistic dogma that blandly ignored the immanence of the Divine Being as well as His transcendence. Rabbinic Judaism interpreted the two Names of God, *Elohim* and *YHVH,* as referring to the "policy of compassion" as well as to the "policy of law." In a deeper sense, these two "policies" reflect the two manifestations of the Divine, as inexorable law and fixed order in the physical universe, and as love, or the intimacy of personal relations, in human nature. This twofold reality of the Divine Being was expressed by the medieval philosopher Halevi as the contrast between "the God of Aristotle" and "the God of Abraham, Isaac, and Jacob." Halevi maintained that by the power of unaided reason, philosophers can arrive at the notion of a transcendent deity who is the prime mover of the cosmos as a whole, but they cannot experience His reality as the ultimate focus of love.[3] To reach the stage of personal religion, one must undergo a religious experience in which the actual presence of the Divine is felt; hence, one must be either a prophet or a son of the prophet-people. Professor Efros, in a fine poetic study, demonstrated the continuity in Judaism of the tension between the "school of holiness" and the "school of glory."[4] The latter stressed the immanence of the Divine in all the aspects of life; the former stressed the *via negativa,* the negation of all that is not truly Divine. Both approaches are dynamic ways of thinking and feeling, which cannot be reduced to the rigid, static systems of mechanical logic. The history of Judaism could well be written in terms of the dialectical tension between the two schools.

Both aspects of the Divine Being were acknowledged in some of our basic prayers. The formula for every benediction includes an awareness of the Divine as a direct, immediate Presence (*Nochah*) as well as a reference to Him as being hidden and beyond our conceptual grasp (*Nistar*). In the High Holiday liturgy, the Lord is addressed as "Our Father, Our King," taking account of our twofold relation to Him. While He is ever our Sovereign, the Source of Law, we can experience His Presence as our Father only fleetingly, uncertainly, and humbly. So, too, in another portion of the High Holiday liturgy, we refer to our ambiguous status in reference to God—"be it as sons or be it as servants."

In addition to this twofold character of the Divine, there prevailed in Judaism the assurance that the "people of God" contained His Presence in a special way; His *Shechinah* dwelt among His people, "even if they were unclean."[5] And whenever the Israelites were exiled, the *Shechinah* was exiled along with them.[6] To be accepted as a convert to Judaism was "to enter under the wings of the *Shechinah*." The patriarchs, the prophets, and the authors of the sacred tradition were generally understood to be the earthly support of the *Shechinah,* its "chariot" (*merkaba*), as it were.[7] In its intense, concentrated form, the *Shechinah* is experienced as the Spirit of Holiness (*Ruah*

41

Hakodesh), which is the source of prophecy as well as of the right interpretation of Holy Writ. The Spirit of Holiness, again, is not an absolute, definable presence, but like the *Shechinah* it appears in various degrees of intensity, as a function of one's life. A great authority asserted dramatically, "I call heaven and earth to witness that whether a person be an Israelite or a Gentile, a man or a woman, free or slave, the Holy Spirit rests upon him in accordance with his deeds."[8]

The recognition of the several aspects of the Divine enriched the concept of the deity and lent intense fervor to the passionate affirmation of His unity. While the human pathways leading to the nearness of His Presence are diverse, He is one and indivisible, for He is the Ultimate Reality. On this point, Judaism never wavered.

Jewish students of primitive Christianity are perplexed by the question of the origin of the Trinitarian dogma. The contemporary consensus among scholars is that the Gospels of the New Testament were virtually complete by the end of the first century. How then did the sectarian heirs of a living Jewish tradition feel impelled to develop the dogma of the Trinity? To this question historians can only give several hypothetical answers. The following are some of the alternative inquiries:

Did the petrified logic of the Alexandrian school transform the protean dynamism of the Rabbinic conception, translating the ineffable experience of faith into the rigid categories of ancient philosophy?

Did the baptismal formula of Rabbinic Judaism include a reference to the tradition of Israel and the Torah as well as to God, and did the early Christians substitute Jesus for the Torah and the Holy Spirit for the community of Israel?[9]

These questions are indeed most challenging and interesting. Whatever the actual course of events, the Jewish and Christian communities went their separate ways until they became not only mutually incompatible but—what is more—mutually incomprehensible. Today, an intense imaginative effort is needed for Jews and Christians simply to understand one another's concepts of God.

Just as Christians must recognize the infinite richness of the Jewish concept of God, Jews must recognize that Christianity is also a monotheistic faith; they, too, affirm the truth of the *Shema*—"Hear, O Israel, the Lord our God is One." As to how the three persons can at the same time be one is, in their belief, a mystery. Historically speaking, Christianity was the social instrument whereby the pagan gods of Europe, from Aphrodite and Cybele to Jupiter and Wotan, were overcome by the God of Israel. Equally with the Jews, the Christians for three centuries were willing to sacrifice their lives rather than throw a few fistfuls of incense on the altars of the pagan gods.

Psychologically, monotheism implies three assertions:

First, that man is not complete unto himself, but that his very humanity derives from that which is beyond himself and beyond the community to which he belongs.

Second, that the ideal aspirations of man, his quest for the good, the true, and the beautiful converge in the experience of holiness, which relates man to the ultimate source of all values.

Third, that this ultimate source of values is also the source of the forces of nature. He is at once the Good and the Almighty, Pure Being and the Soul of All Souls.

On the psychological level, these beliefs of monotheism bring into being a whole-souled effort to create a secular culture and a secular society, since all human values derive from God. Humanism is therefore implicit in the Judeo-Christian tradition. At the same time, the monotheistic mentality generates a deep discontent with things as they are, a capacity to rise above the spirit of the age in the name of the Divine and an ever renewed determination to advance toward the era of perfection, the Kingdom of Heaven. This tension between the way of the world and the vision of perfection is characteristic of both Judaism and Christianity, though not of the petrified forms of the two faiths.

It is this inner polarity within the God-idea that Christians ignore when they rhapsodize on the contrast between the New Testament concept of God as love and the Biblical or Rabbinic view of Him as being jealous and wrathful as well as loving and forgiving. Our ideas must correspond to life if they are to serve effectively as the goals of life. God is the ultimate Being, in whom three quests converge—all of them infinite—the quest for reality, for the realization of goodness, and for the integration of our self within the all-embracing harmony. Love corresponds only to the second of these quests. Insofar as a simple vision of the Divine Being is needed for liturgical or ethical purposes, the rabbis too spoke of God as "The Merciful One" (*Horahman*) and "The Good" (*Hatov*). Furthermore, to promote the ideal of *imitatio Dei,* they enumerated His ethical attributes—His visiting the sick, His comforting the mourners, His concern for all creatures, and His performance of deeds of loving kindness—but they specifically excluded His "jealousy" from the list of qualities that man is bidden to emulate.[10]

In Judaism, emphasis is put on the deed—*naase venishma,* ("we shall do and we shall heed"). In Christianity, emphasis is placed on the affirmation of belief. The difference is real, basic, and all-pervasive. But there is no continuity of good deeds without some beliefs, assumed if not explicit, and there is no genuine faith that does not seek expression in life.[11] The differences are dialectical, variations of line and shade in a spectrum that runs from end to end. The extremists at both ends can only distort the right balance, and those who would reduce the Jewish way of life to the accumulation of merit on a celestial cash register are as biased as those who fail to see the practical and intellectual dimensions of Christian faith.

In regard to Judaism, we can take our point of departure from the investigations of Strack-Billerbeck, who, in their commentary on the Sermon of the Mount, concluded that the good life in Judaism was simply a mathematical summation of so many good deeds, minus so many sins.[12] The fullness of the response to the challenge of life is thus reduced to a simple mathematical calculation, performed in all likelihood by a celestial I.B.M. machine. Some Jewish scholars, persuaded by the massive evidence accumulated by the diligence of these German savants, prefer to phrase the difference between Judaism and Christianity somewhat more ambiguously, as follows: in Judaism, sin is an action, whereas in Christianity, it is a state of the soul. This half-truth is as pernicious as the reduction of Judaism to a mechanical bookkeeping operation.

Let us note, to begin with, the three dimensions of Jewish piety, as summarized by Simon the Just: "The world stands on three things—on Torah, on worship, and on the deeds of loving-kindness."[13] Torah is the pillar of learning. Can anyone rightly maintain that the intellectual concern was neglected in Judaism? At times, the concept of Torah was exceedingly narrow, but at other times, it was conceived as all-embracing—"longer than the earth is its measure and wider than the sea." In the public life of the Jewish community, the intellectual concern predominated. According to an ancient tradition, it was Rabbi Joshua ben Gomla who established universal and compulsory elementary education in Palestine several generations before the destruction of Jerusalem. The houses of Hillel and Shammai are said to have debated for a long time whether learning or deeds were more important, but both schools apparently agreed that good deeds by themselves were of little consequence.[14] "The ignorant man cannot be pious."[15] Hillel went so far as to say that "he who does not learn is deserving of death."[16]

As to the emotional content of the good life, the pillar of worship is intended to cultivate it. "What is the service of the heart? It is prayer."[17] Needless to say, the discipline of prayer is not subject to slide-rule calculations. It is susceptible to infinite depth. Nor are the requirements of "directing one's heart to heaven" in everything one does merely "ornamentations" of the Jewish position, as Strack-Billerbeck insist, for even in the domain of law (*Halachah*), it is asserted that no outsider can tell whether a person is righteous or wicked. Suppose a thoroughly wicked man betroths a woman "on condition that he is a perfect saint." She is then betrothed to him, because in one second he might have repented deeply of all his sins. Suppose again a well-known perfect saint betroths a woman on condition that he is thoroughly depraved, she is betrothed to him, because in one second he might have entertained an idolatrous thought. In that event, all his meritorious deeds would be accounted as naught.[18]

So Rabbi Judah the Prince, editor of the Mishnah, that typical compendium of "narrow legalism," was reported "to weep and say—'Behold, it is possible to acquire one's world in one hour.' "[19]

The essence of the Jewish position is that we tend to become what we do. The inner core of our self is affected not only by our thoughts and feelings but also by everything that we do. So, "one *mizvah* pulls another *mizvah* in its train and one *sin* leads to another *sin*."[20] But the focus of attention remains the individual, scrutinizing himself in the light of God. Saadia Gaon employed the analogy of the soul being an effulgence of light, in keeping with the verse of Proverbs, "The soul of man is a candle of the Lord, searching his inmost parts." With this analogy in mind, he maintained that every good deed adds to the intensity of the Divine light, while every sin darkens its radiance, as it were, but through repentance "sins may be turned into meritorious deeds."[21] Furthermore, as one rises in the scale of saintliness, his responsibility grows in accordance with his enhanced capacity. "The Holy One, blessed be He, scrutinizes the Saints even to a hair's breadth."[22] Reversing Kant's rule, "Ought implies Can," Judaism maintained the opposite rule, "If you can, you ought. . . ." "If a *mizvah* comes to you, do not delay to perform it. . . ."[23] With great men, the Lord is exceedingly strict.

Rabbi Shimeon and Rabbi Elisha were being led to the execution-block for their violation of Hadrian's law prohibiting the study of Torah. Rabbi Shimeon began to cry. Said Rabbi Elisha,

"Why do you cry?" Rabbi Shimeon replied, "I am not afraid to die, but I don't know what I have done that merits death." Said Rabbi Elisha, "Did a woman ever come to you to ask that you judge her case, and you delayed to attend to her grievance because at that moment you were resting or eating? If so, you may have deserved to die for you delayed justice, even if only for a short time. . . ."[24]

As Judaism was not merely a calculus of deeds, Christianity was far more than assent to a creed. Along with faith, it demanded that its adherents live in accord with "the law of the Spirit."[25] It was through Christian influence that the sexual offenses of Roman society were curbed, that the exposure of children and the abandonment of the aged was stopped, and that the gladiatorial games were discontinued. In the Christian list of virtues, faith, hope, and charity go hand in hand. Paul's hymn to charity or love in the thirteenth chapter of the First Letter to the Corinthians is possibly the noblest expression of an ethical ideal, at once Jewish and Christian. And the Epistle of James is widely regarded as being essentially a Jewish work—"Thou believest that God is one; thou doest well: the demons also believe, and shudder. But wilt thou know, O vain man, that faith apart from works is barren?"[26]

There were times in Catholic history when casuistic legalism triumphed; there were also periods and movements that represented the opposite extreme. The history of religion is filled with warning signs—"Don't walk in the ways that I followed."

In any case, we deal here with different positions in a field of force between two poles, not with a logical contradiction. The Jewish bent is probably more pragmatic and balanced than the Christian faith, which was heroic and whole-souled at its best, but one-sided, extremist, and fanatical, at its worst. The Talmud could interpret Jeremiah 16:11, to mean that the Lord, as it were, says, "Leave me alone, but keep my Torah." Christian dogmatics could hardly become that life-centered. But was Walt Whitman Jewish in spirit, when he wrote, "Ah, more than any priest, O Soul, we too believe in God. But with

47

the mystery of God we dare not dally."[27] On the other hand, in the Law of the Talmud, denial of Divine revelation, even in part, was punished by endless tortures in hell, though for all other sins, twelve months in hell was the maximum punishment.[28]

"The old Jewish religion is accordingly a religion of the most complete self-redemption; for a redeemer-savior who dies for the sins of the world, it has no room."

In these words a great Christian scholar summed up his analysis of the Jewish concept of redemption from sin.[29]

Now, it is quite obvious that the second half of the sentence is true. There was no room for a redeemer-savior, simply because the Lord is the Redeemer and the Savior. He certainly would "not have to die for the sins of the world" by way of atonement. To be sure, the Talmud tells of Rabbi Judah the Prince, whose sufferings atoned for the sins of his generation.[30] Great saints voluntarily undertake to suffer for the sins of others.[31] So the ten martyrs, whose story is told on the Day of Atonement, accept the heavenly verdict to die for the sins of the sons of Jacob who sold Joseph into slavery.[32] In a picturesque myth, the Talmud tells of the Archangel Michael sacrificing the souls of saints on a heavenly altar—i.e. saints who suffer for others.[33] All these passages do not detract from the truth of the author's second statement.

But the first statement is altogether false. Does not the Hebrew Bible from cover to cover stress the dependence of man upon the favor of God? Abraham is told, "Walk before Me, and be complete." It is possible for man to attain completeness, but only when he walks "before God," in full awareness of his dependence.

The Midrash contrasts Abraham's "walking *before* God" with Enoch's "walking *with* God" to show the superiority of Abraham. It draws upon the analogy of a person walking with his sons· the bigger boy can walk before his father, the smaller boy needs the steadying hand of his father. The spiritually mature person needs less of God's help in order to walk in His ways.[34]

Still, Abraham is the prototype of the covenanted "believer" who lives by his faith. In Micah's famous admonition, "to do justice, to love kindness, and to walk humbly with the Lord, thy God,"[35] we find again that human goodness is not enough; there must be also the continued feeling of humble companionship.

Commenting on the first of the Ten Commandments, the Tannaitic Midrash declares, "If you receive My Kingship in love, you will receive My decrees."[36] The ethical principles of the Ten Commandments derive from faith in God as the redeemer from enslavement. Paul was simply restating a common theme of Jewish-Hellenistic propaganda when he wrote that the moral perversions and unnatural vice of the pagans were due to their rejection of monotheism.[37]

Rabbinic Judaism cannot, by the wildest stretch of the imagination, be equated with Buddhism, in its original form, when man was expected to work out his own salvation. Not for one moment did the rabbis imagine that they could get along without God or that the precepts of the Torah worked automatically. But they insisted that God is ever ready to help. "He who wishes to become pure, will receive help [from above], he who wishes to become unclean, the doors are opened for him."[38]

That man is free to choose is a basic principle in Judaism, but this freedom is effective only because "God is near to those who call upon him in truth."[39] It was the false Messiah, Shimeon bar Kochba, who, in the pride that comes before a fall, called out, "Don't help us and don't stand in our way."[40]

Anyone who attends the service of the synagogue, especially on the High Holidays, and hears the recurrent calls for God's help and His forgiveness, cannot possibly imagine that Judaism is self-redemptive.

Yet, there is a grain of truth in this statement, a grain that would be evident to one coming from the Christian world. Judaism maintained that man was not condemned to sin or to perdition. Paul's complaint that the Law could not bring salvation because it assumed a strength of will to do the right, a degree

49

of strength that man by himself did not possess, was to the Rabbinic Jew both true and false. Paul's example of not being able to resist the desire to covet was his way of pointing to the infinite upper dimension of Jewish piety. The minimal requirement of external compliance could be kept. How about its outer reaches? Man by himself could not resist the Evil Desire, which doubled as Satan and tripled as the Angel of Death.[41] But the loyal Jew or the righteous convert is not alone. God is with him, and the Torah is the right antidote to the Evil Desire.[42] Through the Torah, man opens himself up to God's help. "Man's Evil Desire renews itself every day, seeking to kill him; were it not for the help of the Holy One, blessed be He, it would be impossible for him to overcome it."[43]

As to how the Torah works to curb the propensity to sin, different views prevailed in keeping with the tensions within Judaism between the mystical and the rationalistic emphasis. To the mystics, the effect of Torah-life was to remove the taint of "original sin." The Talmud asserts: "When the Serpent cohabited with Eve, he injected corruption into her. The Israelites who stood at Sinai, this corruption was taken away from them. The nations of the world, who did not stand at Sinai, this corruption is still in them. As to the converts, their souls were not at Sinai, but the angels of their souls were there."[44]

To the rationalists, it was the active study of Torah that kept a person from sinning. For sin is largely a surrender to folly: "A person commits a sin only when the spirit of folly had entered into him."[45]

The rabbis maintained that the best way to combat the Evil Desire was "to pull him [i.e. the Evil Desire] toward the House of Study."[46] We must remember, however, that the House of Study concerned itself with teaching and philanthropy as well as learning. Instructive in this connection is the high praise accorded to Rabbi Hiyah for the many-sidedness of his efforts in behalf of Torah: he mingled philanthropy and communal leadership with his intellectual endeavors.[47]

In Judaism, as in Christianity, God's help is essential to man's struggle; the difference is in the emphasis on man's freedom and God's evenhanded justice in Judaism, whereas in some Christian faiths the arbitrariness of Divine grace and man's total helplessness are stressed.

As man confronts God, he must be aware both of his own greatness and his littleness. He is Godlike in the gift of freedom that was bestowed upon him so that he can be a "partner in creation." But he is also "dust and ashes," and all the merit that he can gain is as naught. The moment he claims merit, he convicts himself of laboring for the sake of a reward and of pride. Moses was the greatest of the prophets, and yet when he pleaded for the privilege of entering the Promised Land, he used the Hebrew word which recalls the term "an unearned gift." According to the Midrash, Moses confessed that all his achievements were as nothing; he did not deserve any reward at all. He begged for alms.[48]

No contrast between Judaism and Christianity is more frequently invoked than the opposition between the guidelines of law and the spontaneous freedom of love. This opposition is given a new slant in every generation, because in every age the young and the progressive tend to rebel against the fetters of tradition. What is more natural than to identify reverence for law with the old dispensation and to sanction the new ideal as a contemporary expression of the freedom of the elect. In the Age of Enlightenment, Kant described Judaism as a surrender to an alien law. Later, Nietzsche interpreted his attempt to forge a new ethic of freedom for the supermen of the future as a resumption of the Christian struggle against the slavish submissiveness of Judaism. To the "emancipated" ones in the modern world, "free love" had its attractions, regardless of the rhetoric involved. And today, the exponents of "situation-ethic" maintain once again that for the pure of heart nothing is forbidden. Sufficient unto the moment of decision is the spontaneous outburst of liberating love.

51

Here we have an excellent example of the dialectical relationship between two polar principles. In the course of its fulfillment, love seeks to mold itself into an enduring social reality. Those who are truly in love, not merely in the grip of passion, look beyond the moment and beyond themselves to the kind of social structure that will make their love permanent. They enter into a marriage-covenant, even as Israel and the Lord concluded such a covenant. To be sure, the legal bonds of marriage become irksome and even intolerable when the glory of love is gone. So, unlike the Qumran sectarians and the early Christians, the Pharisaic rabbis permitted divorce when a marriage could not be saved. Human relations need to be motivated and exhilarated by love, even as they must be governed by law.

In the Hebrew Scriptures, the people are urged to love the Lord, their God, with all their heart, with all their soul, and with all their might. To guard against the danger of wallowing in the merely sentimental and the merely self-congratulatory kinds of love, the Torah goes on to articulate its meaning. One must establish institutions of learning for the young; one must build his home in this spirit, that it become a sanctuary; and one must bring this elusive and ethereal love of God into the marketplaces and the court houses.[49] (In ancient times, the sessions of the courts were held in the gates of the cities.)

The word "Torah" was translated in the Septuagint as "The Law," but actually it means a body of teaching. Only a small fraction of the Holy Scriptures consists of laws; for the most part it is an attempt to articulate a philosophy of life by way of stories, admonitions, and general principles.

The rabbis of the Talmud were preachers and teachers, as well as legal scholars. They knew that the interior life could not be molded by laws alone, though it is usually necessary to make use of laws in order to foster those social institutions and personal habits that are most conducive to the life of the spirit. They ordained that people should worship three times daily: perhaps the very act of worship would generate the feelings of love and devotion. "Out of their observance of the Commandments, *not* for their own sake, they will come eventually to observe them properly, for their own sake."[50]

In general, the rabbis sought to guard against the desiccation of feeling in the observance of Commandments by stressing the importance of *kavanah* ("the right intention"). It was the special function of the Aggadists to emphasize the importance of the life of feeling beyond the Law. The words of Aggadah "pull the heart." Naturally, the major themes of Aggadic literature reflect the ebb and flow of the various tides of thought at different times—the tides of mysticism, individual romanticism, ethnic romanticism, rationalism, asceticism, and various combinations of these drives.

One basic conviction runs through the diverse periods of Jewish thought; namely, without the firm structure of laws, there can be no room for freedom. "There is no truly free man, except for the one who labors in the Torah."[51] As I mentioned previously, the rabbis recognized the universal Torah of mankind as well as the specific Torah of Israel. The non-Jewish laws may have varied in detail, but they had to correspond to those Divine laws that were firmly fixed in the structure of creation—the prohibition of murder, adultery, stealing, cheating, etc. Once the basic beams of the steel-structure of society were erected, room would be made for the feelings of compassion, love, and forgiveness to ease the strains of society. "Jerusalem was destroyed only because people insisted on their legal rights"[52] (and did not practice compassion). But if the firm foundations of law were not maintained, then society would turn into a shapeless heap and the imagined freedom of the multitude would turn into ashes. In our own day, new laws had to be instituted for the purpose of promoting the status of the Negro, though it is true that the feelings of prejudice can only be overcome by education. But, within limits, the Law itself is an instrument of education.

To be sure, the structure of law must be continually rearranged in keeping with changing circumstances and the abiding concerns of love and compassion. If it is the function of law to serve the goals of stability and justice, it is also the function of lawmakers to respond to the special needs of the poor and the weak with compassion and charity. The rabbis asserted that strict justice must be supplemented by these two principles—"to walk in the paths of the good," and "to do that which is right and good."[53] The Law strikes a balance between contending claims, but the balance must be constantly readjusted.

Some of the debates between Jesus and Pharisaic scholars could have been conducted within the framework of the Law, as it existed at that time. The laws of the Tosefta and Mishnah were compiled several generations later. What kind of healing should be permitted on the Sabbath day, in view of the fact that the Sabbath was made for man, not man for the Sabbath? What should be done if a person abuses the law of vows in order to release himself from the obligation to honor and support his parents? Should the harsh law of the Torah in regard to adultery be applied literally, or should it be suspended? Do those who keep themselves "pure" from defilement and study the Law have an automatic advantage over the humble poor who must work at their trade from dawn to dusk?

The rabbis allowed people to do on the Sabbath whatever was needed "for the saving of a life," even if the danger was exceedingly dubious. They regarded an oath "against a precept of the Torah"[54] as invalid; in the case of a valid vow, they would have compelled the person to ask for an annulment of his vow. The annulment of improper or hasty vows was a Pharisaic invention.[55] Sometime before the year 65 c.e., Rabbi Johanan ben Zakkai declared "the ordeal of the adulterous woman" to be no longer in effect, "since there were so many adulterers."[56] Rabbi Akiba would have suspended the laws of capital punishment. "The rabbis of Yevneh would say daily, after concluding their studies, 'I am a creature and my colleague is a creature. I work in the city, he works in the field. I get up early for my work, he gets up early for his work. As he does not boast of his work, I don't boast of mine; lest you say, I do much and he does little, we have learned, whether one does much or little, what counts is that one direct his heart to heaven.' "[57]

Paul's contrast of the freedom of the spirit with bondage to the Law belongs to a totally different order of belief than that of the rabbis. He believed that his generation was on the threshold of the Messianic Age and that those whom he converted were "baptized by the Spirit." Living in this world, they were already guided by the "law of the Spirit" which was to prevail fully after the coming of the Messiah "with power." The prophecy of Jeremiah had been fulfilled already. The Law was now written on the tablets of the hearts of those who were converted. It was hard for him to face up to the fact that the Second Coming would be long delayed. In his First Letter to the Corinthians, he wrote: "Behold, I tell you a mystery: We all shall not sleep, but we shall all be changed, in a moment, in the twinkling of an eye, at the last trump: for the trumpet shall sound, and the dead shall be raised incorruptible, and we shall be changed."[58]

And in his First Letter to the Thessalonians, he offers a more detailed description, on the authority of Jesus: "For this we say unto you by the word of the Lord, that we that are alive, that are left unto the coming of the Lord, shall in no wise precede them that are fallen asleep. For the Lord himself shall descend from heaven, with a shout, with the voice of the archangel, and with the trump of God: and the dead in Christ shall rise first; then we that are alive, that are left, shall together with them be caught up in the clouds, to meet the Lord in the air: and so shall we ever be with the Lord."[59]

His own age then was an interim period between the First Coming, marking the inauguration of the Messianic Age, and the manifestation of the "World to Come." Apart from his "spiritual" vision of the Messianic Era, we may well inquire whether the rabbis believed that the *mizvoth* of the Torah would be superseded in the "days of the Messiah." We read in Talmud and Midrash about a "new Torah," to be given by the Messiah; also, that nearly all the holidays would no longer apply, that the *mizvoth* would no longer be valid in the eschatological future (*le-atid la-va*), even that the flesh of the pig would then be permitted.[60]

At a later time, Maimonides laid down as a rule that the same laws would still apply in the Messianic Age. But, then, other views may have circulated in the first century.

In any case, the Christian Church did not proceed to live without laws. The Catholic Church built up a more rigid law "for those who would be perfect" than the Pharisees would have allowed, for the latter maintained that in God's design, "there is no man without woman, and no woman without man, and not the two of them without the Divine Presence."[61] In addition to the complex canon laws, the Church took for granted the existence of Roman law.

Therefore, we cannot speak of two contrasting principles, but only of two different emphases and starting points in the same complex of ideas.

In Judaism, the Law is God-given, but it is obligatory for Jews only because they accepted it voluntarily. Generation after generation grow into the same obligation; metaphorically speaking, "their souls had taken the oath at Sinai."[62] Every individual shares in the responsibility of the community, and the community as a whole is sustained by the "merit of the fathers" and burdened by their sins. We live within the stream of history.[63]

To the Reform and Conservative Jews, the Law does not exist as a separable, inflexible entity. It is part of the stream of the living tradition whereby the contemporary community absorbs the spiritual momentum of previous generations. Even as each generation appropriates for itself the lessons of the past, it ingests the "living kernel" and rejects the "dead shell." We have to retain the historical patterns, but improve them, when needed, in order to come ever closer to the vision of perfection as it looms on the horizon. The balance must be kept between the way, as it is legally structured, and the mystical vision, as it glows in the distance.

How does this balanced approach relate to today's "situation-ethics" and the "new morality"? I believe that we face here the perennial challenge of those who see only one side of life. Of course, there are occasions when the spirit of the Law makes necessary the repudiation of the letter of the Law.

Bar Kappara pointed out that there is one verse which encompasses the whole of the Torah: "In all thy ways know Him, and He will direct thy paths."[64] Rava, commenting on the same verse, declared that even through acts of sin, we may on occasion serve God.[65] Those occasions are the exceptions which prove the rule. Basically, the spontaneity of feeling is insufficient because morality consists of structured love and of justly distributed concern. If law is the application of reason to society, ethics is the application of reason to the individual's fund of love—his love of self, of others, and of God. It springs into existence when the judgment of reason impinges on the subjective feelings of love. The spirit of objectivity is rarely present in those moments of temptation and stress, when an act of decision is needed.

A law-structured faith is of its own momentum likely to err in the following directions: in the externalization and desiccation of the interior life of faith, in the substitution of fear and habit for love and spontaneity, in giving the past undue power over the present, and in overemphasizing the role of the community as against the individual. It is liable to these errors, but it can overcome them if it remains open to the challenge of a faith that stresses the opposite emphases. So, too, a love-centered faith may err in the direction of individual capriciousness, of sentimentality, of instability, of irrationality, and of extremism. The challenge of a communal-minded and pragmatic faith is likely to keep it from succumbing to these dangers. And God dwells in this mutual need.

As Christians were wont to glorify their faith by using a caricature of Judaism for their foil, so Jewish scholars were tempted to do likewise. They identified the many-sided historic heritage of Judaism with their own modernist "enlightened" faith, and then they proceeded to contrast it with a primitive or medieval version of Christianity. Of all who indulged in this pastime, Leo Baeck, the saintly rabbi of Berlin and Bergen Belsen, was the fairest and the most knowledgeable. His analysis of the contrast between Judaism and Christianity is therefore of the greatest interest to us.

In his brilliant essay on "Romantic Religion," he distinguishes between two kinds of religion—the classical and the romantic. "Judaism is the classical religion, and Christianity, compared with it, the romantic religion."[66] He takes his definition of romanticism from the writers of the German post-Enlightenment period. F. Schlegel defined the romantic approach as "one which treats sentimental material in a phantastic form." Exultant emotionalism, then, and mythology are the two stigmata of romanticism. Baeck cites as corroborating evidence Schleiermacher's definition of religion as "the feeling of absolute dependence." For a romantic faith, "thinking is only a dream of feeling,"[67] and even its longing is not directed outward toward the community and the world, but it is a form of self-intoxication. All law, all action, all purpose is foreign to its nature. Laws are suspended by the "miraculous"; action is shrouded in mystery and turned into sacraments; there is no purpose in life but to learn to "enjoy" the Divine. In its dream-like universe, ancient images recur again and again, reflecting the dark drives of the unconscious.

In essence, according to Baeck's analysis, the Dionysiac orgies of the pre-Socratic Greek world represented the dynamic core of the Christian religion.[68] In these popular hysterical cults, the individual was given the feeling of being "chosen" by the god, who dies and is reborn. The various Hellenistic "mystery-religions," which tempered somewhat the savage frenzy of the Dionysiac cult, offered salvation or immortality to the individual by arranging for him to share in the life cycle and resurrection of the dying god. In Christianity, the vital essence is still the ancient pagan myth, while the rhetoric of Judaism is only an outer façade. The victory of Christianity, he concludes, was in reality the victory of this romanticism, which glorified "the sentimental myth of the redeeming savior."[69]

In Baeck's view, Paul carried out the "world-historical" mission of fusing the "secrecy-wrapped Jewish wisdom" with the generalized faith of the mystery-religions. "The genuinely romantic Pauline faith with its heteronomy of life, with the passivity on which it is founded, can confront a culture only as an outsider, without any real access to it. . . ."[70]

Admitting that there were stirrings of "social consciousness" in the Christian world from time to time, Baeck attributes them to the impact of the Old Testament. "Many phenomena which seem to refute these assertions are merely the exceptions which confirm the rule; for they have grown on the Old Testament soil of Calvinism and Baptism."[71]

It was the sad fate of Dr. Leo Baeck to endure the incredible horrors of the Nazi frenzy, and as a sensitive scholar, he was aware of the deep roots of Nazism in the romantic movement of the nineteenth century. We can therefore understand why he was so bitterly sensitive to the sickly stigmata of German, especially Lutheran, romanticism.

If our tradition is truly rational and fair-minded, we have to recognize that romanticism and classicism are inextricably blended in Judaism as well as in Christianity. What are the Psalms, if not lyrical expressions of emotional piety? Professor Heschel writes of the "Divine pathos" in the prophetic books. Whatever else the prophets were, they did not confront their contemporaries with Olympian calm and serene, measured reflections. If romantic religion centers on the theme of "chosenness," was not the very core of Jewish consciousness precisely this assurance of being chosen through the patriarchs? As to the centrality of myth, the God of Israel did not die to rise again, but the notion of a suffering people, suffering saints, a suffering Messiah, and even a suffering *Shechinah*, were not alien to Judaism.[72]

The romantic-mystical faith of Paul can be understood only when it is viewed within the perspective of the feverish expectancy of his time. Paul gave his life for what he conceived to be a sacred commandment—to save as many Jews and

59

Gentiles as possible before the final curtain of Judgment Day was lowered. Far from being a Germanic poet, daydreaming about the "beauties of the Night," Paul braved all kinds of danger in order to fulfill his mission. He collected money "for the poor in Jerusalem" and he admonished his converts to abide by the noblest ethical teachings of Judaism. His hymn on love or charity was a magnificent expression of a "great rule of the Torah."[73] Nor did he set out to defy the canons of reason. To be sure, he refused to base his faith on reason and he insisted that his faith derived from an overwhelming experience. He argued against "the Greeks who seek wisdom and the Jews who want a sign," but his letters were magnificent efforts to square his new faith with the reason of the Greeks and the "signs" that were given to the Jews. He was forever struggling against both the Jew and the Greek who dwelt inside of him. And when he spoke of the impossibility of fulfilling the Law, he cited as an example the prohibition of "coveting," a prohibition that belonged to the "duties of the heart," which were infinite in scope. To the truly pious, the Law was unfulfillable, precisely because it contained this infinite dimension of interior feeling. Similarly, on the High Holidays, we acknowledge the vanity of our deeds and affirm that only through the undeserved favor of God can we hope for salvation. In Judaism, too, the saints thought they were sinners and the sinners thought they were saints. I cannot agree that Paul was unconcerned with ethics and with people.

As to primitive Christianity, why overlook the fact that the Jerusalem community was originally founded on the basis of sharing all property?[74] It was, therefore, far from being a group of LSD enthusiasts. After the initial frenzy was dissipated, the Christian Church set out to organize a vast network of philanthropic institutions, paralleling those of the synagogue. According to Harnack, this network of charities did more to spread the faith than any of the dogmas of the Church.

Baeck contrasts the romantic "thou hast" with the classical "thou shalt." The former is a feeling of possession, reveling in its own glory; the latter is a command to act. We may well ask whether this is in fact the way faith is experienced. Is it not always double-edged, affirming a commitment to act as well as a feeling of possession? "For you the Lord has chosen to be unto him a treasure-people . . . therefore. . . . " In another essay, Baeck distinguishes between the components of "mystery" and "commandment" in faith. This distinction is too facile, made to order for the contrast that he aims to demonstrate. Actually, the basic paradox of faith is tension between "possession" and "privation." We know that we belong to a realm of meaning and harmony beyond and above ourselves. But as soon as we begin to spell out that which is "ineffable," to use Professor Heschel's term, we depart somewhat from the central experience. We depart as much by listing ritual commandments as by formulating dogmatic creeds. The ethical and the esthetic, the mysterious and the transcendental, as well as the ethical and the immediate, belong to the creative moment of faith. We may rightly stress the notion of duty and commandment, but we must not forget that Judaism ranked the response of love as the highest form of Divine service. Of all the seven types of Pharisees, the only desirable one is the "Pharisee out of love," who serves the Lord "like Abraham, our father."[75]

The category of a free response is neither "mystery" nor "commandment." It avoids the basic pitfalls of the two forms of Orthodoxy: the one deriving from an excess of legalism, the other from the dark frenzy of mysticism. In responding to the challenge of Divine love, we give expression to our feelings in our own unique way. This kind of piety, beautifully articulated in the writings of Buber, Rosenzweig, and Heschel, is more characteristic of the modern Jew than the one which is patterned after Kant's categorical imperative. Nor was the free response unknown to the Talmudists, though on the whole they preferred the virtue of humble obedience.

M. H. Luzzato explains that a high level of piety (*hasidut*) consists in doing more than is required, "to invent new ways of pleasing his Creator, demonstrating his awareness of the Divine Majesty."[76] The Hasidic movement of the eighteenth century was merely a resurgence of earlier currents of romantic-mystical piety. "Greater is he who does a good deed because he is commanded than he who does it even though he is not commanded."[77]

In general, Baeck's way of contrasting Judaism and Christianity breaks down because it does not take into account the many variations within the two faiths. Baeck himself was a noble exponent of philosophical or rationalistic Judaism, which scorned the myths and phantasies as well as the rites and dogmas of popular religion. But Judaism as a historical faith contained romantic, mystical, and mythical strands as well as those of classical wisdom. Had it been conceived in the wisdom of moderation and classical balance, Judaism would not have produced the saintly martyrs that assured its survival. Was it the serene quest for the golden mean and the avoidance of extremes that led the Jews of the Rhineland to slaughter their wives and children lest they be led to the baptismal fount?

The line of demarcation between Christianity and Judaism consists of a wide and deep gulf, which was carved out by historic forces. It is by no means so simple as the division between the Religion of Reason and the Religion of Sentiment. Actually, according to Harnack, the dogmas of the Christian creed evolved out of the synthesis of Hellenistic logic and Christian piety. In the same way, the legalistic structure of Rabbinic Judaism was due to the combination of scriptural tradition and the logic of Alexandrian grammarians. Both religions are perpetually in danger of succumbing to the disease of fossilization, a disease which in Christianity takes the form of a frozen creed, and in Judaism, the form of a rigid legalism. In both cases, the fresh winds of thought and sentiment are needed if the inherited religion is to function as a living faith.

It is possible for man to assume three attitudes toward the world. He can either assert that he alone is the source of all values, or he can recognize his absolute dependence upon an external power, or he may attempt to maintain an uneasy balance between the two attitudes. The first approach leads to one or another form of humanism, the second leads to an absolutist faith, the third to a humanist faith.

In primitive times, man was keenly conscious of his dependence upon a multitude of natural forces. He needed the bounties of rain, of the winds, of a fertile soil, and he sought protection against locusts, birds, and animals. His religion consisted of the worship of nonhuman and subhuman forces. The rivers, the mountains, the powerful animals, the mystery of fire, were then objects of worship, with the creative play of the imagination generating the myths reflecting this faith.

The birth of civilization consisted in the emergence of organized societies that were able to tame some of the forces of nature and introduce a measure of order, well-being, and security. Thus, in Egypt and in Babylonia, the swamps and jungles of the Nile and the Euphrates were reclaimed by the building of drainage and irrigation canals. This organized effort of a whole people turned the annual overflow of these rivers into a wonderful blessing, bringing a high degree of prosperity to these lands. The individual was no longer utterly dependent upon the caprice of natural forces, but his life was now subject to the will of the king or the state. The result of this new situation was to fuse the worship of nature with the deification of society. The god of one or another natural force became also the god of a city-state, or of an empire, or of a royal dynasty.

With the increase of security and well-being, individual sages began to make their appearance. They were stimulated either by the official wisdom-literature of the temples or by the challenge of competing cultures and traditions. Among the commerce-minded Greeks, these sages discovered a source of authority within themselves. Generally, in each religious culture, the wonder of wisdom was fused with the inherited tradition; but, once discovered, the light of wisdom could not be confined within the walls of tradition. Wherever the priests did not keep abreast of the times, the sages struck out on their own. The splendid explosion of Hellenic philosophy was made possible by the relative weakness of Greek religion. Aside from occasional outbursts of popular frenzy, the philosopher could exult in the independence of his own reason. Protagoras expressed this newly discovered sense of man's importance in the classic formula "Man is the measure of all things, of things that are that they are, of things that are not that they are not." Thus, a self-sufficient, individualist humanism was born.

Socrates rejected both the individualist humanism of the Sophists and the popular gods of his day. He knew that he did not know, but he also knew that objective truth and goodness and beauty existed. He dedicated his life to the search for truth, for "the unexamined life is not worth living." With Socrates and Plato, philosophical religion was born, with emphasis on philosophy.

In Israel, the evolution of ideas followed a different course. Owing to a progressive deepening of thought, from Abraham to Moses, and Moses to Isaiah, the concepts of both God and man were radically altered. Instead of the gods of nature, the Israelite worshiped the God who is beyond and above nature. And man was now regarded, not as a self-sufficient, talking biped, but as a being capable of reflecting the "Image of God."

"Complete thou shalt be with the Lord thy God":[78] man is completely himself only when he is seen in conjunction with his Creator. And God is not simply a mysterious Being, thinking of Himself, as in Aristotle, or contemplating his own navel, as in India; He looks at the poor and the lowly of spirit.[79] His will is a steadfast love of and concern for "all who call unto Him." He is the source of goodness as well as of truth and reality.

Man and God were now brought into a dialectical relation, that is, one cannot think of man without God, or of God without man.

The result of the dialectical tension was to effect a synthesis between man's conscience and intelligence, on the one hand, and the Divine Will, on the other hand. The wisdom of the sage, the moral fervor of the prophet, and the priestly myth and ritual were blended together in one dynamic world-view.

In the moments of its maturity, the Jewish religion was like an electric arc, with its radiant glow arising from the escalation of spirit between the Infinite Being and the infinite depth of human nature. The resultant light was at once humanistic and religious—humanistic in the affirmation of the worth of the individual and of his capacity to reason and to judge, and religious in the assertion of an ultimate focus of loyalty that is beyond man and beyond nature.

But these momentary flashes were invariably unstable. The will of God was either concretized into specific commands, all too specific, or it was enwrapped in a monopolistic mystery, all too monopolistic and all too mysterious. Or, at the other end of the spectrum, various temporary and partial human ambitions, individual and collective, came to overlay and distort the "Image of God" in man.

It is only by returning again and again to the basic elements of our human situation that we can recapture the pristine glow of faith that is the heritage of Christians as well as Jews.

Today, the essential confrontation is not only between the various religions but also within each religion, and between the religions on the one hand and the secular ideologies on the other hand. Within each historic faith, the struggle is on between those who sense its living tensions and those for whom the sanctified solutions of the past are sufficient. The secular ideologies of the day—nationalism, communism, individualism— are so many forms of man's self-worship, for man may worship his own individual self, as did the Sophists, or his collective human family, the nation, or the all-absorbing state.

Between the strident secularists and the absolutists, the men of living faith, be they Jews or Christians, will pursue their endless quest, avoiding the two polar extremes. Aware of their ignorance as well as their beliefs, they will appreciate the unity of the goal and the diversity of the pathways. They will welcome the challenge of differences in religion as the stimulus needed to keep the faith alive and fresh. Jews, Christians, secularists—all need the other's insights. In this need is God.

NEW GROUNDS
FOR A
JEWISH-CHRISTIAN SYMBIOSIS

It is a sad commentary on the tragic momentum of human affairs that in the mid-twentieth century people should still wonder whether a genuine symbiosis of Judaism and Christianity is possible. But then the melancholy records of history remind us that the "interfaith smile" can wear exceedingly thin. In Renaissance Italy, princes of the Church studied Hebrew, Christians occasionally attended the synagogue and listened to learned discourses by rabbis, and Jews at times listened to the great preachers of the Church. Half a millennium later, Christian Europe was still so beguiled by the "mystery" of Jewish existence that large numbers could separate themselves in feeling and thought from the "non-Aryans" and passively tolerate their condemnation to total annihilation. The Hitlerian interlude shocked many people into the belief that the dragon-seeds of mythological anti-Semitism are deeply imbedded in the mass-mind of Christian people.

To be sure, Nazism was essentially as anti-Christian in ideology as it was avowedly anti-Jewish in practice. In fact, it was anti-Jewish only because it was anti-Christian, seeking to substitute the warlike myth of Teutonism for the egalitarian ethics of Judeo-Christian tradition. The basic "ideology" of Nazism in which the Jew figured as a mythical being, who, like Satan, knows God and still defies Him, could only have arisen in a milieu that was haunted by the ghosts of medieval Christianity. Men like Hjalmar Schacht and Von Papen, deeply Christian though they thought they were, could bring themselves to collaborate with the nihilistic Nazis, and even go along part of the way with the anti-Semitic program of isolating the Jews and pushing them back into the medieval ghetto. In his autobiography, Schacht claims that he only knew of the official Nazi program concerning the Jews that called for the removal of their influence from public life. Such a program he could have approved as a "Christian," i.e. a neomedieval Christian who repudiated the liberalism and humanism of the modern world. After all, did the original Nazi program differ materially from the pattern established by the Fourth Lateran Council, 1215 C.E., and continued with only minor variations down to the period of the liberal revolutions? Whether or not his apology be believed, the fact is that good Christians like Pastor Niemöller did hail the coming of Hitler to power as "the end of fourteen years of darkness." We cannot ignore the fact that the underside of Christian myth and symbolism puts the Jew in a special metaphysical category, shunting him "out of this world," as it were, for to it, the Jew is a satanic mystery, assuming in every age the diabolic guise that best suits the hates and prejudices of the populace.

It is therefore by no means an idle exercise for us to consider whether a genuine basis exists for an enduring symbiosis of Judaism and Christianity.

In both Judaism and Christianity, there is an ongoing tension between myth and the living substance of faith. It is not possible for any organized, institutional faith to escape completely the trammels of myth and metaphor, symbol and ritual; hence, the frustration of nineteenth-century liberal theology in both the Jewish and Protestant camps. In relation to the Divine, we can hardly begin to articulate any insight, celebrate any experience, or confirm any values without launching into the realm of mythology. But while a myth adumbrates the Divine Being, it also limits Him. Hence, there is the paradox of faith: it must employ myths and transcend them, at one and the same time. If God cannot be grasped, only pointed to, we must guard against the pointer itself being worshiped. In practice, the tension between the myth-building and the myth-dissolving faculties generates the dynamic thrust for the continued growth of the spirit of faith.

Myth is more than a metaphor, or a parable, or even a whole string of such figures of speech. In the first place, it is collective and traditional in character, not personal, arbitrary, and contemporary. It is the religious language of a historic community, utilizing the imagery of children and appealing to the instincts of the masses. Secondly, it is more than language, in that it points to a reality instead of designating an event or describing a phenomenon. Employing concrete images, myth aims at the penumbra of meaning that clings to its terms, addressing itself to associations, below as well as on the surface of consciousness. Thirdly, myth, like religion, is directed to the whole person, to his will and feeling, as well as to his reason. Thus, its meaning is fully conveyed only after it has been accepted. It must be taken up as if it were true in order that its effective meaning might be embraced.

In this sense, myth is an inescapable phase of religion. It is a concrete representation of the unknowable, an imaginary account of that which passes the imagination as well as the understanding. While it speaks of the transhistorical and the metaphysical, it is immediately and directly related to the deepest concerns and anxieties of our daily existence.

Faith, on the other hand, is the living kernel of a religious tradition. It is the human quest for the reality behind the phenomena, for rootage in the soil of eternity subsisting beneath the flux of time, for valid and enduring moral truth in the midst of changing values. From the human side, it is both possession and privation: a feeling of assurance in regard to the ultimate—of eternity, reality, and truth; a feeling that whatever we have, experience, and know is not ultimate, not eternal, not real, not true. Many different syntheses of the two phases of dynamic faith are possible. As a human experience, faith is a living, progressive event, but at any one time the sacred tradition as a whole is a static body of "certainties"—revealed beliefs, rites, fears, and consolations.

Myths correspond to the possession phase of faith, reflecting the crystallized insights and values of previous generations. They establish the context for the evocation and fortification of the religious spirit. But insofar as it is genuinely alive, a religion is dynamic and progressive. New facts come to light, novel situations emerge. The insufficiencies of the old myths are exposed, and the creative spirit then requires the reinterpretation of the old myths or the creation of new ones.

The tension between myth and faith relates to the three central foci of religion—the nature of God, the character and destiny of the human soul, and the meaning of the good life. That the Supreme Being exists and that His Presence is all-important to us is the first principle of faith; we cannot say *what* He is without entering the domain of mythology. That the human person *is*, we can say, but we indulge in metaphors as much when we speak of souls as when we think of egos and superegos and ids. Finally, we know that as human beings we belong to a larger context of meaning, but we cannot give expression to this conviction of the meaningfulness of our life without surrendering to the spell of some nonrational revelation.

While both myth and faith belong to the life of religion, it matters greatly whether these two orientations are held in balanced tension or not. A religious tradition may be completely hemmed in by the web of myth with the resultant desiccation of all religious feeling. As long as a religion is healthy and well-balanced, its traditional myths will be constantly reinterpreted, revised, and replenished. Without myth and the ritual based upon it, the spirit of faith is hardly evoked, but without the dynamism of a living faith, religion turns into mythology and ritual into magic.

In Christianity, the traditional structure of myth and metaphor contains an anti-Jewish bias, while its substance and dynamic drive are not only pro-Jewish, but so close to the Jewish heritage as to merge insensibly into it. Whenever Christian groups yield to the seduction of the magical-mythical elements in their faith, their anti-Jewish potential is intensified. Also, they become predisposed to carry over the patterns of mythological thought from religion to politics. They tend to interpret contemporary issues in terms of a struggle between God and the Devil, polarizing society into its extremist components. They are then easy prey for political "witch doctors," and pseudo-Messianic adventurers, who promise to solve all problems by exposing and destroying the secret conspiracy of Satan's minions —thus, the Fascists, the Nazis, the Know-Nothings, and the Birchists. The anti-Jewish bias of Christian mythology is part of a general syndrome of emotion-laden symbols that constitutes the primitive underside of Christian civilization. It is significant that Rudolf Bultmann's clarion call for the de-mythologization of Christianity was sounded in 1941, when the vicious perversion of the Christian myth by the Nazis was becoming obvious to the Germans themselves.

On the other hand, the inner impetus of the Christian faith consists of loving surrender to redemptive love, self-sacrifice, austere devotion to truth, a keen and persistent sensitivity to the perennial seductions of self-righteousness, a relentless determination to persevere in the eternal task of the faithful. These ideals are articulated and illustrated differently in the diverse traditions of Judaism and Christianity, but they are mutually supplementary, as are all true ideals, within the context of a common quest for the sanctification of life. While reverence for law is as characteristic of Judaism as trustful submission to love is of Christianity, both traditions are actually permeated with the same ideals, though with different nuances and emphases. The *logos*, consisting of reason and law, is intrinsic to Christianity, while Divine love and forgiveness are of the essence of Judaism. The two traditions, so alike and so different, serve to clarify and reinforce one another. In the realm of ideas and ideals, variety and challenge provide the necessary stimuli to growth. Thought is by its very nature dialectical, that is, it unfolds by way of thesis and counterthesis. Said our rabbis of old, "Who is the wise man? He who learns from all people." Also, "The jealousy of scribes multiplies wisdom."[1]

It follows that the Christian side will be disposed not merely to tolerate Judaism but to attain a genuine symbiosis with it to the extent to which its inner, ideal substance prevails over its mythical-magical outer garb.

By the same token, a similar judgment may be made concerning the tension within Judaism between its living soul and its mythological structure. In Judaism, the structure of myth centers not on a struggle between God and the Devil, but on the supposed act of Divine fiat, God's choice of the "holy seed." In Judaism, as in Christianity, the central myth deals with the deeds of God as revealed and interpreted in a body of tradition. These deeds are not universal, definable in terms that are relevant and meaningful to all, but narrowly focused on a small body of people. The myth of Divine chosenness falls into a dramatic pattern, consisting of a chain of Divine actions, human responses of acceptance and rebellion, Divine retribution, vindication, and ultimately a happy ending. The "Chosen People" is the counterpart to the Apostolic Succession in Episcopalianism, the elect saints in Calvinism, and the hierarchical Church in Catholicism.

Those who are completely enwrapped by the shadowy tentacles of the Jewish myth are as little disposed to a meaningful cooperative dialogue with people of another faith as are some medieval-minded Christian mythologists. For them, humanity is bifurcated into two camps, the Jews and the Gentiles. While they will admit occasional exceptions in both camps, they will tend to force the protean world of common experience into two ready-made molds, with everything Jewish being adored as Divine and everything Gentile scorned as demonic. In matters of practice, they will pit symbol against symbol and rite against rite, accounting it a Divine command to segregate the Jews from the others, as much as possible, and glorying in every opportunity to raise the historical barriers ever higher. They will read the records of history and the daily chronicles in terms of "we" and "they," with all the lines of distinction drawn by politics, culture, and geography fading into insignificance beside the massive Grand Canyon scooped out by the Lord of history between "His children" and the rest of mankind.

71

The Jewish myth undercuts the possibility of any fruitful communication with Christians as effectively as Christian fundamentalism. Even on the plane of secular learning, there cannot be any true understanding. To the founder of Habad-hasidism, the "wisdom of the nations" derives from the unclean shell (*No-gah*) belonging to the realm of Satan and his minions. In the impassioned mood of medievalist separatism, every non-Jewish symbol and religious rite is an offense and a stumbling block. How then can meaningful communication take place?

A genuine symbiosis of Judaism and Christianity can arise only in a situation where both groups move toward a de-mythologization of their respective traditions.

While some scholars in both camps attempted in the nineteenth century to de-mythologize their respective traditions, the masses moved in the opposite direction—they kept the myths but discarded the inner faith.

In the case of Christianity, the emotional patterns of a mythological soteriology are evident in the two "heresies" that have emerged in the twentieth century—Nazism and Bolshevism.

Bolshevism retains the mythological structure of popular Christianity. The objective world of common sense cannot be trusted; the ideas and ideals of humanity are only by-products of dark forces, which subsist below the surface of things. God aims to bring into being the perfect world, but He needs the Devil as His counterpart. As the Devil labors with might and main his foul purposes to perform, he will inadvertently build up the final Armageddon, which will be followed by a return of the Golden Age. Man will re-enter the Paradise which he inhabited before the Fall. He will be redeemed from the power of Satan and, in a recaptured state of innocence, will live happily ever after.

In Marxism, the unidirectional, inexorable flow of history is the counterpart to the belief in Providence. The course of human affairs is driven by its inner dialectic toward a predetermined end. The Devil is the greed of capitalism, which inescapably works its own ultimate destruction, digging its own grave and driving toward the climactic disaster of an all-Capitalist versus an all-Proletarian war. Following that final convulsion, mankind will live in a classless society, as before the Fall, and all the vices of society will have been eliminated.

And as the Church consists of those who, though living in the world, have been "reborn" into the "Kingdom of God" of the future, so the Communist party consists of the "twice born," who have been purged of the evils which distort the thinking of the children of darkness. Again, as the Church contains a body of elite, who alone represent its true genius, so the party, however small in number, represents the true will of the "masses," and the ranks of the party must be periodically purged from heresies; in the last resort, only those who stand in the direct line of apostolic succession from Marx can be trusted. It seemed only natural for Stalin to cap the parallel with the claim of infallibility.

Nazism-Fascism was both an equal and opposite reaction to communism, on the one hand, and a more direct reassertion of the Christian myth, on the other hand. "No man can say Jesus is the Lord, save by the Holy Spirit." But Marxism substituted the quasi-rational analysis of economic production for the seizure of the Holy Spirit. And this quasi-rationality in the area of economics implied a rejection of religion, of national goals, and of all the mores of the "establishment." Nazism-Fascism set out to rebuild the ancient myth with "blood-thinking" as their substitute for the Holy Spirit. The political intuitionism of Fascism and the racial intuitionism of Nazism corresponded in feeling to the psychological and dogmatic intuitionism of blind faith. The authoritarian structure of Nazism-Fascism—the selection of an elite of "believers," who "prove' their beliefs by the intensity of their zeal, and the ranking of corpselike obedience as the supreme virtue of the masses—in all these respects, Nazism-Fascism appeared to be a political version of the Catholic Church.

To be sure, the Church has exalted the role of reason and extolled the prophetic spirit of self-criticism, as well as the

73

virtues of humility, charity, and peace. But this inner soul of Catholicism was precisely what Nazism-Fascism set out to combat through the employment of the *mystique* of the Church and its organizational pattern. By reviling the traditional "enemies" of the Church—reason, liberalism, socialism, communism, Jews—they could give the impression of fighting for the cause of Christianity.

Nazism carried out with Teutonic thoroughness all that was merely implicit in Italian Fascism. It divided mankind into two absolute categories, with the "elect" being destined by birth for paradise, and with the lesser races being condemned to servitude, their life dependent on their usefulness to the blessed saints. Even Hitler certified as Aryans several hundred full- and half-Jews, according to Hannah Arendt. Furthermore, the division between the "sheep" and the "goats" was not based upon such obvious factors as the eye could see or the mind could acknowledge—neither the physical qualities that feed man's natural pride nor the cultural marks of superiority such as the Europeans possessed over the natives. The selection was a matter of faith, asserted in spite of all facts and observations— a belief all the more certain because it was folly to the Greeks, an abomination to the Jews. The subhumans were the *hell-people,* the elect were the *heaven-people,* and in the new dispensation, heaven was built on earth "scientifically," and the hell-people could have no share in it. The transposition of the Christian myth from the other world to this terrestial scene made possible the disposition of rising "beyond good and evil" and consenting to the assignment of entire sections of humanity to hell on earth or to total annihilation. And as the Jew was the symbol of the arch-heretic, outwardly blessed and yet accursed, whose sorry tale was a warning to all who reject the Divine dispensation, so the Jew in Nazism was at once the archenemy and the symbol of non-Teutonic, unredeemed humanity. Clerical anti-Semitism sought political power in Austria, Germany, and France, long before biological nihilistic anti-Semitism appeared upon the scene. By concentrating their

74

attack on the Jews, the Nazis could deflect attention from their program of depopulation and annihilation in central and eastern Europe. They were "safe," hiding behind the protective screen of a symbol of hate that was approved by the religious and conservative classes. In this connection, it is well to recall the official letter from Minister of Justice Otto Thierack, to Himmler, in which the SS are given full authority to implement the program of annihilation. This transfer of authority was made in regard to "Poles, Russians, Jews, and Gypsies," since, the author states, "The Ministry of Justice can make only a small contribution to the extermination of these peoples."[2]

In the Nazi system, purgatory was only a temporary state, while in the Thousand Year Reich there would be only heaven and hell.

Hitler consciously imitated the symbolic panoply of the Catholic Church. He installed himself in the position of the savior, in whose name all personal greeting and public business was transacted. In his propaganda, he concentrated all evil in one satan, that was at once concrete enough and strong enough to be worthy of the cold steel of hate. The Jew was a "metaphysical" target of hate, identified as such by Christian mythology. Everything about him was paradoxical, for he belonged to the realm of "mystery." He was responsible for communism and capitalism, Christianity and unbelief, materialistic prosperity and the depression. "Believe, and ye shall be saved," was his slogan to the German people. Reality, reason, and the ideals that belong to these realms of common humanity were a snare and a delusion. Only if you died to this world and were reborn again, could you be saved.

The frightening aspect of Nazism was precisely the demonstration of the fantastic potency of sheer mythology. Eichmann and the others involved in the atrocities of mass murder claimed that they were bound by an oath of unquestioning obedience to Hitler. Highly placed generals could rank an oath, which was after all merely a symbol, far above all their moral obligations as human beings.

75

Furthermore, both the Protestant leaders and the Catholic hierarchy did not question for a moment that Nazism was more to be preferred than communism. While the Church fought socialism and communism with all the influence it possessed, it resisted Nazism only when its organization was involved. Only when the war was concluded, did Pope Pius XII condemn Nazism as an anti-Christian movement, satanic in its essence. While political considerations perforce restrained the hierarchy from expressing its convictions, the same motives never deterred it from condemning communism, root and branch. Only Pope John XXIII showed a willingness to take a fresh look at communist society.

Indeed, the difference between the two forms of totalitarianism illustrates the contrast between the essence of religion and its mythological vestments. The central goal of communism is, after all, the liberation of mankind from the pall of impoverishment and the injustice of exploitation. It is antireligious, firstly, because it opposes the symbolic-mythical panoply of faith and, secondly, because of its fanatical determination to allow no ideals, rights, or principles to stand in the way of its ends; but it is intensely religious in its essential and ultimate motivation. It is dangerous and destructive by virtue of its fanaticism, its absolutism, its dictatorial methods, and its apocalyptic ways of thinking. Nazism shares these evils, being, in addition, cannibalistic in essence: its purpose is to enslave the vast majority of mankind and to establish an ironclad, conscienceless system of perpetual exploitation. The pattern of Nazi propaganda required not the suppression of the Church, but, what is worse, its suborning by the use of phony slogans, such as a "positive Christianity" or a "German Christianity."

If, then, churchmen by and large chose the party that favored the myths and symbols of the Church, while negating its true import, and utterly condemned the one that favored the inner, ideal content of religion, while repudiating its symbols, does it not follow that mythology is more powerful than religion? Myth and symbol monopolize the channels of communication and establish visible façades, while ideals and values can only be sensed by the inner light of intelligence and conscience. To most people, religion is precisely the outer panoply of myths and rites, not the endless quest for the good. We recall the macabre fantasy of Gogol, in which he tells of a man whose nose separated from his face and then attended all social functions, being welcomed by the guards and recognized by the headwaiters, while the man himself, bereft only of his nose, was treated as an interloper and kicked out in the street.

The tension between myth and ideal in Judaism centers around the meaning of the "Chosen People." As noted earlier, the struggle within the heart of the Jew around this focus turns on the difference between prophetic humanism and sanctified egotism. Down to the opening of the modern era, this issue was somewhat muted, since its resolution was in the hands of God. It was the Lord who "chose" Israel, and the Lord will fully reveal His intentions only in the End of Days. Then and then only will it become clear as to whether there are any tangible benefits for Jews in compensation for their long suffering, or whether their satisfaction will be merely the realization that their cause was vindicated and they were right all along.

In the modern world, the medieval notions of God have been considerably modified, but so deeply had the conviction of "chosenness" penetrated into both Jewish and Christian society that neither group could easily free itself from the feeling that the Jew was unique, different, metaphysically set apart from the rest of the world. To the anti-Semites, Jewish "difference" was merely transposed from the religious to the biological and cultural domains.

In all the arguments about Jewish emancipation, the objection of the anti-Semites was formulated on the ground that the Jews were a nation, not merely a religious community. The liberals countered this argument with the famous slogan of Clermont-Tonnerre: "To the Jews as individuals, everything; to the Jews as a nation, nothing."

Actually, neither the anti-Semites nor the liberals objected to the ethnic character of Jewish being but to that *plus* of separateness, which made the Jews more different than all other ethnic groups composing the modern state. There were Basques, Alsatians, and Italians in France, but their emancipation was not in question, nor was the freedom of the Poles and Danes in Germany ever disputed on the ground of nationhood.

But the characterization of Jews as a nation implied a judgment of the past and an assessment of the future. It meant that the reason for Jewish survival was a peculiarly tenacious "will to live" apart, a misanthropic mood of self-segregation and self-exaltation; hence, a likely expectation that in the future Jews will refuse to amalgamate with the emergent nations of western Europe. While the lines of division between nations were fairly deep, the gulf between Jews and the rest of mankind was deeper by far; indeed, it was impassable.

It is this plus of "difference" that lay at the base of all anti-Semitic calumnies, predisposing the populace to "half-believe" anything about those who were so peculiar. Whether Jews were accused of "poisoning the wells," or "desecrating the host," or using the blood of Gentile children in a secret Passover rite, the common axiom underlying these medieval charges was the *nonhumanity* of the Jew. Such fantastic myths could be true, so the mass-mind reasoned, for, after all, was he not mysteriously set apart from the rest of the human family?

Because of the wide cultural gap between the upper and lower levels of modern society, the medieval mood and the "blood-accusation" were continued well into the twentieth century in Russia (Beilis trial), Germany (Xanten trial), Austria (Hilsner), Poland (Lemberg trial).

The same basic stereotype of a *dehumanized* people was assumed in the "Protocols of the Elders of Zion," where the transition was made from a "religious" to a quasi-secular frame of reference. In the modern as in the medieval world, the fundamental axiom was the utter, absolute "difference" of the Jewish mentality.

The mood and malice of the anti-Semites could have mass appeal only when the axiom of Jewish "uniqueness" was given the appearance of reality by the actual, visible differences that marked contemporary Jewish life. No ghostly myth can endure unless it is given from time to time fresh infusions of the blood of reality. The quaint, outlandish, and self-segregating practices of medieval-minded Jews served to keep alive the sickly phantasies of the anti-Semites. The typical anti-Semitic agitator "liked" the Jewish medievalists, since they fitted comfortably into the narrow molds of his *Weltanschauung*. He could attack them with some degree of plausibility. By the same token, he fulminated most bitterly against the modern Jews, whose very appearance shook the foundations of his entire ideology.

On the other hand, the liberals resented the vestiges of Jewish exclusiveness, especially the tight, interlocking texture of secular organizations clustering around the ghettolike community, because, in their view, these residues of medieval separatism kept the anti-Semites in business. Theodor Mommsen publicly expressed this criticism, which most liberals hesitated to state explicitly. While the anti-Semites roared at the modernist Jews, as does a tiger when his prey is about to escape from his claws, the liberals occasionally protested against Jewish exclusiveness, like shepherds seeking to secure their flock from the roving beasts.

On the Christian side, this myth of Jewish metaphysical distinction, the "meta-myth" for short, was eventually escalated into the fantasy of Aryans and non-Aryans. On the Jewish side, this myth was reasserted as the central dogma of Jewish nationalism by Ahad Ha'am and his school. Whether there was a choosing God or not, the Jews were still the Chosen People. They were "different," not merely as all nations differ from one another, but "different" in a unique and special sense, "different" from *all* the nations of the earth.

As is well known, Ahad Ha'am endeavored for a long time to discover the essence of Jewish ethics, for he was convinced that the "Jewish soul" was most faithfully reflected in the collective vision of the good life. He claimed, as his own interpretation, that Jewish ethics was expressed in the quest of absolute justice, but he added that regardless of any scholar's opinion of the nature of Jewish ethics, one must believe and feel that the Jewish view was somehow uniquely different from that of all nations on the face of the earth.

In the domain of religion, Ahad Ha'am was a thoroughgoing skeptic, but he was eager to appropriate the heritage of the tradition in *feeling*, if not in *thought*. He urged the acceptance of the dogmas of Judaism by the use of the formula *ani margish* ("I feel"), instead of the orthodox version *ani maamin* ("I believe"). Yet, he held on boldly to one dogma—the dogma of "difference."

Ahad Ha'am's philosophy was not an individual idiosyncrasy. It is still a potent social force, because it is maintained by the actuality of the Zionist enterprise and kept alive by the standard "rhetoric of the Jewish religion."

The World Zionist Organization came into being for the purpose of "normalizing" the life of the Jewish people. In the Diaspora, so it is argued, Jewish life was "abnormal," the Jew being stuck like a bone in the throats of the nations. By the establishment of the Jewish State, the Jews of the Diaspora are divided into two groups—both "normal"—the Jews living in their own state, who will reassert their genuine nationhood, and the Jews of the Diaspora, who will "assimilate" and become merely religious communities.

But the partial fulfillment of the Zionist vision implied also the partial frustration of the original thesis. Israel is now a Jewish State, but the World Zionist Organization persists for the purpose of siphoning human and material resources to Israel and in order to prevent the very break between the two communities that Zionism originally set out to achieve. The institutional impact of Zionism is, therefore, calculated to maintain the "abnormality" of Jewish life in the Diaspora and to dramatize the *exceptional* character of the Jew.

At the same time, the religious leadership of the Diaspora

Jewish communities is enmeshed in the traditional rhetoric of the Jewish religion, which celebrates the *uniqueness* of the Jew and his being set apart. The differences between the Orthodox, the Conservative, and the Reform in this regard are not as important as one would think. While the Orthodox are enchained in dogma, the non-Orthodox find it equally difficult to overcome the seduction of ethnocentrism and the historic impetus of Jewish rhetoric. Indeed, many a liberal rabbi will convert his ethnic feeling into an absolutist faith precisely because the traditional pillars of his religion have been shattered. It is sufficient to recall the very titles of some recent books about the Jew in history: *Where Judaism Differed* by A. H. Silver, *The Eternal Dissent* by D. Polish, *The Jew—Natural and Supernatural* by A. Cohen. The accent is on Jewish difference, mysterious, metaphysical, meta-historical.

Largely secularized though it be, the myth of Jewish "chosenness" persists.

Side by side with the secularization of the myths of religion, the opposite process of de-mythologization has also been in progress. In Christianity, the depth of this mighty current is difficult to gauge because its structural unity requires the maintenance of a rhetoric of faith, which clothes its genuine intent in a golden aura of ambiguity. Certainly, the modernist emphasis is far more widespread than dogmatic formulae would allow. In this line of thought, metaphors and myths are recognized as such, though they may still be considered indispensable to the operation of institutional religion. On this basis, the harmful effects of the myth are likely to be suppressed. It becomes an aid and instrument of faith, not its goal and master.

The Catholic Church has begun to face seriously the task of de-mythologization. Pope John XXIII sought to catapult the Church into the twentieth century with such statements as the following:

"While the truth is one, there can be many formulations of it."

"While error has no rights, the people who are in error are the bearers of right by nature."

Formally, the Catholic Church needs to maintain the façade of changelessness, but actually a powerful liberal impetus is at work within it. The elimination of the adjective *perfidious,* as applied to the Jews, from the Easter service is only the best-known step of a steady and consistent process to overcome the dire consequences of the ancient myths.

In Judaism, the extent of de-mythologization is by no means identical with the line of demarcation between the Reform-Conservative movements and the Orthodox community; for the doctrine of the "holy seed" and the "Chosen People" are still passionately held by many Reform and Conservative ideologists, while some Orthodox people seek to combine scrupulous ritualistic conformity with a meticulous openness to the intellectual currents of the day. The central Jewish myth is dogmatic and ethnocentric at one and the same time, namely, the Lord chose Israel from among all the nations of the earth and gave it the one "Torah of truth." While the Orthodox stress the latter part of this formula, the Reform and Conservative leaders are more likely to soften the claim about the "Torah of truth" than to surrender the notion of Jewish metaphysical distinctiveness. An act of decision that transpired within the Transcendent Being, who is the ultimate source of the entire range of existence, accounts for the "unique" character of the Jew and his strange destiny. The key to our life as Jews lies outside the realm of space and time. Ethnocentric fanaticism has become inter-denominational within the Jewish community. Professor Mordecai M. Kaplan deserves the highest accolades for his valiant and lifelong battle against the myth of "chosenness." His influence has been felt in all the official divisions of American Judaism.

Though the pace of de-mythologization has been painfully slow in all the faiths of the Judeo-Christian tradition, we can see certain objective factors that are likely to hasten and deepen this advance of the human spirit.

The objective factors that may be expected to favor the trend of de-mythologization in both Judaism and Christianity are the same developments which in an earlier age were deemed to be "anti-religious." They are the characteristic qualities of the modern mind, derived from the new advances in the fields of physics, history, sociology, and psychology. Each of these areas of research was at one time regarded as a formidable threat to an ethical-religious view of life. It is sufficient to mention names like Darwin, Marx, Russell, Einstein, and Freud. The new ground that they broke appeared at one time to undermine the foundations of morality as well as religion. Yet, today it is becoming clear that the new worlds they opened up provide the perspective for the continued de-mythologization of religion and the vitalization of a living faith.

In the ancient and medieval worlds, the only counterforce to mythology was the kind of abstract reasoning that is loosely called philosophy. The achievements of religious philosophers, like Philo, Augustine, Maimonides, and Aquinas, in limiting the impact of religious mythology were indeed magnificent, but their philosophical armory consisted almost entirely of Aristotle's logic and physics. When "pure" reason was posited as the lone contender against the myths of tradition, the conclusion was soon reached that its scope and penetration was limited. It could not comprehend the ultimate mysteries. Hence, beyond the frontiers of reason, some kind of faith must be asserted, be it the "animal faith" of Santayana, the "practical reason" of Kant, or one of the traditional versions of supernatural revelation. Once this point was reached, the exponents of the several religious traditions could reinstate the entire ballast of their respective mythologies as well as the core of faith. A Maimonides could insist on the rational critique of faith, eliminating the belief in miracles, demons, and saints; but an equally great philosopher, Hisdai Crescas, living in an age of the "failure of nerve," could embrace the entire panoply of mythology—the Messiah, the Resurrection, the "World to Come," and the occult cosmic effects of Jewish rituals—on the ground that "the gates of understanding are closed to us." Since the "iron curtain" of faith must be dropped at some point, there seemed to be some surface justification for those who accepted in toto the dogmatic

83

web of mythology as well as the substance of faith. At times, the absolutist stance of philosophy was even used to harden the dark myths of tradition, adding the rigidity of a logic, deeply rutted and smoothly grooved, to the blind zealotry of inherited beliefs. There were more persecutions for heresy and witchcraft in the scholastic centuries than in the earlier generations of the Dark Ages. If the entire dogmatic structure of the faith could be logically proved, then heretics and Jews must be held guilty of wilfully perverting the truth. When reason became the docile "handmaiden" of faith, then those who would not so believe were "children of the Devil," whose burning was an "act of faith," *auto-da-fé*. In modern times, the rational drive cannot be so easily curbed and restricted, but there are still many for whom the "cold war" between faith and reason is best resolved by an iron curtain or a Berlin wall.

The result is a compartmentalized personality, partly atheist and partly fundamentalist, devoid of the dynamic quest for growth toward the fullness of reality.

In our day, the domain of reason includes an objective approach to the study of history, a new awareness of the depths of the human soul, a new appreciation of the popular follies and zealotries that form the underside of institutional religion, and a new insight into the errors of speech and thought.

In the study of history, both the quest for objectivity and the recognition of the inevitable subjective distortion of perspective are characteristic of the modern age. In the Bible, the prophets regard the peculiar history of Israel as a manifestation of the Divine Will, but their interpretation is inevitably both subjective and selective; they know precisely what history *ought* to prove, hence they ignore the *inner natural forces of the massive events around them, focusing attention only on the ways that their beliefs are "proved" by the course of history.* The "good" kings are immediately rewarded, and the evil kings are punished for their idolatrous ways; when this simple equation appears to fail, they suggest that such pious kings as Hezekiah and Josiah were made to suffer for the sins of their predecessors.

In Greek history, the perspective was broader, encompassing the entire Near East. The moral fervor was less intense; the desire to entertain was greater than the will to take account of all sides, and the sin of *hubris* ("pride") was believed to be the ultimate cause of the anger of the gods. Throughout the Middle Ages, historical writing belonged in the category of moralistic fables.

In the past century, the quest for truth in history was undertaken with the object of *discovering the actual course of events*. History, or the sum total of human experience, became a "scientific" discipline, at least as a conscious goal. Applied to the study of the Bible, the new critical studies resulted in a radical de-mythologization of both Testaments. They are now viewed as human compilations, containing the impact of the Divine nisus, but retaining also the marks of contingent historical circumstances. While there are several schools of Bible study, there are also certain well-established conclusions regarding the slow emergence of Judaism and Christianity. The books of the Bible are now integrated in their historical environment and seen within the perspective of human fears and hopes, follies and phantasies, as well as the human quest for salvation.

At the same time, the inescapable subjectivity of historical writing is now generally recognized. Wiser and sadder than our ancestors, we know now that even the "scientific" historians tend to inject their peculiar blind spots into their view of the past. The great Hegel, who advanced the philosophy of history to its highest pinnacle, ended with the claim that the world-historical idea was embodied in the despotic autocracy of the Prussian State. Karl Marx, a revolutionary disciple of Hegel, made an absolute principle of the subjectivity of all historical judgments, save his own—i.e. all thinking is molded by the bias of caste and class, except that of "historical materialism." Today, we recognize the force of Marx's rule, but we also know the vanity of his claimed exemption.

History, as the quest for objective truth in regard to the past, was long regarded as the most potent challenge to religion. Actually, it served to remove the seal of truth from the myths of religion, but it illustrated and dramatized the indispensability of some myths in the pursuit of man's ceaseless quest for ultimate truth and reality.

The narratives of the two Testaments are understood to be human attempts to express the inexpressible; hence, myths and parables are "true" in terms of what they point to, not literally and not absolutely.

Similarly, "historicism," or the subjective bias of historical writing, does not necessarily lead to total skepticism or nihilism. On the contrary, by liberating our minds from total subservience to tradition, our awareness of the relativity and incompleteness of all historical knowledge makes possible a process of progressive refinement in the search for truth. It sensitizes us to the obsessive sin of religion, self-righteousness, and collective egotism. In his capacity as a historian, the modern researcher fulfills the role of the prophet: he warns us against the sin of self-righteousness, and he cites the errors of the past as a warning to his contemporaries.

In a similar way, the comparative study of religion, which is part of modern sociology, seeks to relate the various kinds of institutional religion to the structure of society as a whole.

The anthropologists have assembled a vast array of parallels for the sacramental rites of Christianity revolving about the death and resurrection of the Savior-God. They have also shown that beliefs regarding immutable ritual laws and dietary taboos are widespread in primitive societies. The newness and greatness of the Judeo-Christian faiths are certainly not to be found in their external rituals and fixed dogmas, for in these respects, both Judaism and Christianity are not distinguishable from primitive, precultural religions and "ways of life." It is in their surge toward the infinite horizons of man's spirit that the Western religions demonstrate their genius; hence, the positive value of all the studies which reveal the encrustations of subjective bias in our history.

Max Weber's studies in this field demonstrate the interrelationship of all social and cultural phenomena, including the rites and dogmas of faith. Such researches illustrate the relativity of all religious developments, even as they prove that the living quest of religion is an integral phase of human societies.

By the same token, the effect of modern "depth-psychology" has been favorable to the inner life of religion, even as it undermined the absolute character of all the external manifestations of faith. On the one hand, Freud and his successors uncovered the psychic roots of many dogmas and rituals, popularizing such notions as the "projection of the father image," the power of "compulsive obsession," the "guilt of the Oedipus complex" and the "projection of guilt upon a scapegoat," the relation of dogmas to the mechanism of repression, and the roots in the unconscious of all lustration ceremonies.

On the other hand, the same researches have uncovered the psychic needs corresponding to the varied ministrations of religion. While the mythological and ritual expressions of institutional religion are not true in themselves, they are true insofar as they serve to help man confront and master the challenges of society and civilization.

Here, then, is a new and potent weapon in the struggle against the corruption and petrifaction of all religions. We can now begin to see how they may be tested, corrected, and evaluated. The gradual accumulation of psychological data will make possible the objective evaluation of institutional myths. We can now foresee the time when man will become the master of his myths, instead of their victim. Thus, "depth-psychology" enhances our appreciation of the psychological role of religion, even as it provides powerful support for those who would de-mythologize the historic faiths of the Western world. Human societies must project myths if they are to satisfy the needs of the individual to feel part of that reality, which overcomes the transiency of life and the negation of death. Pseudofaiths, quasi-political and quasi-scientific, will rush in to fill the void if genuine religion fails to hold its own. But, to serve mankind, genuine religion must be aided to retain its dynamism, utilizing myths and transcending them at one and the same time.

Down to our own generation, Judaism and Christianity confronted each other as mutually contradicting myths. Each faith regarded itself as true, all others as dead wrong. The Jew could expect only the worst grudging toleration at a time when all other heresies were drowned in blood. The so-called Age of Faith was actually the Age of Mythology, with the vitality of dynamic faith being almost completely overwhelmed by the massive chains of dogma and ritual, in both Judaism and Christianity. Each faith was then static, consisting of so many "truths" that could be categorized, numbered, and filed away. The very notion of growth in religion by way of dialectical tension and through a fruitful encounter with another faith was then unthinkable. To secure its hold, each faith sought to obtain control of culture and education.

In the state of Israel, the spokesmen of Orthodoxy are still trying to hold on to positions of power in the political structure of the Israeli nation. Myth-encrusted religious mentalities cannot but identify the life of faith with so many rites, dogmas, and sacraments.

In our age, both Judaism and Christianity have become dynamic fields of force between the polarity of myth and faith. Within each faith, this tension is articulated either by way of an organizational schism or by means of an ideological debate. The leading spokesmen of both religions have come to accept the fact of tension as a blessing, rather than as a curse. No religious groups today would approve of the employment of coercion of one kind or another in order to obtain the sole dominance of their own faith.

Considered as myths, Judaism and Christianity contradicted each other—the one operating on the assumption that the other had been tragically and woefully misled and perverted. The argument centered on the personality of the hoped-for Messiah, and only one group could be right, absolutely so, pure, beloved, "justified," while the other could only be a concatenation of errors, satanic and doomed.

As dynamic faiths, moved by the quest for truth and reality,

Judaism and Christianity can only regard each other as allies in the battle against nihilism and the quasi-religions of our day. Beneath the diverse garments of myth and ritual, the same basic drives are at work in all the religions of the Judeo-Christian tradition.

The actual meaning of each faith is clarified when the external vestures of one faith are juxtaposed with those of another faith. It is easier for Judaism to overcome the dead weight of its mythological encumbrance when it is challenged by Christian ideas. Similarly, every Christian denomination is aided to discover its own genius when the intellectual marketplace is kept from being foreclosed by a single monopoly. Said Thomas Jefferson, "In politics, there is strength in unity, but in religion, strength is found in diversity."

As we look ahead into the future, we cannot expect that the mythologists will be completely overcome—either in Judaism or in Christianity; but, neither are the mythologists likely to prevail in the Western world. The tension within each faith is likely to be maintained, with the prophetic personalities in the several traditions sharing the same ideals and sentiments, and the mythologists manning their barricades in the same fashion. The liberals in both groups will derive strength from one another, while the antiliberal forces will similarly reinforce each other. No longer will the lines of battle be drawn between the several religions, but they will cut athwart all faiths.

The process of de-mythologization in Judaism is likely to be accelerated in the Anglo-American world. The Jewish myth of the Chosen People is challenged daily in a predominantly Christian society. Liberal Jews will interpret their "chosenness" as an *example,* not an exception. They will urge the American nation to regard itself as similarly "chosen," i.e. dedicated to the service of mankind. The Christian myth of the Jews as the mystery-people, at once blessed and accursed, is likely to be dissipated by the progressive normalization of Jewish life in Israel and in the lands of the Diaspora. A de-mythologized Jewish faith will function as a powerful ferment within American society, reinforcing the impact of the universal ideals of ethical monotheism.

Similarly, the challenge of modern Judaism is likely to strengthen the forces working for the de-mythologization of the various Christian faiths. The Jewish challenge is in a somewhat different category from those derived from modern humanistic studies and from secular forces generally. While the latter challenges are unidirectional, negating the validity of the Christian myths, the former challenge is bidirectional, pointing out the vital creative impetus of a living faith that resists the mythological substructure of its own tradition.

Only a generation ago, many Jewish ideologists of "survival" doubted either the validity or the viability of the Jewish religion. It appeared then as if all religions were due to be discarded along with the medieval nightmares of demons and witchcraft. Auguste Comte maintained that mankind had already gone through the two stages of theology and metaphysics and that it was then, a century ago, entering the third and last stage of mathematics, when all human concerns would be formulated in algebraic symbols and then calculated with precision. If, as Voltaire claimed, religion was born "when the first knave met the first fool," then it could be expected to fade away with the progress of culture and the spread of education.

But even if religion in general could be expected to retain a limited position of power and influence, our ideologists feared that the Jewish religion would not be able to hold its own in the Christian lands of the Diaspora. Ahad Ha'am labored hard to provide a national-cultural substitute for religion, convinced that the Jewish faith could no longer function as a fitting instrument of the ethnic "will to live." It became the fashion among our nationalistic writers to denigrate the religious dimension of our heritage. In their eagerness to lay bare the ethnic underside of Jewish loyalty, they went so far as to claim that Judaism "was not a religion at all, but a way of life," or "a strategy for survival," or "the exilic garments" of the ethnic will to live and the national vision of the good life. They were certain that as a religion, ministering to the needs of the individual, Judaism could not possibly survive against the competition of the Christian churches.

Today, it has become clear that in the foreseeable future, mankind is not likely to outgrow the need of institutionalized religion. The individual needs its "staff of life" in order to walk with hope and in charity through the valley of the shadow of death. The community requires its impetus and vision in order to maintain its ethical values and to curb the primitive demons of "blood and soil" that lurk on the threshold of the "collective unconscious." The real choice for society is not between the ancient mythologies of the Judeo-Christian world and absolute agnosticism, but between the myths of religion, with their carry-over into secular life and a dynamic faith, essentially religious but also humanistic.

In the de-mythologizing cultural climate of our day, Judaism can be said to be not only at home, but home at last.

In the past, the novelty and greatness of Judaism consisted in its valiant endeavor to de-mythologize man's thinking. While the philosophers of Greece sought to achieve this goal by rational reflection, the prophets of Israel aimed to purify the faith of the people by mobilizing their moral fervor and by projecting a vision of national greatness. Prophecy and philosophy are two sides of the same coin; both exalt the individual, his conscience, his intelligence, his perception of a fixed order, and his rebellion against the myths of the past.

The prophetic-philosophical current is so massive, ancient, and richly illustrated that one could well claim that after three thousand years its true, universalist genius is first being manifested. It has grown slowly through the ages, accumulating insights from all people, in keeping with Ben Zoma's counsel, "Who is the wise man? He who learns from all people." Within Judaism, the exponents of this trend are willing and able to take account of Christian and secular insights, integrating all that is valid into our growing heritage. A modern rabbi is likely to be as familiar with the thinking of a Niebuhr, or a Tillich, or a Maritain, or a Rabindranath Tagore as he is with that of Hermann Cohen and Martin Buber.

At the same time, a modern rabbi is not plagued by the taunting question that Lavater addressed to Moses Mendelssohn: "Why aren't you a Christian?"

Today, the pluralistic articulation of the religious impulse is taken for granted. As children of history, we take our places within the different contexts of several traditions, though as builders of the future we aim at the same values and goals. To be religious is to work within the stream of history for the sake of the ideals that transcend it. Hence, it is to feel the sense of *vocation*, how best to serve God in the particular circumstances of the particular community and tradition with one's particular gifts at a particular time and place. At the same time, it is to cherish the universal ideals, the Messianic dimensions of our contemporary and particular tasks—the sense of participation in the common advance of humanity and in the building of the great society of the future. The prophet Micah combined the vision of the universal goal with an admonition to utilize the particular web of loyalties and sentiments that belong to our own tradition: "For all the peoples walk every one in the name of his god, and we will walk in the name of the Lord our God for ever and ever."[3]

The opposite of these complementary concepts of *vocation* and *Messianism* is the couplet of religious *indifferentism* and *pseudo-Messianism*. While the Messianist labors within the actual structure of history, the pseudo-Messianist tries to jump the tracks, imagining that by ignoring the grooves of terrestial history he has brought heaven down to earth. The pseudo-Messianist asserts that the "Kingdom of Heaven is here and now." Hence, there is no need for the ancient dispensations. Actually, the pseudo-Messianic mentality is destructive because it is escapist—it runs away from the tension-packed world to the illusion of perfection achieved. The perfection of the redeemed world is, like the receding horizon, always in the future, not a reality, but a goal and a vision.

It is in the light of this universal vision of the good society, one in purpose and diverse in expression, that we see the great vocation of our people. Here is a people that has brought the faith of monotheism to mankind; but, as in the Qabbalistic myth, the vessels were unable to sustain the great light and they shattered under the impact of the Divine light. All human vessels were shattered, the Jewish as well as the Christian, with mythology overwhelming and overshadowing the light of faith. At last, we have begun slowly to arise from under the ruins of both ancient and modern myths. The shades of religious mythology are retreating, assuming new shapes in the light of the new age.

"This is the day for which we hoped, let us rejoice and glory in its salvation."[4]

PERSPECTIVES FOR THE STUDY OF
THE NEW TESTAMENT
AND RABBINIC LITERATURE*

If there is one word that best reflects the essence of modern times, it is the word tension. We know today that to live is to be in tension. The ultimate components of our physical universe can no longer be described as balls in motion, but as gradients of potential energy, or states of tension. The basic mood of modern man, according to Spengler, is the awareness of open horizons, toward which we keep on advancing, but which we cannot reach. Our mood is so dynamic that we no longer know what it means to stand still. It requires an effort of imagination for us to conceive of that simple Ptolemaic universe, in which the earth was stationary and all the points of the compass were fixed, all space was geometrical, all numbers were rational, and all logic was straight-lined and inescapable.

Since one way of looking at religion is to see it as "ultimate concern," in the famous phrase of Paul Tillich, we can hardly expect that it be free from tension. I refer in particular to the tension between the subjective and the objective aspects of religious faith.

This tension confronts us on both a personal and a communal plane. In the realm of personal religion, we know that faith is an intensely individual affair. It is our being as a whole that reacts to the mystery of the cosmos as a whole and to the challenge of the values of life taken as a whole. Since it relates to the interreaction of three systems, the self, the cosmos, the values, faith eludes the grasp of reason. Reason can only

*Address at Woodstock Seminary, 1965.

94

order the components of a system; it cannot go outside the limits of a system. This much we have learned from the existentialists, from Kierkegaard down and up.

"Subjectivity is truth," said Kierkegaard. An earlier theologian, Schleiermacher, expressed it in less technical language when he spoke of religious truth as deriving from "feeling." A twentieth-century writer, Otto, spoke of the "sense of the holy." All these writers pointed to the depths within us as the source of faith. Modern psychology has rediscovered the "depth-dimension," but the Psalmist knew it all along: "Out of the depths I called unto Thee."[1]

Yet, we cannot live in feeling alone. Reason is part of our very being, and if we ignore it, we know that we do so and convict ourselves either of perplexity or hypocrisy. In practice, some people will resolve the tension by "compartmentalizing" their attitudes, rendering unto faith its due in its time and place, and restricting reason to the practical affairs of life. In Judaism, one of the sins for which we confess on Yom Kippur is "confusion of mind."

In our personal life, we are called upon to harmonize our feelings of faith with the rational structure of the world. And this structure is constantly in the process of being reordered, in keeping with the accumulation and refinement of knowledge. The tension between faith and reason must be experienced afresh by every thinking person. It cannot ever be resolved once and for all, if we are truly individuals. Said the rabbis, "All the prophets intended to give but one message, still no two prophets speak in the same style." To the extent that we have our own peculiar styles, we shall sense in our own being the tension between the objective and the subjective approaches. Some of us will incline decisively to either the one or the other orientation, but it will hardly be possible for any sensitive person to ignore completely the claims of the rejected aspect of his being. Those who ignore the depths feel uprooted and alienated; those who close their eyes to objective truth shut out the world from behind their artificial walls, but inwardly

95

they remain uneasy and troubled. Like it or not, it is in tension that the life of faith must be lived.

In the dialogue between members of different historic faiths, we confront the tension between objectivity and subjectivity on another plane. The religious community as a whole affirms truths, which must be related to the universal truths of mankind. Hence, the tension between the communally subjective and the universal mind, which remains our inalienable human heritage, by virtue of our being "thinking reeds," as Pascal put it.

This area of tension is also inescapable. Each one of us is born within a certain tradition, which stamps its peculiar seal upon his basic attitudes to life. A person can no more jump out of history than he can stop the world to get off. We can no more be our own spiritual authors than we can be our own physical ancestors. Yet, apart from our several traditions, we do live in one universe, which presses upon our attention a multitude of relatively objective facts and new challenges. The rival claims and rival truths of our subjective communal traditions must somehow be harmonized with the values and principles of our common universe. The Judeo-Christian tradition has taught us to recognize God in history. The Hellenic tradition found Him in the *logos,* the structure of reason that is inherent in nature. St. Paul recognized the need of harmonizing the truths that derive from these two sources—the communal tradition and the universal mind.

The two orientations of the human spirit are like the two poles of a field of force: they pull in opposite directions, but they belong to the same system. While the subjective perspective seems partial and limited from the objective standpoint, the latter appears shallow and cold from the vantage point of those who are trained in a living tradition. We know that God is revealed in the universal mind of man, but we also know that He draws us to Himself through the diverse textures of ritual, dogma, and sentiment that bear the momentum of previous ages. He who reveals Himself in history in a thousand ways, ranging from the most luminous to the most opaque, appears in nature as the One Principle of universal law. In every generation, the inner unity of the two approaches must be understood afresh if our faith is not to become, as Isaiah warned, "a commandment of men learned by rote."[2] The Talmud speaks of the possibility of diverse theological views being right by recalling that God is the source of life, "these and these are the words of the living God."[3] Life consists of the steady synthesis of opposites.

We have to admit that it is more difficult to accept the tension on the communal than on the personal plane. As individuals, we know our limitations. But on the communal level, it takes a prophet to combine the truth of love, as it is enshrined in our respective faiths, with the love of truth, as it comes to us from the common intellectual endeavors of our day. The most typical quality of the literary prophets was their blending of belief with doubt: "Right wouldst Thou be O Lord, were I to contend with Thee, yet I will reason with Thee."[4]

As Jews, we watched with admiration the marvelous demonstration of faith and courage at the several sessions of the Vatican Council. The call of *aggiornamento* of Pope John XXIII was a ringing affirmation of genuine faith. It was proof of the vitality of the prophetic heritage within the Catholic Church. It was a reiteration of the fullness of faith, and its inner unity, facing up to the tension between an objective universe and a subjective tradition.

In our own tradition, we find this awareness explicitly formulated first in our prophets who questioned and criticized even as they believed and trusted. The two-sidedness of faith was expounded particularly by our great philosophers. Some commentators found it in the central verse of our religion: *Shema Yisroel, Adonai Elohenu, Adonai Ehad,* where the two Names of God are taken to refer to the two aspects of the Supreme Being: as He is revealed in reason and nature, *midat hadin,* the quality of law; and as He is discovered in tradition and in our hearts, *midat horahmim,* the quality of compassion. In other words, it is the same God who reveals Himself to us as Law and Truth, objectively, and as Love and Peace, subjectively.

In the modern world, the task of *aggiornamento* has been carried on for several generations within our faith, since our scholars have had to contend with the new perspectives opened up by modern science and history. There was no agreement among our thinkers as to the manner whereby the tension was to be resolved. As a result, we have today almost the entire spectrum of solutions—from that of an insulated communal subjectivity, or ultra-Orthodoxy, to that of a nonsectarian universalism on the far side of Reform. However, apart from the thin fringes at both extremes, most of us accept the reality of the tension between the way of tradition, which trains and hones our religious feelings, and the way of rational inquiry, which relates us to the objective universe. When we study our sacred Scriptures, we ask two questions: What does it mean in the light of its historic context? What does it teach us about the meaning of our life and about our relation to God and to our fellow man? The two questions are interrelated, yet not identical. The one seeks the truth of contemplation; the other, the meaning of dedication. In the former view, many scriptural tales are at one and the same time products of and reactions against ancient mythology; in the latter view, the Bible as a whole is a collective text of the good life of man and the community in the sight of God. Though it is a product of history, it is also a mirror of eternity. The same words appear in two contexts of meaning. Franz Rosenzweig articulated this tension pointedly, when he wrote: "People understand differently, when they understand in doing. Every day in the year, Balaam's speaking ass may be a legend to me; on the Sabbath Balak, when it speaks to me out of the uplifted Torah, it is not."[5]

Martin Buber pointed to the same truth, when he commented on the verse, "And thou shalt love thy neighbor as thyself, I am the Lord." It is when we love that we find our way to God. Yet, love is focused, directed, structured by tradition, and molded by institutions. In our private life, it centers on one person, on "Thou," and God, Buber asserts, is the "Eternal Thou."

As a historical faith, Judaism includes an interpretation of its own history. This interpretation must be constantly balanced against the new facts and the new perspectives that afford us a fresh understanding of the past. We use the texts of our tradition as cosmic telescopes; we look through them and see the universe and God. We read every chapter as if it were addressed to us. It is in this sense that the Torah comes to life for us anew when we hear it at our services. But in our studies of archeology and history, we also encounter the same verses in a totally different context. Then we see them objectively in the perspective of their own times, insofar as objectivity in history is possible. And there is no wall between the two ways of confronting the Scriptures, only a continuous effort at harmonization, understanding in depth, and, yes, tension.

The Hasidic saint Raphael of Bershad labored all his life at the task of seeing the truth and speaking the truth. He was asked, "Suppose, you are faced with a situation where truth-telling would do only harm, what do you do then?" "Oh," he replied, "then I tell the deeper truth."

It is ever deeper levels of truth that emerge out of the living tension between our communal subjectivity and the objective world.

In our subjective orientations, we can hardly engage in a meaningful discourse with those who belong to another faith. Subjectively speaking, we pray, or sing, or declaim, or exult, or shout at one another, but, apart from the "interfaith smile," we cannot really enter into a dialogue. The moment we retreat behind the dogmatic barriers of our respective faiths, we close the channels of all meaningful communication. We may still speak the same words, but we can no longer intend the same meanings. Each closed "theological circle" generates its own universe of discourse.

Here is where the modern science of semantics is exceedingly helpful. We learn that words do not carry specific meanings at all times, like vacuum-sealed cans. On the contrary, meaning derives from the imposition of a pattern upon an accumulated background of data. The same geometrical pattern, if projected upon an even plane and upon a curved one, will produce different figures. Every person possesses an "apperceptive mass" that determines the effective meaning of a concept for him.

In a historical religious community, every central term is likely to connote a cluster of meanings and a spectrum of nuances that are shared more or less by all its adherents. It is easy enough to carry the same words over into the domain of another tradition, but then their meaning is no longer the same. We see an illustration of this phenomenon in the change of meaning that words undergo when they move from the democratic to the communist world.

It may seem that the Old Testament represents common ground on which believers of the Jewish and Christian faiths can meet and debate as believers. But for the Jew as for the Christian, the verses of Scripture are clothed in the vestments of their respective traditional interpretations. An additional source of misunderstanding is the fact that the literature of the Hellenistic Jews and of the intertestamentary period was not preserved by the rabbis. A complex and subtle array of meanings that for Christians bridged the gulf between the Hebrew Bible and the New Testament was in Judaism either marginal or completely suppressed. A good portion of the original common ground was thus cut out.

In any case, today, words like salvation, faith, the Kingdom of God, Pharisees, the Law, Israel, the elect are central to both the Jewish and the Christian traditions, but their effective meanings in the two faith communities are incommensurate with one another. A good parallel would be two infinite series, in which one consists of all odd numbers and the other of all numbers divisible by three. There would be occasional correspondences, but also situations in which the parallel numbers were completely incommensurate. A more earthy illustration is the tongue-in-cheek remark that the barrier between the British and American mentalities is their common language.

It follows that in the subjective orientation, it is meaningless for Jews and Christians to engage in debates regarding any articles of faith. The disputations in the Middle Ages were, shall we say, religious exercises designed to convert rather than to convince. Conversion, as we now know, is a profound psychic upheaval in which the thin crust of rationality is completely overwhelmed by the upsurge of subconscious forces.

Does it mean then that there can be no true dialogue between Jews and Christians?

Not on the subjective plane. The most that we can expect then is for each community to agree to respect the other religious communities and to refrain from offensive missionary propaganda on the ground that conversion must come from within. Also, and still within the subjective orientation, each community can be expected to make certain that its teachings will not be debased and so distorted as to incite hatred of others, who are entitled to certain rights, even if erroneous abstractions are not.

It is for this reason that some Orthodox Jewish theologians have urged that the Jewish-Christian dialogue be confined to the areas of common social concern. In their view, every historic faith is a closed universe that is completely impermeable to the rays of light that come from other galaxies. If an interfaith discussion should take place on matters of theology, ritual or the Bible, then the discussants will generate ill will, because they will be talking *at* one another, not *to* one another.

This judgment would be irrefutable if religion were only subjectivity, totally excluding the relevance of a universal rational realm of discourse.

But since the objective orientation of the quest for truth is an intrinsic part of the life of faith, a genuine dialogue is not only possible but also mandatory. There is the task of understanding the past, so much of which we, as Jews and Christians, see from different sides; there is more specifically the task of penetrating the myths and stereotypes that have so long dis-

101

posed both communities to see each other darkly through smoked glass; there is the task of developing the intellectual and sociological instruments whereby the spirit of faith might permeate our common contemporary culture; there are the broad areas of social concern in which we can work together.

In the Schema on the Jews, the Vatican Council called specifically for Jewish-Christian dialogues along the objective, as well as the subjective, planes! "Since the spiritual patrimony common to Christians and Jews is so great, the council wants to foster and recommend a mutual knowledge and respect which is the fruit above all of Biblical and theological studies as well as of fraternal dialogues."

In keeping with this policy, we now proceed to describe some of the perspectives that an objective orientation opens up to us.

The first maxim that comes to mind in an objective perspective is a warning to Jewish as well as Christian scholars to reject the stereotypes of a less enlightened age. It is the tendency of communal subjectivism to throw a clear shaft of light in a narrow beam, but as with a flashlight, those outside the beam are cast into utter darkness. They are reduced to the monistic mold of the adversary, taking on all the shadowy qualities of Satan.

As Jewish scholars, we have to beware of flattening out our view of European history, from the Inquisition to the wars of religion, and stamping out a two-dimensional portrait of the Christian that mocks the noblest sentiments of the Gospels. In the study of the New Testament documents, we have to recognize the historic context of every dispute. We are not called upon to keep up the old debates, as if thousands of years had not poured "new wine into old bottles." While as modern Jews and Christians we inherit the impetus of ancient disputes, we cannot but view them differently, because we are different. We repeat old words, but the meaning that we assign to them bears the fresh imprint of our day.

A Catholic scholar, Dominic Crossam, wrote an excellent study, "Anti-Semitism in the Gospel." I should refrain from the imputation of anti-Semitism to the Gospels principally because this psychical complex belongs to an utterly different realm of discourse. The authors of the Gospels were Jews. They did not preach hatred of their own people, though they helped to lay the groundwork for the mythology of anti-Semitism by projecting the view that the Jews, as a collective body, were in league with "the forces of darkness." This way of arguing was part of the rhetoric and mythology of the time. The individual Jew was not blamed—only the collective image. And the image too was ambivalent, blessed as well as accursed, loved as well as hated, marked out for salvation as well as perdition. But if we ignore the context and make no allowance for the heat engendered by the human instruments of the course of revelation, many passages in the New Testament are certainly likely to engender the peculiar malice of mythological anti-Semitism.

The way the term "the Jews" is used in the New Testament is a case in point. In every case, the term stands for a more specific designation, such as the crowd, the mob, the opponents, or some Jews. One gets the feeling that the Jews collectively are all painted with one satanic brush, whereas those Jews who either did not reject Jesus or else did not persecute his followers were somehow not Jews. We know that when Paul was arrested in Jerusalem, he could only describe the Christian community as a "Way." He called himself a "Jew,"[6] and when the accusers under the leadership of Ananias referred to "the sect of the Nazarenes,"[7] Paul repudiated the implication of sectarianism, asserting, "After the Way, which they call a sect, so serve I the God of our fathers, believing all things which are according to the Law, and which are written in the prophets."[8]

Yet, in the Book of Acts, we encounter the use of the phrase "the Jews" without any qualifications as enemies.

For example, in Chapter 17 we read that some of the Jews accepted Paul's message. Yet, the account continues, "But, the Jews . . ." instead of saying, "But many Jews," or "But most Jews . . ."

Manifestly, the Jewish authors of the Gospels or their disciples still operated with a quasi-mythical concept, *Keneset Yisroel*, which was ambivalent from the beginning. On the one hand, it stood for the heavenly counterpart of Israel discoursing with God as her partner in the Covenant. On the other hand, the ideal congregation is also equated with the empirical Jewish people, which comprised many different groups. And the various sects then in existence tended to identify *Keneset Yisroel* with their own group. In the Christian community, the double-faceted concept was repudiated and condemned, with the ideal Congregation being pushed into the shadows and replaced by the Church; as a result, the living Jewish people was now identified with a metaphysical entity that had become satanic. We have no figures regarding the respective percentages of Jews and pagans that became Christian by the time of Constantine. If Gibbon's estimate of the number of Christians at the beginning of the fourth century is at all close to the mark, we have no reason to suppose that in proportion to their populations more pagans than Jews accepted Christianity. Yet, the pagans who rejected the Gospel, even those who threw Christians to the lions, were individuals, while the Jews who acted similarly were embraced in one collective, mythological image, "The synagogue of Satan." They were of their "father the devil."[9]

As students of the history of religions, we know that it is the continuing task of every generation to disentangle the word of God from the illusions and delusions of previous eras. A living tradition is a self-purifying faith, a power, a love, a quest, not a meek simplistic acceptance of all that comes from the past. The follies and phantasies of history belong to the context, not the reality, of faith. Sometimes our awareness of the historic context of Scriptures will liberate us from a slavish letter-bound rendering of Scripture. "For the letter killeth, while the Spirit

104

giveth life." A good example is the obvious need to substitute the proper words for the general designation "the Jews" whenever reference is made to the opponents of Jesus or the Apostles. In translations designed for popular or liturgical reading, the contextual meaning should be given in the translation; otherwise, in a footnote.

The phrase "and all the people" in Matthew 27:25 may perhaps be understood in the light of Rabbinic literature. As it stands, it seems so utterly weird. "And all the people answered and said, His blood be upon us, and on our children." In the past, it was understood to refer to all the Jews of the world. There were Jews then in the entire western world, from Persia to England. Even if the reference is to "the chief priests and the elders of the people" that are mentioned in the first verse of this chapter, it remains incredibly perverse and phantastic that they should thus involve their children. But in the Mishnah,[10] we read that witnesses were warned that the blood of the victim as well as the blood of all the descendants that he might have had will fall on them if their testimony is false. Apparently, they had to respond by accepting this responsibility. Therefore, the reference is to the "witnesses," or to those present "at the house of Caiaphas the high-priest," when the presumed words of blasphemy were spoken. In any case, the phrase "all the people" is either a stylistic inaccuracy or an exaggeration. It can hardly be compatible with the love of truth to let it stand as a convenient peg for myth and malice.

In the Gospel of John, "the Jews" appear as one collective dramatic personality. Here is where the insight of the "form-critics" may be helpful.

That Gospel taken as a whole is not a narrative but a sermon, or a "morality play," and the *dramatis personnae* are not living human beings but incarnations of abstractions. This is all the more reason for us to recognize that it must not be taken literally, as a realistic account of flesh and blood personalities, but as a most powerful work of religious art.

105

Far from being downgraded, its importance is enhanced when it is reverently construed in the sense of its central message, to wit: the love of God and the love of men.

When we attempt to see the New Testament as well as Rabbinic literature in perspective, we recognize at once that some elements that were part of the picture at one time are now missing. Indeed, scholars have realized ever since Charles' basic work, that the Apocalyptic literature provides some of the key elements for the understanding of the world-view of Jesus and the apostles. Early in the second century, the Hebrew Canon excluded the books of Enoch, Baruch, and Ezra IV, as well as the entire intertestamentary literature. It was only through circuitous routes that some fragments of this literature re-entered the stream of Jewish thought. Also, as a result of certain historical developments, the Midrash, which was developed in Alexandria and exemplified in the commentaries of Philo, was not included in the heritage of Palestinian and Babylonian Jewry.

Today, we are able to acknowledge that the common tradition of the early Christians and the Jews of the first century was much greater than had been previously recognized. Nearly all the doctrines and interpretations of the early Christian Church were rooted in the soil of first-century Jewish life, which was far more diverse than Moore imagined when he coined the term "normative Judaism." In the wisdom of Providence, the stream of history was bifurcated, and the two communities were carried into different directions. Judaism became Pharisaic, Rabbinic, Halachic; Christianity became mystical, syncretistic, Catholic. Precisely because they emerged out of one community, the question that divided them took the form "Who is right?" not "What is right?" i.e. which community possesses the Promise and the Hope? And if one community is truly blessed, then the other is anathema. As we look back upon the two long and winding roads, we can see that the identities are as real and as important as the differences.

The ethical message of Jesus does not sound strange to one who is at home in Judaism. On the contrary, with all his originality and power, he stands within the line of prophets, pietists, and sages. His criticism of the Pharisees and scribes is itself in keeping with our Biblical and Talmudic tradition. He pointed to the ever-present paradox of an institutionalized and structured faith. His critique of Pharisaism is a reminder of the judgment to which the moral-religious establishment of every age is subject. The very attempt to raise the standards of piety among the people could not but engender a puritanical scorn for the unlearned and nonobservant—"the multitude without the law." The Talmud, too, warns against this danger and speaks of "seven plagues of Pharisaism," though its authors were disciples of the Pharisaic teachers. The occasional supremacy of simple piety over the scrupulous compliance with the externals of religious observance is illustrated in many Talmudic passages. Within the Jewish community there could be many differences of opinion about various issues of Sabbath observance, of washing the hands and the dishes, and the laws of vows. Compare the spirit of the following two passages.

The first is from the prayer said at the end of every tractate of the Talmud:

> We thank Thee, O Lord Our God and God of our fathers, for setting our portion among those who sit in the House of Study, not among those who gather at corners in the marketplace. We rise up early and they rise up early. We rise for the words of Torah, they rise for things of vanity. We labor and they labor, we receive reward for our labors, they don't. We run and they run. We run to the life of the world to come and they run to the pit of destruction. . . .

The second comes from Berochot 17a:

> The rabbis of Yavne used to say: "I am a creature, and my friend is a creature. I work in the city, he works in the field.

I rise early for my work, he rises early for his work. As he does not boast of his work, I don't boast of mine. Lest you say, 'perhaps my work is great and his is little,' let us remember that we were taught—'whether one does much or little, what matters is that one direct his heart to heaven.' "

If in the opinion of the high-priestly court at any one time one or another group was to be physically punished for their infraction of the Law, the situation could change and a more lenient school of judicial interpretation might come to power. We are told that Rabban Gamaliel, the head of the Pharisaic party, opposed the persecution of the early church. We also learn from Josephus that the Pharisees protested against the execution of James the Just.[11] The people of Jerusalem rejoiced when a school of strict judges was thrown out of office, and they marked the anniversary of that day on their calendar as a day on which one may not fast. In every case, the Pharisees would have acknowledged the propriety of arguing from the standpoint of general ethical principles, as well as in legalistic dialectics, for the Pharisees revered the prophets as well as the Law.

In the broad perspective available to us today, we should be able to resist the temptation to oversimplify each other's position. As Jewish scholars, we dare not close our eyes to the many varieties of Christian faith, in the past and in our own day. By the same token, Christian scholars ought to recognize that even in the first century Judaism was not monolithic. "Normative" Judaism was only a relative composite spectrum, representing the probable consensus of Rabbinic opinion at any one time or place. In the flow of tradition, the diversity and fluidity of scriptural interpretation was encouraged by the zest for creative dialectics. We are told that the famous head of the Palestinian academy, Rabbi Yohanan, complained that a younger colleague agreed too frequently with him instead of challenging his views. The school of Hillel, we are told, would teach not only their own tradition, but that of their opponents as well. In general, the rule was laid down that the views of an outvoted minority must be transmitted in the schools; the opportunity had to be maintained for the minority of one generation to become the majority of the next one.[12]

Even when the Babylonian Talmud was considered complete and unchangeable, the two Babylonian academies, those of Sura and Pumbeditha, nurtured different philosophies, with Sura favoring a mystical philosophy and program, while Pumbeditha remained legalistic and rationalistic.

In the Middle Ages, the mystical, romantic, and rationalistic schools diverged ever more decisively, with disputes becoming acrimonious on occasion. But, apart from the Qaraites, there were no sectarian divisions. It is only in the modern world that the rationalistic school became Reform or Conservative, while the romantic-mystical school developed into the various branches of Orthodoxy.

In brief, the Pharisees of the first century were not all of one mold; the sages of the Talmud were quite a diverse group; the rabbis of the Middle Ages diverged from one another in their basic philosophical orientations; the Jews of today recognize the variety and richness of their heritage, finding their chief inspiration in one or another trend within the stream of tradition.

Looking as a Jew upon the work of Christianity in history, Franz Rosenzweig compared Judaism to the sun and the Christian churches to the rays of sunlight streaming out into space. Judah Halevi, the twelfth-century Jewish philosopher, compared the Jewish faith to a seed thrown into the soil which produces a tree of many branches. Christianity was one such branch, in his view, and when its fruits ripen, the seeds within them will be like the one that was first dropped into the earth. Moses Maimonides considered the growth of the Christian and Moslem churches to be part of the design of Providence to prepare the ground for the ultimate triumph of monotheism and of the ethics of Scripture.[12a]

In all these comments, the underlying principle is the recognition of the essential core of truth in all the faiths of the Judeo-Christian tradition. And the way in which this core is to be identified emerges out of the examination of our own religious tradition in the light of our understanding of human culture and philosophy.

It appears to me that as living traditions, Jewish and Christian ethical teachings differ considerably in emphasis and nuance. Every historical tradition is like a tree, with one stem and many branches, and no two trees are exactly alike. But we may also discern a common Judeo-Christian body of doctrines that is taught in the New Testament as well as in Rabbinic literature.

The principles of the good life are presented to us in the Gospels in two ways—as a vision of perfection and as a body of governing principles. The call to live heroically as a moral being is expounded in the Sermon on the Mount. It is illustrated in the life of Jesus. We are told that to an inquiring young Jew, Jesus offered both a general rule, to love God and man, and also a more specific counsel, in case he wanted to live a "perfect" life, namely, to sell all his possessions and to give them to the poor.

The general principles are expounded in the letters of Paul and James. Contrary to the popular impression, Paul, in his Letters to the Corinthians, insists on the observance of quite a number of moral laws. After all, in the light of history, it is quite obvious that the Christian faith brought about a revolution in human conduct, transforming the ethics of the Greco-Roman world. No one today would summarize the Christian message in the so-called Augustinian maxim, "Love God, and do what you will." The general principles, applying to the lives of all, were to be kept in tension with the injunction to seek perfection by imitating Jesus or his apostles.

In Rabbinic Judaism we find that the good life was expressed in terms of a similar tension between the Law and the call to

110

perfection. The rabbis maintained that "Jerusalem was destroyed only because people insisted on staying within the Law"; that is, they did not go beyond it. The saints of ancient times worked out a series of steps leading to the gift of the Holy Spirit and the power to revive the dead. They set before themselves the task to live like God by following in His steps: "As He is Merciful, so be you merciful, as He clothes the naked, so do you do the same; as He is engaged in deeds of loving kindness, so do you do the same."[13]

But the Law of the Torah was, in Judaism, mandatory only for Jews. "Those who have not been received under the wings of the *Shechinah*" are obligated only to observe the Seven Precepts of the Sons of Noah, and to walk in the ways of God. This is manifestly also the meaning of the decision of the Apostolic Council in Jerusalem.[13a]

In Jewish literature, as in the New Testament, we find a variety of ways in which the Seven Noachide Laws were formulated. There was no agreement on the content of these laws, not even on their number, for it is of the essence of a living core of faith that it remain protean and many-sided, greater than any formulation of its meaning. Since these laws are Divine as well as human, they contain an infinite dimension, a reference to perfection that is out of this world. At the same time, the exigencies of human life may require some tentative and proximate formulations relating to the peculiar problems of the time. But even as we sense the cogency of any one formulation, we must be aware of its incompleteness and its ultimate transcendence. "Perfect, thou shalt be, with the Lord Thy God." And He is always beyond us, yes, even when He dwells among us.

It follows that two of the three phases of Scriptural religion are directly involved in a meaningful interfaith dialogue. The Hebrew Bible consists, according to Jeremiah, of the Torah of the priest, the living word of the prophet, and the rational counsel of the sages.[14] We may recognize these three components in the living faiths of the Judeo-Christian tradition. The priestly component consists of rituals, institutions, and dogmas. The component of wisdom consists of the several sciences of human behavior and history. The prophetic element consists of the living confrontation of all the challenges of the day in the endeavor to face and to overcome the manifold evils of the times. Ideally, the Hebrew prophet was a mystic, a philosopher, and a dedicated statesman at one and the same time. In his great soul, the sheer momentum of the past was overcome. He diverted attention from the fringes of faith, where all friction occurs, to its creative center, where the insights of all saintly and thoughtful men tend to merge. While we have no prophets today, we do possess the inspiration of the prophetic heritage. In modern Judaism as in Christianity, it is a vital force. And it is the prophetic, as well as the intellectual, component of our historic faiths that comes to light in the dialogue.

The doctrines of the Noachide Laws and the imitation of God in Rabbinic literature and their counterparts in the New Testament provide us with the basic framework for the understanding of our relation to people of other faiths.

First, we must distinguish between the dogmatic and ritual structure of our faith, and its essential principles. Second, we must recognize a similar, though not an identical, set of principles under the outer garments of other faiths. Third, we must admit the fragmentary and temporal nature of any attempt to define and formulate the dynamic core of religious principles. Fourth, the endeavor to apply these principles to the concerns of our community and our time is the common task of all the great faiths. Fifth, whatever formulation and application we achieve at any moment must still be under constant review and judgment, for the vision of perfection is always ahead of us, never completely in our grip.

In this way, we avoid the three evils in the domain of religion—imperialism, isolationism, indifferentism.

We do not seek to convert others to our historic faith, though we keep the channels of information open for our mutual enlightenment. Nor do we assume that all religions are equally true, for there is room for the infinite quest in the objective realm, and there is an infinite dimension of depth in the subjective domain, which can neither be weighed nor measured. Nor do we believe that we can exclude other traditions from our understanding and sympathy without blinding ourselves to the fullness of Divine truth. We meet on the common ground of knowledge and prophetic concern in order to know others and ourselves better, and to know our duty more clearly. Out of this deeper knowledge and more embracing sympathy, we may hope to obtain a more penetrating understanding of the dynamic essence of our faith. Perhaps our interlocutors may be similarly moved by these dialogues to arrive at a deeper comprehension of the living core of their faith. For depth calls to depth. "As waters reflect face to face, so does the heart of man to man."

RESPONSE TO FATHER DANIÉLOU'S
DIALOGUE WITH ISRAEL
AND CARDINAL BEA'S
THE CHURCH AND THE JEWISH PEOPLE

This collection of short essays and reviews by the great French scholar Jean Daniélou is entitled by its author *Dialogue with Israel*.[1] It might be objected that the title is misleading, since Jewish authors do not speak for themselves in this volume, except for the beautiful letter of Edmond Fleg. But, then, in a deeper sense, the title is justified in that the author argues with the image of Israel that his marvelous erudition has built up in his own mind. Yet, an image, no matter how carefully it is constructed, cannot take the place of the living reality, because life is dynamic and ever-changing, incapable of being fitted into the neat categories of logic or the rigid formulas of Church councils. In "The Schism of Israel," the author speaks of an "interior knowledge of the Bible" that only Jews can possess. I doubt it, but they certainly possess an "interior knowledge" of themselves as a living historic community.

It seems that a dialogue with Israel is an essential component of the life of faith for every Christian. This circumstance makes us partners in the Divine enterprise. We have to challenge each other to be true to the best of our own heritage and thereby to promote the love of God and man that is our common task. Being human, our very attempt to be loyal to our own historic faith-institutions leads us to close our eyes to the infinite task. We tend to worship the symbols and ceremonies themselves, instead of looking through them to seek Him, who is found only in the quest itself. It is of the very nature of the infinite quest that it be a restless tension between possession and privation—God is *near* unto us, yet He remains *far,* beyond and above all our faculties. Hence, it is in the dialogue situation that the alternating currents of the arc of faith light up and glow.

It is understood, of course, that there is a kind of faith which shuts out the world and, far from being a dialogue, is more like an endless declamation of memorized verses. In the Talmud, the question is discussed as to which verse constitutes the final fulcrum of faith. According to one rabbi it is the assertion of Habakkuk, "And the righteous man lives by his faith."[2] The other rabbi declares it is the verse in which the prophet Amos describes God as saying, "Seek Me and live."[3] To the one, faith is a universe of discourse and practice, complete unto itself; to the other, faith is an ongoing quest. A dialogue is possible only for the disciples of Amos, who recognize the limits of their knowledge and whose faith is an ongoing and endless quest. A great historian who is keenly conscious of the many ways in which the truths of faith have been distorted in previous epochs of history, ever since the Lord spoke to Abraham, cannot feel that the doors have now been barred with absolute assurance against all kinds of error; hence the author's readiness for a true dialogue.

What are the logical prerequisites of a genuine dialogue? Obviously, the first requisite is that the participants talk *to* one another, not *at* one another, that they move within the same realm of discourse. In the first century, this common universe consisted of the Hebrew Scriptures plus many Apocryphal writings, oral traditions that were taught to the general public, and various esoteric teachings and commentaries. Some of these last, like Philo's, were compatible with Orthodoxy, and some, like those of the Qumran caves, were cherished by sectarians.

The first century now belongs to the past. We cannot possibly recapture its mental atmosphere in its fullness. It is only as historians, conscious of the limits of this art, not as dogmatic disputants, that we are today trying to unravel the twisted knots of the primitive Church and its debates with Jews, Judeo-Christians, and Gnostics. From this vantage point it is interesting that the author regards Christianity as continuing the "later Judaism of the last two pre-Christian centuries," including Philo and the apocalypses, while it combats "Judaism after the year 70, to which Pharisaism gives its narrowly legalistic form."[4] Jewish scholars lay claim to Philo and the apocalypses, to the legalists and the preachers, to the philosophers and the mystics. The Law was never cherished in isolation, but along with the prophets and the sages. We do not feel bound to accept any one of the ways of thought that prevailed in the past, certainly not in isolation from the rest of our heritage. For example, the "Spirit of God" in the second verse of Genesis is, according to a commentator in the Midrash, the "Spirit of the King Messiah."[5] But it is one opinion among many others. In the new translation of the Jewish Publication Society, no account whatever is taken of this interpretation, and the verse is translated as follows: "and a wind from God was sweeping over the water."[6]

What then can be the basis of a meaningful dialogue today? I submit that the common universe of discourse today is the objective body of ideas, sentiments, memories, and aspirations that we cherish in common as members of Western civilization in the twentieth century. The objective approach to life is not alien to the Judeo-Christian tradition. On the contrary, the monotheistic faith is precisely the assurance that the compassionate, loving God of our hearts is one with the Divine Being, as He is revealed in the inexorable laws of the universe. This is the deeper meaning of the *Shema,* "Hear, O Israel, the Lord our God, the Lord is One."[7] Paul restates this thesis in the first chapter of his First Epistle to the Romans. His own faith was a heroic endeavor to reconcile the drama of the Incarnation with the moral teaching of Judaism and the rational mind of Hellenism, knowing as he did that without such an effort the Gospel was a stumbling block to the Jews, folly to the Greeks.[8] His personality is fascinating, particularly because of his inner struggle. He battled against the Jews who asked for signs and

116

the Greeks who sought wisdom, but he could not let go of the Jew and the Greek within him.

The objective side of faith is the attempt to explicate the meaning of intelligence and conscience. The ancient world was saturated with myths concerning dying and rising gods, but it did not know the unity of religious faith, ethical insight, and the self-denying intellect. The pagan mentality was fragmentized and compartmentalized. In Jewish monotheism, God is from the beginning the ultimate source of all ideals and all forms of power. He is found in the surrender of faith but also in the assertion of justice and truth, hence, the novelty of Abraham's not sacrificing his son, Isaac.[9] There was nothing unusual in Abraham's initial readiness to sacrifice his son—even ordinary people brought such sacrifices in those days. Thus, Amos insists that the Will of God consists, not in compliance with rituals, but in hating evil and loving good.[10] The Hebrew Bible consists of the Torah of the priests, the word of the prophets, and the wisdom of the sages, reflecting the mystical, ethical, and intellectual phases of a living faith. And in the days of its "narrow legalism," Judaism created the ideal of a Disciple of the Wise, who participated in these three disciplines, being at once somewhat of a priest, an ethical teacher, and a learned sage.[10a] In terms of the priestly rites of our respective faiths, we differ; but we have in common the prophetic quest for God, not merely of the good life and the many-sided wisdom of our common culture.

It is of the essence of the prophetic and philosophic ways of thought that they lead to a reinterpretation of the priestly element, modifying its meaning, even if they do not change its form. On the other hand, popular religion, left to itself, is always liable to degenerate into primitive magic-mongering. It converts God into a tangible idol and projects its own sins on concrete people. In this connection, the author's observation that anti-Semitic pogroms in Christian Europe were popular phenomena, rather than theological exercises, takes on added significance. It is the priestly elements of the Christian faith,

117

the simplistic interpretation of the Crucifixion, of the "curse" resting upon the Jews, and their identification with Judas (an identification which even St. Augustine favored) that provided the sticky tar with which the victims were smeared. The feathers derived from the contemporary scene, spreading heresy, competing with Christian merchants, encouraging luxury, engaging in money-lending, tax-farming, or well-poisoning.

Let us not forget, however, that at times the highest authorities in the Church gave aid and comfort to the perversion of true faith into popular myth and magic. And the Jews were among the first to suffer for the failure of the Church to live up to its high traditions. Nor was this phenomenon confined to the Middle Ages. Soon after the French Revolution, demagogues discovered that they could use for their own nefarious purposes the myths of popular Christianity. All too often, they were assisted by clerical collaborators.

Can the moral-rational phase of religion, which comes to life in moments of true dialogue, prevent the perversion and misuse of the principles of faith? I believe that it can accomplish this end on all fronts—in particular, in respect to Christian-Jewish relations. The moral-rational imperatives do not lead to indifferentism, but they do liberate us from the ancient nightmares of Satan and hell and curses and endless damnation. The debate between the various forms of Judaism and the many varieties of Christianity was peculiarly acute because it was cast in the form, "Who is right?" instead of being merely a question of "What is right?" It seemed that there could be only one Chosen People, and all who were not so chosen would be cast into outer darkness. Today, many of us interpret "chosenness" in the sense of an *example*, not of an *exception*. The more communities that covenant themselves to the Lord, the better. The pagan hunger for the concrete confused the invisible company of saints, "the people of the Lord," with the visible panoply of whichever church prevailed in their area. The Church has now agreed that while *it* can save in only one way, God can bring people to Himself in many ways. The

choice between various forms of faith, all of which are approved
in moral and rational terms, is a choice for oneself between
the good, the better, and the best, not between the One True
Way, leading to heaven, and the several ways leading to hell.

It follows that wherever the New Testament and the Church
Fathers speak of the Jewish faith as being "accursed," it becomes the duty of the teachers to eliminate, modify, or rein-
terpret the relevant passages.[11] This is the main point of
Edmond Fleg's letter: have done with curses! The curse of
Christians that was at one time part of the Jewish liturgy was
removed a thousand years ago. To say, as Father Daniélou does,
"it is sin that crucified Christ, the sin of Israel, but our own
as well," is to continue the identification of the Jew with sin.
This identification is the historical substratum of mythological
anti-Semitism. To fight anti-Semitism with one hand and to
sow its sinister seeds with the other is to act like that general
of Charles V's army who directed his cannonfire against the
pope while praying that no harm might come to him.

Israel's "sin," in Father Daniélou's reply, turns out to be not
the condemnation of Jesus as a "blasphemer" by the members of
the Sanhedrin (they were obligated to do so, in accord with
their faith, he maintains) but the fact that they did not believe
in him as an incarnation of the Deity. Is disbelief then a sin?
Certainly not in a moral-rational world. Father Daniélou offers
to prove that Jesus had indeed fulfilled the requirements of all
the Messianic verses. Some were fulfilled materially, some
"spiritually." He certainly knows the great variety of views
concerning the Messiah that circulated at that time. The Sanhedrin included Sadducees as well as Pharisees. In theological
terms, the gulf between them was immense. Is it sacrilegious
to doubt that even so eminent a scholar as Father Daniélou
could not have convinced the members of the Sanhedrin? After
all, the only real "sign," the "sign of Jonah," was to be given
after the trial and through the action of that Sanhedrin itself—
the Passion, the Crucifixion, and the Resurrection.[12]

The fact is that Paul did not consider the life of Jesus on

earth to be convincing of Messiahship. He said, "No man can call Jesus Lord, save in the Holy Spirit."[12a] If, then, it is God who brings us to Himself and it is agreed that He is not pre-empted by any church, is it not our duty to open ourselves to Him and wait for His guidance?

Jewish scholars do not agree that Jesus could have been convicted on the ground of "blasphemy," since the Halakah specifies that the blasphemer must actually curse the Name of God.[13] The killing of Stephen, in which Paul participated, was manifestly a lynching by an unruly mob. However, a Messianic pretender would be challenged to prove himself through the course of events that his claim set into motion. This was precisely the attitude of Rabban Gamaliel, as reported in Acts. There was no way of attesting the Messiah, save through his success.[13a]

Christians may claim that the wondrous expansion of the Church is proof of Jesus' Messiahship. But they agree that a Second Coming "with power" will bring about the fulfillment of the Messianic hope. We may agree that through Jesus and his apostles a high redemptive purpose of God was fulfilled, though not the achievement of the hoped for Messianic Era, and Fleg quotes Maimonides to this effect. We are ready to welcome into the camp of "the people of God" all who are brought to His service, in word and deed, in accordance with the declaration of Rabbi Meir, an author of the Mishnah, "that a Gentile who labors in the Torah is like a high-priest."[14] The Talmud interprets Torah, in this connection, to mean the Noachide universal principles of religion and ethics.[15] A Midrashic author exclaimed, "I bring heaven and earth as my witnesses: that whether one be Jew or Gentile, man or woman, slave or slave-girl—the Holy spirit rests upon him in accordance with his deeds.[16]

Fleg congratulates Father Daniélou for the latter's emphasis on the doctrine of the Second Coming. It is not for us to enter into a domain where doctors of the Church fear to tread. But apart from dogmatic formulations, Fleg calls upon Christians to think of the future, of the task ahead. There is work aplenty for all of us.

Father Daniélou wonders why some Jewish writers admire and extol the personality and teachings of Jesus, while they refuse to acknowledge him as the Son of God. It is precisely because they admire the teaching of Jesus that they resent the bitter irony of what has been done in his name. He points to the infinite dimension of piety, as against the hollowness of rituals. But were not external rites insisted upon in his name? And did not millions die in the bloody disputes over crossing oneself with two fingers or with three, or celebrating the Mass in one kind or in two? The author mentions Bahya Ibn Pakuda's work, *Duties of the Heart,* which describes this infinite dimension of piety. Then did not he, the Jew, write in accord with what Jesus preached? This work of Bahya's was studied in the synagogues of Poland daily by groups of humble artisans.

According to Protestant scholars, Jesus emphasized man's individual responsibility and the need of breaking through historical barriers in order to open the blessings of salvation to all men. We fully agree with this ideal, whatever we may think of its historicity. This battle against the would-be monopolists of heaven, together with the humble recognition that, being very far from perfection, we can still learn from one another, is precisely what the dialogue is all about.

In his comments on the work of Jules Isaac, the author centers attention on the problem of eliminating the seeds of anti-Semitism from the New Testament. He writes, "A long tradition of texts seems to teach that the Jewish people rejected Christ and put him to death and that their hardship is a punishment for this deicide."

Presumably this sentence was written before the Vatican Council issued its Schema on the Jews. The author in other places disavows the thought that Jewish suffering must be regarded as the punishment for this sin.

In any case, the author takes issue with Isaac, who maintains that "Christ criticized only the abuses of the Jewish observances and did not declare the annulment of the Law itself." Isaac's point is that the moral and spiritual principles of the Torah are eternally valid, as indeed St. Paul instituted the "law of the spirit," as soon as the Corinthians interpreted "freedom" to mean moral license. The Catholic Church maintained in force many laws of the Old Testament: the prohibition of usury, the condemnation of witchcraft, the prohibition of idolatry and of all foods contaminated by idolatrous worship, the degrees of prohibited marriage, and even the condemnation of a heretical city. The essence of Isaac's argument is that Jesus did not condemn the Torah as the work of Satan. Only Marcion did so, and all who along with him condemned the worship of Israel as the "Synagogue of Satan." Isaac would not object to the author's right to claim that Jesus "instituted a new and better cult." It is natural and right for every historic community to assert that its cult is better and even that it is best, but to assert that Judaism is now "of the Devil," as some passages in John and in the patristic writings do, is as vicious as it is ridiculous.

The task of Catholic authors is to remove this dehumanizing stigma from their sacred writings, by means of reinterpretation, as Isaac suggests. For Father Daniélou to require, as a *quid pro quo*, that Jews "recognize what Jesus brought forth as both completing and surpassing that same Law" is to suggest a kind of bargaining that I cannot attribute to Father Daniélou. I therefore assume that he means that Jews shall not regard Christians as living under a "curse," having in mind the ancient curse of the Synagogue, the *birkat haminim*. (Modern Jews learned of its existence, in an anti-Christian form, only since the discovery by Schechter of an ancient fragment in the Cairo Genizah.) He may mean also that Jews should study the New Testament in order to appreciate the noble teachings contained therein and to understand the faith of their neighbors. Many rabbis and Jewish educators have already undertaken this task.

But to ask Jews to recognize in Jesus the "fulfillment of the Law" is to give an excellent demonstration of the folly of transposing the subjective content of one faith into the subjective structure of another faith. We have to remind the reader again that each faith creates its terms out of the fullness of its experience in its own unique way and that the corresponding terms of two faiths are incommensurate, as the infinite series of integers with the infinite series of the same numbers multiplied by the square root of two. It is only in the moral-rational realm of discourse that a dialogue can take place. In the private realm of religious feelings and symbols, comparison involves the fullest analysis of what Catholics mean by "Jesus," by "fulfillment," by the "Law." Then, it is necessary to plumb similarly the primary, secondary, and ineffable meanings of the term "Torah" to Jews. And it is needful to choose one out of many versions of the historical Jesus or one out of many versions of the Christian image of Jesus, and then determine the content of "fulfillment" in respect to Torah and Jesus. It would be easier to move geometric figures into a non-Euclidean world. In view of the depth-dimension of religious terms, is such a task possible? Scripture reminds us, "Man looks with his eyes, but the Lord looks to the heart."[16a]

Father Daniélou points out that Isaac, "in his desire to declare the Jewish people innocent," discovers that the "texts of the Gospel make this argument difficult." The learned Father maintains that the literal meaning of the texts clears only individual Jews of guilt, but the Jewish people as an ideal unit must be considered guilty, or the Crucifixion would be only an "episode" in the life of Israel. From this reasoning, it would follow that a Jew participates in the guilt of "deicide" to the extent that he participates in the living heritage of Israel, that is, when he observes the Sabbath, prays three times daily, fasts on the Day of Atonement, and eats unleavened bread on Passover. If this kind of teaching comes from a friend and a lifelong fighter against anti-Semitism, what is Christian anti-Semitism?

As a student and friend of scholars, I know the anguish that the literal meaning of texts can bring to one whose conscience is as keen and informed as that of Father Daniélou. But here is where the "religion of Jesus" should take precedence over the

123

varied "religions about Jesus"; namely, let the life-bringing spirit prevail over the death-dealing letter. The spirit of Christianity, Father Daniélou will agree, consists in the love of God and of man. Did not St. Thomas already assert that the priority of the spirit to the letter applies to the New Testament as well as to the Old Testament?[17] To follow the logic of the spirit of faith is to accord decisive weight to the moral-rational approach.

In several places, the author speaks of the Jewish people as constituting a special mystery. He adds that Isaac would refuse to consider Jews as just "an ordinary people." I shudder at the term mystery, when it is applied to one people as against the rest of humanity. We should all agree that the ways of God are mysterious and that, in a sense, every person and every historic community participates in His mystery. We were warned that "the hidden things belong to God"[18] and we cannot take His place. To put one community outside the pale of humanity as being at once charged with a metaphysical sin and condemned to an inscrutable fate is to lay the groundwork for the madness of mythological anti-Semitism. Here is the root of Hitler's "non-Aryanism." Some Catholic friends of mine point out that the Church is also a "mystery." Yes, but with positive valence, whereas Israel is in so much Catholic thought shadowed by a "mystery" with negative valence.

I do not know whether Isaac would refuse to consider Jews "an ordinary people," but I certainly regard ordinary people as capable of the highest achievements, if they make use of the heritage of the ages. As Jews, we are more disposed to sense the tragic dilemma of man, so animalic and so Godlike, because we have felt in our bones the fangs of the one and the promise of the other. But it is possible to be a Jew and to be "ordinary," all too ordinary, and to be any other kind of man and quite out of the ordinary. Already in the last generation of the first century, when, according to the author, the foundations of "narrow legalism" were laid, the rabbis decided that "the pious among the nations will share in the World to Come."[18a]

If Father Daniélou and other Catholic scholars understand by the "mystery of Israel" only that which St. Paul conveys in Romans 10, then I suggest that they simply state what they mean, without stigmatizing living people with the mark of metaphysical uniqueness.

Concerning the origins of anti-Semitism, Father Daniélou is quite right in his insistence against Poliakov on the historic facts of Jewish-Christian struggles in the first century. We have only one-sided and garbled accounts of the later struggles, culminating in the joint Jewish-Persian capture of Jerusalem in 614. On the other hand, pre-Christian anti-Semitism developed a massive, myth-laden ideology in the Greco-Roman world, an ideology which differed very little from the complex of motivations that led even good emperors like Marcus Aurelius Antonius to throw confessed Christians to the lions. European anti-Semitism derived its inspiration, strangely enough, from the revival of pagan, classical literature as well as from the Christian world. Pagan in essence, modern anti-Semitism used effectively the popular perversion of the Christian faith.

The Jewish-Christian struggles help to explain the extreme bitterness of some passages in the New Testament. Once their *Sitz im Leben* is understood, these passages should be reinterpreted. If they are read as part of the liturgy, then the translation itself should take account of the contextual meaning. If what is meant is not that "Jews are of their father, the Devil," but those of all races and all times who refuse to open their hearts to love, then why not say so plainly, say so in the name of that love that is the living spirit of Christian teaching? The very least that we can expect of love is that it shall not foment hate. Who today would wish to teach children all that Luther had to say about the popes in Rome and vice versa, or even what Luther and Calvin and Zwingli had to say about one another? These considerations give added force to Isaac's thesis that for the sake of their own integrity, Christian scholars should proceed to eliminate not only anti-Semitism itself, but also the seed-bed of anti-Semitism: the notion of a curse, or the guilt of deicide, resting on the people as a whole.

Lastly, a word about the author's reflections on the "Schism of Israel." What he sees as the separation of Israel from the historic stream, we see as the growth of the Christian branch from the Jewish tree, even as several centuries later, the Moslem branch grew out of the same tree. All three branches, Rabbinic Judaism, Christianity, Islam, have grown from the same trunk. Halevi assures us that, in the fullness of time, the ripe fruits of all the three branches will contain the same seeds.[18b] But we are not living at the end of history. What then shall the relations of Judaism and Christianity be?

Judaism accords to Christianity the status of a congregation that is helping to prepare the way for the Messianic era. Directing its gaze to the future, it reaffirms the message of Micah: "For all the peoples walk every one in the name of his god, and we will walk in the name of the Lord our God for ever and ever."[19] I agree with Father Daniélou that Jews can bring to the common spiritual enterprise a fervent appreciation of the pragmatic, ethical, and optimistic spirit of the Torah. In dialogue with Christians, they tend to keep Christians from succumbing to the simplistic seductions of unworldly mysticism and Marcionite Gnosticism; in turn, our Christian friends tend to keep us from yielding to the lure of many dangers in our religious and cultural life. Without the perpetual challenge of our Christian colleagues, we could hardly expect to keep abreast of all who walk to the mountain of the Lord. We need one another in order to breathe freely and grow straight. Does the Divine "mystery" consist, perhaps, in this very need?

Perhaps I react so strongly to Father Daniélou's words because a recent work I read is still fresh in my mind. It is a short volume by Augustin Cardinal Bea, entitled *The Church and the Jewish People*.[20] In this book, Cardinal Bea, who has earned the deep gratitude of Jewish people the world over, outlines the reasons and considerations that led to the promulgation by the Vatican Council of its declaration on the Jews. He explains why it was decided to put this declaration within the wider context of non-Christian religions.

He states it as the purpose of the Church "to promote the unity of the human family in every possible way,"[21] and he asserts that while the Church can offer salvation only through its sacraments, "God is not so bound and does not limit his activity to these means."[22] More specifically, he attacks the views of those churchmen who assert that the Jews "must be regarded as frankly inferior to all other peoples from a religious point of view, precisely because it is a deicide people, rejected and cursed by God."[23] He maintains that "the members of the Sanhedrin did not know of Christ's dual nature"; their action was "culpable," but their guilt was not unmitigated. He concludes this phase of his argument as follows: "If then the formal guilt of deicide cannot be unequivocally attributed to the leaders, still less can it be imputed to members of the Jewish Diaspora, and again less to the Jews of other times. . ."[24]

Still Cardinal Bea goes on to claim that "the guilt [of deicide] is in the personal order and falls upon anyone who in some way directly associates himself with the 'perverse generation.' "[25] Then he adds, "Generally speaking, refusal to believe in the Gospel and in Jesus is a factor in this judgment, and so, in one way or another, is a free decision to ally oneself with the 'perverse generation.' "[26]

Again, referring to Romans 11:28, he writes, "This last passage simply stresses that while God still loves the people for the sake of their fathers, he holds them as 'odious' because he detests their attitude to the Gospel."[27]

I submit that this characterization of Jews loyal to Judaism either as "odious" or as "guilty of deicide" even while they are "dear to God" is a vestigial remnant of medievalism that is incompatible with the emergent liberalism of the Church and its moral-rational integrity. Even if the Church believes that after the Crucifixion Judaism was no longer "an institution designed for salvation," it is still, from the human viewpoint, no worse than Islam, or Buddhism, or, for that matter, any Protestant sect. If, as Cardinal Bea asserts, there lies upon all of us "the duty of reading the Old Testament intelligently, in order to be able to identify the permanent elements in it,"[28] I ask if we, all of us, are not equally obligated to read the New Testament "intelligently"? If so, is it not our primary obligation as historians and philosophers to take note of the mental context of every generation and to filter out the venom of previous struggles? The demon-ridden world of Jesus' day is not our world, even as the Messianic and pseudo-Messianic tensions of the Jews of that day are foreign to us.

The residual elements of "deicide" and "rejection" may be exceedingly minute in the total view of Cardinal Bea or Father Daniélou, but as long as Father Daniélou retains that hate-soaked rhetoric, he provides a verbal screen behind which pathological and mythological anti-Semites may continue to operate.

The Catholic Church has never officially and legally burned Jews in any *auto-da-fé,* though it condemned to this fate thousands of formerly Jewish backsliders (Marranos), heretics, and Protestants. There is now a growing recognition that Protestants are not to be burned, but rather to be loved as "separated brethren." This is proof that the Church is not fettered by the dead letters of the past. As Jews, we salute the progress of the ecumenical movement because it represents an advance in spiritual maturity, a growth of the capacity to sense inner unity of spirit behind a diversity of external expressions. The hope of the world depends on this Divine gift of empathy, when the love of neighbor ceases to be a self-congratulatory sentiment and becomes a sympathetic understanding of one's neighbors from within. For this reason, we welcome and share the spirit of the ecumenical movement. We appreciate the efforts of Cardinal Bea and Father Daniélou and the vast majority of prelates the world over who, in the declaration on the Jews, opened a new era of mutual trust between Catholics and Jews. This is why we are so disappointed when the pace-setters of the Jewish-

Christian dialogue are apparently so loathe to part with the ghosts of the Middle Ages.

Let us base the dialogue on the firm recognition that many things of the past are no longer valid. We, in appropriating for ourselves the spiritual heritage of our past, do not grant a blanket endorsement to all the actions of our forefathers or to all their beliefs. Our faith at any time is a synthesis of our own understanding and that of our fathers: we address our prayers to "our God and the God of our fathers." On every festival, we acknowledge our collective failures: "and because of our sins, were we exiled from our land." So you, too, liberated as you are from the compulsions of the letter, can afford to follow the counsel of St. Thomas and adopt a "benevolent interpretation" of the status of contemporary Jews and contemporary Judaism—without any quibbling or bargaining.

Part Two
Dialogue with Historians

TOYNBEE
AND JUDAISM*

All readers of Toynbee's monumental work[1] are impressed by
the strong Christian bias that this great historian manifests.
Though he repudiates fundamentalism with the utmost scorn,
he clings to the dogmatic view that the emergence of Christianity has rendered Judaism superfluous. By rejecting its daughter-
faith, Judaism not only stultified its past but forfeited its future.
To be sure, he interprets the dogmas of Christianity in symbolical, psychological terms, denuding them of their literal historical
significance; yet, he persists in regarding Jewry with contempt
if not with malice—as if we were still to blame for rejecting
and crucifying the now purely symbolical Savior. His words are
reminiscent at times of that cynic who said: "I don't believe
that Jesus ever lived, but I still insist that the Jews killed him."

However, on the whole, the scornful references in this great
historian's work to Judaism or the Jewish people are not
essential to his main thesis. They are attributable, for the most
part, to the vein of poetic symbolism in which he prefers to
write rather than to the profound insights whereby he discovers
the articulation of meaning in the bewildering mass of data
furnished by the diverse chronicles of mankind. Seen in the
light of the essential ideas of Judaism, his philosophy of history
is in line with the genuine impetus of the Hebrew prophets
and of the masterbuilders of the Talmud. His monumental
achievement in marshaling facts and inferences from many
different civilizations should be carefully studied by Jewish
scholars and utilized in that transvaluation of popular dogmas

*Reprinted from *Judaism*, Fall 1955.

133

that our generation is called upon to undertake. We can ill afford to ignore the abundant truths that his immense labors and brilliant genius have amassed.

We of the post-Hitler generation are fated to straddle one of the rare thresholds in history, when the opening of a new era permits a relatively large measure of freedom and choice. The disappearance of the Jewish "heartland" in Central Europe, the rise of the State of Israel, and the emergence of American Jewry as the massive center of the global fellowship of Israel are all decisive factors that imply the opening of a new and completely unprecedented era. Challenged as we are to interpret the meaning of the momentous facts for the guidance of our sorely tried people, we must make use of every helpful suggestion and every illuminating remark. The authentic genius of Judaism was reflected in the definition of the sage given in our Ethics—"he who learns from all people." But already it is evident that the superficial bias and the occasional note of scorn in Toynbee's writings threaten to insulate the minds of our intellectuals against the important facts and judgments corraled by his genius. Unfortunately, those sweet-tempered sages who, like Rabbi Meir, know how "to cast away the shell and eat the kernel" are rare at all times, exceedingly rare in our day.

In this essay, the attempt will be made to indicate wherein Toynbee deals unfairly with the Jewish people or with Judaism and then to call attention to the salutary insights that emerge from his analysis of the Jewish situation.

One of the distressing phrases that occur frequently in Toynbee's study is the reference to modern Jewry as a "fossil of Syriac civilization." In his analysis, Jewry is not the only such "fossil," for the Parsees in India, the Nestorian Christians in the Near East, and the Armenians in Turkey and Russia are also "fossils" of the same old civilization. The term "fossil" carries certain negative connotations, which the author, soaring in his Olympian heights, overlooks. A "fossil" is in the first place a category that emerges out of the classification that he employs, having no existence in reality. Thus, if a civilization is defined as a large geographical area, sufficient to be taken as a "field of study" in its own right, then the inner life of the peoples comprising that civilization is relatively unimportant. Indeed, it was while Jewry formed part of the Persian Empire, supposedly its "universal state," that Haman was able to point to it as a unique and intolerable foreign body, thrust amidst the 127 provinces of the Iranian King of Kings. In terms of inner life, the gulf between Jews and pagans was deeper by far than any division between Greeks and Syrians, as is abundantly demonstrated by the fact that the Syrians and Greeks were largely intermingled in the Seleucid era while the Jews remained a "people that dwells alone" even in the heyday of Hellenistic predominance.

In staking out his "fields of study," Toynbee was concerned only with the external phenomena of language, custom, the arts of industry and commerce, and the nature of political and military contacts. Nor was it to be expected that in so colossal an undertaking the author would retain the same attitude at the end of his work as he had at its beginning. In his concluding volumes, he maintains that it is a great religion that gives birth to a new civilization, not a decayed civilization that is saved and guarded by the "inner proletariat" through the medium of a "higher religion." The inner soul of a culture is, after all, more important than the externally observable data of a so-called civilization, for it is the soul that creates the collective "style of life." In terms of spiritual realities, it manifestly makes little sense to speak of Jewry as part of the Syriac civilization.

The term "fossil" connotes not alone a fragment but a lifeless curiosity that properly belongs in a museum of antiquities. This judgment again is justified only in terms of the outer expressions and trappings of a civilization, not in terms of the inner life of Jewry. Judaism did not simply remain fixed and frozen in the ideological molds of the Mishnah or the Talmud. Every intellectual movement that ruffled the European ocean of thought and feeling in the past fifteen centuries stirred similar waves and tidal swells within the bays of Judaism. Primitive rationalism had its champion in a Saadia and religious individualism in a Karaite movement; romanticism came in two fundamentally different versions in Ibn Gabirol and Halevi; ripe rationalism had its noble champion in Maimonides and mysticism its intricate theory and its occult visions in the various trends within Qabbalah and Hasidism. To be sure, in theory what Toynbee designates as the social force of "mimesis" was directed toward the past, but in practice the "past" was reshaped to conform with the changing conceptions of the good life. The "cake of custom" was not only radically broken by overt acts before the rise of Karaism and later the Reform movement, but the spirit in which the same customs were performed reflected the living play of opposing trends within the stream of Judaism. The *mizvoth* may have varied only slightly, but the *taamai hamizvoth* ("reasons for the commandments") were like an unfailing fountain of fresh waters. Even in the case of custom and ritual, the elimination of the whole domain of ritual purity in post-Talmudic days constituted a massive transformation of Pharisaic piety, on a par with the substitution of prayer for animal sacrifices. But the main expressions of the dynamic impetus in Jewish life occured within the interior life, in keeping with the challenge of the contemporary climate of ideas and sentiments.

Jewry could be regarded as "fossilized" only if the intensity of life were measured by the vulgar yardsticks of the world, not if it were assayed in the delicate scales of spirituality. Yet, the basic bias of Toynbee is definitely in behalf of the values of the spirit.

Actually, his judgment derives from an ambiguity in the use of the term Judaism. At times, he equates Judaism with the ethnic culture of Jewry; at other times, he thinks of the Jewish faith as a separable pattern of ideas, which is included more or less in our modern Western culture. The elements of nationality—language, political organization, common sovereignty, sense of ethnic kinship—he regards as a fossilized part of the larger whole of the ancient Syriac civilization. The faith of Judaism is embraced for him within the general context of Christianity, that is, "the consummation of all previous Jewish experience." When he speaks of the four "higher religions," Islam, Hinduism, Buddhism, and Christianity, he assumes that modern Judaism is included within Christianity in the larger sense of the term. More recently, he has begun to speak of Judaism specifically as one of the great religions of mankind. But the ambiguity of his original judgment persists, largely because he does not always bear in mind his own distinction between Judaism as a "higher religion" and the outer civilizational elements of Jewish life. Within the Jewish religion, there was no lack of what he designates as the mark of life, "dynamic movement," occasioned by "creative individual personalities," but up to the rise of the State of Israel in our own day, the civilizational elements of Jewry—the ethnic, popular base, language, residual self-government, and social ways of life—were either retained in a dormant atrophied state or else rejected in favor of corresponding elements borrowed from the environment.

The Jewish people accepted without qualms Aramaic, Greek, Arabic, Spanish, French, German, and Persian as their spoken tongues, creating in the course of time "Jewish" versions out of these languages. Along with the languages of their neighbors, they accepted the outer trappings of civilization, the ways of expressing joy and sorrow, dignity and humiliation that prevailed among their host-nations. Judging all things by the spiritual yardstick of holiness, they esteemed most secular expressions of the "style of life" to be of no consequence. And when in the nineteenth century, Russian and Polish Jews resented so tenaciously the efforts of Nicholas I to foist upon them "German" garments, they clung to garments that were originally Polish—the *kapoto,* the *zhupitze,* the *shtraimel.* Need we be reminded of the fact that it was the advent of the Haskalah, the movement of secular humanism that called attention to the study of grammar, of a "pure language," of

137

decorum and dignity in the "ways of the world"? If the intensity of civilization is assayed in the scales of the spirit, Jewish life all through the long dark ages was of the loftiest pitch, pure and without parallel. The atrophy of the outer civilizational elements in Jewish life, giving the appearance of fossilization to an outside observer, was itself due to the intense moralistic and pietistic standards of value that prevailed within it.

The second judgment in Toynbee's work which is extremely offensive is his comparison of the presumed expulsion of the Arab refugees from the State of Israel with the Nazi crime of systematic extermination of six million Jews. This judgment has already been subjected to scathing criticism by Marie Syrkin and others. No amount of subtle casuistry can possibly equate any wrong done to the Arabs with the systematic extermination of the Jews in the ghettos and the gas chambers. Even to discuss such a comparison under any pretext is in the highest sense of the word sacrilegious.

At the same time, it is important for us to recall points that are overlooked by both sides to the Toynbee controversy.

First, while the majority of Arab refugees left their homes and villages at the behest of their leaders, a goodly number were driven out in the heat of the battle by the Irgunists and others. Also, a considerable number were panicked into fleeing by atrocities of the type of Deir Yassin. These acts of terrorization were performed by individuals who were temporarily frenzied by fear and fanaticism, not by the calm decision of a responsible government. Nevertheless, these facts should not be ignored.

Second, the debt owed to the Arab refugees should be acknowledged by Israel—quite apart from any relations with the neighboring countries. As to how the debt is to be discharged, in view of the changed circumstances in the past years, is a matter of detail. Israel should acknowledge in principle the right of the Arabs to return to their former homes and should offer to cooperate with the agencies of the United Nations in determining the amount of compensation due in every instance. As a matter of inescapable reality, very few Arabs would find any opportunity for reintegration into the economy of the land of Israel. Even in the days of the Mandate, when Jewish immigration was conceded to be a "matter of right, not sufferance," the principle of "economic absorptive capacity" was in force. New homes would have to be found for most of the refugees in Jordan and other Arab countries, or perhaps overseas. But, in principle, it ill becomes us to dispute the right of all the refugees to return to their former villages and to enjoy absolutely equal rights and opportunities in the land of Israel, providing they accept the authority of the government and swear loyalty to it. The funds raised in America and other countries should be placed at the service of all residents of the land of Israel without exception. By no stretch of logic or ethics can the contradictory policy of maintaining that the land of Israel is open for the emigration of Jews from the Western countries, while there is no room for the people who were born and raised in the land be justified. Several times, the State of Israel made overtures in this general direction, but not consistently.

If there is one insight into the long history of our people that is incontrovertible, it is that for us faith and fate are mysteriously one and indissoluble. This is the one valid, vital core of the doctrine of the "Chosen People." Whatever is morally and spiritually true is also practically and politically wise. In the long run, it is hardly possible to doubt that the future of the State of Israel lies in an intimate integration of its people and its economy with that of its neighboring countries. An Israel-Arab partnership is not an unrealistic hope, and such a partnership is completely unthinkable apart from a conciliatory policy, such as is here proposed.

Some of us are beginning to forget—so short is popular memory under the stress of politics—that within the original dream of Zion there was included the aspiration to reclaim morally and culturally the Arabs of Palestine in the spirit of true fraternity. Indeed, this noble ambition constituted part of the vision that lured the early *Halutzim*. Toynbee is dead wrong in speaking of the new Jew in Israel as "partly American technician, partly Nazi Sicarii," forgetting so many other parts, especially the genuine core of idealistic *Halutzim*. But let us ask ourselves if we are always cognizant of the radiant fullness of the original dream, in which the word Zion stood not for a narrow nationalism but for all that was noble and true in our Jewish and humanistic heritage.

Toynbee and Parkes arrive at the conclusion that the Arabs of Palestine were in large part descended from the original inhabitants of the land of Israel. This opinion stated by them in the context of an anti-Israel argument should not be a shocking thought to Zionists. On the contrary, true or not, this theory constituted a major foundation for the belief that a genuine fraternal union of Jew and Arab in Palestine was possible. In a beautiful Yiddish book, *Eretz Yisroel*, authored by the former President of Israel, Ben-Zvi, and the former Prime Minister, Ben-Gurion, the same thesis is presented.[2] Two of the most prominent leaders of the State of Israel maintained that the old Jewish peasantry survived all through the long Byzantine rule, either as nominal Christians or as Jews, and that their subsequent Arabization under Moslem rule was strictly superficial. "Apart from numerous admixtures," they conclude "the overwhelming majority of the inhabitants of Palestine west of the Jordan are of uniform appearance and racial descent, and in their veins there flows without doubt a great deal of Jewish blood. . . ."[3]

In general, the leaders of the "Second Aliyah," which was numerically small but very influential, were eager to elevate the status of the Arab inhabitants of the land. Their zeal for "the conquest of labor" was in appearance only directed against the Arabs. In reality, it was aimed at the prevention of a progressive helotization of the native population. The correlative policy of the insistence on "Jewish labor" was a campaign to raise the living standards of the Arabs and to awaken within them visions of a better life. An eagerness to "bring light to the dormant East" always formed part of the Zionist dream. It is already expressed with romantic fervor in Frischberg's little classic, *L'an* and in the voluminous essays of M. L. Lilienblum. This note began to fade years ago, when the Arab revolt was launched and when the dark clouds of Nazism rendered the Jewish problem so acute as to leave no room for any other ideal. But we cannot consider the dream of Zion as a vision fulfilled as long as the original inhabitants of Palestine live in temporary camps on its uneasy borders—to the State of Israel, a permanent threat, to the conscience of the Jew, a standing challenge.

The third element in Toynbee's presentation which is irritating to the Jew is his persistent reference to religious persecution as Jewish in origin. Thus, he speaks of "Judaic intolerance in the ethos of Christianity" and "Judaically fanatical ferocity," on the supposition that religious persecution was first practiced by the Maccabees when they imposed Judaism by force on the inhabitants of Idumea, Galilee, and several cities of the coast. In reply to this judgment, which Toynbee borrows from Gibbon, Mordecai M. Kaplan pointed to the persecutions of Antiochus, the recurrent persecution of Christians by the pagan empire of Rome, and to the Egyptian persecution of the followers of Ikhnaton. Professor Albright told this writer that Buddhism was driven out of India by persecutions that dwarf all the pogroms of Europe in scale and ferocity. One might also recall in this connection the expulsion of Anaxagoras and the execution of Socrates, the expulsion of the worshipers of Isis from Rome, and the many religio-ethnic civil wars within the Roman Empire.

However, these answers do not dispose of the fundamental question raised by Toynbee, to wit: Does the impetus of intolerance in Western society derive from its Jewish or its Hellenic fountainhead? Although Christianity is the synthetic product of Hebraism and Hellenism, does the Hebraic factor account for the occasional outbursts of intolerance in the Christian world? This question is not altogether academic, reflecting the operation of "poetic justice" in the affairs of mankind. It has contemporary relevance, for history lives within us. If intolerance derives from a Judaic source, then the intensification of the influence of Judaism today is likely to encourage this malignant growth on the body of Western society.

Happily, the reverse is the case. Intolerance in Christianity derives in part from bibliolatry (the belief in the rejection of Israel and in their guilt of deicide), in part from the Greek penchant for the casuistry of dialectics, in part from the Roman imperial drive for syncretism, acculturation, and the final achievement of uniformity. All three elements are weakened whenever the Jewish tradition is appreciated and its impact felt. Historical Judaism is not to be identified with any form of bibliolatry, for its insistence upon the Oral Law negated the worship of the letter. Take the case of Joshua and the extermination of the Canaanites. In the Midrash, the harsh Biblical requirement is softened in many ways. One homily insists that Joshua refused to fulfill the Mosaic command, declaring that the good God could not have ordered so inhuman an act, and that God confirmed, in a vision, the intuition of Joshua.[4] In general, the early Christians reverted to a primitive form of Judaism, because they repudiated the oral tradition. Thus, the entire theology of Paul is based upon a doctrine of sin and atonement by sacrifice that was outgrown in the oral tradition of the rabbis. Hence, the impact of Judaism is away from bibliolatry. Secondly, most of the controversies that divided the Christian world into warring camps hinged on the definition of dogmas. Judaism is notoriously lax in the definition of terms and in the crystallization of dogmatic beliefs. Thus, the controversy with the Arians, the Homoousion-Homoiousion controversy, etc., are hardly comprehensible in Judaic terms. Lastly, the Roman heritage of Christianity is responsible for the kind of zealotry that was embodied in the Westphalian Treaty—*cuius regio, eius religio*, a formulation that reflected the zeal of the politician and the bias of the administrator.

Apart from these and similar inaccuracies, Toynbee's juxta-

142

position of corresponding events helps us to achieve a more comprehensive grasp of the nature of the Jewish people. The great merit of his work consists in the collation of events and developments from many different areas and eras. It is now no longer possible to equate history as such with the particular history of Western Europe—as was done notably by Hegel, Vico, and even Spengler. If history is the record of the self-revelation of the Supreme Being, or of the human mind, then the events to be taken into consideration must include the history of societies in all ages and in all parts of the world. The globe-circling scope of Toynbee's work and his detailed programmatic approach have given a powerful body blow all forms of parochialism.

The writing of Jewish history is particularly susceptible to the distortion of parochialism. All who were raised within the domain of Jewish traditional ideas tend inevitably to regard the "uniqueness" of Jewish being as an axiom. The career of the Jew was different from that of all other historic groups, not only because it was the resultant of a unique combination of causes, but because it bore the impact of a unique mystical factor. While all groups and nations are unique in the sense of being distinguished by a specific combination of characteristics and qualities, the "uniqueness" of the Jewish people was presumed to belong to a different class altogether, for, so the traditional argument ran, the very categories of thought by which other groups are understood cannot be applied to the "uniquely unique" Jewish people. We are not a race, a nation, or a religion, but something *sui generis*—"a people that dwells alone and is not counted among the nations."[5]

This axiom of Jewish "uniqueness" is of course grounded in the language of the Bible, which speaks of the "covenant," whereby Israel became "holy unto the Lord." The prophets and teachers of Israel invariably stressed the conditional nature of the bond thus forged between the people of Israel and the Supreme Being. It is not the Jews that are unique, but the Torah as the Word of God and the Jews as the bearers of the

Torah. "Are you not like the Ethiopians unto me, O people of Israel, says the Lord," the prophet Amos declared.[6] And the prophet Isaiah welcomed "the foreigners who join themselves to the Lord."[7] It is not the ethnic character of the Jew that is unique, but the religious heritage bequeathed unto his charge.

However, there was an inevitable ambiguity in the persistent Biblical references to the people of Israel as the "portion" of the Lord. Israel's choice is dependent upon its loyalty, but God is certain to see to it that this loyalty is eventually re-established. The Lord beholds the people of Israel wallowing in its shame and agony, and He says, "In thy blood, thou shalt live; yea, in thy blood thou shalt live."[8] The ancient covenant cannot be undone. Perforce, the Jews are now "a peculiar people." Thus, the prophet Ezekiel rebukes those who counsel "let us be like the nations," with the stern warning that there exists for the people of Israel no way out: "As I live, says the Lord God, surely with a mighty hand and an outstretched arm, and with wrath poured out, I will be King over you."[9] In the Talmud, we find the rabbis disputing whether the Israelites who do not live by the Torah are still the "Lord's sons." The prevailing opinion is affirmative, declaring that the Lord will cause to arise a potentate like Haman, who will compel the erring Israelites to return to the fold. Thus, the doctrine of the "treasured people" descended into both Christian and Talmudic traditions in a two-faceted form. The "uniqueness" or "peculiarity" of the Jewish people was attributed both to the people and to the tradition. In the Christian religion, the doctrine of the "Chosen People" was transferred to the Church, with "Israel after the spirit" taking the place of "Israel after the flesh." Nevertheless, Paul continued to refer to the Jewish people as the "good olive tree" that will not fail to receive God's grace again once "the fullness of the Gentiles" has been redeemed. This unique status of the Jewish people in the Divine scheme of things made it possible for the Christian countries of Europe to tolerate the existence of the Jewish community in their midst long after all other heresies had been ruthlessly

144

extirpated. In turn, the Jewish people, walled in by the gathering pressures of hate and envy, countered by strengthening the conviction of their innate superiority over the Gentiles. Were they not of the "holy seed," the only legitimate heirs of the Divine promise, to whom belonged the irrevocable favor of the Lord and the ultimate triumph foretold by the prophets?

Thus, it was on the ground of the metaphysical "uniqueness" of their being that Jewish life was predicated both by Jews and Christians. In the course of time, this conviction accumulated ever deeper emotional overtones, so that when the modern age dawned and the theological assumptions concerning Jewish "uniqueness" became vacuous, the feeling of profound cosmic distinction between Jew and Gentile was too strong to be given up. Thus, the modern versions of the "meta-myth" were begun, insisting in their various ways that the Jew was metaphysically, mystically different from the rest of the human race. As the proverbial sneer of the Cheshire cat which remained long after the cat itself was gone, the complex of feelings regarding Jewish "uniqueness" persisted among both Jews and Christians down to our own day.

In the modern world, this emotional complex was sustained by the several ways in which the Jewish situation differed from that of other groups—lack of a territorial center, economic specialization, religious belief, different ethnic origin, etc. To anti-Semites, this "meta-myth" was the axiom upon which the "ideologies," ranging from Fichte to Wagner and from Nietzsche to Rosenberg, were based. To many Jewish romanticists, the "meta-myth" appeared in roseate colors, as a column of light in the wilderness. No longer believing in the dogmas of Judaism, they found a secure anchorage for their feelings in the "unique" qualities of the "Jewish soul." Cultural Zionism of the brand of Ahad Ha'am and Buber embraced the "meta-myth" in their philosophy, contending that the Jewish soul was somehow different from that of other nations. Some political Zionists today still cling to the proposition that the Jew cannot possibly dwell in peace with other nations. Ultimately, they insist, the

Diaspora will be liquidated, because the differences between Jews and Gentiles are radical and irreconcilable. Other national groups may commingle to produce the American nation; but not Jewry, for it is "unique."

Toynbee points out that this appearance of "uniqueness" is due to the form of community organization which arose in the Syriac civilization and which attained its highest development in the Ottoman Empire. In that extensive dominion, everybody belonged to one or another millet—a religio-cultural, ethnic unit. The millets were not divided according to territory, and in many instances, economic specialization accompanied national differentiation and religious allegiance. The head of the millet demanded many-sided loyalty from its members. In turn, he was held responsible for the actions of his people. The impact of Western nationalism upon the millet system was invariably disastrous. As proof, one instances first the fate of the Greeks and then the massacre of the Armenians. Toynbee regards it as a simple law that "the destructiveness of nationalism was proportionate to the degree of discrepancy between the ideal of Nationalism and the local state of existing geographical and political facts. . . ."[10]

On this view, the Jewish community represented a group of people possessing a common ethnic consciousness, a common faith, and preponderantly certain common arts and skills in the economy of the nation. The advent of Western democracy and nationalism rendered the Jewish millet untenable as a form of organization. Both the ideals of freedom and fraternity, which are the essences of democracy and nationalism respectively, militated against the preservation of a self-enclosed group. Thus, the impact of nationalism forced a choice upon the Jewish Diaspora—to become part of the nations among whom they lived, in the true spirit of fraternity and without any political hyphenation or emotional reservation, or to withdraw from the West into Palestine, for the building of the Jewish nation. Both alternatives were embraced by different sections of the Jewish Diaspora. There is logic in either alternative, but not in holding

146

on to both horns of the dilemma simultaneously on the plea that we are a "unique" species. The quality of "uniqueness" is altogether legitimate in the vertical dimension of ideas and culture, for then the achievements of one group are held out as the potential possessions of all groups. But "uniqueness" as an innate quality of being is exclusive in character, invidious in intent, invariably offensive.

As to the State of Israel, Toynbee's low opinion of its prospects are totally unwarranted. In the long memory of the ancient peoples of the Near East, the brief period of its existence is but as the flick of an eyelash. It is still possible to labor for the consummation of the ancient hope of Arab-Israel symbiosis, with the Israeli bringing to the Arab world the technical competence of the West, and the Arabs regaining by these contacts their ancient greatness. The inflamed passions on both sides of a bizarre and precarious border are the inevitable outcome of a war that was never ended. In the long run, however, we may look forward to the reassertion of those fundamental factors that necessarily make for Arab-Jewish cooperation.

Insofar as the Jewish Diaspora is concerned, Toynbee's analysis is happily stimulating and hopeful. In the first place, he looks to the Jews of the Diaspora to make their contribution to the general awakening of religious feeling that he deems to be one of the great needs of mankind. This religious revival must be steered away from dogmatic uniformity and from preoccupation with ritual niceties. It is a rebirth of the spirit of religion that is desperately needed, not the intellectual "hardening of the arteries" that fundamentalists of all stripes mistake for religion. Such a renascence of faith the Jew of the Diaspora helps to bring into being not only by virtue of his spiritual travail, but by his very presence in the heart of the Christian community. The rise of a modern synagogue in the midst of a forest of diverse churches reduces the common denominator of the American faith from the particularistic Christian level to that of an all-embracing religion of humanity.

Within the Judeo-Christian tradition, the strength of the Jewish pole makes for an emphasis on universality, rationality, and interfaith understanding. This role of the Jewish Diaspora is presented in even bolder relief by Toynbee's conception of the creative function of minorities. Humanity rises in the scale of culture through the labors of minorities, who react to the challenge of partial displacement from the general society by projecting a higher level of civilization, in which they can be at home, along with the rest of humanity. Thus, we are bidden to think of the Jewish group as a "creative minority" in behalf of those ideals and instruments that make for a better world.

In the second place, Toynbee points out that the Jewish Diaspora foreshadows the society of the future, helping to project some of the lines along which it is likely to be built up. Certain it is that nationalism cannot bring peace or well-being to mankind. The one world which is even now undergoing its birth pangs will have to allow for the interpenetration of ethnic groups, geographically and politically, with culture and religion becoming the sole preoccupation of the distinctive groups of mankind. Thus, the Jewish Diaspora, if it succeeds in staying free from the virus of nationalism, can help to keep alive the one great hope for the future. It represents the pattern whereby an ethnic group transfers its collective ambition from the domain of politics to the ethereal spheres of culture and religion, from the horizontal pushing of elbows for an ever larger place in the sun to the vertical ascent of the spirit. Jewry can show the way if it avoids the pitfalls at both sides of the highway—if it does not deny its ethnic base and if it places its ethnic consciousness into the service of universal religion.

In the third place, Toynbee regards anti-Semitism as a transitional stage in the mutual adjustment of Jewish and Western society. He sees the contact of the two societies as falling into three stages: stage one, when the host-society is underdeveloped and Jews are welcomed for their skills and commercial enterprise; stage two, when the host-society desperately tries to achieve the same skills and crafts as the Jews

148

already possess; stage three, when the host-society is already highly developed industrially and educationally, no longer being fearful of Jewish competition. In the first stage, Jews are welcomed; in the second, they are resented; in the third, they are accepted since their occupational pattern is no longer significantly different from that of the rest of the population. This three-stage view of Jewish-Gentile relationships may be favorably contrasted with the pessimistic two-stage view that occurs so frequently in European Zionist literature. To Toynbee, Jewish Diaspora existence is not an unnatural phenomenon; most certainly, it is not doomed to disaster. Indeed, it is richly blessed in dignity, in universal significance, and in the opportunities for spiritual growth.

In the most profound and real sense, Toynbee's main theses are faithful to the spirit of our Holy Scriptures and to the spiritual genius of Judaism. When our forefathers gave utterance to their innermost soul by their insistence on the unity of God, they expressed their conviction that the forces of evil, too, somehow play their part as messengers of God. Satan, in the Book of Job, stands among the good angels of the Lord and his activity results in the enhancement of the Lord's work. As the Baal Shem Tov expressed this belief, "evil is a stool for the good." Thus, Toynbee sees the whole course of human events exemplified in that marvelous myth of Eve and the serpent. Mankind in the Garden of Eden is society in its primitive state of passivity ("yin" state). Then, the Devil enters to disturb the peace and to challenge the complacency of the human couple. Their beliefs are shattered, their plodding routine is interrupted. Out they wander into the open world, where by the "sweat of their brow" they produce civilization. It is the distinguishing mark of a vital civilization that it is unconstrained by the straitjacket of habit, it is tense with energy, because its equilibrium has been disturbed, vibrant with visions of the future, because it is aware of ills in the present. In contrast, a primitive society is marked by well-traveled ruts and covered over with the white frost of the "cake of custom."

149

The same thought permeates our sacred literature. While in some Talmudic passages and in the Qabbalah, the sin of Adam and Eve is represented as a catastrophe, which ushered in the twin evils of sin and death,[11] the predominant emphasis in the Aggadah is on the virtue of adversity. "When the Holy One, Blessed be He, said to Adam, 'thorns and briars thou shalt cause to grow in order to eat,' tears streamed from his eyes. 'Shall I and my donkey eat from the same trough?' When the Lord added, 'with the sweat of thy brow, shalt thou eat bread,' he was comforted."[12] Man's very inability to live off the wild vegetation on the face of the earth and his consequent travail in the search of food are the root-causes of civilization.

That suffering is frequently the source of greatness is an authentically Jewish doctrine. In Catholic thought, grinding poverty and widespread pain are not considered to be evil in themselves. In the Protestant emphasis on inwardness, all attention is focused on the career of the individual soul, not on the evils of society. Judaism did not retreat from the turmoil of society to the citadel of the soul, nor did it discount human suffering with Olympian dogmatic assurance, but it taught the possibility of transmuting pain into spiritual greatness. If our suffering is productive of deepened fervor in prayer or a more comprehensive grasp of the word of God, then it belongs to the category of "the pains of love." If not, then our suffering can only be designated as "the pains of rebuke."[13]

Many are the passages in which our sages expressed the historic insight that suffering is the prelude to greatness. "Three great gifts were given unto Israel, and all were granted only through suffering—Torah, the Land of Israel, the World to Come."[14] The Jewish people knew themselves to be the paradox of destiny—"chosen" of the Lord, they were the "martyr-race," as that sorely stricken patient of whose life all doctors despaired but who still awaits the healing Grace of God.[15] "'For I am sick with love'—said the congregation of Israel to the Holy One, Blessed be He—'Master of the universe, all the diseases which Thou bringest upon me are for the sake of causing me to love you.' "[16] In a later chapter of the same Midrash, the Lord is represented as saying of the congregation of Israel, "In the days of her ruin she produced saints for me, while in the days of her establishment she produced for me wicked men."[17] Another Midrash compares Israel to an olive—the more it is crushed, the more oil is produced. And oil in lamps produces light.[18]

This correlation of suffering with spiritual greatness was not merely a homiletic thought hovering on the fringe of consciousness as a conventional palliative of Israel's agony. The central core of the hope for redemption rested upon the innate relationship between pain and purity of soul. As the long enslavement of the children of Israel in Egypt was needed in order to produce a people fit for Sinai, so the travail of the Jewish people in exile was one arduous preparation for the glory of redemption. Hence, the "pains of the Messiah," a virtual crescendo of unprecedented catastrophes, is destined to prepare the ground for the Messiah. No verse was more characteristic of the reaction of our pious folk than this one: "A time of trouble it is for Jacob, and through it he will be saved."[19] It taught them to see the "feet of the Messiah" in the troubles of their day. The Messiah himself was represented as one who was stricken with pain, beyond all men, for it was through his suffering that the light of redemption was generated.[20]

Toynbee's basic conception of the genesis of cultural growth is thus wholly in accord with the fundamental current of Jewish thought. Almost from its inception, but especially in the past twenty-five centuries, Judaism had to contend against the naïve judgment of the man in the street—"a healthy mind in a healthy body." Since the Jewish people were physically weak and militarily nearly helpless, they could not be healthy and strong in spirit. While some attributed Jewish misfortune to the anger of the gods, secularists and others regarded the physical weakness of Jewry as the source of that sickly sensitivity that made Jews "peculiar." But it is precisely our weakness and our increased sensitivity that eventuate in the golden fruits of the spirit if they are seen in the light of our religious tradition.

After surveying the total recorded tale of human travail, Toynbee arrives at conclusions that he did not envisage when he first blocked out his areas of research. In his first six volumes, he assumed as typical the role Christianity played in the decline of the Roman Empire and the emergence of the medieval Western civilization. While Gibbon interpreted the fall of Rome as the double triumph of "barbarism and religion," Toynbee saw medieval barbarism as the nascent form of Western civilization. The role of a "higher religion," he reasoned, was to serve as the "chrysalis" of a dying civilization and as the source of a new civilization. Having formed this picture of the succession of stages in human history, Toynbee found similar processes in nearly all other sections of the world. At the end of his global survey, however, Toynbee found that the process of development was actually the reverse of the one that he had anticipated. The forward process is from a civilization to a religion, with the cycle repeating itself indefinitely. It is when a religion breaks down that a civilization emerges.

This final view of Toynbee's is indeed the logical outcome of his painstaking and many-sided analysis. The first step in the path of culture is the presentation of a challenge. The second is the comprehension of this challenge by the psyche of the people, from which a response is evoked. Culture emerges from a primitive society to the extent to which responses of this type are evoked in every phase in life. Culture grows as long as the succeeding challenges are not too overwhelming in nature and as long as they are comprehended by the spirit of the people. A culture begins to decline when it reacts to a challenge by force, instead of comprehension. The initial external success of a civilization, its creation of a "universal state," is actually its first fatal symptom, for the substitution of force for spiritual creativity is the way that leads to perdition. A "higher religion" that calls upon its devotees to meet the challenges of life by spiritual comprehension holds out, therefore, the assurance of endless growth for any society, provided firstly that the people really live by their faith and provided secondly that the faith is itself uncorrupted either by the cancer of dogmatism or by the Satanic temptations of the fleshpots of this world. Ideally, then, the way upward is from the terrestrial concerns of civilization to the ethereal halls of faith.

This final conclusion of the most monumental survey of human travail is of special interest to us as Jews, for the historical pathway of Jewry has been precisely the one outlined by Toynbee. An ancient civilization was transmuted by a series of challenges into a universal religion. This process was not achieved all at once, but through a series of forward movements and numerous backslidings. Within the heart of Jewry, the tug of war between ethnicism and religion was begun in the nineteenth century—and it is not yet ended. However, we have now passed a bifurcation of two roads which will ultimately resolve the struggle. In the land of Israel, Jewry will become a civilization once again, and, in the lands of the Diaspora, it will become ever more resolutely a precursor of that spiritual orientation that all mankind is striving to attain. The Jew of the Diaspora represents in his person the epitome of human progress—a scion of an ancient civilization he stands as the bearer of an undogmatic, universal faith. If he is true to his own being and to the spiritual potentialities of his historic role, he can, by his very existence, beckon humanity toward the "heavenly Jerusalem," pointing the way from struggle on the plane of politics to the creative responses of the spirit, from civilization to religion. As a Jew, he appears upon the stage, trailing four thousand years of tradition. If he achieves a thorough comprehension of his past and if he learns to embrace the challenge of the present within his soul, he becomes the symbol and the prophet of the future. The tension in his soul is a reflection of the fundamental struggle in the heart of mankind. And this battle is never wholly won. The hands of Moses are heavy, and the Amalekites are fighting in the valley.

TOYNBEE'S LETTER
TO THE HEBREWS*

No scholar, philosopher, or historian has challenged the imagination of American Jews as much as Professor Arnold J. Toynbee. His name has become a household word even in those circles where Amos is known only as the first half of a team of comedians. In the median ranks of the intelligentsia, his name is a kind of litmus paper, separating the romanticists, high and low, from the rationalists, superficial or profound, "those who think with their blood" from "those who think with their brains." The very massiveness of his writings encourages people to seek out the passages confirming their prejudices rather than to view his concept of Judaism against his philosophy of human experience.

Yet, there is a winnowing process in life that carries away the chaff and permits the seed to settle in the soil. I hope to contribute to this ongoing process and to report on my part in his undertaking to re-evaluate his views about Judaism.

Let us first consider the personality of Toynbee. He has always been a crusader as well as a professional historian. He lost his Chair in Greek History and Civilization even before he had a chance to give his first lecture. Touring the Greek countryside after the First World War, he witnessed pogroms of Greeks against Turks which he proceeded to report to the *Manchester Guardian*. Up to that time, the Western world had known only of pogroms of Turks against Greek. The Greek Government promptly obtained his dismissal. For many years, he has been the head of the Chatham Institute, editing an

*Reprinted from *Conservative Judaism*, Winter 1963.

annual survey of international events for foreign-affairs specialists. Far from being a cloistered scholar, he has been an actor as well as a thinker, representing his country at various international conclaves.

He differs from the usual run of professional historians not only in the scope of his work, but also in his concern with ultimate questions. He strives to combine the interests of history, philosophy, and religion, inquiring into the meaning of events as well as into their sequence. Laboring in the prophetic tradition, he confronts professional religionists with the facts of history and professional historians with the insights of religion. By virtue of his critique of institutional parochialism and religious dogmatism, he is an offense to entrenched churchmen; at the same time, he scandalizes academic historians by the introduction of a moral yardstick into their "scientific" domain. Yet, he does not regard the course of history as the vindication of righteousness. To him, military power and an expanding empire are indices of moral failure and social decay, not of creative vitality and healthy vigor. And he dares to maintain that the whole range of human experience is one colossal commentary on the vision of Deutero-Isaiah concerning the "Suffering Servant" and on the central theme of Aeschylus' tragedies, *pathei mathos* ("learning through suffering").

Among professional historians, Toynbee's massive volumes were at first received with cool disdain. In England, *The English Historical Review* of 1956 carried a critical analysis of the first six volumes of *A Study of History*, concluding that it was a "grandiose failure," containing "many excellent ideas which other historians can use as clues in the construction of that intermediate kind of sense which is the most that they can safely try to make of history." Charles A. Beard's judgment of the first volumes was caustic. "Happy are they," he wrote sarcastically, "who know the causes of things."

By degrees, the historians relented, particularly after Somervell's summary caught the popular imagination. Sorokin concluded in *The Journal of Modern History* that the study "was a

155

most stimulating and illuminating work of a distinguished thinker and scholar." The American Historical Association devoted a session of its December, 1955, conference to a discussion of Toynbee's work. The contributors to the volume, edited by Edward T. Gargan, *The Intent of Toynbee's History*, are agreed that "the Study is a monumental achievement of our Century . . . a permanent part of the historical record of this generation's fear and hope."

There is hardly a specialist in any field of philosophical or historical research who, in his domain of competence, is likely to be satisfied with Toynbee's judgments. Shoot a barb of criticism in the direction of this mountainous work, modestly named *A Study of History*, and your arrow will hit something! At the same time, no serious student of human affairs can afford to ignore this work. And the critics generally admit that the abounding insights in the "Study" are invaluable aids. Indeed, the total experience of man is too vast and varied to be comprehended completely by any kind of philosophy. But all of us inevitably create *ad hoc* philosophies of history in our attempts to derive meaning and wisdom from the past experience of mankind. The many interlacing shafts of light cast by Toynbee do not produce a perfect illumination, but they are exceedingly useful to all who seek seriously to achieve an objective, synoptic view of human experience.

Once a scholar achieves renown in the marketplace as well as on the campus, he ceases to be merely a person and becomes an institution. His opinions on all subjects, from the masters of the Kremlin to the "secret persuaders" of Madison Avenue, are given worldwide publicity. He is treated as an oracle of wisdom by the editors of mass-magazines, and his name is invoked frequently at the assemblies of sophisticates, be it in reverence or with contempt.

My correspondence with Professor Toynbee goes back to 1955. It was then that my article "Toynbee and Judaism," which appeared in *Judaism: A Quarterly Journal*, came to his attention. He wrote me that he planned to undertake a systematic re-evaluation of his views about Judaism and the Jewish people and that he would welcome my help in this endeavor. In later years, our correspondence ranged through many domains of scholarship.[1]

In Judaism, there is hardly a historical question that does not reverberate with contemporary overtones. For example, we debated at length this question: Why did not Judaism itself conquer the Greco-Roman world? To Christian historians of the old school, the answer was obvious—Judaism was an "inferior" faith. It had to be transcended by a more "universal" religion. The "jealous" God of the Old Testament, full of "wrath" and "fury," could not be expected to win the hearts of the "gentle" barbarians, while the loving, compassionate God of the New Testament appealed to the "refined" feelings of the Goths and the Vandals. To Jewish historians of the old school, the answer was identical, but with inverse valence—the Gentiles were not "mature" enough for so "pure" and exalted a faith as unadulterated Judaism. Hence, a pagan-monotheistic combination was all that they could grasp.

Contemporary Jewish historians have begun to deal more objectively with this question. Yehezkel Kaufmann attributes the victory of Christianity to the fact that it disassociated itself from the sad fate of the Jewish people. The pagans were willing to accept the monotheistic faith of Jewry, but they hesitated to become part of a defeated and humiliated people. In Christianity, Kaufmann argues, the pagans encountered the monotheism of Judaism in a form that was free from the stigmata of collective failure and humiliation. Kaufmann's argument is well-reasoned, but not entirely convincing. It is true that for most people "nothing succeeds like success" and "nothing fails like failure," and we know from the writings of Tertullian and others that many Christians abjured their faith in periods of persecution. But then the "hard core" of the Christian community was tempered by the flames of persecution. "The blood of the martyrs is seed of the faith." For the proletarian masses, humiliation and failure in this world were heralds of redemption

157

and salvation in the "World to Come." The cross became the symbol of salvation. From the reign of Emperor Nerva to that of Constantine, the Christians endured persecution more frequently, more persistently, and more bitterly than did the Jews. And those were the years of greatest Christian expansion.

Salo Baron's explanation is even less convincing. He postulates a categorical distinction between paganism as the "religion of nature" and Judaism as the "religion of history." Upon these radical abstractions, he sets up the Christian faith as the synthesis of "nature" and "history." It follows that while the pagans found it hard to go all at once from one spiritual domain to its opposite, they could find in Christianity that happy combination, which suited their historic condition. Upon reflection it will appear that when Baron's categories are boiled down to their thin kernels of truth, there is mighty little substance left to explain the course of events. Judaism is a "religion of history" only in an exceedingly limited sense. After all, the Torah begins with the creation of nature, and "history" in the sense of a cumulative tradition, reflecting the word of God, is hardly less characteristic of Christianity than of Judaism. The Christians never gave up the Old Testament, retaining the intertestamentary works of history, including the Books of the Maccabees, which the Jews rejected. And their concept of the Church as the time-conditioned kernel of the eschatological "City of God" was the exact counterpart of the Rabbinic conception of *Keneset Yisroel*, the spirit of Israel insofar as it is oriented to God.

The racists, too, have it easy. All they need to do is to transport the concept of fundamentalism into quasi-biologic terms, for it would appear that the same mood of subjective self-glorification governs the thinkers of medievalist Orthodoxy and modern racism.

Manifestly, the spread of Islam is *hakatuv hashelishi,* the decisive or third verse, in connection with this inquiry. But in which generation did Islam earn its greatest spiritual conquests? Did the Arabs regard themselves as a "chosen people," limiting their missionary activities after the first generation, and did the converted non-Arabs transform Islam into a universal faith? It is apparent that no meaningful answer can be given to our inquiry without taking into account the entire experience of the Judeo-Christian-Moslem world.

In our correspondence, I expounded the views of all the Jewish historians and philosophers with which I was familiar. My own views were certainly clarified and probably modified by these exchanges. The effects of Professor Toynbee's "reconsiderations" were felt in the essays and the lectures that he gave in the last few years. His lectures about the sources of anti-Semitism and its demonic nature, given in German universities, were excellent. His addresses to the Jews of England, on the observance of the Tercentenary of Anglo-Jewry, and to the British section of the World Jewish Congress were remarkable landmarks in the progress of his thought. Above all, he began to refer to Judaism as one of the "higher religions" of the contemporary world. When he completed the two chapters in his volume, *Reconsiderations,* dealing with Judaism, he was kind enough to send me the galley proofs and ask for comment. My letters, discussing three points in his discussion, appear in the book as three Annexes (pages 664-669), dealing with the application of the term "fossil" to Jews, with the axiom of Jewish "uniqueness," and with the continuity of the prophetic impetus in Judaism. The last essay is by far the most important, constituting my reply to his concept of the Jewish "mission." It is also a highly condensed summation of my philosophy of Jewish life.

Anyone who reads this volume carefully will easily find the several areas of disagreement among us. He quotes copiously from my published essays and personal letters, in disagreement as well as in agreement. His intemperate condemnation of the Zionists as "disciples of Nazis" is utterly unjust and hardly debatable. Insofar as the State of Israel and the Arabs are concerned, he finds it difficult to maintain the dispassionate posture of the Olympian observer. He refuses to take account of the intertwining threads in the texture of modern Zionism. So dismal is the bias and drive of nationalism in his view that all distinctions and gradations are obliterated. Apart from the issues of Zionism and Israel, Toynbee's revised judgment of Jewish history and destiny is as interesting as it is challenging.

To be fully understood, this revision must be seen against the transformation that Toynbee has undergone in the past twenty years. As one writer puts it, "Toynbee the Hellene" has become "Toynbee the Christian." While in his earlier work, Toynbee assumed that the function of a "higher religion" was to serve as a "chrysalis" for a new civilization, in his last four volumes he inverted this relationship—religion is the end and civilizations are the instruments for the growth of man's spirit. The ultimate yardstick for the measurement of progress is the state of the souls of individual men and women. To the historians of the nineteenth century, the State was the reflection of God at work in history. Ranke carried this Hegelian axiom to its logical conclusion when he asserted that military power is the index of a society's moral state. In contrast, Toynbee, in his later years, returned to the Scriptural doctrine of God's image in man. History, he now declares, reveals a movement toward saintliness.

The line of progress is from the horizontal form of organization, where men share the same land and the same interests, to the vertical form, in which people share ideals. If a world-state is certain to emerge in the course of time, then the social agencies of spiritual growth will be idea-centered organizations, not language- or area-centered units. On this view, the stateless pattern of Jewish life in the Diaspora represents the "wave of the future." As the Jews have learned to transmute their national loyalties into religious values, making them significant and available to all men, so other national bearers of civilization will have to do likewise. Like Hermann Cohen, Toynbee regards Zionism as a base betrayal of the Jewish ideal and as a surrender to the idolatry of the modern world. Much has happened since the days of Cohen, transforming the Zionist ideal into a veritable lifesaving undertaking. However, thinking as he does of the Anglo-American world, he feels that the movement has outrun the facts of the situation.

Toynbee began his work as a disciple of Gibbon, with admiration of the Roman Empire and with scorn for "barbarism and religion," but he ended by describing the Roman Empire itself as the "universal state" of the Hellenic world. It is the *élan* of the conquered Greeks that lent significance and worth to the conquering legions of the Caesars. The modern era, in his view, stands on the threshold of a religious revival. But religion, in Toynbee's usage, is not the total content of either the church or the synagogue, or the mosque, or the Buddhist monastery but the creative impulse that is occasionally embodied in these institutions. Religion consists in a fresh confrontation of the Divine, akin to the original act of creation. It issues in a breaking through the crust of self-righteousness and a glimpsing of new horizons. He describes himself as a "trans-rationalist" not as a Christian. Let us now examine his views, seriatim:

First, Toynbee refuses to accept the notion that the Jews are "unique," so that the categories of history, ancient or modern, do not apply to them. He points out, rightly I believe, that to set Jews apart from universal history is to deprive them of the universal qualities of nature and humanity. Whatever plausibility attaches to the notion of Jewish uniqueness, he insists, is derived from the theologies of fundamentalist Judaism and fundamentalist Christianity. Many a Jew or a Christian who no longer believes in a God who chooses still asserts that the Jews are a "Chosen People."

In one sense, the subject matter of history consists of unique events, unique peoples, unique faiths, for no concatenation of circumstances and ideas has ever been previously duplicated. In this sense, it is properly maintained that the career of the Jewish people is unparalleled. It is also the task of the historian to discover similarities, repetitive patterns, ideas, norms, and laws within the flux of events, or he could hardly describe, much less explain, the course of human affairs. To assert that

161

the Jews are unique in this sense of defying analysis is to indulge in theological mystification, not in historical analysis.

To reject the axiom of Jewish uniqueness is to repudiate the notion that the Jew is immune to the laws of society and history. Since it is the business of social philosophers to assign arrows of direction to the processes of history, they cannot exempt Jews from their general evaluation. Hence, liberals and rationalists will extol the Jewish emancipation as a mighty advance of freedom and justice, contending that Nazism was an atavistic ephemeral reaction. Anticipating a fairly steady trend toward an orderly society, they will deplore Zionist romanticism and racism. On the other hand, romantic and racistic historians will be prone to describe anti-Semitism as "natural" and Zionism as healthy and inevitable. (Did not Edouard Drummond, notorious leader of French anti-Semitism, ask to be invited for inaugural ceremonies of a Jewish state?) But their argument will lead them to question the foundations of Jewish life in the Diaspora. In sum, without the axiom of "uniqueness" we are bound to arrive at a program of normalization of Jewish life, negating the claim of some Jewish leaders to a status of "exceptionalism."

Christian dogmatists, anti-Semitic mythologists, and Jewish romanticists concur in postulating the mystical uniqueness of the Jew. I consider this myth to be a dangerous delusion, the source of endless mischief, and agree with Toynbee that the Jew is not exempt from the universal processes and laws of history.

In Part Two, Chapter 3 of this volume, I elaborated my thesis, contrasting its implications with those of other historians. In greater detail, my views are expounded in my book *The Meaning of Jewish History*. Briefly, my point is that the history of our people may be described as unique in the sense of a chemical compound, but not in the sense of a chemical element. In other words, Judaism may be analyzed into components, which are operative everywhere. Furthermore, the usual categories of religion and

162

nationalism are as inadequate for the understanding of Judaism as they are generally unsuitable for the analysis of other peoples and faiths. Both categories are actually composed of bipolar fields of tension. Accordingly, Judaism is a "quadripolar" field of consciousness, with one or another polar aspect predominating at any one time, within one or another segment of the Jewish community.

Toynbee quotes the following thesis from my essays and letters, illustrating their application within his own perspective— namely, the concept of "the dynamic ideas of history as vertical fields of force between an ideal and an instinctive drive" and the interpretation of Judaism as a "quadripolar field of consciousness." Each of the four poles of Jewish consciousness—the self-transcendence of religion and its self-satisfied dogmatism, the spiritualization of national feeling and its degeneration into nihilistic chauvinism—could achieve dominance in the soul of the Jew."[2]

Broadly speaking, Jewish history strikes the observer as being unparalleled in the following domains: the genesis of monotheism, the survival of Jewish communities in the midst of dispersion, the emergence and persistence of anti-Semitism as a kind of *Weltanschauung* centering round Judeo-phobia, and the two great mass-movements of return to Zion.

The interpretation of these phenomena, in the light of the repudiation of the axiom of "uniqueness," was discussed in our correspondence. It is the subject of my book.[2a]

Second, is modern Judaism a continuation of Syriac civilization? Leaving aside for the moment the implications of the odious term "fossil," we may inquire whether the religious culture of the Jews may be understood as a branch of the civilization that flourished on the Syrian plateau in early Biblical times, including the Hebrew-speaking Israelites, Canaanites, Moabites, Edomites, Ammonites, and Phoenicians, as well as the Aramaic-speaking and Persian-speaking peoples.

Manifestly, a semantic issue is involved here. What is a civilization? Toynbee maintains that behind every civilization

163

there looms a vision of the good life, some ideal essence or soul. In this volume he quotes approvingly the observation of Whitehead, "In each age of the world distinguished by high activity, there will be found at its culmination, and among the agencies leading to that culmination, some profound cosmological outlook, implicitly accepted, impressing its own type on the current springs of action."[3]

As such, a civilization is a psychological unity, even if it is not an organism. Certainly, when we speak of Western civilization, we have in mind a certain body of ideals and values as well as a cluster of technical skills and a pattern of economic organization. Did the Syriac plateau possess a similar unity of ideas, ideals, religious myths, and technical skills? We should hardly care to dispute this assertion insofar as it refers to the period of the patriarchs. The Torah reflects the sense of kinship that the early Israelites possessed for the Arameans.[4] The Canaanites transmitted their language as well as many cultural-religious rites and myths to the Hebrews. Ever since the decipherment of the Ugaritic tablets, we have come to realize the indebtedness of the Biblical authors to Canaanite literature. Throughout the Biblical period, the Israelites and the Phoenicians were united by cultural as well as commercial bonds. But the religion of Israel emerged as a *protesting movement* against Canaanite-Phoenician-Syrian culture and religion. The "creative minority" of Israel, to use a Toynbeean term, were the prophets, scribes, and sages who transformed the debris of previous cultural elements into the massive structure of Judaism. A new civilization, Toynbee maintains, is the achievement of such a "creative minority." In any case, the lines of meaning within Judaism were no more intelligible to the Syrians in the Second Commonwealth than to the Greeks. Josephus assures us that the women of Damascus were more or less converted to Judaism, but he also tells us that when the chips were down the Syrians tended to make common cause with the Greeks against the Jews.

Toynbee does not underestimate the revolutionary impetus of Hebrew prophecy. On the contrary, he suggests that Zoroastrianism may have arisen as a result of the impact of Israelite refugees upon the religion of the Persians.[5] It should also be noted that recent archeological discoveries have revealed Canaanite parallels with Biblical ideas and customs that were previously unsuspected. Nevertheless, I feel that the assumption of a Syriac civilization that includes the Jewish faith is totally spurious. While the bricks and field-stones comprising Judaism were gathered on the Aramean-Mediterranean plateau, the design, the mortar, and the steel-structure were the fresh creation of a new elite the remnant of Israel, *shêrit Yisroel.* This inspired group evolved a universe of meaning and a kind of self-awareness that were set in radical opposition to the entire pagan world. In terms of the vision that looms behind the charade of ways of living and ways of thinking, post-Biblical Judaism could hardly be squeezed into the mold of a Syriac civilization.

Naturally, the crucial question at this point is, What do we consider to be the central core of Judaism? If the civilizational elements of the tradition are pre-eminent in our estimation, as they are to secularists, then it is correct to relate "Jewish culture" to the Canaanite-Syriac world. To some of our people, the Hebrew language is not a key to the Temple of faith but the *kodesh hakodoshim* of our heritage. I once heard a Hebraist at a public meeting invoke the "deity" of Hebrew—*Elohai ho-ivrit.* Even in our religious tradition, Hebrew is extolled as "the language of creation," with the angels in heaven being ignorant of so cognate a dialect as Aramaic.[6] Less than a century ago, Samson Raphael Hirsch, the sainted founder of neo-Orthodoxy, laboring under the influence of Schlegel as well as the Midrash, elaborated a whole cosmology on the basis of the interrelationship of Hebraic roots.[7] It is good for these worshipers of Hebrew to be reminded that it was the language of the Canaanites. It may well be that many religious rituals were borrowed from Syriac culture and incorporated within the texture of Judaism. But neither language nor ritual constitutes the heart of Judaism.

To me, Judaism is essentially a body of ideas and sentiments as well as a living memory of their genesis, growth, and application in varying circumstances. In terms of its ideal core and subjective memory, Judaism was anti-Canaanite, from its earliest beginnings. Yehezkel Kaufmann's argument is apropos at this point. The prophets show a total lack of comprehension of the higher reaches of pagan mythology. They do not orate as revolutionaries within the pagan Syriac world, but as sheer aliens to the culture of the Near Eastern peoples. On the other hand, the possibility of relating Jewish practices and ideals to their pagan context was suggested by the medieval Jewish philosophers. Maimonides postulated that most Jewish rites were developed in conscious opposition to pagan Near Eastern observances, though he admitted that some primitive taboos, notably those relating to women's menstrual periods, were incorporated within Judaism in slightly modified form.[8]

Third, concerning the application of the term "fossil" to the Jews of today. In Volume XII, Toynbee apologizes for the use of this word, though he insists that it carries no derogatory connotations. His intention, he declares, was to point out that the peculiar combination of ethnic and religious elements in Judaism was structured and fixed in an alien milieu, before the thought categories and the society patterns of the Western world had been evolved. Perhaps, he suggests, the symbol of a *coelocanthus,* that amphibian fish which retains the features lost by nearly all other creatures in the process of evolution, is illustrative of his meaning.[9]

Actually, both symbols insinuate the value-judgments of "social Darwinism" into the understanding of history. As several other critics have noted, Toynbee consciously combats the biological bias of Spengler and the romantics. Yet, now and then he slides into this slippery realm, where the achievements of culture and the values of man's spirit are measured by their potency in the struggle for survival. In the perspective of evolution, the only virtue is flexibility, the only sin is rigidity, and the supreme folly is refusal to "adjust." But it is well to recall the insight of Plato and the prophets as to the nature of the "realm of ideas"—it is essentially transhistorical and self-validating in all its changes. As a Conservative rabbi I refuse to regard either antiquity or modernity as patents of truth and nobility. Truth has its own standards, and they are ideally timeless. In one of my letters, I wrote: "Religious societies pre-eminently and national societies generally are both value-centered and survival-centered. The philosopher of history is justified in applying biological categories to societies, only insofar as they are survival-centered. Universal values, reflecting facets of truth, beauty, goodness, or holiness are essentially imperishable."

The fundamental question is whether loyalty to a cherished pattern of communal life was so powerful among Jews as to render them insensitive to the ever-changing spiritual panorama around them. That single loyalty, if this question be answered in the affirmative, led Jewish leaders to raise ever higher the barriers of the inner ghetto, excluding the outside world and its vast horizons. This is the real meaning of the judgment that our people became a fossil.

Understood in this deeper sense, it is apparent that many Jewish and non-Jewish scholars believed that the Talmudic sages deliberately set the goal of ethnic survival above every other consideration. For them, the "carapace of Law," so delicately structured in the Talmud, was not the articulation of Jewish piety but a social instrument of the collective will to live. Thus, Ahad Ha'am described the *mizvoth* as "exile garments." James Parkes writes in a recent volume of Rabbinic Judaism as the "religion of survival." To Toynbee, such an interpretation would make Jewish life liable to the charge of being "an idolization of an ephemeral self."

Now, it is simply untrue that in Judaism, the "will to survive" triumphed over the "will to be true." Survivalism is a modernistic goal, retrojected into history. It reflects a Darwinistic way of thinking, which was totally alien to ancient and medieval Jews. Furthermore, the Law did not create Amishlike ghettos, where the outside world was seen "through a glass darkly." Whenever circumstances permitted, Rabbinic Jews engaged in philosophy, science, medicine, literature, industry, commerce, and painting. A fraction of the Jewish community resisted these interests in the past as fringe-elements still do today; but so do backward elements in all cultures. Saadia, Israeli, Ibn Gabirol, Ibn Shaprut, Samuel HaNagid—they were all Rabbinic Jews. The entire complex of ideas is erroneous—the Law did not exclude intellectual and artistic activity; it was not an expression of the "will to survive" but of the "will to be true to God"; it was not blind obedience to rigid ordinances but the opposite —an openness to new ideas and new ways—that enabled the Jew to overcome the various hurdles of his history.

Toynbee is not alone in maintaining that the thought-processes of Judaism are those of the Semitic world of long ago, not of the modern European West. Jewish romanticists have insisted for a century that our standards of judgment are "different." For instance, it was said that the Jews identified themselves by the term *"am,"* which is peculiar and untranslatable. Also, we were told, Jews cannot comprehend the meaning of the separation of nationality and religion. All this is typical romantic nonsense—as likely to be claimed by diverse and sundry German or Russian romantics as by Jews. As I see it, geography and chronology do not determine the categories of culture. Various communities exist among us today, both Christian and Jewish, whose thought and feeling bear no relation whatever to that of twentieth-century Western civilization. Such Jewish enclaves, preserving either the medieval ghetto or the Syriac millet or the ancient, self-governing polis, are still to be found among us. But they are not representative of the spirit of the modern Jew, who is an integral part of the West.

Thus we come to the next question raised by Toynbee, the

fourth in our reckoning: Does the Jew belong to the West? Toynbee's answer is actually ambivalent. Historically, he asserts, the Jew is not part of the West, but it is his mission and destiny to sink his roots in the West and to divest himself of the impediments that prevented him in the past from becoming fully integrated in European society. At this point in our discussion we are concerned with the first part of this argument. Is the Jew part of the West?

I maintain that the right answer is the affirmative, without any qualification. It has been the common bias of French and German romanticists, on the one hand, and of Jewish racistic visionaries, on the other hand, which gave rise to the distorted view of the Jew as the alien and the outsider. Neither the Jewish romanticists nor the Gentile anti-Semites saw the European Jew as he was, but as a mythical figure of the mysterious Orient who had just stepped out of the pages of Scripture. Even as perceptive a philosopher as Lord Balfour was so far beguiled by these dreamy illusions as to write in his Preface to Sokolow's *History of Zionism* that the Jew was like an alien thorn thrust into the bodies of European peoples. The moment the veil of illusion is torn away, it becomes obvious that the European Jew is as Western as any component element of European society—indeed, more so because of the concentration of Jewish people in large metropolitan centers. No European philosophical, artistic, or cultural movement was devoid either of Jewish participation or of Jewish counterpart—not even anti-Semitism. Jewish sons and daughters gloried briefly in the Italian Renaissance, endured a Jewish counterpart of the Counter Reformation, experienced a mystical upheaval which undermined the authority of the rabbinate, burst into the sunlight of the rationalistic *Aufklärung*, and pulled back into the shadowed recesses of the romantic reaction. In the nineteenth century they faced up to the need of liberating secular life and thought from the encumbering chains of communal unity and the deadweight of a petrified tradition. If some sections of European Jewry resisted the nineteenth century, so did some

169

sections of Catholic, Protestant, and Greek Orthodox European society. If some Western Jews toyed with the illusion of retreating from the West to an imaginary dreamworld suited for the "ineffable" character of their "national soul," they only imitated slavishly the flights of fancy of romantic Frenchmen and Germans, Poles and Russians. At the inception of the modern world, Spinoza and Mendelssohn were among its intellectual architects. And in the twentieth century, who can number the titans of the spirit who were Jewish in respect to the impetus of tradition, if not in personal faith? Only racistic mythology and fundamentalist dogma could create the illusion that the European Jew was an alien to the West.

This discussion sets the context for the examination of Toynbee's final message to the Jews:

Fifth, what is the "manifest destiny" of the Jews in the Western world? As Toynbee sees it, the Jews of our generation are pulled in opposite directions by their melancholy memories of persecution, on the one hand, and by the inner core of their religion, on the other hand. Shall they take the Nazi holocaust to be the last gasp of Gentile savagery or shall they regard racist genocide as the "wave of the future"? The nationalistic component of Judaism was, in Toynbee's view, responsible for the failure of the Jewish religion to convert the Greco-Roman world. In modern times, this nationalistic barrier was the major underlying cause of anti-Semitism. Now, following the establishment of the State of Israel, this nationalistic impetus might be steadily cultivated and exaggerated by the political heads of the state in order to strengthen their global position and influence, "exploiting" the Diaspora politically and financially for the benefit of the "homeland." If the Jews of the Diaspora should heed the siren call of nationalism, Toynbee feels, they would build trouble for themselves, in the first place, and, in the second place, they would lose their historic opportunity to convert millions to the "religion of Deutero-Isaiah."[10]

By the "religion of Deutero-Isaiah," Toynbee means the universal core of "ethical monotheism," abstracted from the nation-

170

alistic entanglements of ethnicism and the legalistic "carapace" of ritual. He is convinced that our age is ready for a universal religion that addresses itself to all men and that is rich in memories, experiences, and reflections. Having suffered from the barbs of ethnic arrogance and religious fanaticism, the Jew is uniquely qualified to rebuke these sins in the accents of Isaiah. At the same time, the rationalistic component of Judaism is likely to resist fresh outbursts of obscurantism and mysticism. Toynbee calls upon the Jews of the West to become missionaries for this prophetic religion. In this counsel, he follows the lead of the classical reformers. It was Abraham Geiger who first called attention to the unique qualifications of Reform Judaism to serve as a "universal religion" in the modern world. Reform Judaism is nondogmatic, yet historical; rationalistic, yet centering around the God-intoxicated prophets; rooted in one ethnic tradition, yet open to the inspiration of all fresh "winds of doctrine." In recent years, the American Reform movement has been stirred by earnest calls to renew missionary activities to the Gentiles.

In my view, the "religion of Deutero-Isaiah" is an illumination of mind and heart within any and all of the faiths comprising the Judeo-Christian tradition. It occurs at the narrow edge, when one transcends his religious tradition by penetrating to its deeper meaning, or when he transcends his sheer ethnic loyalties by reaching down to their deepest humanistic intent. Religion is not advanced by cynicism, but by the prophetic spirit; even so, nationalism is not purified by cosmopolitanism, but by the affirmation of a universal "national purpose." Hence, it is never a static possession but always a dynamic event, as the striking of a spark, "when the hammer shatters the rock." The people who subscribe to this faith constitute what may be called an "invisible synagogue," for to all appearances they belong to different faiths. By its very nature, the prophetic power to evolve universal truths out of particularistic events cannot be institutionalized or inherited. Since the prophet attains his fulfillment by transcending the bonds of ethnicism and the rites of faith, he belongs neither to a people nor to a religion, but to all men, at the cutting edge of their spiritual growth. Prophecy cannot be "given"; it can only be rekindled afresh. To live in accord with the "religion of Deutero-Isaiah" is to live in tension—within a people and beyond it, within the seductive sacraments of faith and also above them. If he no longer feels the embrace of parochial loyalties, he cannot transform them, but if his horizon is bounded by them, he is not even "the son of a prophet."

For this reason, I conceive of the Jewish "mission" as being fulfilled in a similarly "invisible" way. Whenever we rise in faith beyond the static forms and sanctified rituals to the point of seeing them objectively and rendering them more meaningful in universal terms, we carry out our "mission." Whenever we dare to see the faults and failures of our own and rebuke them in love, we fulfill our "mission." But is not this, too, the "mission" of all our neighboring faiths and peoples? Precisely. Our "mission" is not an exclusive treasure, but the vocation of all historic communities. All of us stand equally before God as individuals and as communities. All of us are equal in obligation to Him. All of us are equal in His love. But the summons of opportunity knocks now here, now there. It is for us to hear it in the turbulence of events, the press of action, and to respond in heart and soul—as individuals and as communities.

TOWARD A PHILOSOPHY
OF JEWISH HISTORY*

More than in any previous period, thinking people today are history-minded. Having lost the easy optimism of the early decades of this century, we know now that failure and doom are possible. Modern man is neither passively fatalistic, so conscious of his frailty as to await with impotent resignation the inevitable knell of doom, nor naïvely fundamentalist, so confident of God's beneficent guidance as to repose no faith in human initiative, nor even buoyantly positivistic, so certain of the potency of science and the inevitability of progress as to look forward with untroubled serenity to the triumphant advance of freedom "from precedent to precedent." We know all too well that the fundamental facts of human nature are only organized and cultivated, but not metamorphosed by the advance of civilization. Below the calm of the surface, demonic fury slumbers in the unfathomed depths of the soul. The catastrophes of the past remain perpetual possibilities in the future, hovering on the horizon like dark and ominous clouds.

But as we turn the pages of history for some augury of the future, we become keenly conscious of the relativity of all historical judgments. Ours is the age of scientific psychology, when the hidden springs of human actions and ideals have been exposed to view. We have learned to prick the bubbles of proud pretense and to recognize the humble biological roots of all absolute judgments. The domain of history affords immense sway to the creative fancy of a searching mind. Indeed, the great historical writings of every generation tell us as much

*Reprinted from *Judaism*, 1956 and 1957.

about the *Zeitgeist* of the author's milieu as about the spirit of the age he describes. A perceptive, interpretive study of the past is inevitably a projection of philosophy against the background of time. We learn far more than a multitude of facts when we read a great historian's account of the French Revolution, the Protestant Reformation, or the American Civil War. The connective tissue in which the objective events are imbedded is woven out of the historian's subjective insights and preconceptions.

If all interpretations of history are inescapably marked with the ephemeral seal of contemporary bias, it is doubly difficult to achieve an objective understanding of the Jewish past, for a philosophy of Jewish history constitutes a part of the Jewish faith. The first of the Ten Commandments describes God in terms of an interpretation of the exodus of the Israelites from Egypt. By the same token, every modification of the monotheistic faith has implied a divergent explanation of Jewish history. The worshipers of the "Golden Calf" attributed the deliverance to the bull-god, and the feminine votaries of the "Queen of Heaven," who remonstrated with Jeremiah, offered their own account of the reasons for the rise and fall of Jewish fortunes. In modern times, the rise of every movement in our life, from Reform to Zionism and from Haskalah to socialism, involved a reinterpretation of the fundamental factors that are operative in Jewish existence. Thus, a philosophy of Jewish history is an integral portion of our faith, and faith is an intimate, subjective phenomenon.

The situation is further complicated by the circumstance that we live in the midst of the Christian intellectual world, which harbors its own interpretation of our history. A negative explanation of Jewish survival is part of the Christian pattern of beliefs since, in their view, Judaism was "fulfilled" in the emergence of the Christian message. This denial of any justification for Jewish existence was not an abstract intellectual judgment, but a deeply felt and widely disseminated article of faith—an emotion-laden attitude, the impetus of which was transferred from fundamentalist Christianity to its modernistic version and even to presumably anti-Christian philosophies. Thus, Voltaire combined a goodly measure of anti-Jewish bigotry with his crusade against Christianity.

Caught in the vise of emotional pressures, the would-be interpreter of Jewish history is strongly tempted to adopt an "existential" explanation; that is, to allow his "total being" to proclaim its "overwhelming truth" in a "moment of decision." By an "authentic" reaction of this sort, the historian becomes in effect the mouthpiece of historic forces rather than their judge and analyst. Jewish theologians like the late Franz Rosenzweig and our contemporary Will Herberg substitute the mystical entity of the "congregation of Israel" for the person of the Christian Savior in the "existential" situation, arriving at a conception of history that they call "theological" and that bears little or no relation to reality. I should not have mentioned these esoteric flights of fancy but for the circumstance that most people do, in fact, that which the "existentialists" affirm in theory; namely, allow their sentiments to fashion their understanding of history.

Jewish history is more than an artistic recreation of the past. A right understanding of the record it unfolds is essential for planning our future. Hence, arduous as the task may be, we cannot afford to rest content with the seduction of subtle sentimentalities. The realities of Jewish life are harsh and rugged. If in our absorption with subjective satisfactions, we dare overlook them, we court disaster. An objective understanding of the total panorama of Jewish life through the centuries should be our prime concern.

Can this task be done? I believe that it can be done with relative, if not absolute, success. The dynamism of a vital faith consists in a continuous oscillation from the intimacy of personal feeling to the cold austerity of objective judgment. We do not ever rise completely beyond the reach of personal preconceptions, but we achieve greater objectivity and deeper comprehension as we learn to make allowances for the involvements of our objective situation. Relative objectivity is all we can hope for, but even this limited goal is of tremendous concern to our life as Jews. We know now that we cannot afford to repose blind faith in the automatic functioning of the forces inherent in our situation. If we merely rest on our oars, the tides of history, for all their seeming quiescence at this moment, may well sweep us once more against the rocks.

Three mighty phenomena combine to give us the vantage point for a re-examination of the character of our history. First, the massive rise of racial anti-Semitism in the nineteenth and twentieth centuries, culminating in the cruel massacre of the six million, teaches us to appreciate the magnitude of the demonic forces that lurk beneath the surface. Second, the rise of the State of Israel demonstrates the extent to which a conscious program of rebellion against the automatic momentum of Jewish history can succeed in overcoming its impetus and reversing its direction. Third, the rise, prosperity, and spiritual vitality of Jewry in the Anglo-American countries demonstrates that the tragic fate of Central European Jewry is not the inevitable outcome of Diaspora existence. These three outstanding events of our time, taken together, underscore the folly of an uncritical acceptance of the ideological impetus of the past. Those who cannot rise above history are doomed to repeat it.

What is a philosophy of history? It is the endeavor to plot the curve of human experience in order to hazard an educated guess concerning its probable course in the future. A philosopher might discover one basic formula whereby the entire curve might be plotted in the future as in the past. Thus, Oswald Spengler predicted the decline of the West, and his Nazi disciples promptly undertook to prove his thesis. A less ambitious philosopher might aim at discovering the relations between various factors in history, thereby accounting for certain critical turning points in the evolution of human society. Employing the language of mathematics, we should say that a philosophy of history might consist of an "integral" formula, or of a series of "derivatives." The "integral" concept proposes to account for the overall direction of the curve of history, while the "derivative" concepts offer explanations for the curvature of the line at certain special points. Hegel's majestic interpretation of history as the self-unfolding of the human mind is a good illustration of an "integral" philosophy, while Toynbee's meticulous analysis of the psychological factor, "challenge and response," is an instance of the "derivative" approach. Ideally, these two types of philosophy of history are mutually supplementary.

Applying these observations to the understanding of Jewish history, we find that our objective is an all-embracing "integral" formula, capturing the dynamic impetus of Jewish life and its distinctiveness. This "integral" conception is then likely to lead to a series of "derivative" explanations, accounting for the important turning points in the life of our people. The overall formula must reflect the distinctive quality of Jewish existence and the motive power of its inner development, not merely offer a static description of the Jewish situation. The "derivative" explanations will account for such crucial consequences as the following: the sense of "difference" which both Jews and Gentiles feel concerning the nature of Jewish being, the return of the exiles from Babylon and the transformation of the "religion of Israel" into Judaism, the "rejection" of Judaism by the pagan world, the vigor of Jewish creativity in spite of the pressure of persecution and the lure of assimilation, the genesis and the growth of the Hydra-headed monster of anti-Semitism, the paradoxical nature of Jewish "alienism" in spite of seemingly complete assimilation, the persistent longing for Zion capped by the wonder of the State of Israel.

As I remarked above, the Jewish faith, from its very inception, proposed to account for all the vicissitudes of Jewish life. With the rise of nationalism and the scientific spirit in the modern period, the naïve conceptions of Orthodoxy lost their validity and charm. The stage was set for a fundamental re-evaluation of Jewish life and history. Thus, the "science of Judaism" was launched soon after the walls of the ghetto were leveled in Western Europe. The modern Jew commenced to apply all the insights of modern philosophy and historical criticism to the interpretation of his own past and the understanding of his destiny.

Broadly speaking, there emerged in the modern period four types of Jewish philosophy of history, which we might designate as the idealistic, the nationalistic, the synthetic, and the economic.

Idealistic philosophies of Jewish history constituted part of the ideology of Classical Reform. These philosophies were formulated by different Jewish thinkers in a variety of ways. Samuel Hirsch expounded his conception in terms of the Hegelian philosophy of life, Solomon Formstecher based his analysis on Schelling's "philosophy of the spirit," and Solomon Steinheim presented Judaism in the categories of Kant's critical philosophy. Abraham Geiger was eclectic in his metaphysical thought and Hermann Cohen provided the fundamental concepts of his own profound "philosophy of culture" for the interpretation of the nature of Judaism. Leo Baeck, in our own day, brought this philosophy up to date and gave it a contemporary ring. Different in technical idiom as these philosophies of Jewish history may appear to be, they all join in recounting the Jewish adventure as the story of "monotheism and martyrdom."

The following are the essential doctrines of the idealistic school:

1) Out of the totality of Jewish life and experience, all that matters is the pure *essence* of Judaism, the ideas of ethical monotheism. God is one and unique in the quality of His Being, different from all the forces and phenomena of nature. Man participates in the nature of Divine Being. He is free to choose good rather than evil and destined to be a partner of the Lord in the creation of the Kingdom of Heaven. God's will is completely congruent with the promptings of the human conscience, even if the Divine will transcends the bounds of human comprehension. While the forces of evil lurk perpetually beneath the surface, the scales are balanced in favor of the

good. The ethical and spiritual commands of the Holy Bible constitute the living kernel of true religion. All else, such as national memories, ancient rites and customs, symbols and ceremonies, feasts and fasts, belong to the outer shell.

2) Whether the ideas of "ethical monotheism" arose in Israel by the agency of Divine revelation or by means of a gradual evolution, the fact is that already in the first stage of Jewish history we behold their gradual advance and ultimate triumph among the people of Israel. This first stage corresponds roughly to the Biblical period, when the "essence of Judaism" needed to be defended against the impact and encroachments of the spirit of paganism. On this view, paganism was not merely the belief in many gods and a multitude of rites relating to the worship of gods and demons. Arrayed against the "essence of Judaism" was the "essence of paganism," embodied as it was in the diverse cultures of the ancient world.

The core and substance of paganism is the apotheosis of the forces of nature. The divine beings of the ancient world were fanciful elaborations of various natural phenomena—such as the powers of vegetation, of the ocean, of winds and clouds and thunder, of human genius, lust, and triumph. Since in nature both good and evil are found in profusion, the essence of paganism includes a recognition of the eternal battle between the gods that favor human life and the demons that account for all that is evil in the world. While the religion of Zoroaster stressed this dualism more than the other faiths of the pagan world, all forms of paganism included a perception of this timeless struggle between the good and evil forces in the occult world.

For the pagan mentality, man was part of nature, determined in his character and in his destiny by forces that were beyond his control. While the gods were somewhat humanized and spiritualized in the higher forms of paganism, the ultimate nature of the universe was altogether amoral and indifferent to human weal and woe. Above the struggles of both gods and men, the net of fate was suspended with its iron meshes pressing

179

cold, dark doom upon all forms of life. The gods were not the ultimate sources of being. For the most part, the gods for whom shrines were built were of the second or even third generation of Divine beings. Out of the chaos they emerged, and, in spite of their "immortal" nature, they were doomed to perish in the final conflagration, the "twilight of the gods."

This "essence of paganism" included rites and forms of worship that were not essentially different from the practices of magic. There was no moral element in the pagan propitiation of the gods. The central core of pagan piety was the enhancement of vitality, not the cultivation of moral and spiritual values. Paganism knew of "negative confessions" in which worshipers purged themselves of "guilt," but pagan cultures did not develop either a sense of true moral contrition or the feeling of utter devotion and absolute dependence that distinguishes the worship of true monotheists.

3) After the "essence of Judaism" won the battle against the "spirit of paganism" within the soul of the Jew, rigid laws were needed in order to provide a secure barrier against inroads from the outside world. The flowers of Judaism, so fresh and fragile, needed to be protected by an iron fence against the intrusion of aliens. For this reason, the Jews accepted the laws regulating their diet and interposing high barriers against their free association with the outside world. Jewish "separatism," which aroused the ire of Haman and his ilk, evolved not out of religious zealotry or ethnic pride, but out of the need of protecting the pure doctrines of ethical monotheism. Deep within the soul of the Jew, there lived the conviction that he was the chosen bearer of Divine Truth and that he must accept willingly the isolation and hostility that is inevitably the fate of prophets.

On this view, the sense of difference between Jews and Gentiles in the ancient world was a direct corollary of the triumph of monotheism in the soul of the Jew, while the rest of the world still groped in the twisted paths of polytheism. Anti-Semitism was the reaction of non-Jews to Jewish "separatism." Thus, Philo attributed the hostility of Gentiles to the "austerity" of Jewish laws and to the "perfection" of the virtue inculcated by them. At the same time, he recognized that the Law isolated the Jews from their neighbors and put them "in the position of an orphan compared with all other nations in other lands." Unable to join their neighbors in social activities, the Jews failed to obtain allies in their battle for survival, while non-Jews, "by reason of their frequent intercourse with other nations, are in no want of helpers who join sides with them."[1]

Thus, too, the Roman orator Cicero spoke for many of his countrymen when he assailed Jewish people on the ground that "the practice of their sacred rites was at variance with the glory of our empire, the dignity of our name, the customs of our ancestors."

As long as the sad fortunes of Israel appeared to contradict the notion of its being the chosen object of Divine favor, there could be no mass-conversions to Judaism. Thus, the Book of Esther tells that, following the triumph of Mordecai, "many of the peoples of the land became Jews." And Philo expected that all nations would accept the laws of Moses, once the Messiah had succeeded in retrieving the fortunes of Jewry.[2] In the meantime, the people of Israel were compelled to pay a severe price for their glorious role as a "prophet unto the nations."

4) Why, then, did Christianity succeed in converting the Gentile world? Did not the early Christians, too, outrage the convictions and feelings of their pagan neighbors? The answer of the idealistic school of Jewish philosophers is that Christianity constituted a blend of the pure monotheism of Israel with the cults and ways of thinking of the pagans.

Thus, in Paul's letters, sin is conceived as an inescapable contagion of the soul, not so much a moral failing as a metaphysical necessity. In early Christianity, "sin" was imputed by definition to all who did not accept that belief in Christ, "which was folly to the Greeks, and to the Jews, a stumbling block." The considerations of the "Categorical Imperative" were shunted aside in favor of a deity that predetermined some for salvation and some for perdition. Conceived in these nonmoral terms, "sin" took on the pagan connotations of "guilt," which could be washed away by mysterious rites.

By the same token, the Christian concepts of God and the Son of God partook of pagan thought and feeling. While the Messiah was the Son of the One God of Israel, he was also understandable in terms of the myths and concepts with which the pagan world was familiar. The later developments of this doctrine of God, which led to the emergence of a virtual Christian pantheon, with a Son and a Queen of Heaven, stirred memories in pagan souls that were ancient and tenacious.

Similarly, the substitution of "salvation by faith" for "salvation by works" was, in primitive Christianity, not a spiritualization of religion, but its very opposite. Faith at that time did not mean humble surrender to the will of God, but the acceptance of an irrational dogma. Tertullian's declaration "I believe because it is absurd" was a triumphant affirmation of freedom from reason and from the dictates of conscience. It goes without saying that "faith," in this sense, is far easier for the vulgar than a life of "good works."

In opposition to the prevailing views of Christian historians, the philosophers of this school point out that primitive Christianity did not substitute the pure kernel of piety for the shell of the Law. In Catholic Christianity, the Sacraments took the place of the Law, and the mechanical effectiveness of the sacraments was a concession to pagan rituals and a retreat from the high pinnacles of prophetic Judaism. The Sacraments were believed to function as quasi-natural forces, not as symbols and vehicles of monotheistic piety. Taken in conjunction with image-worship and saint-worship, dogmatic fanaticism and zealotry, early Christianity had little in common with its enlightened forms in our day. Thus, at every point where the spirit of paganism collided with the "essence of Judaism," Christianity occupied the mediating position. It was therefore excellently equipped for its historic role as the agency whereby the teachings of monotheism were to be disseminated—hence, Rosenzweig's image of Judaism as the sun and Christianity as the radiation of the sun throughout the world. But, for this very reason, Christianity could not take the place of Judaism in the souls of Jewish people. In the advance of the human mind, monotheism was destined to supersede paganism, but for Jewish people, Christianity constituted a descent from the lofty reaches of their faith, since it compromised at so many points with the pure faith.

Through the dark and torment-filled centuries of the medieval era, the Jews guarded the pure flames of monotheism, repudiating by their very presence the notion that all truth has been pre-empted for all time by the Lord's vicar on earth. As the Jewish faith guarded the pure essence of monotheism, the Jewish people constituted a standing challenge to the compromises of Christianity, leading the Western world to an ever more enlightened faith. The Reformation was stimulated, at least in part, by the Jew, acting as the eternal, unyielding protestant, and the Enlightenment which ushered in the age of science and democracy was aided by Jewish dissent from the "cake of custom" in European culture. Paradoxically, religious faith is a powerful force for good only when it is continually questioned and challenged. Did not modern democracy emerge from the womb of Christian Europe only after Christianity was softened by the rays of the Enlightenment? Only in tension is the life of the spirit productive of good, and Judaism provided the counterpoint for Christianity in all the long dark years of medievalism.

5) What then is the role of the Jew in the future? According to this idealistic school, it was the "mission" of the Jew to exemplify the doctrines of pure monotheism and to treasure these doctrines in behalf of all mankind. Several philosophers of this school maintained that the Jew was endowed with a unique "genius" for religion, akin to the marvelous gifts of the ancient Greeks for art. But even those who did not postulate this racial principle affirmed that Judaism was in possession of the only pure faith. In His wisdom, God dispersed the people of Israel

among all the nations of the world in order that they might scatter the seeds of monotheism everywhere and thus lead to the consummation of the vision of all nations speaking "a clear language," with the Lord being One and His Name One.

For the philosophers of this school, the dispersion of the Jewish people was not a sign of Divine anger, but a mark of His favor. They loved to expatiate on this comment of an ancient Midrash: "The Holy One, blessed be He, did not bring about the dispersion of the Israelites among the nations for any other purpose, but that converts might be added to them."[3] It was the historic mission of the Jew to bring pure monotheism to all men, and this mission will end only when all men will learn to live by the truths of the "essence of Judaism." While some Jewish theologians dared to dream of the ultimate acceptance of Judaism by all the nations of the earth, most philosophers of this school did not go so far as to envisage a terrestrial fulfillment of this Messianic hope within the course of history. However, they all affirmed it to be the duty of the Jew to live as a prophet of true religion unto all mankind. Thus, Hermann Cohen repudiated the ideology of modern Zionism on the ground of its proposing a retreat from the historic role of the Jew. To him, as to all the exponents of Classical Reform, Zionism amounted to a denial of the worth of Jewish life in the Diaspora. The Jew should accept the sting of anti-Semitism as the price he pays for loyalty to the clear call of duty. For Jews to capitulate to the anti-Semites and to retire to their ancient homeland would be tantamount to religious treason. To Cohen, Zionism was essentially a materialistic movement, in that it rejected the mission which Providence assigned to the Jew. "They want indeed to be happy," he remarked contemptuously.[4]

What about the problems of anti-Semitism? To the idealistic philosophers, all manifestations of Judeo-phobia were simply vestigial remnants of the dead past, which mankind was certain to outgrow. As liberals, the theologians of this school believed that human progress was steady and irresistible, with the light

184

of reason banishing all the creatures of darkness, as the rising sun on a cloudless day. Anti-Semitism was born out of the resistance of the pagan mind to the truths of monotheism. This pagan mentality is not yet completely overcome. People still dream of being God's favorites by virtue of a primeval act of creation rather than because of their own visible merits— hence, the pride of the Aryan. People still hunger for a badge of superiority, which is meaningful only when a badge of inferiority is placed in contrast to it—hence, scorn for the non-Aryan. The pagan mind is still engrossed by the polarity of "guilt and expiation" rather than of "sin and repentance"—hence, the search for a scapegoat, who "will bear the burden of their sins." In many and diverse ways, the advance of reason is still held back by the momentum of mythology and by the persistent distortion of self-centered emotion. However, reason and conscience are but two sides of the light of God in the human soul. Their triumph is assured and irresistible. "Grass withers and blossoms wilt, but the word of the Lord Our God will endure forever."[4a]

6) As I remarked above, this idealistic interpretation of the Jewish past was expressed in diverse philosophic idioms. Rationalists like Hermann Cohen saw the "essence of Judaism" in those maxims and principles that reflected "pure" reason, while intuitionists like Steinheim conceived this "essence" to be the contradiction of reason by the truths of revelation. And both classes of philosophers could find in the rich armory of Jewish tradition ample weapons for their purpose. Our tradition is complex and many-sided, containing Halevi as well as Maimonides, offering the comforting shades of Quabbalah and naïve piety to pale mystics and turbulent romanticists as well as lofty palaces of enlightened faith for humanists and rationalists.

The weakness of this idealistic interpretation is thus its inveterate abstractionism. The history of the Jewish people is more than the adventure of an ethereal "essence." In the first place, it is inescapably arbitrary to select one expression of Jewish thought as the kernel that is all important and then

185

to press the history of a whole people into the mold implied by that one idea. What is only a "shell" from one standpoint may have functioned in the exigencies of history as the "kernel." Just as so many Christian historians imagined that primitive Christianity was "essentially" identical with their own philosophy of religious humanism, castigating the Jew for his failure to realize that the fulfillment of his tradition depended on the teaching of the Christian Savior, so the idealistic Jewish historians identified their own enlightened faith with the "essence of Judaism," which the actual history of Christian dogma and life negated. Both schools are guilty of the sin that William James dubbed "vicious abstraction," substituting one aspect of experience for its totality.

The mighty labors of the historians of this school are extremely valuable for the understanding of the Jewish past, but in themselves they are woefully insufficient, either as an "integral," formula for Jewish history as a whole, or as a series of explanations for the crucial turning points in the evolution of the modern Jew.

To the nationalists, the Jewish people were simply a nation. The story of the Jew is a recital of the adventures and vicissitudes of an ethnic group that happened to be wonderfully gifted with spiritual insight. On this view, Jewish history falls into three easily discernible stages. In the first stage, commencing with the patriarchs and ending with the Great Revolt in 67 c.e., the Jews were a "normal" nation, rooted to the land, battling against its neighbors for its place in the sun. In the second stage, lasting from the destruction of Jerusalem to the opening of the modern period, the Jews were an "abnormal" nation, preserving its identity and cherishing its institutions under the protective covering of a religious faith. In the third stage, which opened with the rise of the Zionist movement, the Jewish people rediscovered their nationhood and determined to regain their ancient homeland, in order to become a "normal" nation once again.

When the totality of Jewish experience is interpreted as the triumphant achievement and tragic suffering of an ethnic group, then a radiant metaphysical aura is inevitably ascribed to the inner being of the Jewish people. What was previously attributed to God is now credited to the genius of the nation. Hence, a paradox: the very effort to see Jews as another nation makes them appear to be a unique ethnic group, different in kind from other races and tribes, since their character and destiny were so obviously different. Thus, the three outstanding philosophies of this school ascribe to the Jewish people a peculiar genius or a unique capacity for culture that continues to set them off from the rest of mankind.

Krochmal, the first philosopher of Jewish history in modern times, represented a unique blend of ideas derived from Jewish and German thought. Along with Herder, he viewed the history of nations in the categories of biology. Every nation, like a plant, goes through the stages of rapid growth, massive maturity, and the stage of slow senescence, culminating in decay and death. In its prehistory, an ethnic group resembles the seed of a plant, pushing its roots into the soil and only barely visible above the surface. With the passing of time, a nation acquires self-consciousness and begins to assert its cultural character. It commences to scatter the blossoms of its culture to the winds and it lends character to the total panorama. This first stage in the life of a nation may be said to end when it attains its maximum development. During the second stage, corresponding to the years of maturity in the life of a tree, the nation manages to hold its own against the ravages of time and the assaults of its neighbors, continuing to produce those fruits of culture that are characteristic of its peculiar nature. Every nation is an individual plant, evolving a culture that is distinctive and unique. In the third stage of its growth, a nation ages and declines, gradually losing its vitality and creative power, remaining on the scene, if at all, as a desiccated monument to its ancient glory.

This biological figure of speech is so facile and fascinating that one tends to forget the obvious truth that an analogy is not an explanation. In Krochmal's mind, this biological conception was combined with the thesis of Hegel that history is the unfolding of the Universal Mind. On this view, the reason for a nation's decline is, first, the circumstance of its cultural fruits becoming the property of universal civilization, and, second, a kind of fatigue of the spirit, manifesting itself in lust, pride, and materialistic value generally. As soon as the unique contributions of a people attain general acceptance, it ceases to have any reason for continued existence. Consequently, it endures merely by the power of momentum, passing slowly into the shades of oblivion.

To this double contribution of Herder and Hegel, Krochmal added the thought that occurs frequently in Rabbinic literature, namely, all nations have "angels" in heaven, while the "angel" of Israel is the Lord Himself. An "angel" in this connection refers to an ideal quality, such as beauty, orderliness, legality, freedom, fraternity, or hierarchy. All the nations that rose and fell in the course of time embodied in their characteristic cultures one or another of these qualities that represent a phase of the totality of goodness comprised in the will of God. The Jewish people are unique in that their national soul has as its characteristic content the ideal of piety, which is all-inclusive. The Jew is dedicated to the Absolute Spirit; hence, his contribution will not be fully assimilated before the "earth is filled with the knowledge of the Lord as the waters cover the sea."

To be sure, the Jewish people, too, underwent several cycles of youth, maturity, and old age, for in every age they were subject to the weaknesses of flesh and blood that pull a people down from the heights of idealism. Thus, the first cycle of growth and decline began with Abraham and ended with the Babylonian exile. The second cycle began with the return to Jerusalem and ended with the disaster of the Bar Kochba revolt in 135 C.E. The third cycle began with the editing of the Mishnah and terminated in the middle of the eighteenth century.

In Krochmal's own generation, a new period had opened up. Common to all the cycles in Jewish history was an indissoluble attachment of the people to the Supreme Being; yet, in each cycle, a different phase of Jewish piety constituted the living core of the national culture.[5]

Did Krochmal believe that the Jewish national soul *possessed* the idea of God in all its perfection? Or did he assume only that the Jewish people had dedicated themselves to the *search* for the Absolute Idea? The distinction between these two interpretations is the basic barometer of the nature of Jewish piety, as will be demonstrated later. At this point, we can only state that Krochmal assumed that the Absolute Idea became the possession of the entire people by the end of the first cycle of Jewish history.[6] Intuitively, the Jewish people acquired the Absolute Idea in all its purity, though the intellectual articulation of the Idea depended on the philosophical idiom of the age. Krochmal shared too the fundamental feeling of distinction between Jew and Gentile that runs through the Holy Scriptures. All the "nations of the world" were ranged on one side of a cosmic gulf, while the Jews stood on the other side. The Absolute Idea, or the one God, is an elusive goal to the "nations," who glimpse only fleeting facets of its nature from time to time, while the Jews are already standing at the final goal post of the human race, waiting for erring, groping mankind to catch up with them.

Asher Ginsberg, better known by his pen name, Ahad Ha'am, was by all odds the most influential Jewish essayist of modern times. By his reinterpretation of the Jewish past, he evolved a satisfying program for his contemporaries and a blueprint for the future. While his primary concern was the solution of the problem of Jewish homelessness, he dealt with a re-evaluation of the lessons of Jewish history, for, as I remarked previously, a philosophy of history constitutes part of the living faith of the Jew.

To Ahad Ha'am, the impetus of the "Jewish national soul"

189

consists in the aspiration for absolute justice. In contrast to the generation of Krochmal, the contemporaries of Ahad Ha'am no longer believed implicitly in God. The eternity of the Jewish people could not therefore be postulated on the basis of attachment to the Absolute Idea. But, if the Jewish idea of God arose out of the search for righteousness and ethical perfection, is not this search itself a permanent and enduring quality of the Jewish national soul?

To Ahad Ha'am, the ambiguous lessons of history were viewed in the categories of biology. All nations are motivated by the "will to live," which is not always expressed in conscious terms. The military and political battles of history reflect this conflict of ethnic groups. But there is a spiritual dimension in the lives of human beings, and, in the realm of ideas, the struggle among nations takes the form of a rivalry among different sets of values and opposing cultural movements. Corresponding to the quasi-biological "will to live" of nations, there are the national ideas reflecting the national souls of different ethnic units.

On this view, it is not the totality of the religious tradition of Israel that is important for the future, nor the consciously formulated doctrines, comprising the "essence of Judaism," but the underlying "spirit of Judaism"—that is, the dynamic psychic impetus of the national soul that generated the ideas of monotheism. Ahad Ha'am maintains that the quest for Absolute Justice is the distinctive quality of the Jewish soul. The feeling of profound difference between Israel and the nations is retained in this philosophy and attributed to the inability of non-Jews to appreciate the loftiness of the Jewish Idea. The purpose of Zionism is to revive the Jewish "will to live" and to establish an ethical-cultural Jewish community in Palestine that would evolve a new expression of the Jewish Idea, giving fresh form to the eternal quest of the national soul for an Absolute Moral Order.

Ahad Ha'am, too, saw the history of Jewish people as falling into three periods: first, the Biblical period. During these centuries of normal growth, the Jewish genius was able to unfold freely, with the result that the Holy Bible was produced. In the pages of the Bible, we find the record of a continuous conflict between priest and prophet, the priest representing the congealed heritage of the past, the prophet functioning as the living voice of the national soul. The vagaries of mythology and the complexities of ritual were merely effects of contemporary culture. The distinctive quality of prophetic teaching was a sense of amazement at the reality of evil and an unquenchable passion for righteousness. The ethical ideal was conceived in terms of social welfare and national greatness, for when the national "will to live" functions normally, the individual is not overly concerned with his personal fate.

The second era embraces the long period of exile and national paralysis from the exile in Babylonia to the rise of the Zionist movement, a period of political prostration broken only by a hundred years of resurgence under the leadership of the Hasmonean rulers. The weakening of the national spirit led to the emergence of the individual as the new focus of attention. To sustain the morale of the individual, the doctrines of immortality and resurrection were evolved out of the depths of the national soul. To enable the Jew to live in the agonizing isolation and the menace-filled loneliness of the ghetto, the "spirit of Judaism," operating through the scribes and sages, produced the rigid ritualism of the Talmud. The undue emphasis on legalistic niceties in the Talmud was historically necessary in order to create an artificial Jewish homeland, protected by high barriers from the influence of the outside world. The cumbersome rites of Judaism constituted the "exilic garments" for the bruised body of the national soul.

During the long dark night of exile, the motive power of Jewish life, pulsating beneath surface stratagems and devices, was the "will to live" of a mature people. This dynamic impetus was aided on the plane of ideas by the "contempt of the Jew for the power of the fist" and his reverence for the high values of the spiritual life. Because of his love of rationality, the Jew was able to apply the scalpel of criticism to competing philosophies of life and thus to reassure himself of the superiority of his tradition to that of his neighbors. Because of his high esteem for moral values, the Jew did not succumb to the lure of the pomp and power of his mighty neighbors.

In the middle of the nineteenth century, the thinking Jew found himself surrounded by inveterate enemies and stripped of the protection of his "exilic garments." The rites and myths of religion no longer enthralled him, while the ethical-spiritual impetus of his national soul was assaulted by a medley of materialistic philosophies which were frequently only rationalizations of the primitive urge for domination and brutality; hence, the need for a return to the homeland, where an ethical-spiritual community would be built in accord with the prophetic passion for Absolute Justice and the Maimonidean love of pure reason. In the "cultural center" of the homeland, only a fraction of the Jews of the world would live, but out of that dedicated community there would issue the rays of moral fervor to the most distant corners of the Diaspora, infusing them with the longing for ethical purity and national loyalty.

This, then, was the philosophy that suffused the Zionist movement of national rebirth with a Messianic aura of spiritual greatness. In the early twenties, Dr. Chaim Weizmann, a genuine disciple of Ahad Ha'am, refused to allow mass-immigration into Palestine of Polish Jews for fear of turning Tel Aviv into "another Nalevke" (the Jewish section of Warsaw). He insisted on a period of indoctrination and moral preparation to make certain that the new settlement would be morally elite in character. In the light of contemporary events, it is difficult for outside observers to realize that Jewish nationalism was not atavistic and narrow, being motivated by high and universal ideals of service to mankind. The "cultural," or, better, "spiritual Zionists" aimed to make the "house of Israel" strong and secure like unto the dwelling places of "all other nations," but only for the purpose of reviving the moral greatness of the Jewish soul and contributing to the spiritual regeneration of all men.

We need hardly subject this philosophy to the rigors of criticism, since it is so obviously compounded of many half-truths. Its credibility and potency were due to the mentality of a generation of transition that had lost the dogmatism of religious faith but retained its pathos and its spiritual fervor; a generation that no longer believed its own religion to be true but was convinced of the falsehood and futility of the faiths that challenged it; that believed Jewish life in the Diaspora to be a national tragedy and a thing of shame and cast about for ways of redeeming it. Various critics have already pointed out that concepts like "national soul" and "will to live" were mythological illusions, not sociological realities. And the craving for the purity of "Absolute Justice" is attributed by all "patriotic" historians to their own respective races.

Professor Simon Dubnow, the great historian who was murdered by the Nazis, based his construction of Jewish history on still another concept of nationality. He drew a clear line of demarcation between nationalism, the striving of a nation for the control of its own governmental machinery, and national loyalty, which is the effort of a historic group to retain its own cultural character. Taking as his vantage point, the struggle of the small nations of Central Europe for cultural autonomy, Dubnow saw the Jew of history as the protagonist of this battle for nationality rights, from the days of the Babylonian Empire to the present day. The uniqueness of the Jewish fate was due to the fact that it attained cultural self-consciousness long before the society of mankind was ripe for any such concept as a plurality of cultures dwelling within one political unit. It was the great achievement of the prophets to insist that national life can flourish without the protection of the state. "The nation is the kernel, and the state is no more than a shell; when the shell breaks, the kernel is saved. If the kernel is healthy, the nation can maintain its distinctive character against the influence of the environment and become 'a banner unto nations,' a living demonstration of spiritual power."[7] Dubnow entitled his main work *Weltgeschichte des Jüdischen Volkes* to suggest that the Jews had long ago become a "world-people," a nationality capable of prospering apart from a native soil, apart from a unifying government, and without the aid of a unifying religion. He arrived slowly and by degrees at this conception of "secular nationalism" being influenced chiefly by the movement for national autonomy in the period following the First World War.

In this development from a nation living by the sword to a nationality aspiring for cultural autonomy, the Jewish people anticipated the progress of other ethnic groups. Hence, the welfare of mankind depends on the fate of the Jew, for, as the dimensions of our globe shrink into one all-embracing society, the example of the Jewish Diaspora will provide the model for a world at peace, in which many nationalities dwell side by side without recrimination and rancor. Thus, Toynbee's conception of the Diaspora as a "milletal" community, demonstrating the possibility of cultural diversity going hand in hand with political unity, was anticipated by Dubnow.

But the very magnitude of Dubnow's research demonstrates the folly of endeavoring to compress the whole of Jewish historical experience within the confines of nationality struggling for self-preservation. The question, Why did the Jews alone strive for self-preservation? is answered by the supposition that they were "more cultured," or "more self-conscious." But the Greeks of old were "cultured" and the Egyptians were deeply "self-conscious"; yet, their diasporas disappeared in short order. In the mind of Dubnow, it was a high moral ideal for a nationality to strive for self-preservation. This axiom is not native to the human mind, nor does the tradition of Judaism affirm it as a general principle, while the experience of the American "melting pot" refutes it altogether. The national principle accounts for only one phase of Jewish life. It is related to the fullness of Jewish history as a shadow is to its three-dimensional object.

The insufficiency of the nationalistic "integral" concept is best demonstrated by a study of the explanation it provides for the crucial turning points in Jewish history.

The first and most important fact that a philosophy of Jewish history must seek to explain is the sense of difference between Jew and Gentile that was manifested with disastrous consequences long before the rise of Christianity. To Krochmal, this sense of difference was due to the superiority of the Jewish God-idea. At this point, his explanation is a theological one. To Ahad Ha'am, this feeling of differentiation, amounting almost to an awareness of cosmic distinction, was due to the moral superiority of the Jew. This is a flattering dogma for Jews, but there is no awareness on the part of the non-Jews of the pagan era that the difference was one of an ethical philosophy of life. The ancient world was familiar with moralistic societies. What it resented in Jews was this feeling of difference or self-isolation, which they interpreted as "misanthropy." The arguments between Jews and Gentiles were conducted on the plane of theology, with such practices as sodomy being mentioned as consequences of polytheism, not as things evil in themselves. To Dubnow, the sense of difference was simply the feeling of one nation that another cultural group is alien to it. But the conviction that the Jews are somehow different, for better or for worse, was the one silent assumption in which both Jews and Gentiles shared. In his reflections on the character of his destiny, the Jew of Biblical and Talmudic times thought of his lot as being different from *all* other nations. In this judgment, the preachers of anti-Semitism in Roman times concurred. Seen from the standpoint of an enthusiast inside the Jewish community and of an enemy watching it from without, there was a high and rugged barrier that set the Jew apart from the rest of mankind. The expulsion of children born of mixed marriages by Ezra was motivated by a zeal for the purity of "holy seed" that reflected the feeling of Jewish difference. Although converts were accepted in large numbers, in the generations following Ezra the feeling of difference was intensified and widely disseminated. Anti-Jewish feeling was frequently exploited for the partisan purposes of demagogues. But it was not invented.

Anti-Semitism was even in ancient times too deep-rooted,

long-lasting, and widely distributed a phenomenon to be understood simply as the "dislike of the unlike."

Leo Pinsker, one of the forerunners of the Zionist movement, sought to explain the phenomenon of anti-Semitism as the reaction of non-Jews to the fact of Jewish dispersion. A people living in the interstices of other ethnic groups gives the impression of a "ghost nation"—a thing frightening and unreal. In the ancient world, there were many diasporas. While we read of struggles among ethnic groups in the Roman world, we encounter nowhere a bitterness so universal, a hostility so deep and enduring, a passion at once so popular and so intellectualized. National rivalries and battles have taken place since the dawn of time, but a *philosophy* of hatred, directed against one people, is a thing new and unprecedented. Therefore, anti-Semitism is not understandable on the supposition that the Jews were just another nation.

The series of disasters, beginning with the Great Revolt in 68 c.e., continuing with the catastrophic riots in Cyprus, Cyrenaica, and Egypt in the years 111-113 c.e. and culminating in the Bar Kokba rebellion of 135 c.e., are not fully explicable in the narrow formula of a nationalistic conception. Such Roman emperors as Vespasian, Trajan, and Hadrian are ranked by historians as having been among the best imperial rulers in history. Roman policy was on the whole tolerant of national distinctions and religious preferences. Why were the Jews convulsed again and again by suicidal revolts against Roman power?

Professor Klausner in his history of the Second Commonwealth makes every allowance for the superb patriotism and political sagacity of the Zealot leaders. Yet, he concludes sadly that the catastrophic revolts were at least in part due to a chain of misunderstandings. "The Romans did not understand the Jews, and the Jews did not understand the Romans."[8] That multiple misunderstandings led to the outbreak of the Great Revolt is also suggested in the Talmud.[8a] The history of anti-Semitism is one long account of the accumulation of misunderstandings and falsehood, rising layer by layer like glaciers on high mountains and cascading down from time to time with devastating power. Why should the Jews have been so signally liable to misunderstanding and misrepresentation?

The spectacle of anti-Semitism in modern times is even more instructive, pointing to another factor that is overlooked by the nationalistic theory. Anti-Semitism became an independent factor that was almost unrelated to the circumstances of living Jews. Compounded of atrocious lies and macabre phantasies, anti-Semitism was nevertheless capable of functioning as a powerful political force in modern Europe. This quasi-mythical mass-movement was hardly due to the actions of Jewish people, or to the character of their being. When political anti-Semitism attained its first triumph in modern Germany, its strength was centered in provinces where Jewish people did not reside at all. The same phenomenon is repeated in the United States, with the Jew being most feared and hated in the areas where he is only a legendary figure, not a living presence. The miasma of anti-Semitism, whatever its historic sources might be, is part of the living heritage of our Western world. And anti-Semitism in its dark, romantic phase is largely a spiritual malaise that is only tangentially related to living Jews. Thus, a French socialist like Fourier and a careful scientific sociologist like Karl Marx attacked Jews as mythical, symbolic figures of capitalism, rather than as actual, living contemporaries.[9] Yet the actual Jew suffered the brunt of the attacks directed against the mythical figure.

It follows that national rivalry in itself does not account either for the failure of the Jew to understand other nations or for the failure of other nations to understand the Jew. The barrier between Jews and their neighbors is compounded of material that is not caught in the meshes of nationalistic theory.

The survival of the Jew in the face of overwhelming obstacles is similarly not understandable on the basis of the nationalistic hypothesis. Ahad Ha'am's supposition that the Jews had contempt for the "power of the fist" is altogether insufficient to account for their resistance to the sections of pagan society that were relatively cultured and ethical. The "will to live," in Ahad Ha'am's or in Dubnow's formulation, deriving from biological and social sources, operated presumably with equal potency in other groups.

Dubnow poses the thesis that the prophets anticipated the modern social theory of "cultural autonomy," assuring the Jews that they could continue to live as communal groups in exile. But a social philosophy can only offer form and guidance to social forces. It cannot evoke them out of the void of chaos. The prophets could tell the people that they could live as minorities, but why should the people want to live so? The dynamic power of survival had to flow from the "will to live" of ethnic groups. And this is just the point that is so frequently overlooked—the "will to live" of a social group is gradually dissipated. Why then was the Jewish will to live not dissipated? Dubnow declares, "in foreign lands, the national will to live is intensified."[10] This observation is certainly true of the Jews in exile, but it is hardly an explanation of the phenomenon. By consulting the words of the prophets themselves, we find that they supplied motivation for Jewish survival. And this motivation had nothing to do with the glories of "cultural autonomy."

Dubnow persists in treating the religious motivation of Jewish life as only a peripheral and conventional expression of subterranean ethnical forces, but his generalizations do not mesh with the actual data of Jewish experience. Summing up his understanding of the inner drive of Jewish history, he asserts: "And this living and eternal people battled at all times and in all places for its distinctive existence in communal life and in all other domains of culture."[11] It is simply not true that Jews strove to preserve their *cultural* identity apart from their religious concern. Is not language the most distinctive expression of a national culture? Yet, the Jews did not try to keep their language in circulation, yielding first to Aramaic and then to Greek, in the ancient world. The phenomenon of Jewish survival is remarkable precisely because cultural assimilation was so readily accepted in all spheres that were not distinctively religious. Jews accepted with alacrity and eagerness the vernacular tongue in all its subtle variations, the various art forms, the ways of celebrating joy and expressing mourning, the patterns of commercial life and the techniques of industry, the styles of clothes and the fashions of manners, the hierarchy of social concepts and the popular forms of entertainment. In a word, all that we call culture, the Jews in their wandering from country to country donned and doffed with relative indifference.

Nor was self-government an important aim of the Jewish people, save insofar as it was needed for the practice of their faith. The Hasidim, forerunners of the Pharisees, were willing to accept the suzerainty of Syria and to desert the leadership of Judas Maccabeus as soon as their religious freedom was safeguarded.[11a] When Pompey came to the borders of Palestine, the "party of the people" pleaded with him not to recognize either one of the two Hasmonean brothers, Hyrkanos and Aristobulus, but to appoint a Roman governor for their affairs.[11b] Rabbi Johanan ben Zakkai, founder of the Academy at Jamnia, was, in the eyes of the Zealots of his day, a deserter of the national cause. In the Talmud, the Zealots are described as little better than bandits, and the noblest of all the Hasmonean heroes, Judas Maccabeus, is not even mentioned. In the Middle Ages, the appointment by a potentate of a *Naggid,* Exilarch or Chief Rabbi, was motivated by the ruler's desire to exert control over the Jewish community rather than by the desire of the people to govern themselves. Jewish law does indeed encompass the whole of life, but this fact is due to the religious drive for the hallowing of every aspect of life, not to a high estimate of secular self-government. A code of law that stipulates the proper manner of lacing one's shoes, could it leave out of consideration the manner of administering justice in any walk of life?

To assume that Jewish survival was due to the indomitable will of the nation to preserve its cultural identity is to attribute to the Jews of the ancient and medieval world concepts that derive from the secular thinking of modern times. National

199

cultures attained the rank of supreme values only when the religious hierarchy of values was shattered. The Jews in the Rhine provinces, who killed their sons and daughters in order to keep them from being forcibly converted by the Crusaders, were not motivated by the will to preserve their "distinctive, cultural autonomy," but by the belief that they exchanged the transitory goods of this world for the eternal bliss of the "World to Come." To think otherwise is to fly in the face of the facts and to attribute to our ancestors the sin that Toynbee designates as the "idolization of an ephemeral self."

Why did the Jews "reject" Jesus and the message of Christianity? While the idealistic philosophers answered this question by pointing to the "compromise" of Christianity with the mentality of the pagan world, the nationalistic historians explained this rejection in terms of nationalistic ideals. Jesus and his disciples were guilty of deprecating the worth of Jewish nationhood and betraying the national cause. Thus, Professor Klausner stresses the absence of a nationalistic note in the teaching of Jesus. "His ethical philosophy is separated from political and social life." Furthermore, he continues, "Judaism is not only religion and not only ethics. It is the totality of the needs of the nation, based as they are on a religious foundation. A religion, centered round a universal doctrine of God and an ethical message directed to all men, burst through the fences of nationality, consciously or unconsciously."[12] Though Klausner recognized that all the sayings of the Gospels were duplicated in Rabbinic literature, he insisted that there were nonnationalistic overtones in the words of Jesus.

In line with this thought, Klausner explains the opposition of the Jews to the preaching of Paul, especially his declaration, "There is now no Jew and Greek, no slave and freeman, no male and female, but all are one in the Messiah."[13] "Judaism," declares Klausner, "made converts out of pagans, transforming them into 'sons of the covenant,' and absorbing them into the body of the nation. Paul erased the boundaries of nationality, causing the Jews to be absorbed into the pagan body."[14] Klausner accounts for Paul's lack of a nationalistic emphasis by pointing to the fact that "he was an uprooted Jew, a Diaspora Jew." His doctrine was "a contradiction of the Jewish faith and a negation of the Israelitic nation." The Christians and the Jews fell apart into "two separate worlds," according to Klausner, because the Christians deserted from the battle against Rome in the Great Revolt.[15]

In exactly the same vein, Dubnow undertakes to account for the break between Christianity and Judaism. The novelty in the message of Jesus was the "emphasis on the sharp distinction between inner faith or individual ethics and communal religion or an ethics that is geared to a particular situation in the life of the nation."[16] The activist or Zealot Pharisees saw in the message of Jesus a challenge to their entire program, while the quietistic Pharisees "saw in the new teaching a hidden intention of opposition to nationalism."[17] Hesitating on the verge of the abyss before plunging into the Great War, the people were shown three roads: the Zealots said, "Let us fight by the sword to save the State"; the Pharisees said, "Let us arm ourselves by faith to save the nation"; the Christians said, "There is need neither for the sword of the Zealot, nor the shield of the Pharisees, for it is right to fight neither for the state, nor for the nation, but for the salvation of the soul of the individual."[18]

Strangely enough, the explanation of the nationalistic historians concurs at this point with the standard interpretation of anti-Jewish historians like Wellhausen. Judaism, it is maintained, was narrowly nationalistic, while Christianity burst the bounds of ethnicism to become a truly universal faith. Actually, both the Christian and the nationalistic interpreters saw in the mirror of the past a reflection of their own beliefs. There is no basis for the assumption that Jesus was less nationalistic than his opponents, the Pharisees. In the whole vast range of Talmudic literature, we find no such contemptuous reference to the other nations as is attributed by the Gospel of Matthew to Jesus.[19] Pharisees are described in the Gospels as being eager to bring converts to Judaism. Halakah, or Jewish Law, knows of no barriers between Jews and Gentiles "under the Torah," even as Paul sees none "in the Messiah," though this generalization does not hold true for all the opinions expressed in the Talmud. Certainly, the Hillelite wing of the Pharisees was friendly to converts, and Talmudic legends ascribe non-Jewish ancestry to the most outstanding sages, to Rabbi Meir and Rabbi Akiba, to Shmaya and Abtalion.[19a] Even the question of admitting converts, without requiring circumcision, was debated in the Talmud, with Rabbi Joshua ben Hananiah accepting the proposition —the dispensability of circumcision for proselytes—that almost divided the infant Christian Church.[20] The question of the validity of the Torah had nothing whatever to do with nationalism, and the hope of "all flesh" acknowledging the One God was not given up at any period of Jewish life. Can anyone acquainted with the mentality of the Talmudic sages doubt that they would have accepted Jesus if they were convinced of his Messiahship? Conversely, can it be doubted that, being persuaded of his not being a heavenly messenger with power to save and transform the world, they would have rejected him even if he had spoken in an approved nationalistic style? The folly of this approach becomes manifest as soon as it is examined in the broad light of day.

Inadequate as the conceptions of nationalism are for the understanding of ancient Jewish life, the history of our people in the period of the emancipation is to the nationalists a perpetual affront and humiliation. How could the Jews of western Europe accept so readily the status of a religious community when, according to Dubnow's theory, this was in fundamental contradiction to their essential being? Yet, the Jews, who not only welcomed this status but fought for its attainment, were rooted in the tradition and eager for its preservation. They were not uprooted intellectuals, misled by abstractions, nor romantic "returnees" who fled from an illusion and returned to a dream, nor worldly men of wealth who were moved by the prospect of material gain. The ambitious, the uprooted, the easygoing, and the Philistines chose the path of outright conversion. Those who remained in the fold were prepared for a life of arduous sacrifice. Yet, they willingly gave up their residual remnants of "nationalistic autonomy," while they clung with might and main to their religious heritage.

This choice, demonstrating the nature of the hierarchy of values in the soul of the Jew, was made not once but many times and in different parts of Europe. There was first of all Napoleon's "Assembly of Notables" and his subsequent "Sanhedrin," which renounced any aspirations for national autonomy and expressed the eagerness of the Jews to become part of the nations among whom they dwelled. The "Sanhedrin" at Paris believed that it concluded a solemn compact, by means of which the Jews had given up their quasi-national status and their longings for a return to Zion, and had become part of the "great nation" of France.[21] They ceased to be that which their enemies and Napoleon stigmatized as a "nation within a nation," and had become Jewish Frenchmen, willing to bear arms in defense of their fatherland. To Dubnow, the "Assembly of Notables" was "guilty of denying the national unity of the Jews." But the "Assembly" and later the "Sanhedrin" included some distinguished rabbis who saw no contradiction between the new "covenant" and the sacred tradition.[22] In the Duchy of Poland, the sect of Hasidim led the fight against the complete civil emancipation of Jewry—but for religious, not national, reasons.[23] In the provinces of Germany, the foremost fighter for full Jewish emancipation was Gabriel Riesser. Seeing that Jews were deprived of "civil rights" on the ground that they were a "nation," he sought to prove that Jews were not a nation, but a religious group. "The Jewish question is only one of freedom of religion. . . ."[24] "The battle which our fate imposed upon us was not that of a nation against nations, but the struggle of a faith, pursued by zealotry, of the freedom of the spirit against compulsion, of humanity and ethics against barbarism. . . ."[25] Dubnow agrees that Riesser was the foremost Jewish leader of his day. Yet, the remnants of ghetto autonomy that Riesser dubbed as "a shameful blot upon Jewish life," Dubnow extols as "the distinguishing sign of a living nation."[26]

In the discussions of Jewish emancipation throughout the nineteenth century, the anti-Semites maintained that the Jews were a "nation," that is, a self-isolating group cherishing the myth of its own "difference," while the liberals, from Macaulay in England to Mommsen in Germany, maintained that post-emancipation Jewry was a religious community. To be sure, some Gentile writers regarded such practices as the dietary laws to be not religious disciplines but national boundary markers.[27] Truly amazing is the extent to which the rites of Judaism were occasionally misrepresented. Thus, Charles Fourier, founder of a school of socialism, wrote: "This refusal to eat [non-Kosher] . . . proves patently that there is truth in the accusation that Jews consider themselves free to rob Christians with impunity."[28] The resurgence of anti-Semitism in the late seventies of the nineteenth century was given tremendous impetus on the intellectual front by the German historian Treitschke, who pointed out the powerful nationalistic overtones in Graetz's *History of the Jews.* "Our state," he declared, "always saw in the Jews only a religious society and granted them civil equality on this assumption and in the expectation that they will become like the other citizens of the state. But if the Jews should now come and demand recognition of their nationality, the legal ground is removed from their equality. For the fulfillment of this desire only one road is open, to go out and found a Jewish state someplace outside this land. On the soil of Germany, there is no place for a twofold nationalism."[29]

While Graetz, in his replies to Treitschke, denied any partiality for Jewish nationalism, Professors Hermann Cohen and Moritz Lazarus strove, with all the subtlety of their mighty intellects, to prove that Graetz represented only a residual remnant of German Jewry. The Jews of Germany, outside a small and insignificant "Palestinian party," considered themselves to be Germans in nationality, Jewish in religion.[30]

Does the circumstance that the Jewish nationalists and the

anti-Semites concurred in the same concept of Jewish existence mean that the doctrine of Jewish nationhood is erroneous? This inference is obviously unwarranted. But it is fair to conclude that the entire mentality of Western Jewry throughout the nineteenth century was echoed faithfully by Gabriel Riesser when he complained bitterly "against the nationalism that is being foisted upon us." Before European nationalism came to be based upon racist doctrines, it was possible for both Gentile and Jewish liberals to maintain that nationalism is a "plebiscite that is voted daily," a voluntary act of identification in thought and sentiment whereby the Jews of Western Europe transformed themselves into the nationals of their respective countries. The argument between Treitschke and Cohen was over a question of fact, whether or not the Jews of Germany had already become Jewish Germans. Gradually, German nationalism came to be based upon the Teutonic race-consciousness, in which the Jew could have no part. Soon this racist note was echoed by Jews.

The racist foundation of nationalism was assumed implicitly, though it was not always affirmed explicitly, by nationalists like Hess, Lilienblum, Ahad Ha'am, and Dubnow. In the context of Jewish life in the Diaspora, opposition to the integration of the Jew into the national life of his native land could only be based on the ethnic phase of nationalism; cultural values are additive and noncompetitive. In the vertical dimension of ideals, neighborhood cultures achieve a synthesis through the impetus of their inner logic and implicit merit, not by way of a struggle for survival. On the assumption that Jews were like other people, any resistance to the normal processes of cultural assimilation and social integration could be justified only as a temporary measure. Natural and unforced assimilation is ponderous and slow-moving. Thus, the Yiddishist nationalists in Russia and the Jewish section of the Bolshevik party held to this view. Any attempt to justify Jewish national existence on a permanent basis, in spite of the absence of a natural basis for Jewish life, had to be based on the assumption that Jews were somehow different. The normal processes of national commingling and integration do not apply to Jews, because a deep, cosmic gulf yawns between them and "the other nations of the world." The unconscious assumption of a quasi-metaphysical distinction between Jews and Gentiles derives its plausibility from the folk traditions of both Judaism and Christianity. But popular plausibility is not a valid measure of worth. The massive danger inherent in any such assumption was demonstrated by the perverse mass-madness of Nazism, which founded its cannibalistic ideology on the racial mythology of Aryan and non-Aryan. It is the task of philosophers to analyze traditions into their component elements and to prevent the errors of the past from becoming the bane of the future.

The massive popularity of the doctrine of "historical materialism" made it almost inevitable that attempts would be made to interpret the whole of Jewish experience in terms of economic factors. To any thoughtful scholar today, these attempts are manifestly no more than curiosities, symptoms of a sickly age. Yet, the influence of the Marxist school of history was too great to be ignored.

Karl Marx set the fashion for this type of historical interpretation by his articles on "The Jewish Question." In his eagerness to explain all processes of consciousness by material facts, he turned attention away from the "Sabbath Jew" to the "weekday Jew," the "Jew of the marketplace." And he was persuaded that by this change of focus it was possible to perceive clearly the inner nature of the Jew and his impact upon Gentile society. The Jews are, economically speaking, the bearers and the agents of capitalism. Judaism is simply a translation into spiritual terms of the mentality and character of the exploiter and the money-man. The sense of "difference" between Jew and Gentile is simply the reaction of people in a less advanced stage of economic development to those who represent for them the juggernaut of capitalistic civilization. The Jews were transformed into money-mad capitalists long before the rest of Western society. Anti-Semitism is a concealed form of resistance to the bacillus of capitalism, of which the Jew was first the victim, then the master, and lastly, the agent. Therefore, the "Jewish problem" will be solved only when the capitalistic order of society will have been overturned.

"Let us consider the actual worldly Jews, not the Sabbath Jews, as Bauer does, but the everyday Jews. Let us not search for the secret of the Jews in their religion, but for the secret of their religion in the Jews. What is the worldly basis of Judaism? Practical need. Selfish utility. What is the worldly cult of the Jews? Haggling. What is his worldly God? Money. Well, then emancipation from haggling and from money, that is, from real practical Judaism, would be the self-emancipation of our time."[31]

This fantastic equation of the Jew either with capitalism or with money generally enjoyed immense popularity in Western Europe. Dr. Joseph Bloch tells in his autobiography that in the eighties of the nineteenth century, anti-Semite agitation among workers harped upon the theme, "the Talmud trains the Jews into capitalistic ways of thinking."[32] In those decades, it was widely believed by leaders of socialism that "anti-Semitism is only a prelude to the movement that is now taking shape. Its conclusion will be anticapitalism."[33] Only by degrees did socialistic theoreticians realize that anti-Semitism could easily become a tool in the hands of reactionaries. By that time, nonsocialists took up this belief. Werner Sombart set out to prove that the Jewish mentality conceived the fundamental thought patterns of capitalism and later invented the basic instruments of modern banking and commerce.[33a] The fact that modern industrialism coincided in most countries with the process of Jewish emancipation and with the loosening of the hold of the Church upon the power of the State was taken to be positive proof of the inner unity between Judaism and capitalism.

In all these discussions, an unreal image of the Jew as banker and moneylender was substituted for the real, breathing, struggling Jew, who was a thousand times more likely to be

207

impoverished and many more times likely to be a manual worker. The Jews of the nineteenth century were concentrated in the eastern provinces of Russia and in Austria-Hungary with hardly a banker of note to a million of them. Yet, the phantasy of the Jew as an "unproductive element," a representative of the "exploiting class," was extremely potent among the socialists of Western Europe.

The followers of Fourier in France, who hated bankers as the most vicious caste of capitalists, concentrated a double dose of their venom upon the Jew, who symbolized for them the practice of usury. On the other hand, the ardent disciples of "Saint-Simonianism," who esteemed banking as the noblest and most creative profession, admired the Jewish people and looked forward to a "new Christianity," which would be a blend of both Judaism and Christianity. Needless to say, both the Fourierists and the Saint-Simonists dealt with a European stereotype, not with the living Jewish people.

When the French socialist Pierre Leroux was taken to task for identifying a whole ethnic group with a class of usurers, he replied that he merely followed the usage of the French language. Even the official dictionary of the French Academy assigned to the word Jew the meaning of loan shark and usurer.[34]

The impact of Marxist thought upon the Jews of Russia was expressed in the rise of a philosophy of rebellion against the religious tradition which learned to live with those conditions. This eagerness to transform the life of the Jewish masses and to render them into a "productive" class was divided at the beginning of the twentieth century into the "Bundist" stream, which aimed to "normalize" Jewish life in the Diaspora, and the Zionist-Socialist stream, which sought to create a new socialist society in Palestine. The dominant note in both movements was evocative of the old dream of a Messianic society. Though the philosophy of historical materialism was granted official homage by the ideologists of both schools in the form of diatribes against the "unproductive" and the "exploiting" character of Jewish life in the Diaspora, the chief emphasis of Jewish socialism was on the idealistic, hopeful side of Marxism.

"Marxism is not only a doctrine of historical materialism concerned with the complete dependence of man on economics; it is also a doctrine of deliverance, of the messianic vocation of the proletariat, of the future perfect society in which man will not be dependent on economics, of the power and victory of man over the irrational forces of nature and society. There is the soul of Marxism, not in its economic determinism."[35]

It is this idealistic and hopeful quality of Marxism that found expression in the history of the Zionist-Socialists. Bitter notes of condemnation of the "unproductive" character of Jewish life in the Diaspora alternate with paeans of praise for the idyllic quality of Jewish life in pre-exilic days. Following the defeat of Bar Kochba, the Jew came to live on "a bitter illusion, empty pride, and deception." The essence of exilic life was the readiness to depend on the labor of others. The basic cause of anti-Semitism was the "deproletarization" of the Jewish people. "Universal hatred was rooted in the hearts of the nations toward those who came to them from afar, prepared to use their productive achievements, and at the same time, setting themselves apart." Jewish life in exile was "immoral," since it was not based on manual labor. "The question of Judaism is the question of the lack of productive labor for the masses of Jews, who have become like floating dust, unable to work."[36]

This passionate revulsion against nearly two thousand years of Jewish history coincided with the Zionist rebellion against continued life in the Diaspora. The Zionist-Socialist élan was expressed in an ardent endeavor to idealize labor and to mobilize the floating feelings of Jewish piety for the effort of converting the wastelands of Palestine into blooming gardens. A new gospel of a "religion of labor" was preached by A. D. Gordon, one of the apostles of the kibbutz movement. It was through "deproletarization" that the Jewish problem emerged, and only through a "reproletarization" in a socialistic homeland will it be solved.

Among the historians who sought to achieve a synthesis of nationalistic and religious forces, Graetz, Baron, and Kaufmann are of pre-eminent importance. They concur in the recognition of the complexity of Jewish being, but they differ in their interpretation of the play of forces within the soul of the Jew.

Graetz wrote his brilliant essay *"Die Konstruktion der Jüdischen Geschichte"* in 1846, when the influence of Hegel predominated in the German intellectual world. Hence, he stressed the idea of the state as the goal of historical evolution and he thought of the massive flow of universal history as the slow and steady unfolding of thought. "History is the reflex of the idea." Within these limitations, Graetz's conception is remarkably relevant even today. We may summarize it in the following theses:

1) Judaism is not simply a set of ideas about God, humanity, and nature, howsoever those ideas be expressed. Every abstract idea reflects a phase of the complete structure of Judaism, which is an organic reality. As a fact of history, Judaism is many-sided and complex.

2) Essentially, Judaism is a blend of political and religious ideals. As a protest against paganism, which idealized the forces of nature in plastic art, in a naturalistic ethics, and in a colorful pantheon of gods, Judaism idealized man's spirit. Hence, it lavishes its love upon the miracle of speech, which is the medium of communication between souls. The only authentic Jewish arts are music, poetry, and prayer. The Jew is an "ear-man" rather than an "eye-man." The basic concerns of Judaism are the attainment of freedom and the values of ethics. Not the achievement of perfection for the individual, but the consummation of the good life for the community is the ultimate good.

"For Judaism is no religion for the individual, but for the community." In an age when intellectuals disdained excessive preoccupation with the concerns of the individual, Graetz was moved to say, "In the strictest sense, Judaism is no religion at all—if by this be meant the relation of man to his Creator and his orientation in life—but it is a constitution for the state." In the evolution of Judaism through the ages, he saw a continuous tension between "knowledge of God and social well-being, religious truth and state interests."

3) The periodization of Jewish history follows naturally from this conception. In the Biblical period, the political phase predominated, with religion functioning in the background. In postexilic life, religion predominated, with the individual emerging as a focus of interest. Following the destruction of the Temple, "Talmudism" set out to "isolate" the Jewish community so that the political phase of the Jewish ideal could be put into practice. During the long dark years of the medieval period, "Talmudism" was counteracted by the universalistic emphasis in Jewish philosophy. Within "Talmudism," the attraction of the wide world was acknowledged only in the abstract command to acquire knowledge and understanding.

4) With the opening of the modern period, "Talmudism" had to be discarded. Henceforth, the whole world should become the object of the ambition to establish a "Kingdom of Heaven" on earth. "The task of the Jewish God-idea is to organize a religious constitution for a state that is coextensive with the whole world, in its concern and activity."

The shortcomings of Graetz's conception are obvious. His formulation bears the stigmata of his generation. The individual is not overlooked in pre-exilic Judaism (behold the prophets and the psalmists!) and ethnicism or nationalism was the "counterweight" to religion rather than the political ambition for a "state." Not "politics," but the yearning to explore, to the last detail, the implications of God's word for the building of the "Divine society" was the motivating drive in Jewish legalism as it was hammered out by the Pharisees. To these masters of "normative Judaism," a Jewish secular state was of no consequence, and a Roman procurator was preferable to both Hyrkanus and Aristobulus, descendants of the glorious Hasmoneans. Nor was Graetz faithful to the corollaries of his own conception when he wrote his monumental *History of the*

Jews. Treitschke launched a movement of "higher anti-Semitism" in Germany after reading Graetz's history and inferred from its pervading nationalistic bias that Jewish ethnicism was as powerful as ever. Though Graetz protested officially against the imputation of a nationalistic viewpoint to his work, his disavowal of Jewish ethnicism sounded hollow and unconvincing. In the latter years of his life, he oscillated between a Diaspora-oriented, universalist Judaism and a Palestine-centered, self-enclosed neo-"Talmudic" conception of Jewish life.

Professor Baron seeks to account for the entire career of the Jewish people in terms of the contrast between "history" and "nature." The Jewish people were history-minded, while the nations against whom it struggled were nature-minded. The essence of Jewish monotheism is its historical reference. The Supreme Being is "God as revealed to the patriarchs," not "God who created heaven and earth." It is this association of religious ideas with historical events and personalities that is the "essential contribution of Israel's religion to the history of human creeds."[37]

The three pilgrim festivals in the Jewish calendar were at one time "natural" festivals, but in Judaism, they were transformed into historical commemorations. "History is the all-pervading dominant sanction of the most fundamental ideas, including the concept of messianism, the chosen people, the covenant with God and the Torah."[38] The centrality of law in Judaism is understandable as "the necessary consequence and instrinsically consistent form of an historical monotheism";[39] hence the relative unconcern of Judaism with the fate of the individual.[40] The Jewish people understood their destiny to be the subjugation of "nature" by "history." For this purpose, a select body of men is needed; hence, the doctrine of the "Chosen People."

In the light of this distinction, Baron proposes to explain the crucial turning points in Jewish history. Judaism "rejected both the localized Baal and incarnation as anthropomorphisms of a natural order, but tenaciously clung to the historical anthropomorphisms of God the Father and King."[41] All during the Biblical period, the sense of difference between Jews and Gentiles was sustained by this fundamental dichotomy of approach. "Little wonder that again and again the Bible draws a sharp distinction between the nations, who worship nature in some form or other, and the Jewish people, whose chief concern is their central position in history."[42]

The downfall of the two Jewish kingdoms and the exile to Babylonia are to be understood in terms of this distinction. "This tragedy is a necessary consequence of the revolt of nature against history."[43] The return from Babylonia and the establishment of the Second Commonwealth constituted a "defiance of nature."[44]

Christianity did not triumph among the Jews because it constituted a break with history. "With the realization of the messianic expectation, so he [Jesus] taught, nationalism had largely completed its task and should give way entirely to the universalistic aspects of the Jewish religion."[45] Yehezkel Kaufmann disproves this thesis most convincingly by pointing out that Jesus, as a folk-Pharisee, was far more chauvinistic than the rabbis of the official schools.[46] But Baron follows the iron tracks of hypothesis all the way down the line. Concerning Paul he writes, "In many ways, however, Paul sacrificed history to nature." "His non-Jewish approval of nature, however, led Paul to the opposite extreme of opposing nature."[47]

By now, the ambiguity of Baron's conception is fairly clear. However, to complete the picture, we might cite Baron's explanation for the revival of the observance of Rosh Hodesh among the Hasidim of Russia and Poland. "The quasi-revival of that forgotten holiday by modern Hasidism is simply another back-to-nature aspect of that movement."

Manifestly, in his laudable eagerness to do justice to the complexity of Jewish being, Baron employs a term that is so multifaceted in its meaning as to be entirely meaningless. History means many different things. In its opposition to "nature," it may mean the impulsions of the human spirit and of humanistic values. It can hardly be argued that paganism

213

did not accept any of these values. Professor Fritz Baer makes a good case for the interpretation of authentic Jewish ethics as being "according to nature."[48] Does the contrast between the values of the spirit and a naturalistic ethic account for the Babylonian exile, or for the rejection of Christianity by Jews, or for the continued millennial struggle of Judaism against Christianity and Islam? Does this presumed dichotomy in philosophical thought account for the "Chosen People" idea? Is is not an undoubted fact that philosophic ideas and ethical philosophies were generally propagated by a school of disciples rather than by a people?

A second meaning of the term "a people of history" is a self-conscious nationality. But the Jews were not the only nation of antiquity that had traditions concerning its past. There is hardly any justification for assuming a deep chasm between Jews and Gentiles on the question of the rightfulness of the idea of nationality. To be sure, the Jews did not yield to the solvent powers of the Persian, Greek, and Roman empires, but then their resistance to assimilation was not due to their reverence for the idea of nationality. They believed themselves to be in possession of the one true faith, and they urged the acceptance of their Law upon their pagan neighbors with all the zeal that they could muster.

A third meaning of "a people of history," and indeed the only legitimate connotation of this term, as an explanation of Jewish life, is the possession of a historical consciousness. In this sense, Professor Baron's reference to the historical explanations of the festivals are in order. But, then, as a matter of fact, the Jews were hardly a history-minded people. The festivals were not related to actual historical events, but they were related to God's redemptive act. Already, in the days of Philo, Yom Kippur was the most observed festival, though it had no historical reference. For the Biblical historians, the deeds of the kings and the great events of their reigns were relatively unimportant, and they are brushed aside with the deprecating reference "Now the rest of the acts of Solomon. . . ."[49] To judge by the Book of Kings, the expansion of the Northern Kingdom, under Jeroboam the Second, was a minor event. So unhistorical was Jewish consciousness in its most authentic period that Judas Maccabeus is not mentioned even once in the Talmud, and the typical nineteenth-century rabbi, who was kept away from secular learning and educated strictly upon the approved literature of European Orthodoxy, could hardly be expected to know the most important dates in Jewish history. The Talmud accounts for the destruction of the Holy Temple by telling several myths and fables that make sense as religious homilies, not as historical explanations. In fact, a historical consciousness, in the sense of viewing every particular event in the broad, universal perspective of the evolution of mankind, was precisely what the Jews lacked. Brilliant flashes of insight are to be found in the prophets, but the Talmud proscribed the study of "Greek wisdom," relegating the study of non-Jewish life to "the hour that is neither day nor night."[49a]

Judaism taught a ready-made *interpretation* of history, but not an objective understanding of it. So profoundly were the Jewish people convinced that the will of God accounted for all events that their interest in the actual events of history was all but extinguished. God's will is the sole and sufficient explanation of every disaster and every triumph. What more is needed? Only in the framework of a legal question were some of the victories of the Hasmonean rulers recorded in Megillath Taanith. In modern times, the Talmud may be studied by historians for the facts that it reveals more or less indirectly; but in its own terms, this mighty compendium of Jewish law is as unhistorical, or better, transhistorical, as the will of God.

Professor Baron uses the term "history" in all these connotations at once, so that it glosses over the mysterious chasms in the tortuous millennial road of the Jewish people without plumbing their depths. As an explanation of the riddle of Jewish destiny, the attempt to contrast "history" with "nature" is too ambiguous to be useful.

Yehezkel Kaufmann's critical analysis of "exile and alienism"

215

is the first serious study of the fundamental sociological factors that are operative in Jewish history. His basic theses may be described as follows:

1) Monotheism arose among the people of Israel as a mighty original conception, drying up the roots of all pagan thought in the early days of the Biblical period. Thereafter, it became impossible for the Israelites even so much as to understand pagan myths and ways of thinking. All residual idolatry among Israelites was of a vestigial, archaic nature that did not challenge the triumph of monotheism. The great prophets, in their perfectionist zealotry, grossly exaggerated the extent of pagan deviations in Judah and Israel.

2) There resulted in the post-Biblical period a unique combination of a perfectly universalistic religion with an intensely nationalistic ethnic group. The broad universalism of the Jewish religion was not narrowed down by the feverish fervor of nationalism, for the two factors were associated historically, not systematically. In theory, there was no reason why other ethnic groups should not accept Judaism; though, as an actual historical fact, the Jews knew themselves to be the sole bearers of monotheism.

3) Christianity did not come to prevail among Jews, because its historic "role" was to disseminate the doctrines of monotheism, and it could not fulfill this role among the Jews who were already monotheists. In the pagan world, Christianity triumphed, even as Islam did many centuries later, because it became the historical bearer of the banner of monotheism. In the advance of humanity on the ladder of culture, monotheism is a higher rung than paganism, and progress in thought is well nigh inevitable. Christianity could appeal to the pagan world better than its ancient rival, the religion of Judaism, because the latter was inevitably associated in the public mind with the sorry fate of the Jewish people.

4) Following the emancipation in Western Europe, the Jews consented to assimilate, but only in a national-culture sense. They were willing to give up their "separatism," they were

anxious to forge bonds of fraternity with their neighbors. But, in spite of their eagerness to divest themselves of any distinctive national ambitions, they clung tenaciously to their ancestral faith. Thus, their halfhearted bow toward the Nirvana of assimilation ended in failure, for the Jewish religion maintains automatically the wall of ethnic alienism between Jew and Christian. Since the Jewish religion may be expected to endure indefinitely, the Jew cannot achieve the fullness of assimilation.

5) In the absence of a final consummation of assimilation, the sense of national or ethnic distinction between Jew and Gentile will remain forever in the Diaspora. And this feeling of difference is a sufficient basis for the irresistible rise of anti-Semitism, which acquires momentum by feeding upon itself until it attains its culmination in extermination camps. Anti-Semitism is not a peculiar or mysterious phenomenon, it is simply another instance of the universal and "natural" fight of nations against nations. In the case of the Jewish people, this struggle assumed a unique form only because of the extremely exposed character of Jewish settlement among the nations.

6) Hence, there is hope for Jews only in the land of Israel. In the lands of the Diaspora, a dark doom of ruthless destruction awaits those who do not manage to escape the avenging sword of ethnic anti-Semitism while there is still time.

Every one of Kaufmann's theses may be questioned. For the purpose of this study, however, I find it best to indicate my disagreement with his assumptions and conclusions in the course of outlining my own interpretation of the philosophy of Jewish history.

Having passed under review the leading philosophies of Jewish history, we are now prepared for a synthetic approach that would embrace the genuine insights of all the great interpreters of our past. The fragmentary nature of the interpretations that we have examined is quite obvious from the vantage point of our contemporary cultural position. We know that the idealistic school did justice to the occasional peaks in Jewish thought, but

217

not infrequently it overlooked the actual mentality of empirical Jewish people, in all their human weaknesses and limitations. Yet, it was on the level of mass-culture that fateful friction between Jews and their neighbors was generated. Similarly, the nationalistic school observed with clarity the sociological context of Jewish life; ignoring, however, the reality of the conflict on the plane of ideas, in both Jewish and Gentile minds. And the unrelenting need of countering the barrage of poisoned barbs of hate from the anti-Semitic underworld has imbued many of our writers with an excess of injured pride, lending an air of polemics and apologetics to the works of both schools of interpretation. As to the economic school of historians, we cannot but regard any attempt to explain the whole travail of Judaism in economic terms as no more than a conjurer's trick in the domain of ideas. Economic factors enter into the making of every concrete situation. Every time an industrial economy entered into an expansive period, Jews were tolerated, while they were squeezed or expelled if the economy underwent a significant shrinking. Still, the economic factor in itself misses the core of the problem. The Jews never constituted a distinct socio-economic caste, occupying the same position in all lands. The peasants and sharecroppers of Babylonia, the sailors of the African seas, the intrepid merchants of the early Middle Ages, the humble artisans of Poland, the scholarly winegrowers of northern France, the harried moneylenders of Germany, the apathetic beggars of North Africa, the peripatetic peddlers and old-clothes dealers of nineteenth-century America, the proud bankers of Vienna, and the bold builders of the mighty "Jewish" unions in New York—how could one economic concept embrace them all and account for their destiny as Jews?

A synthetic concept is obviously needed for the understanding of Jewish history, but at this point we must caution against a mechanical combination of the two basic concepts—nationalism and monotheism. Such a mechanical combination could easily give the semblance of an explanation for every crucial event by shifting attention from one vantage point to the other. This

218

approach overlooks the unitary nature of Jewish consciousness. After all, the living people who are the subjects of our inquiry possessed hearts and minds, which were not subdivided by airtight compartments. Nationalism and monotheism can exist side by side only in a state of continuous interaction and tension. This state of tension is our starting point.

We recognize that the history of every people takes place in three dimensions—in struggles against nature, in relations with other people, and in attitudes toward the realm of ideas. In the case of Jewish history, the first or physical dimension relates only to the first or Biblical period. The later history of Jews qua Jews is not organically related to the attempt of man to control the forces of nature. The distinctive pathos of Jewish life consists in a struggle against other groups of men, coupled with the tension of contending ideas in the realm of thought. Thus, the two coordinates leading from blind ethnicism to pure humanism and from primitive mythology to absolute monotheism describe the field of tension for the curve of Jewish history.

As long as the mighty currents of philosophical idealism determined the course of human speculation, it was assumed that ideas were "pure" entities, dwelling like immutable stars in the incorruptible heavens and determining the affairs of men by means of their innate power and their inherent logic. In the twentieth century, this intellectual illusion was shattered by the combined criticism of philosophical pragmatists and empirical depth-psychologists. William James strove valiantly against the notion that ideas were Olympian gods dwelling "between the worlds" in splendid isolation. Freud uncovered the vast sea of the unconscious with its primeval tides and subterranean currents surging restlessly beneath the surface of rationality and providing an underside of instinctive power and motivation beneath the ideal façade. The disciples and opponents of Freud widened and deepened our knowledge of the unconscious, and C. G. Jung discovered that it was a treasury of intuitive truths as well as a repository of repressed lusts.

With the complexity of human nature being thus revealed,

it becomes necessary for us to envisage the dynamic ideas of history as vertical fields of force between an ideal pole and an instinctive drive. Ideals are not pure essences sailing serenely in an abstract realm of their own; they are psychic forces that are subject to the inescapable rhythms of life, and that oscillate between a pole of true nobility and an instinctive satisfaction, with the ideal emerging at times as the master of the instinctive quest and reverting at other times to a subordinate position, when its aura is used to glamorize instinctive impulses. In logic, ideals can be defined with precision, but in life, ideals that are capable of moving men to action come enveloped in a magnetic field of instinctive forces with which they blend insensibly. The age-old debate between the idealists and the materialists can only be resolved by the recognition that both philosophies are right at different times, for in the tension between the universal idea and the self-serving instinctive drive, there is no static point where the equilibrium is permanently held. In the life of all human beings, individually and collectively, this restless polar tension is articulated in a ceaseless oscillation along the invisible line from instinct to idea and back again, with the lofty power of the intellect alternately justifying the raw instinctive drive and sublimating it. It follows that a philosophy of history must take account of the depth-dimension of every historical ideal and of its rootage in the instinctive soil of human nature.

Both nationalism and religion constitute powerful historical forces that reach down to the most fundamental needs of mankind and up to the most exalted ideals. Nationalism emerges as a distinct ideal only when the people become conscious of the cultural bonds that unite them and set them apart from other human groups. There can be no national unity without some ideal factor, which makes the people feel that their national character is of supreme value. In the primitive state, an ethnic group tends to assume that only its own members are human. As they climb up the ladder of civilization, people come to recognize the worth of human groups other than their own and to interpret the supremacy of their own nation in terms of the needs of humanity as a whole. This conviction gathers momentum, depth, and pathos as the nation gears itself for defense against enemies. If enemy pressure is prolonged and relentless, national consciousness is raised to a pitch of feverish intensity.

Thus, it is through the double action of universal values and the harsh needs of group defense in the battle for survival that nationalism as a distinctive ideal emerges. Manifestly, it is a depth-ideal, with the ideal elements of self-transcendence being held in polar tension with the instinctive forces of self-assertion. There is hardly a nationalistic movement worthy of note that does not contain an idealistic or humanistic impetus. The forms of the nation's culture, its language, mores, and memories, are sacred because they concretize some high ideals that are of momentous concern to all mankind. It hardly matters that a Mazzini attributes to the genius of Italians precisely what a Fichte does to the intuitive reason (*Vernunft*) of the Teutons; a Mickiewicz to the character and destiny of the Poles, a Dostoevski to the genius of the "Slavic soul," and a Buber to the spirit of the Hebrew nation. All these writers postulate that the salvation of the world is ultimately dependent upon the triumph of their respective nations. At the same time, they affirm that it is for the sake of humanity that their compatriots must live. On the one hand, the "Chosen People" are extolled as a kind of superhumanity; on the other hand, the "Chosen People" are chosen for the service of mankind.

As to what nationalism "really" is—whether it be a subversion of the idea into an instrument of national survival, or a self-transcendence of the nation for the sake of an ideal purpose— one can only say that the answer depends on the selection of representative individuals within a particular nation and on the particular period in the life of the nation. Take the American of today who conceives of the ideal of universal freedom as being the dynamic essence of the "American dream." For some Americans, the American people as a whole constitute a dedicated group devoted to the "American way of life" and to its ultimate expansion into a universal society of free men and women. For other Americans, the ideals of freedom and democracy constitute only so much "window dressing" which the national struggle for survival and greatness requires. Yet, both groups of Americans will use the same slogans, with the shoddy jingoists mouthing the high ideals of the groups more vociferously than the refined idealists, for whom the national slogans truly have meaning. In every case, the scalpel of analysis must be employed to determine the nature of the scale of values that is implied.

A religious group is one that is banded together in the service of the Supreme Being. The common purpose of the group is not to win the goods of this world, but to gain the approval of the Deity, though the rewards of piety might include not only the "dew of heaven" but also the "fat of the land." In a religious community as in a historical nation, we encounter the same tension between self-assertion and self-transcendence. Every organized religious group lays claim to Divine favor and approval, maintaining that these virtues belong to their very structure. To some members of the group, this claim to "chosenness" serves not as an inducement to noble living but as a socially approved means of bolstering their sense of importance and pride. God has "chosen" *them!* This is the decisive fact. Whether they are "chosen" because of their good fortune in being born to the proper parents, or because of their believing the right beliefs and undergoing the right sacraments, or because of their experience of "conversion" and reception of "grace"—all these dogmatic differences are important from a historical, not a psychological, viewpoint.

Decisive in the psychic makeup of the individual is the question whether the group was selected for the sake of universal ideals, or whether those ideals were important because they emerged out of the life of the group. The feeling of "chosenness" is inescapable in a religious community, but it makes all the difference in the world whether the reason for this "chosenness" is conceived to be the innate goodness of the group or whether the "chosenness" of the group is conditioned upon its dedication to the service of high ideals and the universal society of mankind. When we are told in the Book of Deuteronomy that the Israelites were chosen because God loved them and their forefathers, we have an example of the instincts of self-assertion subordinating the ideals of self-transcendence.[50] When Isaiah describes for us the mission of Israel as the "suffering servant" of mankind, we encounter the outreaching ideals of Judaism at their best, sublimating and transmuting the instincts of ethnic loyalty.[51] In the Talmud this issue is debated by Rabbis Judah and Meir. Said one, "Children are ye to the Lord, your God, *if* you do His Will"; said the other rabbi, "Children are ye to the Lord, your God, *whether or not* you do His Will."[52]

For the sake of clarity, we might designate the tension in the national ideal as oscillating between the two poles of *ethnicism* and *humanism*. In the case of religion, the two poles might be designated as *humble piety* and *proud dogmatism* respectively. In both domains, the tension cannot be broken since the ideal ceases to exist as a massive human drive when it is severed from its corresponding instinctive gratification. It may be paradoxical, but it is incontrovertible that no one may cultivate the ideal of humility without taking pride in it, or aspire to the heights of piety without savoring the seductive delight that is the portion of those who can say, "The Lord is my strength and my song."

When Israel Baal Shem Tov, founder of Hasidism, was about to depart this world, his disciples asked whether he would name his successor. He replied that his successor should be that disciple who would teach them how to overcome the sin of pride. Following the death of the master, one disciple after another was confronted with this question. No one could give a completely satisfying answer, until Rabbi Dov Ber of Mesrich said, "How can we expect to overcome the sin of pride in the service of God, since the Lord Himself wears pride as his garment, as it is said, 'The Lord reigneth, He is clothed with pride.'" Thereupon, the disciples elected Rabbi Dov Ber as their teacher.

It follows from this analysis that nationalism and religion may merge and blend together at both their lowest levels and their highest reaches, flowing in separate channels only in the course of their imperfect development. In a primitive society, it is hardly possible to distinguish between a national culture and its faith. The elements of self-transcendence are lacking in both primitive religion and primitive ethnicism. The earthly prosperity of the nation is the ultimate goal, both in relation to the occult forces of the cosmos and in respect to struggles against other ethnic groups. When nationalism emerges as a conscious struggle for survival, with the "fig leaf" of idealism being used to cover the nakedness of the raw struggle for power, we have a perfect parallel to the situation of a religious group when "chosenness" is attributed to the group for its own sake. On the highest levels of nationalism, when the group is conceived as the bearer of a high ideal that is taken so seriously as to serve as a standard of critical evaluation of the life of the nation, we have a direct parallel to a "higher religion" in which the community of the "chosen" is truly and self-critically regarded as the instrument of redemption for all mankind. But though idealistic nationalism and a universalistic religion are parallel phenomena, they are not identical, since, in the one case, the qualities of the group, and, in the other case, the ideals bequeathed to their charge by the Supreme Being constitute the vantage point for a way of life.

In all cases it is not the verbal apologia *pro vita sua* that determines the quality of a group's religion or nationalism but the total posture of the group as it is articulated in an organizational structure and in a program of action.

With the foregoing analysis of the nature of nationalism and monotheism, we are prepared to understand the fundamental concept of Jewish history. In the consciousness of the Jewish people, monotheism, with its profound sense of radical difference from paganism, and nationalism, with its deep pathos of historic self-consciousness, were blended together into one multi-faceted awareness. Thus, there emerged a quadripolar field of consciousness, which was both unprecedented and unparalleled. A simple ethnic awareness on the primitive level is nearly always associated with a pagan earthbound religion. The emergence of a national culture and a historic self-consciousness among the Greeks was not accompanied by a sense of radical difference in religion but by the cultivation of an attitude of philosophic detachment and easy tolerance. In the case of the Jewish people, all four poles of consciousness in religion and nationalism were dynamically represented and tempered with the "strange fire" of being set apart.

Monotheism contains within itself the seeds of eternity. In the quest of the human mind for the comprehension of the cosmos, the postulate of unity projects the ultimate goal. In the endless search of the human spirit for the triumphant vindication of its values, the assertion of Divine goodness acts as a perennial spur to the tackling of social problems. To be sure, monotheism can be the source of intellectual attrition and petrifaction, as well as of endless growth. If the will of the One God is dogmatically asserted as the sole and sufficient answer to all questions and problems, there can be no challenge to man's imagination and no advance in thought, only a continuous circling round the same all-silencing pole of dogma. Hence, the specter of slow stagnation and even fossilization is always present in Jewish life, as a warning and as a challenge. But monotheism by virtue of its insistence on the rationality and ethical character of the Divine will is capable of inducing an endless revolution, aiming at the transformation of the world in keeping with the creative impetus of the higher faculties of human nature—reason and the moral will. Its genius consists in the "internalization" of every historic event; that is, a social or a political problem is converted into an intellectual challenge. Men are led to search their souls for the answer to their difficulties, and wrestling with one's soul is the beginning of all true progress.

The conclusion of the Covenant with the One God, howsoever it may have taken place, set the endless task of humanity as the peculiar vocation of the people of Israel, transforming them into an "eternal people." Not because the "eternal verities" were given over into the safekeeping of the Israelites; for, humanly speaking, there are no "eternal verities," only yearnings for the understanding of His eternity and aspirations for His "nearness." These yearnings were translated into intellectual concepts and norms of conducts in keeping with the spiritual complexion of every age, but at no time were they frozen with absolute finality. In asserting the oneness of God and His justice, the Israelites made certain that their reach would always outdistance their grasp. So rich and complex were the implications of the "Divine discontent" stirred by the basic axioms of the Israelites that their task could not but remain unfinished until the advent of the millennium. Every historical happening became for them a spiritual problem, every human disaster a reminder of His sovereignty, every social upheaval a call for preaching His word. As His children, the people of Israel were personally involved in the total travail of the endless human quest for ultimate truth.

At certain times, it was entirely correct to speak of Judaism as "religious ethnicism," in the sense that ethnic feeling was then substantive and fundamental. But this descriptive phrase of Professor Baron's would not apply to the religion of a Maimonides, who, in his magnum opus, hardly mentions the "chosenness" of Israel. Maimonides, in his final chapter, accords to the pious philosophers of all nations a superior position to that of the learned, loyal Talmudists. Kaufmann's conception of Judaism as a universal religion which *happened* to be associated historically with the life of a specific people is a correct description of Maimonidean faith, as it is expressed in his purely philosophic work, but it is hardly adequate to account for the Jewish consciousness of a romantic philosopher like Halevi, who regarded the Jews as a spiritual "superhumanity." Halevi and Maimonides represent two of the several different forms in which the tension within the Jewish soul could be resolved. In theory, each of the four poles of Jewish consciousness—the self-transcendence of religion and its self-satisfied dogmatism, the spiritualization of national feeling and its degeneration into nihilistic chauvinism—could achieve dominance within the soul of the Jew, drawing the other foci of loyalty into its service. What is "shell" for one philosophy is "kernel" to the other, with the protean character of our sacred tradition providing the inner field of tension and the outer façade of unity. The differences among Jewish thinkers of any one generation may be fully as significant as the differences in nuance and emphasis that occurred during the long evolution of the Jewish faith. The periodization of Jewish history must not be pressed at the cost of overlooking the diversity of trends within the same portion of the historic stream.

Neither the ideal of nationalism nor that of monotheism could be maintained by the Jewish people in the past without the admixture of negative attitudes toward the nations around them. In both ideals, there was an inescapable implication of uncompromising opposition to the opinions of the rest of mankind. Monotheism pronounced a scornful judgment of annihilation upon the gods of other nations, while nationalism asserted the rights of the Jewish people in the struggle for the goods of this world. Every action produces a reaction. In the pagan world, the nations reacted to the Jewish challenge by a double polar tension of their own. Toward the assertion of the One God, they responded by a psychic tension between the recognition of its truth and their natural conservative tendency to continue worshiping their own gods. In the realm of worldly struggles, they responded by a tension between admiration of Jewish genius and a double dose of resentment against Jewish pride. On the spiritual plane, the pole of truth proved far stronger than the attraction of a decadent paganism, while in the domain of national struggles, the power of bitter resentment prevailed, with the result that the main ideas of Jewish monotheism were taken over by Christianity and Islam, though the specific tradition of Israel was condemned either as "misunderstood" or as "perverted." The message was twice accepted, but the messenger was twice rejected.

By the confluence of these two polar ideals the unique character of Judaism was forged, and it was through the inevitable reaction to this double challenge that the unique phenomenon of anti-Semitism was born. Jewish history consists of the interaction of the double polar tension within the soul of the Jew and the corresponding double tension prevailing within the cultural and social environment in which he lived. Generally speaking, a favorable, tolerant climate of opinion evoked the universalistic elements of Judaism, bringing about an efflorescence of the spirit of rationalistic piety and gentle humanism. When the Jewish community was walled in by hate, it reacted by reverting to the earthly poles of its historic consciousness, those of sanctified ethnicism and zealous dogmatism. In several periods of our history, the small upper crust of Jewish society reacted in one way, while the masses were impelled into the opposite direction. Such a development occurred in Alexandria, following the destruction of Jerusalem by the Romans, and in Christian Spain, following the widespread persecutions of 1391-1412.[53] Thus, it is not possible to understand Jewish history completely from within, nor is it possible to envision it solely as the record of reactions to a changing environment. Both factors of polar loyalty from within and recurrent hostility from without operated together, each reacting not only to a contemporary stimulus but also to a historic tradition.

The "chosenness" of the Jewish people is the concept whereby monotheism and nationalism were joined together in the soul of the Jew, and anti-Semitism, which is a philosophy of hatred singling out the Jew as the demonic force of history, is manifestly the doctrine of "chosenness" with inverse valence.

The argument of this section is not that Jewish attitudes and actions are to be *blamed* for the emergence of anti-Semitism. The term "blame" has moral connotations. There was a causal historical connection between the Jew and the peculiar brand of hate that was directed toward him. Obviously, if Jews had not seemed to be "a peculiar people," there would have been no anti-Semitism, which is a peculiar hatred. But the Jew was no more to blame than an intellectual living among benighted folk, or a reformer in a rock-ribbed reactionary town, or an iconoclast among believers, or a wealthy man among the poor is to blame for being what he is.

Secondly, the character of Jewish life is determined very strongly by the momentum of ideas and sentiments from the past, so that any one generation can slightly affect but not altogether shape its destiny. Thus, it is no refutation of the thesis herein propounded when it is pointed out that Nazism arose in Germany, where Jewish nationalism was officially disavowed. This phenomenon will be discussed in detail in its place. Suffice it here to note that anti-Semitism is now a historical impetus in the minds of Gentiles which is capable of combining with diverse sociological factors and which is only partially affected by the actions of a contemporary generation of Jews. It should also be noted that German and Polish propagandists made good use of Zionist literature to prove their point that the Jew is forever an alien and that he cannot ever feel himself to be a national of any country except Palestine.

As a reaction to the ethnic character of the Jew, anti-Semitism expresses ethnic zealotry and arrogance; as reaction to the religious "heresy" of Judaism, it expresses the spirit of religious dogmatism. In its two phases, it fulfills a psychic need of those who suffer from inner doubt and inferiority, requiring a sacrificial victim for the "abreaction" of fear and hate. The well-known judgment that anti-Semitism is the "socialism of fools" is true only in part. Pathological anti-Semites are more neurotic than foolish, finding in the propagation of their phobia an approved outlet for hate that is nearly identical with the psychic outlet of war, which is so exceedingly exhilarating for certain psychological types.[54]

In any one generation, Jewish life is not merely a product of the living thoughts and convictions of that generation of Jews and non-Jews but is also the resultant of the accumulated burdens of the two traditions. Anti-Semitism is not only a reaction to the "chosenness" complex of the Jewish people in its own age, but it is itself a product of a long and varying tradition. It is activated and stimulated by a variety of causes, only some of which are related to the actions of living Jews. When anti-Semitism first appeared as a political force in Germany, the deputies that were elected to the Reichstag on an anti-Semitic platform came from sections of the country where no Jews lived.[55] It was the stereotype of the "historic Jew" in folktale and folk-memory that the anti-Semitic demagogues sought to evoke. And this historic image was created, in the first place, by way of resentment against the Biblical portrait of the "Chosen People." This doctrine, as it was popularly understood, served to lend a cutting edge to the vague residual feelings of Jewish alienism in the age of the emancipation. It implied that Jewish alienism was more thorough and deep-seated than that of other ethnic groups. As Jewish loyalty partook of both ethnic feeling and religious conviction, hostility to Jews consisted of the condemnation of the people and their faith.

In his monumental work, Professor Toynbee points out that barbarians living beyond the peripheral boundaries of a civilization generally accept a heretical form of the culture of the nuclear people.[56] As the faith of a civilization radiates to the barbarians by way of commercial intercourse or military conquest, the latter accept it in the form of a heresy, so as to satisfy both their admiration for and their hatred of the people of culture. Thus, the Goths accepted Christianity in the heretical form of Arianism and the Persians accepted Islam in its heretical form of Shiism. In the domain of religious culture, the Jewish people constituted a radiating center of considerable power. While many millions of Gentiles were influenced by the Jewish religion, the faiths that ultimately prevailed in the non-Jewish world were Christianity and Islam, both of which were essentially Jewish heresies. It is the distinguishing quality of a heretical faith to be of the parent-religion and bitterly against it at the same time, claiming exclusive possession of the true interpretation of the traditions of the parent-people, and asserting that the people of the radiating center either abused or distorted their own tradition. Heaping abuse upon the parent-people is an integral element of the psychological complex that is expressed in the acceptance of a heretical faith by a trans-peripheral people. Islam, too, arose as a heretical faith of both Judaism and Christianity, especially of Judaism. In this case, the Arabs constituted the "external proletariat" of Judaism, both culturally and religiously. In keeping with this psychological law, Mohammed maintained that Christians and Jews falsified their own Scriptures, eliminating or distorting the passages that foretold his advent.

Modern anti-Semitism attempts to retain the sinister complex of hate and admiration that was embodied in Christianity, apart from the dogmatic foundations upon which it was first based. As Jewish loyalty shifted by degrees from the domain of religious convictions to that of ethnic solidarity, so, too, obeying the same historical forces, anti-Semitic feeling moved gradually to the new ground of racial hatred.

Both the unique strength and the peculiar weakness of the Jewish people derive from the perfect blend of the two polar ideals in their tradition. Jewish loyalty is like a double-pronged anchor, which cannot easily be pulled out. A religious challenge is countered by nationalistic feeling, and a challenge to national survival is opposed by an upsurge of religious feelings. In other national groups, religion occasionally fulfilled the functions of a protecting wall, shielding and sheltering national aspirations. Thus, among the Poles and the Irish, who were battling against the superior power of Russians and Englishmen respectively, the Catholic religion merged insensibly with ethnic loyalty, adding immeasurably to the strength of the anti-assimilationist sentiment of those minorities. Yet, the union of nationalism and religion could not be as strong among the Irish and the Poles

231

as it was among the Jews, since Polish and Irish ethnicism went back to pagan days and Catholicism was the religion of many millions of non-Poles and non-Irishmen. Among the Armenians of the Near East, who are frequently compared with the Jews, national memory goes back to pre-Christian days. Perhaps only the Parsees of India are comparable to the Jews of Europe in the perfect blending of their nationalism and their religion. The Parsees, too, represent a combination of extreme religious tenacity, economic specialization, and cultural proficiency, though it was not the sad lot of the Parsees to live among a people committed to a "heretical" form of their own faith.

Because of the double nature of Jewish loyalty, the exiles in Babylonia were not assimilated during the long predominance of Persia, when national ambitions were ruthlessly suppressed while religious loyalties were permitted and even encouraged. It was as a Temple-centered community that Judea re-emerged upon the scene of history, but the Hasmonean dynasty was nevertheless enabled to build a national state upon the impetus of rebellion against religious oppression. Later, when the two great rebellions against Rome were drowned in blood, it was ostensibly as a religious community that the Jews lived on in the latter days of the empire and all through the long centuries of the medieval era. But under the surface of religious loyalty, national ambitions and feelings surged mightily, finding expression in Messianic hopes and pseudo-Messianic movements. Nor was the ethnic origin of Jewry forgotten in the Christian world, since it was only as "children of the stock of Abraham" that Jews were allowed to live, when all forms of Christian heresy were cruelly extirpated.

When religious toleration became the order of the day, following the French Revolution, the Jews were felt to be in a unique category. In all the lands of Western Europe, opposition to the civil equality of Jews was motivated by the charge that they were somehow "different," being a self-segregating nationality as well as a religious community. Minority ethnic groups as

232

well as minority religious groups were granted rights of equal citizenship, but the Jews appeared to fall in a category all their own. As the anti-Semites saw them, they were a self-isolating national community, with the gulf between them and their neighbors being of a quasi-mystical order. The survival of the Jewish people appeared to be so contrary to nature as to suggest a streak of unique willfulness amounting to "misan-thropy." Jewish loyalty seemed to be a mysterious phenomenon —more than religious conviction and more than national loyalty. Thus, there emerged the "meta-myth," a vague belief that Jews were separated by a cosmic, metaphysical chasm from "all the other nations of the world."

During the nineteenth century, the Jewish fighters for civil emancipation in Western Europe attempted consciously to divest themselves and their religious culture of any residual national-istic sentiments. They hoped to break the historic bond between religious exclusiveness and national separateness, a bond that determined the fate of the Jewish people.[57] However, this process of denationalization within the Jewish community was counteracted, firstly, by philanthropic Jewish sentiments; sec-ondly, by occasional outbursts of anti-Semitism; and, thirdly, by the intimate association between religion and ethnic feeling in Judaism. The organization of the Alliance Israelite Universelle in 1860 was an instance of the former trend and the emergence of German cultural anti-Semitism in the eighties presaged the future development of Nazism. Graetz's monumental work, *The History of the Jews,* furnished ample evidence to the mind of the German historian Heinrich von Treitschke that the Jews of Germany did not yet accept the spirit of German nationalism. Anti-Semitism, he declared, was the "natural reaction of the German folk-feeling against an alien element." And this "folk-feeling" resents the intensity of Jewish isolationism, not the racial character of the Jew.[58] Though Graetz himself main-tained formally that the religious emphasis should predominate in the mind of the modern Jew, he could not but relate the history of German Jewry in such a manner as to offend German nationalists. Thus, Martin Luther was to the German nationalists a great hero, since he liberated German religion from foreign influences; but from the standpoint of Jewish experience, he was a vile anti-Semite. It was significant that the Association for the Study of German History refused to accept the "Palestinian Jew" Graetz in its midst, in spite of his illustrious achievements. The appetite of German nationalism proved to be insatiable. For the German nationalists, the written works of Graetz were a revelation of the residual ethnic zealotry in the soul of the German Jew.[59] From an objective standpoint, it can be stated that in Western Europe the denationalizing process within Jewry was retarded, while in Eastern Europe it was never started.

The Zionist movement arose as a reaction to European anti-Semitism, but it managed to gather massive momentum only because it was able to mobilize the authentic impetus of Jewish tradition. Zionism embraced two contradictory mental attitudes. Realists like Herzl and Nordau rebelled against the automatic forces of Jewish history, against the anomaly of Jewish "alienism," resulting from the pristine unity of ethnicism and religion. They sought to overcome the "abnormality" of the Jewish status, so that the Jewish individual and the Jewish group would be liberated from the "peculiarities" of Jewish life and destiny. In their view, a Jewish state was to solve the problem both of those who would become its citizens and those who would stay in the Diaspora. The latter would have a chance to demonstrate their disavowal of Jewish nationalism by staying outside the Jewish homeland. But the romanticists, chiefly the Zionists of Russia, gloried in their "uniqueness" and "distinctiveness," seeking to give fresh vigor to the automatic forces in Jewish life. Zionism was, for them, not a rebellion but a continuation, an invigoration of ethnic zealotry, a reassertion of ancient loyalties, leading to the emergence of an inner world of hypnotic certainty, in "defiance" of any objective evaluations and considerations.

Modern Jewish nationalism was therefore not a new con-

234

trivance, except in form. The tension within the two poles of nationalism was quickly manifested. Cultural or spiritual Zionism was projected by Ahad Ha'am, embraced with ardor and sincerity by thousands of intellectuals and pioneers, and applied on the political scene by Dr. J. L. Magnes and his associates of the "*Ihud*" group. But nationalism under the violent impact of cannibalistic anti-Semitism revealed also its earthly pole of zealous ethnicism. That Jews were so ineradicably different from "all the nations of the world" that they could never live at peace among them became the basic thesis of many Zionist intellectuals and politicians. Anti-Semitism is the "constant shadow which follows the Jewish people as long as and wherever it moves."[60] Thus, the "meta-myth," the unconscious assumption of a deep cosmic chasm between Jews and Gentiles, took on a Jewish guise in both literature and political organizations. Since Zionism revived the ethnic phase of Jewish consciousness in both its ideal and instinctive directions, it intensified the pitch of tension within the soul of the contemporary Jew, so that following the establishment of Israel the two types of Jewish nationalism began to pull toward opposing orientations. The spiritual nationalists now find themselves completely at home in the American status of a "religious community," which conceals not infrequently an ethnic foundation. Will Herberg, writing of American religion, concludes, "But, then the religious community itself, as a social institution, tends to revolve about an ethnic rather than a dogmatic axis."[61] For the spiritual nationalists this status is altogether satisfactory since in their interpretation of Judaism, religion is substantive and national feeling is adjectival. On the other hand, Jewish chauvinism and ethnic zealotry, based on the "meta-myth," and proclaiming either the untenability or the unworthiness of Jewish life in exile, permeate a goodly portion of Zionist literature and propaganda. Organizationally, it is expressed in the endeavor to bring about a total "ingathering of the exiles" and in a persistent negation of Jewish life in the Diaspora.

There is no element of strength in social life without a

corresponding weakness. The union of monotheism and nationalism brought the aid of ethnic feeling to the ideal content of religion and it added the supreme sanction of the Divine will to the instinctive drives of nationalism. But this combination served also to isolate the Jew from his neighbors by a double wall, giving rise to the dark dogmatism of the "meta-myth." This attribution of a unique cosmic status to the Jewish people militated against their mundane well-being, not only by provoking the ugly specter of anti-Semitism, but also in diverse other ways. It lessened the ardor of Jewish missionary efforts, for example. The Jewish religion was as universalistic in its teaching as Christianity or Islam, but the tension of ethnic loyalty within the soul of the Jew directed his energies largely, though not exclusively, to the salvation of his own people. Thus, there were times when Jewish missionary efforts were vigorously and successfully pursued, but not in a sustained and consistent manner. The varying attitude of Jewish teachers to proselytes reflects the tension between ethnicism and religion in Judaism.

This polar tension was manifested also in the confusion of self-identification that has marked Jewish life from the very beginning. While the prophets representing the mainstream of Judaism sought to win national greatness in the domain of the spirit, there appeared countercurrents from time to time, led by men who sought to redirect Jewish energies toward the goals of political power and national independence. In modern times, of course, this divergence in the interpretation of the nature of Jewish being is most in evidence. At this very moment in America, Judaism has not gained as much as other faiths from the massive movement of religious revival, chiefly on account of the confusion of self-identification in the mind of the Jew.

Another weakness that resulted from this blend of monotheism and nationalism was the failure of the Jewish people to extend their truly remarkable philanthropic institutions and high code of ethical conduct to their non-Jewish neighbors. The record on this point is not altogether clear, since it is not difficult to assemble an impressive array of maxims, teaching the extension of loving-kindness to all the children of man. On the other hand, the Talmud operates consistently on the supposition that a deep line of distinction must be drawn between the rights of Jews and of non-Jews. And the net of Jewish philanthropic institutions reflected at all times this gulf between the in-group and out-group, the line between *Binnenmoral* and *Aussenmoral*, in the language of Max Weber. The chief menace of this pernicious doctrine within the Jewish community consisted in the encouragement that it provided for the belief that the "Gentile mind" cannot possibly understand the "Jewish mind." Jews and Gentiles belonged to two incompatible mental worlds operating with concepts that were mutually incommensurate. Again, it is easy to document this view in literature and to recognize its expression in the organizational policy of some Jewish groups. Historically, this undefined but powerful axiom led to situations in which Jews made not the slightest effort to understand the minds of their neighbors. This failure to take account of the categories of thought of the non-Jewish world is one of the enduring factors in Jewish history, resulting in tragedies that were manifestly avoidable. Again, Jewish experience merely brought to a high pitch of intensity the universal tendency of ethnic groups to put themselves on a pedestal and to dramatize their own achievements as the works of a national genius so transcendent as to be inevitably beyond the comprehension of "lesser breeds without the law." This axiom of ethnic zealotry, common though it is to all nations, especially to those that have been thrown on the defensive by the accidents of history, proved to be more potent among Jewish people because it was re-enforced by the self-centered pole of religion. While the self-transcendent pole of monotheism directed Jewish ethnic feeling into universal channels, the self-centered pole cast the mantle of dogmatic smugness upon the nakedness of injured pride, effectively isolating the Jewish mentality from any channels of communication with the outside world.

Before proceeding to illustrate this concept of Jewish history

237

and to indicate the ways in which it supplies a comprehensive context for the totality of Jewish historic experience, it is helpful to indicate briefly how this formula applies to the contemporary Jewish scene. There are at present three areas of Jewish life— Soviet Russia and its satellites, America or the English-speaking countries generally, and the State of Israel. In Soviet Russia, the nationalistic ambitions of small nations, especially of those with connections outside the iron curtain, are virtually proscribed. Religion is discouraged, though not actually prohibited. Anti-Semitism is still alive, but it is officially discountenanced. Hence, we may expect the gradual dissolution and disappearance of all that is distinctively Jewish in the lives of the three million Jews of Russia and Eastern Europe.

As between the State of Israel and America, the current of Jewish life is presently bifurcated, with Jewishness in Israel being primarily a national quality and Jewishness in America becoming ever more decisively a religious characterization. In neither country will monotheism and nationalism be completely separated, for the massive labors of history cannot be undone. Yet, the Jewish Israeli thinks of himself predominantly as part of the Jewish ethnic group, though he is forced to include within his purview the Berber Jews of Northwest Africa and the black Jews of Northeast Africa. By the same token, the American Jew thinks of himself as a member of a "religious community," but he interprets this term broadly enough to include all members of the Jewish ethnic group, who have not converted to other faiths. Neither his religion nor his ethnic character carry any negative valences, stamping him as "peculiar" and "set apart," for American religion is becoming steadily less fundamentalist and American nationalism is not founded on the feeling of racial unity.

In both America and Israel, however, this divergence of orientation between religion and ethnicism is supplemented by the tension between the poles within each ideal. Within the State of Israel, the significant alternatives are to be found between a type of nationalism that is conceived in the universal

238

and moral terms of the "spirit of ancient Israel" (*ruah Yisroel sava*), and a kind of nationalism that is self-centered, blood-based, and chauvinistic. Only the spiritual brand of Israeli nationalism will make possible a genuine acceptance of the Arab minority within the Israeli nation. Also, this brand of nationalism blends insensibly into the ethereal realm of religious idealism, providing a channel of communication between Israel and the Diaspora.

In America, too, the fundamental dichotomy within the soul of the Jew will not be the tug of war between monotheism and nationalism, a tension which fixed the issues in Jewish ideology for more than a century, but the perennial pull between the poles of open, outreaching genuine piety and a self-enclosed narrow dogmatism. The earthy, fundamentalist type of piety merges insensibly into ethnic zealotry, with hardly a hairline of separation, while an enlightened faith, conceived in the universal terms of man's conscience and intelligence, will have no difficulty in refining and redeeming the vestigial loyalties of the ideal phase of Jewish nationalism.

In both America and Israel, the tension within the Jewish soul is likely to be no longer distinctive and "peculiar," but rather of a universally human character. As American Jews move steadily away from the entrapment of ethnicism and as the bigotries of dogmatic religion give way progressively to the tolerant spirit of liberalism, we may expect the gradual fading of the "meta-myth." The "Jewish problem" cannot be solved altogether because of the factor that sociologists call the "cultural lag," which is the inability of all the people to ascend the heights of spiritual nationalism and nondogmatic self-transcending religion. In contrast to the realistic trend in Zionism, which sought to cut the Jewish Gordian knot by a vertical line, sundering nationalism from religion, we look forward to the elevation of Jewish consciousness above a horizontal line, in which the ideal phases of both nationalism and religion predominate. In American society, composed of diverse ethnic strains and founded consciously on the "Judeo-Christian Tradition," the Jew is likely to become less and less of an alien, either physically or spiritually. Similarly, as the Jews of Israel acquire sufficient confidence to stand on their own feet, they will learn to regard themselves more and more as "normal" nationals of the Middle East. This twofold trend cannot be completely consummated, however; nor is it altogether certain that it will not be reversed, for there are still powerful forces in our midst that are not restrained by the realization of the tragic potentialities in Jewish life. If the manifold ethnocentric efforts, reflecting the automatic impulses of our history, should prevail, then American Jewry will become an isolated enclave and the State of Israel will be grievously burdened and hampered in its international relations. This result may not be intended by any significant group today, but history is fashioned by the logic inherent in actions, not by the weight of good intentions.

Part Three
Dialogue with the New Atheists

RESPONSE TO THE
"GOD IS DEAD"
MOVEMENT

The "God is dead" movement is a unique phenomenon, characteristic of the aimlessness of our time. It has nothing in common with that coarse corrosion of the Divine within man that leads the wicked to "say in his heart, 'there is no god.'" The exponents of today's atheism are deeply troubled and intensely ethical personalities. They would not imitate the Grand Inquisitor of Dostoevski and proceed to kill him whom they knew to be their Lord on the ground that people love order, fixed habits, and slavish submission. On the contrary, they are disgusted with the staid complacencies of the theistic faiths. They want to arouse and mobilize the dormant energies of modern man, making possible a new birth of creative freedom.

But they are not really Nietzscheans either, though they emblazoned on their banner the words coined by Nietzsche— "God is dead." Nietzsche lived at a time when the men of the West had taken a big bite from the apple of the Tree of Knowledge, and before they had felt its bitter aftertaste. In the latter half of the nineteenth century, there seemed to be ample ground for boundless optimism. There was no problem that the educated elite could not solve, and when they spoke of the nobility of man, they meant those made in their own image. Neither the "internal proletariat" of Europe and Africa, nor the "external proletariat" of the impoverished colonies had as yet voiced their protests. Marxist socialism was then still buoyant and fresh like the dawn. They knew of only one Dark Age, a joint product of "barbarism and religion." The crude, perverted myths of anti-Semitism appeared to be only the vestigial nightmare of a moribund medievalism. Today, after Auschwitz, the atomic bomb, and blatant preparation for a third world war by the militarists of both sides, there is hardly any justification for any kind of naïve faith in man. Both the intuitive wisdom of the masses and the integrity of the intelligentsia have been found wanting.

It appears that the paradoxical religious atheism of our day derives from three sources—the dead end of erstwhile existentialism, the failure of religions to date to curb the evil urges of man, and the resurgence of mythological thinking.

Let us begin with the third source. In the past two decades, theologians became keenly aware of the "depth-dimension" of ancient symbols and rites. The myths of ancient religions were not the products of an idle and undisciplined imagination, but like floating icebergs, their center of gravity was far below the surface. All modernists agree that the ancient myths were associated with diverse abuses. If mythology is the "natural" form of religion, then the irreligion of modern man can be overcome only by a resurgence of the mythmaking faculty. Is it possible to revive an ancient myth and restructure it to serve the ideals of our day?

One of the most tenacious myths of the pagan world was the legend concerning the "dying god," which was found in diverse forms throughout the ancient world. It corresponded, on the one hand, to the annual rhythm of the seasons and, on the other hand, it reflected the inner contradictions of human nature. Faith is, to many people, not the outgrowth of experience but the attempt to overcome it. Faith and reality are mutually contradictory to this way of thinking. Oswald Spengler describes religion as "the waking-being of a living creature in the moment when it overcomes, masters, denies and even destroys being."[1] In this view, religion is born when reality is stilled. The Buddhists and the primitive Christians discovered that when "they die to their old self," they can face life with courage and say, "O death, where is thy sting?"[1a] Surrender has its own kind of sweetness, more consoling and enduring than the triumph of the proud.

In the first centuries of our era, the Christian apostles and fathers grafted the myth of the dying god into the long cherished eschatological "hope of Israel." The result was an unbeatable combination: the fusing of Jewish moral activism with pagan mythological fervor. But, the radical theologians assert, the Christian synthesis is presently no longer effective. It no longer speaks to modern man in terms of his present needs. It does not stir us to our depths. Its imagery is no longer gripping. It speaks of God's heaven and man's spirit at a time when heaven has become "outer space" and the spirit has become the vast dark basement of the unconscious, filled with Freudian complexes and Jungian archetypes.

A new form of the ancient myth is needed. How shall it be produced? Manifestly, a myth is powerful and effective only when it springs spontaneously out of the collective psyche of an age. If it is consciously constructed, it is not a religious myth but a lifeless tissue of illusions. To bring the new myth into being, it is necessary to enter into its vital rhythm and submit to its unconscious vigor.

Therefore, the neotheologians reason, it is essential to dramatize and identify with the first part of the life cycle of the god. If people die with him, shall they not rise with him?

The neotheologians do not state their case in this blatant form, since the absurdity of their position would become patent. Mythology belongs to the childhood of the race. Those who still live under its spell will resent any new version of a subtle "deicide." On the other hand, the educated elite, having become emancipated from its archaic tyranny, will scorn any new effort at re-mythologization. In effect, such a reconstitution of the old myth would open the gates wide to the unpredictable tides of the unconscious.

Altizer argues against the notion that mythology can be excised from religion: "When logos and mythos are interpreted as antithetical categories, the victory of the new mode of under-

245

standing is seen as banishing mythos to the archaic world of primitive men. Thereby it is assumed that the higher forms of religious understanding and belief must be a-mythical. But this assumption obliterates the tension between the religious and rational consciousness and assumes that religious faith and understanding are founded upon an understanding and affirmation of the world. Yet, this interpretation is manifestly untrue of the higher religions of the world. All of them in one way or another are world-negating, world-dissolving, or world-reversing."[2]

To Altizer, primitive Buddhism and primitive Christianity are "higher religions," whereas Rabbinic Judaism and philosophical Christianity are weak and unstable compromises with reality.

Judaism performed the majestic "world-historical" mission of combating the mythological way of thinking. In Judaism, the resurgence of spirit takes the place of the rhythm of life. The categories of spirit—truth, goodness, holiness—are set over against the categories of life—death, rebirth, new life. Still there is no gulf between spirit and life. The theme of all festivals is, "Thou shalt rejoice in thy life." But neither is spirit simply the reflection of the drives of life. Spirit is the vertical dimension of life. Man cannot in his lifetime attain the "vision of the Lord." To be sure, God is called *Mehaye Hahayim* ("the vitalizer of life"), but He performs this role by virtue of His being above the vicissitudes of life. He is not the surge of a blind life force in the universe, but its upward movement, its outreaching toward the textures of spirit.

In essence, the radical theologians seek to reopen the unconscious springs of human nature. In their view, religionists have been unable to curb the vicious instincts of their followers because the religious message is now articulated solely on the surface level of the conscious ego, whereas power dwells in the dark depths of the psyche. As long as religionists direct their appeal to man's intellect and conscience, they cannot endow their word with the magic potency of a mystical *kerygina*. The sense of the holy points to the depths of human nature, but in our life today, it has become staid and decent, pale and lifeless—hence, the necessity of a mythological shock therapy.

In reply, let us examine wherein religion failed in the past century. Did it err on the side of rationality or of mythology? In the first part of the nineteenth century, the spokesmen of religion were overly concerned with emotional "conversions" and almost totally uninterested in alleviating the plight of the working people. By and large, the clergy ranged themselves on the side of the powers that be and concentrated their fervor on the maintenance of the orthodox dogmas. Science was the enemy or secular "enlightenment" generally. In the latter part of the nineteenth century, "godless socialism" and Darwinism were condemned while the "Social Gospel" was conspicuous by its absence. In the first half of the twentieth century, most religionists blessed and sanctified the various forms of nationalism. The alliance between nationalism and religion seemed to be "made in heaven," since both movements sought their inspiration in the romantic glorification of mass-feeling and mass-mythology.

It was not for lack of mystical potency that religion failed, but because its spokesmen refused to support the fragile shoots of rationalism and liberalism. In Russia, the Church supported the Czar, not the liberal Cadets. In Germany, it called for the worship of throne and altar. In France, most of the clerics were ranged against the Republic and against its liberal, revolutionary heritage. In all countries, mythological anti-Semitism found its most fertile soil in the "religious" sector of the population. The recent Glock-Stark study of anti-Jewish prejudice uncovered a similar situation in this country.

In our own day, it was Hitler who confronted the churches with their "moment of truth." In terms of the myths and rites of the Church, he pretended to be a friend. He attacked its age-old "enemies"—rationalism, liberalism, socialism, even individualistic capitalism; above all, he was the enemy of the Jews, who symbolized all these "sins" of the intellect and of the liberal West. He could persuade many churchmen that he would

247

support "positive Christianity," and that his inauguration would mark a rebirth of the myth and mystique of the faith. Had the churchmen thought in terms of the prophetic impetus of the Judeo-Christian traditions, they could hardly have been beguiled by Nazi offers to bolster the attendance, membership, and stability of the churches. It was an axiom for all churchmen that Nazism was preferable to communism. This was the crux of Pope Pius' conviction. Yet, after all, in terms of despotic terror, both were alike; while in respect of the core of doctrine, communism stood for the equality and well-being of all men, Nazism sought to establish a "master race" in control of a horde of Slavic and other subhumans, and it did not hesitate to condemn millions to extermination.

We are driven to the conclusion that if there is failure in religion, it is not due to the absence of mythology. We are still suffering from its superabundance.

The sudden popularity of religious existentialism immediately after the Second World War was due to a massive rebound from the anguish of human failure. If our moral-rational self is weak, there is invincible strength in our deeper nature. The religious existentialists stressed the nonrational character of man and insisted that whatever was understandable in religion was both false and idolatrous. It substituted the polarity "depth to depth" for the previous polarity of man and God. The depth-dimension in man is suprarational, said Tillich, and susceptible only of imaginative and intuitive perception, while the Divine Being was "the God beyond the god."

While the existentialist emphasis is true in its analysis of the human craving for the Divine, it is easily distorted and thrown out of balance. In their eagerness to prove that life is more than reason, the existentialists frequently came near to saying that reason is hardly relevant in the life of faith. A God whose will was understandable became for them an idol, hiding the inconceivable, just as rational man was in their eyes a monstrosity.

The genuine function of existential literature is not to exalt irrationality but to point to the transrational in man and in the universe. When reason is set aside as irrelevant to the life of faith, the floodgates to irrationality are thrown open—the irrationality of radical empiricism that lives in and for the momentary experience at one extreme, or the irrationality of fundamentalism at the other extreme.

It is the former type of irrationality that is now represented by the radical theologians. Having abandoned the world of realism and reason, they seek to stir enthusiasm on behalf of man's self-worship. "God is dead. Long live mankind."

But the feelings of religion arise precisely out of man's recognition that he cannot worship himself. He feels the inexorable rush of time driving him to oblivion and he seeks contact with eternity; he senses the meretricious and the superficial in his own existence and he longs for the assurance that he is embraced in reality; he is only too keenly aware of his moral frailty and he seeks to become one with the good. In these three dimensions of religious feeling, we aim at the source of all that is human, not at humanity as a collective entity.

Existentialists have always claimed to be pragmatists. It is in place therefore for us to examine the practical consequences of any form of man's self-worship. We know the evils of its individualistic form—every man for himself. Ibsen, in *Peer Gynt*, pointed out how easily the counsel "to thine own self be true" is twisted into the egotistic principle "to thine own self be enough."

As to the collective forms of self-worship, has not history provided us with an abundance of illustrations—the worship of the god of the city-state, the worship of the king or the emperor, and in our day, the worship of the class, the state, the nation, or the race. In fact, the secular ideologies of the twentieth century—nationalism, communism, racism, and Darwinian individualism—are nothing but variants of the "God is dead" theology. None of the radical theologians would favor any one of these ideologies. They are all humanists, if not liberals. But the social consequences of an idea derive from its own inherent logic.

The strongest challenge to faith comes from those who claim that, in practice, God is today a meaningless word. The pragmatic meaning of faith in God depends upon the kind of belief that is affirmed. Faith in a supernatural God is inevitably associated with one or another tradition which spells out His will. In this sense, faith belongs within a definite historic context —Jewish, Catholic, Protestant, Moslem. On the basis of this belief, one cannot complain about the absence of empirical consequences. The inferences from this belief are certainly clear and practical—all too clear and all too practical.

The argument of meaninglessness has some relevance to the nonsupernaturalist concepts of the Divine. If God is either nature as a whole or a force within nature, then we may well question whether the use of this age-old term serves more to confuse the faithful than to enlighten them. The pragmatic test is relevant to all concepts and it is of decisive significance in the case of the most fundamental of all ideas. If it should appear that faith in God makes no detectable difference in the life of some people, then this concept is indeed meaningless to them.

They may have to repeat the test again and again, but in theory we may agree that if faith in God turns out to matter little or not at all in the lives of people, this faith is probably of no meaning to begin with. The pragmatic critique is thus far entirely in line with the prophetic current of thought in Holy Scriptures. To do justice and to love mercy are ranked by Micah ahead of walking humbly with the Lord.

Does this pragmatic test condemn as irrelevant all non-supernaturalist conceptions of the Deity? Suppose you do not assume that one or another transgression will cause a thunderbolt to strike you, or that an angel will hurl you down for so many years into the black fires of purgatory. Is faith in God meaningless?

By no means. There are many ways in which such faith can be effective, apart from such crude metaphors. We who affirm a liberal faith are justly challenged to prove that our faith is not simply a hollow phrase, but the pragmatists, in their turn, must beware of rushing to conclusions.

For example, several studies indicate that the activists on the college campuses are not drawn predominantly from the ranks of those who are committed to faith in God. If the cause of civil rights, or de-escalation in Vietnam, or free speech is the modern equivalent of "doing justice and loving mercy," does it not follow that religion makes no difference? The answer is that the implications of faith are so many and varied that no one test is adequate. "Ten times, our ancestors in the wilderness tried the Lord. . . ."[2a] While "civil rights" is of the essence of a good society, any specific suggestion for coping with a contemporary problem may be open to just criticism. The supreme pragmatic value of faith is precisely the fact that it is so all-embracing as to guard against the precipitate exaltation of any one cause as if it were the be-all and end-all of life. No social ideal or cause is so absolute as to deserve that fullness of devotion which blinds us to the worth of the many and diverse values that are entangled in any concrete situation. Secularists generally and young enthusiasts in particular are apt to plump for whatever cause is highlighted at any one moment. Their revolutionary ardor, for all its usefulness in effecting needed reforms, is on balance exceedingly dangerous for society. Normally, society requires the conservative pull of strong roots more than it needs the fervor for radical changes. Manifestly, our heritage from the past contains *so* much more good than any single generation can appreciate, or even conceive, much less create afresh out of its own resources.

The concept of God that I assume is neither naturalist nor supernaturalist. It is not the personification of the forces of nature, or of a force standing over, against, and beyond nature. Its starting point is not force, but the human spirit. While man is part of nature, he is capable of reflecting a Being that is supreme in reality, truth, and love. By centering his life round the effort to appreciate this reflection and respond to it, man attains the fulfillment of his own being.

Faith is not a denial or a killing of one's self, but the integration of one's own personal life into the realm of spirit and the projection of that realm into the infinite—or if existentialist language is preferred, into the ultimate ground of reality. We come to feel that our true self consists in our participation in the eternal life of spirit. And this life in turn represents the will of God.

Since the human spirit is our starting point, we have to begin with an analysis of this term. Is spirit an independent reality, a kind of substance or soul-force? No. As pragmatists, we do not deal with substances or essences, but only with relations or potential movements. Spirit is a realm of relations in respect of meaning. In turn, meaning is the relation of any one event to a class, and that class, in its turn, to a more inclusive whole, reaching up to the ultimate Being that is God. In this way, spirit is the polar opposite of a mechanical universe. While the latter is ideally understood through the interaction of the smallest conceivable particles, the former imposes the reign of meaning through the operation of the whole upon each of its component parts.

As I write now, moving my pen across the smooth paper, my action can be interpreted in both mechanical and spiritual terms. Mechanically, the motion of my fingers is the result of some interaction in the brain cells, setting off certain physiological changes in the nerve tissue and the muscles of my right hand. This physiological explanation is not complete. Ideally, we have to know how the message travels from the brain—the chemical processes involved in the action of the brain, the nerves, and the muscles. Even so, the explanation is incomplete, for the chemical processes have to be interpreted in terms of the basic qualities of matter. Since matter is now known to be congealed energy, we have to go beyond protons and electrons to the ultimate tremors of physical reality, the simplest waves that undulate at the edge of existence. Throughout this chain of explanations, the assumption in every equation is that nothing new has happened. The novelty of the new is explained away by the mechanical-mathematical equations that reduce all events to the final infinitesimal quintessence of reality.

The spiritual explanation of my writing begins with the idea that I seek to express. It is that one idea which embraces the myriad physiological and chemical activities involved in my action. In turn, this idea needs to be explained by reference to the totality of my personality, my frame of mind, my history, my limitations. This explanation would be incomplete without the further attempts to interpret my ideas in the light of the spirit of the age, and to judge the spirit of my age in the light of the Universal Mind or Spirit.

The simple act of writing can be led downward to the infinitesimal mechanical quantum of energy and upward to the Infinite Mind. Faith consists in the persistent upward quest of the human mind and heart.

Since human faith cannot reach its ultimate goal of total identification with the will of God, we may well ask whether there are any objective grounds for the validity of its upward orientation. Philosophers have long known that God cannot be proven, but grounds for faith may be given. In one way or another the philosophers of the classical tradition have pointed to the ascending ladder of wholes in the universe. The infinitesimal burst of reality is matter and energy at the same time; it is and it is not; it is itself and its dissolution. As we rise in the scale of existence, even more complex wholes arise, from the atom to the molecule, to the crystal, to the living cell, to multicellular organism, to the plants and the animals. In man, there is a further ascent to the complex whole of consciousness, whereby multitudes of things that do not even exist may be brought into the field of action. And beyond consciousness looms the self-regulating domain of spirit.

Here we come to the second ground of faith, the human quest for the transcendent. As the individual emancipated himself from the "collective thinking" of the primitive clan, he became aware of his personal identity and its precariousness. He now faced the mystery of life in fear and trembling. Gradually, his fear and anxiety were mellowed by the projection of humane feelings unto the Divine beings that controlled his destiny. The mysterious reality was a paradoxical blend of feelings—the apprehension of the holy. In many cultures, the feeling of the holy was cultivated apart from the intellectual and ethical dimension of spiritual life. Even in the modern world, there have been frequent reversions to the dichotomy of the human spirit, with the champions of the realm of holiness guarding their domain as "wholly other" against the intrusion of the other faculties of the human spirit.

In Judaism, the holy is one with the quest for truth, goodness, and beauty; for in these quests, man reaches out to the Transcendent Reality. In all the domains of spirit, we fulfill ourselves by identifying with a realm of being that is not ourselves. We come to participate in a kind of life that is nonphysical, nontemporal, and structured according to its own laws.

The feeling of the holy is a blend of love and fear: love, for it relates us to our deeper self; fear, for it confronts us with that which is not ourselves. The holy is mysterious, the Transcendent; yet, it is also the inner light "that searches our Transcendent; yet, it is also the inner light that searches our inmost parts."[2b] It is "wholly other" and "wholly ourselves" at one and the same time. Its key word is not "either/or," a demand for our unconditional surrender, but "this and that," a call for our personal growth through participation in the realm of the Divine.

The holy, then, is our intuitive apprehension of belonging to a whole that is related to our selves, as mind is to life and as living wholes are to the dark tremors of an electromagnetic field of force.

In social life, the sense of the holy divides as it develops, becoming a hunger for truth, an ardor for justice and mercy, a passion for the construction of harmonious wholes in art, in industry, in the organization of society. Thus, culture in all its diverse forms is an articulation of the component elements of faith. But the equation cannot always be reversed. All that is cultural is not religious. Religious energy generates the dynamic impetus for the varied arts of culture, but these arts then develop lives of their own. They may indeed bring about the fragmentation of the human personality, for each of the three currents of culture is by nature "jealous" of its "purity," resisting the imposition of standards that are not of its own making. We have "pure" esthetes, "pure" saints, and "pure" scientists, but the three quests are one at their source, our personal integrity and our sense of the holy, as well as one in their goal, the Supreme Being.

In worship, we aim to regain this unity of the varied quests of our spirit. The oneness of God that we assert is a reflection of the oneness of our self. We seek to bring together philosophic reflection, moral fervor, and esthetic ecstasy in one effort of outreaching that is at the same time the fearful "existential" cry of the deepest level of our being. God is the Infinite Being, which our apprehension of the holy assumes intuitively. At the same time, He is the goal of all our self-transcending quests. We conceive of Him as the one goal of the three infinite progressions of reason, of ethics, and of esthetics. He is therefore true being, love, and harmony.

Since God is the intuitive response to our existential "fear and trembling," as well as the ultimate goal of the three "pure" quests of reality, we face the constant danger of fragmentizing His reality. Primitive people will fear Him as a blind force or as a self-willed autocrat. Moralists will close their eyes and extol him as pure love. Scientists will think of Him as mind, and artists as the principle of harmony. But in truth He is all these and more. He is immanent in mind, heart, and creative imagination, but He is also a transcendent being in whom all quests are fulfilled and negated at one and the same time.

Altizer writes in explanation of the "God is dead" theology: "Thus, in the modern world religion is doomed to wear the cloak of idolatry if only because modern man can grasp no reality that is not a reflection of himself."[3]

As he sees it, the chief characteristic of modern man is historicism, the awareness that all judgments are conditioned by time and circumstance. We know, then, that to some extent all our views of the external universe will be affected by the prevailing winds of doctrine. This does not mean that we live in a self-created world of phantasy. It is precisely because we seek the Transcendent in all its "purity" that we are so keenly aware of the distorting effects of our subjectivity. The way to God consists in the progressive overcoming of this distortion, not in following Kierkegaard, who, in a fit of rebellion against human finitude, asserted that "subjectivity is truth."

The valid core in Kierkegaard's thesis is that truth is the product of our personal orientation as well as the external reality. This stance of our self consists not in a rejection of the rational or the ethical, but rather in the convergence of all our outreaching faculties, the fusion of our quests for goodness, truth, and harmony in the awareness of the holy. Spirit is not a reflection of man as he is, but as he seeks to become, in his noblest moments. In turn, the realm of the holy is not an independent world, but simply the awareness of the inner unity of the tasks of truth-seeking, community-building, and imaginative creativity. The holy is therefore inherent in all our creative efforts.

We may now inquire, What is the purpose of cultivating the sense of the holy by means of religious rites if its implications can only be articulated through the three areas of humanism? The answer is that the quality of holiness provides the cement of unity for the individual and for society.

The individual learns to find the focus of his being in the realm of spirit with its three dimensions, to integrate his faculties and to orient them toward the Transcendent. In this way, he achieves an inner unity of personality, a deep sense of oneness with the Transcendent Reality in which his personal being is rooted, and an active participation in the ongoing task of building the realm of spirit in this world.

Deep in the heart of man is the need for belonging—belonging not only to a family, a circle of friends, a nation, a faith-community, but to the Ultimate and the Enduring. There may be a biological reason for this longing, since man is the only living being that knows of his impending death. He cannot be content with the unconscious assurance that his life continues in the endurance of his species. In the primitive mythical world, the emergent consciousness of man was lulled into acquiescence by the magic of an imaginative re-entrance into the womb of Mother Nature. The various rites of the nature-gods and the occasional orgies of the fertility festivals served to recreate artificially the pristine unity of man and nature. Later, the emergence of the city-gods or clan-gods fulfilled a similar function in preventing the awareness of an individual consciousness. The fear of death was allayed because it was only the individual that perished, and the individual did not yet learn to esteem his own identity.

The individual made his appearance in two cultures—in Hellas and in Israel. In the Hellenic world, he emerged by virtue of the discovery of the critical intellect. In Biblical Israel, the individual appeared as the custodian of God's commandment—hence, as a being, responsible for his actions. The mystery religions of Greece, Asia Minor, Egypt, and Canaan were devices for the intoxication of the individual, his "dying to his former self" and his "second birth" in the life of a resurrected deity. The wild outbursts of the Dionysiac celebrations were, therefore, comparable to the LSD flights from reality in our day. The marriage of Hellenic reflection and Hebrew monotheism produced first Rabbinic Judaism, then philosophical Christianity, finally the consciousness of the modern religious humanist.

Through his moral responsibility, his intellectual and his esthetic integrity, the religious man comes to feel the holiness of his life. He, as a man of spirit, belongs to the God of eternity, who is also immanent in all the endeavors of a religious culture. In moments of genuine worship, the wholeness of his being is stirred by the sublime feelings of holiness. New life from the "vitalizer of all life" is poured into his being, his right hand is reinforced, and he knows the blessing of being embraced in the peace that "passes understanding." His individuality is "fulfilled" in the life of God that is the Universal Spirit. And it is fulfilled in this life, without being submerged in the sea of mob excitement.

GOD AND
THE CATASTROPHE

The singular fate of the Jews in Nazi Europe is so shattering that only now are we beginning to face up to it. The popularity of Shirer's book, *The Rise and Fall of the Third Reich*, of *The Diary of Anne Frank* and its dramatization, and of *The Deputy* indicate increasing interest in the tragic fate of the six million. Now that refugees from the Nazi terror are no longer a practical problem, the attention of the world is drawn to the intellectual challenge of ideological mass-murder and totalitarian genocide.

The theological aspect of this soul-shattering tragedy cannot be ignored by either Jews or Christians. First, the very idea of setting the Jews apart from other peoples, as if God had created two species of humanity, is a central theme in the religious heritage of the Western world. It would hardly be possible for a Chinese to think in terms of Jews and Gentiles. Second, the elaboration of this distinction in the popular theology of Christian Europe created a demonic image of the Jew, an image that disposed the masses to believe so many canards concerning the Jews. Third, the emancipation of the Jews took place under the banner of secular liberalism, with the result that the religious reactionaries, the conservative economic classes, and the nationalistic romanticists became used to the idea of directing their enmity at Jews along with liberals and rationalists. When the left-wing of liberalism turned first to socialism and then to communism, this fear-born hatred became more and more irrational and hysterical. Fourth, anti-Semitism was invariably rooted in the mood and sentiment of the Christian

259

political parties, even when the official party platform did not contain a specific anti-Jewish plank. It can hardly be doubted that the religious traditions of the Western world provided the stake and the faggots for the execution of the six million. The Nazi criminals merely had to bind the helpless victims to the stake and light the match.

The theological challenge of the six million is rendered even more acute by the circumstance that they died as the initial sacrifice of an anti-Christian crusade. The Nazis sought to suborn Christianity and to transform it into a neoprimitive creed of Teutonism. They directed their venom at the Jewish base of the Christian ideal in order to subvert Christianity from within, to stand it on its head, as it were. This was perhaps the first time in history that Jews died for the Christian as well as the Jewish faith. While some historians still question the wisdom of recognizing the unity of the Judeo-Christian heritage, the Nazis had no such doubts; they joined the communists in providing the malice and the fury to prove it.

For the Christian, then, the travail of the Jews in Europe during the Second World War is an inescapable theological challenge.

To us, as Jews, the fiery ordeal of the six million is like an open wound which we dare not forget, even at moments of our "chiefest joy." It is a personal loss, a bereavement so intimate and so unnatural that it cannot be eased.

At the same time, it is an ideological challenge that cannot be dismissed simply as another instance of the problem of evil. In Judaism, the life of the Jewish people has always served as an epic of salvation—*Heilsgeschichte*, ("redemptionist history"). We are taught to look at the travail of our people and see the redemptive hand of God in the affairs of men. Our central symbol is not Man-God but the *Congregation of Israel*. Its tragedy and its destiny are, for us, gateways to the mystery of the Divine will, windows opening onto the heavens. What, then, do we make of this latest and greatest *hurban*?*

---

*Great destruction, like that of the two destructions of Jerusalem

We cannot be content with the old clichés, rehearsing the "sins" of our people and reveling in visions of Messianic glory. Nor can we point to the "miracle" of Israel as the counterweight to the tragedy of the six million. The scales do not balance, however much you try.

If we are not to throw our hands up in despair, stating *les din v'les dayan* ("there is no justice and no judge"), we seem to have only three possible ways of relating God to the greatest catastrophe of our generation.

We may assume that though God is both all-powerful and all-good, His ways are mysterious; we cannot fathom them.

We may assert that God is indeed all-powerful, but not good, i.e. He does not have any purpose or set of purposes. He is the dynamic cause of all creation, but there is no final cause.

The third alternative would declare that God is all-good, but by no means all-powerful. He is the source of all values, but His potency is restricted to the power that He exerts within the human heart and mind.

Let us examine each of these assumptions.

The first assumption is, of course, that of traditional monotheism, where it is combined with a body of revelation, explicating the will of God. To believe that God is the "Lord of history" is to project Him into every historic situation, leaving no loophole for the blind operation of the laws of nature. If He is the Lord of nature, interfering with the laws He laid down only at rare moments, the massive evils of history must still be somehow consistent with His purpose. The question of an anguished conscience is then changed only in formulation, from "Why did He cause it?" to "Why did He not prevent it?"

If, as Nahmanides interprets Leviticus 26:41, God occasionally leaves the world to the play of contingent and mechanical forces, it is still His decision. If, as Isaiah asserts, the Lord "hides" Himself to punish a generation for its sins, what were the sins of the six million, or of their generation?

Those who believe they know the will of God cannot but attempt to fill the limbo of mystery with their dogmas. This theological exercise is particularly easy in the case of the Jewish people, whose character and destiny have always been enveloped in the web of theological phantasies and popular myths.

Fundamentalists, be they Jewish, Catholic, Protestant, or Moslem, will have no difficulty in numbering the sins of the hapless victims, though they will differ radically over the character of these sins.

I cannot conceive of a more sinister approach to the problem of evil in general and to the agony of the six million in particular. A people that is the "mysterious" whipping boy of a mysterious Lord will attract the myth and malice of all the fanatics who fancy themselves to be the chosen instruments of a mysterious Providence. The Jewish people already have the highest M.Q.(Mythological Quotient)of all historical communities. Have we not been the peculiar target of every myth in recent human history, from the anticapitalist illusions of the utopian socialists of France to the anticommunist fulminations of the national socialists, from the agricultural myth of the American Populists to the racial myths of the Teutons and the technocratic myths of the disciples of Henry Ford?

The cloud of mystery hanging over the heads of the Jewish people set them in a world apart, where the normal laws governing the human race were suspended, where the abnormal was the rule. Is it any wonder that even the most incredible accusations were half-believed when directed against our people?

The inkblot test in modern psychology teaches us that people see in a mystery images that reflect their subconscious hates and fears as well as their suppressed desires. To blur the image of our people in surrealist fashion is to expose them to the collective myth and malice of the populace. Yet such a deliberate blurring has long been the policy of both Christian and Jewish image-makers. The Christians have had their myth of deicide, and the Jews that of the suffering servant, which is the Christ-myth collectivized.

An illustration of the seductive myth of mystery, which relates an omnipotent Providence to the colossal crimes of Hitler, is provided in the play *The Deputy*.

The Cardinal expostulates with the idealistic, self-sacrificing German, Kurt Gerstein:

Cardinal

Tell me one thing Herr Lieutenant—how on earth could the Germans forget the mission that God had given them in the center of the West?

Gerstein

Eminence, that cannot be. God would not be God, if He used such a man as Hitler. . . .

Cardinal

Yes, yes, most certainly He would . . . indeed, was not Cain, his brother's murderer, also the tool of God? . . .

It is important to bear in mind that Hitler, too, thought of himself as a "world-historical figure," in Hegel's interpretation of the term. While he did not believe in the Judeo-Christian God, he invested his own demonic ambitions and Wagnerian dreams of Teutonism with the mysterious aura of Divine Providence.

The fundamentalist mentality views the demonic destroyer as the active partner of the Lord. Thus the unfortunate victim inescapably becomes either a sinner or a sacrificial lamb, a scapegoat. Inevitably, people are driven to number the "sins" of the victim. It is one thing for the sufferer to blame himself and to search his soul, in keeping with the admonition of our sages—*yefashpesh b'ma-asav.** It is quite another for others, even the fortunate survivors, to point an accusing finger.

Sin-mongering, let us not forget, is easily transferred from one universe of discourse to another. The Orthodox may blame the six million for their laxity in the observance of the *Shulhan Arukh.†* The Zionists will blame them for not having been clairvoyant, for not having seen the inevitability of a Hitlerian

---

*"let him search his deeds"

†"The Prepared Table," a Code of Jewish law

holocaust. The communists will excoriate them for not having glimpsed the Marxist light in time. And all the while, half-demented demagogues wait on the sidelines.

The second alternative is to think of God as the totality of all forces in the universe. It is the assumption of the physical scientists, for whom all the ideals of the ego and the superego are so many variations of the basic instincts. In their turn, instincts can be seen to be physiological processes, which are chemical reactions, resulting from the combinations and permutations of the ultimate building blocks of the universe.

Spinoza endowed this view of the universe with intense religious emotion. In our day, the Communists seem to think that a thoroughgoing material philosophy can generate the energy needed to hasten the advance of mankind toward the Marxist millennium.

What light can this way of thinking shed on the martyrdom of the six million? In the first place, it is helpful in searching for the hidden motivations of human conduct. Freud has certainly done more to expose the immense complexities of man's behavior and anxieties than all the moralists of our Western tradition. He has advanced mightily our understanding of the range and depth of moral problems. Similarly, building on a materialist hypothesis, Karl Marx has exposed the "social unconscious" in our contemporary affairs. It is hardly possible to write history today without taking into account either depth-psychology or the sociology of opinions.

But the materialist world-view offers scant comfort to those who contemplate the martyrdom of the six million. We are urged to recognize that the wheels of history grind without mercy, that it is the height of folly to resist their inexorable advance. In the Marxist view, the Jews are essentially remnants of an economic class, or caste, that is rapidly being "liquidated," caught as they are between the upper millstone of cartel-capitalism and the lower millstone of the revolutionary proletariat. Their salvation lies in yielding to the course of history and, in the language of religion, making the will of God their will. Any attempt to cling to their identity, whether ethnic, cultural, or religious, is basically evil, since the only measure of goodness is consonance with the march of the inevitable.

We must not minimize the menace of the Marxist challenge, for it confronts us in the Western world as well as behind the iron curtain. Those who reduce ideals to instincts cannot but degrade humanity to the masses. Man becomes a dot or a dash on an IBM machine, measurable, predictable, subject to manipulation and control, harnessed securely to the chariot of the God of history. This view pushes into limbo those who do not yield quickly enough—sentimental traditionalists, the thoughtful few, the sensitive elite, the incorrigible idealists. They are slow to see the mind of the Eternal in the marching feet of their contemporaries. They presume to look for the rational, the moral, and the beautiful in their own minds and in the great creations of humanity, instead of learning from Hegel and his disciples that "the real is the rational and the rational is the good." They are ready-made children for the firing squad.

The third alternative, the view of God as being all-good but not all-powerful, seems to be particularly appealing when we view the catastrophe in the light of our contemporary knowledge of man's primitive heritage. God is the name for that moral force that slowly is asserting itself in the human breast during the course of man's evolution. In such a millennial process, occasional relapses are to be expected. On the time scale of human history, going back a million years or so to the day when the first apelike creature began to walk erect, civilization is but a few hours in a man's life, cannibalism was the rule two hours ago, children were sacrificed to the gods or exposed to the wolves an hour ago, entire populations were massacred in the name of religion, and women were burned as witches a few minutes ago. And it is only minutes since cash prizes were offered by American states for the scalps of little Indian boys, since slaves were hunted like mad dogs in the "land of the free."

The smoking chimneys of Auschwitz are but another atavistic outburst against the rule of God. They remind us of the constant need to combat the primitive within us. In this view, God is young, and it is through us that He grows in strength and in stature.

Genuine moral ardor can be generated by this approach. If God can function only through our own good right arm, dare we stay aloof from any struggle in which moral issues are involved? Our sages spoke of man as "a partner in the work of creation." If man is the only active partner, the burden of progress rests upon him. The manifold evils of our day demonstrate the great need of rallying under this banner in order to hasten the day when His Kingdom does in fact prevail over the whole earth.

At the same time, there is no reason for us to despair of man's future. After all, the Nazi challenge was met and overcome. We are now wiser, even if a bit sadder. The forward march of mankind has been resumed. Behold the emergence of Israel, the rise of the oppressed nations, the birth of new hope in the breast of billions. Were Isaiah living today, he would not hesitate to proclaim to all who dream of the Divine rule, "Arise and shine, for thy light has come."

Faith in the God Who Becomes is now popular among would-be sophisticates. Gittelson's *Man's Best Hope* and Robinson's *Honest to God* reflect this trend. The difficulties inherent in this view become apparent when we return to the basic human situation out of which the belief in God arises. Please note that I do not appeal to the testimony of any particular religious experience. However one describes the nature of the religious consciousness, one cannot ignore the yearning toward, or the possession of, the Eternal, as against our time-conditioned secular affairs; the longing for, or the possession of, Reality, as against fleeting shadows on the surface of things; the straining for, or the possession of, Absolute Truth, as against the parade of falsehoods that is the tissue of our worldly experience.

These components of the religious consciousness are not so

many "feelings" which are peculiar to mystics or to prophets or to their latter-day pontifical successors; they are essential to its very nature. Religious faith contains these "moments," as the Germans would say, quite apart from any poetic elaborations, mystical disquisitions, metaphors, myths, or dogmas. For religion is essentially a turning away from the temporal, the unreal, the untrue, the wrong—hence, a turning toward their polar opposites, the eternal, the real, the true, the good, or the Absolute Being.

How does the concept of the God Who Becomes meet the religious needs of man? It seems to me that only one dimension of the religious realm is constituted by this view, namely, God as the good or the moral ideal emerging through the process of evolution. But even this one aspect of the Deity is vitiated by its rootlessness and vagueness. If that which emerges is good, then success is the only criterion, as indeed it is in the evolving animal kingdom of the Darwinian universe.

Suppose now that Hitler had won the war that he had launched! Would not his phantasies of "race" purity have commended themselves to most people as being the last word of evolutionist ethics? As a matter of fact, the Nazis' entire way of thinking is a projection on the political level of the biological categories of Darwinism. "Young nations" have the right to make room for themselves. Their "world-historical" career is far beyond the reach of the ethical categories of "good and evil." As romanticists and even mystics, the Nazis were "religious," in an evolutionist way, believing that God reveals Himself in their "pure" German blood. He speaks in Teutonic accents, shouting *Sieg Heil* across the bloody cannonades of the battlefield. Indeed, the gas ovens of Auschwitz might be considered the altars of the Moloch of evolution.

If God himself evolves, where are the standards of right and wrong, good and evil, the holy and the profane?

We have found each of the alternatives to be untenable, but each one answered to a line of inquiry or concern. What then is the conclusion to which we are driven?

Is it not true that each alternative corresponds to a phase of our nature? The view of God as all-powerful and all-good responds to our religious stance, when the whole of our being is set over against the ground of all existence. The concept of God as limited but good reflects our quest for the good. The view of God as the morally indifferent force that runs through all things is the silent assumption of our quest for objective knowledge. In each case, the concept of God is a projection or an extrapolation of an inquiry that begins with man and—however far it advances—cannot reach its goal.

I would suggest, then, that each of our alternative views of God is right in a limited way, right in one of several realms of inquiry and as basic postulates. These lines of inquiry converge in our soul, as the five senses bring their data to our mind. The pursuits of logic, of ethics, and of religion pull us in seemingly divergent directions, disturbing our "peace," for it is man's fate to live in tension and ultimate uncertainty. This does not mean that we postulate three truths, as some medieval scholastics preached the doctrine of "two truths," philosophical and religious. In the latter case, each of the body of truths was absolutely valid. Hence, the theory cannot be sustained. What I am suggesting is not the static coexistence of different kinds of truth, but their dynamic interaction, it being understood that each hypothesis is valid for us, but in a qualified, limited way.

We begin with the religious viewpoint. God is all-powerful and all-good, but not in terms that can be divested of the darkness of mystery. The entire range of creation and the course of human history have their dynamic source in Him. Some things and events are merely His work; other things and events reflect His will. When an artist builds a wall, laying the bricks and the mortar in certain patterns in order to hang a picture on that wall, we can discern a gradation of purpose, the message of the picture being the essence of the artist's will. Even so, there are gradations of purpose in nature and in history. But in the religious mood, we are aware of our finitude and of the infinite mystery of Divine Providence. We sense the presence of that which we cannot grasp in the nature of God, in the relation between His will and His work and even in respect to the nature of our own life; hence, the paradox in the religious stance: it is both possession and privation. It is the assurance of ultimate worth and the deep awareness of total worthlessness. We are like "sheep" putting their trust in their shepherd, but also like "sons," members of His household (Psalm 23).

In this religious realm, the tragedy of the six million is one of the mysteries of Divine Providence. We do not know the nature of life; perhaps life extends into domains of existence where the injustices of this life are somehow balanced. We do not know the mystery of the Divine purposes; perhaps the fulfillment of His will on earth requires a host of sacrifices. We do not know the ultimate sources of evil; perhaps Satan, too, does the work of God in his own perverse way. But with all these dimensions of ignorance, we also have the assurance of the sacredness of human life, of the infinite worth of every individual in His sight, and of the meaningfulness of the human career on the face of the earth. We affirm Him in the spirit of *af al pi ken* ("in spite of it all"), a spirit that every convert to Judaism is expected to possess.*

The "mystery" then is in the nature of Providence and of the human fate. *It is not in the peculiar destiny of the Jewish people.* As the "Chosen People" of our theology and of the Christian world, we exemplify and demonstrate the *all-human* tragedy. We are bidden to read our history not as a *trans-natural current,* coursing through the sea of mankind, but as a demonstration of the human predicament. We consider ourselves to be "chosen," in the self-same way we consider other communities to be similarly "chosen," namely, by way of dedicating ourselves to the service of God. We are chosen as an example, not as an exception: *B'ni b'khori Yisroel* ("my eldest son, Israel").

---

*"Shulhan Arukh," Yore Dea, Hilchot Gerim

In this sense, the six million died for the sanctification of the Name of God, the God of all mankind. And the mystery of their martyrdom is not the "peculiar treasure" of the Jews, but the inescapable challenge to the emergent conscience of humanity.

This basic meaning of the Jewish tragedy is to be illuminated by the other two approaches that I have described.

First, God is all-good but He is not a physical force. Whatever be the documents and the events of revelation that we accept, we cannot but insist that the ethical imperative *is* the will of God. We dare not so treat rite, myth, and dogma as to blur His revelation in the conscience of men and women, when they are in a position to be impartial and fair. In fact, the greatness of Judaism has consisted precisely in the fact that it did not allow the myth and magic of ancient times to distort its vision of the good, as the one invariable purpose of God.

In our rapidly changing times, it is particularly necessary to recognize certain unchanging ramparts. Fast as we may move, we cannot be catapulted beyond the standards of "good and evil." No "leap" in the dark, be it in the name of religion or nationalism or some other ism, can ever carry us beyond its reach.

The conviction that a Divine purpose does not inject itself in human affairs is also inescapable, when we set ourselves the task of investigating the actual nexus of events in history. As men of reason, we assume the permeability of all events to the light of reason. There are no transcendent domains, certainly no transcendent people in whole or in part. When we ask the question "How did it actually happen?" we shatter all mystical barriers and shun all subjective valuations. We then become single-minded Spinozists, monks, who renounce all that is their own in their total surrender to the spell of events as they are. Absolute truth may never be reached, but truthfulness in our search for truth is itself a religious imperative.

The religious approach is an attempt to bring together the

270

two quests of our spirit, for truth and for goodness. Both are infinite in reach, moving independently of one another. Yet they are one in their ultimate essence. This is our faith, for God is the ultimate source and the final purpose of both quests.

Was not this, too, the deeper meaning of our ancient sages when they spoke of the two Names of God—Elohim and YHVH? The first had the same numerical significance as nature (*teva*). It represented God as the author of the invariant laws of existence (*midat hadin*). The other reflected His Being as it appeared in the conscience of our great men, our patriarchs and prophets. Its chief quality is compassion (*midat harahamim*) or steadfast love (*hesed*). Our sages were not unaware of the polar tension between the two aspects of the Divine Being; they questioned how Moses could conjoin His truth and His abundant, steadfast love (*rav hesed veemet*). But they insisted, in the intensity of their faith, that these two realms of the Life of Spirit were ultimately one. We can do no less.

What then is the conception of God that emerges from our discussion? It is not the concept of a supernatural being, manifested in miracles, in arbitrary revelations, and in mythical flights of fancy. Such a concept is discontinuous with His revelation in conscience, in intelligence, or in our quest for harmony and peace. Neither is it simply the concept of one who is immanent here and now in all that makes for righteousness. Half of religious feeling is the recognition of the insufficiency of the world as it is. He must be ultimate and supreme in being as well as in value. Hence, He is transcendent to the three quests of the human spirit, even as He is immanent in them. They reach out to Him and merge in the mystery of His nature.

"I am first and I am last"—God is within us as the driving power of spirit, which divides into the three quests of the true, of the good, of the holy, and He is also without us as the Ultimate Being, in whom all spiritual yearnings find their fulfillment.

Part Four
Dialogue with Secular Ideologies

MASS-CRIME AND THE
JUDEO-CHRISTIAN TRADITION*

It was a radical rebellion against the Judeo-Christian tradition that made possible the great atrocities of our time. The brutality of the Bolsheviks toward their nobility, peasantry, and later the deviationist elements in their own party, shocked the civilized world. The trampling of human rights by the Fascists was not openly anti-Christian. But when the Fascists began their Ethiopian adventure, intervened in the Spanish Civil War, and reached their final culmination in an alignment with the Nazis, their frank repudiation of the Christian ethic could hardly be denied. Nazism, officered by the "blonde beasts" of the SS, with its extermination camps, *Einsatzgruppen,* and its ambition to enslave the masses of mankind, carried the banner of "positive Christianity" for a long time.

Hitler succeeded in fooling major sections of the Protestant and Catholic faith by his presumed hostility to communist "materialism" and "Jewish" capitalism. Today, the bitterly anti-Christian animus of the Nazi ideology is clear and indisputable.

Nevertheless, we must confront the shocking fact that these three ideologies of violence arose out of the soil of the Judeo-Christian tradition. Our problem is not solved either by castigating "sin" in general or by analyzing the particular manias and phobias of Hitler and Stalin. So infinite are the possibilities of human nature that almost any individual monstrosity is conceivable. But the degeneration of a people proves the decay of an entire culture. In Fascism, Nazism, and Bolshevism alike, a rich religious culture formed the matrix for the revolutionary philosophy of ruthless brutality.

*Reprinted from *The Minnesota Review*, Winter 1963.

Each of these revolutionary movements was essentially a rebellion against the Judeo-Christian tradition. Yet, this is not the way things looked to the people. Rebels can no more liberate themselves from the total impact of their tradition than people can jump out of their skins. Mass-movements can be set in motion only by well-known popular motifs. Even when a people rebels against some elements of its tradition, it continues much of the impetus and some of the outer context of its collective heritage. In a real sense, communism, Fascism, and Nazism are *heresies* of the Judeo-Christian culture of the West, to use a Toynbeean phrase. The communist heresy substitutes its utopia for the Kingdom of God, its concept of historical materialism for the guidance of Providence, its commissars and party line for the Church and the apostolic succession. Fascism and Nazism, worshiping Caesar and Wotan, made use of the symbols and dogmas of the Church, though they stabbed at its very heart. They bettered the example of communism, retaining the outer façade of religion but suborning it to their own purpose.

Can it be that the Judeo-Christian tradition itself contains the dragon's teeth which have given rise to the moral monstrosities of our age? If so, it is essential to recognize the germs of disaster before it is too late.

To begin with, we need to take account of the fact that mass-ideas carry their own momentum. A constellation of such ideas in one ideological context may be broken up, with the consequent dissolution of some ideas, while the rest of the constellation is eventually incorporated into another context. The best example is the mythology of ethnic anti-Semitism, which incorporated the mass-myth concerning the Christ-denying Jews into the context of an Arian, God-denying faith. The gods and the sacraments changed, but the demon and the scapegoat-offering remained the same. It is easy enough to find Gentiles who disbelieve that Jesus ever lived but who still assert that the Jews killed him, or Jews who disbelieve in a God who chooses, but still assert that they are the Chosen People. Mass-ideas, like floating icebergs are only partially exposed to reason. Evidently, the Judeo-Christian galaxy of myths and ideas contains elements that can be dissociated and recombined into ideologies of violence. Let us list the components of the Western religious tradition.

Most scholars rank the belief in the sanctity of the individual as the chief component of the Judeo-Christian tradition. This idea goes back to the Hebrew doctrine of man being made in the image of God and to the Hellenic doctrine concerning the divinity of the human soul. As Henri Frankfort points out in *Before Philosophy,* the Hebrew and Hellenic religious cultures were distinguished by an estimate of the individual which was unparalleled in other cultures. The philosopher in classical Hellas and the prophet in Biblical Israel broke through an encrustation of myth and custom. The philosopher celebrated the quest of the individual for truth. His maxim was either Gorgias' "Man is the measure of all things" or Socrates' "Know thyself." The prophet sought righteousness and holiness. His maxim was either the Mosaic command "Thou shalt love the Lord, thy God with all thy heart" or the precept of Amos, "Seek Me and live."

The second main idea of the Judeo-Christian tradition is the belief in the all-pervasiveness of a Divine law. The law of God is as fundamental in Scriptures as physical law is in our modern world. He who set the sun and the moon in their fixed courses is also the author of the laws which man is commanded to observe in order that "he might live by them." In the Hellenic world, the concept of an immanent law of reason was proclaimed by the Stoics and elaborated by Roman jurists. In the Western tradition, this concept of a "natural law," Divine in origin, was the polar complement of the doctrine of the sanctity of the individual. Liberal humanism retains the same polarity, albeit in secular terms. It glorifies man's quest for self-fulfillment and the texture of ideals belonging to humanity as a whole.

In addition to this polarity, the Western tradition contains the tension between the collective conviction of being Divinely

277

chosen and the dedication of a people to the service of mankind. These two ideas are frequently so involved and interwoven that they can be separated only with the greatest difficulty. As polar concepts they imply one another; yet, they can be as far apart as the two poles.

"Chosenness" is the natural pride of a people, transposed into religious terms and projected against the screen of universal history. The whole of humanity becomes the backdrop for the stage on which this one people enacts its Divinely appointed role. The masses of the nonelect are assigned the role of suppliants or disciples, servants or cheerleaders, doomed foes or humbled hangers-on. In any case, they stand in the dark, while the spotlight of history is trained upon the chosen. This belief is rooted deep in the collective psyche of a people, and it is perennially reinforced by its public ceremonies and standard rhetoric.

While the Chosen People doctrine is rooted in the Hebrew Scriptures, it is by no means restricted to Judaism. All Christian denominations reassert it, in many different forms. Every Christian group believes itself to be "Israel after the Spirit," the heir of the promise and the blessing. The classical Hellenes, with their contempt for the uncouth barbarians, added their peculiar tang to the quality of this Western faith. All the faiths of the Western world nourish the peculiar pride and passion, the dignity and the impetus, the love and the hate which the conviction of being numbered among the elite of God brings to the soul of man.

Dedication to the service of mankind is a rational Judeo-Christian ideal, accepted in the broad light of day. Mankind in all its variety is taken as the frame of reference, determining the areas and forms of service. In the light of these human needs and ideals, the destiny and vocation of each nation or religious community may then be assessed. Each group ought to render the particular service in which it is most competent at any one time and in respect of the needs of others. But no eternal covenant is made with any people that it might monopolize a specific vocation for all time. Humanity and its ideals are the enduring realities, while in the flux of history, nations and communities fulfill now one role, now another. In this pattern of thought, the permanent reality is the universal structure of values, and every historic group is the object of judgment, not the source of judgment.

Whereas both "chosenness" and humanism are components of the Western tradition, the former is the sentiment of the masses while the latter is the ideal of the intelligentsia. Such a differentiation is virtually inevitable, since mass-feelings have high momentum, while the advance of thought is slow, painful, and restricted to the few. In the Hellenistic tradition, the elite thinkers were the Stoic philosophers, who reinterpreted the myths of religion and expounded the goals of national life in terms of service to humanity. In the Hebraic tradition, a similar function was performed by the classical prophets, who combated the myths of ethnicism as well as the follies of idolatry. If the philosophers were more intellectualistic than the prophets, the latter were more intensely moralistic. It is as important for would-be prophets to subject their fervor to the scrutiny of reason as it is for philosophers to temper their intellect in the fire of an alert social conscience. In any case, the Judeo-Christian prophets and the Hellenic philosophers fulfilled the same function in society, clarifying the import of universal idealism and rebuking the proponents of mass-religion and mass-ethnicism.

What is it that the modern ideologies of violence have in common? The brutality which they evince is not primitive, animal-like, naïve, and unself-conscious. It is a complex *Weltanschauung* in which the following ideas seem to predominate:

1) The concept of a *transrational* law, governing the course of human affairs. In the case of communism, the commitment to an irrational law of becoming is not obvious at first glance. Do not the Marxists regard themselves as the proponents of "scientific socialism"? Indeed, the word "science" carries in their vocabulary the occult overtones of a mystical revelation. Inas-

much as they take the rational processes of man to be epiphenomena, by-products of a deeper current of being, they look beyond reason for the understanding of society. The great obstacle to mutual understanding between the communist and the noncommunist worlds is precisely this scorn for objectivity. Communists do not agree that human beings can be trusted to think truthfully and to judge honestly, regardless of their class interest. Their basic argument is directed *ad hominem* to all who are nonproletarians—hence, their suspicion of all neutral commissions and their resentment of any world court; hence, too, their refusal to be drawn into a genuine dialogue, where they might be forced to emerge from behind the ramparts of their inwardly consistent dialectics. Reason, for them, is the froth on the surface of the heaving tides of economic forces; these social forces in their turn are massive and impersonal, impelled by an immanent "law," as inexorable as gravitation and equally as indifferent to human weal or woe.

A similar transrationality lies at the base of Mussolini's Fascism. The adoration of the power of the state and of the glories of the nation was justified on the ground of a collective instinct, as it were. Essentially, Fascism was a reaction against the rational values of liberalism and the materialistic dialectic of Marxism. To the liberals, individual man is the focus of all values; to the socialists, the advancing proletariat is the source of all truth and genuine productivity. Against these axiomatic starting points, Fascism set up the nation as the "natural" unit, in terms of which individual concerns, class-interests, and all-human ideals are "disruptive." And the "nation" is not the product of a "social compact," molded by a confluence of comprehensible ideas and identifiable sentiments, but it is a metalogical entity. Its will is the supreme law; morality and intelligence are the black lifeless lava of the elemental volcanic surge of the nation's vitality.

The transrational source of "law," in Nazism, is the factor of race. For centuries, Teutonic pride has been at work building up a glorious "self-image." The translation of Tacitus' work on the ancient Germans at the beginning of the sixteenth century was a milestone in the romantic emergence of nationalism. It was taken to be an accurate description of a guileless and sinless people, instead of a visionary glorification of a primitive race. Already Luther could base the success of his Protestant movement upon the mighty rock of Teutonic pride. But it was the Romantic movement of the early nineteenth century that virtually produced all the component elements of German racism. Pre-eminent among these was the resentment of reason in social life as the source of evil. The rationality and egalitarianism of the French Revolution resulted from the "conspiracy" of the French and the Jews against the Germanic world. Schleiermacher, the great theologian of the Romantic movement, did not hesitate to condemn the English, the French, and the Russians, along with the Jews, as being incapable of sensing the reality of the Divine. Fichte divided mankind into two categories—those of *Vernunft*, who know truth and righteousness intuitively, and those of *Verstand*, who are fated to grasp vainly at the empty charade of appearance. Naturally, again, the Jews and the Frenchmen were pre-eminently people of *Verstand*, while the awkward, stolid, seemingly dull Teutons were in reality those in whom the transrational "reason" of the cosmos was revealed.

It is easy enough to trace the self-laudatory phrases of the ideologists of *Deutschtum* throughout the nineteenth century and on into the muddy waters of Nazism. We can see the architects of this philosophy at work, evolving "myths" and promptly embracing them in "faith." For to believe "because it is absurd" is to the mystics of ethnicism proof of racial "purity," as a similar capacity was to St. Paul and Tertullian proof of the operation of the Holy Ghost. There is Hegel, now viewing the entire cosmos from the detached viewpoint of an Olympian sage, now asserting with a straight face that the Prussian State is the final "revelation" of the world-idea and believing it too. Gobineau began his massive work with the frank intention of glorifying the Teutonic race in order the better to condemn French democracy; in dutiful piety, he came to have "faith" in his own myth. There is Wagner, the myth-creator, with his "heroes" and his ax-wielding forest- and mountain-gods, disavowing anti-Semitism in his sane moments, but whenever the racist frenzy took hold of him, preaching that the Jew is the "plastic demon of the decline of mankind." There is Treitschke with his "philosophy" of Germanism, consciously built up to promote unity, and Chamberlain hailing the twentieth century as the time when the German dream will be fulfilled. And always anti-Semitism is interwoven with the myth of Teutonic superiority, for if there are "supermen," must not "sub-men" be there to balance the picture? And if the "supermen" are the bearers of the new revelation from the ancient Teutonic gods, should not the "sub-men" be those who bear the old revelation in their blood? And if the Gospel of love needed a Satan to fight against, how much more did the gospel centering on the "will to hate"?

2) Along with the concept of a transrational law, the ideologies of violence assert that an *existential precondition* is needed for the apprehension of this supreme reality. In their normal or "corrupt" state, human beings are incapable of recognizing this transrational Reality. They must "awaken" (*Deutschland erwache!*), for the rational consciousness puts the occult primitive passions of the nation into a state of sleep. People must "die" to their old ways, recognizing the vanity of rational and moral values, in order to be "reborn" to the new way of thinking. In this view, all rational discussion and debate is beside the point. The "unredeemed" may be "prayed into" one's ideological communion, or "clobbered into" it, or lured to it by stirring spectacles and torchlight parades. Between the believers and the unbelievers, there can be at best only a state of "cold war," in which people talk at each other, not to each other. And "little wars," strikes, riots, street brawls, are but so many rehearsals for the big war. Reason is not a universal faculty of all men, providing the common ground of mutual understanding and conciliation; it is but an instrument, capable of serving either the corrupt intellect or the glorious transrational faculty. To reason

is to shoot pellets of ideas into the brains of the opposition. Normal reasoning, such as is common to all men, is a "Jewish," or a "French," or an "English" technique of propaganda. The "authentic" ideologist consults his "feelings" and does not permit the paltry considerations of mere reason to influence either his actions or his beliefs.

This insistence on an irrational, ecstatic path to a self-contained realm of truth is obviously common to all these ideologies of violence. The communists assert that workers must become "conscious" of the dialectics of the social process. Intellectuals have to be converted; they are always liable to be persuaded by the logic of the situation and to stray from the curving pathways of the party line. From the Stalinist viewpoint, Jewish intellectuals were especially suspect since they tended to think in "cosmopolitan," all-human terms. The successive blood-purges of the Stalin era, which convulsed Soviet society with ever-mounting agony, were, on this basic assumption, absolutely essential for the preservation of the one saving truth. Since those who deviate, however little, from the party line cannot be persuaded to alter their opinions, they must be eliminated. "'All who enter in it do not return'—that is heresy," says the Talmud. The truth is one and exceedingly "jealous;" any departure, be it ever so tiny, proves that the person is no longer attuned properly. It is therefore "right" to anticipate the future and to judge opponents as if they were already traitors.

Mussolini's Fascisti introduced "persuasion by violence" into the politics of Central Europe. His goons would administer castor oil to their opponents, proving their point by the suffering of their victims. He set the fashion for the successful suborning of the Church to the foul cynicism of his brutalitarian ideology, utilizing for this purpose the surface similarity of a hierarchical structure of authority and the more significant fact that both the Church and the party possessed common enemies in the spirit of liberalism and in the socialist parties. Mussolini justified his right to leadership on the ground that the true will of the nation can only be discerned by the elite. And those who

283

rally to the call of national greatness prove that their heart is in the right place—they are the elite.

It was left for Hitler to concentrate all the poison in the European body-politic. The transrational reality can only be intuited by those who *think with their blood*—and this blood must be racially pure. With the German penchant for a *Weltanschauung,* no ideology could hope to win which did not contain a "philosophy of history." Gobineau's racial theory, attributing all the gifts of culture to periodic infusions of Nordic blood, was an excellent tonic to ethnic pride. Now the Teutons could again be made to march, devastating the declining West which is the modern replica of ancient Rome, and they could feel that the God of biology was on their side. "Blood-thinkers," they need not be deterred by the considerations of common sense. They could believe *because* it was absurd, and they would believe whatever they were told, as soon as the people of alien race, with their logic and their individualism, were silenced and then exterminated. Those who still thought with their brains could be re-educated in concentration camps where they would be literally shocked into the new consciousness. The capacity to believe the myths of race is itself proof of its own authenticity. Faith, as in religion, marvels at its own steadfastness, even when all the facts are stacked against it. Hitler in his last testament to the German people and Goebbels in his diaries wrote as if they believed the lies that they themselves originated. Strange indeed are the ways of faith, when it is transposed into the key of politics. Violence becomes an act of faith that is self-justifying. Anti-Jewish verbal and physical outbursts fulfill the role of orgiastic exercises ("enthusiasm," in the original meaning of the word, "in God"). Participation in them is a sacred rite, like the festive *autos-da-fé* of Spain.

It is interesting to note that the myth of racial unity did not issue in a call for Aryan, or Nordic, much less European, unity. Its primary import was to intensify German nationalism and to place its imperatives beyond the reach of reason. Hitler found it compatible with his racial conscience to plan the virtual biological extinction of Britain by the removal of its male population, ages fifteen to forty-five; to order the depopulation of vast stretches of Russia; to plan for the annihilation of the entire Polish intelligentsia and the expulsion of half the Czech populace. By any physical standard, the Slavs approximate the Aryan type far more than do the Germans. Yet, all Slavs, by the logic of German nationalism, were to be treated as subhumans. The gypsies, whom Hitler consigned to total extermination, were also an Indo-European race.

The point is that no scientific principle, however unfounded, guided the Nazi mind, but a passionate determination to evolve a self-glorifying myth and then live by it, amending it to the needs of the hour. Here is "existentialist" politics with a vengeance.

American "Know-Nothingism" is an exceedingly mild phenomenon by the side of the European ideologies of violence. It is still completely nested within the Judeo-Christian tradition; yet, the telltale stigmata are quite apparent. "Americanism" is supposed to be a philosophy that grows out of the soil. The "regular" guys who cheer the ballplayers from the grandstand know the right instinctively. Anything that is evil is the importation of "foreigners," and whatsoever is "alien" is evil. The old agricultural myth of the American countryside that represented the city slicker as the archvillain has been transformed only superficially. In urban America, the image of the city slicker has been replaced by the egghead, the liberal, and more particularly, the communist. Senator McCarthy's claim that he could "smell" a communist was entirely in keeping with this mood—hence, his popularity. An undercurrent of anti-Semitism derives from this suspicion of all who have not been fused into the melting pot—in particular because the Jew symbolizes the superego and the intellect in the symbolic imagery of American prejudice.[1]

The very designation of disliked ideologies as "un-American" is an expression of this fundamental axiom that the right ideas spring out of the minds of the right people, those who have attuned their minds to the proper transrational currents of being. Ideological differences are not matters for rational discussion, but reflections of certain kinds of people. Ideas are not so much right and wrong, good and bad, as they are *of* the right or *of* the wrong people, of the good or the bad people. The mass-mind is shy of intellectual distinctions. For it, the decisive question is not "What is right?" but "Who is right?"

3) This point leads to the third component of the "ideologies of violence"—the doctrine of *one* people, or race, or class, being chosen to bear salvation for all mankind. Chosenness, as we have seen, is a peculiar complex of altruistic motivations superimposed upon collective egotism. But while the altruistic ideals refer to a distant future, the drives of self-exaltation apply to the here and now. Hence, an immense impetus may be generated by the mobilization of mass-enthusiasm through the arts of self-glorification, while all qualms of conscience are silenced by the official bows of the leadership toward the hazy utopia at the end of the rainbow. The very splendor of the idealistic vision lends wings to the ruthlessly selfish campaigns of the present. How can anyone criticize the evils of today, however harrowing they be, if the nation's policy is designed to eventuate in happiness and blessedness for all?

The idea of being chosen by a transrational being in order to bring happiness to the future society of mankind may be divided into two component elements—the notion of one's group being superior to others, and the notion of the group being dedicated to the service of mankind. These two components are by no means mutually exclusive; it is the pattern of their union that is decisive. The first notion is one that is generally meant when the doctrine of the Chosen People is stigmatized as "collective egotism." But in itself this doctrine is as generally human as it is usually harmless. All tribes and nations believe themselves to be superior to the generality of mankind. Even the most primitive societies observe moral laws, which, however, are limited to those who belong within their closed society. The alien and the outsider are, to primitives, fair game.

The primitive nation is not generally harmful precisely because it is so obviously primitive. In the broad vistas of the modern world, primitive nationalism can hardly assert itself without ridicule. While nations may build up glorious self-images in their elementary textbooks, they tone down the bold colors on the high-school level. By the time the intelligentsia achieves its world-view, the egotistical image is generally reduced to the point where the rest of humanity may live with it.

Chosenness becomes a problem for humanity because it combines idealism and egotism. This synthesis protects the popular belief from the solvent effects of criticism. A whole people can rarely be moved to action by egotistical appeals—however flattering. But when idealism as well as egotism are blended together and conjoined in a crusade on behalf of all that is glorious, an irresistible appeal is generated. Yet, the humanistic component may well be relegated to rhetoric and window-dressing, while the egotistical impulses are indulged far beyond the dreams of a primitive cannibal. Such a complex of motivations is contained in the three ideologies of violence.

In the Bolshevik movement, the proletariat is in theory chosen by the inner forces of history to bring about the millennium. In practice, the Communist party considers itself to be the one authentic representative of the proletariat. Those who join the party are taught to feel that they are in step with the "Power, not ourselves, making for righteousness." And those who are not with it are against the irresistible forces of the unfolding future. At the same time, the chosenness of the proletariat is not intended in theory to create a master class but a "classless society," in which all the evils of the bourgeois world will disappear. Thus the Communist parties in the non-Communist world were able consistently to exact terrific sacrifices from their adherents. Fanatical monks, demanding much from themselves, invariably demanded much from others. Communists did not hesitate to condemn immense masses to starvation or to sacrifice millions of people to the advancing juggernaut of partisan politics. Seeing the events of the passing day against the total panorama of the distant future, they could not but allow little weight in their calculations to the actual sufferings of living people. Of what worth is the passing hairline of the present against the vast infinity of the future?—hence, the Stalinist contempt for the agonies of mere people. The catch, of course, lies in the fact that the future as a whole is beyond the bounds of anyone's knowledge. And the immediate future grows out of the momentary present, with evil means leading to evil ends.

Indeed, all forms of romantic nationalism in nineteenth-century Europe included the peculiar paradox of chosenness—all were dedicated to the "saving of mankind" and all set the "liberation" of their own people as the indispensable precondition for that longed-for salvation. So, to Mickiewicz, the Poles were more than a nationality; they were a Messiah-people, with the promise and the blessing for humanity certain to come from the agonies of the Polish soul. So, to Dostoevski, the Russians were the Chosen People, destined to repudiate the shallow superficialities and the deep corruptions of the West. And the more exalted the high ideals and the noble vocation of these chosen peoples, the more they felt justified in suppressing the "lesser breeds without the Law."

As to Nazism, the paradoxical complex of chosenness was so potent within it because its roots in romantic nationalism were nourished and cultivated for many generations. The opening phrase of the national hymn echoes a widespread popular conviction: *"Deutschland, Deutschland über alles."* And the maxim *"Am Deutschen Wesen wird die Welt genesen"* ("the world will be healed by the character of the Germans") is as well-known as the shout of the Hitlerite crowds, "Today Germany is ours, tomorrow the world."

The Nazi purpose to establish a "New Order" throughout the world was not merely a slogan but a detailed plan, the initial stages of which were put into operation in all the conquered lands. The "racial" policies, which are now increasingly regarded as the peculiar aberrations of Hitler and his henchmen, are actually logical, if perverted and brutalized, developments of romantic German nationalism.

4) The fourth "religious" component of the ideologies of violence is the axiom of *absolute* distinction between the "redeemed" and the rest of mankind. In life, all distinctions are gradual and overlapping. No reasonable policy is either radically right or radically wrong. As long as we move within the realm of common sense, the gray realities of human life check the wild flights of philosophers and impose an empirical balance upon conflicting theories. In these circumstances, the strife of politics is moderated and restrained. Those who win attain only a fleeting, relative, mild victory, and those who lose the election retain the power to win another day.

In the ideologies of violence, the absolutism of fundamentalist religion, with its unyielding polarity between the "saved" and the "damned," the "sheep" and the "goats," enters into the domain of politics. Wide is the road leading to hell and many do follow it, but narrow is the road leading to heaven and few walk in it. For these twentieth-century quasi-religions, heaven and hell are here on earth—but they are still matters of faith. Those who are right are so utterly and without reservations, and those who are wrong are dead wrong. In fact, the "deviationists" are not merely wrong, they are dehumanized, no longer entitled to the merest human decencies, condemned even before they are tried.

Lenin, not Stalin, penned these words: "We repudiate all morality that is taken outside human class concepts. We say that this is deception, a fraud which clogs the brains of the workers and peasants in the interests of the landlords and capitalists."

It was also Lenin who set the pattern for that incredible intolerance which Stalin later perfected into a system: "The Mensheviks say, 'We have always said what you are saying now; permit us to repeat it again' . . . we say in reply: 'Permit us to put you up against the wall.'"

Fascism and Nazism adopted the same basic attitude, directing their fury at all who deviated from their dogmas. Ostensibly "anticommunist," they would not and could not recognize any of the mediating positions in the political spectrum. All parties, other than their own, were not just partly wrong, but altogether "damned." And those "who were led by Providence," in Hitler's terminology, remained forever immaculate and "unspotted of the world," even while they waded in the blood of innocents.

Manifestly, the four facets of the ideologies of violence correspond to the four essential principles of the Judeo-Christian tradition. When we extol the benign influence of this tradition in the evolution of Western democracy, we refer to the conception of a Divine law, supervening above all human legislation; to the capacity of man to reflect the Image of God either by way of faith or by way of obedience to that law; to the doctrine of chosenness, applying to a body of people and reflecting their collective vocation; to the quality of absoluteness that characterizes the Divine will and His judgment. In the latter-day quasi-religions, these ways of thinking persist, albeit in altered, perverted form. Apparently, the ideologies of violence continue the momentum of the Judeo-Christian tradition, its subjective orientation and its structure of sentiment, its pathos and its *élan*, even if the formulation of ideas and their application in practice are so utterly different. *If this is so, then the Judeo-Christian tradition itself must be regarded as an ambivalent heritage, capable of generating the right atmosphere for freedom, under certain conditions, but also of fostering the mythological underbrush of sanctified egotism.*

The resemblance of the communist ideology to a Judeo-Christian faith has long been noted. While the Bolsheviks are bitterly atheistic, their own ideology contains many aspects of an evangelical religion. In the past, communist movements emerged out of the Judeo-Christian tradition—the Essenes in the first century, the early Christian community in Jerusalem, the Anabaptists in the sixteenth century and the monastic orders in both the Eastern and Western branches of Christianity. Historical circumstances imposed an anti-religious mold upon the communist movement, though some observers claim that the stamp of the Greek Orthodox faith is still evident in the structure and operation of the Soviet system.

Fascism and Nazism appeared to many brilliant and sincere clergymen to be "spiritual" movements, "antimaterialistic" rallies for the defense of the faith. The saintly Martin Niemöller hailed the Nazi triumph in 1933 as the end of "fourteen years of darkness" and the beginning of a "national revival."[2] Otto Dibelius, who was to fight against the Nazis at the end of the war, saluted the Hitler triumph in April, 1933, after the first assaults against communists, socialists, liberals, and Jews had already taken place—"In the conviction of the renaissance of nation and Reich . . . the Church expresses its joyful union with the leadership of the new Germany."[3]

The German Evangelical Church, fostered and led by a government appointee, contained the majority of the Protestant pastors. They chimed in with the declaration of Bishop Marahrens, "The National Socialist conception of life is the national and political teaching which determines and characterizes German manhood. As such, it is obligatory upon German Christians also."[4]

The Protestant pastors proved their "Germanhood" by swallowing the doctrines laid down for them—"God's Will reveals itself in German blood . . . True Christianity is represented by the party . . . The Führer is the herald of a new revelation."[5]

Could primitive paganism be stated more frankly? Yet it was not until the tide of battle turned at the end of 1943 that the majority of Protestant pastors found the courage to protest against the annihilation of Jews: "Our people oftentimes regard the sufferings which they must bear from the enemy fliers as retaliation for what was done to the Jews."[6]

Nor was the Catholic Church at all opposed to Nazism in the early years of its triumph. Cardinal Faulhaber, who was to lead the battle against Nazism in later years, thought it right, in 1933, to justify the "anti-Jewish" core of the Nazi *Weltanschauung*, drawing a clear line of distinction between the Jews of B.C. and those of A.D.[7] The Jesuit organ *Civilta Cattolica* followed the Nazi line in 1936, calling for the institution of ghettos, yellow badges, etc. It was only after the Nazi fury was turned full-blast at the Catholic priests and population, that Pope Pius XI declared sadly: "Late, too late have I discovered that the dangers to the Faith do not come only from one side; they come also from the other side. Henceforth, I shall devote what remains of my life to helping my sons partake of this my discovery."[8]

Even so, the death of Pius XI led to the reinstitution of a policy of "neutralism" by his successor, Pope Pius XII, which was terminated only at the end of the war. Even when the Vichy government looked to the Vatican for moral support against Nazi pressure for the delivery of Jews to extermination camps, none was forthcoming. It was only in 1945 that the Pope condemned Nazism in the strongest words as "the arrogant apostasy from Jesus Christ, the denial of His doctrine and of His work of redemption, the cult of violence, the idolatry of race and blood, the overthrow of human liberty and dignity."[9]

The fact remains that subtle and saintly men long regarded both Fascism and Nazism as allies of religion, though both movements articulated their *Weltanschauung* in thousands of pamphlets and speeches, in street riots and at "secret" conclaves that were not hidden from the keenly observant eyes of the Vatican. No greater indictment of religious leadership can be envisioned than the actual demonstration of its blindness to the brutalitarian ideologies of our day—a blindness that was not a temporary aberration but a long, historic phenomenon, being in fact an extension of traditional attitudes.[10]

How explain this phenomenon? I believe that the psychological similarity of the mythological undercurrent in the Judeo-Christian tradition and the pseudoscientific mythology of the Communist-Fascist-Nazi ideologies is the root-explanation. There is the same sinking of individuality into the mass, the same submission to an irrational mystery, the same clinging with desperate fanaticism to a saving myth, the same orgiastic reveling in self-righteous cant, the same unloading of guilt on a luckless scapegoat. Long ago, Émile Durkheim postulated the identity of religious feeling and the sense of solidarity with the herd. Later, Henri Bergson pointed out that Durkheim's observation applied only to one phase of religion—that of the "closed society." As he saw it, prophets and mystics represent a phase of piety, which liberates the person from the spell of the collectivity, breaking the bounds of the "closed societies" and projecting forward the standards and goals of universal humanity. In keeping with the metaphysical context of his thought, he described the mystics as the bearers of a fresh revelation of the *élan vital*.

Apart from its metaphysical encumbrances, Bergson's insight is directly relevant to our discussion. If the mythological piety of a "closed society" provides the fertile soil for the ideologies of violence, the rational piety of the questing individual, facing the mystery of being in all immediacy, provides the antidote. The Judeo-Christian tradition records the travail of prophetic spirits, who represented the "active" moral-rational phase of religion. Within it, we recognize the multiple tensions between the philosopher and the saint, the prophet and the priest. It reflects the recurrent rebellions of the sacred collective egotism of the people against the dedication of great men to ideals transcending their time and place. Prophetic religion and critical philosophy inspired in our day the saintly men and women who resisted the crushing power of totalitarianism. It is to the fortification of *these* elements of our Western faith that all who oppose ideologies of violence should now dedicate themselves.

The classical prophets in ancient Israel transformed the faith of the Judeans and endowed it with marvelous dynamism. Similarly, though less effectively, the philosophers of Greece built up the framework for Western thought. The Judeo-Christian tradition contains the element of mass-faith along with the genius of prophecy and the ferment of philosophy. The ideologies of violence constitute the transposition of primitive mass-faith, minus its prophetic and philosophic components, into the secular terms of politics.

The essence of the prophetic mood is the identification of the Divine will with ethical fervor. Religion was, for the classical prophets, not surrender to a transrational will, but an insistence that the will of God and the voice of conscience are indeed one. While the prophets emerged out of an ecstatic tradition of cultic enthusiasts, they fought for a rational and a humanistic concept of the faith. They excoriated the various nighttime faiths, which reveled in orgiastic frenzy, and ministered to the quest of emotional "peace." They rebuked the reliance of the populace on cleansing rites and lustrations that appealed to the underworld of human nature. For them, religion was not an escape from either reality or rationality, but a daytime dedication to truth and goodness within the vaulting pressures of life. While the source of the Divine imperative is transcendent, its content is spelled out in human, rational, and moral terms. Thus, the prophets condemned myth and magic as well as the excesses of ritualism and ethnicism. Their faith was a dynamic balance between mysticism and rationalism, between humble, trusting piety and arduous, ethical action.

The philosophers of Greece performed a similar function in their attempts to reform popular religion. Xenophon, Socrates, Plato, Anaxagoras—all, in their different ways, sought to purify and to elevate the faith of their contemporaries. Like the prophets', their teaching was essentially a synthesis of contradictory moods. On the one hand, the official rites and the mystery cults retained the allegiance of the populace. On the other hand, the Sophists preached the glory of unrestrained individualism. Protagoras proclaimed the principle "Man is the measure of all things, of things that are that they are, of things that are not that they are not." The Homeric sagas were then so variously interpreted as to be virtually devoid of authoritative guidance. The Athenians had no difficulty reconciling their murderous policy toward the Melians in 416 b.c. with glib references to "the gods." If Moses Hadas was right in phrasing the ethos of *The Illiad* in this maxim "to strive always for excellence, and to surpass all others," then the Sophists represented authentically the latter half of the Homeric spirit. The philosophers, beginning with Socrates, maintained that the heart of reality was somehow one with the heart of the individual, who strives for excellence. In theological terms, man encounters God if he pursues steadfastly the quest for self-knowledge. Plato's judgment of the "golden" age of Pericles exemplifies the prophetic approach: "They have filled the city with harbors and dockyards and tributes and walls, instead of with righteousness and temperance."

The Stoic teachers combined the moralism of the prophets with the rationalism of the classical philosophers, evolving the concepts of humanity, equality, indwelling reason, and natural law. The parallel between the teachings of the prophets and the philosophers was clearly apparent in the first centuries of the Hellenistic era, when Jewish sages and Greek philosophers engaged in dialogues at the Ptolemaic court of Alexandria. Indeed, the legend arose that Plato was a disciple of Jeremiah. The philosophers combatted the crude mythology of their contemporaries by the weapons of reason, while the prophets appealed to man's moral nature; yet, the moral emphasis was strong among the philosophers, just as the prophetic message is essentially rationalistic.

The Judeo-Christian tradition contains both the ethical impetus of prophecy and the rationalistic criticism of philosophy, as well as the tradition of submission in faith to a supervening, transrational, transmoral will, which, in human terms, could well be cruel and even paradoxical.

In the prophetic tradition, Abraham, in Genesis, reasons with God, maintaining that the "Judge of the whole word" cannot but be just, while the impulse of popular religion may be recognized in the command, in Deuteronomy, to annihilate all Canaanites.

If mythological ways of thinking could capture the minds of millions in our day, it is because this dual trend of thought is contained within the religious heritage of the Western world. To be sure, the mythological view of life and history is, within our tradition, balanced by prophetic, ethical, and humanistic ardor and by the restraints deriving from philosophical dedication to the austere canons of objective truth. But, then, much of what passes for religion in our day is devoid of prophetic and philosophic components. It is in effect a reassertion of nighttime faith, reveling in paradoxes and absurdities, preferring the mythological explanation of history as the battleground between the "sons of light" and the "sons of darkness" to any rational confrontation of interlocking causes and ideals.

Goethe remarked, *"Der kleine Gott der Welt ist stets derselbe Schlag"* ("The little god of the world is always of the same stripe"). Popular religion is always likely to sink back into mythology, with its demonic theory of evil and its self-image of a chosen people, with its orgiastic bloodletting, its irrational pieties, its absurd paradoxes, and its quest for scapegoats. The Judeo-Christian tradition imposed the discipline of reason and the ethical fervor of prophecy upon the tides of popular faith.

Our age, however, suffers from an excessive "division of labor" in the domain of the spirit. Our would-be philosophers drift into academic research and instruction, while our would-be prophets enter social work and governmental administration.

All too often, this diversification of effort, profession, and discipline makes it appear that "religion" consists only of the nonprophetic and the nonphilosophical components of the Judeo-Christian heritage. In a world of proliferating specialties, the clergyman and the academician must stand for the vision of the whole, relating the pulsation of the individual's fears and hopes to the accumulated wisdom and moral insight of humanity. Unfortunately, the clergyman in our society is frequently driven to become one of many specialists, a supervisor of liturgy and an administrator of the temple, dealing with the yearnings of men to be shriven of guilt, to resolve all frustrations by a refurbishing of the old myths, to attain "peace of mind" or "peace of soul" by taking a pleasant, accommodating, patriotic god into "partnership," as it were.

This tendency of the clergyman is reinforced by the prevailing posture of academicians and administrators. They, too, seek to carve out domains where the categories of investigation are clear and distinct, extending beyond the campus, unbemused by poetry and faith. Our philosophers are specialists, concentrating on the analysis of words, the involution of ideas in the distant past, and the complexities of symbolic logic. The quest of a synoptic vision of the whole is as rare today as Plato's legendary philosopher-king.

Is it any wonder then that fresh mythologies are again sprouting here? At a well-attended meeting in Long Island, Robert Welch told a seemingly sane, well-dressed, and wildly cheering crowd that "Communism is an evil imposed upon the masses across the world by the millionaire class." He explained his principle of reversal, according to which things are the opposite of what they seem. (It is the "sinners" and the "publicans" that are saved). He asserted that "the United States Supreme Court secretly approves communism." (The first shall be last and the last shall be first.) His villains were the "respectable" leaders of the people, "the Republicans, the Democrats, Earl Warren, urban renewal, the United Nations, and Franklin D. Roosevelt."

The John Birch Society, with its thousands of well-heeled supporters, is still floundering today, for it has not yet discovered the strings of mythology that possess resonance for the American people. But it is a sorry symptom of our age.

If the withering of the prophetic and philosophical components in the Judeo-Christian tradition predisposes the populace to revert to mythological ways of thinking, then we need to call for a reinvigoration of the impetus of prophecy and the discipline of philosophy in our colleges, seminaries, churches, and synagogues. If our philosophers have become specialists and our prophets have gotten lost in a labyrinthine bureaucracy, then we need to return to a vision of the whole. Jerusalem and Athens, Golgotha and Parnassus have their tensions and polarities. But in the face of the tide of primitive barbarism and popular mythology, they must stand together, defending the dynamic equilibrium that is our noblest heritage.

FREEDOM AND THE
JUDEO-CHRISTIAN TRADITION

The term "Judeo-Christian" is a creation of modern sociologists
and historians. It crops up particularly in works dealing with
those elements of Christianity that constitute the source and
inspiration of our culture. In earlier generations, historians would
speak of the Christian faith as the matrix of American or Western
ideals. The change from the use of the term Christian to that
of Judeo-Christian in this context is motivated in part by the
laudable motives of liberals to foster the mood of tolerance and
to reject the implication that Judaism, as a non-Christian faith,
did not in the past contribute to the evolution of Western society
and does not now nourish the roots of our culture. In nineteenth-
century Europe, the "Christian" political parties were pretty
generally closed to Jews, even where they were not distinctly
anti-Jewish. These parties were consciously antiliberal and anti-
socialist, seeking their inspiration in the religious tradition and
the feudal patterns of social conduct that prevailed in pre-
Enlightenment Europe. For them, the very emancipation of
the Jew was associated with the "Goddess of Reason" of
Revolutionary France and the Age of Rationalism. Also, in many
cases, the prevailing Christian faith, be it Lutheran, Catholic,
or Greek Orthodox, was intertwined with the national ethos,
excluding the Jew as an alien by a barrier that was ethnic as
well as religious.

In addition to the repudiation of these negative connotations
of the term Christian in the context of our society, the sociologists who preferred the term Judeo-Christian sought to em-

phasize the rational-universal elements in our spiritual tradition. They would trace our "public philosophy" to the affirmation of our faith in a Supreme Being and His concern for mankind, rather than to the specific dogmas concerning the redemptive power of the blood of the Savior, the role of the Virgin and the potency of the Sacraments. In their view, it was the common tradition of the Church and the Synagogue that generated the ideals of our society, not the distinctive beliefs of diverse denominations, which interposed many divisive and twisted barriers across the face of our nation.

Manifestly, Jewish leaders could only applaud the motives of the social scientists who introduced the term Judeo-Christian into their discussions of the spiritual roots of our society. Yet, even now, many a journalist or rabbi entertains some reservations about the usage of this term. Some writers question whether it stands for any substantial body of ideas. Some would argue that to conjoin Judaism with Christianity is to put together two opposites. Others express the fear that our marginal people might opt for the Christian faith once they were assured that the ethical-social ideals of Judaism are shared, in one form or another, by their Christian confreres. Many of this generation of our people have been brought up to believe that Judaism is not a religion at all, but a "way of life"—whatever that may mean. Our nationalists, according to their several kinds, consider the very comparison of Judaism with Christianity to be a denial of their thesis. The dogmatists of both the religious and the ethnic variety regard it as an axiom that the Jew is "unique," "different," "set apart"; hence, it is "sinful" to speak of common ideas or trends of thought.

We cannot dispute about tastes and desires. Those who yearn with masochistic passion for the status of "aliens" in the West will not be convinced by any discussion of historical trends and sociological studies. Those who believe themselves able to keep from our people the facts, which it is not good for them to know, are living in an obscurantist dream world of their own.

Some three hundred thousand of our boys and girls attend the colleges of our nation every year. In respect to the basic issues of life, they are likely to consult the same authorities as their Christian friends. They are more likely to be familiar with Jefferson, Locke, and Rousseau than with Mendelssohn, Krochmal, and the Vilner Gaon. Their Jewish heritage can be meaningful in their lives only if they are aware of its intimate association with the ideals and sentiments of the Western tradition. Their personality is likely to be fortified by the knowledge that as Jews they are not mendicant suppliants lately come to the fountains of learning, but heirs in body and soul of those who nourished the springs of our common culture. Their Jewish awareness is likely to deepen their sense of at-homeness in American culture and their feelings of fellowship with their Christian neighbors. By the same token, their appreciation of the many cultural and social facets of the Judeo-Christian tradition is likely to enhance their loyalty to the wellsprings of their own faith.

It was only the rare philosopher who, in the Middle Ages, could speak of a Judeo-Christian tradition. Medieval Jews and Christians thought of one another as antagonists. To most Jewish authorities the Christian adoration of icons and the "transsubstantiated" host appeared to be little short of idolatry. It is important to recall that the founders of Protestantism shared the same view. Some medieval rabbis anticipated the view of the Enlightenment. Rabbi Menahem Meiri specifically exempted the Christians from the Talmudic category of pagans, but he represented a philosophical approach that other Talmudists did not share. By the same token, medieval Catholic authorities insisted that "there is no salvation outside the Church" and that Jews were destined for hell. At best, they were destined for endless peregrinations in a shadowy "limbo," along with other unbelievers. Though Judaism was not a heresy to be crushed by the sword, it enjoyed a precarious status of dubious toleration. Every time a prince of the secular realm or of the Church experienced a twinge of his dogmatic conscience, the Jews were likely to be expelled as "enemies of the Lord." To the medieval-ist mind, the Jew was worse than a pagan—he was an adversary of the faith.

This dogmatic hostility was compounded for both groups by a long memory of mutual recriminations and attacks. The popular tales of Lives of Saints abounded in references to Jews as persecutors. The Jews, so it was believed, instigated the riots of the Roman populace against the Christians. They engineered the persecutions that resulted in Christian martyrs being thrown to the lions; they circulated a false gospel portraying Jesus as a sorcerer, scoundrel, and false prophet; they continued to "de-fame" the Savior in their Talmud and to "plot" against Christians in their synagogues. The medieval Jews were totally unaware of the rivalry between the two faiths in the Roman Empire, but in each generation they could cite numberless instances of Christian malice and cruelty.

Indeed, as long as both Christians and Jews stressed the external expressions of their respective faiths, one could hardly speak of a common core of these faiths. However, even in the Middle Ages, there were occasional flashes of rationalism and humanism. Thus, a Maimonides could write of both Islam and Christianity as mediating movements, preparing the world for the true faith. And Halevi could project his famous allegory of the seed and the tree, i.e. Judaism was at once the true seed planted by God and the trunk of the tree that grew from it; Christianity was one massive branch of that tree and Islam was another; when in the fullness of time the fruit produced by both branches will ripen, the seed in the heart of Christian and Moslem fruits will be the same as that grain of Abrahamic faith that God first implanted in the soil of the Holy Land.

The dubious and indecisive victory of rationalism in the nine-teenth century did not result in a recognition of the essential unity of the Judeo-Christian tradition. For the most part, the friends of Jewish emancipation were found among the rational-ists and the skeptics. Few indeed were the clergymen who dared follow the example of Abbé Grégoire, the enlightened

301

champion of the Jews in the period of the French Revolution.

The Jews of Central and Western Europe generally looked to the antireligious liberals for support. On the other hand, Christian thinkers sought aid and comfort in the recurrent waves of romanticism and anti-intellectualism. Politically, the clericalist parties drifted to the extreme right, clinging to the remnants of the *ancien régime*. The use of anti-Semitism as a political weapon was as congenial to the clerical politicians of Greek Orthodox Russia as it was to the antiliberals of Germany during the *Kulturkampf* and to the Catholic Action leaders in France.

The rise of nationalism in the nineteenth century served to blur the image of Judaism as a universal faith. Christian historians were wont to interpret Jewish ideas as peculiar expressions of the Jewish national soul—hence, of no value for mankind generally. In their view, Biblical Judaism began as the private religion of an ethnic group; then, the great prophets introduced the *élan* of a great universal faith, but this universalist faith was encumbered by the Pharisees and by their disciples, the rabbis of the Talmud, with a heavy armor of laws that quenched its light. On this view, the medieval Jews were not the bearers of universal ideas but simply a self-glorifying Chosen People, determined to survive until the coming of their Messiah. The prophetic heritage of Judaism was "fulfilled" in Christianity, while Judaism itself was left to wither on the vine. Judaism survived, but no longer as a universal faith—only as a kind of "sanctified ethnicism."

To be sure, the rise of the Reform movement protested against this perverted picture of Jewish history. The founders of Reform Judaism considered their movement to be a revival of the prophetic tradition. In their view, the prophetic faith was transmitted as well as traduced in both Judaism and Christianity; in Judaism it was overlaid by a network of laws, and in Christianity it was strangled by the interlocking chains of dogma, sacrament, and hierarchy. Some Reform leaders looked forward to the time when both Judaism and Christianity would be

302

divested of their extraneous empty hulks, making possible the emergence of the kernel of faith from the shell of legalism in Judaism and from the encumbrance of dogmatism in Christianity. Then, the prophetic faith would become the universal religion of the West.

Some of the great founders of classical Reform did not realize that the prophetic faith is meaningless, apart from a specific context of communal life and historic tradition. There can be a prophetic emphasis within Judaism and there can be a prophetic emphasis within Christianity, but these emphases become meaningless abstractions if the traditions within which they have arisen are completely negated. The prophetic spirit is a way of dealing with a religious tradition and with a pattern of inherited ethnic loyalties, but it is not itself a disembodied faith. In the light of prophecy, the Law becomes a Divine instrument for the Jew and the sacraments assume a similar function for the Catholic. Without the concrete patterns of faith, prophecy is meaningless.

It was left to the enemies of faith to demonstrate the reality of the Judeo-Christian tradition. Nietzsche, who sought to evolve a supermorality for his supermen, rebelled in beautiful prose against the "slave-morality" of both Judaism and Christianity. While his argument was so involuted and paradoxical as to lead nowhere, he did project the question of whether the age of Darwinism requires a new morality. Since in the world-view of evolution, the standards of perfection are neither in the past nor in an external unchanging realm of ideas, should not the norms of good and evil be related to the requirements of a future presumed state of perfection? This question challenges the central axioms of the Judeo-Christian ethic—the principles of equality and justice, of fraternity and compassion, of gentleness and peace. It introduces a mystique of scientism in place of the ancient mystique of religion. All the subsequent justifications of mass-criminality in the name of a hypothetical "wave of the future" derive their inspiration from Nietzsche. Richard Wagner, who was at one time the idol of Nietzsche and later his *bête noire,* agreed with him on the need of overcoming the Judeo-Christian ethic. But instead of looking to the distant future for inspiration, Wagner harked back to the legends of the early Teutons in the attempt to evolve a new Germanic mythology and Aryan religion.

Not all the prophets of the new racist faiths centered their attacks on the common core of Judaism and Christianity. Most Teutonomaniacs preferred to hide their ideas behind the official façade of Protestant Christianity. They spoke of "positive Christianity," as did Hitler, or of "German Christianity," as did a considerable segment of the Evangelical Church. It is indeed amazing that so discerning a man as Pastor Niemöller could have hailed the coming of the Nazis to power as marking "the end of fourteen years of darkness." Niemöller atoned amply for his early adoration of the modern Satan. He was carried along by the tide of popular emotion. Even today many are fascinated by the curious logic of hate—"the enemy of my enemy is my friend." Since Nazism was the antagonist of communism and the adversary of Judaism, it just had to be pro-Christian!

Today it is clear that the quasi-religions of modern man are arrayed against the central core of the Judeo-Christian tradition. Fascism in the sense of adoration of the totalitarian state or in the sense of nationalism grown radical, ruthless, and intolerant, is certainly as anti-Christian in its essential impetus as it is nearly everywhere openly anti-Jewish. Communism, in its worship of the party and of the process of dialectical materialism that propels it in history, is a quasi-religion that draws no distinction between Judaism and Christianity. Anticommunism of the Know-Nothing, home-grown variety that is rapidly emerging as a quasi-religion, with a twisted mythology all its own, has already begun to undermine the faith of the people in Protestant preachers and Jewish rabbis. It bids fair to confront thinking Americans with some searching questions concerning the ambivalence of popular religion and popular patriotism.

The "public philosophy" of our democratic society contains certain basic convictions that are essentially antithetical to the quasi-religions of communism, fascism, and Know-Nothingism. Our world-view is not one faith, but a wide spectrum of faiths, teaching certain basic affirmations. This American spectrum ranges from humanism to liberal orthodoxy. It is the heir of the European religious tradition, but also of the rationalistic movements that refined that tradition by passing it through the fires of criticism. The patterns of freedom can prevail only within a fairly balanced field of tension. This tension is itself the noblest quality of the European religious tradition. The polarity of humanism and religious faith generates a dynamic equilibrium, in which freedom grows and flourishes.

Did not democracy arise in Europe only after such an equilibrium was established? In the medieval world, islands of freedom floated precariously across the waves of fanaticism wherever conflicting sources of authority generated a temporary balance. The humanism of the Renaissance and the conflicts of the Reformation made possible the partial neutralization of dogmatic faith and the consequent emergence of the era of Enlightenment. Amidst the tension between the fanaticism of faith and the lure of the new rational ideal, the spirit of democracy was born, first in England and then in France. The glorious ideals of the French Revolution nearly died aborning because the revolutionaries tended to turn reason itself into an idol. The fortunes of freedom trembled in the balance as soon as either brand of fanaticism threatened to achieve total dominance. In the two centuries that have elapsed since the European "enlightenment," the dominant circles of Western religion have come to accept a measure of rational criticism as part of their own being. The liberal emphasis within religion has become fairly well entrenched in Western Europe and in America, save for certain islands of fanaticism where the fundamentalist spirit still reigns supreme.

It is to be hoped that the quasi-religion of communism will not take two centuries to soften its brand of fanaticism. Already voices are heard behind the Iron Curtain calling for the recog-

305

nition of the mystery and the sanctity of the individual. In any case, the banishment of the ghost of Stalin will not of itself establish the patterns of freedom in the Soviet system. The collective devotion of a society must be molded and directed in keeping with the structure of authority prevailing within it. Since in communist doctrine, the individual is denied intrinsic authority, the enthusiasm of the society must be directed to the governing elite.

Popular religions inevitably degenerate into "personality cults" —witness the glorification of heroes in mythology, the veneration of messiahs, old and new, the deification of the Roman emperors, the worship of saints in medieval Europe, and the adoration of the Führer in the first cult spawned by racist scientism.

The communists will find their way back to Western society when they learn to balance their monolithic doctrine with an affirmation of the ultimate sanctity of the individual.

What is the "public philosophy" of democratic society? Nearly everyone will agree that the doctrine of the sanctity of the individual forms its central core. Religionists will quote Genesis, "in the image of God created He him."[1] They might also quote the Declaration of Independence. While the framers of the American Constitution, notably Madison and Hamilton, were aware of the manifold evils imbedded in human nature, they were also convinced of the possibility of countering these tendencies and developing man's infinite potentialities for good.[2] The Magna Charta of Britain and the Bill of Rights of the American Constitution stand out as landmarks of freedom and the rights of the individual. When we come to the threefold slogan of the French Revolution, liberty, equality, and fraternity, we notice that the third ideal certainly contains implications that limit the range of the first one, and that the second ideal might also contain such connotations. Since human beings are born with unequal talents, the ideal of brotherhood imposes obligations upon the swift runners to assist those who falter in the race, and the ideal of equality might be so construed as to imply the obligation to maintain an artificial equality over and against the inequality of nature.

Manifestly, the sanctity of the individual cannot by itself constitute an adequate philosophy for any organized society. Its logical result would be sheer anarchy. The very term sanctity implies the existence of a structure of norms and values supervening above the individual. Thus, we actually have a polarity between the individual and a universal realm of law. The rule of law could be identified either as Divine, natural, or rational. In all cases, it is this normative focus that balances the emphasis on the individual in democratic society.

The history of freedom in the West could be written in terms of this polarity. Whenever the inalienable sanctity of the individual monopolized public attention, the ideal government was believed to be the one that governs least. But then man's responsibilities toward his fellow man were neglected, and there resulted grave inequalities of fortune that tormented the conscience of the citizen. The shift of the pendulum of public opinion toward the focus of the all-embracing law inclines the scales toward the goal of the "welfare state." It is easy to see that this emphasis can lead to the steady attrition of the rights of the individual and his freedom. It is always in the name of a "higher law" or a "greater good for the greatest number" that the rights of the individual are abridged.

As a matter of fact, the prevalence of any one philosophy or religious tradition is virtually certain to lead to tyranny, for in embodying a set of norms that are inwardly consistent, it inevitably releases an all-consuming leviathan that leaves no room for the free individual.

If the law is conceived as the word of God, then the ecstatic mystic or the fanatical priest is its font on earth; if the law is viewed as the operation of reason in society, then only the legal scholar can interpret it; if the law is that of an organic body, then the charismatic Führer can best sense it; if the law is that of a machine, then the technocrat is the master. In no case can there be room for the individual's free choice. On the basis of

307

any such monolithic principle, freedom can only mean the freedom to submit to the supreme law of existence. This semantic satisfaction did in fact please many scholastic and modern philosophers, but it is actually a poor substitute for political and social freedom.

We know that when a religious tradition is fully dominant and consistent, the individual is forced to conform in mind and body. This is as true of ancient Judaism as of Calvinist Geneva, of Catholic Spain as of Communist Russia. Nor are philosophers far behind religious fanatics, for any self-enclosed system is easily perverted to the uses of tyranny. In Plato's Republic, there could be no freedom for the vast majority. In Rousseau's conception, the "general will" of the community—that which most or all would want if they clearly knew their own minds and their total interests—could in actuality be represented by a small group of elite. Robespierre sincerely believed that he was not a tyrant but an executor of the "general will." Similarly, in Hegel's political theory, a "world-historical" figure may well represent the unfolding idea of reason, even as he sets out to destroy the freedom of everybody else in the state. Hitler, we are told, consciously modeled himself after Hegel's "world-historical" figure.

The doctrine of "natural law," which is adumbrated in the Declaration of Independence, could serve as a liberating force only when it was set against the conflicting tradition of political "legitimacy." In itself it could be used to justify diverse enormities such as slavery, feudalism, the right of conquest, the prohibition of moneylending on interest, etc. Even today, the Catholic Church regards contraception devices as contrary to "natural law."

In sum, freedom prevails only when a dynamic tension extends between the individual and a supervening law. Both sides of this polarity are anchored in a dark and impenetrable mystery —the unknowable individual and the inconceivable source of the universal law. Various syntheses of these two polarities are embodied in the several traditions of the Western world, some emphasizing the inviolate sanctity of the individual, others stressing the all-encompassing law. Freedom thrives best when these traditions are mutually balanced and maintained in a dynamic equilibrium.

Western democracy arose as a result of the challenge presented to the religious traditions by the rising spirit of humanism. Both the religious and the humanist traditions contained an uneasy balance between universal law and the individual's conscience, but this balance was heavily weighted on one side or the other. The humanists opposed the law of reason to the laws of the Church, and the judgment of the rational individual to the concept of the Divine soul implanted in man. This opposition restored the state of equilibrium in Western society. Neither dogmatic faith nor secular humanism by itself would have produced the kind of ordered freedom that prevails in a democracy. Auguste Comte, the French philosopher, sociologist, and founder of modern positivism, revealed in his utopia, *System of a Positive Polity*, the frightening image of a society based on mathematical logic. Comte's utopia was closer to a Stalinist society than to a democracy. Yet, it was patterned after the Catholic Church, with a hierarchical priesthood that was superior to temporal authority, with a positivist catechism, a series of sacraments, and even a calendar of saints. Only instead of God, there was to be worshiped the Great Being— i.e. humanity, past, present, and future.

The rule of reason, abstract and absolute, is inevitably tyrannical and hierarchical, whether the dialectical process be conceived *à la* Marx, Comte, or Hegel. By the same token, every fundamentalist faith imposes shackles upon the human spirit. But when the two traditions are sustained in a state of mutual criticism and opposition, the spirit of democracy comes into being.

The humanist emphasis is itself only the temporary and fragile by-product of the clash of two religious or quasi-religious traditions. What can the preciousness of the totality of human nature mean? We do not confront a situation where human life is in competition with physical nature. If human life is "sacred," it is so in the context of comparison with human values, such as freedom, prosperity, or equality. The "sacredness" of human life can only mean the assertion that all human ideals are of relative significance in comparison with human life itself. But humans have not hesitated to advocate revolution and war in order to attain the goals of freedom. In a deeper sense, humanism is not an independent faith but a protest against the abuse of an established faith. In the sense of a preference for man's higher values, humanism is manifestly part of a metaphysical system, ensconcing those values either in an eternal "realm of ideas" or in the will of God.

Apart from such metaphysical anchorage, either in theology or in Platonism, humanism is a truncated philosophy depending on the spiritual residue of a religious tradition. Hence, it appears as a massive popular force only when a broad no-man's-land extends between conflicting traditions.

Thus the spiritual roots of our "public philosophy" go back to the conflicting religious traditions of the Western world and to the humanist philosophy generated by this clash.

These roots are (1) the sanctity of the individual, transcending reason, and (2) the universal law of God, understandable by reason.

To this polarity, we may now add a third element—not a principle or an idea, but a mood or a method, recognizing creative tension as the cutting edge of man's spirit in its quest for the fullness of truth. From the side of religion, this is the mood of the prophet purifying his faith in the light of its human and universal intent. From the side of secular life, this is the calm insight of the philosopher who rises above the partiality and relativism of our contemporary intellectual-moral judgments. Both prophecy and philosophy imply the vision of expanding horizons and the courage to explore them.

The role of classical prophecy in the evolution of Judaism is variously understood. The prophets certainly differed on many significant issues. As a class, they worked within a religion and advanced it to new levels. Mystics, in the sense of feeling the immediate presence of the Divine, they were yet rationalists, in the sense of identifying the call of God with the voice of reason and with a humane conscience; they rose beyond the forms of faith by virtue of experiencing the direct pulsation of a living faith.

Another side of ancient prophecy impinges directly upon the secular-political concerns of our society. The prophets transcended ethnicism as well as ritualistic formalism, and ethnicism is the all-pervasive idolatry of our time. In many diverse forms, the bias of ethnicism is expressed in the tendency to exalt and to glorify the interests, policies, and aspirations of the nation or the state. People tend to idealize their collective interests, to forget the heavy, earthy underside of their national policies, and to see only the flattering sheen of the surface. They are perennially tempted to treat relative balances of good and evil as "pure" issues between God and the Devil. Overlooking the limitations of time, place, and circumstance, they see absolute truths and eternal distinctions where only the gray ambiguities of human existence are to be found. The prophet's bold vision and the philosopher's calm objectivity resist this popular perversion, restoring the dynamic, creative equilibrium of our Western tradition.

Returning now to the task of nourishing the spiritual roots of Western democracy, we note that the Judeo-Christian tradition is an apt term for that turbulent heritage, with its multiple tensions, that provided the fertile soil for the emergence of the fragile plant of democracy. Within the Jewish tradition itself, the free flowering of the democratic spirit was constantly threatened by legalistic rigidities and ethnic exclusiveness. Within Christianity, mystical other-worldliness, exaggerated sentimentality, and dour dogmatism were easily capable of quenching the gentle light of a humanistic society. But Judaism and Christianity are prone to correct each other's errors, while yet they belong to the same intellectual tradition and operate within the same realm of discourse.

311

Judaism evokes the prophetic-humanist emphasis from its daughter-faith. In respect to faith, the Judeo-Christian dialogue places the God of all men in the center of things, not the Savior of that fraction of humanity that believes in him. Faith must be conceived in human, universal terms, not in the molds and patterns of one historic tradition. In terms of the goals of life, the good life here on earth becomes the basis of discussion, not the salvation of the soul in the hereafter. The dialogue is focused on life and action, even while it explores the relative priority of good deeds as against the good will, the love of God, or the experience of "conversion." Both the rigidity of dogma and the inflexibility of the Law yield the center of the stage to the ethical-spiritual core of both traditions. The Old Testament with its theme of earthy men and women, struggling to be worthy of God's gifts, becomes the central text of our civilization.

At the same time, the Christian challenge weans the Jew away from the seductive shadows of ritualism and ethnicism. It evokes the haunting plea of prophets, philosophers, and pietists for emphasis on the inwardness of piety and for the recognition of the all-human dimension in the Jewish tradition. The Christian philosophy borders most closely on the Jewish mystical tradition, insistently calling attention to the dark mystery of things, the nigh-magical potency of love, and the saving power of sacrifice.

It is the challenge of Judaism in literature and in life that evoked the spirit of liberal Christianity, first in the evocation of medieval philosophy, then in the stimulation of Bible-centered heresies culminating in the rise of Protestant movements, then through the gradual seepage of the Protestant spirit into Catholic circles. By the same token, it is in Christian lands that the Jewish family was reorganized along monogamous lines. It is there too that the Jewish communities abandoned the patriarchal patterns of Oriental society and pioneered in the development of institutions of self-government along democratic lines. In Christian lands, the Jewish sermon was developed to a high degree of excellence, largely as a reaction to the influence and attraction of monastic preachers. The anti-intellectual current in Jewish thought of such thinkers as Crescas and Arame was greatly indebted to Christian influence, even as Christian rationalism was perennially stimulated by the works of Maimonides and Gersonides. In modern times, it was the stimulus and influence of a reformed Christianity that has generated the miracle of liberal Judaism. No such movements existed in Eastern Europe or in the Moslem world.

From all the above, it is clear that the Judeo-Christian symbiosis generates a creative dialectic in both camps and encourages the rise of the humanist philosophy in the country as a whole. In this field of tension there grows and flourishes the bipolar spirit of democracy, maintaining a dynamic balance between the sanctity of the individual and the supremacy of the Divine Law.

What are the conclusions that flow from this analysis of the relationship of freedom to the Judeo-Christian tradition? There is hardly an aspect of Jewish life or experience that is not freshly illuminated in this perspective, from the place of the Jew in the civilization of the West to the function and destiny of Judaism in the Diaspora. The consequences of this argument for the formulation of educational policy on the academic level are of greatest interest to us at this time.

Religionists have long maintained that freedom and democracy can grow only in the soil of a firm rich religious tradition. They managed to build an impressive argument for their case—hence, a network of religiously oriented schools from Yeshiva University in the East, through hundreds of Catholic colleges dotting the country, to Southern Methodist University in the West. With some notable exceptions, the concept of religion in these schools hovers perilously close to fundamentalism.

On the other hand, some secularists are firmly convinced that the essence of democracy is the separation of Church and State. For them, the references to God in the pledge of allegiance or to a Creator in the Declaration of Independence are remnants

313

of antidemocratic reaction. They turn a similarly jaundiced eye on the government's support of chaplaincies in the service, on the swearing in of government officials, and on the exemptions from taxes that are granted to religious institutions. Naturally, they explode with righteous indignation at every incursion of religion into the program of tax-supported schools. They assume that democracy came into being when the forces of religion were beaten down. The several religious traditions in our country are, in their view, organic bodies that are allergic to one another, and the institutions of democracy are allergic to them all.

From our standpoint, these two extremist positions delineate the outer boundaries within which freedom flourishes. Neither fundamentalism nor secularism is, in our view, the foundation of freedom, but the Judeo-Christian tradition taken as a whole, together with the humanist philosophy resulting from their mutual tensions and from the challenge of the scientific spirit. Hence, it would be most desirable in our colleges to expose the students to the entire range of the Judeo-Christian tradition. Instead of permitting a situation to continue wherein religion is either conveyed in fundamentalist terms or else is altogether ignored, we should encourage the teaching of all the major religious traditions within the objective, academic context of the university.

The utility of such a program for the uprooting of tenacious prejudices is obvious. No one who has ever participated in the teaching of such a course at a university can fail to sense the deep gratitude of students and their sense of relief at being unburdened from the oppressive weight of inherited bias. Every empty lot will soon be filled with weeds, while good grass requires patient cultivation. In view of so large a percentage of our young people being exposed to college education, we have the opportunity at long last to weed out those poisonous plants of prejudice that have bedeviled our people for so many centuries. It is in the universities of Germany that the battle for the minds of youth was lost, before it was lost in the marketplace and in parliament. It is in the universities of America that the battle for the minds of young people can be won for the future. One department of religion in a great university, offering objective courses in each religious tradition, is worth thousands of meetings for goodwill and brotherhood. The B'nai B'rith Hillel foundations deserve hearty commendation for their labors in this domain. But much more remains to be done.

Quite apart from the negative effect of countering prejudice, the teaching of the three major forms of American religion in an academic context provides a sound foundation for the spirit of religious humanism that is our "public philosophy."

Religious humanism, as we have shown, depends on a delicate balance between opposing forces. In our day, it is challenged by scientism, which is not so much a philosophy as an antiphilosophical impetus, deriving from the staccato rhythms of our machine-civilization. In the last decade and a half, the science and engineering faculties of our universities were greatly and disproportionately expanded in order to "keep up" with the Russians. The great heresies of Western civilization—namely, communism, nazism, and fascism—are actually forms of scientism. In each case, a core of myth and passion is enveloped in a pseudoscientific pattern of ideas. The myth may be changed, but the essence of the challenge remains: how to transform society after the image of a self-regulating machine. This challenge becomes dangerous only when it is unchecked by a similar and opposing emphasis on the values of liberal religion. We need to foster a positive appreciation of the three indispensable components of freedom—the sanctity of the individual, the supremacy of the Divine Law, and the prophetic-philosophic passion for a continual rethinking and refeeling of the traditions of yesterday.

JEWISH PHILOSOPHY
AND
WORLD TENSIONS*

Every generation believes that it stands at the final edge of history. In our case, this feeling is far more than a fond illusion. Today we already possess the means of total self-destruction, while the instruments of peaceful coexistence are yet to be invented. The evil impetus of ancient wrongs is still unspent, but the peacemakers dare only dream of "negotiations about negotiations." Armageddon is no longer a nightmare of hysterics, but a series of detailed plans kept at the Kremlin and the Pentagon. The Horsemen of the Apocalypse are now driving with the speed of jets. Where is the wisdom and the vision by which tensions might be allayed and disaster overcome?

Religious teachers are wont to give easy answers. "Love your neighbor," or "believe in God," or "obey the moral law"—these maxims fairly leap at us from pulpit and pew, but they are adored in the abstract, while our times demand hard thinking. We are sufficiently sophisticated in the sad lessons of history to know that satanic personalities never hesitated to drape their weapons in the buntings of love, faith in God, and belief in a higher law. As a matter of fact, the bloodiest wars were religious crusades in which both sides fought for the love of God or country, and in the name of an all-sanctioning Divine Law. The Civil War of a century ago, to which attention is now drawn by a series of commemorative exercises, was motivated on the Northern side by appeals to the "higher law of God," and on both sides by religious zeal and unreal myths. No ethical ideal is more easily frustrated in international affairs than the love

---

* Address at Theodor Herzl Institute, April 1962.

316

of neighbor; warmakers gladly swear by this principle, providing they alone will paint the image of the neighbor. Did not the German army of World War I proudly proclaim on its banners the pious legend *"Gott ist mit uns"?*

We need to build up a national ethos that will maintain our dedication to the high ideals of humanity and, at the same time, keep us free from the pious cant and the narrow fanaticism that have stultified such national aspirations in the past. In the past few years, some of our best writers addressed themselves to this need and sought to define our "national purpose." For all their occasional brilliance, these attempts to articulate the implications of the American dream were self-defeating.

The greatness of America is precisely the fact that it is not weighted down by the burden of a single national or religious tradition. Its greatest gift is a negation—the negation of the sufficiency of any single faith or ethnic heritage—hence an openness to the new horizons of the open frontier. Yet, the American mind is not a *tabula rasa,* but the meeting ground of the diverse traditions of the entire Western world.

It is a truism that the ethos of America was fashioned out of the Judeo-Christian tradition. This essay is an attempt to uncover the import of this tradition from the standpoint of Jewish philosophy. While we cannot presume to solve the multiple tensions of humanity today, we can contribute to the creation of that climate of discussion wherein solutions become possible. Our purpose is to stimulate a fresh awareness of our heritage, demonstrating its relevance to the great issues of our time. By regaining hold of the creative impetus that sustained the spirit of a hundred generations of our people, we may be enabled to cast new light on the grave tensions of our era.

What is it that the term "Jewish philosophy" comprises in the context of our discussion? Manifestly, the term is controversial. To some scholars, Jewish philosophy is *shatnez* ("illegitimate mixture"), because, as they see it, whatever is Jewish is not philosophy and whatever is philosophy is not specifically Jewish. Those who maintain that Judaism always contained a certain metaphysics generally insist on their own interpretation of that world-view. Current versions of Jewish philosophy run the entire gamut of modern thought, from the "critical" philosophy of the neo-Kantians (Hermann Cohen) to the mystical existentialist view of Buber. And all these interpretations correspond to authentic trends in our tradition. Contrary to a widespread impression, Judaism is not a monolithic body of ideas; it is not even a single, authoritative approach to the practical problems of life. It is a broad, winding river, composed of many and diverse streams, and given to a variety of moods. Different writers may prefer one or another of its confluent currents, designating it as the "mainstream," but in truth, the choice of a "mainstream" is a matter of academic taste.

Perhaps the broadest current in the river of Judaism is the one for which there is no exact equivalent in the vocabulary of philosophy. We might best think of it as "Halachic pragmatism"—i.e. a pragmatic approach to metaphysical problems, coupled with a Divinely revealed Law that contains implicitly certain ethical principles. In this school of thought, it is assumed that the great issues of metaphysics cannot be solved by human effort; hence, it is best to leave them alone. The good man will "respect the honor of his Creator" and will not venture into the treacherous domain of speculation, inquiring "what is above, what is below, what was before, what came after."[1] Instead, he will be concerned with the building of the good life here on earth—hence, the indifference to philosophy of most Rabbinic authorities and their single-minded preoccupation with the intricacies of the Divine Law. Like its American counterpart, Rabbinic pragmatism was optimistic, melioristic and tolerant of diverse approaches.

While the rabbis were mainly concerned with the promotion of obedience to the Divine Law, they recognized the rational-moral faculties as the expression of the Divine image in the human personality. The *neshamah* ("soul") is God's gift to man. and it is man's duty to foster its fullest development. The Torah

318

is not merely God's command; it is also His redemptive activity. All creation groans and travails with the aspiration to reach Divine nearness.

"An angel is assigned to each blade of grass, which beats it, saying 'Grow'!" In the case of man, this cosmic thrust is expressed in "Torah and good deeds." Said the great salvager of Rabbinic Judaism, following the burning of the Holy Temple in 70 C.E.: "If you hold a sapling in your hand and you hear people shouting, 'The Messiah has come,' plant the sapling in the ground first, and then go out to look for him."

But while the current of "Halachic pragmatism" is long and massive, there are other streams of thought, which no concept of Jewish philosophy can exclude. One can speak of "normative Judaism" only in a particular period and in a specific country. Who can ignore the mighty surge of Jewish rationalism that was represented so brilliantly in the works of Maimonides? And Jewish ethnic romanticism, as elaborated in the works of Halevi and Maharal, was extremely influential at various times. Mysticism, with all its heaven-storming ardor and its imaginative myths, was virtually ignored by the rationalistic historians of the nineteenth century, but it is a long and deep current, deriving from the earliest generations of Judaism.

In view of the confluence of diverse currents, we cannot speak of one mainstream of Jewish thought. However, the fact that a variety of approaches was tolerated is significant. It indicates that the concept of Jewish philosophy was generally conceived so broadly and tolerantly as to leave ample room for diverse pathways up the slopes of the "mountain of the Lord."

Doubtless, many of the architects of Judaism suspected that ultimate truth is beyond the ken of all philosophies and all visions, including the revelation of Moses. "Never did the *Shechinah* come down to earth, and never did Elijah and Moses ascend above."[2] We shall return to this thought in a moment.

Another way of capturing the import of Jewish philosophy is to fasten attention upon the one or more elements that are peculiar to our tradition. The term "Jewish" is then restricted to that which is distinctive to it and is not shared by other faiths and cultures. We recall that Samuel David Luzzatto believed the spirit of "compassion" to be characteristic of what he called "Abrahamism," in contrast to Atticism. Ahad Ha'am, on the other hand, maintained that an absolutist, rationalistic ethics was the essence of Judaism. More recently, scholars have spoken of the concept of unidirectional history as the living core of Judaism.

We doubt the wisdom of identifying the heart of Judaism with that which, in the opinion of one or another scholar, is peculiar to it. Aside from the questionable character of such judgments, this morbid preoccupation with peculiarities is hardly likely to do justice to the fullness of Jewish thought and its variety. This approach is vitiated at best by an excess of apologetic zeal and at worst it is marred by the astigmatism of bigotry. In the past, the cult of peculiarity was understandable, even if it was not desirable. As long as Jewish writers knew themselves to be on the defensive, challenged to prove their right to a separate communal identity, it was natural for them to seek to prove that Judaism was unique and irreplaceable. But once we value differences, peculiarities, and unique characteristics for their own sake, we open the gates wide to romantic exaggerations and we launch ourselves on the slippery incline of the "beatnik." The healthy-minded person strives for integrity, while the alienated nonconformist makes a fetish of being different. If the pressures of conformity vulgarize, the seductions of nonconformity distort and even pervert the uniform tenor of personality.

Fortunately, Jewish people today no longer feel that they are perpetually on the carpet, challenged to prove their right to exist. Now that the State of Israel is a vigorous and heartwarming reality, even de-Judaized Jews enjoy a sense of "normalcy." Their identity is assured; their "self-image" is clear; they stand on solid ground. Their existence is no longer a function of a "peculiar treasure."

In actual fact, without straining to be different, every great tradition constitutes a channeling of energies, a molding of hopes, and a patterning of values that are not likely to be duplicated by other faiths. All historical movements are unique configurations of sentiments, ideals, and memories. But the elements composing these configurations are shared by other faiths and cultures, for they are carved out of the same stuff of human hopes and fears.

If the impact upon contemporary society is our main concern, then we need to focus attention on the continuing impetus of the tradition, providing such a dynamic core can be discovered. Tempting as it may be, we cannot begin our investigation by laying down axioms, however pleasing or venerable.

We do not follow Ahad Ha'am in assuming the existence of an ethnic psychical entity, a "national soul," which determines the style of a culture and evokes its vision of the good life. Happily this myth of nineteenth-century romanticism is now totally discredited. Nor do we follow the fantasies of C. G. Jung in postulating a "racial unconscious," which manifests itself in dreams, visions, and myths, determining the deepest foundations of a people's life. Nor do we assume that the ideal of "peoplehood," the will of people to battle together for the goods of this world, is in itself calculated to generate universal ideas or ideals. Nor yet do we operate on the assumption that any fixed body of ideas constitutes the treasury of salvation for the Jewish people or for mankind as a whole. Ideas are by their very nature universal, insofar as they are true, good, or beautiful, and the human mind is one.

In every great tradition, there is embodied the momentum of certain sentimental aspirations and spiritual orientations that are real enough to be transmitted from generation to generation, yet protean enough to be variously articulated at different times. Dynamic, creative, and continuous, this inner impetus of character and aspiration is incarnated in all the varied facets of the ongoing tradition—in its prevailing mores and styles of living, in the values that are silently assumed, and in the elemental

321

patterns of behavior that enter into the making of a culture. In the long run, it is the inner spirit of a living tradition that counts, *Torah Shebalev*, to use Ahad Ha'am's phrase, in contradistinction to the outer shell of Torah that is visible to the naked eye. To avoid being detoured into the tortuous pathways of biology and mythology, we must remember that the subject of our inquiry is the great tradition of Judaism, not either the mental or the sentimental qualities of Jewish people. It is really *lev ha Torah* ("the heart of Torah") that we seek to discover, not the collective spirit that presumably dwells within the hearts of the people.

In Bible and Talmud, there occur many beautiful and succinct statements of the essence of Torah. Yet, there is one passage in the Talmud that appears to be corroborated by the entire gamut of Jewish experience. Maimonides built his theory of revelation upon it, and his judgment in regard to the heart of Torah was sustained by Krochmal and Ahad Ha'am, by the endless battle of the common run of Jews against idolatry, and by the subtlest philosopher of modern Judaism in the twentieth century, Hermann Cohen. It reads: "The two Commandments, 'I am the Lord, Thy God,' and 'Thou shalt have no other gods' we heard from 'the Power.' "[3]

While the other eight of the Ten Commandments and all the hundreds of precepts in the Torah were presumably spoken by Moses, the Israelites apprehended the first two Commandments by an immediate intuition, from the Lord Himself, as it were. This distinction between the principle of monotheism and the various precepts of the tradition is certainly sustained by the insistent emphasis of the prophets, the martyrdom of our saints and sages, and by the readiness of even ordinary Jews to die for His unity. By general consent, the one sentence that all Jews remember and treasure as their affirmation of faith is the *Shema*—"*Hear, O Israel, the Lord our God, the Lord is One.*" The total repudiation of idolatry and image worship is but the inevitable corollary of the assertion of Divine unity.

322

Yet, the matter is not quite as simple as it appears—neither the concept of unity, nor the rejection of the slightest taint of idolatry to the point of proscribing the symbolic use of any and all images. On the face of it, to say that God is One is to utter a tautology. Why then did this affirmation become the rallying cry of Israel? Manifestly, its real import cuts deep.

In ancient times, the gods of men fell into two categories—those that represented the forces of nature and those that adumbrated the diverse faculties of human nature. With the advance of religious sophistication, the unity of nature's laws became apparent. Also, the gods that, as Xenophon well knew, reflected the shifting images of human nature tended to be fused together. Yet, the fundamental cleavage between the God of man's highest ideals and the first cause of nature's laws could not but be felt even in ancient times. The God of love, compassion, and freedom, which human nature at its best reflects, however dimly and sketchily, is utterly different from the God of absolute necessity, who holds the heavens in thrall, governing the world with infinite majesty—more immovable than the universe itself, as implacable as death.

The cosmic gulf between necessity and freedom, law and love, force and compassion, the "God of Aristotle" and the "God of Abraham, Isaac, and Jacob," has continued to occupy the attention of all religious philosophers. In Judaism this paradoxical dichotomy was transcended by the genius of faith and turned into a polarity—God is One, working in the necessities of nature and in the freedom of human nature, in the iron inexorability of universal law and in His loving concern for particular people and groups of people. "To plant the heavens and to found the earth and to say to Zion, 'Thou art my people.' "4 The significance of the *Shema* consists precisely in this affirmation of the ultimate unity of the Cause of all Causes and the Soul of all Souls.

The unity of God projected the possibility of the good life here on earth—"and they shall keep the way of the Lord, to do justice and righteousness." Man, as the "Image of God," is not an alien to the realities of earthly existence—a pilgrim, a perpetual wanderer, a citizen of another realm. But this assurance of the unity of ethics and physics was by no means a simple identification of the two realms. After all, the mystery of infinity was implied in this unity. God's Name will ultimately be articulated in human society—but when? In time to come "His Name will be One," but meanwhile it must be *believed* that He is One in spite of an apparent contradiction. He is the sovereign of nature, *Elohim*, and He is also *YHVH*, the compassionate Father.

It was easy enough to shatter the polarity of this concept, so as to be relieved of the severe tension that it generates. Nature's God and man's Ideal Father could be separated and the sweet, self-denying god of love would then be considered as only "a finite force, not ourselves making for righteousness." A god that sustains and fortifies man's ideals, but is not almighty, cannot be held responsible for the multiple evils and agonies of existence. This solution appealed to the Persians of old and to many modern thinkers, from John Stuart Mill down, but it is too easy, hence, also unworthy of serious men and women. There is order and unity in the cosmos with all forces, however evil, and all ideals, however gentle, cohering in one system, with every tremor of a lightwave being felt to the ends of space. If God be only a limited force for righteousness, then there must be a more ultimate principle providing for the co-existence within its purview of both this God and of those forces which resist His work—hence, a God behind the God and that which is not God.

It is possible, too, to resolve the tension by the assertion that it is not for man to question the nature of the Divine unity. If the very being of God is paradoxical, then His will too must seem dark, impenetrable, yes, even absurd, to the puny mind of man. He may condemn innocent infants to eternal damnation in hell, as Jonathan Edwards maintained, while opening the gates of heaven to His backsliding favorites. And the pious will acclaim His wisdom and His goodness without question, for the "gates of reason are closed," as Crescas warned insistently.

As Judaism rejected both the easy solutions of the "little God" and the "God of paradox," it rejected also all attempts to dissolve the God of mercy and compassion into the substance of the God of necessity and force. This pantheistic solution allows the dark forces of necessity to swallow up the light of freedom, reserving for man only the privilege of assenting to the inexorable course of events. Rationalistic and pragmatic Judaism fostered the active, earth-transforming piety of man as "the partner in the works of creation," as well as the passive piety of resignation, humility, and obedience. Since He was immanent in conscience and intelligence, God could be served by a moral-rational law, but since He was also transcendent, He was manifest in a vision of infinite appeal that could be fulfilled only in the End of Days.

Maintaining the inconceivable unity of God, Judaism taught that it is man's duty to bring about a similar harmony of freedom and necessity here on earth. Again two opposing duties were laid upon his shoulders—to identify his own best insights with the will of God, but at the same time not to convert his ideals, however beautiful, into idols worthy of worship in their own right. Thus, the patriarch Abraham laid down the principle that the prophets were to develop and apply in later generations— God cannot but be good and just. "Can it be that the judge of the whole earth will not do justice?" Trusting man's understanding, they asserted that God must will that which is good; yet distrusting it, they prohibited man from worshiping his own creations. The faltering steps of man on the highway of civilization must not be turned into sacred resting places. The light of God shines out of beautiful things and out of sainted, heroic personalities, but it is the light that is holy and its source, not the reflecting surfaces. All things "in heaven above and in earth below" are only the temporary holds of mountain climbers. Even the holiest of men can falter and sin—yes, even Moses. And his greatness consisted precisely in his recognition

325

of his frailty. Says the Talmud, "How do we know Moses from the Torah? Because it is written, 'for that he is flesh.' "[5]

Thus, the Bible sets up heroes of faith but also insists on their fallibility. The prophet speaks with great authority, yet even if his predictions should prove true, he must not be followed blindly. "For the Lord tests you. . . ."[6] The priests are anointed of the Lord, yet Aaron, their ancestor, made the Golden Calf. King David, symbol of the perfect King Messiah, was not without sin; Jacob-Israel, the ancestor-hero of the twelve tribes, wrestled with an angel and prevailed, but he emerged a cripple from the ordeal.

A daring vision of faith coupled with a sustained mood of searching, doubting, and questioning—this is the creative genius of the Jewish faith. God is mysteriously One, so we must believe, but it is also our duty to reason and even to argue. "Right wouldest Thou be, O Lord, were I to contend with Thee, yet will I reason with Thee."[7] The duty of obedience is inculcated in the Scriptures from cover to cover, but along with obedience there is the obligation to love, with all one's heart and soul and might, and to seek the knowledge of the Lord.[8] In the Talmud, piety and humility are highly esteemed, but intelligence or good sense is prized even more highly. "Every person in whom intelligence is found, it is as if the Holy Temple had been built in his day."[9]

Faced with the task of articulating the Jewish faith in the language of philosophy, Philo stressed both aspects of this polarity. On the one hand, he maintained that God functions through the Divine logos, the principle of intelligibility and order. On the other hand, the Lord Himself transcends the logos; hence, He remains unknowable. His unity can be understood only by a few blessed souls.

Maimonides retains this polarity. He, too, insists that God is to be reached by systematic study and rational reflection. In his famous allegory, describing the five categories of pietists, he puts the meticulous observers of Talmudic Law outside the palace, while he places the philosophers inside the palace,

milling in their diverse ways through its labyrinthine halls.[10]
For Maimonides, reason provides the channel of communication
between God and man, with the Divine Torah serving to
facilitate the establishment of the kind of society that is congenial to philosophic meditation. Yet, for him, too, the unity of
God is a supreme mystery, possessing only a most tenuous
relation to the kind of unity that is conceivable by the human
mind.

He concludes that God can be approached only by way of
the *via negativa*—i.e. by the comprehension of all things which
are not God. At the same time, man fulfills himself only by
loving God, and to love God, says Maimonides, is to seek to
know Him. Thus, man's task is to reach for the unreachable,
to affirm his faith in love as an infinite quest, and then to
articulate its meaning in rational reflection, step by step.

This polarity of faith and reason, the affirmative vision and
the negative way, is expressed in the social philosophy of
Judaism. Man is free to choose between good and evil, between
life and death, between the blessing and the curse. While all
Israelites are responsible for one another, the individual remains
an ultimate reality, a universe unto himself. For even as God
is unknowable in His essence, so there is a Holy of Holies
within every man. Even God cannot lay down the law for a
person and hold him to it, unless he had accepted it for
himself.[11]

On the whole, the radiance of the infinite vision dominated
the minds of great Jews in the Biblical period, with the prophets
dramatizing the terror and the majesty of the "day of the
Lord." In time to come, the unity of God's creation and His
purpose will be manifest to all. "The Lord will be One, and
His Name One."[12] Peace and harmony will reign supreme, for
He is both first and last.

Yet, even in the Bible, the "way of the Lord" is identified
with the principles of justice and righteousness that human
beings discover by their own efforts: "That they may keep the

327

way of the Lord to do righteousness and justice."[13] The civil laws of the Bible, we now know, were either restatements or amendments of the common law of the Near East. Yet even those who were aware of this historical character of the laws could think of them as Divine, for the best efforts of man to live the good life are holy in the sense of direction and intention, as so many steps along the infinite path. The ritual laws of holiness are virtually all prohibitions. It has been noted that the Book of Holiness (Leviticus 19) consists of a recital of what one must not do—a ritualistic version of the *via negativa*.

In the literature of the Talmud, the vision fades into the background, and the details of the way move into the foreground. The Law was formulated by the rabbis in accord with the rational principles of their day. The leaders in the Second Commonwealth were neither visionaries nor mystics, but reasonable legislators. To be sure, they operated within strict dogmatic limits—"a law I laid down, a decree I ordained—you do not have permission to question it."[14] Yet, in actual fact, the rabbis questioned, argued, and debated in the belief that it was their meditations and cogitations within the borders of the Law that God desired. Virtually all Rabbinic decisions were made on the basis of rational discussions and realistic considerations, not in response to the prompting of the Holy Spirit (*Ruah Hakodesh*). The Talmud tells of several instances when the "echo of a Divine voice" was specifically rejected by the scholars of the Academy.[15]

While the image of the Biblical prophet has won worldwide acclaim, that of the Pharisaic sage has been generally scorned and even ridiculed. But in Jewish tradition, the Talmudic sages, building the patterns of the good life, were the direct heirs and counterparts of the prophets, who sought a living confrontation with the Divine mystery.

Actually, the rabbis were not merely legislators. As Aggadists, they continued the prophetic tradition. "If you wish to know Him Who Spoke And The Universe Came Into Being, study the 'Aggadah.' "[16] In the course of time the deeper concerns of the

Aggadah split into two streams—rationalistic philosophy and Qabbalah. The prophetic goal of a living confrontation with the Divine is the central theme of Maimonides' great work, *The Guide for the Perplexed*. In Qabbalah, the sober world of reality is regarded as merely a pale copy of the "higher worlds." The *Shechinah* is in exile, the entire universe is "fallen," and it is up to the pious to overcome the "shells" in their own life, to reach the highest levels of their souls and then bring about the "unification of worlds." Through Qabbalah or through philosophy, the tension between the vision of the prophets and the Law of the rabbis was reinstituted. Still, there is always the danger in Judaism of the tension snapping with the result of either the Law or the Messianic vision usurping the fullness of loyalty. In the event the Law is regarded as self-sufficient and of absolute authority, the community is ossified and the Jewish personality is denied the opportunity to confront the fresh horizons of the growing intellectual and esthetic worlds. In the event the Law is rejected and the dynamic impetus of Judaism is shifted toward the pole of Messianism, diverse forms of pseudo-Messianism are likely to captivate emotional youth.

The vibrant tension within Judaism is best reflected in the concepts of the Messiah and the "Kingdom of God." On the one hand, the rabbis insisted that the "Kingdom" was definitely of this world. It is the task of man to "improve this world by means of building the Kingdom of the Almighty." "Jerusalem that is above" is intimately associated with the actual, troubled city here on earth.[17] To love God is not to indulge in solipsistic rhapsodies but "to make His Name beloved in the world"[18]— hence, the pragmatic temper of the rabbis and their passionate concern with all the contingencies of life. This sober mood was countered by a passionate expectation of the coming of the Messiah. Virtually every generation of Jews believed that the Messiah would come within their lifetime or that of their children. Rabbi Levi Yizhak of Berdichev invited his friends to attend the wedding of his daughter in the courtyard of the Holy Temple in Jerusalem, but he added, as if in an afterthought, "If perchance the Messiah does not come, then the wedding will be held in Berdichev."

In spite of this daily expectation, the vision of the Messiah loomed so large in the folk-imagination that no earthly person could ever match it. The Messiah was expected, at the very least, to gather the exiles, establish Israel's supremacy, and win dominion over the "principalities" of this world. The arrival of the Messiah was to inaugurate a wondrous era that would culminate in a universal Judgment Day, the resurrection of the dead, and the glories of *Olam Haba* ("the World to Come"). The vision of the Messiah was at once of this world and of a realm of existence, surpassing our comprehension[19]—hence, the dynamic tension in the soul of the Jew. He was to keep the heavenly vision alive and exciting in his mind, but he was also to labor steadily and realistically in this world. And at all times, he was to remember that no earthly king or potentate could claim the dignity of the Messiah. True, the Messiah will come "today, if his voice you will heed"; but then again, if he is here, he is no Messiah.

The tension between the heavenly vision and the pedestrian way was too much for the mentality of a large portion of the Jewish people. This is why pseudo-Messiahs could win large numbers in so many generations. Harassed in both body and soul, many could not stand the agony of the tension. The Messiah had to come, here and now, if indeed God ruled supreme. The false Messiahs ranged through all the colors of the Messianic spectrum—some were ascetics, like Sabbattai Zevi, others were mystical visionaries, like Solomon Molcho, still others were military heroes, like Bar Kochba, still others charlatans, like Jacob Frank—most of them were paradoxical personalities sharing in several or all of these contradictory qualifications.

A popular Hasidic tradition tells of a *Zaddik* who was told that the Messiah had arrived. He went to the window and saw the people hurrying to their work. "No," he said, "by the

330

rush and the clamor of the crowd, I can tell that the Messiah had not yet arrived."

So, too, the Jewish people living in Christian countries were told on all sides that the Messiah had already arrived. They looked at the marketplaces and in the battlefields of the world and they could not but conclude that the Messianic era had not yet begun. At the same time, those who remained loyal to their heritage insisted that, tarry as he will, the Messiah would surely come one day. Otherwise, the travail of the centuries is meaningless. Rabbi Moshe of Ohel in Hungary spoke for millions of the faithful when he addressed the Lord on Yom Kippur as follows: "O God, I know that I am full of sins, but one virtue I do possess—all my life I search for truth. And now I tell you truthfully that I could live every year of my life only in the expectation that the Messiah would indeed come before the year was over. So, at the beginning of each year, you led me on, and now I am an old man. . . ."[20]

Like the *Zaddik* of Ohel, every generation of Jews believed that the Messiah would come in their day. Yet, so many-splendored was this vision that it could not possibly come to pass. And the Jewish dilemma was merely a concrete demonstration of the human predicament—the vision of God's Kingdom on earth must ever loom before us, fascinating and reassuring, but we must know that the way toward its realization is slow and hard.[21]

The fullness of the human personality is reflected in the polarity of Judaism; hence, the perennial appeal of Judaism and its claim to eternity. The paradox of human nature consists in the fact that the ideal of self-mastery is set over against the ideal of self-transcendence. To master oneself is to achieve a harmonious blending of all one's power; to transcend oneself is to locate the focus of devotion and meaning outside the self. Both ideals are articulated respectively in the symbols of philosophy and religion.

The bewilderment of our times in respect to problems of personality derives from the breakdown of the two self-images

331

that in the past supplemented one another—the classical Hellenic concept of the rational self and the religious concept of the soul as a spark of the Divine Being. For centuries, these two concepts served to maintain for the peoples of the West a creative polar tension. The religious view nurtured the feelings of mystery and sanctity, pointing to a transnatural realm of resplendent glory. At the same time, for practical purposes, Western man operated with the classical ideal of the self as an entity, complete unto itself. The great works of Rome and Greece, which were used to educate the elite of the West, interpreted the ideal of the self-sufficient personality, harmonious and well-balanced, contemplating life with poise and assurance. The well-poised statues of the classical era, the rounded arches of its great buildings, the measured cadences of its rhetoric—all these symbols of harmony reflected the ideal of the ancient wise men of Athens—"nothing in excess" and "know thyself," in the sense of knowing one's limitations. Of the four "cardinal virtues"—courage, justice, temperance, and wisdom—the latter three are reflections of harmony and order, while the first one is the drive for self-assertion. Lacking are the ideals of reverence, love, and compassion, which relate man to his fellows and to God.

This so-called Apollonian ideal or self-image has been undermined by many factors: the discovery of man's animal ancestry (Darwin), the recognition of the dark and heaving depths of human nature (Freud), the awareness of the distortion of environmental and economic factors (Marx), and the progressive restriction of freedom of action in today's highly organized world. At the same time, the Biblical view of man's self, encrusted with many accretions of myth and superstition, was shunted into the shadows by the rational, empirical emphasis of the modern mind.

An important factor in dimming the spell of the Apollonian ideal was in all likelihood the rapid pace of change in the modern world. An ideal of static perfection seems out of this world to people who are catapulted from one age into another in less than a decade. The atomic age and the television age gave way in the fifties to the hydrogen age and the jet age. In our world, nothing feels real unless it be on the run. Modern man is likely to concur with the Talmud that humans must be thought of as being on the move (*holechim*—literally, "goers") in contrast to angels who are designated as standing still (*omedim*).

The dynamic impetus in Judaism should be felt in the reconstitution of a meaningful tension between the Apollonian and the God-centered view of personality.

Both are phases of the one self. Man is "alienated," as our literati complain, and properly, as much when he repudiates the "love of God" as when he denies the rational order. It may be true that "hell is other people," as the popular proverb has it, but it is even more true that to live in utter isolation without personal love or a high purpose is worse than hell—it is death in life.

On the one hand, man is not complete unto himself, but he is part of the texture of ideas and ideals, embracing his entire being and laying claim to his allegiance. In religious terms, man fulfills himself when he "faces God." "Walk before Me and be whole,"[22] said the Lord to Abraham. The concept of living "before God" is the Biblical answer to Protagoras' famous maxim, "Man is the measure of all things, of things that are that they are, of things that are not that they are not."

On the other hand, the Apollonian concept of the harmonious and the rational needs to be reconstructed. Religionists who delight in the discomfiture of reason must remember that the breakdown of rationality is far more likely to release man's demonic powers than his Divine potencies. Have not we of this Hitlerian generation learned this lesson to our great sorrow? Nietzsche's proclamation that "God is dead" did not result in the coming of superman but in the atavistic resurgence of subhumanity.

The vision of religion must be related to the rational, moral, empirical standards of man. A Karl Barth and a Rudolf Bultmann, asserting that "God is all, man is nothing," are as guilty

333

of breaking the tension of spiritual life as the agnostic and the atheist. In fact, the two extremists prepare the way for another. If the Biblical author complained of "a slave who becomes king," we of a sadder and subtler generation have cause to complain of communists who become fundamentalists and atheists who are yet orthodox. When the intuitive vision and the rational way are in creative tension, we remain aware of incompleteness and movement. The way is not fixed, final, and absolute; the vision challenges as a symbol, a parable, a promise. The vision may be represented in the vestments of the past, but it is a herald of the future; it may be transrational, but not anti-rational; it is the "pillar of light" that leads us on, but God is not in its fire, or wind, or terror.

As seen from our perspective, existentialist novelists, poets, and mystical rhapsodists are right insofar as they demonstrate that man is more than his physical, concrete self, but they are wrong when they proceed to tell us precisely what that "plus" is. It is by faith that we attain the fullness of freedom—that is the import of the First Commandment. But that faith is a recurrent endeavor to confront anew the Divine mystery. Once this faith is spelled out in images, symbols, rites, and beliefs, we violate the Second Commandment, prohibiting the worship of concrete things presumed to be Godlike.

We tend to think of the aberrations of pseudo-Messianism as belonging to our storied past. Actually, this menacing mentality achieved its greatest power and popularity in the first part of the twentieth century. As we have seen, its essence is the snapping of the tension between the vision of perfection and the gradualistic way, in the belief that the promised Savior is here and now. The worship of the ultimate and the absolute is transferred to a concrete person or plan. The objective, tentative approach of the reasonable man is, for the pseudo-Messianists, the primary sin, for it is the "Holy Ghost" that picks its followers. "No man can say Jesus is the Christ, save by the Holy Ghost."[23] Thus, reasoning gives way to the charismatic preaching of "world-historical" figures. Those who will not see the light are children of Satan. If they cannot be "converted," they must be eliminated. In fact, "monosatanism," the attribution of all evil in society to the opponents of the Savior, is the most telling of all the stigmata of the pseudo-Messianic malady.

Individualism, nationalism, socialism—each of these visions of human well-being is of high worth and dignity; yet, each ideal has also been transformed by excessive zeal into a destructive ideology. This melancholy distortion is most evident in the case of socialism. No modern ideal evoked as much genuine devotion and altruistic ardor as socialism. In the latter decades of the nineteenth century and in the first two decades of this century, socialism bore all the lineaments of the Messiah. It provided a total transformation of all values, a reinterpretation of the entire tragic travail of the past, and a glorious vision of a "world that is all good." It spoke in the accents of "scientific" certitude and it assured all men of their inherent dignity, for Providence in the shape of "historical materialism" wrought unfailingly in behalf of the poor and the disinherited. The promise was sure to come, the Messiah was around the corner.

How grievously this ideal was destroyed by the zealotry which it evoked! It shattered the rational realm of discourse by the dogmatic assertion that all ideas and ideals were merely the froth on the tides of economic class-interests. Thus, reasonableness and tentativeness were merely the marks of the weak and the naïve, with propaganda, subtle or ruthless, taking the place of education and enlightenment. Above all, it substituted the mythology of monosatanism for the faith of monotheism. All evil was due to the lust for private possessions, from the corrupt rhythms of degenerate music to the murderous adventures of fascist dictators. Since the Bolshevik leaders were, by definition, free from the bourgeois virus, they could do no wrong. The spirit of self-criticism is the sinister serpent in the Paradise; hence, the repression and the terror, the awesome self-righteousness and the steel-shuttered minds, the police-state and the rising crescendo of blood-purges, corresponding to the human sacrifices of old.

335

Nationalism, too, began as a resplendent liberating ideal. It would restore to every man the dignity and the solace of his historic communal "self-image." Some form of "pooled pride," as it has been called, is certainly an essential ingredient of the good life. Yet, consider the havoc it has wrought in the heart of Europe! Both fascism and nazism were essentially radical versions of "pure" nationalism, the former stressing the worship of the state, the latter proclaiming the Messiah in the shape of the master race. Again, objective reasoning was of no avail, only the pallid propaganda of the bloodless intellectuals. The "voice of the blood" was articulated in the elemental struggles of races for mastery. The "children of light" were those who, hearing the message of salvation, "converted" and hailed the Messiah riding on the donkey (symbol of the "masses"). The "children of Satan" were those who either could not or would not accept the new faith. They were the cause of all the manifold evils of life. Never mind any "logical" contradictions. To a good ideologist, what is "logic" but the desperate dialectic of the damned?

That individualism can serve as a pseudo-Messianic frenzy is not easily apparent. Does not the very ideal of individual freedom preclude the mass-delusion of salvationism? True, but then the insidious consequences of this philosophy appear when it is associated with the belief that perfection is here already. It then follows that the enemies of society are those who would change the status quo. In America the identification of all social goals with political freedom has led to the dogma that communism is the root of all evil. Domestically, we still have "inverted communists," for whom "anticommunism" is a sole and sufficient philosophy of life. The "social Darwinists" of a generation ago who identified the fang and claw of raw competition with the "Law of God" are a vanishing species on the national scene. But in international affairs, many of our diplomats act as if there were only one evil in the world—the communist conspiracy. The very fair-mindedness of the American people leads them to feel that the communist challenge should be met in the same way as the Nazi-Fascist bid to conquer the world. The simple fact that the two evils are different in their essential nature is difficult to accept, since it runs counter to the lure of mono-satanism.

The readiness of some of our military strategists to resort to a "pre-emptive" nuclear war in defense of freedom is proof of the powerful appeal of the pseudo-Messianic mentality. In the first place, the multiple shapes of "the good, the true, and the beauti-ful" are rolled together and concretized in the one goal of freedom. And the many forms of freedom in society—economic, educational, social, and political—are reduced to the simple equations of the two-party system. In the second place, the multiple evils of society are reduced to the curtailment of freedom, and this curtailment is in turn simplified as the "lust for power" of a "clique" in the Kremlin. This entire monosatanic myth is then embraced as the "faith of America," believed because "it is absurd." And the proof of its truth is to be offered in the shape of human sacrifices, tens if not hundreds of millions of them, in keeping with the grandeur of this glorious vision!

How did the noble ideals of individual freedom, social enter-prise, and national greatness become perverted into devastating ideologies? This is the central question of our generation. For many of us, this is now a *postideological* era. We have seen the great ideologies rise and fall. Our primary concern is to tell how they can be used, without being abused. Our analysis of the Jewish philosophy provides the perspective for the solu-tion of this problem.

Each of the great ideals of the modern world arose out of the matrix of humanism. Such was nationalism in the romantic philosophies of Germany, Italy, Poland, and Russia. We tend to forget that Marxism was originally an intensely humanistic move-ment, aiming at the liberation of the human personality and the promotion of its growth. After the Renaissance, individualism was one of the goals embraced in every forward, uplifting movement. How then did these ideals become antihumanistic, in the instances I cited previously?

337

Apparently, it is not enough for ideas to be associated together. As in the Newtonian laws of momentum, ideas become disassociated and recombined. Thus, the myth and malice of anti-Semitism, originally combined with Christian fundamentalism, was, in our world, separated from its Christian matrix and then recombined within an anti-Christian, positively pagan philosophy of racism. In our view, all social ideals constitute part of the gradualistic way whereby man advances his society toward the religious vision of infinite perfection. In a healthy society, the inner tension between the way and the vision generates the ardor for advancement without precipitating the seductive madness of pseudo-Messianism.

An instructive parallel with the philosophy of Maimonides comes to mind. His *via negativa,* the contemplation of things that lead to God but are not God, suggests a similar procedure for the ideologies, the quasi-theologies of our time. On the one hand, we should cultivate the vision of man's potentialities and glorify the infinite dimensions of human happiness and greatness. This a great faith achieves through its rites and beliefs, which symbolize the endless reaches of the Divine. The rhapsodic language of religion suggests the effort to break through the boundaries of the expressible and even the conceivable. On the other hand, the very splendor of the vision is set off against the pedestrian, sober, melioristic qualities of the way which the men of any one generation must follow. The absoluteness and infinity of the vision imply the relativeness and the finitude of all that belongs to the immediate and the proximate, the here and the now.

The fascination of the ideologies consists in their apparent certitude and finality. As Erich Fromm pointed out in his perceptive book *Escape from Freedom,* most people shun the responsibilities of self-guidance. They want to surrender to an authority, becoming part of a being that possesses the qualities they lack. Greatness is possible for most people only through the coalescence of their spark of selfhood with some blazing flame. In a living faith, this passion "to die in order to live"

338

is directed toward the "Kingdom of God" on earth and to the "way of the Lord" leading up to its realization.

Man's craving for absoluteness and certitude is projected unto the vision, awakening his hope and sustaining his faith, while in the actual world he labors with instruments that are historical, hesitant, tentative, and melioristic. He keeps his faith in the Messiah fresh and strong, but at the same time he follows the earthly road (Halachah). His attention to the problems and concerns of his day affects the character of his faith, preventing it from hardening into dogmas, while the transcendent Messianism of his vision keeps him from absolutizing and finalizing the strategies of the hour. Diversity of approach and rational-empirical discussion constitute the life of the earthly phase of faith.

How then are the vision of hope and the way of relative rationality to be kept from fusing together, generating either the fanaticism of fundamentalism, or the frenzy of pseudo-Messianism? Only through the recognition of the total perspective, generated by the polarity between the vision and the way. God in Himself remains hidden from us, but He is revealed fragmentarily in two ways—the rational-moral quest of man, formalized in the norms of the way, and the ardor of hope, the intuition of inspired seers formulated and symbolized in the promise of the End of Days. It is man's fate to live in tension, articulating his faith in rational terms and opening his soul to that which is beyond the horizons of his present knowledge, guarding against the seduction of pseudo-Messianism, on the one hand, and legalistic stand-patism, on the other hand. The ultimate implications of religion for social life are suggested by the first two of the Ten Commandments—a vision of perfection and a warning against the usurpation of Divine perfection—hence, an openness to change and a readiness for self-examination. The issues that divide mankind today are tactical and strategic, belonging to the pragmatic realm of the way, though they are frequently articulated in the absolutist rhetoric and symbolism of the vision. But only the vision is our ultimate goal; the way must not be turned into an idol.

TOWARD A PHILOSOPHY OF HOPE*

The quality of hope is the acid test of a healthy philosophy of life. The Talmud tells us that when a person is brought before the bar of judgment in heaven, he is asked first, "Didst thou deal faithfully with thy fellow man?" and then, "Didst thou hope for salvation?" Similarly, in an ancient version of the Pandora legend, we are told that when she opened the box, all gifts but the one of hope flew away. But because hope remained, all other gifts were regained in time.

All surveys indicate that the college youth of today are strangely sober and even melancholy. The shadow of an all-annihilating hydrogen bomb weighs heavy on their horizon, blighting the natural gaiety of their age. While they dutifully discharge their obligations, they are troubled by the feeling that all their work is of no consequence. Of what use are all the subtleties of science in the post-Big Bomb world? A remark of Albert Einstein comes to mind. He was asked to describe the weapons that will be employed in the next war. Said he, "I cannot tell what weapons will be used in the next war, but I can tell you which weapons will be used in the war after the next one—bows and arrows."

The present generation sees its statesmen approaching the brink of ultimate disaster again and again. How then can it have faith in the future? For a while it appeared as if the "balance of terror" would make any all-out war unthinkable and obsolete, but this hope has been nibbled away by a concerted effort to get the people to take a nuclear war in their stride. What if fifty million or one hundred million should perish in the first day? Victory may still be won, however hollow or

*Address at a Cornell University convention, Fall 1959.

340

shadowy. All normal weapons are even now being replaced by nuclear armaments, and the governor of New York is urging the construction of basement shelters. Homo sapiens has not hesitated in the past to sacrifice millions of lives for symbols, shadows, and slogans. How can we hope that nations will not do so in our day? Thus, despair looms large on the horizon today.

This despair is aggravated by a persistent feeling that the agencies of hope have failed to truly function in our time.

In two directions, man discovers the inspiration and incentive of hope: in the objective realm, through the study of the outside world and the gradual mastery of its secrets; in the subjective realm, through the upwelling of new faith and fervor out of the mysterious springs of the soul. The rainbow of hope attaches either to the rational values and moral harmonies of life, endowing them with endurance and power, or it clings to that protean exuberance and love of life, which subsists beneath all our conscious planning. In the daylight struggle for existence, man's instruments of hope are the philosophies and ideologies of the time as well as the pedestrian progress of science and industry. Ideologies reduce the chaos of existence to order, and technology opens fresh horizons for man's mastery of nature. On the side of feeling, the agencies of the flow of hope from the recesses of inner being are the institutions of religion, art, and poetry—chiefly, those of religion.

I submit that both these agencies have failed to kindle the light of hope for modern man. The ideologies of our day—and our age has been called the Age of Ideology—lie strewn in the dust, discredited and discarded: Socialism, nationalism, scientism, democracy—we can recall the time when each of these ideals was acknowledged to be the herald of a new and golden age for mankind. There are few, indeed, that would care to place their entire faith in these ideologies. Socialism appeared on the horizon of the nineteenth century as a mighty force of liberation; today, it is revealed to be one of the beasts of the Apocalypse. Nationalism was, at one time, the hope of a new and glorious order—all nations governing themselves, determining their own destiny and laboring for the common good; today we know it to be one of the mightiest forces of delusion in all the backward areas of the world.

The ideal of self-determination of nations is still piously invoked from time to time, but with a mournful undertone, for we know that many a nation offers less freedom and less hope to its people after it has attained self-determination than before. We still project the ideal of a free world, but we know that in many areas of the world the freedom of those governed may not at all be related to the freedom of those who govern.

Many great and glowing spirits were once wont to say, "Science is my shepherd, I shall not want." Its light will banish the fears and phantasies of the past, ushering in an age of abundance and happiness to all. Today we know that science is not enough. It has created a Frankenstein of horror without giving us the means to control it. Even the light of democracy is beginning to pale. Country after country has retreated from its precepts, resorting to modifications or restrictions that nullify its extent and meaning. France, the birthplace of democracy, has begun to beat the drums of retreat, and in the new countries of Africa, as in the old countries of Central America, the radiant promise of democracy quickly turns to ashes. All down the line, the ideologies of our time have ended in frustration.

The subjective agencies of hope—art, poetry, and religion—have also failed to generate the elixir of new vigor and inspiration. I shall not speak of art and poetry but of religion. We live at a time when people are returning to religion. This return is the demonstration of a need, not the discovery of an answer. People flock to churches and to synagogues in quest of a new accession of faith and inspiration. But all too often, they are fed the straws of dogma, not the heavenly manna of Divine inspiration. The religion that college students bring with them to the campus is all too often a batch of disjointed dogmas and rituals, not a unifying philosophy of life. These religions of the students are frequently nullified by the free commerce of ideas that prevails on the campus, where the dogmas and rituals of one group are canceled by those of other conflicting tradi-

342

tions. Religion today thrives on the disappointments and dis-illusionments of modern life, but such religion is only an escape into the night. It speaks in dark and mysterious paradoxes, promising "peace of mind" and "peace of soul"; it affirms and negates at one and the same time, reveling in contradictions; it rebukes man's "pride of reason," thriving on every failure of the human mind and heart, but it does not offer the firm solace of an abiding faith. We have faith in faith, a hunger and a thirst for the word of God, but no articulation of the meaning of the word. Such explication as we do have in church and synagogue is imprisoned in unacceptable dogmas or encased in meaningless platitudes. We cannot believe that God intervenes suddenly in the affairs of men, pulling them back from the brink of disaster, nor can we draw strength from the hallowed formula, "Believe and thou shalt be saved."

The wellsprings of hope have become "broken wells." This is the central challenge of our generation.

Let us examine precisely what is meant by hope. We want to triumph rather than fail, to attain the high plateaus of achieve-ment and glory, and to escape the manifold ills that beset our path. But who are we? What is it that we mean by our self, the subject of hope and despair, of triumph and failure?

Manifestly, we arrive at two different answers to this question, depending on whether we pursue the objective pathway of knowledge or the subjective clues to the meaning of self. Sub-jectively, we probe into the nature of our being by excluding progressively from our consciousness all that is external, tem-porary. We remove from view all the data of experience, one by one, shunning the relations between objects as well as the objects themselves. We arrive by this analytical pathway at a bare vacuous mystery, which David Hume and his followers declared to be nothing at all. The empiricists of this school assert that there is no self and no soul. By means of a similar line of thought, they concluded that there was no substance and no God. On the other hand, romanticists and mystics find the true kernel of reality in this naught that is at once nothing-ness and pure being. For them, the self, abstracted from all experience, is either pure will, or pure freedom, or the *élan vital* in all its unpredictable majesty, or the mysterious ground of all reality.

There is no doubt that the views of the romanticists and mystics correspond at this point with the feelings and judgments of what is called "common sense." When we do not sail on the wings of abstraction, we identify our self with the mysterious subject of all our experiences. Though we cannot tell what we mean by our self, we want "it" to win in the battle of life; though we could conceivably part with any phase of our empirical self, we want the unknown within to triumph. The doctrine of immortality is a reflection and symbol of this hope. Even more patently, the doctrine of bodily resurrection reflects the impetus of hope in all its dark subjectivity. According to several forms of this hope, the resurrected body would be totally different from the garment of flesh and blood that clothes our self in this world; it will be a radiant body, made out of the substance of the heavens. And according to the Qabbalists, the soul, too, will not be the feeble, uncertain, flickering "candle of the Lord"; purged in the black, primal flames of "the river of fire" that flows from under the Throne of Glory, it will carry no remembrance of the ills of this world. Yet, in spite of the absence of any tangible marks of identification, the new body and the new soul of the World to Come represented the height of the fulfillment of the blind subjective craving for sheer life.

If we now reverse direction and pursue the quest for the identity of the soul along the lines of objectivity, we note that the self grows out of experience, achieving fullness of stature and richness of personality through the processes of life and learning. But the self is not merely a collection of memorized data and fixed judgments induced by experience, like a marvelous Univac. It has a flow of feeling, a pulsation of will, a quest for truth, a hunger for beauty. In brief, it confronts us with a surge of interpretations and a hierarchy of values, more or less reasoned, more or less qualified by universally applicable judgments of right and wrong, more or less in accord with firm standards of fitness and unfitness that are shared by the spirit

344

of humanity as a whole. If we pursue the analysis of these superpersonal judgments still further, we find that the values, through which the self is concretized, become steadily more universal, more abstract, more devoid of entanglement with actual agonies of the living person.

The triumph of the self, in this view, is therefore the assurance of victory for the values of the self. The visions of hope, inspired by the objective quest of the human mind, center on the ultimate achievements of the totality of man's ideals and values. In Judaism, this hope is reflected in the prophetic vision of the "Kingdom of Heaven," when peace and justice will prevail among all men and when the "Word of the Lord will fill the earth as the waters cover the sea." In the Augustine system, this objective version of man's hope is designated as the "City of God." In the philosophies of the modern world, this hope was transmuted into a secularized dogma of continuous progress. As the ancient Messianic hope of the Judeo-Christian tradition came in apocalyptic and nonapocalyptic forms, so in the modern secularized philosophies of inevitable progress, we encountered a catastrophic as well as a noncatastrophic type of expectancy. In the philosophy of Karl Marx, the perfect, classless society of universal peace and justice will be ushered in only after a series of ever worsening catastrophes, precipitated by the ruthless struggle of the dominant class to keep the proletariat from attaining its ends. In the philosophy of Herbert Spencer the noncatastrophic version of linear, inevitable progress is outlined, in keeping with Anglo-American experience, "with freedom slowly broadening down, from precedent to precedent."

In sum, the meaning of hope is twofold—the triumph of our personal self, in all its mysterious oneness, and the triumph of our values, in all their diversity and impersonality. Both the subjective and the objective expressions of hope are part of our conscious lives. For the most part, we effect a temporary synthesis between the two phases of our spirit, for we cannot permanently rest content with only one phase of being. Thus, the hope of immortality through the life of one's children, or one's nation, or one's cultural tradition, is an expression of this synthesis of two orientations. Every such synoptic vision possesses a temporary plausibility and even a measure of validity, but there is no ultimate or final synthesis that integrates for all time the two orientations of the human soul. There are two sides to our nature, and we are fated to approach reality, like the mythical denizens of Jonathan Swift's Laputa, with one eye directed toward the starry heavens of eternal truths and the other eye directed inward.

Both categories of human hope are challenged today. The subjective craving for personal existence is threatened by the specter of a nuclear war; it is also negated by the experimentalism of modern psychology, the skepticism of philosophy, and the clash of contending dogmas in the free world. The objective yearning for the triumph of our universal values is challenged once again, firstly by our failure to discover a common universe of discourse for the free world and the communist countries. It is also challenged by the philosophies of doom that have become fashionable in our day. We have been subjected to a continuous harangue about the decline of the West and the imminent collapse of our civilization. In a reaction against the radiant optimism of the nineteenth century, we have been told more recently that decline and death, not growth and progress, are truly inevitable; that the taint of "original sin" corrupts and frustrates all our efforts; that we are galloping down the hills of history to the abyss of destruction.

If hope is to spring anew in the human breast, we need to evolve a faith that will deal truly with the issues that threaten our personal existence. At the same time, we shall have to see how, on the subjective plane, universal values can be asserted and made to grow, in spite of all the philosophies of doom. Both needs are one at their source, for the human mind is one. We need a religion that will deal realistically with the issues of the day and a renewed faith in rational reflection that takes account of the totality of experience.

The slogans and clichés with which spokesmen of religion confront the challenges of today are more meaningless than they are wrong. We are told to repent, to have faith, to live by the law of love. But how does this repentance, or faith, or love deal with the menace of the bomb? Nearly all religionists tell us to "keep our powder dry" and to eschew the pitfalls of pacifism. What do these slogans mean then? When we are told that we should know ourselves to be sinners, doomed to frustration by virtue of "original sin" and laboring perpetually under the judgment of God, how does this counsel help us to hope? In fundamentalist religions, repentance was in a way proof of being chosen for salvation. The road to the peaks of hope led through the valleys of despair, and the ultimate goal was clear. The prophets spoke of the horrors of the "Day of the Lord," which allow only the merest remnant to survive, but their disciples could feel assured of belonging to that remnant. In the New Testament, the apostles spoke of the "Day of Judgment" that would condemn the majority of mankind to perdition; still, by implication and for their hearers, theirs was a message of "good news," since the community of believers were persuaded that they were numbered among the chosen saints, destined for the glories of salvation.

Today, spokesmen of religion continue to speak the language of despair, but the implication of hope and redemption no longer reverberates in their charismatic thunder. Neither the hope for subjective immortality nor the hope for the objective grounding of human values is furthered by the pleas for "leaps of faith," by the starry-eyed adoration of the "ineffable," or by acceptance of the logically absurd and the patently paradoxical. Today, it is no longer possible to repeat Kierkegaard's formula, "subjectivity is truth," and to believe it—at least, in the academic world. The smooth sayings of much that passes for religion is not so much untrue as irrelevant. Thus, it fails to inspire hope.

By the same token, the disciplines that represent man's quest for the values of objectivity do not speak in unison. The totality of human knowledge is today so vast that hardly ever is the attempt made to correlate the data from all fields of study to provide a unified structure of values. We have many more bricks of knowledge and a far better cement of methodology than was possessed in past ages, but we have no vision of the design of the sanctuary, which Philo and St. Paul called the "temple of the soul." We have mountains of knowledge, but not the architecture of wisdom.

Traditionally, it was the task of philosophy to discover the categories and point out the ultimate lessons to be derived from the totality of human knowledge, but very little of this genius of philosophy is in evidence today. By and large, philosophers are divided in two camps—the existentialists and the positivists. Neither group takes account of the totality of the human quest for truth. The existentialists turn their back upon the objective orientation of the soul as being coarse and common, smacking of the marketplace of commerce and industry. The positivists study language, logic, and the multiple errors of mankind.

Hence, from the philosophical realm of essence, too, there does not emanate today a voice of courage, an all-embracing vision, and a deathless hope.

To achieve a meaningful and hopeful outlook of life and the course of history, it is necessary for us to recapture the eternal meaning of faith, on the one hand, and, on the other hand, to re-establish the liberal philosophy of progress that has been so sadly shaken in recent years. We need a reasoned faith and a faith in reason.

Every attempt to investigate the nature of religion involves a paradox. The religionist is predisposed by his convictions to reflect his own subjective estimate of its character. The non-religionist is self-exiled from the paradise of faith, so that he can only speak of the revolving swords at the gate. Thus, we have two categories of definition: those that define religion in terms of feeling, experience, the inner life of the soul, and those that summarize sociological data on the role of religion in society. In the former category, we have the word of God spoken to prophets, the visions and ecstasies of mystics, and the many-hued "feelings" of romanticists; in the latter category, we have definitions ranging from Whitehead's description of "what the individual does in his solitariness" to Durkheim's concept of religion as group-awareness and Malinowski's interpretation of it as the celebration of the values of the community and the affirmation of its "*sancta.*"

In addition to this basic dichotomy in the comprehension of faith, there is the question of the extent of its boundaries. Since religion in itself tends to embrace the whole of life, while other social forces tend to limit its domain, it is possible to conceive of religion, in terms of its inner tendency, as embracing the totality of civilization; and it is also possible to limit it to the specific area where other disciplines have not yet penetrated. Thus, art, science, government, and charity institutions were at one time or another part of religion. In primitive societies, there is no aspect of life that is free from the dominion of religion, though even there, certain gradations of relevance are recognized. As Malinowski has pointed out, even the most primitive societies recognize certain skills and activities as relatively secular. History proves abundantly that when religion absorbs the whole of life, the many-sided energies of society are either atrophied into insignificance or absolutized into crystalline, dead dogmas. On the other hand, when religion is confined to moral sentiments and metaphysical speculation, it loses touch with reality and sinks into desuetude. Manifestly, both tendencies are right only in part. An alternating rhythm of "contraction and expansion," to use a Qabbalistic phrase, lies at the heart of faith.

To do justice to the totality of faith, in all its manifestations, we must take account both of its subjective character and of its articulation into subjective institutions and values; of its yearning to embrace the whole of life's adventures and of the growth within it of relatively independent domains of activity and valuation. Our initial starting point is the human spirit, in its totality. But then we soon note that much of our enterprise is concerned with techniques and tools that are needed for the daily business of living. Separating these utilitarian activities from our definition of the spiritual domain, we are left with the ends and aspirations that appeal to us as right and true

349

in themselves. Faith deals not so much with what we need as with that which needs us.

In its yearning for unity with the substance of things, as distinguished from the colorful charade of fleeting appearance, the human soul can turn either inward to seek the essential core of its own being, or it can turn outward to discover the ultimate sea of being, the enduring substance beneath the fleeting veil of phenomena. The consciousness of man is suspended precariously over the darkness of the deep, and its surface reflects the undulations of inner turbulence as well as the shifting storms of the outer world. Countless experiences bring home to man the flimsiness of that thin membrane of objective existence extending between the two massive infinities, the inner and the outer deeps of chaos. He feels the impetus of the driving will within himself, its inherent contradictions and frustrations. And he recognizes the immense mystery of the outer world, looming beyond the luminous circle of man's scanty knowledge.

However, man's awareness of his limitations contains also an assurance of the possession of truth. In feeling we somehow contain that which we try to reach in thought. Every particle of being contains the mystery of the whole. While our mind sails out on the surface of existence into the vast horizons of infinity, can it not proceed in the contrary direction, embracing the mystery from within? The firm soil of reality, in all its mystical charm and potency, is within as well as without. Hence, man's ultimate quest, the driving hunger for "that which does not fail," must move in two opposite directions—the rational quest for objective knowledge for its own sake and the romantic-mystical yearning for contact with the inner current of reality. Detachment is the hallmark of objectivity, while the individual's quest for roots is the distinguishing drive of the subjective quest for reality.

These two phases of faith appear only at the frontiers of the expanding horizons of human culture. The pursuit of knowledge for its own sake appears as a moving ideal among few people and at rare moments; similarly, the purely religious yearning for inclusion within the Divine harmony is rarely apprehended in isolation. The values and ends of the human spirit, be they esthetic, ethical, or religious, arise out of the free play of the intellect and imagination. Hence, they are not necessitous products of natural pressures and impulses. Born in freedom, they evolve a distinctive structure, an independent realm of purpose and judgment. All the values of human culture arise slowly and haltingly out of the prehuman and the precultural. When they emerge into consciousness, their inner logic and inherent impetus determine their development.

Man pursues his quest for reality in two directions. In rational reflection, he seeks to overcome all that is personal and subjective, canceling out the self-centered bias in his mathematical equations. Man needs to surmount the charm of the things that are characteristic of himself and of his group, learning to view the human scene from the impartial lofty heights of heaven, as if he were a disembodied spirit. In his quest for objective knowledge, man needs to love truth, above all, to shun every manner of falsehood, to cut off ruthlessly the "offending arm" of the self that habitually seeks aggrandizement; he needs to cut off the "offending eye," which seeks to glorify him at the expense of reality. He needs to sacrifice all that is his own—his pride, his family's glory, his tribe's interests, his nation's ambitions—in order to see reality, true and whole.

The domain of morality, originating in the feeling of love and sympathy, expands along with the quest for the fullness of an objective truth. The essence of the ethical imperative is to view all actions from an objective viewpoint. In its outgoing orientation, the human self is capable of seeing itself as others see it and arrives at the rule "Do unto others as you would have them do unto you." This Golden Rule, which Hillel phrased in a negative and Jesus in a positive formula, is found implicitly or explicitly in all great faiths. Immanuel Kant gave this rule its classic formulation as the reflection of perfect objectivity when he phrased it, "Act so that your action may be a standard of action for all others." Intellectual objectivity is, in essence, the application of the Golden Rule to the sphere of knowledge.

To be sure, ethical action is not merely the quest for objectivity. It constitutes a blend of feeling and reason, of subjective sentiment and objective reflection. In fact, impersonal thought can reach such heights of objectivity as to be utterly unconcerned with the fate of the individual. Mathematical thought, in its concern with masses and averages, may become the servile instrument of totalitarian ruthlessness and amorality.

We stand today at the end of a long evolutionary process that brought the glory of conscience into being through the gradual extension of rationality and the slow ripening of the feelings of love. Whether the ethical sense arose through the expansion of family feelings or through the growth of co-operative sentiments in the evolutionary process, we cannot tell. We do know that the moral sense is neither feeling alone, nor will, nor reason alone, but a composite of all these elements, the mature product of the interaction of the two orientations of the human mind. In both ethics and religion, the quest of the soul for objective truth is balanced and deepened by the movement of spirit into the shadowed recesses of inner life and feeling.

The inward orientation of the soul is also a quest for the fullness of reality. After all, we do not merely see and know, we also *are*. If we could only probe deeply enough into the nature of our own being, we should discover not only our own self, but the heart of being itself. We are part of being; in our conscious mind, the surface of reality is reflected, but in our deeper self, or will and feeling, the dynamic substance of reality is vibrantly alive. It is in our own deepest layers that we transcend the realm of appearance and achieve contact with truth and reality.

This quest for inner depth and refinement of feeling is the other phase of the life of faith. It is an inverse direction but not a contradiction of the search for objective truth.

Logical formulas may be contradictory, but orientations of the soul are not. As human beings, we are fated to live in continual tension and alternation, with the two truths of total selflessness in contemplation and total withdrawal of the self into its own oceanic depths of passion contending against each other. The mystery of being reveals to us only fleeting glimpses. We fit our fragmentary insights together like a jigsaw puzzle, and in every age, we strive all over again to attain a philosophy of life. But the growth of objective knowledge and the refinement of subjective feeling are progressive and cumulative in their effects. The truths of objectivity need to be embraced in feeling; the varied sentiments and judgments that flow from our communion with our deepest self need to be subjected to the light of objective criticism.

Revelation is not the product solely of the intuitive, non-rational quality of our nature, but of its mysterious creative energy as it is refined and clarified by rational reflection. The voice of God is one but our hearing is twofold; we hear his voice in the austere call of truth and in the gentle charm of whole-souled devotion. The prophet, medium of revelation, is in part mystic, in part sage, altogether a social reformer.

In all our discussion of religion thus far, we did not speak of the command or word of God. Eschewing the clash of dogmas, we can only examine religion from the human point of view. To man, the call of God for unity or harmony comes in two forms—the call to know the truth, and the call to love the source of all life. Man's response to this double call is accordingly also twofold, a hunger for the purity of truth and a love of God that seeks the refinement of purity and the singularity of devotion.

Knowledge, in its ideal perfection, is the outgoing coordinate of the human soul, along which man's confusions and prejudices may be plotted; love, in its ideal perfection as the extension of man's empathy, is the inner coordinate of the soul, and all the variations of feeling are but diverse modifications of it. Both the quest for truth and the yearning to be embraced in a cosmic harmony of love are limited and modified by the objects of knowledge and the objects of affection that are encountered early in the history of human life. But the multiplicity of human modifications and even perversions should not blind us to the unity of the core of man's spiritual adventure.

If the key word to man's objective orientation is knowledge, and the key word to man's inward pathway is love, then it is well to reflect on the fact that in Hebrew both words have the same root, *yodea;* for to know is to seek in love, and to love is to seek to know. The two orientations of man's spirit are opposite in direction, but one in their living source.

We speak of religion as the "cutting edge of man's quest for reality," implying that behind that edge we find the whole of man's cultural attainments. As the "cutting edge" advances, diverse skills and data become relatively dissociated from the domain of religious tension. We can then speak of these activities as secular in character. On the other hand, the quest for totality and integration tends to sweep into the maelstrom of religion virtually everything that swims into the human ken. Thus we find that in its subjective orientation religion absorbs and transmutes the manifold paradoxes of human feeling—fear and anger, sense of guilt and expiation, love of one's ancestors and fear of their avenging ghosts. The inner life borders on the realm of dreams, in all its protean mystery and tension. The swing of the pendulum of consciousness toward the outer world may either "project" an internal experience into the trappings of materiality or it may expose that experience to rational scrutiny. In the initial stages of man's growth, the first eventuality is far more likely than the second. The offering of expiatory sacrifices in which the animal "carries the sin" of the worshiper upon it is a perfect example of the phenomenon of "projection." The perennial search for a scapegoat, even in modern times, is proof of the relatively obdurate character of man's nature and its resistance to the fullness of rationality.

Many theories concerning the origin of religion have been propounded since the days of Democritus and Euhemerus. Religion has been caused by man's fear, man's perplexity and anxiety, man's attempt to understand the world, man's eagerness to control it, man's pristine sense of kinship with the animal world and with his ancestors, man's reverence and awe for the mighty events in nature. To all these ancient theories, the sociologists have added the consciousness of society, its values, hopes, and its need for self-preservation; the Freudians in our day have added the concept of mass-neuroses as a way of deflecting the tensions produced by an inner sense of guilt. The Jungians have pictured man's subconscious soul as a mighty, intuitive faculty, operating by means of myths and symbols and producing a language of salvation, consisting of "archetypes" and "collective representations."

All these hypotheses need to be taken account of in the actual study of the evolution of religions, but the adulteration of the human spirit by the multiple dross of myth and magic should not blind us to the emergence of the nonutilitarian, the self-giving dimension of culture. Far from overlooking the multiplicity of factors in the emergence of culture and religion, our point is that the human soul absorbs a variety of subjective factors and outer pressures in its alternation from the recesses of feeling and mystery within its own being to the contemplation of external reality. Many and diverse are the steps along this undulating wave of spiritual growth. When the curtain of history opens on the human adventure, the mind of man has already undergone a vast development. But, at any one time and in any one place, the vitality of religion is to be found at the "cutting edge" of man's quest for unity and harmony.

The concept of the "Holy" has given theologians a firm fulcrum for their faith, especially since the appearance of Rudolf Otto's *The Idea of the Holy*. Actually, it is only a restatement of Schleiermacher's *Gefühl* and, in a larger sense, of the grand course of Christian Protestant thought, going back to St. Paul and St. Augustine. In "normative" Judaism, the Holy is neither feeling only, nor thought only, nor action only; it is the "seeking of the Lord" through each and all of these avenues —learning, prayer, and deeds of loving-kindness. It is the outward movement toward objective clarity, as it is the inward orientation of the soul to depth and worth, and our life is in the tension between them. Objectively, God is the order of the infinite universe—"He puts on light as a garment." Subjectively, He is the infinite reach of the soul of man, the "candle of the Lord."

Some Protestant theologians speak of a depth dimension, or of a "higher category of reason" which is contrasted with the "calculating" reason of normal speech, or of the incursion of the "suprarational" or the supranatural power of grace, or of revelation, into the stream of history. These efforts to glorify the retreat of the soul into subjectivity are both right and wrong: right insofar as they insist on the insufficiency and relativity of man's reason at any one time, but wrong insofar as they restrict the essence of faith to the appearance of the nonrational. "Higher reason" or the "depth dimension" turn out to be euphemisms for those "paradoxes" that were in earlier ages labeled frankly as dogmas, without the haze of equivocation. Faith is not the defiance of, or the transcendence of reason, for the part does not stand over against the whole, not even in a "dialectical" relation. But faith is the insistence on the *wholeness* and the *oneness* of man's spirit, which oscillates between the inner and outer poles of reality. Faith is related to both feeling and rationality as the mind is to the senses, not as the diverse senses are to one another.

The actual institutions and rites of religions are the instruments of this quest, dramatizing the relevance of the infinite goal, which is unreachable. Sometimes these instruments work effectively, bringing people to a fresh confrontation of inner or outer reality; sometimes these instruments merely record the vast momentum of the past. But religion in itself is a protean, momentary phenomenon, the very life of which is movement. It is never finished and complete, even as the pathway from man to God is infinite. It is always tension, eagerness, and quest, an overcoming and a surmounting, not a placid, peaceful possession. The depths of feeling may be plumbed by psychologists *ad infinitum*, but the task of self-knowledge must forever remain uncompleted, since the very act of self-probing changes the self that is studied. The vast mysteries of the external world keep pace with the expanding horizons of man's knowledge. There is no limit to man's quest in either direction. The task of religion is never done. There is no external truth; only an endless quest. "The righteous," says the Talmud, "have no rest either in this world or in the World to Come."

It is difficult for us to become accustomed to the idea that religion is in essence a dynamic wavelike movement, not a specific body of ideas, nor a specific religious experience, nor anything that is fixed and definable for all time to come. But upon reflection, we come to realize that dynamic tension is the substance of all things. The ultimate building blocks of the universe are now seen to be waves of one sort or another, not concrete balls of solid matter. The more we come down to the rock-bottom facts of existence, the more we find reality dissolving into a dynamic system of undulation. As physics teaches us to see matter as a bipolar field of tension, so logic teaches us that the realm of mind is a field marked by the two poles of universality and particularity. In every logical definition, in every proposition, in the very act of thinking, this duality of meaning is inescapable. We tell the meaning of a particular datum by pointing to universals; we tell the meaning of universals by pointing to particulars. Since religion is the endeavor to deal with the ultimate facts and values of existence, we can hardly expect it to be other than a dialectical confrontation.

The mystics have always contended that religion is a series of wavelike ascents and descents of the soul, aiming at the confrontation of the soul with God and culminating in an ecstatic experience of unity with the Divine Being. On the other hand, the common religion of all rationalists has always been the conviction that reality is reached only through the repudiation of all that is personal and subjective, and the total submission of the soul to the compelling logic of objective existence. We consider the opposing goals of both rationalism and mysticism

357

as constituting the two phases of the life of the soul. Both are phases of religion. Neither goal is ever reached, and it is our human destiny to live in perpetual tension between the insight of the soul and the generalizations of reason, achieving a temporary synthesis of them for the guidance of one or more generations.

All of human progress in the realm of cultural values is motivated by the life of faith. Out of objective contemplation *ideas* are born. If these ideas have any bearing upon human life, they are turned into *ideals* when the soul, in its inward orientation, comes to invest the data of contemplation with the powerful undergirding of emotion. Ideals, by reason of their emotional appeal and intellectual charm, tend to grow into historic forces, becoming articulated in institutions and mass-movements. Society, thus ennobled by the ideals of the past, makes possible the emergence of individuals *who seek and obtain* further glimpses of objective truth. Thus do the wheels of history grind painfully forward. If this creative process could be continued indefinitely, there would be no ground for despair. The feelings of hope would open up even more beautiful vistas. But somehow the creative alternation of man's spirit grinds to a halt from time to time; the two phases of man's spirit pull apart and become mutually incommunicable; the language of hope becomes irrelevant; religion ceases to charm and begins to thunder; despair sets in.

What is it that stops the movement of the human spirit, causing religion to become petrified and to congeal into dead certainties? On the objective plane, there is the peril of fragmentary truth. In the subjective world, we encounter the fragmentation of loyalty through the multiple fascinations of self-flattery. The two forms of fragmentation act as brakes, halting the advance of human thought and sentiment.

First, the fragmentation of universal truth. It is our fate, as human beings, to accumulate knowledge bit by bit, and every new discovery looms so large as to obscure the rest of the horizon. Our abstractions glance off the roundness of reality like tangents, touching it and moving beyond it at one and the same time. As subsequent generations build upon the tangential abstractions of their predecessors, they move farther and farther away from the turbulent depths of existence. A reaction against the "life of reason" then takes place in the name of the logic of life itself. The pendulum of the soul swings inward until the partial truths are integrated and absorbed, readying the soul of the age for new ventures into abstract, objective knowledge. But an age may be so fascinated with its limited truths as not to dare venture into new domains. This is especially true when the fragmentary visions of reality have had a hard struggle to win acceptance. Ideas cannot become mass-ideals unless and until they have become invested with powerful emotional valence, but this very mass-appeal generates mass-pride, which prevents the mind from contemplating any fresh truths.

This relationship of the faith of the individual to that of the community constitutes one of the inveterate paradoxes at the heart of religion. It is the social function of organized religion to fortify and celebrate the values of society. In this aspect, it is a powerful, conserving force. On the other hand, insofar as it is the "cutting edge of the soul in its quest for reality," it seeks freshness of approach, novelty of insight, new levels of creativity. Hence, every forward step in the life of faith takes the form of rebellion. Nothing new in faith is born without social tension between those who behold new horizons of objective truths and those who nurture the glowing embers of subjective pride and the self-exalting sentiments of a parochial tradition.

Reinhold Niebuhr has called attention to the paradox of "moral man within an immoral society." It is the very enthusiasm and devotion of man that leads him to exalt a communal ideal, but the massive stature of this ideal prevents the emergence of a more objective, more valid, concept of social welfare. For instance, patriotism frequently bars the road to the more universal ideals of humanity.

We thus arrive at the major obstacle to progress, the fascination of collective self-flattery. The brevity and precariousness of life demand the aura of certainty so that insights are quickly turned into dogmas. Within every society, the affirmation of its objective values is quickly associated with the assertion of the supreme worth of the existence of the society itself. The passions of ethnicism, once aroused on behalf of any truth, prevent any effort that would limit the worth or range of that truth. Dogmatism and ethnicism are the twin obstacles of the dynamic life of the soul. Both carry the "Name of God," but in vain. Their aim is to "magnify and sanctify" an existing society or a time-conditioned ideal, not to magnify and sanctify the One, "whose seal is truth." It is the function of all organized religions to preserve the intellectual insights and the moral values of the past for the guidance of contemporaries. To discharge these functions, religions tend to endow these insights and values with the aura of eternity and absolute truth so that fragmentary truths are converted into "infallible dogmas" and values of relative merit are transformed into inflexible commandments of infinite duration.

The paradox of religion then consists in the fact that its own negation as a living quest is implied in its affirmation as a social reality. Does it follow that the quest of religions is forever frustrated and that any hope for mankind cannot be found in the annals of man's organized faiths? Several investigators have arrived at this conclusion.

Let me recall the thinking of a great Russian philosopher, Nicholas Berdyaev. He pointed out that *culture*, the totality of man's great ideas, is always the creation of the few, and that culture quickly degenerates into the dead molds of *civilization*, since ideas can be sold to the masses only by appeals directed to their emotions. But the utilitarian ambitions and self-seeking sentiments of the people transmute ideals of universal meaning and value into symbols of collective pride and arrogance, undoing the arduous labors of saints and philosophers. Such is the pessimistic philosophy of Berdyaev, reflecting the despair of great minds with the shoddy standards of the populace.

If we are to find the dawn of hope in the bloody tale of blundering and stumbling that is the history of mankind, we must be persuaded of the possibility and practicality of two tasks: first, that a conscious and mighty synthesis of objective knowledge with subjective feeling, of science and religion, remains a reasonable possibility and a valid goal at all times; second, that the masses of people can be persuaded to accept the practice of rational-moral self-scrutiny and self-criticism as a religious imperative.

Rationalists find the principle of evil in the resistance offered by the populace to the rigors of thought. In their view, society can achieve perfection only if the aristocracy of the intellect is wedded to political power. Since the consummation is not apparently possible in a democracy, they see little hope ahead. Mystics seek a harsh and lonely road to salvation, which only a few can take. Romantics idealize the people and excoriate the pride of reason. For them, the principle of evil lies in the rootlessness of the intellect. Since leadership in the modern world is so utterly dependent on intellectual progress, they find salvation only in idle dreams of retreating into the dark caverns of the past. To us, the principle of evil lies in the imbalance of the human spirit and in its failure to grow by way of the dynamic dialectic of intellect and emotion. Our hope is centered on the attainment of a dynamic equilibrium between reason and faith, and between the religions of the masses and the insights of their leaders.

Let us consider closely these two desiderata of a hopeful philosophy of life; the possibility of a fresh synthesis of man's objective search for knowledge and his subjective quest for harmony with the final ground of all existence. All too often this question is presented in the framework of controversy, as if the rightness of either science or religion implied the wrongness of the other. Actually, the very possibility of meaningful progress is at stake, since the advance of the human spirit in either

361

direction exclusively marks the defeat of mankind. Those who are trained to maintain the objective orientation of the human mind sometimes forget that the retreat of the soul into a shadowed inner world is part of the inescapable rhythm of life. If the subjective realm is ignored, all the manifestations of primitive myth and self-aggrandizing superstition are certain to come back with a vengeance.

In the modern world, dogmatism has been declining steadily in power since the seventeenth century. In its place, ethnicism has been rising in inverse proportion. Dogmatism derives from the investing of subjective formulas with objective certainty. As religious dogmatism gave way before the advance of objective knowledge, the vacuum in the interior life of people was gradually filled by the growth of nationalism and racism in all its forms. On the threshold of the nineteenth century, the German Enlightenment had shattered the chains of dogma, and the Romantic movement arose to forge the new chains of mystical nationalism. While ethnicism is a primitive feeling, modern nationalism suborned into its service the diverse objective disciplines of history, anthropology, biology, etc. Yet, all these data of objective knowledge were employed selectively, subjectively, and with malice aforethought, in order to flatter the resurgent pride of primitive instinct. The modern period has made *autos-da-fé* unfashionable, even as the medieval period had ruled out human sacrifice as an abomination, but the sacrifices to Moloch were not only continued but multiplied in both the medieval and modern eras. The subjective fanaticism of nationality has taken the place of the subjective pathos of religion. In the Soviet world, a new dogmatism deriving from nineteenth-century science and a new ethnicism masquerading as hostility to the "cosmopolitanism" of the West have arisen to fill the psychic vacuum left by the official banishment of religious dogmatism and nationalism.

We live in an age of marvelous and rapid growth of knowledge, but the unitary architecture of wisdom is lacking. The massive mountains of data are not related and brought together.

We suffer from a dichotomy of the soul, with the subjective values of religion being kept apart from the discrete facts of objective knowledge. The voice of religion is stifled and made irrelevant by the dead weight of rituals and dogmas with which it is associated, while the pathos of subjectivity drives mankind from one dungeon of fanaticism into the other.

The seeds of hope cannot be nourished in a society where the values of religion are unintegrated with the insights of objective research. The pathos of subjectivity is then wasted on rituals and dogmas, while the tender texture of society is left to its own devices. Man's objective powers grow apace, but the *ideas* of the few are not articulated into the *ideals* of the many. The prophets of knowledge glare at the priests of sentiment, and never do the twain meet, while primitive passions forge illegitimate unions with the fragments of unintegrated knowledge that are strewn about. Can religion come to glorify the insights of objectivity? Can religion which ministers to our subjective needs once again embrace the goals of reason and lead the battle against the Molochs of the modern world? The central question of our time is whether the masses of mankind can ever learn to accept criticism of their collective actions as a religious imperative. The distinction between the values of the "creative minority" and the passions of the masses has always led learned men to despair of the future. This is why Goethe insisted that "*Der kleine Gott der Welt ist stets derselbe Schlag*" and Plato foretold the ultimate ruin of a democratic society. Soviet philosophy assumes that the masses are moved only by economic pressures and that all idealistic creations are irrelevant and useless. We have already mentioned the pessimistic refrain of Berdyaev, insisting that only the few create the pure, self-authenticated values of "culture," while the masses transform these values into the coarse coin of utilitarianism and materialism.

The rise of the Hebrew prophets provides the one answer to the two questions: the possibility of a synthesis between the objective and subjective phases of the human mind, and the hope of the people accepting the practice of self-criticism as a Divine command.

The double character of the Biblical prophets is rarely appreciated. Commonly the prophet is regarded as a "charismatic personality" who was governed by the mystical feeling of being guided by Providence. To be sure, the prophets were mystics and they certainly believed that their words reflected the will of God. But at the same time the prophets were philosophers, attempting to apply the rational-moral conscience to the events of their day and to the heritage of tradition. It is interesting to note that the earliest interpreters of Judaism to the Greek world described the Hebrew prophets as the teachers of the Hellenic philosophers.

Every creative advance in the history of both Judaism and Christianity constituted a return to the freshness and originality of the prophets, though different movements emphasized the diverse facets of the prophetic consciousness. The prophet is the representative of classical religion as it seeks to achieve a dynamic equilibrium between the mystery of subjective inspiration, the call to objective reflection, and the challenge of focusing the light of rationality and the fervor of piety upon the ethical issues of the day.

By the nature of his task, every prophet brought a fresh nuance into his interpretation of the word of God. He was not a mere child of tradition, even when he preached the virtue of loyalty to tradition. He was not the practitioner of ancient arts, as were the other representatives of faith and virtue in Biblical times. Jeremiah insists, "There will not be lost Torah from the priest, nor the word from the prophet, nor counsel from the sage."[1] Both the sage, teaching the international wisdom of his day, and the priest, guarding the specific ritual of his tribe and its hallowed tradition, were professionals. They were apprentices for many years, learning their "trade" and relying on the authority of their masters. Also, their place in society was fixed— the one cultivating and training the intellect, the other ministering to the devious ways of the human heart.

The prophet was the agent of the living synthesis of wisdom and piety. Moreover, he added an original emphasis of his own which highlighted the relevance of both the priest and sage. Stressing the centrality of the ethical issue, he brought the shrine and the lecture hall into the dusty marketplace. Ethics, as we have seen, is made possible by the amplitude of the wave of man's spirit as it oscillates between the two poles of objectivity and subjectivity. In the shifting circumstances of social life, new challenges are presented daily to the custodians of the human spirit. The prophet as the man of action stood between the sage and the priest, harmonizing their respective traditions and applying them to the varying needs of his time. For this reason, the Jewish religion, continuing the prophetic tradition, stressed consistently the rightness of deeds rather than the correctness of creeds.

The prophets must be distinguished from the "prophetizers," who practiced the arts leading to mystical frenzy and ecstasy. As prophets, they were also separate and distinct from the sages, who taught "wisdom," and from the priests, who guarded the sacred rituals and scrolls, though some of them may have come from the ranks of these functionaries. Their characteristic feature was the conviction that the "still, small voice" of conscience was also the voice of God. As mystics, they watched intently for the light of guidance to appear in their souls; as philosophers, they identified the art of rational-moral criticism with the Divine imperative. They were agents of revelation in both its intuitive and rationalistic phases, and in the domain of ethical action, which derives from the synthesis of love and reason.

They were passive, like the mystics, conscious of the vanity of all human attainments, but they were also active, in relation to God, pleading, demanding, storming the heavens. They withdrew from public life, trying to shun the unholy fires, the restless tremors, the driving storms of social affairs; in the privacy of direct communion of the alone with the Alone, they shut out the noise of the marketplace and hearkened to the word of God, but at the same time, they always came back to the community as faithful messengers and leaders of public affairs. Who more than they knew the emptiness of human wisdom and the frailty of man's intellect? Yet, they dared confront God with their reasoned arguments, their ethical assertions of right and wrong, their rational-moral insights. Abraham exclaims, "Can it be that the Judge of the whole earth will not do justice?" And Jeremiah cries out, "Just art Thou, O Lord, but judgment I shall speak with Thee—Why is the way of the righteous prosperous?"[2] There was a dynamic equilibrium in the soul of the prophet between his self-surrender and his self-affirmation in regard to God.

The prophets represented, therefore, a perfect synthesis between the two orientations of the human soul, proving that the objective values of reason can be turned into luminous ideals for a whole people and that the sacred heritage of a people can be elevated and refined by rational-moral criticism. All that is truly great in the Judeo-Christian heritage goes back to this essential unity of objective thought and subjective feeling in the teaching of the prophets.

This unity is seen, firstly, in their critique of ritualism; secondly, in their transformation of ethnicism.

In several ways ritualism is an expression of man's retreat from the gray world of reality. Firstly, every rite is based on ancient tradition, which was absorbed in childhood. As man probes his inner soul, he encounters the experiences of childhood and the impact of tradition within the core of his being. Secondly, most rituals, but especially those of sacrifice, articulate the philosophy and pathos of the unconscious—sin is a quasi-physical taint that can be washed away by priestly lustrations or projected unto scapegoats. Thirdly, all rituals symbolize by their very irrationality the dark, unreasoning depths of human nature; hence, they channel the yearnings of the mysterious soul within us for unity with the great mystery above and beyond us. Ritualism is thus the symbol and vehicle of the subjective phase of religion.

By the same token, nationalism transfers the focus of devotion from God to the collective being of the ethnic group. It is "my people," "my blood," "my mystical, inner, national soul" that is extolled and magnified. Nationalism is utterly subjective and romantic, while devotion to the public welfare, conceived in the rational terms of statehood and citizenship, is objective and strictly utilitarian. Nationalism glorifies the invisible and the intangible self-image of the people, which is frequently only vaguely related to the actual facts of the situation.

Living at a time when sacrifices and religious rituals pervaded the whole of life, the prophets dared to assert that God is not mollified by such devices, but that He seeks the offering of a "broken spirit." Though heaven is His chair and the earth His footstool, He looks to the "poor and the lowly in spirit." A thousand different ways lead to His nearness, and in every place where people gather in sincere worship, howsoever they call on their god, incense is offered to His Name. His will is expressed in this classic formulation: "He hath told thee, O man, what is good; and what the Lord desires from thee, but to do justly, and to love mercy, and to walk humbly with the Lord, thy God."[3]

Greater by far than their transcendence of ritualism was their refinement and transformation of nationalism. Time and again, they reminded their people that the principles of right and wrong were far more important than the material advantages of any policy. A nation should seek greatness by the knowledge and the love of God, not by way of pursuing the worldly ambitions of wealth and power, fame and cleverness. The prophets courted martyrdom at the hands of the zealous patriots of their day. But, in their own way, they were fervent patriots, loving their people with every fiber of their soul. Precisely because they loved their people they sought for them the highest possible distinction, that of assuming the role of a "prophet-people," bringing "light to the nations." Their people were to seek greatness through service, blessedness through conferring blessings upon the whole of mankind, redemption through liberation from sin, and dedication to the ideals of God. The acme of Israel's glory was to be its role as the "suffering servant" in the drama of mankind.

The greatness of the prophetic achievement was not merely its transcendence of ritualism and ethnicism, but the fact that they preached this message in the name of God and through the agencies of faith. In Greece, there were several schools of philosophy, and some of them managed to attain the same triumph of the rational-moral faculties over the impulsions of blind faith and ethnic pride. But the philosophers, representing the objective orientation of the mind, had hardly a common bond with the Greek people, with their day-by-day faith, their feelings, and their hopes. Pagan religion, where it was most effective, glorified the mystery of life and catered to the subjective needs, fears, and superstitions of the people. Pagan philosophy represented the arduous efforts of the mind in its search for truth. Between these two articulations of the human soul in its quest for reality there was no inner, necessitous connection. In the later centuries of the Greco-Roman world, when attempts were made to bridge the gap between philosophy and popular religion, the two domains were so far apart that any association between them could only appear to be artificial and contrived.

Because philosophy in the post-Socratic and post-Platonic era lacked the moral fervor of faith, it could not keep its own disciples from wandering off into the blind alleys of cynicism, epicureanism, and mysticism. Lacking any intimate contact with the religion of the people, philosophy could not generate a sustained movement for the amelioration of the social ills of the day.

Paganism in the classical world was Janus-faced, compounding myth and magic, cruelty and slavery, desperate sensualism. and hopeless despair on the popular level, along with flashes of philosophical humanism in all their diverse forms. The refinement of philosophy was socially powerless as the mythology of the people was rationally untenable.

The spirit of melancholic despair that pervaded the classical world appears strange to moderns, but the men of reason in the ancient world knew themselves to be hopelessly isolated. The mythology of the people articulated the anxieties and fears of man's "collective unconscious," which is deeply pessimistic. All mythologies reflect the blind power of fate that crushes all human efforts to overcome the manifold obstacles of life. Mythology interprets the world in terms of the categories of *life*: the love interests of the gods account for human affairs; the world has come into being as the result of some conflict among the gods; the rhythm of spring and autumn is due to some process in the life of the gods; man finds salvation by identifying himself with the god that dies and is reborn. With biology providing the basic key to the mystery of existence in pagan mythology, despair is inevitable, for all that is born is fated to die.

By contrast, the prophets brought to their people a message of hope and consolation in the bleak days of defeat and disaster. They saw the "Spirit of God" as containing the values of man's spirit in their perfection. "Grass withers, blossoms wilt, but the word of God stands forever." Their concept of God was an ideal extension of the soul as it is aware of the mystery of its own being, and as it views the validity of its values. Maintaining a dynamic equilibrium between mystical faith and rational reflection, they were enabled to transform the life of their people and to generate undying fervor on behalf of the rational-moral ideals of the life of wisdom. They transformed the arts of self-criticism into a Divine exercise. Opposing the impulses of ethnicism, they persuaded the people to subject their actions and judgments to scrutiny in the name of a higher, Divine Law. They refined the faith of the people with the acid of objective values and standards, and they fortified these attainments of objective reflection with the help of religious fervor.

369

The dynamic equilibrium of the prophetic consciousness gives us the meaning of spirit in action. It stands for the unity of man's essential values. That which is true is also good, also beautiful, also a compelling summons to social action. Today the term "spirit," or "spiritual," has a hollow ring because the awareness of this unity is now extremely rare. In every generation, this unity of spirit needs to be re-experienced precisely because the quest of reality is oriented in two opposite directions. Spirit does not exist *in* man, but, like light, *between* man and reality. Spirit is one, in its source, the human soul; it is asserted and apprehended in the exalted moments of religious experience; its unity on the open horizons of every age is always a goal and a vision, not an accomplished fact.

This is why the prophets insisted so universally on the unity of God. That God, as seen in nature and in human nature, is One means that the values of humanity, in their objective rationality, and in their subjective depth, are one in essence. To overlook the unifying source of the "Spirit of God" is to exalt truth at the expense of goodness, or beauty at the expense of both. But these fragmentized values are idols, false and misleading. Says the prophet Isaiah concerning Abraham, "For one I called him and blessed him."[4]

What is it that we learn from the example of the prophets concerning the spiritual perplexities of our time? Is the prophetic synthesis at all relative to our problem? I believe it is directly relevant, for the culture of our time draws its inspiration from both Hebraic and Hellenic sources, with neopagan elements contending against the Judeo-Christian heritage of the prophets. We, too, are Janus-faced, with philosophy moving off blithely in one direction and religion in the other. Only today, popular religion comes in diverse forms of ritualism, ethnicism, the neomagic of pseudoscience and the neomythologies of romanticism. And philosophy is divided into many branches that know not one another.

Of ritualism, we need hardly speak. Clearly, a large portion of our public thinks and lives as if the symbolic and dogmatic shell of faith were its soul and substance. This observation applies to all faiths. Even many thinking people identify religion with the rites and myths that they absorbed in childhood. They grow in many different directions, but their religions remain swaddled in nursery garments. More importantly, perhaps, the objective domain is now pre-empted by a thousand different disciplines, and only subjectivity, in its diverse expressions, appears to be the proper field of religion.

Ethnicism is very largely a form of religion in our time. The editors of our papers consider it their duty to extol the actions and policies of our State Department almost automatically and without criticism. When Senator Mansfield came out with a remarkable appraisal of our foreign policy in reference to Berlin and West Germany, a well-known editor of one of our largest dailies commented: "He spoke as if he were a representative of the United Nations." This was the senator's ultimate error—he dared to think in objective terms, as a citizen of the world! But, is not objectivity the very quality that we should most seek in all discussions of foreign affairs?

Unhappily, Kierkegaard's "subjectivity is truth" has been translated for more than a century into the collective and secular terms of nationalism. The massive wars of the twentieth century were brought on by this perverted piety that affirmed objective truth and the rational criticism of national policy to be mankind's "original sin." In spite of the enormous slaughter of the Second World War, which was caused by the deliberate determination to think with one's blood instead of one's brain, we still have not reached the point of recognizing objectivity itself as a Divine imperative. Religion is still expected to "magnify and sanctify," bless and extol, whatever is affirmed to be national policy, not to generate enthusiasm for a supranational, all-human approach.

The difference between religion and magic has been variously understood. Professor Frazer pointed out that religion *persuades*, while magic *compels;* i.e. the worshiper implores God to help him, while the magical practitioner manipulates the occult powers to achieve his private ends. To the religionist, God is mystery, standing beyond all human grasp; to the magician, He is a thing that can be turned this way and that. To the man of religion, the *values* that he and God share are all-important; his own fulfillment is envisioned against the background of a hierarchy of values that is both human and Divine. To the practitioners of magic, ancient or modern, values are of no account, and man seeks to achieve "success," in terms of the marketplace.

Much that passes for religion in our time is neomagical. The "power of positive thinking" is described as something concrete, pliable, capable of serving human ends. The "bitch-goddess of Success," in the language of D. H. Lawrence, is elevated to the highest pedestal—all else is but a means to this supreme goal. Religion is not conceived as the quest for unity with reality, but as an instrument for getting on, sitting on the important boards, manipulating God and influencing people.

Along with the perversion of "positive thinking," there prevails today the vogue of "peace of mind." In an age when "tranquillity pills" are consumed by the millions, it is natural to think of religion, too, as a kind of "pill," which through the combination of Bible and Freud brings on the boon of peace.

Prophetic religion was neither magical nor medicinal. It did not transform God into a portable battery of mysterious power, nor did it seek to charm people into bland tranquillity. On the contrary, the opponents of prophecy, we are told, made it their policy to shout "Peace, peace." The true prophets preached the glory of continuous tension, for it is in tension that the "cutting edge" of the spirit is brought to light. Theirs was a heroic, manly faith that extolled the strenuous virtues, not those that relax, comfort, and beguile. The prophets called men to act in the daytime world with courage and resolution. Theirs was a *daytime* faith of action and vision, not solely a *nighttime* faith of self-hypnosis, of "leaps into faith," of auto-intoxication with the "dark speech" of theologians.

Popular versions of depth-psychology provide the veneer of

science for the neomagical types of religion. Religion today must embrace the truths of psychology, as it must take account of truth wherever it is found. But religion possesses its own values and its own genius. While the psychiatrist aims at the goals of "health," or "adjustment," or "contentment," the man of religion aims at goodness, greatness, the love of man, and the love of God.

Apart from the channels of organized religion, certain myths arise, from time to time, in the shadowed recesses of subjectivity. These myths may well become powerful social forces if the objective orientation of the soul is denied the powerful support of religion. We tend to think of myths as creations of the primitive era of human life, but the primitive mind is reborn in every generation. Spiritual values must be transmitted by the process of education, but primitive ways of thinking spring naturally and, as it were, automatically, into being.

The mythologies of nationalism are the clearest examples of the tendency in modern times to create fresh myths. They are all characterized by the assumption of a dark and mysterious "national soul," which is apprehended in intuition; by an attempt to explain the whole history of mankind in terms of this "national soul" and the opposition to it by the forces of Satan; by the tendency to attribute all that is good and noble to the mysterious operation of this "national soul" and all that is evil to its opposite. The ideology of nazism, as worked out by Alfred Rosenberg, was a conscious attempt to promulgate the "Aryan myth" as the basis for a resurgent and invincible German Empire. The Jew was assigned the role of devil and scapegoat in this attempt to evolve a perverted philosophy of life out of the natural subjectivity of nationalism. Few people realize that the Nazi ideology had deep roots in German culture. Rosenberg's *The Myth of the Twentieth Century* was actually only a restatement of Fichte's *Characteristics of the Nineteenth Century*. The philosopher of German nationalism at the threshold of the nineteenth century already divided mankind into two classes: those who use their intellect (*Verstand*) and are always wrong, generating the manifold evils of modern industrial society; and those who use their intuition *(Vernunft),* which is their exclusive, inborn gift, and are always right, creating all the great achievements of culture. Naturally, according to Fichte, the Germans were pre-eminently the chosen people of *Vernunft,* as the Jews and the French could only make use of *Verstand.* To trace the line of development from Fichte to Rosenberg is to write the history of German romanticism in all its multifarious manifestations.

But the Germans were not the only creators of national mythologies. There was Adam Mickiewicz with his concept of Poland as the Messianic people. There was Danilevsky with his interpretation of the whole of world history as a contest between Germanic-Latin Europe, on the one hand, and the Russian-Slavic world, on the other hand. The pan-Slavic movement of Russia was a powerful reactionary force dedicated to the concept of Russia as the Messiah of mankind. Dostoevski devoted his magnificent talents to this doctrine, and Walter Schubart added the weight of his learning to the assertion that Russian culture was an expression of the "Messianic soul."

Nor is mythology the peculiar product of European cultures. Hofstadter describes the "agrarian myth" in his fine study of the Age of Reform, *Social Darwinism in American Thought, 1860-1915.* The dragon's teeth of anti-Semitism are scattered the world over, and they are compounded of myth and hate and frustration in equal proportions. New myths are arising even now in Africa and Asia, with the white man taking on the role and disguise of the devil. Communism began its career as a scientific analysis of European capitalism, but it has long ceased to base its appeal on purely intellectual arguments. Today it draws its strength from the dark underworld of mythology, where the shining white knights of the proletariat battle incessantly against the fat, grinning black-coated devils of capitalism. And "free enterprise," too, has its mythology, one that has been aptly named "Social Darwinism."

374

In the seventies and eighties of the nineteenth century, Darwin's and Spencer's ideas were utilized as a demonstration that *laissez-faire* economics was the invariable law of nature, hence, the law of God. The competitive struggle in society was only an expression of the operation of the law of "natural selection," and any interference with it was both futile and immoral: futile because natural law cannot be resisted, immoral because it tended to make for the "survival of the unfittest." This argument held sway for nearly a generation, and when it was finally overcome, the racist interpretation of "Social Darwinism" came to the fore in a brief but feverish flirtation with "Anglo-Saxonism" and its "manifest destiny." However, American infatuation with the myth of Anglo-Saxon supremacy came to an end in the First World War. The brutal abuse of the racist myths by the German militarists brought on a revulsion of feeling and a return to the liberal philosophy of the American tradition.

All the mythologies that have ever convulsed the fevered imagination of man share one quality in common. They all operate on the analogy of *life*—the processes of biology determine the categories of judgment. All of culture and religion are merely subtle forms of the struggle for survival. The dumb, unconscious dynamic will of man underlies all the sophisticated creations of the human mind, determining their shape and form; hence, the "biologism" of the Darwin-Spencer era and the *psychologism* of the Freud era, and the "class struggle" of historical materialism, of Marx, Lenin, and the communist world.

All philosophies which draw their categories from the events that make life possible, rather than from the values that life makes possible, are bound to be *dehumanizing*, for they degrade that which is human and mental to a plane of reality, which is prehuman, at least, precultural. They are also bound to be pessimistic, for the melody of life always ends in death.

All "organismic" theories of society are essentially subjective. While they may marshal any number of data in support of their

375

thesis, they direct their appeal to instinct, intuition, and native enthusiasm, rather than to mind, morality, and objective judgment.

In contrast, we plead for a "spirit-centered" conception of man and society. By "spirit," we do not mean a rigid body of rational laws, principles, and religious doctrines, but the unity of all values as they are unfolded in the course of man's quest for reality, a quest that alternates between the depths of subjectivity and the furthest reaches of objective reason. Spirit is celebrated in worship, but articulated incompletely in the diverse patterns of culture. The reality and validity of human values, esthetic, ethical, and religious, is the basic axiom, though the content and nature of any one value may be periodically re-examined. This axiom may also be called an assertion of faith, but it is that residual minimum of faith that our human nature invariably contains as it confronts the mystery of existence. When we search for truth, in all its mystery and complexity, we face the world with a double attitude—a willingness to let the outer facts of reality impress themselves upon our minds and a whole-souled listening to the truth already contained within our self. This double orientation of the human mind outward and inward is the primary starting point of all "spirit-centered" philosophies. Their content is never completely spelled out, though they will be articulated anew in every generation. Their common quality is a way of thinking—asserting the truth and validity of man's inner life, while driving toward the noblest peaks of disinterested contemplation. Such philosophies contain the seed of hope, for they assume and express the validity and triumph of human values in the scheme of things.

What then is the import of a "spirit-centered" philosophy of life to the men and women of our day? How does it combat despair and elicit hope in the peculiar circumstances of our time?

376

Its message is twofold: it issues a call for the return to faith, and it challenges us to embrace the objective approach to all social problems as a Divine imperative.

The first message of a "spirit-centered" philosophy is the assertion of its own worth. The hunger for knowledge needs no utilitarian justification; it is true to human nature and to the universal symphony of creation. Similarly, the yearning of the self for unity with the Divine will is a fundamental source of values. The concern of the human soul with its place in the Divine scheme of things is ineluctable. If the religious phase of life is ignored, myth and magic rush in to fill the vacuum thus created. The "mystiques" of nature and of the tribe take up the psychic energy that an irreligious generation leaves unused.

At the same time, our call for the return to religion does not imply a rejection of the rationalistic approach. On the contrary, religion in its dynamic essence contains the pathos of philosophy and the ideal of contemplation as well as the feelings of mystical piety and the ideals of philanthropy. Faith and the transcendence of ritualism and dogmatism imply each other, as the swing of the pendulum in one direction implies its eventual return to the opposite direction. A faith that fails to embrace the criticism of its own sources and institutions is no longer a living reality.

Out of the subjective life of religion, the values and ideals are born that endow the life of the individual with supreme worth, counteracting the collectivist pressure that modern life generates even in a capitalistic society. As we are herded together by massive social forces, we might well become a form-less, faceless herd, unless we learn to guard the citadel of privacy in our soul. And that citadel is the soul, as it confronts the dark, mysterious source of its own being.

The second message is the plea for the acceptance of the objective approach as a Divine imperative. He, too, prays who wrestles with his soul, or researches in the laboratory, or fashions

377

new patterns of beauty. This means, above all, the pursuit of knowledge and the esthetic domains of culture, not for their utility, but as ends in themselves. We are to envisage a domain of spiritual values as supervening above the stresses and strifes of our competitive world. In this realm, our soul may find a secure anchorage of meaning and purpose.

But the most important expression of objectivity in our life today consists in the need to surmount the perpetual fancies and myths of ethnicism. The tendency to glorify all that is "our own" is an expression of man's inalienable subjectivity, but if subjectivity is embraced in the dynamic equilibrium of religion, it should be possible to emulate the prophetic example and to deflate the recurring myths of ethnicism as promptly as they arise.

The great challenge to our way of life is presented by the surge of communism. This global movement derives momentum from the nature of our machine civilization, on the one hand, and from the "mystique" of the machine, on the other. The mounting pressures of economic life tend to build up the values and ideals of mass-culture, leaving little room for the individual. At the same time, the communist "mystique" takes the machine as the basic analogue of life, considering all ideas and ideals to be only subjective. The communists do not recognize in theory that there can be objective judgments of right and wrong, true and false. All that is "idealistic" and "spiritual" is to them secondary and suspect.

It is always tempting to fight subjectivity with subjectivity—this is how the bloody wheel of war was kept awhirling in its gory rut, century after century. To combat communism by an intensification of subjectivity means to oppose everything that they favor with equal zeal and blindness, to foster that which they combat, and, with unbounded devotion, to counterpoise the two forms of modern fanaticism, that of religion and nationalism, to the impassioned zeal of the communists. It means, in short, to make of nationalistic anticommunism a religion.

378

Our analysis calls for the contrary approach—the celebration of the ideal of objectivity. In spite of their materialistic philosophy of life, the communists retain a high degree of objectivity. Their emphasis on education and the sciences inevitably produces a mentality that cannot be utterly constrained by the chains of dogma. As against a truly free world, where the myths of ethnicism and dogmatism are subjected to scrutiny, the communists have no real defense. Victory, then, benefits all and harms no one.

In recent years our nation has led the world in the direction of objectivity—through the founding of the United Nations and through the projection of the principle of giving assistance to underdeveloped countries. We still have a long way to go in the development of a body of international law, in the acceptance of the authority of the World Court, in the development of a type of public servant whose loyalty is to the society of mankind as a whole, not to any particular country. If citizenship of the world is to be accepted as a worthy ideal by all, some people must be allowed to choose such citizenship as their career and their way of life.

This method calls for the unlimbering of the processes of growth in the human spirit by deepening the wells of inspiration in our personal life and by expanding the horizons of objectivity in the affairs of our nation. These processes generate the radiance of hope in two ways—by refreshing the fountains of renewed life through the instrumentalities of religion, and by concentrating attention on those faculties of the human mind which alone can dissipate the clouds of danger that darken the vistas of our generation.

In other words, we call for the rebirth of both a liberal faith and a faith in liberalism. So many of the preachers of faith in our time have found it necessary to shatter the spirit of liberalism and to undermine its faith in the perfectibility of human society. Also, many liberals have withdrawn from the official creeds, with the result that the voices of dogmatism and ethnicism, of neomagic and neomythology, are loud in the land.

A liberal faith that cherishes the rhythms of the interior life, reverencing the institutions of organized religion but transcending them, will revive the vital powers of faith and bring them to bear upon the problems of our day. Similarly, renewed faith in liberalism holds out the possibility of bringing into being the magnificent vision of the prophets—a world united in freedom, in truth, and in justice.

If one happy and creative world is to emerge out of the travail of our multiple crises, the resources of both faith and reason will need to be mobilized. The approach of dry reason alone cannot win the hearts of men, and the self-exalting genius of nationalism cannot by itself create a universal society. This many-splendored vision can become a reality only if we learn to bring together the subjective love of national greatness and the objective faculty of self-criticism in terms of universal values. To let our spirit move in two opposing directions, in a tension that is perpetually resolved and renewed again, is to revive the conditions that make possible the hope of the ages.

Several surveys have indicated the defeatist mood of our young people today. They no longer sense the charm of heroism. The heroes of the past no longer enthrall us—the saint of the medieval era, glorying in suffering; the philosopher of the classical world, retiring into the ivory tower of contemplation; the scientist, uncovering the mysteries of matter; the engineer and the technocrat, perfecting the machines of automation. Our generation is not altogether happy with the rapid progress of science and it contemplates with anxiety the advance of automation. Can we expect young people to be enthused by the prospect of making comfortable people still more comfortable? Actually, the horizons of heroism are wide open.

Actually, our time calls for a new surge of the heroic spirit, for we stand at the narrow threshold of a new age, while the abyss of chaos yawns on all sides. In a way, we have outlived the age of heroes, for ours is the century of the common man.

But the vision of a true hero can endow the life of every one of us with new zeal and purpose.

The heroic vision of our time should be the prophet in his ideal dimensions, for he encompasses in his many-sidedness the great visions of our past. He is, at once, philosopher and mystic, patriot and universalist, man of spirit and man of action. He is the foe of self-glorifying ethnicism, of self-sanctifying dogmatism, of human arrogance in all its subtle variations. He stands for the love that rebukes, criticizes, and chastises as well as the love that blesses and sanctifies. He focuses the insights of reason and the wisdom of feeling upon the social problems of the day. Above all, he is the reviver of the free flow of the human spirit toward the mystery of the good and toward the sunlight of reality. And because the two poles of spiritual tension are equally potent in his soul, he sees all things fresh and radiant with the golden promise of tomorrow.

Part Five
Dialogue with Judaism

THE PROPHET IN
MODERN HEBREW LITERATURE*

Every culture is the collective effort of a human society to rise above the sheer pressures of life and to attain a victory, however small, of spontaneity over routine, freedom over necessity, love over callousness, spirit over matter. While the content of the human spirit and the nature of the resisting matter undergo endless variations, the contest is usually represented in symbols and images that are concrete enough to appeal to the popular imagination. Always, the underlying impetus of any culture is visualized in the guise of a hero, who has already attained, and in the fullest measure, that which the group as a whole sets as its goal. The hero is the underlying *élan* of a society, incarnate and resplendent. In ancient societies, the hero usually belonged to the misty caverns of the past, but, whether of the past or of the future, he represented at all times the consummation of the dearest hopes of his society.

The central hero-image in Jewish religious culture is the prophet. Around this image are concentrated the memories of Israel's greatness—Moses and the exodus from Egypt, the emergence of those religious ideals that made possible the return from Babylonia, and the genesis of the two daughter-faiths of Judaism, Islam, and Christianity. Upon the assurance of the prophetic words, the hopes of the Messianic future rested, and the Kingdom of God was to be marked by the universal attainment of prophecy, or at least by every Jew's achieving this rank.

The Messiah too was to be a prophet (Sanhedrin 93b).[1] In addition, the great pietists during the medieval and early

---

* The Goldenson Lecture of 1957 at Hebrew Union College

modern period dreamed of attaining some of the lower degrees of prophecy. In modern times, the prophet was the symbol of Jewish originality, since he articulated the deepest longings of the people in the days of their sovereignty, and he battled valiantly against the incursions of foreign influence. Creative originality is almost inevitably envisaged in the terms of the prophetic situation—the hero who disdains the clamor of the crowd and shatters the idols of the marketplace, listening with single-minded zeal to the "still, small voice" within his breast that is the voice of God.[2]

The central significance of the image of the prophet in the evolution of Judaism can be understood only when it is compared with the hero-images of other cultures. Without presuming to be exhaustive, I limit my survey to the Western world and call attention to the hero-image of the philosopher in Hellenism, the saint in Catholicism, the artist and the engineer of modern times.[3] To understand the similarities and dissimilarities of these hero-images, we shall do well to envisage the three co-ordinates of the spiritual life. These three lines of intellectual and emotional dynamism converge upon the soul of man, and all the variations in the history of human culture can be plotted in this three-dimensional space. The three coordinates are the channels leading from the soul to nature, either to the elements of nature within the human personality or physical nature generally; from the soul to human society, either a limited group of people or humanity as a whole; the avenue leading from the soul to God, either God as the transcendent absolute or a lesser god reflecting a more primitive stage of religion. Along each of these three coordinates, the soul might be conceived as a recipient of values or as a progenitor of standards and goals; i.e. the human soul might be in an active or a passive position.

Plotted on this spatial graph, the philosopher is active or outgoing in respect of nature. He seeks to impose the logical order of mathematics upon physical nature and, within the human personality, he seeks to enthrone the reflective and free sovereignty of the soul by means of rigid training and self-discipline. He is both active and passive along the coordinates of human society: active, in that the ideal philosopher is either the ruler or the teacher of rulers; yet, also passive because the philosopher's strength consists in his ability to withdraw from the pulls and pressures of society. The coordinate of human society was in Hellenic literature at first limited to Greeks and, within the Hellenic world, to one community or *polis*. But this limitation was overcome by the early Stoics, and the philosopher was envisaged as a citizen of the universe. In respect to the third coordinate, the philosopher was conceived as active, attaining knowledge of the Divine by means of active, sustained search. The philosopher was an athlete of the spirit reaching by gradual ascents the highest levels of contemplation of the Supreme Being.

The saint is active in respect to his own human nature, striving constantly to subdue it to God's service; yet, he is also passive, disbelieving in the sufficiency of his own powers and acknowledging that success in this endeavor is an act of grace. While the classic philosopher maintained that truth was possible and the Stoic sage asserted that virtue was possible and the Epicurean master claimed that happiness was possible, the saint contended that none of these goals was attainable without the gift of grace. The saint responds in a passive manner to the challenge of physical nature, seeking to withdraw from it, not to master it. His attitude to human society is both active and passive: active, in that he seeks to convert people to his ways of piety; passive, in that, for the most part, he withdraws from society into a limited or nuclear City of God, whether it be the church or the monastery. In regard to the coordinate leading to the absolute, the saint is totally and typically passive. Therein the burning focus of his personality is to be found. He is completely and without any reservations submissive, yielding his mind, his feelings, his moral judgment, and his will to God.[4] He sees no source of values other than that which God dictates and, at his best, is completely the passive vessel of the Divine will. At the loftiest peaks of his religious experience, the saint is a mystic, feeling himself governed from without, led about hither and thither, almost without a will of his own.[5]

The predominant feature of the artist is his passivity toward nature. As a craftsman, the artist is a perfect seer and hearer of the plenitude of impressions that impinge upon his consciousness. As an artist in the Western world, he does not, like a spider, spin silken threads out of his own peculiar fancy but selects, for emphasis, the aspects of nature that are particularly meaningful to the people of his time. When art is turned into a philosophy of life, human nature in all its fullness is celebrated and afforded expression. The ideal of "living according to nature" emerges into full view. The artist does not seek to reform society, and the tension within the soul of Tolstoy is an illustration of this point. In respect to the coordinate of pure being or God, the artist again is passive, allowing validity neither to man's reason nor to man's conscience, seeking to grasp the fullness of existence as a unity; i.e. he employs intuition, arriving at philosophies like those of Bergson or of Schelling.

The hero-image of the engineer is still in the making. It is active along all three coordinates. Physical nature is to be molded at will, and human nature is to be fashioned eventually according to precise specifications. The society of mankind must be run according to a unified all-embracing plan. Even God is to be treated pragmatically and employed insofar as He "works." As passivity along all three coordinates is the mark of the artist, activity is the distinguishing feature of the engineer, who is the emergent cultural hero of secular civilization.

The prophet is both active and passive along all three coordinates. He is both artist and engineer, both philosopher and saint, so that perpetual tension and dynamic restlessness are the characteristic marks of his being.

He is both active and passive in regard to the Supreme Being, submissive in his function as a messenger of the Lord but assertive in his insistence on the validity of the promptings of his conscience. The distinguishing feature of the Hebrew prophets is not their submissiveness to the ecstasies of mysticism, which was a familiar phenomenon in the ancient world, but their firm conviction that the voice of conscience somehow merged insensibly into the Divine will. Not that conscience alone was a sufficient guide. The prophets were mystics as well as humanists, yielding alternately to the Divine command and to the ethical challenge in the unshakable conviction that the two imperatives were somehow one in the ultimate mystery of the Divine will. Thus, the prophets could on occasion remonstrate with the Deity. They sensed the peace that passes understanding, even as does the mystic, but they did not focus attention on their feelings. The word of God was for them a supreme command, transcending all rational understanding but, paradoxically enough, continuous and congruous with the voice of conscience.[6] In contradiction to Kierkegaard and his neo-orthodox followers, as well as in opposition to liberal humanism, the point in the tale of Abraham's sacrifice of Isaac was double-pronged. Abraham was to obey the Divine command even when it seemed irrational, but, in the final analysis, the Divine will merges and coincides with the rational promptings of man's own nature. The ideal prophet is solicitous both for "the honor of the son as well as the honor of the Father," i.e. for man as well as for God.[7]

The prophet is also both active and passive in regard to human society. He is concerned with the task of bringing God's word to the children of man, establishing the Kingdom of Heaven in time and on earth. Yet, the prophet is not a futurist seeking to rush mankind by forced marches to the ideal goal. Unlike a revolutionary reformer, he is humble enough to wait for God's own time; and unlike a pseudo-Messianist, he holds that the drama of redemption takes place within the human heart. He envisions the future as clearly as if it were within reach, yet in saintly humility he bides his time, praying for the favor of Him who at times "hides His face."[8] His message is not of the moment and not directed to one individual. The prophet assumes that all his hearers can tell the authenticity of his message, for God speaks to all men, though more clearly to prophets. Those who act as if they did not hear God's word deliberately shut their ears. The appeal of the prophet is to a kind of "intersubjective hearing" and judging.

This twofold attitude to human society is best seen in the attitude of the prophets to the two societies in the Divine scheme—the people of Israel and humanity as a whole. Ultimately, God's will is to prevail throughout the world, but He will achieve this consummation in His own good time. The prophets do not undertake missionary journeys among the nations, save one, Jonah, and he reluctantly. Their vision of a redeemed humanity is to be achieved neither by universal conquest, nor by the infectious enthusiasm of a worldwide preaching tour, but in quietude and resignation. However, within the community of Israel, the prophets assume an active, even aggressive role, insisting that the "vineyard of the Lord" be kept utterly free of weeds and be made immediately to produce luscious fruits. The prophetic message to the people of Israel could well be summed up in that famous motto, which could be made to serve several different philosophies of life, "To thine own self be true." In the genius of the prophets, Israel was to be true to itself in such a manner as to be for that very reason true to the universal soul of mankind. This is the deeper meaning of the prophetic conception of the Covenant.[9]

In respect to the coordinate of nature, the prophet again is both active and passive. Having grown out of the institution of "sons of the prophets," the prophet was doubtless originally a person who practiced some form of ascetic self-discipline. Elijah was obviously an ascetic. Yet, in contrast to the prophets of the Baal, his preparatory exercises were predominantly prayer, earnest contemplation, and whole-souled listening to the voice of God. In later Judaism, the ideal image of the prophet involved an arduous ascent on the ladder of self-conquest. Rabbi Pinhas ben Yair lists a series of steps leading to the gift of *Ruah Hakodesh,* and Maimonides describes *Ruah Hakodesh* as the lowest of eleven degrees of prophecy.[10]

At the same time, the prophets take account of the fullness of human nature. They do not advocate either celibacy, or mortification of the flesh, or incessant struggle against the impulses of nature, or resistance to the advance of civilization. A deep appreciation of the dignity of the human personality is embraced in the prophetic message.[11] Jeremiah commends the Rechabites for their loyalty to their ancestral way of life, but he does not demand that the Israelites should give up city life. In all their descriptions of the future world, there abound earthly joys and the healthy fragrance of fields and forests. Their motto is "life according to God's will," not "according to nature"; yet, they do not demand that which is against nature.

It follows that the hero-image of the prophet has affinities with the hero-images previously described. Alike to the philosopher in the coordinates of nature and mankind, the prophet differs in respect to his attitude toward God. Alike to the saint in respect of society, he differs in respect to both God and nature. The artist and the engineer represent one-sided images of him, for they are either wholly passive or wholly active along all three coordinates, while he maintains a dynamic, tense equilibrium and a sense of balance in all three domains of the spiritual life. Yet, the artist as poet and the engineer as social planner or reformer reflect tangential aspects of his towering personality.

In one essential respect, the prophet differs from the other hero-images. As a rule, prophecy is regarded as the peculiar gift of God to Israel. While occasional passages maintain the occurrence of prophecy among other nations, this opinion is confined to certain personalities mentioned in the Hebrew Scriptures. The predominant opinion in our sacred tradition is that only Israel is the people of prophecy. In a sense, all sons of Israel are "sons of the prophets." The Jews beheld in the image of the prophet an ideal representation of their own collective being. Thus, the ambivalence of pride and dedication that is implicit in the concept of chosenness was focused on the image of the prophet. On the one hand, the prophetic ideal reflected the noblest aspirations of the Jewish people, their dedication to the task of bearing the knowledge of God to the nations. On the other hand, the calling of the prophet lent an aura of superiority and self-worshiping adulation to Jewish consciousness. The tension between these two polar attitudes within the heart of Israel contributed in no small measure to that peculiar awareness of isolation which is the soul of its tragic history. The vision of the prophet towered high like the mountain of Sinai with the cloud of glory resting upon it; the masses of the people saw chiefly its earthly base and stood at a distance, while only a few brave souls ventured like Moses into the cloud, up the steep slopes and toward the holy summit.

As the prophetic ideal receded into the mists of the past, Judaism entered the phase of crystallization, making do with the leadership of lesser personalities. The first Hasidim still preserved the pattern of prophetic piety, at least as an ideal. Along the coordinate of nature, puritan zealotry made its appearance; along the highway to mankind, the wide vistas were narrowed and high barriers were raised; along the gateway to God, submissive feeling was threatened by the frost of formalistic obedience, and the assertive spirit was curbed.

The descent from the peak of prophecy is implicit in the ideal itself, for prophecy is a momentary phenomenon. The prophet is not "transfigured" permanently, as in Buddhist or in some Christian theologies. When the lightninglike moment of the dialogue with God is over, the prophet can only seek to recall the golden moment and yearn for its recurrence, hence, the lyrical pathos in his utterances. Also, he brings the ineffable fluid content of ecstasy into the light of his intelligence, where the protean glow of belonging to the infinite is transformed into the firm assurance of a binding, permanent relationship, the awareness of being "covenanted" unto God. The "covenant-relationship" is the ecstasy of the dialogue experience translated into sober terms and projected outward into the external world of time and space. By degrees, this relationship is spelled out in a series of general principles and specific laws. Thus, the prophet, descending from the summit, becomes successively a preacher, recalling the Covenant; a sage re-examining the life of his day in the light of Divine first principles and against the background of his vision; a priest seeking to preserve the element of mystery in the Divine encounter and to dramatize this mystery in a series of rituals; a scribe preserving the laws, the crystallized expressions of fluid moments of inspiration, counting the letters of sacred Scriptures and transmitting the tradition to successive generations.

It follows that these hero-images of Judaism were not anti-prophetic, but representations of the prophet, in his sober uninspired moments. Aaron, the priest, is the spokesman and pragmatic—alas, at times, too pragmatic—interpreter of Moses. The conflict between Amos and the high priest of Beth-el, however, is not as typical as the nearly unbroken record of collaboration between prophets and priests. In later Judaism, the high priest was vouchsafed the privilege of approaching the *Shechinah* once a year. Ezra, the priest, was also the scribe par excellence. His function was to count the words and interpret the meaning of previous revelations, but he was not completely devoid of the prophetic aura. "Ezra was worthy of being the agent for the Almighty to give the Torah, but Moses preceded him."[12] The sages of later years were frequently said to be worthy of the *Shechinah's* resting upon them, for prophecy was taken from the prophets and given to the wise.[12a] Great rabbis were believed capable of ascending to heaven for conversations with heavenly beings.[13] They were believed to be effective intercessors for the people, providing they possessed a "broken and humbled heart," as well as an immense store of sacred learning.[14]

Still, the hero-image of the prophet was never completely forgotten, and whenever it reappeared on the horizon, a renascence of Judaism took place. We recognize the lineaments of this vision in the personality of Hillel and in the movement he led to base the oral Law on the foundation of an implicit, inner logic and by recognition of the golden rule as its central core. We recognize the prophetic ideal in the life and thought of Philo and in the great movement of philosophical Judaism, which seeks to recapture the essential tension of true religion in both its active and passive phases, i.e. the tension between piety and ethics, mysticism and rationalism. Fragments of this ideal are recaptured in the Essenic societies, in the circles of proto-Qabbalists and Qabbalists. As we approach the modern age and the rebirth of Hebrew literature, we encounter once again the heroic image of the prophet on the threshold of the new era.

The first titanic figure of modern Hebrew literature was a prophetic personality of many and diverse talents. Rabbi Moses Hayyim Luzzatto shared in the ecstatic visions of the Hebrew prophets, in their sense of total identification with the life of the people, in their overwhelming sensation of the overpowering nearness of the Divine Being, in their hunger for purity of soul and the perfection of love, in their lyrical quality of poetic composition—above all, in the power to see all things with the freshness of a creative imagination. Compelled to interpret his immense gifts, psychic upheavals, and volcanic imagination in terms of the complex and rigid dogmas of his day, Luzzatto believed that saints of long ago and winged seraphim conversed with him, dictating to him magnificent works of sacred lore. In the prevailing concepts of his generation, the protean events of his great and restless soul could no longer be described in the simple formula of the Biblical prophets, "thus spake the Lord." During the Talmudic and post-Talmudic period, the normative conception of God in Judaism became ever more decisively transcendent. In the official Targumim, the Word (*Memra*) or the Presence (*Shechinah*) or the Glory (*Kavod*) of God was interposed in those places where the text read God. In the Mishnah, no angels are mentioned at all, except for the quasi-angelic figure of Elijah. In the Talmud and later Midrashim, ecstatic and mystical experiences are pressed into the mold of a "revelation of Elijah." As the subterranean stream of Qabbalistic mysticism burst into the open in the latter half of the thirteenth century, "prophetic Qabbalah" made its appearance in the erratic career of Abraham Abulafia. Elaborate schemes were worked out for the attainment of interviews with diverse heavenly beings, ranging from the imaginary characters of the Zohar to a class of anonymous *Maggidim,* or "revealers."

Pressed within this dogmatic context, the prophetic consciousness degenerated into a feverish catharsis of self-exaltation. In the *Maggid Mesharim* of Rabbi Joseph Karo and in the *Sefer Hahezyonoth* of Rabbi Hayyim Vital, we look in vain for the stirring of a noble passion or the insights of a creative imagination. Virtually the sole content of both books revolves around the wondrous greatness of the two authors, describing the amazing delights that await them in heaven.

Though Luzzatto's *Maggidim,* heavenly "revealers," conformed to the general type, there were remarkable and fresh overtones in his writings. The Hebrew style of his writings is chaste, simple, precise, and responsive to the logic of modern grammar. Whatever the nature of his inspiration, the quality of his literary creations is uniformly high. In him, the lyricism of the prophets is reborn as well as their ethical fervor and their genius for distinguishing the kernel of piety from its shell. His "revelations," for all their superstitious framework, open up a new era. Themes borrowed from Italian poetry blend naturally with ideas and symbols deriving from Qabbalah. The love of God takes on, in his dramas, the charm and gentleness of earthly love. Mundane life and love are seen fresh and new, as if they were bathed in heavenly radiance. The human personality in its yearning for beauty and the fullness of expression moves back into focus and the great movement of Jewish humanism is launched.

Different aspects of Luzzatto's personality appealed to the different builders of the Hebraic renaissance. The *Maskilim* were enthralled by his poems and dramas, seeing in him the first author of secular literature in the new era. The Hasidim loved and studied his marvelously lucid expositions of Qabbalistic metaphysics and psychology. The "lovers of Zion" expatiated on the symbolic significance of his journey to the Holy Land, since his visions could be considered pure and holy only if they occurred in the ancestral land of Israel. The Gaon, Elijah of Vilna, himself a center of renewed interest in secular wisdom, admired above all Luzzatto's ethical-pietistic classic, *Mesillath Yesharim*. He who so cruelly castigated the Hasidim for their exaggerated adulation of their *Zaddikim*, is said to have declared, "Had the author of the *Path of the Righteous* been still living, I should have set out on a pilgrimage to learn the ways of piety under his guidance."[15] The opinion of this pre-eminent scholar coincided in this instance with the feelings of the unlearned masses, who formed societies for the study of this little volume.

Indeed, the *Path of the Righteous* is a reflection of the prophetic consciousness, at its best. In this volume, the vagaries of mystical feeling are brushed aside so that the relation of man to God might be presented in all its chasteness and sublimity, its heaven-storming aspiration and its earthly practicality. Truly remarkable is the absence in this work of that dismal phantasmagoria of superstitious piety centering round Satan and his hordes, the "outsiders" who plot the downfall of man in this world and stoke the fires of hell in the hereafter. Suffice it to bring to mind two popular ethical-pietistic works of the same genre, *Kav Hayashar* and *Reshith Hochma*, to note the uniqueness of Luzzatto's work. The first work is replete with malicious devils, tales of horrible punishment for the least infraction of any ritual law, and instructions regarding various devices for the overcoming of the "other side." Man was created "to observe the Torah, the laws, and the commandments," and woe betides him, if he is neglectful.[16] Elijah di Vidas' work, *The Beginning of Wisdom*, commences its exposition of piety with the "gate of fear," detailing the injury done to the sinner's personality, to his higher soul, and to the *Shechinah* by every infraction of the Law.

396

It describes the horrors of *Hibbut Hakever*, the beating of the dead at the grave as well as the terrors of the various caverns of hell, adding for good measure the fear of being reborn in this hateful world.[17]

In contrast to this fear-born jungle of fantastic horrors, Luzzatto's world is fresh and sunny, high as the heavens and open on all sides. Hell is not even mentioned and its dark, ubiquitous minions are brushed aside. The purpose of man's life is defined not in the servile terms of blind obedience, but in the accents of happiness and fulfillment. "Man was created for the sole purpose of delighting in God and basking in the radiance of His *Shechinah*, for this pleasure is the greatest and most genuine of all joys in existence."[18] To be sure, the goal of man's life is set in the hereafter, but it is a bright and beautiful vista, in which all men may share to the extent of their merit. Nor is the radiance of the *Shechinah* totally removed from the ordinary concerns of our mundane existence, for the Spirit of Holiness (*Ruah Hakodesh*) may be attained in our lifetime. Not only the pre-eminent Torah scholars but every ordinary artisan may aspire to "direct his heart toward the goal of clinging truly unto God, till a spirit from above is poured upon him, the Name of God is bestowed upon him, even as the Lord acts toward His saints. Then he will become actually like an angel of the Lord with all his deeds even the lowliest and the most material being accepted as sacrifices and offerings."[19]

The piety of Luzzatto is prophetic in the brightness of its spiritual horizon, in the goal of quasi-prophecy that it sets for the pious, and in the powerful ethical quality of its teachings. A child of his age, he could still write that "forbidden foods introduce real uncleanliness into the heart and spirit of man so that the holiness of the Lord removes itself and departs from him."[20] Nevertheless, his predominant emphasis is purely ethical. He reflects the spirit of the Renaissance in his call for a principle of balance and harmony to govern the aspirations of piety.[21] Thus, he allows that the pious must take account of the way their deeds impress men and women outside the fold, refraining from actions which excite ridicule.[22] If Luzzatto's sage advice had been followed by the Hasidim of Poland, the tragic battles regarding the *kapotes* and the *yarmulkes* would not have been necessary. While Luzzatto did not embrace all of mankind in his purview, he did accord some weight to the opinions of non-Jews. To the veritable horror of his Rabbinic judges, he studied the secular and Latin cultures of his day, and in his literary works, he strove for grace and precision of expression. Remaining within the walls of the Law, he concentrated attention on its spiritual kernel. And, going beyond the Law, he called for new and creative ways of serving God, to articulate in original actions the dynamic spirit of piety.

Luzzatto was a lonely and exotic reincarnation of the ideal image of the prophet. His tragic career proved the impossibility of the resplendent ideal for the European Jews of the middle of the eighteenth century.

In some of the Western countries, the fresh breezes of a new world were beginning to be felt, consigning to oblivion the mystic muses of Qabbalah. In the East, Rabbi Hagiz, the leading persecutor of Luzzatto, aroused widespread support with his motto, "Whatever is new is prohibited by the Torah." When the unitary stream of European Jewish history was bifurcated into Western and Eastern currents, the prophetic ideal was fragmentized in both areas of Jewish settlement. And, in both East and West, the respective fragments were sufficiently potent to win a massive popular following.

In Western Europe, a significant fragment of the prophetic vision was recaptured in the ideals of the Haskalah. In the horizon of the classical prophets, the Jewish people were seen against the background of mankind as a whole. God was concerned with the salvation of Assyria and Egypt even as He strove for the redemption of Israel. The Jewish people did not monopolize the entire horizon of the prophets, who interpreted the Jewish task in the light of the needs of all mankind. This synoptic vision, all but lost in the dark centuries of persecution, was now made the central focus of Jewish interest. In the philosophy of Mendelssohn, man is the object of Divine concern, not solely the people of Israel. The Torah, Divine though it be, is not really necessary either for the good life in this world or for salvation in the hereafter. The *mizvoth* were interpreted as ceremonies, binding upon the Jew, because God willed it so, but not intrinsically of significance to the rest of mankind. Furthermore, it is through the realization of all the potentialities of man's nature, especially his love of beauty and his faculty for reasoning, that God is best served.

N. H. Weisel propagated the ideals of Haskalah in pamphlet after pamphlet, calling for the acceptance of the "Torah of man," i.e. humanistic values and goals. Yet, his humanism was profoundly religious as well as ethical and esthetic. In his campaign for a new program of education, he stressed the prophetic approach, i.e. emphasis on the spiritual core of religious life. Neither Mendelssohn nor Weisel followed the counsel of the Talmud to limit the pursuit of secular studies to the twilight hour, "which is neither day nor night."[23] They considered philosophy, literature, and culture to be part of the "Torah of man." The *Maskilim* translated into Hebrew the apocalyptic literature, and in their schools they stressed the teaching of the Scriptures, as against the Talmud. Their followers composed moralistic tracts along with literary creations, and the greatest achievement of the German *Maskilim*, appropriately enough, was the long epic of Weisel on the life of Moses, the "Master of the prophets."

Another fragment of the heroic image of the prophet became a dynamic force among the Jews of Eastern Europe. Rabbi Israel Baal Shem Tov, virtually a contemporary of Luzzatto, rediscovered the full pathos and splendor of mystical piety, thereby launching the magnificent mass-movement of Hasidism. To be sure, the *Zaddikim* did not claim the rank of prophecy, but they averred that they were blessed with the wondrous gifts of the Spirit of Holiness (*Ruah Hakodesh*), which Maimonides describes as the first level of prophecy.

So successful were the *Zaddikim* in the early years of the movement in attaining high states of mystical ecstasy that they wondered why it was so easy in their day to commune with the *Shechinah*, whereas in earlier ages it appeared difficult. The assertive aspect of prophetic piety was exemplified in the bold innovations of the Hasidim, chiefly, their insistence that the unlearned man could reach the highest places in heaven and their declaration that it is the soul of Divine service that matters, not its external forms. In folk-Hasidism, Rabbi Levi Yizhak of Berdichev emerged as the great protagonist of the people of Israel who, in the ardor of his defense, dared to challenge the justice of God Himself, as it were.

Hasidism was in many ways a revival of popular prophetism. The attainment of mystical ecstasy was consciously set as the goal of all *Baalei Madregah* ("those who aimed at high levels of achievement").[24] While some Hasidic groups envisaged this goal in the crude terms of the ancient bands of prophetizers and modern backwoods revivalists, other groups developed exceedingly refined and subtle forms of mystical contemplation. On a less ethereal plane, they rediscovered the meaning of prayer as a dialogue with God and the possibility of worshiping him in new and unconventional ways. Along the highway of the soul to man, they developed a new communal form, the voluntary community centering round the saint. On the plane of human nature, they combated the ascetic tendencies of an earlier era, cultivated the arts of singing, dancing, and storytelling, and stressed the joys of fellowship and conviviality.

The *Zaddik* of the Hasidim was a prophet in miniature. Some *Zaddikim* were modeled after the wonder-working early prophets, like Samuel, Elijah, and Elisha, while the truly great teachers among them sought to exemplify in a small way the careers of the classical prophets. Rabbi Nahman of Bratzlav taught that the "true *Zaddik* of every generation was in the category of Moses-Messiah."[25] Through him, the flow of Divine grace was channeled from heaven to earth. Even so intellectual

a teacher as Rav Shneur Zalman taught that the people generally derived their "sustenance" through the agency of the saints
of their day.[26] While the *Zaddik* was not an agent of revelation,
he was himself a representation of Divine revelation, since the
non-Divine soul in his personality was completely transformed
into a Divine entity. Accordingly, even "the way he put on his
stockings" was Torah. In other Hasidic writings, the *Zaddik* was
exalted to such dizzying heights, as to surpass even the hero-
image of the prophet. Thus, Rabbi Elimelech of Lizensk
asserted that the "eyes of God are in the *Zaddik*, so that it is
within his power to open the eyes of the Creator, blessed be
He, upon Israel."[27] The *Zaddik* was thus elevated to the rank
of a mediator, for it is through him that not only God's word,
but His sustaining vitality is channeled.[28] No achievement is
beyond his power, not even the final redemption. "The *Zaddik*
can bring about all things, including the advent of the
Messiah."[29]

The fragmentation of the prophetic hero-image ended in
frustration and tragedy for both branches of European Jewry.
In the West, preoccupation with esthetic goals and humanistic
values lowered the barriers of the inner ghetto walls to the
point where total assimilation became a mass-movement. The
one-sided emphasis of the German Haskalah on the "Torah of
man" awakened longings for immediate union with the nations
of Europe to end the long travail of exile. For the sake of an
emergent new humanity in Europe, many a Jew was willing to
sacrifice the consolation and comfort of his traditional heritage.
The men and women who led the way to the baptismal font
in the nineteenth century were not always sick souls, afflicted
with self-hatred (the term was not yet invented), but in many
cases, idealists who were lured by the universalistic facet of
the prophetic vision. Many of them did not forsake their people
with cold, calculating callousness, but they allowed their Jewish
loyalties and sentiments to be sacrificed on the altar of their
new faith in humanity and European culture. Men like Heine
and Börne, Friedrich Stahl and Edward Gans, were not vulgar

401

materialists. Some of the best sons of our people belonged to the tribe of which Heine sang, "those who die when they love." Dazzled by the bright prospect of one humanity, they could see no purpose in Jewish survival and, as they severed their last ties with their past, they imagined that they helped fulfill the vision of the prophet. "Yea, at that time I will change the speech of the peoples to a pure speech, that all of them may call on the name of the Lord and serve Him with one accord."[30]

Thus, the fragment of prophetic vision in Haskalah led to its own decay and disappearance.

Similarly frustrating was the fate of that fragment of prophetism that was embodied in Hasidism. While the German Haskalah saw only the man in the Jew, the Hasidim saw only the Jew in the Jew and mighty little else in the world beside the Jew. From the sacred writings of Qabbalah, the Hasidim received the belief that only the souls of Jews were derived from God.[31] Non-Jews possessed only sparks of the various "shells," whence too, Satan and his demonic cohorts were derived.[32] Operating with this fundamental principle of "psychology," the Hasidim allowed no room in their world either for humanity or for human values. Their religious life, for all its intensity and nobility, was therefore exceedingly narrow, benighted and utterly unworldly.

In the mists of folk-legendry enveloping the figure of the Baal Shem Tov, we can recognize occasional glimmerings of a wider horizon. Thus, we are told that, in one of his ascents to heaven, he learned that the heavenly tribunal was planning severe decrees against the Jews, because of the sins of Jewish peddlers in cheating the ignorant peasants.[33] There are extant, too, literary versions of folktales extolling the virtue of kindness to gentiles.[34] But, on the whole, the Hasidim ruthlessly limited the horizons of their world to the concerns of Jews and things Jewish. With misplaced zeal they fought against the efforts of the Russian government to have them wear European garments.[35] With the redoubled fanaticism of the hopeless and despairing, they conducted a holy war against secular education and against the intrusion of humanistic values.[36] Within two generations, the Hasidic movement lost all the creative *élan* that it ever possessed; the light of originality was quenched for want of fresh air, and the smoke of fanaticism grew ever more dense and acrid.

The moral failure of Hasidism to take into account the wide horizons of humanity and the hard facts of reality generated the mood of widespread rebelliousness among the literary *Maskilim* in Russia. Levinson, the "Mendelssohn of Russia," protested against the prevailing spirit of unreality, the inability of the pious masses to take stock of their opportunities in the fields of agriculture and skilled labor. So unworldly were the masses and so visionary were their leaders that it was necessary for quasi-heretics to urge the people to engage in agriculture and in physical labor.

Most of the Hebrew writers in the first part of the nineteenth century were satirists and protestants. The target of their bitter criticism was the hero-image of the prophet, distorted as this image had become in the shadowy world of Hasidism. Isaac Erter and Joseph Pearl attacked the image of the *Zaddik* directly in their clever parodies. Other *Maskilim* fought the battle for humanism on the front of education, proclaiming as their motto, "Be a Jew in your tent, and a man when you go out." Publicists and novelists, in their several ways, bewailed the abuse of the "prophet-people" conception.

The leading figure of Russian Haskalah assailed the image of the prophet, which he beheld in the guise of the Orthodox rabbis, who by his time had made common cause with the Hasidic *Zaddikim*. Thus, J. L. Gordon, foremost spokesman of Haskalah, capped his career with a long poem of bitter invective against the prophet Jeremiah. In *Zidkiyahu beveth Hapekudoth,* the last King of Judah is heard lamenting,

But wherein did I err? What is my guilt?
Because to Jeremiah I did not submit?
The soft-hearted man, of soul cringing,

Who counseled shame, servitude, yielding.
But I refused his counsel to take,
For I said, iron should iron break . . .
This, too, he a new covenant for Judah proposed,
All the people, young and old
Should study bookish things and teachings.
Every man should say, I'll not plow, I'll not harvest.
A son am I of a kingdom of priests and a holy people.

Gordon's protest against the prophetic hero-image reflected the struggle of the enlightened against the wizened Orthodoxy of both the Hasidim and the Mithnagdim. Weak echoes of the debate on religious reforms in the West appeared in Hebrew literature, but the predominant concern of the *Maskilim* was to make room for secular and humanistic interests within Jewish life. Their tragedy was the absence of any objective foundation for a secular culture. A prophet-people Israel could be, but not just a people. In the sixties and seventies of the last century, Russian Haskalah saw itself in the strange position of winning a battle and losing a people at one and the same time. Masses of Jewish people heeded the call of the *Maskilim* all too well, and rebelling against the narrow horizons of Jewish life, plunged into the wide ocean of Russia, leaving behind them the new Hebraic literature as well as their ancient faith.

The fragmentation of the prophetic ideal into mysticism and humanism ended in tragic futility in both East and West. But it was not long before the prophetic ideal in its fullness was rediscovered in the West, making possible a subsequent revival of prophetism in Russia.

In Germany and Austria, the rise of liberal or nondogmatic Judaism with its two wings, the "prophetic" and the "historical," recreated the original conception of the prophet and the prophet-people. The builders of Reform Judaism recognized the error of Mendelssohn in reducing the specific area of the Jewish religion to the domain of rites and ceremonies. If what is essentially Jewish is the ballast of rituals that an advancing

404

people steadily leaves behind it, there is no justification for Jewish existence. Judaism must be seen as a call to cooperate in building the future, not as an archaic remnant of a "Jerusalem" that once represented the will of God.

Geiger and his associates discovered that, in terms of essential religious ideas, Judaism was far more congruent with the mature modern mind than Christianity, for in Judaism, the relation of man to God is active as well as passive, a stirring call to the daytime tasks of building the Kingdom of Heaven, not merely a soothing whisper for nighttime rest in the comfortable assurance of salvation. The hero-image of Judaism is the prophet, while the hero-image of Christianity wavers between the saint and the mystic, the crusader and the monk. If Judaism asserts its authentic message in the accents of the contemporary world, Christianity, too, is drawn away from the blandishments of its pagan components and toward a genuine prophetic faith.

Thus, the call of Reform was for a return to the prophetic faith all along the line. Judaism was to become prophetic in stressing the inwardness of faith, in affirming the central ideals of ethical monotheism, and in preaching the essence of religion to all men. Prophetic, too, Judaism was to be in the sense of taking religion to be that which is alive within the heart of its people, hence, a willingness at all times to make a fresh effort to see all things synoptically, combining facets old and new. Dedicated to their ideals, the Jews can once again assume the destiny of a prophet-people. In liberal Judaism, the hero-image of the spiritual leader was shifted from that of priest-sage-scribe to that of sage-preacher-prophet. It was no longer to be the function of the rabbi to be the custodian of the laws and the guardian of the tradition, but like the prophet of old, he was to become the instrument through whom God manifests the forward thrusts of His purpose.

The proponents of "historical Judaism," Frankel and Graetz, entered the lists against Reform. Yet, when seen from the distance of a century, their efforts served to fill in the details of the prophetic hero-image. While the Reform wing emphasized the rational and assertive elements of the prophetic mentality, the Conservative wing stressed the passive situation of the individual within the massive processes of history, which include the fortuitous, the irrational, and the national elements. The historians uncovered the connecting tissue between prophetism and rabbinism, proving the existence of an organic unity between prophecy and peoplehood, between inwardness and reverence for Divine Law. Thus, while one wing of modern Judaism stressed the message of the prophets to mankind, the other called attention to the psychic background of national soil and cultural context, out of which prophecy emerged. Later Conservative writers were to complete the prophetic image by focusing the spotlight of research on the mystical elements which enter into the prophetic consciousness.

Thus, the fullness of the prophetic hero-image was reconstructed. Once again, the Jewish people could be seen against the backdrop of past and future and within the context of competing cultures and clashing ideologies. The Jew was to live not merely by the compulsions of a Divine mandate which, for the doubting and the hesitant, begged the question, but for the sake of a high purpose which could be read out of the historical experiences of mankind. This purpose was conceived in terms so lofty as to transcend the actual reach of any generation. New this concept of a prophet-people was, in its nonritualism and its nondogmatism. The content of the prophetic message was not a list of commandments but the spirit of love, faithfulness, and truthfulness. The appeal of this vision was direct and immediate. Liberated from the dross of the ages, it evoked fresh loyalty and renewed enthusiasm among the Jews of the Western world.

In Krochmal's philosophy of Jewish history, this revived conception of a prophet-people was projected, albeit sketchily and vaguely. A people is formed by loyalty to a great ideal. In the unfolding of the Divine purpose, one ideal after another enters into the actual process of history and merges gradually into the total, eternal treasury of mankind. Along with the rise of an ideal, the people embodying and representing it emerge upon the stage of history, and when the ideal sinks into eternity, the people lose their inner cohesion and descend from the stage. The Jewish people, in their worship of the Absolute Spirit containing the totality of ideals, are as eternal as the Divine plan for mankind. Subject to the laws of nature and history, they too rise and fall, along with the ideals of their faith, but phoenix-like they emerge from the ashes and rise again with the dawn of the new ideal that is for them but a fresh facet of Him whose seal is truth. Every ideal is but a revelation of the Divine truth to which the Jewish people are dedicated.

In the progressive emergence of new ideals, the Jew constantly rediscovers his own faith.

The steady and massive growth of the new concept of "prophetic Judaism" in Germany and Austria slowed down, though it did not completely halt, the tide of frustration and despair in the Western world. The influence of this concept was also felt most powerfully in Russia. There, however, for many sociological and ideological reasons, the focus of attention was shifted from the message of the prophet to the national base for his pedestal. This shift of focus was occasioned, at least in part, by the rise of Romantic nationalism among the nations of Europe.

Romantic nationalism is the ideal of the prophet-people reversed and stood on its head. The seductive suggestion is put forward that the healthy and abundant life of the people produces authentic life-giving ideals, as a healthy tree produces the fruits of its own peculiar kind. This apparently innocent observation converts the prophetic ideal into a self-righteous, jingoistic slogan on the banners of the nation. The life of the people, not its ideals, becomes the supreme purpose. We need to concern ourselves only with the cause; the effect, it may be assumed, will take care of itself. Thus, we move from the realm of ideals to that of sociology. Since the ideal is the natural product of the life of the people, the vitality and purity of the nation are elevated to the highest moral rank. The national message or ideal seldom checks the excess of chauvinism, for its nature is shrouded in the mythical vagaries of intuition and its time is in the future. But the self-righteousness and the self-exaltation of the prophetic posture remain. The life of the nation itself is magnified and sanctified, instead of the Name of the Lord. The nation itself is glorified, not made to serve an ideal or the glory of God. So subtle is the distinction between the prophetic and romantic concepts that it frequently escapes detection. In certain circumstances they coalesce, for, on occasion, what makes the life of a people possible must take precedence over what the life of that people makes possible. Indeed, the paradox is inherent in the very nature of prophecy. Since the prophet speaks for God, how can he, save by his uniquely keen conscience, avoid self-exaltation and self-sanctification? Must not his powers of self-criticism be fully as great as his intuitive vision? Objectively, the only acid test of authentic prophecy is the relation of a person to other individuals and of a nation to other human groups, the capacity to rise above the narrowness and blindness of sheer nationalism. The true prophet demands more from his own than from other nations, loving his people passionately but with open eyes and a generous spirit. The inner life of a prophet therefore balances on a hairline drawn taut between heaven and hell. Thus, the Baal Shem Tov was uncertain to the end of his life whether he would land in highest heaven or in deepest hell.

Romantic nationalism appears to be a modern recasting of the Biblical concept of prophet-people but, in actuality, it is a radical inversion of the heavenly ideal. Ends and means are subtly reversed, and the pretentious stance of the prophet takes the place of the substance of his message.

How penetrating was the insight of the Qabbalists when they maintained that the archetypal hierarchy set up by Satan parallels in every respect the one set up by God, except that the arrangement is reversed!

Whether it is Mickiewicz writing for the Poles, or Mazzini

for the Italians, or Fichte for the Germans, or Dostoevski for the Russians, the emphasis is uniformly on the life of the people, on the assumption that its concrete prosperity will redound in a general way to the benefit of humanity in the abstract. The concept of a prophetic mission is employed not as the standard and measuring rod of the acts of the nation, but as a fig leaf hiding the nakedness of sheer national aggrandizement. So clever is the camouflage on occasion that only the keenest analysis can separate prophetism from its satanic counterpart.

At one and the same time, the romantic and prophetic conceptions of peoplehood burst upon the horizon of Russian Jewry. The tension between these conceptions is the major theme of Hebrew literature from the time of Ahad Ha'am to the present.

Ahad Ha'am was looked upon by contemporaries and disciples as a veritable prophet, announcing a fresh revelation. Hayyim Nahman Bialik articulated the feelings of all Hebraic intellectuals, when he wrote:

And suspended midway between these twain magnetic poles
The vague inchoate feelings of our heart then yearned for
    a prophet,
A true prophet who would touch the channels of our heart,
And kindle on high, above our heads his star,
His spirit becoming the fountain for ruminations
In many hearts hidden as dreams, vague aspirations.
While still toward the clouds our looks were fixed,
While still we wandered, desperate, disbelieving,
Loitering at crossroads, inquiring, "Whither?"
Behold, your star appeared and modestly beckoned,
Calling and leading us out of the darkness,
And under your single star all of us were gathered.

Several writers maintain that Ahad Ha'am regarded himself as the modern incarnation of a Biblical prophet, standing at the

409

crossroads and pointing the way leading to salvation.[37] While this assumption is unwarranted, we cannot doubt that Ahad Ha'am regarded the prophet as the ideal exponent of the spirit of the nation. He founded the secret society of "Sons of Moses" as an instrument for the revival of the prophetic ideal of Jewish life, and in his essays he wrote of the prophet as the one who, in his search for absolute truth and justice, gives expression to the underlying spirit of the people.[38] In keeping with the prophetic and Hasidic tradition, Ahad Ha'am stressed the "inner Torah" in contrast to the visible Torah of precepts and commands, and insisted that spiritual redemption preceded, as an indispensable condition, the redemption of the people. Like Isaiah, too, Ahad Ha'am argued for a return, not of all the people, but of the chastened remnant. Like Jeremiah and Ezekiel, he looked forward to the birth of a "new spirit" and a "new heart" in the land of Israel, which will generate new ideals and life-giving forces throughout the Jewish Diaspora and among all men.

In striking contrast to the nationalists of his day, he recognized the marks of the prophetic spirit in the passionate devotion of the Talmudists and medieval scholars to every detail of the Law. While he disapproved of the pedestrian piety of the Shulhan Aruch, he saw in its very extremism proof of the continued vitality of the prophetic spirit. The prophet is an ethical absolutist, unyielding and uncompromising.

But the prophetic tone and message constituted only one side of the complex thought of this philosopher of Hebraic renaissance.

Actually, the philosophy of Ahad Ha'am was a synthetic union of Hebraic prophetism and nationalistic romanticism. Like all the romantics, he maintained that the nation as a biological organism (not the Torah) is the "tree of life," producing the ideals and ideas of its own peculiar kind, and giving good and ripe fruits only when the conditions of soil and climate are ideal. He even spoke of a "nationalistic pantheism," as if all things produced by the nation were holy.[39] His central emphasis on the building of a homeland, which would function as a "spiritual center" of world Jewry, is essentially romantic, i.e. it operates with the image of Israel as a biological organism. Only in its own native soil can the tree of Israel strike roots, and only when the tree is healthy and secure will its fruits be ripe and life-giving. It is important to note that Ahad Ha'am did not believe that any ideal presently conceivable could endow Jewish life in the Diaspora with the golden radiance of a supreme purpose. He criticized caustically the "mission-theory" of Reform on the ground that the ideas of monotheism were in modern times the possession of mankind. But he advocated a "mission-theory" of his own, founded on the romantic principle of the essential unity of blood, soil, and spirit. Out of the reconstituted homeland, a new ideal will emerge that will correspond to the instinctive character of the Jew, awaken the loyalties of the scattered people who no longer believe in the Jewish faith, and also bring fresh vision to mankind. While the liberal rabbis of the West thought of the Jewish mission in terms of religious teachings presently understandable and available in classic formulations, Ahad Ha'am thought of the "mission" as the emergence of a doctrine, presently inconceivable. This fresh dawning of a new light will be made possible through the efforts of national rebirth. While the nature of the new ideal cannot now be foretold, we may safely assume that it will constitute a fresh embodiment of ethical absolutism, devoid of the mystical fetters of religion. Religion was to him, in his positivistic moods, both futile and outworn, the discarded "garments of exile." The "national spirit" needs fresh garments, and these will be found only in the national homeland. "For only where the national ideal was first created can we look for it again." In exile, "a living national idea, a great national ideal, cannot be created."[40]

If Ahad Ha'am had been only a Romantic nationalist, he could not have awakened the quasi-religious fervor of the Zionist movement. To the pious sentiments of nationalism, he added the modernized conception of a prophet-people, blending the two so skillfully that they could hardly be told apart. Adopting the Reform-Conservative conception of "ethical monotheism" as the heritage of the prophets and the living kernel of the Jewish faith, Ahad Ha'am carried the process of discrimination one step further, asserting that religious faith in its totality was the shell of which the living kernel was the "national ethics." Loyalty to this ethical ideal is the first duty of a national Jew.

As to the nature of this ethical ideal, Ahad Ha'am attempted to define it more than once. It was the spirit of absolute justice, perfectly abstract and unemotional, concerned with the welfare of the group as a whole, not with the happiness of the individual, and disposing society so as to produce from time to time "saints" that, like the Nietzschean "supermen," stand beyond "good and evil," beyond the ordinary rules of ordinary people.

Though he reiterated this formulation time and again, he remained dissatisfied, for well he knew, firstly, that there was nothing Jewishly distinctive about any aspect of this formulation and, secondly, that other scholars had formulated Jewish ethics in exactly opposite terms.[41]

At this point, Ahad Ha'am again had recourse to instinct. Jews know by instinct that their ethics are different. Scholars may define this difference in various ways, as they choose, but they are obliged to maintain that a deep and impassable gulf yawns between the ethical insights of Jews and Gentiles. This obligation to believe in Jewish difference is a kind of "national imperative," a patriotic form of thinking. Thus, the Romantic nationalist dogma of being somehow and essentially different was substituted for the dogmas of religion.[42]

The prophetic side of Ahad Ha'am was manifested in his being the first leading Zionist to recognize that Arabs, too, live in Israel and that the early colonists were occasionally unjust in dealing with them.[43] Along prophetic lines, too, was his insistence on the need to choose for colonization in Palestine men and women of the highest idealism and moral integrity. This principle, only partially implemented, was doubtless in-

412

strumental in setting a high moral tone for the early pioneering colonies. A. D. Gordon's "religion of labor," expressing the mystical and devotional spirit of the self-sacrificing *Halutzim* may be considered as a continuation of the prophetic phase of Ahad Ha'am's philosophy. Productive labor takes the place of "mortification of the flesh" in mystical piety and the surrender of personal ambitions, the place of the Biblical "We shall do and we shall listen." However, it was in the Hebrew University of Jerusalem that Ahad Ha'am's moral heritage was most zealously guarded. The greatest proponent of his prophetic ideal of "absolute justice" was a stranger from the West, a rabbi and a rebel, a man of peace who was always at war with the people he loved most, for he could see the ideal towering above them— Judah Leib Magnes.

In the progressive descent of the Zionist ideal from heaven to earth, it was Rabbi Magnes who for a full generation protested against the subversion of moral principles to the pressures of political expediency. While in any study of modern Hebrew literature the name of Magnes is not likely to be mentioned, his voice and personality cannot be ignored in any analysis of the struggles within the soul of the modern Jew. Amidst unparalleled desperation and against a rising tide of violence, he stood for the right, boldly and immovably clinging to the prophetic banner at all costs. Around him, the remnants of a prophetic conscience in Israel were gathered, building up a claim on eternity for the Jew more enduring than any army or any government. While patriots around him glibly employed the prophetic posture as a cover for the resurgence of "sacred, collective egoism," he cherished the soul of prophecy and nurtured it with his life's blood, even when, like Jeremiah, he was assailed as a traitor.[44]

The brilliant essays of Ahad Ha'am dominated the intellectual horizon of his generation, but the prophetic hero-image which he re-created and imposed upon the substructure of Romantic nationalism was not captured in its fullness by any one of the

413

writers in modern Hebrew literature. Once again, the dazzling vision illuminating the skies for a brief moment came crashing down to earth in fragments. The Qabbalists peered deeply into the tragic mystery of human nature when, in describing the process whereby a heavenly ideal is clothed in the flesh and blood of reality, they spoke of the "breaking of the vessels." As in the mid-eighteenth century, the prophetic vision was fragmentized in the post-Ahad Ha'amist era, with only broken facets of it being found here and there.

Hayyim Nahman Bialik believed himself to be a faithful disciple of Ahad Ha'am. His wondrous poems of national resurgence betray the posture, tone, and pathos of a prophet. His earnestness was so overpowering that the Hebrew reading public did not resent his wrathful rebuke of the Jewish people for their defenselessness and passivity during the pogrom in Kishineff. His readers felt that the national poet spoke for the newly born sense of dignity in their own hearts. Seldom in history did a poet exert as much influence as Bialik did in the first decade of the twentieth century.[45]

Several of his poems were written in conscious emulation of the style and stance of a prophet (his Hebrew poems, *Davar, Achen Gam Zeh Musar Elohim, Hozeh Lech Brah*; his Yiddish poems in *Lieder*). In his *Songs of Wrath*, he protests against God in terms verging on the blasphemous, but in the spirit of one who finds it impossible to assume His indifference to human woe. Like Jeremiah, he pleads, "Righteous art thou, O Lord, but judgment I shall speak with thee,"[46] though unlike the ancient prophet, he fails to state his basic premise. As the poet of national continuity and rebirth, he both glorifies and lays to rest the ideal of the *Mathmid*, the hero-image of a bygone generation. For the guidance of his contemporaries, he re-creates and transfigures the legend of the "Dead of the Desert," the heroes who dared defy Moses and God. Though they failed and perished, a magical aura of heroism pervades their camp and evokes the tribute of awed reverence from the wanderers of the wilderness. This glorification of the impatient rebels against the authority of Moses was intended to inspire a similar rebelliousness in his own day against the spirit of pious resignation to the will of God. The message of the poem is a call for the substitution of aggressive force for quiescent piety. Thus, the dead, momentarily revived in a storm, shout

> We who are heroes,
> Last of the enslaved and first of the redeemed are we!
> Our hand alone, our mighty hand,
> From our proud neck the heavy yoke hath removed.

But the spirit of rebelliousness is tempered by the feeling of belonging inescapably in the entourage of the *Shechinah*. The poet sees the Divine cause as being nearly defeated and deserted, but he remains with God even if only to bemoan the tragedy and to lament over the desolation of His Kingdom (*Al Saf Beth Hamidrash Hayashan* and *Levadi*). The cause of God may suffer temporary setbacks. The Almighty, as it were, may be "wounded," but He cannot be defeated (*Yadati Beleil Arafel* and *Lo Timah Bimherah Dime'athi*).

Within the soul of Bialik, the earthly spirit of Romantic nationalism vied for supremacy against a genuine spark of prophetism. This titanic struggle within him, he represented symbolically in the beautiful prose poem *Megillath Ha'esh*. The young refugee from Jerusalem is torn between two fiery forces, the one deriving from the last flicker of holy fire on the altar of the Temple, the other issuing out of the subterranean black flames of hell. With this titanic turmoil in his restless soul, the young hero wanders disconsolately, unable to achieve inner harmony and peace.

Bialik failed to represent the prophetic vision in its fullness chiefly because he did not rise above the immediate national needs of his people and did not glimpse the human and the universal vistas of existence. In his poem *Be'ir Haharegah* he does not attempt to look beyond the horrors of the programs to the people that perpetrated them. To him, the rioters were simply inhuman beasts. He fails to take note of the tragic conflict of ideas, the whirl of interests, malice, and misunderstanding that led to the slaughter. In the "Dead of the Desert," he ascribes the defeat of the defiant rebels to God, not to the Canaanites defending their homes, while the exodus from Egypt he attributes to the "strong hand" of the Israelites, thereby reversing the order of explanations in the Torah. For him, the Canaanites (read: Arabs) did not exist. Though he sensed the prophetic hunger for inner purity in the sight of God (see especially his poem *Halfah 'al Panai*), he lacked the prophetic passion for universal ideals and the moral strength to behold mankind as a whole.

In Saul Tchernichovski, we encounter Bialik's rebelliousness without the latter's firm faith in, and reverence for, tradition. Like that lonely rebel of the Mishnah, Elisha, son of Abuya, Tchernichovski knows the Jewish hero-image and rebels against it. In behalf of his people, the poet apologizes to the Greek god Apollo (*Lenochah Pessel Apollo*) for the sin of rejecting "the light of life" and the crime of binding with thongs of *tefillin* the primitive impulses of the flesh. In contrast to the enfeebling piety of the true prophets, he extols the unabashed love of life of the "false prophets." Above the crown of Torah and heroism (*Mehezyonoth Nevi Hasheker*), he sets the crown of beauty (*Sheloshah Ketharim*). In his version of Dinah's parting words, he reverses the scale of values in the Blessing of Jacob (*Parashath Dinah*), praising natural vengefulness and raw courage rather than quietude, ethical principle, and moral restraint.

In the massive writings of M. J. Berdichevski, the spirit of rebellion against the prophetic hero-image is given poignant and moving expression. Yet, in his passionate avowal of the supreme worth of the individual, we can hear a distinct echo of the prophetic voice. Since Ahad Ha'am attributed to prophetism an exclusive concern with the community, Berdichevski believed his own emphasis on individuality to be a revolt against the tradition of Hebrew prophecy. Actually, the reverse was true. The Hebrew prophets rejected the totalitarian tendency of paganism, insisting on the responsibility of the individual, the supremacy of the ethical imperative, the sole rightness of the "still, small voice" of conscience, the substitution of the holy remnant for the holy people, and the duty to oppose the national interest in the Name of God. Deeply steeped in the mystic lore of Hasidism, Berdichevski centered attention on the direct bond between man and God. By arguing for the fullness of the life of the individual, he, for all his avowed rebelliousness, articulated a genuine prophetic demand. In all his writings, one senses the horror and mystery of the "hound of heaven" theme. He rebels against monotheism, against Judaism, against "spirit," against "the book"; but, even when he strikes the pose of a "blonde beast," he remains inescapably a man of the book and a son of the prophets. His heroes find themselves held fast by the chains of Israel's peculiar, prophetic destiny, even when they set out boldly to act the part of Nietzschean "supermen."

Another broken fragment of the prophetic soul we find incarnated in the writings of J. H. Brenner, who combined supreme emphasis on the free individual with the ideals of socialism. In addition to its inherent apocalyptic elements, socialism hit Jewish youth with the impact of a pseudo-Messianic movement, promising the glory of regeneration through identification with the proletariat. All that is ugly and unworthy in Jewish life will be magically transmuted, all problems will be solved, all yearnings will be stilled. For the "national theology" of Brenner and his fellow ideologists of the Histadruth, socialism spelled inner and outer redemption. "The new Hebrew individual of our generation enters with but one simple word on his lips—'labor.' "[47] The magic of labor will cleanse the Jewish soul of its "sin" and of its "shame," incurred through centuries of a capitalistic life in "exile."[48]

Labor assumed a quasi-Messianic guise in the life and literature of the new Israel, and the *Halutz*, with open blouse and khaki pants, spade in hand and song at heart, was its forerunner. The intellectual who, surrendering individual ambitions and the modern cult of success, bows his back to the unyielding soil and sacrifices the joys of privacy to the rigors of communal discipline is the hero of the "religion of labor." Originally Tolstoyan in inspiration, the new "man with the hoe" became the bearer of the promise of national rebirth and fulfillment. His renunciation of bourgeois comforts offered a psychological equivalent to the saints' fasting and ascetic exercises, the prophet's escape into the wilderness, the artist's retreat to the garret, and the knight's donning of his heavy armor. "This love of Zion movement is to embrace all the parts of the nation that are capable of repenting of the sins of exile and to accept the penance of labor."[49]

Still another tattered shred of the prophetic soul is incarnated in the muscular verse of Uri Zevi Greenberg, the favorite poet of the Revisionists. Greenberg mourns over the fate of Hitler's victims, calling for bloody vengeance. He evokes the saintly figure of Levi Yizhak which, brooding over the devastation wrought by the Nazis, gives up prayer and demands revenge. For him, "the nations," all mankind with hardly a significant distinction, are embraced in one category. And Israel, the "holy people," is the perpetual victim of "the nations."[50] In the ardor of longing for national dignity and power, Greenberg attains lyrical climaxes of purest chauvinism:

None are purer for dominion than Jews, none more beautiful,
None nobler or deeper among the nations, more heroic, melodious or brighter,
Not one in the world more worthy of carrying a kingly crown.[51]

The saintly figure of the Berdichever *rebbe*, Levi Yizhak, is utilized by another great poet, Jacob Cohen, for the purpose of symbolizing the rejection of the prophetic mission for the Jewish people. The poet makes use of the legend concerning the ten martyrs, who learned that their death was decreed by God Himself. If they cry out against this decree, the Lord will

418

return the world to chaos. The ten martyrs accept God's will and do not protest. They know that up in heaven the Archangel Michael offers the souls of saints in sacrifice in order that the Divine purpose may be fulfilled. The poet knows that the prophets have taught the Jews to look upon themselves as the suffering servants of the Lord, the "martyr race," who bear upon their pain-racked backs the sins of mankind. But he also knows that, in his generation, the ten martyrs have grown into a vast mass of nearly six million hapless victims of the satanic rebellion against the Divine Kingdom. Levi Yizhak, the loving advocate of Israel, is prepared to utter that "third cry" which might turn the world into chaos, for even chaos is preferable to so colossal a crime.[52]

In Greenberg's verses, rebellion against the prophetic spirit attains its acme. The garments of the prophet-people are still worn by Israel, but only as drapery and disguise for the newly raised national flag.

The antiprophetic outbursts of Greenberg can hardly be matched in recent Hebraic literature. However, he is by no means alone in his endeavor to substitute resurgent nationalism for the ancient faith. Significant is this final verse in the popular poem by the late David Shimoni:

And in this dreadful darkness, in this darkest of all nights,
Let our exultant song go up out of the night:
"Hear, O Israel: Israel is our fate, Israel is One."

In the last line, the most fundamental assertion of Jewish faith by prophets and martyrs of all ages and climes is transformed into a slogan of national unity. Israel takes the place of God in the Scriptural declaration of faith.[53]

A glowing spark of the prophetic flame shines out of the mystical writings of Chief Rabbi Kuk. While the fullness of prophetic stature cannot be ascribed to this gentle saint, since he lacked a clear comprehension of reality, a genuine vision of mankind and a deep appreciation of its universal values, we can see in him the man who lives in "two-aloneness" with God. The prophets were more than mystics; for, disdaining to speak of their intimate feelings, they concentrated on bringing the Divine message to mankind. The Jewish literary tradition, following the example of the prophets, discouraged any descriptions of the ineffable ecstasies of mystical delight and terror. In Kuk's writings, this literary genre makes its appearance.[54] A charming note of freshness pervades his poetry in prose, reflecting a remarkable synthesis of Hasidic mysticism and Western romanticism. Perhaps, the central message of his books is best conveyed by the motto which he coined, "The old shall be renewed, the new shall be sanctified."

Motifs of religious mysticism occur frequently in the Hebraic poetry of our generation, reflecting the unspoken yearning of the Jewish soul for the reconstruction of its prophetic hero-image. The union of people and land inevitably makes the storied characters of the Hebrew Bible take on the vividness of flesh and blood. The great theme of our Holy Scriptures, the eternal dialogue between man and God, becomes inescapably the fundamental theme of Hebrew literature. Though we have now scarcely passed beyond the threshold of the new Israel, we can already discern beautiful expressions of longing for the wholeness of the Jewish soul through its service of God.

Abraham Shlonsky expresses the inchoate, vague piety of a whole generation in this hymn to labor in the new land:

Clothe me, purest of mothers, in the resplendent coat of many colors.
And lead me to toil at dawn.
My land wraps itself in light as in the prayer-shawl.
New homes stand forth as do phylacteries.
And like phylactery-bands, the highways, built by Jewish hands, glide.
Thus, a town beautiful recites the morning prayer to its Creator.[55]

Except among the Orthodox writers, who are separated from the rest of the population by a forbidding barrier of dogma, the sense of dedication to high ideals is still restrained by the rebelliousness of the preceding generation. The literary world of Israel has not yet experienced the stirring phenomenon of the return of the "third generation" to the spiritual wellsprings that were repudiated by the second generation of immigrants. The contrast between two poetic treatments of the same theme is instructive. Richard Beer-Hofmann, living in Vienna, celebrated the wondrous destiny of the Jewish people in the hauntingly beautiful dramatic poem *Jaákobs Traum*. Jacob is warned by Satan that his children will be "chosen" for untold agonies and be marked for lonely wretchedness if they should accept the proffered Divine mission to be "a prophet unto the nations." Yet Jacob, in full realization of the immensity of the price and the multitude of yawning pitfalls, accepts the Divine command, even as every poet and every great man accepts the obligations implied in the insights granted to him. Yizhak Lamdan, expressing the spirit of a sadder generation, makes Jacob protest against the imposition of a yoke which deadened his senses to the joy of life and made him an orphan among the nations:

But now heavy are the heavens of a sudden;
The soil burns my soles, till they hurt;
Like a serpent biting heels, every path in it and trail.
Uplifted with bigness I awoke and bowed down by fear and
    orphanhood.

In Lamdan's version, Jacob is quite willing to accept a revelation of God in nature, but not a special human task that will set him apart and single him out.

Let me be! I will not be dragged perforce any more
To the gallows of thy love, O Lover and Seducer!
As one, the only chosen one, I am called to thee,

And by the time I come—I am misshapen—crippled;
"Jacob, Jacob!" No I will not come and listen,
And be once more scorned of man, yet beloved of God.
  If you have some matter to impart to me, a great and
    precious matter of love—
Stretch it at my feet as a verdant carpet of spring;
Light it up over my head as a blazing morning-rose.
Let its music sing in a myriad voices that all, that all, may
    hear:
Bejewel it with thy stars at night; thy sun by day,
And let the butterflies of all the world frolic with it.[56]

But even when the prophetic mission is repudiated, its haunting spell remains pervasive and powerful. The peculiar tragedies of Jewish history hammer home the realization that, bereft of the prophetic garb, we stand before the world naked and shamed. Caught in the serpentine coils of Romantic nationalism, the prophetic vision may be perverted, but not utterly dissipated.

The dramatic poet Matithyahu Shoham re-creates the image of the prophet Elijah. Addressing the dying King Ahab, who was sincerely devoted to the military greatness of the Northern Kingdom, Elijah says, "Forgive me, my king, but the Lord has led me far beyond the boundaries of your Kingdom." Contrasting Ahab's vision of national power with the prophetic vision of Israel's true greatness, the poet asserts:

We are called to triumph, as a nation
        within man and before God, sworn to salvation.
And cursed be all who sneak away, all who deny
Pristine purity and ultimate redemption.
Let the panicky prophets of other nations
        preach their counsels of escape; for us
        the word of greatness
        for the generations of man on earth.[57]

Our survey of the prophetic image in modern Hebrew litera-ture ends on a mixed note, trembling uncertainly between the haunting spell of the ancient vision and its rejection in whole or in part. The debris of the mighty Biblical figure lie littered in all directions, but its organic unity is lost. The voices of anti-prophetism are as loud in the land as the scattered echoes of prophecy.

Since literature is the mirror of life, we can hardly expect any other result; for the worldwide mass movement of Zionism, which revived Hebraic literature and created the State of Israel, was compounded of two spiritually contending forces—the one quasi-prophetic in nature, the other, opposing and contradicting it. Also, the mentality of those Jews who aimed to root them-selves heart and soul in the lands of the Diaspora was similarly compounded of the same opposing forces.

Within Zionism, the heritage of Ahad Ha'am was opposed by the "realists" who thought of the goal of the movement as the attainment by Jews of "normalcy" in order to become "like unto the other nations." A stateless people takes on the aspect of a ghost, evoking fear and hatred from the naïve masses. To be-come "normal" once again, the Jews should learn to fight for the things of this world and give up all pretensions to the mission of prophecy which made of them a "peculiar people." The one cure of all afflictions consisted in the dissociation, clean and complete, between people and prophecy, between the nation and its faith. In the land of Israel, the people would attain earthly salvation by ceasing to strive for heavenly bliss and by arising to confront the world as just another secular nation. The world refused to honor the people with the Book; they will be forced to respect the people with the sword. This antiprophetic mood was obscured at times by the ambiguous verbiage of Romantic nationalism, which tended to employ the prophetic posture and occasionally to use its central symbols, though with opposite intent. Self-glorification and self-sanctifi-cation to the point where the nation takes the place of God is

423

altogether in keeping with the "sacred egoism" of modern nationalism. Of the subtle seduction of this malady of the spirit, both life and literature offer ample substantiation.

In Diaspora Judaism, too, we recognize a similar tension between prophetism and rebellion against the Divine mission. On the one hand, the ideologists of classical Reform and Conservatism re-created the image of the prophet as the protagonist of "ethical monotheism," proclaiming its "eternal verities" to mankind. On the other hand, Zionist critics were not altogether off the mark in pointing to the assimilationist trends within modern Judaism. It cannot be denied that this domain shades off gradually into the no-man's-land of indifferentism and ultimate disappearance. A liberal faith does not delimit itself by rigid boundaries and does not impose sanctions upon its marginal adherents. Hence, the outside boundaries of its following are not defined. Conversionist assimilation blends insensibly into its opposite, prophetic Judaism, and the two forces are interlocked in an embrace that is also an unending struggle. In the Diaspora, it is not the group as a whole, but many individuals, who seek the nirvana of "normalcy" by dissociating themselves from the faith and destiny of the Jewish people. These seekers of oblivion employ the symbols and banners of prophetic religion, though their purpose is to reduce Jewish loyalty to the minimum. The tensions of Diaspora Judaism are, of course, sensed and interpreted by the Hebrew writers in Israel.

If we hazard a guess concerning the future, it is this very contact between Hebrew literature and Jewish life in the Diaspora that leads us to foresee the possibility of a revival of the prophetic image in Israel. Twice in the period of two centuries, the vision of prophecy was re-created through the stimulating influence of an outside cultural force. Humanism in Italy helped to produce the peculiar genius of Luzzatto, and nineteenth-century rationalism brought into being the philosophy of modern Judaism. May it not be that the same event will be

424

repeated once again, the re-emergence of prophetism in the Diaspora being followed by a corresponding resurgence of the prophetic image in the literature of modern Israel?

Two factors appear to make for such a revival. First, to recapture the synoptic vision of prophecy is indispensable for the very life of the Jewish community. Without the dynamism of a supreme purpose that is universal in scope and transcendent in quality, the Jewish community cannot long continue to thrive. Second, the overwhelming majority of Diaspora Jewry reside in America, where the spell of Romantic nationalism, that satanic counterpart of prophetism, is bound to become progressively weaker. America is the classic land of liberal statism as Germany was the classic land of Romantic nationalism. Furthermore, American culture is more hospitably disposed toward the Hebraic prophetic image than toward the competing images of saint or mystic, artist or philosopher. In this land, there is no conflict between Judaism conceived in prophetic terms and Americanism interpreted in the light of its prophetic tradition. Hence, the prophetic miracle is, to say the least, a possibility in this country—the miracle of being so authentically true to one's own being as to reflect at the same time the soul of mankind.[58]

If American Judaism rises to the magnificent challenge of its time and circumstance, modern Hebrew literature will be sensitized to discriminate between the stance of prophecy and its substance, between the allurements of romanticism and the call of God.

In the worldwide struggle of the Jewish soul to recapture its heroic vision, the decisive engagement is being fought here and now. It will not do for us to imagine that the prophetic fire is rekindled in us automatically the moment we recount the achievements of the prophets of old. Salvation is not "over there," in the past, all packaged and ready. We are not the proud custodians of "eternal verities" unavailable to others, but only the humble seekers of a Divine mystery that is never fully grasped. The genius of prophecy may be described, the mantle of prophecy may be institutionalized, but the spirit of prophecy cannot be manufactured at will. In keeping with the Qabbalistic ideal of gathering the scattered sparks of Divinity, we should aim at that synoptic vision that is always being built but never completed. We cannot claim to be among those who know all about God, but we can proclaim the supreme virtue of the unending quest. Let our motto be, "Those who seek the Lord shall not lack aught that is good."[59]

Nor will it do for us to await complacently the rebirth of a new prophetic vision in the land of Israel on the romantic assumption that prophecy is like the fruit of a tree, ripening best in its own native climate. Salvation again is not "over there," in the storied rocks and freshly poured cement of Israel. Always and everywhere, salvation comes from within, consisting in the sparks that fly when the hammer of God beats upon the anvil of the soul.

FAITH AND LAW*

The nature of the theme requires that we begin with some conception of the essence of faith, but it is hardly possible to commit oneself to any one definition of faith without projecting the outlines of a whole set of inferences, nor does the luminous core of faith lend itself to investigation by the methods of empiricism, though any meaningful conception must be inferred from the recorded experiences in the great documents of religious faith. We have to accept the fact that we are dealing with a subject where reasoning is inevitably circumscribed within a closed circle. The recognition of our subjectivity must be our sole concession to the claims of objectivity. It is faith within the Jewish religion, or the Judeo-Christian tradition, that engages our attention. We are concerned with a certain kind of faith—faith in a God who is both immanent and transcendent, immanent in our self and transcendent to all our experiences.

The medieval distinction between faith as assent and faith as trust has been revived in our day by Martin Buber. As assent, faith is primarily an event on the plane of knowledge. A proposition which may or may not be true—say, that God spoke in so many words to Moses on Sinai—is affirmed to be true by virtue of an act of will on our part. Such volitional decisions may be termed acts of faith. They are essentially expressions of obedience, submission to the authority of an institution, a book, or to the impetus of tradition as a whole.

As trust, faith is an event on the plane of personal relations. It is not an arbitrary acceptance of a narration from the past, but

---

*Address at American Conference on Jewish Philosophy, 1964.

a living reaction to a contemporary phenomenon. We respond to other people in a manner that affirms them to be more than objects and somehow related to our own inner self. Faith belongs to the realm of interpersonal relations, which is *sui generis* and not to be confused with the calculations of force and utility that prevail in our mass-society as a rule. As trust, faith is more closely related to love than to any other emotion. Genuine love, as we know, is both an assertion and a surrender; it is both self-fulfillment and self-denial. Faith as trust is thus ambivalent in tone, while faith as assent is simply a negation of human power.

Buber's analysis centers on his basic insight concerning the supreme distinction between the "I-Thou" and "I-it" relations. When he proceeds to identify the notion of faith as trust with the central idea of Judaism and the concept of faith as assent with the character of Christian faith, he resorts to the vice of abstraction in regard to both communities. The personal element of direct confrontation was always a central note in Christianity, while surrender to the authority of Scripture and Talmud was always of central importance in the Jewish religion.

Furthermore, if in Judaism the concept of God as a living person is the basic axiom, we also find the continuing insistence that He is not a person. After all, the desperate struggle of the patriarchs and prophets against the seduction of pagan images revolved around this point—no image, however glorious, could suggest, let alone capture, the nature of the Supreme Being. Philosophers, eager to note the distinction between the "God of Aristotle" and the "God of Abraham, Isaac, and Jacob," have tended to overlook the crucial battle, that of the one true God against the various pagan deities. Yet, it was the latter struggle that reflected the real clash between the two world-views. The Hellenistic Jew thought of the philosophers as being basically allies in their ongoing war against the seductions and illusions of the pagan masses.

In the Judeo-Christian tradition generally, and in Judaism particularly, God was not-person as well as person at one and the same time. In the formula of benedictions, the Lord is addressed as "Thou," in the opening clause, "blessed art Thou," but then the language is changed to the third person, "Who has."

There is an alternation from direct confrontation to the feeling of impersonality and hiddenness—*nochah* and *nistar*. When the Biblical authors express the feelings of trust, they frequently stress the nonpersonal character of the Divine Being. "God is not a man that He should lie, neither the son of man that He should repent."[1]

Reliability is more often than not expressed by way of impersonal imagery: "He is the Rock, His work is perfect, for all His ways are justice; a God of faithfulness and without iniquity, just and right is He."[2]

The so-called doctrine of *imitatio Dei* is not stated directly in Scripture. In the Talmud, it echoes the accents of Plato, but even there no effort is made to draw more than some homiletic inferences from it. Even so, the Midrash insists that God's "jealousy" must not be emulated by man.

To me it seems that the basic note of faith in the Judeo-Christian tradition is the apprehension of unity and polarity. It is the awareness of a bond of unity in some sense, along with the realization of categorical separateness and disunity. It is a reaching for that which cannot be grasped; hence, it is always an anticipation and a goal, as well as an assurance and a possession.

To be sure, faith as assent to an intellectual proposition and faith as trust in the Supreme Person, the "Judge of the entire world," are also embraced in the glowing moment of unification. The quest of the meaning of the encounter between man and God is part of the encounter itself, and it emerges to the forefront as soon as the momentary presentness of faith turns into a fact of memory.

The unity of faith consists of three unities: the unity of self, the unity of the cosmos in the will of the Supreme Being, and the unity of the pathways leading from man to God. In the glow of faith, these unities are felt in the silent beat of reality: I am a person, not merely a bundle of reflexes and emotions; the universe is not merely a sprawling chaos but the embodiment of one law, one mind, one will, that is akin to my self at its deepest level; and the meaning of my life is found in my relation to this One God.

A good illustration of this three-dimensional unity of faith is afforded in the Midrashic explanation of the manner in which Abraham attained his faith: "It is as if a person saw a beautiful palace, with the windows lighted and the lawns tended, while the various servants came and went, attending to their respective tasks. Said he, 'Is it possible for this palace to be without a master?' Then, the master of the palace glanced at him and said, 'I am the master of the palace.' "³ Abraham, as we learn from other legends, was a restless seeker of truth. He broke the idols in his father's house in his quest for the meaning for life. He thus appears as a bold individualist, eager to think and feel for himself. This, then, is the first unity of the man of faith, his own personality. He proceeds to determine the nature of the external universe. Is it run by many forces, as the people of his day thought, by the stars, the sun, the moon, or perhaps by an "assembly of the gods"? No, there is the seal of order, the mark of design, the intimation of a supreme harmony, hence, there must be a master of the palace. Thus, we have the second note of the ring of faith—the unity of the cosmos. The story goes on to relate of the "glance" of the master—a glance which assures Abraham that the master of the palace is a friend, whom one could love and serve, and discover in the search for blessedness. Here, then, is the third and final note of faith.

The character of faith as unification attains explicit affirmation in the piety of the Qabbalists, who formulated the intention for the performance of a *mizvah* as follows: "For the sake of the unification of the Holy One, blessed be He, and His *Shechinah*, in the realm of mystery and in the name of all

Israel." The *Shechinah* is the immanent phase of the Deity, immanent in the hearts of man, while the "Holy One" is transcendent to humanity, but still immanent in the cosmos. Israel represents the work of God in history. One could not perform a *mizvah* properly without the prior process of "unifying" one's self by the elimination or the purification of "strange thoughts," and then unifying oneself with Israel and with God in His two aspects.

While this aspect of piety was explicitly formulated only in the later stages of Qabbalah and in Hasidism, we find intimations of it in the earliest documents of the faith.

The festive affirmation of Divine unity in Deuteronomy is followed immediately by the command to love the Lord "with all your heart, with all your soul, and with all your might." The unity of the cosmos is set forth as the preamble of Torah in the story of creation. The unity of man, in spite of his sinfulness and weakness, is illustrated in the story of Adam and Eve and Cain and Abel—it is always possible for man to start afresh and to attain the fullness of his own destiny. The unity of man and God is given concrete representation in the doctrine of the Covenant, which is concluded first with Adam, then with Noah, and later in a more specific way with Abraham, Moses, Joshua, and others.

Faith in Scripture is not one aspect or one insight or one line of activity among others; it is the totality of man's devotion, comprehension, and his sense of honor—hence, the persistent harping on Divine jealousy. There simply is no room for interests and concerns apart from faith. Thus, the rabbis commented that the judgment "behold, it is very good," which the Lord rendered when he created man, meant that man's evil desire as well as his good desire were praised. In faith, it is man as a whole that confronts His Creator. Abraham, the archetypal man of faith, was praised by the prophet for being one, that is, whole: "For one I called him and blessed him."[4] We are told that the Divine command to Abraham was "Walk before me and be complete."[5] Faith as the outreaching of man's entire

431

being toward the Divine is a blend of several lines of effort—
the rational, the moral, the esthetic, the holy. These quests in
their turn are given additional drive by the failure and frustration
of man's occasional endeavors to run away from God—in pride,
selfishness, idolatry, the seduction of momentary pleasures, in
fear and superstition with their thousand faces.

The three unities that blend together in the fullness of faith
are themselves creations of faith; that is, they are not the kind
of realities which our partial faculties can encompass. Reason
may analyze all portions of creation, but it cannot envision the
whole of the cosmos, be it finite or infinite. Neither can we
visualize the self, nor understand the coherence and consistency
of the several pathways of man's quest for reality. How do the
disparate ways of reason, ethics, esthetics, and holiness come
together when each way is "pure" and genuine only when it
is unmixed and single-tracked? Yet, we assert in faith that they
are one in their infinite goal as they are one in their mysterious
source. Faith projects the three unities as a task that we have
to bring to realization. "On that day the Lord will be One and
His Name one."[6] But it does more than set a goal; it also
bequeaths an assurance that the ultimate unity is already here,
in the depths of reality or in the mind of God, as it were.
Hence, it issues in two opposite feelings—a glow of euphoria
and a dynamic restlessness.

Tension is of the essence of living faith; there is hardly any
phase of it that is not a reflection of a polarity, but it is a
dynamic tension, expressed in a rhythmic oscillation of feeling
and orientation, rather than a passive position wherein the
opposing forces are set over against one another and thereby
neutralized.

We begin with the three unities of which faith is the
momentary meeting. The unity of the self is a restless synthesis
of character and spontaneity. A person is not merely subject
to the laws of physiology, but insofar as he is a personality,
he abides by certain regulations—there are certain things that

he will *not* do. These are not of his own private invention; on the contrary, these are the laws of our society, for the most part, objective and fairly universal. On the other hand, a personality is not merely an incarnation of laws; he is also the bearer of a spark of freedom, whereby he might go beyond the laws, for good or ill. He cannot be understood as being simply the sum total of impulses and ideals; he acts as an individual. Insofar as a human being attains the quality of personality, he brings into the dynamic equilibrium of consciousness the laws whereby he, taken as a whole, guides his conduct and that protean *élan* by which he on occasion transcends these laws or transgresses them.

Naturally, some people are blindly conformist, rebelling rarely, if at all, against the established patterns of society or the ingrained habits of their own life. They are self-conscious personalities only in a marginal sense, even if in 1984 all of us may turn into similar mesmerized mechanisms. On the other hand, some individuals may so cherish the inner surge of their moral energy that they refuse to abide by any man-made laws. But freedom is meaningful only as it relates to a firm character who acts consciously and who brings the totality of his being to bear upon any decision. Otherwise, a person's choice would be not freedom, but caprice and chance. The very concept of self, then, is an ideal synthesis, which is attained only occasionally and ephemerally.

A similar synthesis of regularity and novelty is apparent in the cosmos. Through the massive achievements of the human mind, the iron meshes of inexorable law governing the universe are steadily being uncovered. But there are also manifold evidences of a cosmic energy controverting the momentum of entropy and driving toward ever greater complexes of freedom. The cosmos contains a graduated series of "wholes," rising in complexity and in the variability of response, from the inorganic molecule to the one-called organism and from the amoeba to an Aristotle. The capacity of a system to react as a whole is not in direct conflict to the mechanistic laws that govern all phenomena; a new factor is simply added to the situation, the organism as a whole. If life, mind, and spirit are not to be explained away, our evolving universe must be understood as four-dimensional, with the fourth dimension measuring the ascent of being on the scale of wholeness and freedom. The cosmos throbs with, and surges toward, a higher unity.

Nevertheless, it is clear that our self is pretty close to the pole of freedom, though it is subject to the laws of physiology and sociology as well as to the self-imposed laws of personal conduct. The external universe, on the other hand, is quite close to the pole of an absolute and unbending law, though it does contain the ascending hierarchy of wholes. As we push our efforts to explain the phenomena of the external cosmos, we tend to reduce all qualities to quantitative measurements and to strive toward an Einsteinian general field-theory that would embrace the secret of existence in a mathematical formula of identities.

The concept of God in the Judeo-Christian tradition is a synthesis of the unities of self and cosmos. God is the Ultimate Being, in whom we and the universe find our source. He is the source of the free personality and of the laws that govern the physical universe. He is our "Father" as well as our "King"—two titles that are nearly always juxtaposed in our liturgy. He is the infinite self, so that man merely reflects His image, however dimly and spasmodically. But He is also the Intimate Being, the unfailing "I am" of Exodus, "The cause of all causes" in medieval philosophy, the qualityless undetermined infinite (*en sof*) of Qabbalah.

The assertion that God is the creator of the universe and of man can be taken in two ways—either that there is absolutely no relation between the Creature and the Creator, which is comprehensible from the creature's side, or that the relation is "projectible" though not conceivable. Employing a mathematical analogy, we may present the alternatives as being the relation of a finite series of integers to an infinite series of integers, or alternatively a finite series of integers to an infinite series of irrational numbers, such as $\sqrt{-2}$, $\sqrt{-4}$, $\sqrt{-16}$, etc. The decision between the two alternatives cannot be made by us with any degree of certainty. At this point, it is clear that the temper of the believer is crucial. If it be of a life-affirming nature, then a person will stress the common dimension between the human self and the Deity. On the other hand, those who come to God by way of rebounding from the frustrations of life are likely to stress the incommensurability of the minds of man and God. On the whole, faith in historic Judaism inclines more to the pole of religious humanism than it favors the "leap in the dark" variety.

Since God partakes of freedom as well as of necessity, we cannot identify Him with the projection either of self alone or of cosmos alone. By whichever pathway we approach him, we can only offer an intimation of His Being. We cannot assert His "otherness" without removing Him completely from our comprehension, but neither can we project His identity with our self without having Him disappear into the mystery of our own selfhood, thereby ceasing to be God. It follows that faith by its very essence involves a negation as well as an affirmation.

It is this paradoxical quality of faith that our Scriptures enshrine. The true God is unknowable. Fetishes do not enclose Him, images do not represent Him, sacraments do not embrace Him, temples do not enclose Him. Yes, even the "father of all prophets" could but glimpse His glory, from behind, as it were. At the same time, He is revealed in righteousness, in love, in holiness, in the pristine harmony of creation ere it was disturbed by human sin, and in the ultimate consummation of peace in the End of Days.

Faith is an assurance of possession; somehow we are embraced by His power, because "The eternal God is thy dwelling place, and underneath are the everlasting arms."[7] But God, if He is truly God, eludes our grasp; He is infinite and stands beyond the circle of the comprehensible. If light is the symbol of intelligibility, He is the source of light, hence, beyond it. "For with

Thee is the fountain of life, and in Thy light do we see light."[8]

It follows that the living moment of faith issues in an awareness of privation as well as possession. Our values, when integrated and fused together, lead us to the assurance of His reality, but also to the consciousness of their fragmentariness, their incompleteness, their excessive, prideful boldness—yes, their sinfulness. Each of the directions of spiritual life tends to be "pure" and self-sufficient. The pride of the man of reason, the scorn of the esthete, the jealousy of the lover, the blindness to this world of the mystic—all are expressions of one facet of faith. Because of its one-sidedness, each is unbalanced on the side of possession.

On the side of negation, too, there is the one-sidedness of those who deny and despair—the skeptic, the cynic, those who close their eyes to the manifold beauties of this world, those who are so deeply aware of frustration and failure that salvation can be conceivable to them only as a total break with the normal order of this world.

True faith is an unstable, dynamic equilibrium in which we feel the reality of the Divine presence, but also its remoteness from our grasp. The two aspects of faith are not mutually canceled, but instead they are acted out in life. The note of assurance is translated into a positive program of religion in action, while the note of aspiration is maintained and reaffirmed in humble recognition of ignorance. Though we act on faith, we remain open to doubt and self-criticism. In this way, the restless tension of religious life generates an active devotion to earthly goals, even as it keeps alive the feeling that these goals are somehow inadequate, because the pathway to the Divine is infinite. "For as the heavens are higher than the earth, so are my ways higher than your ways, and my thoughts than your thoughts,"[9] says the Lord.

Naturally, there can be no perfect synthesis between the claims of possession and privation, at least none that would adequately reflect the temper and the need of every age. At times, it is out of the depths of despair that one finds his way to God;

the pendulum of the spirit is set moving powerfully from one end to the other. But the even tenor of sober piety that marks the lives of those whose lot has fallen in pleasant places must not be despised on account of its placidity and lack of violent alternation. We may err in both directions. In a discussion of the basic principles of the Jewish faith, one sage of the Talmud[10] suggests that Habakkuk summed it all up in the one verse, "The righteous shall live by his faith"—that is, faith is a possession of the righteous, which they seek to protect. Another sage asserts that the one fundamental verse is that of Amos, "Seek me and live"; that is, religion is a perpetual quest for the fullness of life. It is an awareness of privation; the goal of our own fulfillment is beyond us. We may conclude that both Amos and Habakkuk were right, for as we seek God, we find the "peace that passes understanding" but also the discontent that drives us onward. "The disciples of the wise can find no peace, neither in this world, nor in the next."[11]

The feelings of assurance and possession are crystallized in Judaism in the concept of the Covenant, the "signs" by which it is expressed and the "laws" by which an action program is governed. The vision of Abraham is the archetype of Jewish faith. Abraham is assured that God favors him: "Those who bless thee will be blessed, and those who curse thee I shall curse."[12] But he is not chosen for his own sake; the Divine intent is to bless his ideal self—that which he will transmit to subsequent generations. "For I have loved him in order that he may command his sons and his household after him, that they shall keep the way of the Lord, to do justice and righteousness. . . ."[13] (Rashi's interpretation of *Yedativ* is included in the translation.) The ideal self cannot be achieved once and for all, nor can it be maintained in static perfection by a detailed regimen. Hence, the Divine imperative is stated in general terms—"and be thou a blessing." In later years, this all-embracing imperative was translated into a series of laws, which were intended to spell out its implications for Jewish and general society at any one time and place. But the supremacy of the general principle was affirmed as late as the time of Hillel and Akiva: "Whatever is hateful unto you, do not do unto others" and "Love thy neighbor as thyself."

It follows that the correlative of faith is not any one law, but the principle of law: we are bound to the one God in a Covenant, as it were, and we are called upon to express by action, personal and communal, the import of our consecration. Laws are the standardized programs of action for a community, some of the laws will be "signs," outward symbols of an inner reality, and some will be corollaries of the principle "to be a blessing," "to love our neighbor as ourselves," or of the collective destiny of Jewry, "Ye shall be my witnesses."[14]

The feelings of privation in Jewish faith were expressed in the continual admonitions of the prophets and in the willingness of the people to heed the cruel taunts of the prophets: "we have become like Sodom, we are like Gomorrah."[15] The prophets stressed the inwardness of genuine piety: "and with their lips they honor me, but in their hearts they are far from me."[16] They also insisted on the primacy of the ethical imperative within the religious framework. Above all, they kept alive the awareness of the open horizons of a living faith. We are favored, yes; but then, do we live up to the full implications of the Covenant? These implications are infinite in degrees of intensity and as varied as the ever-changing kaleidoscopic pattern of society. The rutted grooves of the past are not enough. We need to renew the Covenant, to write it afresh on the tablets of our hearts.

In Judaism, faith is articulated in both "the Law and the prophets"; that is, in the specific patterns of action—which are to be observed *as if* they were eternal laws—and in the living protesters against the soulless piety of mechanical compliance with the same laws. In Deuteronomy, the Law is not described as unchanging in its perfection—a prophet like Moses is supposed to arise, who could continue the revelation at Sinai.[17] When the high court is stated to be the highest authority—"Thou shalt not depart from what they tell thee, to the right or to the left"—a

Rabbinic comment insists that this is so only "if they tell you that your right hand is your right and your left hand is your left."[18] It is the sectarian Book of Jubilees that asserts that the Law is a copy of the one eternal law that is inscribed on heavenly tablets. Later, this idea reappears in Qabbalah, where the Torah is said to be written in heaven "with black fire on white fire," though there it is differently scanned.[19]

Perhaps it was unfortunate that the earliest translators spoke of Torah as the Law. Actually, laws constitute only a small fraction of the Holy Scriptures. In Pharisaic Judaism, the living tradition was designed to balance the written Law. Philosophic Judaism continued the tradition of the prophets and the Pharisees, interpreting the intent of the laws in accord with the universal principles of ethics.

Maimonides drew the distinction between "true ideas" and "necessary ideas."[20] The latter notions are needed for the maintenance of the Jewish community. It appears clearly that whereas his general concept of prophecy belongs to the first category, his insistence on the unique status of Moses is purely dogmatic, i.e. it is a postulate that, in his judgment, is essential to the life of the community. This distinction is reinforced by his interpretation of many ritual laws as being merely concessions to the primitive feelings of the Jewish people at the time of Moses.

The ritual law in Judaism is, as Hermann Cohen taught us, a metaphorical representation of the eternal, moral law. Cohen esteemed the principle of "lawfulness" as the essence of "culture-consciousness." But even before he came to the notion of a personal "correlation" between man and God, he insisted that the starting point of all culture and religion is the feeling of "truthfulness" (*Wahrhaftigkeit*)—a personal confrontation of the mystery of being in the search for truth. All positive law can only aim at conformity with the ultimate law.

Reverence for law is one of the polar expressions of faith, the other pole being the free and personal relation of man to God.

439

This polarity arises out of the very concept of God as the source of both man and the cosmos. In the universe all our efforts at comprehension aim at the discovery of the ultimate laws of being, while in the case of man, freedom is the soul of personality. Jeremiah speaks of the Covenant, not the laws, as being firm and eternal as "the laws of heaven and earth."[21] A covenant is quite different from a contract; for whereas in a contract, specifications are set against specific rewards; in a covenant, specific undertakings are supplemented by the spirit of love, which is whole-souled and indivisible. The whole of personality includes one's intellectual, ethical, and esthetic faculties. Faith is not the repudiation of any phase of our being, but the unification and completion of our self, which by its very nature points beyond itself. The revealed Law is in the Talmud regarded as subject to the reasoned judgment of the rabbis.[22]

It is possible to trace the dialectical tension between the two polar articulations of faith in the history of Judaism. Such a study would expose the hollowness of the dogma that the Jewish faith is reducible to the flat assertion of a revealed law, as Moses Mendelssohn had maintained. Suffice it to point out that in the twentieth century, the two giants of the Jewish faith, Hermann Cohen and Martin Buber, articulated the two phases of faith. Cohen stressed the ideal of the Law and Buber that of personal confrontation. Yet, in spite of their mutual antagonism, both knew that their philosophies supplemented one another. That luminous spirit that rose suddenly, like a comet on the horizon, Franz Rosenzweig, knew himself to be a loving disciple of Cohen's and an ardent co-worker of Buber's.

The strictly religious tension between freedom and submission reflects the larger tensions within the realm of culture as a whole. Apart from the domain of religion, modern man must choose between submission to the regnant ideologies of his day or withdrawal from the world in order to find his soul. Often enough, to be authentically himself, a truly sensitive person must become an alien and a pilgrim. Indeed, alienation is regarded by many authors as a peculiarly modern phenomenon, deriving from the breakdown of ancestral traditions.

If the life of faith is to reflect the tensions of our existence as a whole, then certainly the picture we have presented of the rhythm of faith is an adumbration of the dilemma of the free individual in our society. By the same token, the recognition of the rhythm itself as the core experience of faith provides the basic answer to the social polarity between self-assertion and self-surrender. We find our self in both orientations of our spirit, in our withdrawal from society as in our total identification with it. Even as we move in the one direction, we bear the conviction that our self truly belongs in the opposite direction as well. We surrender to society, but not totally; only in order that we might with redoubled effort tear ourselves away from it and see it objectively, from without. And when we retreat, it is for the purpose of returning with deeper love.

Is this oscillation of the spirit an artificial combination, utterly alien to the basic simplicities of nature? By no means. The contrary is the case. Have we not learned from modern physics that the building blocks of the universe are essentially not so many billiard balls, but waves, tremors in a polar field of force? Why then expect that our awareness of the surge of creation— that is, faith—should not be similarly structured?

JEWISH
ETHICS

If the unity of God is the central affirmation of the Jewish religion, the unity of man is the central theme of Jewish ethics. Indeed, a good case could be made for the thesis that the theological doctrine was a reflection on the metaphysical plane of the Jewish concept of human nature. In its most basic form, this concept asserts that man must strive to become a fully harmonious being—one in himself, one with mankind, one before God.

The first principle is therefore an act of faith. In our experience, man is pulled in opposite directions by the conflicting forces within his being. The good desire (*yezer tov*) and the evil desire (*yezer hora*) are perpetually at war within our breast. On the plane of philosophy, this conflict is reflected in the polarity between the concept of man as a self-sufficient entity and the view of him as a dependent creature inherently related to a metaphysical realm or being. Then, as we turn to the realm of social relations, we encounter the opposition between man as a political animal, who discovers his identity in the state, and man as an independent source of judgment, whose conscience is perpetually and properly in polar tension with the laws and judgments of the community.

In our experience, then, man is in tension, in the three dimensions of existence—psychologically, metaphysically, and sociologically. The fundamental assertion of Jewish ethics is that man can and ought to achieve a harmonious resolution of these tensions, for they derive from God, who is One. "And be ye holy, for I the Lord your God am holy."[1] Man is to *become* holy, while God *is* holy.

Psychologically, it is the function of the good desire not to overcome and crush the evil desire, but to embrace and sublimate it. Commenting on the Divine assertion that "man is very good," the sages affirm that "good is the good desire, very good is the evil desire."[2] The depths of passion within us make possible superlative levels of achievement, levels that must be transcended almost as soon as they are attained.

It is our duty to guard our personal well-being, to enjoy the legitimate pleasures of life, including "wine, women, and song," and take delight in all the gifts of life; but we must also know that we belong to God, not to ourselves, and voluntarily deny ourselves some permissible indulgences—"Sanctify yourself by means of that which is permitted to you."[3]

Philosophically, man is a thinking being. It is his task and destiny to reflect on the whole of creation, assigning "names" to all creatures and discovering their essences.[4] Wisdom consists in classifying all things, putting them into their respective categories. In human relations, the quest of philosophy is to achieve a design of life in which every impulse and every ideal is accorded its proper place. This quest is opposed by our numinous feeling, or our metaphysical intuition, which insists that the essence of our being eludes the meshes of reason. Human nature cannot be fitted into the system, because it contains a dimension that transcends the knowable world. In this polarity, too, Jewish ethics embraces both horns of the dilemma, asserting both the rightness of humanism and the need of transcending it. "Complete, ye shall be *with* the Lord thy God."[5] To render justice to the whole of human nature is right, but this task cannot ever be finished, since apart from his reference to the Supreme Being, man is not complete.

Sociologically, man is a "political animal," incapable of self-fulfillment in isolation. Hence, it is his duty to submit to the laws of the community and to obey the law, even if his life be required. But man may also discover the Divine will in his heart, the inner depths of which are beyond the reach of the state. Every man faces God directly, and when the commands of God collide with those of the State, the latter must yield. "The words of the Master, and the words of the disciple—whose word shall be followed?"[6]

Some scholars describe the central motif of Jewish ethics as being the "sanctification of life." This phrase is extremely suggestive, but also ambiguous. Is life holy, or must it be made holy? In reality, both answers are given. Human life, in all its many-sidedness, is good, but not as it is in the raw—only insofar as it is directed toward God. The task of so directing it is never completed.

In the pagan world, man's yearning for ethical perfection was fragmentized because the deity was conceived under the aspect of many and warring gods. Certainly, the promptings of conscience were reflected in the literature of ancient Egypt and Babylonia. Wisdom, or philosophy, was cultivated by sages and formulated in memorable maxims. The priests of the "official" religions and of the private "mystery" cults catered to man's sense of the numinous. The law of the land was proclaimed with all the authority of gods and kings. But these disparate ideals were not fused into one flame of idealism. The priests plied their trade, the ecstatics impressed the populace, the men of wisdom trained the bureaucrats, and the kings proclaimed their laws in the names of the gods. Since the diverse disciplines were not related to one source, there was no dynamic dialectic. When philosophy emerged in full bloom in the schools of Athens, its principles and practice were quite independent of the rituals of the city-cult and the laws of the civil government.

In the Biblical world, the wholeness of human nature and its transcendent dimension were affirmed; hence, the tension between instinct and ideal, between the rituals of tradition and the individual's awareness of the Divine word, between the laws of State and Temple and the insights of human wisdom. This tension is not between the Divine and the demonic, but between the several embodiments of the Divine. Therefore, the tension

444

is resolved only through a series of compromises, which extend throughout man's history, attaining the perfection of peace only in the End of Days.

In the Hebrew Bible, we are given many examples of the creative character of this ongoing tension. The life of Abraham is paradigmatic. He is represented as the great ancestor, "the father of a multitude of nations";[7] yet, by Divine command, he leaves his aged father in search of a new destiny. Like the good and pious men of his age, he is prepared to offer his son, Isaac, as a sacrifice, but, in advance of his time, he affirms that God abhors human sacrifice and demands only man's inner obedience; hence, animal sacrifices are quite sufficient. He is not merely the "knight of faith," but what is far more significant, the defender of a faith that is rational and moral, even as it is a commitment to the transcendent God. He preaches the justice of God, on behalf of the individual, and in his plea for the Sodomites, he insists that God must not destroy the just along with the wicked.[8] Yet, on behalf of his descendants, he accepts the state of slavery and torment for four hundred years, as long as this period of trial will eventuate in the emergence of a "great nation."[9]

The Jewish faith unites man's moral and rational faculties with the mystical feelings of surrender to the Divine will, hence, its inner dialectic. The very concept of a covenant implies a realm of existence in which God and men enjoy a fundamental mutuality. It is true that God lays down the law for His creatures; but not as a willful autocrat. The purpose of His laws is to enhance life and to bestow wisdom.[10] The "way of the Lord" is not a mystical *Tao,* but it is "to do justice and righteousness."[11] In his God-given freedom, man rethinks the thought of God in respect of the true, the good, and the holy.

Some scholars have maintained that Judaism is a "classical faith," in the sense of harmonizing all of man's faculties.[12] This classicism is balanced by the nonclassical recognition that human nature points beyond itself to the Divine Being, whose thoughts are not our thoughts. Hence, not man in himself but

445

"man as he stands before God" is the "measure of all things." To face the Divine is to remain open to new insights, even as one bows to His will, which is revealed in Torah and wisdom.

The Hebrew Bible is the work of three religious personalities —the priest, the sage, and the prophet. This is how Jeremiah envisaged the sacred tradition, "For there shall not cease Torah from the priest, nor counsel from the sage, nor the word from the prophet."[13]

In all religions, the priest is the guardian of the tradition. He performs the sacred rites that symbolize man's dependence upon the Divine Being. Priestly rites are nonrational and even irrational, for their function is to minister to man's sense of the numinous.

But the Torah of the priests is balanced in Scripture by the living word of the prophet, who confronts the social realities of his day with a fresh awareness of the Divine will. The prophet is a moralist, insisting that the core of the Divine will is goodness and mercy. The sage adds his "counsel," which consists of the lessons of human experience and reflection.

Although they speak with different voices, the priest, the prophet, and the sage together reflect the will of God. The wisdom of the sage is Divine in origin, as are the admonitions of the prophets and the teachings of the priests.[14]

The basic virtue of the sage is justice in society and temperance in personal life—"giving all things their due," and refraining from "excess" in all the spheres of life. The central virtue of priestly piety is charity or love—the love of God and the love of man—self-surrender to God, and self-giving to man. The prophet accepts both counsels, and he fuses them in the mystical fire of Divine confrontation; hence, the entire tradition becomes problematical to him. He adds the quality of humility, which derives from the awareness of the infinite dimension of man's task—thus Micah's summation "to do justly, and to love mercy, and to walk humbly with the Lord thy God."[15]

In the post-Biblical era, the nature of Jewish ethics could best be described as loyalty to the teachings of the Law and the prophets.[16] It was not sufficient to comply with the requisites of the Law; one had to embrace also the "prophets," who represented the heritage of critical and inspired reflection on the *meaning* of the Law. While the Law set the norms of conduct for the community, the pious individual was bidden to go "beyond the line of the Law" and to meditate on its governing principles.[17] He was also commanded to defer to the conscience of civilized humanity (*derech erez*), for Torah is founded on the obligations of humanity.[18] The Jew was therefore expected to share in the virtues of priesthood, prophecy, and universal wisdom.

Out of the blending of these three Biblical hero-images, there emerged the Rabbinic hero-image, the Disciple of the Wise. He took upon himself the obligation to abide by the priestly regulations of purity. To the extent that he merited it, the "Holy Spirit" directed his Torah-reasoning. It was his responsibility to care for the sick, the widows, and the orphans. He was the judge, the teacher, the social-service worker, and the preacher, doing the Lord's work without pay, "even as the Lord takes care of our needs without any compensation."[19] He practiced his trade for many hours a day in order to provide for his wife and children, but he set fixed hours for prayer and Torah-study. He was an athlete of the spirit, endeavoring to climb the ladder of forty-eight virtues, whereby the Torah was acquired and the gift of the Holy Spirit was merited.[20] But he was not an ascetic. To be sure, he "sanctified himself by denying himself the things that were permitted," but only with moderation. Like the ancient philosophers, he esteemed learning as his chief pleasure, but his learning was inseparable from the practice of charity, the pursuit of the "ways of peace" in the community and the raising of his family. "A man whose wisdom exceeds his deeds, to what may he be compared? To a tree, the branches of which are large and the roots of which are small. When the southern wind comes, it is uprooted and turned over."[21]

Above all, in his quest for the vision of perfection, his ultimate goal was beyond time itself. While no more was required of him than to follow the way of the Torah as it was formulated in the oral Law, he required of himself the unrelenting endeavor to achieve perfection. Every day he was to say to himself: "When will my deeds reach the level of Abraham, Isaac, and Jacob?" In the face of the infinite demand, he could not but be humble and discontented with his spiritual attainments: "The Disciples of the Wise cannot rest, either in this world or in the next one."[22] Yet, he knew that in "matters of the heart," achievements could not be calculated mechanically. In pride, all may be lost, and in true repentance and humility, a "person may acquire his world in one hour."[23]

The Disciple of the Wise was not distinguished from the people by any formal ordination. To be a disciple was the popular ideal in Rabbinic Judaism, an ideal that was "professionalized" in part only in the later Middle Ages. At different times, one or another aspect of this ideal personality was emphasized. Saadia Gaon stressed the need of balance and harmony—we must not allow any one ideal to distort our personality, not even the "love of God."[24] Bahya was far more single-minded, assenting even to the virtues of the monastic life.[25] Maimonides was more even-handed. He retained the polarity of the "golden mean" and the "intellectual love of God."[26]

On the threshold of the modern age, the Hasidim emphasized the virtues of religious enthusiasm, of unquestioning piety and limitless zeal in the practice of charity. They revived and adopted ancient Pharisaic *Haburah*, binding themselves by special covenants to be loyal to a saintly leader. In their fellowships, joy and piety were inseparable, as they sang and danced and drank "for the sake of heaven." Their motto was the Psalmist's injunction, "Serve the Lord in joy, but rejoice in trembling."[27]

The *Mithnagdim* ("opponents") stressed the intellectual component in the hero-image of Disciple of the Wise. To them, the noblest virtue was diligence in learning. The ethical movement that arose in their midst (*Mussar*) sought to achieve ever higher levels of perfection through the regular practice of self-criticism and self-examination.[28]

When the boundaries of Orthodoxy were breached by the impact of modern thought, the impetus of the ethical ideal was directed largely toward classicism. This tendency was enhanced by the circumstance that the friends of Jewish emancipation were generally liberals. Nevertheless, various Romantic currents exerted a powerful pull in the past century.

Under the joint influence of Zionism and utopian socialism, there emerged the hero-image of the *Halutz*. Both Martin Buber, with his famous theory of interpersonal relations, and A. D. Gordon, with his romantic glorification of agricultural labor, contributed to the emergence of this ideal. The *Halutz* achieves "self-realization" by the surrender of any personal ambition for gain or fame; he fulfills himself in the service of the nation and as a servant of the life-giving soil; yet, he does not "retreat" from the world; he marries, and his children are given a good education in the kibbutz; he overcomes the "self-alienation" of bourgeois society by becoming part of a collective, which is the nucleus of the ultimate, worldwide socialist society. He shares in the cultural as well as the political aspirations of the nation. He is a peasant-scholar-soldier and a man of culture. He is a Disciple of the Wise in a new guise.[29]

THE CONCEPT
OF ISRAEL*

Israel is at once the name of a people, a state, a religious community, and an ethereal ideal. A certain ambiguity characterized the term "Israel" from the very beginning. Jacob's name was changed to Israel in order to indicate his elevation to a high cosmic status. He was on a par with angels, "for thou hast struggled with God and men, and hast prevailed."[1] Philo interprets Israel to mean "he who sees God," that is, the man of Divine visions.[2] Certain it is that from the moment of its historic genesis, the people of Israel considered itself to be "covenanted" unto the Lord. A covenant is more than a love affair, no matter how impassioned, since it cannot conceivably be terminated at the whim of either partner. It is rather like a marriage, as marriage was originally intended to be: exclusive, enduring, indeed eternal.[3] Accordingly, the people of Israel are also called "sons of the living God," or the "firstborn son," or the treasure-people.[4]

It is not possible, in any case, to speak of the historic community of Israel without taking note of its special relation to the God who was different from all other gods, a Being unique and alone (*Ehad*). A people that is lifted out of the mass of struggling humanity by the One God, set apart from all other nations and given a unique cosmic status, cannot but deem itself radically different. When the elders suggest to the prophet Ezekiel that it might be wise for "the house of Israel to become like all the nations," he storms at them, "It shall not be."[5] The very thought is absurd. The children of Israel are not at liberty

---

*Address at symposium of theologians at the St. Vincent Archabbey, Latrobe, Pa., 1965. Torah & Gospel, Sheed and Ward, Inc., New York, 1966.

to mold their own destiny. They are committed. They "belong" to God, who will rule over them as their "King," with "wrath outpoured," whether they will it or not.

This feeling of *radical difference* from the Gentiles became a powerful historical force. It affected the policy of the last kings of Israel. So Hezekiah resisted Sennacherib, pinning his faith on the One God, for whose sake he inaugurated a reformation. Josiah carried forward that spiritual revolution and centralized all sacrificial worship in the Holy Temple of Jerusalem. Though he died on the battlefield, his reform was not undone.[6] In time, the feeling of being radically different penetrated into the depths of the national psyche. Jeremiah phrases in Aramaic the message that the exiles were to bring to Babylonia: "So shall ye say unto them, 'The gods that did not make heaven and earth will pass away from the face of the earth.'"[7]

In this formula, Jeremiah articulated the uniqueness of the One God of Israel. He is not merely one, but He stands above and beyond the whole of creation as its master. He transcends the battles between the diverse gods and the empires that worship them. But this God, who is alone, is not simply the God of the universe that all can find and worship in their own way. He, too, is committed, covenanted, bound by His spoken word. He is wedded to Israel, as it were; He had sworn an oath to the patriarchs; He had spoken to all the Israelites at Sinai; He had revealed to them His Torah. Thus was the import of Israel's message given a more personal tone and a cutting edge: "It is *our* God, the God of Israel, who is the One God of the universe."

It is this double message that demonstrates the two-sidedness of the concept of Israel. The self-image of the historical community reached up to the universal realm of metaphysical entities. It "corresponded" to a heavenly reality.[8] But this self-image also contained a written history of a living people, its poignant memories, its agonizing anxieties, its bread-and-butter needs, its flesh-and-blood desires and hopes.

The two-sided character of the Jewish self-image and its resultant sense of radical difference from all other nations

451

evoked a corresponding reaction among the non-Jewish population. How could they help but react with an extra measure of hostility to a people that considered itself especially set apart from all others, separated by a distinction that ranks far and beyond the usual differences that separate all human groups? If they acknowledged the unique status of Israel and its message in an affirmative way, they became either converts, semi-converts, or sympathetic hangers-on.[9] If they reacted against either the cogency of the message or the claim of Israel's election, they came to regard the Jews as "the most odious race of mankind." Here was a people that insulted and assaulted their gods and arrogated to itself an exalted cosmic rank. In many cases, admiration and scorn were combined in a puzzling complex of hate. Thus, classical anti-Semitism emerged as one of the responses of the pagan world to the twin challenges of Israel and its monotheism. In their turn, the Jewish people felt the loneliness of their situation to be a direct consequence of their covenanted status.[10] If God had chosen to make them different, their destiny in history must also be different. When the nations are uplifted, they are degraded; when the others are defeated in the End of Days, then Israel's turn will come.

In periods of bitter rivalry and persecution, the notion of being chosen as *against* the rest of humanity tends to take the place of the feeling of being chosen *for the sake of humanity*. The eschatological vision becomes zealot, narrow, and exclusive, a vindication of Israel rather than the triumph of its teaching.[11] Thus, the actual situation of Jewish people at any one time helped to shape the outlines of their collective self-image. Their earthly misery and their cosmic power, their martyrdom in the present and their Messianic glory in the future lent vitality and vividness to one or another aspect of the traditional concept of Israel.

One trinity of ideas remained unbroken throughout the long history of the Jewish people down to the emergence of our secular age: the presumed unity of the conceptions of Israel,

Torah, and God. Israel was covenanted to the Lord, and Torah was the bond that united them—the contract which stipulated the terms and conditions of a union that could be cruelly stretched, but never entirely severed. It is in the Zohar that this unity is formulated in the most incisive way: "Israel, the Torah and the Holy One, blessed be He, are one."[12]

The Qabbalistic author assumed that each of the three entities in this triad was a cosmic current that extended all the way from this lowly earth to the highest heaven. The glory of God fills the world, but in His essence the Lord is infinite, transcending all humanly conceivable categories. The designation "the Holy One, blessed be He" corresponds to the aspect of the Divine Being that is directly concerned with the administration of earthly affairs.[13] In a similar way, the Torah is in this earthly life a body of laws, principles, and narratives; but up in the heavens it is an ethereal essence, "written in black fire or white fire," and consisting of an articulation of the Names of the Lord.[14] So, too, the people of Israel "correspond" to a heavenly essence that merges at its source into the effulgence of the Divine Being.[15]

This mystical concept of Israel illustrates the extent to which the collective self-image of the Jews was an integral part of the prevailing theology. Its contours varied in accord with one's philosophic approach. Accordingly, we may best describe the concept by filling in the details in the several self-images as they appear at the rationalistic pole of thought and at the mystical pole. It will then be possible to indicate the degree to which one or another concept predominated in the minds of the legalistic authorities, who steered generally a middle course between the two extremes.

Already in the Talmud and Midrashim the mystical character of Israel is suggested. "The image of Jacob is carved into the throne of Glory,"[16] we are assured, and, when the patriarch enjoyed his famous dream, the angels went up and down on the heavenly ladder, comparing the upper image with the lower one.[17] The Throne of Glory symbolizes the aspects of Divine power that relate to the administration of mundane affairs. We are told that this Throne of Glory "hovered over the deep" before the creation of the cosmos.[18] The souls of the righteous are kept there after death until the Messianic redemption, the resurrection, and the World to Come.[19] Another passage tells us that "the Patriarchs—they are the Divine Chariot"[20]—that is, they are part of the mediating channel of Divine grace. Abraham, in particular, had a continuing function in heaven. His prayers and that of the other patriarchs keep the scales of mercy weighted against those of justice.[21] Also, he stands at the gates of hell in order to prevent those who are circumcised from being thrown into its yawning abyss.[22]

The close mystical association between Israel and the Divine Being is adumbrated in the concept of the *Shechinah,* the Divine Presence. In one sense, the *Shechinah* is found where love, compassion, and devotion abide.[23] In yet another sense, "ten persons who steadily engage in the study of Torah, the *Shechinah* rests with them . . . even five . . . even three . . . even one. . . ."[24] In a more potent, more openly manifest way, the *Shechinah* was found in certain synagogues in Babylonia.[25] But in a special and more immediate sense, it dwelt in the Holy Temple, and it departed thence prior to the destruction of its abode, although, according to some authorities, "the *Shechinah* did not move away from the western wall."[26]

The Holy Temple "corresponded" to the sanctuary in one of the heavens, and the Archangel Michael offered "lambs of fire" on the heavenly altar, matching the sacrifices of the high priest. Now that the Holy Temple is in ruins, Michael continues to sacrifice on his altar the souls of the saints.[27]

The sanctuary in the wilderness and later the two Temples were visible habitations of the Divine Presence, but even when these were destroyed, the *Shechinah* did not depart from Israel. "Wherever the Israelites were exiled, there the *Shechinah* too went into exile."[28]

Indeed, Moses was assured that the *Shechinah* will be asso-

454

ciated with Israel, and Israel only. "Said Rabbi Johanan in the name of Rabbi Yose': Three things did Moses ask of the Holy One, blessed be He, and He granted them to him—that the *Shechinah* shall abide in Israel . . . that it shall not abide on the 'worshipers of stars,' and that he might know the ways of Providence. . . ."[29]

Explaining the superiority of the pure-blooded Israelite in regard to the capacity to intuit the Divine Presence, the philosopher Halevi writes: "The *Shechinah* which is visible to our eyes is presently lacking, for it is revealed only to the prophet or to the people generally only in the selected place, and this is the meaning of our prayer for the return of the Lord to Zion, 'and may our eyes behold when Thou returnest unto Zion.'

"But the hidden, spiritual *Shechinah* dwells with every born Israelite, who is also a believer in the true faith, whose deeds are pure, whose heart is true, whose soul is attuned to the God of Israel."[30]

This association was so commonly accepted that to be converted was described as "entering under the wings of the *Shechinah*."[31] In the course of the discussion concerning the non-Jewish identity of Job, some rabbis in the Talmud argue that he could not have lived after the death of Moses: "After Moses died, did the *Shechinah* abide on worshipers of stars [that is, non-Jews]?"[32]

The bond between Israel and the *Shechinah* was so close that every worshiper was "to feel as if the *Shechinah* were opposite him."[33] So deep was this awareness that some rabbis considered it sinful to walk erect, or with head uncovered: "It pushes the legs of the *Shechinah*."[34] This mystical consciousness of the Divine Presence heightened the tone of Jewish piety: "He who commits a sin in secret, it is as if he pushed the legs of the *Shechinah*."[35] The Divine Presence was a comforting reality to the downhearted: "The *Shechinah* rests on the heads of the sick";[36] "When a person is troubled, how does the *Shechinah* speak—'my head hurts, my arm hurts.' If the Holy One, blessed be He, is so pained by the blood of the

455

wicked, how much the more so by the spilled blood of the righteous?"[37]

In their prayers, Jews were admonished to think of the "exile of the *Shechinah*" or of the "anguish of the *Shechinah*," rather than of their own troubles.

After detailing the mystical effects of evil deeds in closing the channels of mercy, an Orthodox pietist of the nineteenth-century describes the function of prayer: "Though the law of the Talmud permits a person to bring to mind his own troubles when he prays, the core of his intention must not be the petition to assuage his own sorrows, since it is through suffering that his sins are purged . . . But the essence of his intention must be the need on high, for there might be an involvement of his Name, if the honor of Israel is involved . . . But even if there be no desecration of the Name, the Divine Presence feels his pain, and if the worshiper forgets his own pain in his intense concentration on the anguish of the Lord, then indeed his sins are forgiven. . . ."[38]

The ideal "congregation of Israel" (*Keneset Yisroel*) is often treated in Talmud and the Midrashim as an interlocutor with the Deity. It presents the case of the empirical people to the Lord and the demands of the Lord to the people. Anyone who partakes of the pleasures of life, without a prior offer of thanks (*berocho*), "it is as if he robbed the Holy One and *Keneset Yisroel*."[39] The benedictions were formulated and instituted by the rabbis, acting in the Name of God. So *Keneset Yisroel* is the heavenly counterpart of the sacred tradition.

"Said *Keneset Yisroel* to the Holy One, blessed be He—acknowledge this as my favor to Thee, that I made Thee known to the mighty in the world [that is, in the discussion, to the Jewish people]."[40]

Here, too, the ideal congregation is regarded as distinguished from the actual, living people of Israel. Referring to the symbolism of the Song of Songs, which portrays the Lord and Israel as a lover and his bride, a Talmudic sage says, "I am a wall, that is *Keneset Yisroel*, 'and my breasts are like towers,' these are the synagogues and houses of study."[41]

Naturally, even in the first centuries of our era some Jewish people frequented the circuses and theaters of their cities more than the synagogues. Yet, the ideal congregation is imagined to speak as follows: " 'I did not sit among players.'[42] Said *Keneset Yisroel*, 'Master of the Universe,' I have never gone to theaters and circuses of the nations of the world, and played with them."[43]

To the mystics, the revealed Torah was only an earthly shadow of the heavenly entity.[44] Since the written and oral laws refer almost exclusively to the people of Israel, an intimate association had to be assumed between the Divine Being and the ideal congregation of Israel. I have already referred to the unity of the triad—God, Torah, and Israel.[45] At times, Torah is left out, and a dual unity is asserted: "The Holy One, blessed be He, and *Keneset Yisroel* are called one."[46] The image of a lighted candle is often used: "Israel is the wick, Torah is the oil, the Divine Presence is the flame."[47]

The pre-existence of the heavenly Torah was a widespread assumption in the literature of the Midrash. From this belief it followed almost inevitably that the congregation of Israel, its acceptance of the earthly Torah, its destiny and its eventual redemption through the Messiah, were also previsioned. "If the Holy One, blessed be He, had not foreseen that after twenty-six generations the people of Israel will accept the Torah, he would not have written in it—'Command the children of Israel.' "[48]

The Torah was the goal of creation, since it represented the *will* of God, while all creation was merely the *work* of God. Hence, the Midrash asserts that the Torah furnished the design for all creation, and the "Holy One, blessed be He, looked in the Torah as He created the world."[49]

It follows that Israel, the people of Torah, occupies a central role in the administration of this world, not merely in the World to Come. On its account, the sun shines, the rains come down to bless the soil, and the golden harvest ripens at summer's end. By the same token, however, the failure of the empirical people to abide by the precepts of the Law causes the order of nature to be disturbed, with dire consequences for all mankind. If the nations had only known of this relationship, "they would have appointed two policemen for every Jew," to make certain that he observed the entire Law.[50] All earthly gains are due to the merits of Israel; "even boats that travel from Gaul to Spain are blessed only for the sake of Israel."[51] On the other hand, the catastrophes of nature and history are also due to Israel."[52] While the constellations of the stars and the ministering angels usually and largely control the affairs of "the nations of the world," the people of Israel are lifted above this natural order and governed directly by God. "There is no *mazal* ["determination of stars"] for Israel."[53] They are "beloved more than the ministering angels."[54]

Even while they glorified the congregation of Israel as an ethereal "City of God," the mystics allowed that not all living Jews were equally exalted. The Talmud asserts that "all Israelites have a share in the World to Come" and "will not see the face of hell."[55] Yet, the Zohar, which concentrates and magnifies the mystical streams in the ancient tradition, declares, "Not all Israelites are alike, for some of them are princes, deriving from the Holy Kingdom [*Shechinah*], and some of them are slaves, deriving from the side of the slave [Satan]."[56] Also, "Israel is called man and beasts; if they merit, they are man, fashioned after the one above; if they do not merit, they are called beasts."[57]

The notion that the people of Israel contain a vital core of saints who are closely associated with the Divine administration of the world is rooted in Talmudic literature, though it was left for the Hasidic movement of the eighteenth century to provide concrete institutionalization of this belief.

We read in the Talmud that "the Holy One, blessed be He, decrees, but the Saint repudiates it"; also that "the Saint decrees and the Holy One, blessed be He, abides by this decision." These saints suffer for the sins of their people, and their anguish is accepted as a sacrifice of atonement for their contemporaries. Since the order of the world depends upon these saints, "no

Saint perishes until a Saint of equal stature is created."[58] While the world may exist even for the sake of one saint, it was widely believed that "there are never fewer than thirty-six saints who confront the *Shechinah* every day."[59]

The Qabbalists deepened the gulf between the pneumatic saints and the ordinary scholars.[60] The power of the saints is felt even after their death, when their souls enter into hell in order to redeem the wicked who were attached to them in some way.[61]

The Hasidic movement created many saint-centered societies on the supposition that each saint was an embodiment of the redeemed world. In him, the evil desire and the impulses of material nature had been transmuted into forces of holiness. Even the occasional sin of the saint is due to a holy impulse. "The Holy One, blessed be He, in his Mercy impels the Saint to sin, so that he might fall from his high level and descend to that of the public; then, later, when the Saint raises himself to his holy height, he uplifts the people along with himself."[62]

The emphasis on the ideal of sainthood did not lead, in the Hasidic movement, to the weakening of the ethnic element in Jewish piety. The saint was never thought of in isolation, but as the living center of "all Israel." His prayer is focused on the "exile of the *Shechinah*," and in behalf of all Israel.

In the mystical stream of thought, the Jewish people were a unique metaphysical creation; hence, they were biologically different from the rest of mankind. We read in the Talmud: "Why are the worshipers of stars unclean? Because they did not stand at Mount Sinai. Because when the serpent cohabited with Eve, he threw uncleanliness into her. The Israelites had their uncleanliness removed at Sinai. The worshipers of stars, not having been at Sinai, their uncleanliness was not removed."[63]

We have here a version of original sin, which is purely racistic, assuming that Jews are free by birth from the corruption which is the lot of humanity. Yet, this racist emphasis was contradicted by the law which admits Gentile converts into the holy community. The Talmud assumes that, in the case of converts, "though they were not present at Sinai, their *mazal* was there."[64] This means that they were included in the Holy Community, but in a category of their own ("under the wings of the *Shechinah*," as against "over the wings of the *Shechinah*").[65]

The Romantic philosopher Halevi assumes that even in the Messianic era, the descendants of converts will be distinguished from those of pure Israelitic lineage in this, that only the latter will be endowed with the gift of prophecy: "Whoever clings to this way, will participate along with his descendants in our nearness to God. But the convert will not have equal standing with the Israelite by birth, since only the Israelites by descent are suited for prophecy. . . ."[66]

In the Talmud, the gift of prophecy is further restricted, even in the future, only to those whose line of descent is completely unblemished: "The Lord causes His *Shechinah* to rest only on the pedigreed families in Israel."[67]

The racist dogma permeates the mystical stream in Judaism down to the present day. Halevi stands close to the center between the mystical and rationalistic currents, for he admitted the worth of the other monotheistic faiths: "We deny to no man the reward for his good deeds, no matter which creed he belongs to. But we see the perfect good which comes to the people that are close to Him, in their lifetime. . . .

"But our destiny it is to cleave to the divine quality in prophecy and in states of mind that are close to it . . . ."[68]

The belief in the dogma of Jewish centrality and supremacy in the Divine scheme of creation became more deeply rooted in the popular mind in the late Middle Ages as a result of the decline of rationalism and the growing influence of Qabbalah. In fact, the medieval era continued for the Jewish masses of Central Europe down to the twentieth century. We find the most extravagant formulations of the holy character of Israel in the last few centuries. Israel should properly be the "portion of the Lord," because "the Perfect One should have the perfect."[69] A sixteenth-century pietist wonders why the physical appearance of Jews is so much like that of non-Jews, seeing that their souls are drawn from radically different heavenly realms. The founder of the Liubavich dynasty of Hasidim asserts that of the two souls of every Israelite, one is a Divine portion of the Lord Himself, and the other derives from the shell of *nogah* (radiance), which is both good and bad, while the souls of the other nations are formed "out of the unclean shells, which have no good at all."[70]

A nineteenth-century Hasidic author wrote: "Every nation has a certain holy spark, even as it possesses vicious qualities, since 'Thou givest life to them all,' and this is the purpose of the Jewish exile, to absorb these sparks. . . .

"As the root of *Keneset Yisroel* is the love of the Israelites for God, so the root of all the nations is their love for the pleasures of this world. . . ."[71]

So deeply rooted is this dogma in the tradition that even some of the modernist reformers of the nineteenth century could not resist its impact. Thus, Geiger, the architect of Reform Judaism, spoke of a Jewish "genius" for religion.

The mystical temper predominated in Jewish life only in the darkest periods of political oppression and cultural stagnation. Whenever the warm winds of enlightenment mellowed the hostility of the Jews' neighbors, the Jewish spirit regained an equilibrium between the insular mentality of self-glorifying myths and the open horizons of theistic humanism. In such open cultures as those of the Hellenistic era, of the Moslem Renaissance, of Christian Humanism, and of the Age of Enlightenment, the rationalistic threads in the web of tradition came to light.

Contrary to a widespread impression, the Talmud contains significant components of a moral-rational approach to the understanding of the Jewish character and destiny. A broad definition of what it means to be a Jew is offered on a purely intellectual plane: "Everyone who denies idolatry is called a Jew."[72]

"Said Rabbi Elazar, The Holy One, blessed be He, exiled Israel among the nations for the sole purpose of adding converts

461

to their number. So, it is said 'and I shall sow it in the ground.'[73] Doesn't a person sow one measure only in order to harvest many more?"[74]

According to this view, the dispersal of Israel was not due to an outburst of Divine wrath, but, on the contrary, to His concern for the redemption of mankind. The "chosenness" of Israel was, therefore, to be interpreted not as an exclusive privilege, setting Israel apart from the nations, but as a task, to bring hosts of men and women to the service of the Lord. Israel is the "firstborn," but not the only child. In the Torah, the "firstborn" cannot lay claim to the whole inheritance, but only to a portion double that of his brothers. Israel's vocation is to be an *example*, not an *exception*, to the other nations. It is not set apart, but set ahead, and ordered to work for and with other peoples.

Elaborating on Israel's task to "witness" unto the nations, the Midrash applies the law in regard to those who withhold testimony from judges: " 'If he does not tell, he shall bear his sin'— if you will not explain my Divinity to the nations of the world, I shall punish you. . . ."[75] This missionary task was imposed upon Israel from the very beginning: "The Holy One, blessed be He, gave the Torah to Israel in order that they might bestow its merit upon all the nations."[76]

Naturally, the people of Israel are not alone in this task. The wise and the pious, wherever they may be, are allies of Israel. They are "priests," so to speak, individually, as the people of Israel were designed to be a "people of priests": "The Holy One, blessed be He, will grant to the pious among the nations a share in the life of the World to Come . . . because they are priests to the Holy One, blessed be He. . . ."[77]

The duty to "bring people under the wings of the *Shechinah*" is treated as a supreme *mizvah*. Said the leading sage of third-century Palestine, Rabbi Johanan: "Why was Abraham our father punished and his children were enslaved in Egypt for two hundred and ten years? Because he separated people from entering under the wings of the *Shechinah*. As it is said, the king of Sodom said to Abraham: 'Give me the souls, while you take the

462

property' (and Abraham returned the captives, without converting them)."[78]

For this reason, it was mandatory for masters to convert their slaves; they, in turn, were then obliged to observe the practices that were obligatory on Israelite women. Upon liberation, these slaves would become full-fledged Israelites, qualifying to be counted in the prayer-quorum of the synagogue.

The interpretation of a Biblical verse offered the great Rabbi Johanan ben Zakkai an opportunity to illustrate and to condemn the chauvinism of his disciples.[79] In Proverbs 14:34 (usually rendered, "Righteousness exalteth a nation, but sin is a reproach to any people"), the Hebrew original puts the last two words in the plural—"the nations"—and it seems to draw the line between the one people—Israel—and all other nations. The zealous disciples vied with one another in finding an interpretation that would exalt Israel and scorn the Gentiles, namely, "even the charitable deeds of the nations are imputed to them as a sin, because of the impurity of their motives or their arrogance."[80] Then the aged master points out the true meaning of the verse: "As the sin-offering would bring forgiveness to Israel, so does charity bring forgiveness to the nations of the world."[81] This interpretation is the one favored by Abraham Ibn Ezra in his commentary.[82]

We may assume that this discussion took place after the burning of the Temple, when the Israelites, too, could count only on deeds of charity, along with prayer and repentance, for the expiation of their sins. Jew and Greek became one in their need for forgiveness. When the same rabbi was apprised of the burning of the Temple, he said, "We have a nobler means of atonement—righteousness and charity."[83]

The tension between the moral-rational and the romantic-mystical interpretations of the difference between Israel and the nations can be recognized in the many debates in the Talmud in regard to such issues as to whether Torah should be taught to slaves or not;[84] whether those who accepted Judaism and were baptized, but did not undergo circumcision, were to be

463

considered full-fledged members of the community;[85] whether the laws of the Torah, barring intermarriage with the neighboring nations, were to apply to their descendants at all times, or possibly even be extended to all Gentiles, as Ezra and Nehemiah inferred, or whether those laws were no longer valid because "Sennacherib came and mixed up the nations."[86]

There was also the theological question of "exclusive salvation," that is, whether the Gentile who accepts the "Seven Principles of Noah," and is classified as *a ger toshav,* must do so in the presence of three learned Israelites and on the basis of a dogmatic acceptance of the Torah of Moses.[87] Finally, we encounter the well-known dispute as to whether or not "the pious of the nations have a share in the World to Come."[88]

The lines of demarcation are frequently blurred, particularly since dialecticians always endeavor to impose systematic consistency upon ancient controversies. The same Midrashic work might contain views that are in diametric opposition to one another. In an honored Midrash we encounter a dramatic affirmation of the equality of all men in the sight of God: "I call heaven and earth to witness that a Gentile or an Israelite, a man or a woman, a slave or a servant-girl—the Holy Spirit rests upon him only according to his deeds. . . .[89]

"Is it conceivable that the Lord will discriminate between a Gentile and a Jew, between a man and a woman, between a slave and a servant-girl? No, whatever *mizvah* one does necessarily brings its reward, for it is said, 'and Thy righteousness is like the mighty mountains.' "[90]

But we also find in the same Midrash the assumption that, in point of fact, only Israelites are "God's children," and they alone are due to share in the glories of the World to Come: "Though everything is His, and all are His creatures, He does not delight in all, but only in the seed of Abraham. . . .[91]

"Once, as I was going from place to place, I met an old man. Said he to me, 'Will the nations of the world exist in the days of the Messiah?' I said to him, 'All the nations of the world that tortured Israel and oppressed Israel will come and behold its joy, then return to dust and not ever be revived. But all the nations and peoples that did not oppress or torment the Israelites will become the peasants and vineyard-keepers for the Israelites. . . .' But this is only the days of the Messiah, not the World to Come. . . ."[92]

We need add only that the zealous author discriminated among Israelites as well. He praised the Lord for choosing the sages and their disciples "to the end of all the generations," assigning to the "sinners in Israel" the dubious distinction of being destined to be burned within the "Great Synagogue and the Great Academy of the Future."[93]

While the Aggadic material of the Talmud varies greatly, containing even crude insertions by vulgar hands, the Halachic material is more organized and consistent. In Talmudic law, Ezra's insistence on the "Holy Seed" is definitely repudiated. Converts are warmly welcomed after due warning of the hardships they may expect to encounter: "When a person comes to be converted, we say to him, 'Why do you wish to convert? Don't you know that Israel is at this time driven, distressed and troubled?' If he says, 'I know, and I am not worthy to join them,' he is immediately accepted. He is then told the roots of the faith—the unity of God and the prohibition of idolatry, elaborating on the meaning of these principles. Then, he should be told of the *mizvoth,* the light and the awesome ones. . . .

"And he should be told that by means of those *mizvoth* he will merit the life of the World to Come, and that there is no complete Saint, except for the wise who know and observe these *mizvoth.* He should be addressed as follows:

"Be it known to you that the World to Come is kept only for the saints, and they are Israel. The circumstance that in this world Israel is troubled is really a favor to them, for they cannot receive an excess of favors in this world, like the worshipers of stars, lest they become arrogant and err, losing the reward of the World to Come. But, the Lord does not punish them too severely, that they might not disappear. For all the nations will perish, but they will endure."[94]

In the eyes of the Law it was a *mizvah* to induce a person to accept the Jewish faith. "Whoever brings one person under the wings of the *Shechinah,* it is accounted to him as if he had fashioned and brought a person into the world."[95] To be sure, some of the converts reverted to their pagan ways, causing all Israel to be guilty of sin in accordance with the principle that "all Israelites are responsible for one another."[96] Some of the rabbis protested for this reason against "those who accept converts."[97] Still, the legal authorities considered that all the nations will be converted in the time to come.[98] Once converted, a person has the same privileges as those who were born Jewish, except that he may not be a judge or a king over Israel. [99] He is expected to think of Abraham, Isaac, and Jacob as his ancestors, for "Abraham has been called 'the father of a multitude of nations.' "[100]

Hellenistic Judaism, to judge from the writings of Philo, was conspicuously liberal in its interpretation of the concept of Israel as the vanguard of humanity. Although Philo speaks of the Jewish people as "sons of God," he maintains that all who have knowledge of the universal Father are "children of God."[101] The people of Israel represent symbolically "those who have a vision of God."[102] Prophecy (in the highest or dogmatic sense), resulting in laws, was reserved for the Israelites of the Biblical period, but the message of the Scriptures is universal. Indeed, Philo indentifies Plato's "philosophic frenzy" with one of the phases of prophecy. "For what the disciples of the most approved philosophy gain from its teaching, the Jews gain from their law and customs, that is, to know the highest and the most ancient cause of all things."[103] Out of Abraham "there issued a whole people, and it is of all nations the most beloved by God, for, as it seems to me, to them priesthood and prophecy were given for the benefit of the entire human race."[104]

Philo describes proselytes as being related to Jews "by kinships of greater dignity and sanctity than those of blood."[105] Praising the proselyte "who comes to God of his own accord," he adds, "in order that all men who behold this example may be corrected by it, learning that God receives gladly virtue which grows out of ignoble birth, utterly disregarding its original roots."[106]

The semiproselytes, or the "spiritual proselytes" (to use Wolfson's term), are included in the Mosaic polity of the "sons of God." They are the philosophers and the righteous men who share the monotheistic philosophy of life. Thus Philo speaks of "the blameless life of pious men who follow nature and her ordinances" and of "all who practice wisdom either in Grecian or Barbarian lands and live a blameless and irreproachable life" as belonging to the ideal community.

The Torah itself was, to Philo, not a mystical entity and a supreme source of values, but an educational instrument conveying the saving truths that God had built into human nature. The Sabbath is a covenant between God and mankind, not merely between God and Israel. It is a call for men to share in the Divine activity of contemplation. In his listing of ten festivals, Philo leaves out Hanukkah and Purim, possibly because he regarded them as national observances. He listed "every day" if it is lived as a holy day. In Philo's judgment, Passover was not so much a festival of national freedom as a perennial call on all men to "pass over" from a life of passion to the life of yearning for God. Similarly, Sukkot was not a symbol of Divine concern for the Israelites, but rather a symbol of the equality of all men and of the duty of cultivating the virtue of gratitude.

For Philo, therefore, the empirical community of Israel was still the most beloved community, but ideally its boundaries shaded into a twilight zone, embracing those who in various degrees dedicated themselves to the love of God. Philo, too, looked forward to a Messianic era when Israel would triumph, but then all other nations would merge with it: "I think that each nation would abandon its peculiar ways and, throwing overboard their ancestral customs, turn to honoring our laws alone, for when the brightness is accompanied by national prosperity, it will darken the light of others as the risen sun darkens the stars."[107]

The rationalistic and mystical streams in Judaism diverged more decisively in the Middle Ages than they did in the Talmudic and early Gaonic periods. For a century the Jewish world was torn by a long and bitter controversy between the followers of Maimonides and the antirationalists. Both schools included in their category of Israelites the "righteous proselytes," that is, those who were fully converted to Judaism. However, regarding those who worshiped the one God in purity of thought and in ethical action, the romanticists and the legalists hesitated to make use even of the category of *ger toshav* ("semi-proselytes") of the Talmud.[108] As was earlier noted, some maintained that the *ger toshav* is one who accepts only the "seven *mizvoth* of the sons of Noah" on the basis of Mosaic revelation and by way of a formal declaration in the presence of three learned men. Others added that this category applied only "at the time when the Jubilee institution was in effect."[109] In this school, even the "pious of the nations" were merely peripheral to the only bearers of salvation, the empirical people of Israel.

On the other hand, the rationalistic school in nonlegalistic works projected the concept of a spiritual elite, who, apart from any rites and ceremonies, advance ever closer to the Divine Being through the service of mind and heart. For them, the empirical people of Israel were significant only insofar as they were likely to produce a greater number of such philosophical saints.[110] The "Torah-society" was designed and ordered to stimulate the emergence of men and women who love God and ceaselessly meditate on the wonders of His creation. But it is not the *mizvoth* in themselves that generate holiness or "nearness of God," but their presumed effect upon the moral character of the individual and the peaceful order of society. This effect is by no means certain or even likely in the case of the majority of the people. Saintly philosophers may arise among all nations, and only a few Jews may qualify for the honor. The living people of Israel were, therefore, in Maimonides' view, by no means coeval with the spiritual elite, those who approach most closely to the Divine Being. It was a good school, indeed the best possible school, designed by the Lord Himself. But even in the best schools some students will be no wiser on their graduation than on their initiation. And students of poor schools have been known to excel. Salvation or fulfillment is an individual achievement.

Isaac Arame, whose work *Akedat Yizhak* was long a popular source book for preachers, manages to combine the view of individual judgment, on the one hand, and the collective salvation of Israel, on the other. He maintains that "one is truly designated as *Yisroel* [an Israelite] only if he is a saint [*Zaddik*]," for an Israelite and a saint are synonymous in respect of their tasks. " 'All Israelites' [that are assumed to have a share in the World to Come] means those who fulfill the obligations imposed upon an Israelite." The Torah, according to Arame, is so designed as to lead all its devotees to salvation. Writing in the last decade of the fifteenth century, Arame saw hope only for "the remnant" of the nations that will accept the Torah: "For He scattered and subordinated Israel among them, in order that they [that is, the nations] should be encouraged to learn to know the Israelites, their customs and the ways of their Torah, so that they will desire and accept it [the Torah]. In this way, Israel will cause a remnant of the nations to be saved, that they might call on the Name of God. But they see and do not take it to heart . . . interpreting the verses of Scriptures as they desire. . . ."[111]

Maimonides maintained that only "true ideas" lead to God, but those ideas are accessible to the human mind and are readily deducible from first principles. They comprise the doctrines of God's unity and incorporeality, the first two of the Ten Commandments. All the other *mizvoth* are principles of training for the individual and of a properly ordered society. He summarizes his view of the various categories of religious people in a famous passage: "I will begin the subject of this chapter with a simile. A king is in his palace, and all his subjects are partly in the country and partly abroad. Of the former, some have their backs turned toward the king's palace, and their faces in another direction; and some are desirous and zealous to go to the palace, seeking 'to inquire in his temple,' and to minister before him, but have not yet seen even the face of the wall of the house.

"Of those that desire to go to the palace, some reach it, and go roundabout in search of the entrance gate; others have passed through the gate, and walk about in the antechamber; and others have succeeded in entering into the inner part of the palace and being in the same room with the king in the royal palace. But even the latter do not immediately on entering the palace see the king or speak to him; for after having entered the inner part of the palace, another effort is required before they can stand before the king—at a distance or close by—hear his words, or speak to him.

"I will now explain the simile which I have made. The people who are abroad are all those that have no religion, neither one based on speculation nor one received by tradition. . . .

"Those who are in the country, but have their backs turned toward the king's palace, are those who possess religion, belief and thought, but happen to hold false doctrines . . . Because of these doctrines they recede more and more from the royal palace, the more they seem to proceed. . . .

"Those who desire to arrive at the palace, and to enter it, but have never yet seen it, are the mass of religious people, the multitude that observe the Divine commandments, but are ignorant.

"Those who arrive at the palace, but go roundabout it, are those who devote themselves exclusively to the study of the practical law; they believe traditionally in true principles of faith, and learn the practical worship of God, but are not trained in philosophical treatment of the principles of the Law, and do not endeavor to establish the truth of their faith by proof.

"Those who undertake to investigate the principles of religion have come into the antechamber; and there is no doubt that these, too, can be divided into different grades.

"But those who have succeeded in finding a proof for everything that can be proved, who have a true knowledge of God,

470

insofar as a true knowledge can be obtained, and are near the truth, wherever an approach to truth is possible, they have reached the goal, and are in the palace in which the king lives.[112]

In Maimonides' gradation, the philosophers of the nations who seek God are far ahead of the masses of the empirical people of Israel, coming nearer to God than the zealous Talmudists who only go around and around the palace of the king. A commentator expressed the views of many shocked pietists when he wrote, "Many of the wise rabbis said that this chapter was not written by the master [Moses Maimonides]. And if he wrote it, it should be hidden or, better, burned. For how could he say that those who contemplate the laws of nature are on a higher level than those who busy themselves with the duties of religion?"[113] Maimonides did not list the belief in the Chosen People among his principles of faith. He welcomed genuine converts most warmly, writing in a famous letter to a convert: "You may say, 'our God and God of our fathers,' for Abraham is your father. Since you have entered under the wings of the Shechinah, there is no difference between us and you . . . Let not your pedigree be light in your eyes . . . If we trace our descent to Abraham, Isaac, and Jacob, you trace it to Him who spoke and the world came into being."[114]

However, in his popular and legal works, Maimonides employs the imagery and rhetoric of the people, in the belief that the maintenance of the Torah-society requires that certain popular opinions be stated by the philosophers as if they were true. (In his letter to the Jews of Yemen, he asserts that those who leave the fold are not descended from ancestors who stood at Sinai.) These "necessary truths," as he calls them,[115] help to bridge the gap between the philosophers and the populace, creating an enduring, vital community in which the few guard the many from gross errors, and the many help the few to attain human fulfillment.

Divine Providence, in the judgment of Maimonides, was not focused on the people of Israel except insofar as the Messianic

471

age was predetermined, but normally the degree of Divine guidance depended on the extent of attachment to the Divine Being by single individuals. However, to placate his opponents, Maimonides reintroduced the belief in the resurrection and in the World to Come as predestined events at the end of history.

The radical intellectualism of Maimonides was repudiated by many of his successors. Arame postulates a special miraculous form of Divine Providence that is distinctive for Israel as a people. In turn, there are several levels of Divine Providence in Israel, depending upon degrees of piety.[116] Some felt that "nearness to God" was more a matter of love or of faith or of Divine grace than of sustained reflection. But the axiom that the way to holiness is infinite and that it is reached by inward meditation and self-scrutiny was accepted by many popular preachers and pietists.

The axiom that the pathway to God runs through the intentions of the heart and the further realization that this pathway is infinite could, in theory at least, blur the distinction between the "people of Torah" and those without the Covenant. It is this emphasis on inwardness that, in the Hasidic movement, served to elevate the dignity of the unlearned masses. The application of the same principle to non-Jews was already foreshadowed by Rabbi Judah the Prince, editor of the Mishnah, who upon being told of a Gentile who offered his life for God wept and cried out, "Indeed, it is possible for a person to acquire his world in one hour." Albo added the principle that the Lord may well give different Torahs to various peoples. "Even when the Torah of Moses was valid for the Israelites, there was the Torah of the sons of Noah for all the other nations. There is no doubt that people would attain through it their fulfillment as human beings, since it was Divine, though it was not of the same degree of attainment as the Israelites could obtain through the Torah . . . So we see that it is possible to have two Divine Torahs at one time, but for different peoples."[117] Since the "chosenness" of Israel was effected by the Torah, which specifies the terms of the Covenant, it could no longer be regarded as an exceptional phenomenon. To be sure, in Albo's view, the merit of the Mosaic Torah consisted in the fact that "human perfection could be attained by means of even one of the *mizvoth*. . . ."[118]

All through the Middle Ages the intimate association between ethnic feeling and religious loyalty in the concept of Israel was not questioned. The rationalists might recognize the relative holiness of other faiths, but only for non-Jewish groups. They might interpret the purpose of Israel's existence in terms of the education and ultimate redemption of all mankind. "For indeed the earth belongs to me, and the pious of the nations are precious to me, without a doubt. 'But, ye shall be unto me a kingdom of priests.' In this respect, you will be my treasure—you will be a kingdom of priests to instruct and to guide the entire human race, that they might all call on the Name of God and serve Him together, shoulder to shoulder, as Israel will be so transformed in the future."[119]

Even the mystics thought of Israel as the vanguard of the redeemed portion of humanity in that it is the Jewish function to gather the "Holy sparks" that have become imprisoned by the "shells of uncleanliness" throughout the world. These holy sparks must be rescued before the appearance of the Redeemer. The Messianic redemption of Israel would justify the Divine intention in the creation of man; through Israel's triumph, the human race would come into its own and attain fulfillment.

For Christian theologians as for Jewish thinkers, the ethnic separateness of the Jewish people was axiomatic. The place of the Jew in the medieval world was determined by the fact that he was of the "stock of Abraham." Socially, too, the Jews were nearly a self-governing enclave. They were outside the feudal system, not as individuals, but as a corporate body. Taxes were nearly always levied upon the community as a whole, and it was up to the Jewish authorities to distribute them. In the Spanish communities, Jewish authorities had the right to impose severe corporal punishments. In the German and Slavic areas, similar, though unofficial, means of discipline were frequently available. Furthermore, the semi-autonomous Jewish communities had in common the same basic laws and religious literature. The local variations, considerable as they might be—especially those between the monogamous society of Ashkenazic Jewry and the polygamous society of Sephardic and Oriental Jewry— did not prevent the Rabbinic authorities from moving freely throughout the Diaspora and speaking in the name of a common sacred tradition.

Those in Moslem or Christian lands who left the Jewish faith might still be considered members of the Jewish community in the first generation on the ground that they were irrevocably committed by the oath that their souls took at Sinai. "Once Israel was chosen to be God's people, no Israelite can become a member of another nation. They belong to God's people, even against their will and even if they leave the fold of their religion. Therefore, said the prophet, 'When thou passest through the waters, I will be with thee.' This is an allusion to the angry waters of baptism through which pass all those who accept their religion [Christianity]".[120]

The travail of the Marrano families in both Christian and Moslem lands is well known, but in the course of time they disappeared from the Jewish community. Even the Frankist Jews who joined the Catholic Church *en masse* in 1759, with the intention of retaining their own collective identity, did not leave more than a nostalgic memory in the first half of the nineteenth century, when Adam Mickiewicz, the poet laureate of Poland, was their most illustrious descendant.

It was through the changes in their religious convictions as well as outside pressure that some Jews left the fold. Their rationalist views might lead them to feel that the various monotheistic religions are so many social expressions of one philosophy, so that a change from Judaism to Catholicism is not very different from the change of one language to another. In their view, those differences that were left were not worth the cost of lifelong martyrdom.

On the other hand, Jewish pietists might be led by the impetus of the mystical tradition to feel that the Christian faith was the logical development of Biblical Judaism. Abner of Burgos, Spain, who was converted in 1321, was a famous and ardent convert, and he addressed many books and pamphlets to his former co-religionists, calling upon them to emulate his example. His arguments were directed chiefly against the rationalists.

"Abner began with a critique of the rationalist interpretation of Judaism, cultivated by the Jewish intellectuals who were his friends—and for this he found ample support in Qabbalistic doctrine—and moved ultimately to a position of complete identification with the Christian ideology."[121] The majority, however, retained a balanced faith, rejecting the extremes of both rationalism and mysticism.

The modern period opened with the dawn of the Age of Reason. The intelligentsia began to glory in the balancing of religious tradition by rational and moral enlightenment. At the same time, the feudal age with its corporate bodies began to evolve into the modern State, which consists of individual citizens.

The new ideals and circumstances confronted the Jewish people with the task of reorienting their own self-image to suit the new categories of social thought. Spinoza met this challenge by calling for the complete dissolution of the Jewish community. Reducing the core of Jewish faith to a few principles that could be applied in diverse historical religions, Spinoza maintained that the vast body of Jewish law applied only to a self-governing community, living in its own land. He did not rule out the possibility of the emergence of a Jewish state in Palestine, but, insofar as the Diaspora was concerned, he declared that only the essential principles of faith in Judaism were valid. As to the people of Israel, they were no more "chosen" than any other nation that accepts its lot with gratitude and seeks to make the most of its heritage for the benefit of mankind. ". . . We have shown that the divine law, which renders man truly blessed, and teaches him the true life, is universal to all men . . . ingrained in the human mind."[122]

Although Spinoza lived as a lonely Titan on the border of the

Jewish community, his philosophy exerted enormous influence on the Jewish intellectuals who remained within the community. Yet his contention that the State had the right to regulate all the actions of its citizens, as distinct from thoughts and feelings, ran counter to the emerging liberal philosophy of government.

For a century Jewish statesmen in the West allied themselves with the dominant ideology of liberalism. Religion and State must be separated; the State should abolish the corporations and estates of feudalism and base itself on a free and equal citizenry; all institutions, including those of religion, should be subjected to the scrutiny of reason. The concept of Israel, argued Moses Mendelssohn, should not be taken as an example of the ideal unity of religion and civil government. For ancient Israel was a unique creation, intended for the meta-historical, especially chosen people of the Biblical period, and reserved also for the meta-historical period of the Messianic era in the future. In historical times, the laws of reason, common to all men, must govern human society. Religion, consisting of the free interaction of the Divine mind and the human heart, cannot be subject to the coercion of the State. Also, in historical times, the Jews were simply a religious community, with the hope for a return to Zion being merely a transworldly, pious dogma, affirming an action on the part of God, not on the part of the empirical community. "This state existed only once in the world. Call it the Mosaic society by its proper name. It has already disappeared from the earth. Only God knows in which people and at which time we shall again see a similar situation."[123]

Mendelssohn agreed with Spinoza that the Torah was a revealed law of action intended for a specific community, but he maintained that the Jews of his day were still individually obligated to abide by the Torah insofar as a personal observance of ritual laws was concerned. Mendelssohn also agreed that the ideas necessary for salvation were placed by God in the hearts and minds of all peoples, that they are in no sense, therefore, a monopoly of Israel. The loyalty of Jews to their Law is due to the impetus of the past. They were born into the Torah-community, but the salvation of mankind does not depend upon them. All men are judged by God as individuals, and as individuals the Jews should enter the State. The concept of Israel, for Moses Mendelssohn, was dual in nature: total separateness and a metaphysical dimension in the distant past and in the mythical future, but social integration, in all ways except religion, in this mundane realm.

Mendelssohn's concept of Israel was a logical development of the rationalist stream in Jewish thought; it implied a complete repudiation of the romantic-mystical currents that removed the empirical community of Israel as well as the ancient and eschatological ones from the common course of human events. His viewpoint was certainly shared by the upper circles of Jewry in Western Europe, but in the long belt of Jewish mass-settlements, extending from the Baltic to the Black Sea, the influence of Qabbalah was reinforced by the rise of Hasidism. The wall between East and West, established by the division of Poland and the policy of the Czarist Empire, was supplemented by a cultural-religious schism between the rationalist philosophy of Western Jewry and the mystical isolationalism of Eastern Jewry. Although this wall was constantly breached by the flow of immigrants from East to West and by the return of young men from the universities of the West, it nevertheless remained an obdurate social factor down to our own generation.

In the West, the exponents of Judaism were aware that the ancient Covenant of Israel with the Lord needed to be complemented by a second covenant between Israel and the nations. The new covenant would be far more than a business transaction, but, like the ancient one, it would involve a total reorientation of heart and mind. Unlike the various agreements of the Middle Ages, the new society called for the attainment of "fraternity" with the host-nations. No longer was the Jewish status to be that of an alien enclave, tolerated by the sovereign under certain conditions; the Jews were to become members of one unit—the Nation-State—which, on the surface, was a legal-rational entity and, below the surface, an idealized fellowship

477

which reached down to the dark bedrock sentiments of a blood-brotherhood. So it was that the Grand Sanhedrin of Paris was asked whether the Jews would regard Frenchmen as their brothers.

Because the rationalists had already subscribed to a concept of Israel that included the fellowship of the right-thinking, it was but a small step for them to identify the fellowship of the right-thinking with the society of the enlightened in the eighteenth century, with German *Kultur* in the nineteenth, with the French homeland of liberalism, and with the architects of a free society in England and America. Although they could not join a blood-brotherhood without physical assimilation, they could become part of the new cultural fellowship as well as its political expression, excepting only religion.[124] "The Freedom of the Jews," noted a French-Jewish author, "has put an end to our exile."[125]

This trend of thought within Western Judaism was reinforced by the rising tide of liberalism in Europe that aimed to separate the Church from the State, that is, the fellowship of culture and politics from the traditional institutions of religion. The liberal world was based upon the association of individuals, sharing cultural values as well as political loyalties. The Jewish individual could become part of this new fellowship, since his specifically Jewish loyalties were restricted to the transworldly realm, the mythical past, and the eschatological future.

But the liberals within Judaism, as well as similarly minded men and women in the Catholic and Protestant worlds, were pulled back by the residual, romantic-mystical forces in their respective traditions. The European nations of nineteenth-century Europe were Janus-faced, now turned toward the liberal vision of an open society, now facing back to the older plan of a closed society associated with one or another religious tradition, and going back through the mists of prehistoric time to the primitive, yet potent, feelings of blood-brotherhood. The religious romanticists, who called for a Catholic France, a Protestant Germany, a Greek Orthodox Russia, were allied psychologically with the ethnic romanticists, who idealized the Slavic or the Russian soul, the Teutonic character or the Gallic spirit.[126] Both kinds of collective romanticism were engaged in fighting the same, all-pervasive enemy, the rational spirit in philosophy, the egalitarian spirit in politics, the progressive *élan* in culture and in social legislation. Soon enough the emancipated Jew became the symbol of the hated age of liberalism to the romantic lovers of the good old days. To the protosocialists and economic romanticists the Jew symbolized the rising industrial era, with all its vulgarity and corruption, causing the coarse and uncultured *nouveau riche* to usurp the leadership of the wellborn and the well-bred.[127] To the ethnic romanticists, the ideal age antedated the historic era, when an alien Christianity and a citified culture were imposed upon the guileless noble savages, whose innate culture was too inward and too refined to be noticed by the earliest chroniclers with their monkish minds. To the religious romanticists, the emancipated Jew was also the symbol of the passing of an idealized age, the great Middle Ages, when religion dominated the private as well as the public life of the country, separating the faithful flock from the goats who would not so believe, and putting the latter in their proper places.

In each of these three phases of romanticism, a distorted image of the Jew was constructed around a grain of truth. Jews were predominantly an urban people, participating actively in the creation, first, of a commercial and, later, of an industrial society. They were long the one and only tolerated religious minority. Their ethnic roots went deeper into the past and farther into distant lands than did those of their neighbors. Moreover— and on this point the three kinds of romanticism concurred again, though, on the whole, they were mutually contradictory —the Jew was a child of mystery, doomed by a dark destiny to dwell apart from, and in opposition to, the rest of humanity.

Thus, the "meta-myth" of modern anti-Semitism was born— the mythological notion of the Jew as being metaphysically set apart from the rest of mankind. Between the Jew and the rest of the nations of Europe the gulf was cosmic, eternal, and unbridgeable. This myth, deriving from both Jewish and Christian dogmatism, was now set up in three dimensions: religious romanticism, ethnic culture, and the economic sphere.

In Europe of the post-Enlightenment age, religion was rooted in "feeling" rather than in supernatural revelation. Thus the dogmatic image of the Jew was transposed into the language of "feeling"; his "Semitic" nature could not possibly appreciate the noble sentiments of Christianity. In this view, the Jewish non-acceptance of the Christian faith was transposed from theology to biology. In the realm of politics the same myth implied that the Jew could enter only into superficial alliances with the host-nations, since, in moments of national crisis, the Jew would listen to the voice of his blood. He belongs to a unique species of mankind, a mystical category that is *sui generis,* an international nation.

In the dimension of economic life this myth projected two images that reflected the same animus, although they were mutually contradictory. In the literature of proletarian rebellion and antibourgeois propaganda, the Jews took on, collectively, the lineaments of Shylock, that caricature of the heartless capitalist.[128] In the reactionary literature of those who struggled against the exploding age of industry, the Jew was the economic radical, the new Messianic enthusiast, who had no roots in or love for the ancient virtues of aristocracy.

The one meta-myth combined the feelings of traditional religion, the "pooled pride" of ethnicism, the resentments of the military aristocracy, and the militant malice of the new proletarian radicals. It is easy to see that these diverse elements could be given a spurious façade of unity through the meta-myth of anti-Semitism, though this development did not appear until the rise of the Nazi movement.

Echoes of the meta-myth abounded in the Jewish world, since writers in the Western as well as the Eastern world were exposed to the same influences that produced the Romantic reaction to the liberal revolution. Samson Raphael Hirsch reasserted the claims of Orthodoxy along the romantic-mystical lines of Judah Halevi. His vision of a *Yisroel-Mensch* imposed the luminosity of humanism upon the image of a unique ethnic group segregated supernaturally from the Gentile world. Even Geiger, the rationalist, taught that the Jews were endowed with an ethnic genius for religion. Krochmal wove a new pattern of Jewish history around the ancient dogma that, while the Gentiles worshiped certain angels, the people of Israel were alone dedicated to the One God. Ahad Ha'am asserted that in the domain of ethics the Jewish national soul was at work. And it was unique, incomparable, unlike that of all other nations.[129]

Even the Jewish writers who left the fold shared in some of the manifestations of the myth that was torn from its Judeo-Christian context. Disraeli viewed the Jews as not merely another ethnic group but a Messianic race, bearing the seeds of universal salvation.[130] To Marx, the Jew was the capitalist par excellence, the class enemy that had to be overcome. Moses Hess, the one-time socialist, projected the vision of a Jewish utopia in Jerusalem reborn. Even to Léon Blum, the Jew was uniquely disposed to bring into realization the glorious utopia of socialism.[131]

Jewish secularism, however, did not appear as a worldwide movement until the year 1897 when the World Zionist Organization came into being in Basel and the nucleus of the Jewish socialist movement was formed in Vilna. From that time to the present, the variety of Jewish self-images did not change drastically. The revolutionary events of the past two generations —the transfer of the center of gravity of the Diaspora from the Old World to the New, the replacement of czarist oppression by communist repression, the annihilation of Central European Jewry, the rise of Israel, and the virtual liquidation of the Diaspora in Moslem lands—all these developments have been fitted into the following spectrum of shades and nuances, marking the contemporary concept of Israel.

Going from right to left, we have, first, the ultra-Orthodox group, which is small in numbers but intense, even feverish, in devotion. Theirs is an airtight world that rejects the underlying categories of the secular age and employs the ancient axioms of the romantic-mystical school of medieval Judaism. They regard the State of Israel not as a Messianic-eschatological event, but as simply another framework within which the people of Torah may live or not, as they choose.[132] While they agree that it is a *mizvah* to live in the Holy Land, they insist on viewing this *mizvah* within the perspective of the ancient commentaries as if there were no State and no ingathering. Indeed, in their view, the Jewishness of the secularists and the socialists who control the Government of Israel is so woefully attenuated as to border on the meaningless. The Torah—and the Torah alone—is the sole yardstick of belonging to the "people of God." The Messianic-eschatological State is one in which the Torah is the constitution, the Holy Temple is brought down from heaven or built up, the Sanhedrin is reconstituted with the help of the Holy Spirit, and the Messiah is revealed. All else belongs to the historical world, where the loyal remnant of the meta-historical people must make do, waiting for the coming of the Promised One.

The moderate Orthodox (*Mizrahi*, or Religious National Party, or the modern Orthodox in the Diaspora) assume that the concept of Israel is bipolar, national, and secular as well as religious and fundamentalist. They participate in the government of Israel, recognizing the Jewishness of all ethnic Jews who have not broken away from the fold officially and flagrantly. They regard the State of Israel as the "beginning of the growth of our redemption." They look upon the present situation as the twilight between the night of exile and the day of Messianic redemption, the borderland between history and meta-history. They have not given up the hope for the fullness of redemption, but they feel that its course must not be plotted in advance.[133] Hence, it is the duty of all Jews to work for the upbuilding of the land, the ingathering of the exiles, and the sovereignty of Torah within the limits of a modern State. They waver between the teaching that it is a meritorious deed for a Jew to settle in Israel and the doctrine that it is the bounden duty of a Jew to live in the land of Israel. This indecision is due only in part to practical considerations; essentially, it is a reflection of the feelings of tension between the compulsions of our temporal existence and the claims of the meta-historical realm that is even now taking shape. Were not the excesses of twentieth-century anti-Semitism, culminating in the Nazi "final solution," precisely the "pains of the Messiah" that the ancient tradition foretold? Was not the flight of the Arabs from Israel in 1948 a miracle that made possible the ingathering of the exiles? Do we not live in a world where the light of redemption and the night of exile are commingled? If so, how is one to tell whether any issue is to be seen in the sober perspective of everyday existence or in the wondrous mirror of the days of the Messiah? For the present, there is no answer to this question.

The ideology of the national-religious movement in Israel was expressed most profoundly by the great Orthodox mystic Rabbi Abraham Isaac Kuk. While he esteemed all forms of nationalism to be fragmentary and partial expressions of the holy dimension, he considered Jewish nationalism to be clearly and fully Divine, the "foundation and essence of Judaism."[134] "Torah and Zion are two sanctities that supplement and imply each other."[135]

The Divine quality of the "congregation of Israel" is not due to any achievements of the empirical people, but to the free act of God.[136] But the living people can bring its Divine endowment to fruition only when it is healthy, physically as well as spiritually. "The wisdom of holiness shines only in the land of Israel. Whatever is envisaged in the Diaspora is nothing but the corollaries of the understanding and its branches. . . . In the land of Israel, the spiritual fountain of the inwardness of holiness, which is the light of the life of the soul of the congregation of Israel, flows spontaneously."[137]

In the mind of Kuk, the yearning to live in the land of Israel is itself proof of the activity of the Holy Spirit that functions primarily only in the Holy Land. "The Holy Spirit received in Palestine continues to function, even if the recipient should by chance go to the Diaspora, either through an error or for some compelling reason. . . . The more difficult it is to bear the atmosphere of the Diaspora, the more one feels the spirit of uncleanliness of the unclean soil, the more true it is that the soul has inwardly assimilated the holiness of the land of Israel and that the grace of the Lord did not desert it. . . ."[138]

Yet, Kuk believed that the redemption of Israel would bring salvation to all mankind, since there was an inner correspondence between the spirit of Israel and that of humanity. "Original Jewish creativity, in thought and in the practical achievements of life, is not possible for Israel, save in the land of Israel . . . and this is a great boon for Israel and the world. . . . Judaism of the Holy Land is salvation itself."[139]

This last statement is a neo-Qabbalist doctrine, equating the "secrets of Torah" with the course of redemption.

In Israel there is no organized religious ideology apart from the Orthodox and the ultra-Orthodox. The secularists fall into two categories—the romanticists who continue to use the traditional categories of thought, albeit with new meaning (for example, substituting "the Rock of Israel" for "the God of Israel"), and the humanists or leftist socialists who seek to build a state that will in no way differ from other progressive countries. The romanticists intend to retain the bond between the Synagogue and the government of Israel because they consider the Jewish religion to be the matrix of Jewish culture and inseparable from the life of Jews. For them, too, a Jew who converts to another faith cannot be designated as a Jew. They do not necessarily believe in a God who chooses, but they do affirm with impassioned zeal that the Jews are the Chosen People, somehow separated from all the nations, set apart and charged with a Messianic vocation. They sound the tocsin for the ingathering of the exiles, specifically for the immigration of American Jews, partly because they feel so insecure and partly because they can see no future life for Jews in the Diaspora. Thinking in nationalistic terms, they consider the Hebrew language to be the key to the tradition, and the mark of assimilation to be the nonuse of Hebrew.

Yet nationalism does not exhaust their concept of Israel, since their national awareness is forged in the crucible of the meta-myth. By itself, the national ethos does not inspire a process of global concentration; the Irish do not leave the "fleshpots" of America; the Italians are not deserting the sidewalks of New York; and even the French Canadians with all their bitterness against the English and the Protestants show no signs of emigrating *en masse* to *la patrie*. It is nationalism plus the protean cloud of myth and mystery that extends to the heavens, appearing as a "pillar of flame" by day and a "pillar of smoke" by night. The Jew feels, in the light of his history, that his is a special glory; but he also feels that he is dogged by a massive satanic hate which can never be overcome. Even after Israel has been established, the Jew is still not among the nations, but unique, as against them all. Certain it is that if the gates of Russia were opened, many thousands would flock to Israel and to the West in order to be able to affirm their unity with the millennial stream of Jewish history—this in spite of the fact that the present generation of Russian Jews received hardly any religious or even Hebraic instruction.

Romantic secularist nationalism is a real factor in the life of Jewish people today, even if it seems irrational to liberals and humanists. It enshrines the feelings of identity that were nourished by the religious tradition, though it negates the central faith of the heritage. It is a reaction to, or the Jewish counterpart of, the meta-myth in the Christian world. It is the equal and opposite reaction to the nationalist frenzy in the twentieth century. Finally, it reflects the awareness of Jewish history that throws a vast shadow on our age. Three thousand years cast a strange spell, like a heaven-piercing pyramid so massive that it seems to be part of the inner structure of the universe.

Romantic nationalism in Israel is balanced by the ideals of

humanism and socialism that European Jewry embraced so heartily. It is these ideals that impel the government of Israel to undertake a program of foreign aid that is far out of proportion to its size and resources. More than fifty new and underdeveloped nations are being assisted by technicians and scientists sent out of this small state of barely 2,565,000 people. Scholarships by the hundreds are made available to students from Asian and African nations. The Histadrut (Organization of Workers) maintains a year-round institute for the training of African industrial managers and secretaries of cooperatives. Toward the Arabs in Israel, the Histadrut directs a number of projects with the purpose of developing the skills of these people and of furthering their integration into the economy of the land.

The lamentable rift between Israel and the Arabs was not due to the absence of a humanist approach in the ideology of Zionism. On the contrary, the vision of Zion (rebuilt in the writings of Herzl, Ahad Ha'am, Lilienblum, and Borohov) included the native Arabs of Palestine in the idyllic picture of a noncompetitive, nonexploitative, nonaggressive utopia. The "exiles" would go back to awaken the East, as returning natives armed with the technical skills of the West. They would embrace the Arabs as long-lost "brothers," descendants of Abraham, laying the foundation for a joint renaissance of the two kindred nations.

That the Arab phase of the Zionist ideology went so tragically awry was due to a number of factors. The returning Jews were actually Europeans, in the cultural sense, and "Semites" only in their own dreams and in the eyes of anti-Semites. The rhythm of their life was centuries away from that of the Arab masses, while the Arab leaders could gain standing in the eyes of the mandatory government only as nationalist agitators and revolutionaries. A generation later, to sit for a few months in an English jail was a prerequisite for any would-be savior of his country. Again, the contending ideals of romantic nationalism and liberal humanism did not move on the same plane. The former aimed at making the life of Israel possible, while the latter detailed that which the life of Israel would make possible. As Herbert Spencer pointed out long ago: in a crisis, the necessities of life will always prevail over its ideals. The rebuilding of Israel was effected by way of an uninterrupted series of crises.

The renowned religious thinker Martin Buber traced the mystical dimension of the Zionist idea from the dim beginnings of Biblical history to the present day. A modernist and an antitraditionalist in the field of ritual, Buber was essentially a mystic, though with reservations. He did not aspire to achieve unity with God or to overcome "selfhood," but he was perpetually aware of a Divine Presence, a Divine call that may address us in diverse ways. While his mystical or existentialist philosophy is shared by few people, his interpretation of the Zionist ideal is resonant with the undertones and overtones of Jewish history: he spoke of Zionism as an age-old religious and popular reality, adapted to the universal form of the national movements of the nineteenth century. This reality was the holy matrimony of a "holy" people with a "holy" land, the local point of which was the name of Zion.

"In other respects the people of Israel may be regarded as one of the many peoples on earth, and the land of Israel as one land among other lands; but in their mutual relationships and in their common task they are unique and incomparable. And, in spite of all the names and historical events that have come down to us, what has come to pass, what is coming and shall come to pass between them, is and remains a mystery. From generation to generation, the Jewish people have never ceased to meditate on this mystery."[140]

Buber regarded this "mystery" as an objective phenomenon, by no means comparable to the similar illusions of other nations. In the case of Israel, the "mystery" was embraced in authentic faith. It was given by the Divine Commander: "The essential point is that Israel heard the will of the Lord of the world at the beginning of its expedition to Canaan and conquered the land in the perfect and well-founded faith that it was accomplishing His Will . . . at all times there have been peoples who have given divine labels to their passions and interpreted the acts of violence born of their own greed for possessions, power, and destruction as commanded by these divinities . . . but, so far as we are able to judge from the record, no other people has ever heard and accepted the command from heaven as did the people of Israel. So long as it sincerely carried out the command, it was in the right and is in the right insofar as it still carries it out. Its unique relationship to its land must be seen in this light. Only in the realm of perfect faith is it the land of this people. . . . Where a command and a faith are present, in certain historical situations, conquest need not be robbery."[141]

Coming down to modern Zionism, Buber showed how the "love of Zion" steered the quest of Jewish leaders for a haven of refuge toward Palestine, regardless of rational and pragmatic considerations that pointed to other territories. Such westernized intellectuals as Pinsker and Herzl wavered, but the instinct of the masses was sure and firm. Ahad Ha'am, rationalist though he was, recognized the mystical dimension of the land of Israel and projected the ideal of a cultural center. Yet Ahad Ha'am did not go far enough when he wrote of the "power of the historical feeling that unites the people and the land." For Buber, the bond between the people and the land was not merely subjective feeling. "The decisive question is the objective reality which is mirrored in the historical feeling." He asked, "Is it merely a historical reality, transient like all merely historical things, capable of being annulled by new historical facts like all merely historical things? Or is what has befallen this people in its encounter with this land, and this land in its encounter with this people, the token and expression of a suprahistorical relationship?"[142]

For Buber, there was no question that a "suprahistorical" reality is incarnate in the Zionist enterprise. He quoted approvingly from the writings of A. D. Gordon, the revered *Halutz* and mystic. " 'It seems as if the whole nature of the plenitude from on high that is poured from all worlds into the soul of man, but especially into the soul of the Jew, is entirely different from what it is in the lands of the Diaspora.' "

Gordon was a mystical poet, but not religious in a formal sense. He apotheosized the spirit of the land of Israel because of its intimate union with the people of Israel. "David's harp can only regain its power here in the land of Israel." And the land speaks, as it were, to the people. "It is not we, it is our land that speaks to the people. We have merely to express and intimate the words spoken by the land, and we say to you, to the whole people: 'The land is waiting for you.' "[143]

Buber's ascription of a mystical dimension to the people Israel and to its bond with the land of Israel is based upon two sources: the romantic folkism of his youth and the testimony of the Hebrew Bible. Though he had disavowed the mystical racism of his early writings, he had continued to glorify the primitive sense of direct communion with God, nature, and folk.

All who are able to see through the web of romantic illusions must recognize that if we posit sanctified "feeling" as our guide, there is no way for mankind to keep from repeating the bloody errors of the past. The elimination of the context of rational culture from the quest of reality puts all ethical considerations on a secondary plane. To reassert Biblical nationalism as unique, because the Israelite conquest was kept within the framework of a divine command, is to open the floodgates to similar feelings and similar consequences.[144]

Buber did not believe in the literal revelation of the Divine will in the Hebrew Bible. It is the light of meaning that a person experiences when he studies the Scriptures that is Divine. Like Spinoza, Buber regarded the entire Law as invalid, but unlike the great rationalist, he looked to the feelings of devotion for guidance, and he esteemed the "mystery" of Israel as a "spiritual reality" that is objective and normative.

The mystical concept of Israel, in all its variations from the Qabbalists to Buber, contains several dynamic tendencies that

489

might lead to the self-transcendence of the individual and the nation. First, the emphasis on inwardness in the service of God.[145] In comparison with the supreme significance of the intention of the individual, the boundaries between the various systems of serving the Lord lose some of their dogmatic rigidity. If the whistle of a shepherd boy could open the heavens, why not the Gregorian chant or the cry of the *muezzin?* There is an undercurrent of antinomianism in any upsurge of mysticism. Second, the projection of an infinite dimension in the cultivation of religious feeling reduces the finite variations among diverse sects to insignificance. Third, the awareness of an ever-present mystery militates against the need of dogmatists to direct the events of history by their own power and do God's work for Him, as it were. The overtones of skepticism toward the affairs of this world introduce a healthy detachment from the plausible panacea of the moment.

As we move from the romantic-mystical side of the spectrum to the rational and humanistic views, the concept of Israel tends to break along the line between religion and nationalism.

The nationalists, like Dubnow and Ahad Ha'am, regard the Jewish religion as one of the historical expressions of national culture. While there are no radical breaks in history, the creative energies of the people may be expected to seek new expressions in keeping with the spirit of the times. Both Dubnow and Ahad Ha'am were convinced that the age of religion had ended. The Jewish people, who had formerly lived within the protective walls of the "inner ghetto" of law and myth, must now rearrange their life in order to be a "cultural," or a "spiritual," people. Ahad Ha'am saw the future Jewish world-community as one organic body, with its heart in Israel and its scattered limbs in the Diaspora. He maintained that this "center and periphery" arrangement would sustain the Jewish sense of being radically different (the meta-myth in our analysis), and would halt the "normal" processes of assimilation.

Dubnow portrayed the entire panorama of Jewish history as of a "spiritual nation," a people that learned long ago to confine the drives of nationalism to the domain of culture and self-government. He fought for the principles of autonomy in behalf of all minority nationalities. In the interim between the two world wars, Dubnow's philosophy became the basis of the minority clauses of the Versailles Treaty as well as of the organization of the Jewish communities in Eastern Europe. Long before the holocaust, the currents of life had ebbed away from the secularist communities and all their agencies. The community organizations of the large Polish cities were torn between the two irreconcilables—the Bundists and the Orthodox. In the Soviet Union, the Yiddish organizations lacked popular support, with most Jewish parents preferring Russian schools and cultural fare. It was not the Yiddish language that appealed to them in the first instance, but the ideals and sentiments of the literature—ideals that the communists did their best to undermine. The impassioned will to live as a Jew falters and fades away in the atmosphere of secularism.

In America, the philosophies of Ahad Ha'am and Dubnow were brought up to date and revised in the Reconstructionist movement, founded by Professor Mordecai M. Kaplan. Religion is not a temporary dispensable "garment" of the enduring genius of the people, but it is the crown and glory of every civilization. Religion is the "firstfruits" of the evolving civilization of the Jewish people.[146] It should change in accord with the changing patterns of the life of the people, reflecting their collective hopes and ideals. Organizationally, Israel should be constituted as a world-community centered in the Holy Land, where its civilization is dominant, and extending into the Diaspora, where Jews will live in "two civilizations." Liberal in religion, Reconstructionism is romantic in its concept of the "organic community." But, unlike Ahad Ha'am, Kaplan disavows the "chosenness" and the uniqueness of the Jewish people. The meta-historical phase of the concept of Israel belongs to a supernaturalist world-view that should give way to a naturalist philosophy of religion and to a concept of Israel that reintegrates it into the evolving society of mankind.

At the extreme end of the nationalist spectrum, the attempt was made to remove the ethnic plane entirely from the concept of Israel. The Jewish community was simply a religious community—nothing more. This view emerged with some hesitation, even in the ranks of the classical Reformers. Abraham Geiger still postulated a Jewish racial genius in the domain of religion. At the turn of the century, classical Reform was radically opposed to the Zionist view of Israel as a nation. The Jews ought to take on the national character and the specific culture of the nations among whom they live, retaining only their own distinctive faith. Their mission to humanity consists in the promotion of "ethical monotheism."

Perhaps the most profound thinker among the ideologists of this school was Hermann Cohen, who thought of Israel as the vanguard of humanity. Its religion consists of the glorification and sanctification of pure ethics. Its collective purpose is to help establish the "Kingdom of Heaven," the perfect society of universal justice for all mankind. Its destiny is to be the "suffering servant" of humanity, since all chauvinists and zealots, sensing in the Jew the harbinger of the time to come, vent their fury upon him.[147]

Cohen combated the Zionist ideal not on the ground of its impracticality or its utopianism, but because it was a deliberate attempt to reject the noble role of martyrdom. "They do want to be happy," he complained of the Zionists.

Cohen's disciple, Franz Rosenzweig, veered sharply from rationalism to existentialism. He believed in the revealed religion of Judaism, not in a "religion of reason," and he thought of the people of Israel as a community formed by Divine will and lifted out of the course of history—a meta-historical people. But Rosenzweig's view was remarkable in that, for him, the Christian community was engaged in fulfilling Israel's mission. The people Israel was like the sun; the Christian community was the effulgence of Divine rays permeating the nations with the spirit of monotheism. The boundary line between Judaism and Christianity was not along the plane of intellectual thought, since the Divine Being could be caught only figuratively or symbolically within the meshes of human reason. Existence is prior to thought in the life of the community, as in the experience of the individual. Our role is determined by our place within the unfolding charade of world history. Specific functions were assigned by Providence to each community: the cultures of India, Greece, and China to prepare the ground; the people of Israel to preserve the heavenly fire; the Christian community to convert the pagan world. Both communities are the agencies of Divine redemption, since "salvation is from the Jews."

Rosenzweig based his conception upon the assertions of both Halevi and Maimonides that Christianity and Islam are "preparations" for the coming of the Messiah and the ultimate triumph of Judaism. Yet his view is a distinct advance, for they operated within the context of a literalist faith. Hence, the deviations from the "pure" faith were grave sins. At the same time, Rosenzweig moved within the thought-world of modern Judaism, where diverse religions are so many pathways to the one goal. For him, the being of God was the ultimate truth, and deviations were only distractions that were unavoidable in any case.

Rosenzweig saw the course of revelation in the actual processes of history, inverting Hegel's dictum, "The rational is the real." For him, "The actual is the way to Truth." Thus anti-Semitism, embodying Christian resentment of the metaphysical character of the Jews, was, in the view of Rosenzweig, part of the Divine revelation, as was the defiant stubbornness of the Jew, his indomitable pride in possessing the fullness of truth, believing himself to be standing at the goal toward which others only stumble and fumble—a self-assurance that exasperates and offends.[148]

Rosenzweig felt that Judaism was both "more and less" than nationality and also "more and less" than a religious denomination. It was unique, meta-historical in the present because of its meta-historical roots in the past and the persistent incursions of Divine grace within the stream of history. He conceived of the

493

Zionist enterprise as being in the same relation to Judaism as socialism is to Christianity. Both social movements operate on the basis of opposing ideologies, but historically they fulfill the real purpose of religion: the establishment of a just society here on earth.[149]

The position of classical Reform is still maintained by some ideologists, but it is now largely defunct, chiefly because the course of events has rendered it academic. The Jews of the Western countries could not shed their nationality in one century when the Eastern Jews were so obviously reasserting their ethnic character and their determination to reconstitute themselves as a nation. The triumph of racist anti-Semitism in Germany made all theories worthless. For a while, at least, the vision of one humanity had turned into a cruel mirage.

Yet, in spite of his temporary successes and his slaughter of six million Jews, Hitler failed. His downfall served to clear the air and to usher in an era rich in hope and boundless in promise. The apostles of hate have retreated into the shadows, and concerted efforts are made in many parts of the world to overcome the dragon's teeth of bigotry still embedded in the soil of contemporary culture.

No concept can be understood apart from the historical context in which it is placed. In the past generation, the Nazis provided an object lesson of the powerful momentum of ancient hatreds. At the same time, the rapid realignments in the postwar world, projecting the vision of a Europe united, demonstrated the range of freedom in human affairs. It is not written in the stars that France and Germany must forever fight against each other. Nor is it written that the Jews must be forever homeless wanderers. The rise of Israel through the voluntary effort of individuals in the course of two generations is perhaps the greatest demonstration of the range of freedom in the history of mankind. Its foundations were laid by individuals from many parts of the world, and they received their inspiration from books; they labored for several decades to realize a vision that

494

appeared to be hopeless, but which was, for them, the quintessence of spiritual rebirth—a blend of hope, faith, and love.

If we should now proceed to project the concept of Israel into the future, we must take note of the following considerations.

First, the continuity of trends in Jewish history. As a community that is constituted by reverence for a sacred literature, we cannot ever dismiss any of the major movements of antiquity. We may expect that there will always be fringe-groups, and by no means only in isolated communities, that will cherish ancient myths and legends, however antiquated they may seem to those who are in the mainstream. We do not have an authoritative body to define the faith for all Jews. We may regret many passages in the Talmud, and we might want to edit some of its discussion. But as a collection of notes and a record of ancient disputes, it belongs to the past. To the Conservative and Reform, it is a literary monument of the past to be studied with ardor and devotion, but not as a guide for our times. Still, there will always be some pietists who will insulate their minds from all contemporary winds of doctrine and force their living souls into the frozen molds of ancient times.

For this reason, the entire spectrum of opinions from the past looms as a perpetual pageant of potentialities for the future.

Second, the gradational character of the concept of Israel. Whether Israel is defined primarily in ethnic or in religious terms, allowance must be made for those who will associate themselves with it partially or marginally. In the domain of religion, we run the gamut from ultra-Orthodoxy to total skepticism, stopping short only at the lines of express atheism. In the domain of ethnic loyalty, we have the Canaanites of Israel at one end and the Councilites of America at the other. Ethnic assimilation can be as gradational and near-total as an asymptotic line.

Third, the interaction of the concept and the complexities of life. The equilibrium of tensions within the Jewish community is naturally responsive to the changing forces in the general society. Every flare-up of anti-Semitism is likely to frustrate the liberals and to strengthen the isolationists. Every intellectual movement in philosophy, as in statecraft, will challenge either the religious or the ethnic phase of the concept of Israel and evoke a corresponding response. The self-image of the Jew is too intimately enmeshed in the texture of life to be kept pure and inviolate, "unspotted of the world."

Fourth, the diversity of views within Israel. The diversity is too great to permit any kind of meaningful, communal unity. Jews will agree that anti-Semitism is evil and that a united effort to combat it is possible. They will also respond to campaigns for refugees and for the relief of whatever branch of Jewry is sorely threatened at the moment. But short of the necessity to combat the physical threat of annihilation, Jews are unlikely to act in concert or even to share a vision of the future. On the other hand, a persistent threat, maintained for a long time, might well call into being an association of organizations representing world Jewry, a quasi-community that might continue to exist for years, by the impetus of sheer momentum, after the emergency has passed.

Fifth, several tendencies that might eventuate in the expansion of the scope of the "invisible Synagogue" and the identification of Israel with the moral-spiritual vanguard of humanity. The strong component of rationalism within Judaism focuses attention on the moral-spiritual core of faith, the "religion of reason"; in this view, the diverse faiths of our time incorporate this core in varying degrees.

The rites and ceremonies of the different denominations are only so many varying instruments. It is not the instruments, but the manner in which they are used that matters.

The mystical trend also favors the view of a greater Israel, insofar as it deprecates the criteria of ritualistic conformity, and it points to the infinite dimension of religious intention and enthusiasm. The "intersubjectivity" of the realm of feeling corresponds to the objective standards of the rationalistic philosophers.

On the ethnic plane, the secular version of Messianism implies an active commitment to the task of building the "Kingdom of Heaven" here on earth. This goal may well go hand in hand with the warning that emerges out of so many pages in our tradition—the warning against the varied seductions of pseudo-Messianism. Jewish Messianists are cautioned by their history against the assumption that any project or plan or person represents the final hope of mankind. The Messiah is up in heaven; he is a vision, a goal, a hope; in historic times, he is not here and now.

The secularized version of Jewish Messianism was embodied in the past century in three movements, each promising redemption for the Jew and claiming to be the final form of Judaism in the End of Days.

The first ideal which appeared in this light was that of individualistic liberalism. All men were to be torn out of their historic context and left to float in splendid isolation within the ethereal realm of absolute law. The Jews in France and Western Europe were indeed emancipated by the upsurge of liberalism. As we have seen, to many of our nineteenth-century philosophers, the "religion of reason" was indeed the soul and substance of Judaism.

The second ideal to acquire the deep pathos and ringing resonance of Messianism was the vision of socialism. It was represented as a contemporary "scientific" version of the prophetic quest of righteousness, of the "Kingdom of Heaven" on earth. At the same time, it would liberate the Jews from the historic hates of anti-Semitism which—so it was proven again and again—derived from the "inner contradictions" of capitalist society.

The third ideal which appeared to be the light of the Messiah was that of Zionism. The Jew would be redeemed from the crushing burdens of hate, and his faith would be revitalized in the land of its birth.

We can now say without fear of contradiction that these three secular versions of Messianism represented different colors in the ideal spectrum, but that none of them constituted the final revelation. Each movement achieved fulfillment in the modern world, but each also eventuated in certain frustrations of its own.

Here, then, we have concrete illustrations of the dangers of pseudo-Messianism.

Two major events are likely to intensify the attraction of the movements at the two ends of the spectrum. First, the rise and rapid growth of the State of Israel is likely to dramatize and re-invigorate the ethnic base of Israel. Second, the growth of the ecumenical movement is likely to strengthen the humanist trend in the concept of Israel, transforming it into the vision of the invisible fellowship of all who seek the Lord with heart and soul. This development is likely to gather additional momentum if Moslem intellectuals should fall into line. We may expect some deep and sustained soul-searching among Jews, and this will result in according full recognition to the latent universalism within the Jewish faith.

Will the universalist trend be opposed by the resurgent national loyalties centered on the young and fragile state? The State of Israel is dominated by secularists, though the Synagogue is not separated from the government. To the preponderant majority of Israeli, the concept of Israel is largely that of a na-tionality united by sentiments of affection and concern with the nuclear center in Israel—largely, but not entirely. The bond between nationality and religion has been hammered out by the forces of history. The nonreligious have approved of the law prohibiting the raising of pigs, or disqualifying the "Jewishness" of a Brother Daniel.

The secularists may embrace their religious heritage in one of two ways. They may esteem the Jewish faith to be an asset and instrument of the national ethos, in which case they will stress the doctrines and customs that confer a mystical aura upon the national being. Consciously or not, they would seek to revive and glorify the meta-myth. On the other hand, they may spurn the manipulative and cynical approach toward the Jewish re-ligion and, in their earnest search for spiritual roots, discover

498

and make their own the prophetic core of Judaism, the eternal quest of the soul for truth and holiness. In that case, they would strengthen the unifying thread between their historic past, their vision of the future, and their bold social experiments that are designed to follow the narrow pathway between Messianism and pseudo-Messianism.

In sum, the "chosenness" of Israel remains a tantalizing challenge to Jewish people, whether they be secularist or religious. The dogma derives not only from the many-sided tradition that we have analyzed, but from two sources that are perennially replenished: the wonder of Jewish history and the personal experience of the Divine.

Within the complex course of history, the role of the Jew has been particularly conspicuous. His past appears to be unique as the agent of monotheism, as the target of hate, as an object of mystery, as a pioneer, and as a pariah. Many secularist Jews will find in the experiences of their own day subjective confirmations of the meta-myth, which they are likely to articulate in the literary-cultural terms of their day. Strange as it may sound, the secularist mentality has had no difficulty in accepting the status of "chosenness," while rejecting belief in a God who chooses. The resources of the mythological imagination are endless. It would be easy to cite abundant evidence from contemporary "mystics of Jewish history," who reassert the metaphysical uniqueness of Israel, though in all other respects they are realists and pragmatists.

At the same time, "chosenness" is a phase of the individual's experience of grace. As we move in thought and feeling away from the outward appearance of things and yearn for the "nearness of God," we do get on occasion that flash of illumination which is the basic quantum of religion. It is at once a feeling of surrender and of assurance. As we yield in trust, we feel the upwelling of the Divine within us. We are accepted, we are loved, we are anointed, we are commissioned—these are various ways in which our grateful reception of Divine favor is

499

expressed. This sense of possession that accompanies all religious experience is so close to the notion of "chosenness" as to merge with it. To be sure, religious experience also leaves us with the feeling of privation—we know that we do not know—hence, its inexhaustible dynamism.

Thus, personal religious experience, in the case of Jews, is likely to seek confirmation in the rhetoric of the Jewish tradition and in the collective experience of the Jewish people. In turn, the ancient doctrine in all its variations acquires the fresh resonance of contemporary experience from the mystical fervor of deeply religious people.

Rooted in the sacred tradition, in history, and in religious experience, the "chosenness" of Israel, however it is interpreted, will long continue to intrigue the imagination of Jews and non-Jews alike.

FAITH
AND
INTERFAITH

The fundamental dichotomy in our experience is the cosmic gulf between the world of things and the realm of spirit. Looked at from without, the universe consists of things marked by space and time, and enchained by laws that establish an identity between the two sides of a formula describing an event. The more we succeed in comprehending external phenomena, the more the complexities of experience are reduced to simple things. Quality and spontaneity disappear. Sights and sounds are no more. At bottom, there is only matter in motion.

Looked at from within, our mind reveals to us ideas, sentiments, memories, and hopes. Entire galaxies may be envisioned in the sweep of one idea. The past with all its wonders is ordered, cherished, and embraced in concepts that include and transcend time. Our thought discovers myriads of new relations, and there appear to be no boundaries to the creative play of our imagination. Freedom and spontaneity characterize the realm of spirit, as space-time fixity determines the world of things.

How are the two realms related? This is the central problem of philosophy, but not of philosophy alone, for in crude, incipient terms all men are philosophers.

Religion is the self-awareness of man's spirit. Conscious of being the bearer of a realm that is not of this world, man reacts in fear and hope—fear that his precarious self is nothing more than an ephemeral bubble on the heaving waves of matter, hope that he might be related to a world of which his own self is but a premonition and an anticipation.

The Greek philosopher Democritus noted that religion derives from two sources, fear and reverence. We might carry this observation further and note that these two basic sentiments derive from the contemplation of the outside and inner worlds respectively. If the outer world of matter is all in all, then the self and its seeming freedom is the froth of illusion. If the inner world is the final truth, then the charade of material phenomena is no more than a delusion of the senses. The pressures of everyday living give the edge to the outer world, imposing the limits of things on the brave thrusts of the spirit.

If history teaches us anything at all, it is the erratic, fumbling, and stumbling course of human progress. Nothing emerges full-blown into reality, and religion, reflecting the totality of man's self-awareness, is certainly no exception.

The sporadic rays of light that we behold in history are enveloped in dark and billowy clouds. We note a persistent tendency to reduce the protean *élan* of faith to the concrete dimensions of matter.

In itself, faith is the self-affirmation of man's spirit, its assertion of its own reality and truth. Spirit contains its own laws, standards of value, a hierarchy of essences. In moments of inspiration, man senses that his spirit is oriented more truly to ultimate reality than the multitude of things around him. Insofar as he shares in the life of spirit, he is a spark of eternity and reality.

When the fleeting moment of inspiration passes, he faces the need of translating his newly won assurance into lasting terms. Inevitably, he tends to convert the free and protean nature of spirit to the concrete and static forms of matter. At best, concrete things serve as reminders of and pointers to that which is other than matter. At worst, all experience is reduced to material phenomena. The surging tides of spirit are frozen into a lifeless arctic landscape.

Fetishism is the simplest illustration of this transformation of spirit into matter. But the same process is also at work in the higher forms of religion. Totemism associates a living community, a tribe or a clan, possessing an incipient tradition, to an animal species. A higher stage is reached when the nature of spirit is refined and individualized. The subhuman vital energy of animism graduates into individualized, anthropomorphic deities, and these deities are then further moralized and spiritualized. But until the coming of monotheism, the gods remain concrete personalities, moved by human—all too human—motivations of anger and jealousy, lust and caprice.

In monotheism, the human spirit affirms its ultimate goal. Unity is the ideal of all directions of spiritual energy. Thought aims at the reduction of all phenomena into a series of interconnected equations. Einstein's "generalized field-theory," beginning with the ultimate building blocks of the universe, running through all physical, chemical, physiological, and psychological realms, and ending with Einstein himself, a formula-producing formula, would be the final achievement. Such a goal, too, is always to be approached, but never to be reached.

Similarly in the directions of ethics, esthetics, and the quest of the holy, we have thrusts toward ever greater systems of unity: unity of the individual as a free being, completely the master of the chaos within him; and unity of the individual with the overarching unities in which society is integrated—the family, the tribe, the state, the nation, the society of mankind. Ethically speaking, the varied goals of integration are in tension with one another. This is also true in esthetics, for the needs of harmony exclude more than they include. Yet, the esthetic drive aims at the achievement of a total harmony.

The sense of the holy emerges at the cutting edge of man's spirit, when the self as a whole confronts the universe as a whole—that is, in the living moments of faith. Here, too, unity remains a goal, not an achievement. Man tends to associate the holy with only one of the aspects of the spirit—only with the quest for truth, for the good, or for the beautiful, or for the awesome and the mysterious. At a lower level, the holy is associated with the needs and impulses of life—food, sex, the inter-unification of the feelings of life in orgiastic exercises.

On the one hand, the holy aims at the establishment of integrated selfhood; on the other hand, it aims to relate man to Him, who is the infinite ground of man. Tension is, therefore, at the heart of the experience of the holy.

Being neither prophets nor mythologists, we do not speak of what God is in Himself. We try to see the situation from the human point of view. To us, therefore, monotheism is the human endeavor to reach out to God. It is the assertion of the intimate relation of our spirit to the Spirit of the universe; at the same time, it is the recognition that He remains beyond our grasp. We can serve God, but we can never achieve possession of Him.

Faith, in monotheism, is two-sided—an affirmation and a negation. Its *that* is clear; its *what* is symbolic, pointing beyond itself. In relation to God, the self affirms its *possession*, its sense of rootedness in the Divine, but also its *privation*, its incapacity to clarify its meaning in the full light of day. In relation to life, faith is articulated in deeds and in creeds; but if it is alive, it also is painfully aware of the ineptness of all its representations and the inadequacy of all its applications.

In the Hebrew Bible, the elusiveness of a living faith is demonstrated again and again. Jewish scholars, long before Philo, asserted that the entire Torah is embodied in the Ten Commandments. A certain Rabbi Simlai maintains in the Talmud that only the first two of the Ten Commandments were spoken by the Lord to all the Israelites, while the rest of the Commandments were formulated by Moses. All of Judaism, then, rests on the first two Commandments, the one affirming the Lord as the source of freedom, the other denying that He can be adequately represented in any image, shape, or form. *That* the freedom of our spirit is brought into being by the Infinite Spirit, we dare not doubt; but, every one of our attempts to reflect the Spirit in any concrete fashion must be denied, for it is ultimately false. Hence, the paradox: faith is fully alive only when it is articulated; yet, every concrete representation or application is true only as a step forward, not as a final resting point. The living spirit generates forms and passes beyond them, for it is essentially self-transcending.

The Psalmist reflects this thought in the famous verse, "For with thee is the fountain of life, and in thy light do we see light."[1]

As life rises above matter by introducing a realm of potentiality and spontaneity, so the Lord rises above nature. Compare a pebble and a seed. Both can be measured, weighed, contained, but the seed possesses the potential of becoming an oak tree or a thorn bush. New ranges of creative potentiality flow from the Being of God. Light is the best symbol of His Being, but no more than a symbol, for it exists only *between* things, not in things, opening them to one another.

The Twenty-Third Psalm is very popular because its imagery reaches down to the depths of our being. It begins with the recognition of man's utter dependence and creatureliness. We are like lambs, watched over and led by the Shepherd. All we can do is submit and yield and trust. But as we yield in faith, we rise with renewed strength. We know ourselves to be no longer sheep but princes, members of the King's household, sitting like equals at His table. As we overcome our egotism and reach the depths of our being, we attain the realm in which God and man communicate.

Within Judaism, the persistent danger has been the reduction of the Divine will to a concrete, detailed law. Law is the articulation of the moral-spiritual approach; it is "reason in action," but, even at its best, it is not in itself the full expression of the life of spirit. Generally, its concreteness makes it liable to subversion. At its worst, it is a caricature of the spirit, regulating human actions but ignoring intentions. Indispensable as it may be, it can contain the spirit as poorly as a sieve can hold water.

Hence, the Hebrew prophets continually protested against the external piety of their contemporaries. They did not resent the sacrificial system so much as the naïve piety of the people, for whom the elaborate rituals of the Holy Temple were not aids to piety, but the sum and substance of religion. Micah summed up the message of classical Hebrew prophecy in the oft-quoted verse, "He hath told thee, O man, what is good and what He requires from thee, but to do justly, and to love mercy, and we walk humbly with the Lord thy God."[2] Ethical action, according to the Law, spontaneous love beyond the Law, plus— and this *plus* reflects the persistent negation of living faith—the feeling that we must go forward, using human stepping-stones, but always with the knowledge that we do not know. The Talmud calls attention to the prophets' use of the phrase "to walk," commenting that angels stand still, but human beings must never be content to remain transfixed in the belief of knowing it all. But this dynamic quality of faith was often forgotten in Judaism—especially, in times of stress.

The major emphasis in the preaching of Jesus was a new and vigorous expression of the prophetic conscience. Jesus protested against sheer legalism in his arguments with the Pharisees. He stressed the infinite dimension of true piety and its protean, measureless character. His entire career as a teacher was devoted to a fresh recapturing of the two aspects of a living faith—our assurance of Divine help and our ignorance of the precise details of God's will.

The open horizons of faith were never entirely lost either in Judaism or in Christianity, though neither stream was always true to its source. In Judaism, the prophetic heritage was maintained by the philosophers of medieval Judaism, who faced the challenges of pagan skepticism, Moslem nationalism, and Christian criticism.

In Christianity, the prophetic heritage is strongly articulated even by St. Paul, who, it was said, first transformed "the religion of Jesus" into "the religion about Jesus." With all his emphasis on the finality of the religious experience in baptism by the spirit, he cautions his disciples as follows:

"Though I speak with the tongues of men and of angels, but have not love, I am become as sounding brass, or a tinkling cymbal.

"And though I have the gift of prophecy, and understand all mysteries, and all knowledge; and though I have all faith, so that I could remove mountains, but have not love, I am nothing.

"And if I bestow all my goods to feed the poor, and if I give my body to be burned, but have not love, it profiteth me nothing.

"Love suffereth long . . . love envieth not . . . seeketh not its own . . . rejoiceth with the truth. . . ."[3]

The word "love" in Hebrew means the quest for truth as well as dedication to the service of God. It is an apt reference to the spontaneity of spirit. Similarly, St. Augustine's maxim, "Love, and do what you will" is not a formula of action, but an attempt to articulate the paradoxical nature of a living faith.

Yet, in Christianity, as in Judaism, there was the perennial need of fresh challenges in order to keep faith from freezing into rituals, dogmas, and an assorted variety of spirit-killing, dead certainties. The Protestant Reformation was a massive protest against such a degeneracy of faith. Within the Catholic Church, the Jansenist movement in France served a similar function.

For a long time, religious leaders believed that they could only protect the "purity" of faith by silencing the opposition. During the sixteenth and seventeenth centuries, both Protestant and Catholic governments endeavored to utilize the secular arm in their struggles against one another. Actually, religion thrives best when it is challenged; otherwise, the Second Law of Thermodynamics begins to operate. Entropy increases; the free energy of religion is blocked; spirit congeals into things.

In our day, the cause of freedom is allied with the fortunes of faith. The communist campaign embraces atheism principally in order to undermine the ideological foundations of Western democracies. If there is any hope of preventing the disastrous slide of a technological society into despotism, we can find it only in the insistence on freedom as the expression of man's inherent dignity, indeed his divinity.

But as long as the dominant religions in European lands were not challenged by each other and by the consequent emergence of widespread skepticism, the champions of liberty, equality, and fraternity found no succor among the institutional defenders of religious Orthodoxy.

The "religious revival" of our generation, insofar as it is real, is actually an anguished cry for help against the apparent horrors of a world in which "God is dead." People look to religion to provide the counterballast to the impending reduction of man to a cipher in the production machine. In a sense, our vast universe and complex economy bring home to man his total "negation." He looks to religion for the restoration of his spiritual balance, the feeling of worth, the validity of the realm of spirit in which, if he so wills, he might be naturalized.

In any case, it is through the piercing of our complacency that we lay ourselves open to the awareness of the Divine reality.

It follows that we become fully aware of the meaning of our heritage only as we learn to understand with sympathy the religion of our neighbor. This is particularly true of the several religious streams within the Judeo-Christian tradition, for their realm of discourse is one—the field of the tension between the infinite mystery of the cosmos and the reflection of it in our souls.

We have only one life to live, and being raised in one tradition, our soul enters into an inheritance with many insights, but also, unfortunately, with many blind spots. In the dark night, we cannot throw the beam of a flashlight in one direction without casting the rest of the environment into impenetrable obscurity. Through learning in love to understand one another's faith, we learn to surmount the drag of entropy in our own faith, achieving new life and light.

As the great Hebrew prophets saw it, the purpose of learning to know one another is not mutual conversion, but a mutual stimulation and partnership—yes, even a walking together toward the same goal, though not along identical pathways. The advance of my neighbor in his way helps me find my own way.

The prophet Micah, after picturing the vision of the ideal future, adds, "For all the peoples [shall] walk every one in the name of his god; and we will walk in the name of the Lord our God for ever and ever."[4]

THE ENDURING
TENSIONS
IN JUDAISM

Eternal is man's quest for the eternal. All that is alive and human is subject to change, but amidst the protean flux of phenomena, man clings to a vision of the permanent and the Divine which supervenes above the rushing currents of life. Conceptions of ultimate reality may and do change, but this reality in all its infinite mystery will ever challenge and even tantalize the minds of men. Confined as we are to the human view of reality, we apprehend the eternal as a limitation and negation—the ultimate is beyond our grasp. The metaphysical quest —be it an illusion or an intuition, the response of the deep to the deep, or the idle reach for the unattainable—is the essence of the feeling of eternity and the heart of Judaism. This quest may be articulated in different ways.

The human base of the Covenant has been variously designated as the "holy seed" (zera kodesh), the "community of the Lord" (kehal hashem), the "people of God" (am hashem), the "congregation of Israel" (Keneset Yisroel), or "those who abide under the wings of the Shechinah." But while the concepts of the people and of the object of their worship are variable, the Jewish people are constituted by the correlation between these two "eternal" realities—God and the ideal people of Israel. It is the Covenant, reflecting this correlation, that forms the living core of Jewish consciousness and its claim to eternity.

Three propositions are implied in this statement, namely, that God is both known and unknowable, that the empirical people of Israel is not identical with the ideal community that is the counterpart of the *Shechinah,* that the Covenant between God and the people must be expressed in two ways—a pattern of living and a dream of perfection. The concepts of God, Israel, and Torah are polar in character, extending from the concrete and finite to the ideal and the infinite.

The first proposition need hardly detain us long. It has long been recognized that in Judaism God is both near and far. We know that in contrast to pagan myth and ideas, the One God was conceived to be transcendent to the whole range of creation, while His power was immanent in it. The forces of nature were fashioned by Him; the angels sing hymns of adoration to Him; He is first and He is last.[1] While His glory is revealed in the heavens and in the wonders that are daily with us, He is beyond all things that are in heaven above and on earth below. "The Holy One, blessed be He, is the place of the world, but the world is not His place."[2] It follows that His thoughts are not our thoughts and that His ways are not our ways.

But this remote and unknowable God is also revealed in and through those who turn to Him in heart and mind. He loved Abraham and chose the people of Israel, though they did not merit His grace. He is revealed in the quest for justice, the hunger for freedom, the feelings of compassion. His "image" is in man, so that man attains the Divine dimension when he realizes his deepest self. As the prophetic formula puts it, "Holy, holy, holy is the Lord of hosts, the world is full of His glory."[3] Holiness, as Professor Leon Roth points out, is expressed in negations and prohibitions. It suggests the sublimity and inconceivability of God, while His glory is articulated in the events and experiences that we experience as evidences of the Divine Presence. "Taste and see that the Lord is good."[4] God is both in man and beyond him at the same time. How, then, is His will to be expressed among men?

It can only be reflected in a polarity between a relatively practical pattern of laws and a surge of idealism that aspires toward a goal of perfection that is beyond man's present grasp.

Divine immanence is articulated in the norms and mores of an empirical community, somewhat transmuted by the passion for justice and righteousness, while Divine transcendence is reflected in a vision of the Kingdom of Heaven (*Malchuth Shomayim*) so resplendent as to be unearthly. The Covenant relationship with Him who is at once far and near is articulated in both a vision and a way—a prophetic vision of the End of Days when the Divine Law will be inscribed on the tablets of the heart and a pedestrian, practical way of justice and righteousness (*derech adonai*) for the slow and stumbling advance of an existing parochial community.

"Without vision, a people perishes," but they cannot live on vision alone; they need the "pleasant ways" of Torah, mapped and measured by masters of the Law.[5]

Similarly, in the concept of the people, this polarity of the Divine will was articulated in a tension between the belief that a living people was chosen in love and the assertion that it is the Torah of Israel that forms the object of God's love. While the life of a people is certainly related to its ideals, this relationship is neither necessary, nor unvarying, nor exclusive. Ideals are inherently universal, transcending parochial loyalties to the extent of their validity, be it of the intellectual, moral, or esthetic order; hence, the tension in every generation and in most countries between the patrioteer, championing the life of the people, and the humanist, championing its ideals. In Judaism the essential debate is the one held between Rabbi Judah and Rabbi Nehemiah—whether Israelites are called "sons" of the Ever-Present only when they comply with the will of their Father in Heaven or whether they are "sons" in any event (*ben kach uven kach atem keruyim bonim*).

The assertion that it is the threefold polar tension within Judaism that constitutes its enduring core needs to be proven, first by an examination of the tradition and then by an analysis of the general human situation.

In respect to Jewish experience, we recognize the tension

between Torah as ideal vision and Torah as existing, somewhat amended law in the struggle between priest and prophet during the Biblical period. No matter how we read the account of the evolution of the religion of Israel from Moses to Ezra, we cannot escape the conclusion that the prophets were most instrumental in uncovering the full implications of monotheism. The priests were the guardians of Torah in the sense of a compilation of laws, while the prophets expounded the principles that underlie the law.

While the Hebrew prophets emerged out of a brotherhood of mystical ecstatics, their genius was of the opposite order. They were essentially moral philosophers, criticizing and reforming the laws and the ways of their contemporaries. While the ecstatics raved and the mystics poetized in dark speech, glorifying and sanctifying the prejudices of the people, the classical prophets reasoned and admonished. Their ecstasy was of the formal order, while their vision of new ethical and intellectual horizons was the substance of their message.

To translate the word "Torah" by the Greek term *nomos* or the English word *law* is to do justice only to the Samaritan concept of Torah, since the Samaritans rejected the mighty currents of prophecy. But the Torah, as it has come down to us, consists of principles as well as laws. It was to be administered by prophets and kings as well as by priests. The Hebrew Bible contains in its three parts the contributions of priests, prophets, and sages (Tenach or Torah, Prophets, Writings). Jeremiah speaks of the three callings as constituting together the leadership of the community. "For there shall not cease Torah from the priest, nor counsel from the sage, nor the word from the prophet."[6]

The crucial issue in the interpretation of the history of Judaism is the relation of the Pharisaic sage to the Biblical prophet. Did the scribes and sages, who sat "in the seat of Moses," continue the prophetic tradition, or were they degenerate deviationists? Was the relationship of the Pharisees to the prophets analogous to that of a ripe fruit in the late summer to the blossoms of the spring, or was the crystallization of prophecy into Pharisaism comparable to the artificial preservation of flowers by pressing them within the covers of a book?

This question was manifestly a central issue in the ongoing debate between Judaism and Christianity. As the Christians saw it, Jesus was the "fulfillment of prophecy," not only in his person but also in his message. In his critique of the Pharisaic emphasis on the minutiae of the Law, he continued the ancient struggle of the prophets against the priestly veneration of ritual. In his day, the *mizvah*-cult of the Pharisees had taken the place of the "rams and the rivers of oil" at the time of Micah. The creative current of Judaism, in this view, flowed from the prophets to Jesus and Paul; whereupon it was again crushed by the sacramentalism and the dogmatism of the Catholic Church, only to be rescued by the heralds of modern Protestantism. This is how liberal Protestants view the relation of prophet and sage, or the vision and the Law.

From the Jewish view, Christianity broke the inner creative tension in Judaism by repudiating the Law and the earthly pathways in general in order to still the unquenchable yearnings of the people for the immediate realization of the ultimate Messianic goal. For the early Christians, the Kingdom of God was already on earth. The Law was no longer needed. In actual practice, the vacuum created by the rejection of Jewish Law was quickly filled in by Roman law, by various sacraments, and by the introduction of Greek philosophy. In the philosophy of St. Augustine, the original tension was reconstituted, to some extent, with the "City of God" looming above the stumbling world of reality. All too often, however, the "City of God" was identified not with an ideal vision of human perfection but with the actual hierarchy of the Church. Only in liberal Christianity of the modern world was the pristine Jewish polarity reconstituted, fragmentarily and sporadically.

To many Jews, the evolution of the prophet into the Pharisee was comparable to the growth of an academic philosopher into a practical statesman or legislator. To translate ideals into laws is to lend them the impact of concreteness and the substance of

513

reality. In actual practice, the Talmud bulked larger at various times in the consciousness of Jewish people than did the Bible. On the other hand, the renaissance movements in Judaism involved a return from the Talmud to the Bible, as, for example, in Babylonia of the tenth century, in the Golden Age of Spain, in the Italian Renaissance and its offshoot in Holland, and in the Haskalah movement of the nineteenth century.

In truth, the Law of the rabbis and the vision of perfection painted by the prophets were in polar tension with one another. This relationship was symbolized by the requirement to read the prophetic Haftorah along with the reading of a Torah portion on the Sabbath. More often than not, the Torah reading and the prophetic message were contradictory, on the surface at least, and this juxtaposition was intended to dramatize the difference between the two strands of the one tradition, for they are in fact both mutually supplementary and mutually contradictory. Ideals should be crystallized into laws, but the wisest legislation of any one generation may become the spiritually intolerable yoke of another generation if the community lacks the capacity to return to the first principles of faith and ethics. The quest for righteousness and the sin of self-righteousness go hand in hand; hence, the never ceasing need for prophetic conscience, the prophetic capacity for self-criticism, the prophetic vision of the unattainable glory.

The Pharisaic sages are to be congratulated on their rejection of the Book of Jubilees, which represented the laws of Judaism as being engraved on eternal, unbreakable tablets in heaven. But, then, some of the Midrashic assertions of the sages came close to this view. Indeed, we can recognize an awareness of the tension between Law and vision within the Talmud itself, and certainly within the larger stream of the tradition as a whole. To some rabbis, the ideal scholar was the faithful transmitter of the Law, "like a lime-covered pit, which does not lose a drop"; to others, the ideal was a more creative type, like a living "upwelling fountain."[7] In his first analysis of Jewish history, Heinrich Graetz recognized the Aggadah and later Jewish philosophy as the countervailing pressures against the rigidity of the Law. Contrast the Talmudic principle, *mizvoth ain tzerichot kavanah*, with the opening up of an infinite dimension of piety, consisting of "duties of the heart," by the philosopher Bahya Ibn Pakuda.

Indeed, we find the reconstitution of the tension between the way, which is practical, rational, and moral, and the vision, which is transrational, transhuman, transnatural, in the philosophies of the three greatest philosophers of Judaism—Philo in antiquity, Maimonides in the medieval era, Hermann Cohen in the twentieth century.

Philo identified the Torah with the Logos, which is the principle of intelligibility. The will of God is amenable to human understanding and articulated in the order of nature. Yet, God Himself is unknowable—"unlike" all things in nature and in human nature.[8] He is "superior to virtue, superior to knowledge, superior to the good itself and the beautiful itself."[9]

Maimonides regarded reason as the pathway deriving from God and leading to Him. More than any one of his predecessors he identified the rational with the Divine. Yet, he insisted that God could only be reached by the negation of the things that seem most Godlike, the so-called *via negativa*.

Hermann Cohen was a superrationalist, as it were, for he asserted that reason must deduce the totality of being completely out of its own resources, without aught that is "given" by the senses. He was a champion of "Pure Reason," "Pure Will," "Pure Feeling." Yet, in respect to God, Cohen maintained that the idea of God stands outside the systematic coherence of all other ideas. This idea appears in the mind of man with the apprehension of the call to truthfulness (*Wahrheit*), which is the source of the demands for purity in the three currents of "culture-consciousness." This idea asserts the inner unity of reason, ethics, and esthetics, while it also projects the final vision of the End of Days, when the unity of this trial will indeed be realized in fact.

For all three philosophers of Judaism, despite the vast differences in their world-views, the Divine is represented in a transrational and transhistorical goal as well as in a rational, moral, historical way. There is good reason for this coincidence of opposites, since it is actually implied in the central doctrine of Judaism, the belief in the One God. This unity, it has been abundantly argued, is not merely an arithmetical dogma. It is an assertion of the ultimate identity of the two avenues leading to the idea of God—the process of reasoning from nature and the way of reflecting on human nature. Needless to say that the gods of polytheism are also the products of such a synthesis of elements, some human ideals and some forces of nature. But in Judaism, both avenues are projected toward their ultimate end. The entire range of creation is God's handiwork, and human nature at its best is the image of God. But the essence of nature is reason, mathematics, self-contained laws. The essence of human nature is to aspire toward that which is more than human, to "be like unto the gods, knowing good and evil."[10] The doctrine of the One God, then, projects a faith which can never be proven, yet one which man will never stop trying to prove, for God is in the surge of the spirit toward metaphysical reality, as He is in the yearning for self-transcendence. In His transcendence, He is the ultimate goal of love, but in His immanence, He is reason, ethics, law. He inspires the many-splendored vision of perfection as the goal of history; yet He is reached by the methods which reflect the orderliness of nature, its limitations, its rationality.

Rabbi Simlai said in a famous passage, "Only 611 *mizvoth*, out of 613, were spoken by Moses, the other two were spoken by God directly. They are, 'I am the Lord thy God, and thou shalt have no other gods beside me. . . .' "[10a]

The First Commandment sets up the reality of the Unknowable, who can only announce and reveal Himself. Yet, the quest for His nearness is man's freedom, for man is truly human only when he hungers for the Divine. The Second Commandment is a direct corollary—while man must tread the pathway to perfection, it is the direction that is Divine, not the temporary resting places. We are called upon to cultivate that which is Godlike in us and about us; yet, the Godlike is not God. To stop on the way is to deny His call; hence, the vision of the prophets, announced in peremptory tones, in accents which brooked no contradiction. The vision must be conceived by man as perfect, the seal of the Absolute. The sages who explored the Law and the way, at their best relied on reason, on practical good sense. "*Lo bashomayim hi*" ("It is not in heaven"). They even dared to deny the right of a Divine voice to announce a final decision. They respected differences of viewpoint, for the way must be rational, empirical, tentative. The Lord Himself studies the Torah of mankind as follows: "Rabbi Jonathan, my son, says this. Rabbi Joshia, my son, says the opposite."

As this polarity constitutes the life of Judaism, the temptation to break it amounts to its dissolution. The pseudo-Messianists embrace only the vision, either in its mystical or in its political form, repudiating the rational-empirical way as obsolete and false. The Law was, for St. Paul a "schoolmaster," which was no longer needed when the vision itself had become a reality. A similar antinomianism was contained in all pseudo-Messianic movements, from Abu-Isi of Isfahan to Jacob Frank of Turkey and Poland. Generally, the mood of "realized eschatology" requires some tangible symbol that involves the violation of the Law; hence, the repudiation of circumcision by St. Paul, the sexual orgies of the Frankists, the minor gestures in this direction of the Hasidim—namely, slaughtering with "polished" knives, changing the *nussah* of the prayers, postponing the time of the services, substituting contemplative exercises and convivial fellowship for the austere discipline of Torah-study.

By the same token, Judaism ceased to be a dynamic spiritual movement when the sheer dialectic of the Law was regarded as the sole permissible content of the faith. The criteria of growth are, after all, unfolded by the process of growth. In the eras when the Jewish mind was entirely absorbed in the pages of the Talmud, the disciplines of reality, as well as the arts and norms

517

of the esthetic order, were forgotten almost in their entirety. Even the principles of ethics were painfully distorted by the bias of ethnicism. Thus, the Talmud and its literature contain many regrettable statements, despite the intensely ethical concern of nearly all its discussion. The "man of Halachah," as he is revealed to us in the literature of the Talmud, was great in many ways, but his humanity was severely restricted, primarily in the esthetic and intellectual domains, but also in the broad field of human relations. The heralds of the enlightenment were compelled to inaugurate a spiritual revolution in the name of humanism, seeking support in the dynamic personalities of the Bible against the rigid dogmatics of the Talmud.

In the Mussar movement, the Law of the Talmud was recombined with the heroic ideal of ethics, with the result that fresh wellsprings of devotion were tapped. But the esthetic element was given only scant recognition, and the intellectual challenge was ignored altogether. The Mussar masters contented themselves with the theosophic speculations of Qabbalah. The German Neo-Orthodox movement stressed the esthetic as well as the ethical dimensions in Judaism, combining them with the strict observance of the Law. Their slogan was *"Torah im derech erez."* To counter the intellectual challenge of modern disciplines, they embraced the new myths and new fervor of German romanticism. In general, ethnic romanticism was always employed as a countervailing influence to sustain the one-sidedness of the Law.

The modern Jew needs to recapture the ancient balance between the infinite vision, accepted in faith, and the rational-moral way. The vision lifts him above the entangling prejudices of the present, so that he can recognize the tentative and the limited truth of the norms and standards of his day. At the same time, the insistence on everyday patterns of living keeps him from an impatient surrender to a romantic vision, as if it were a reality, here and now. The vision of an all-human perfection keeps us from sanctifying our present society, our ethnic boundaries, our economic structure, our social mores. The focus on the immediate reality and its intricate patterns keeps us from yielding to the phantasies of those who believe that the Messiah is here already. The tension between the vision and the way makes for a pragmatic dedication to the highest conceivable human goals, along with the recognition that our goals too will change as we move ahead on the infinite pathway. It is the advance itself and the direction that are eternal, not the visible goal and not the concrete steps on the way to perfection.

We have assumed that the eternal content of the Covenant is that which is essentially human. All that is inconceivable in universal terms, or that which does not commend itself to the general conscience, belongs to the temporary and accidental domain. Is, then, the tension between the vision and the way a universal category of human life? To my mind, this tension is the Jewish contribution to the understanding of man's nature and destiny.

Two major conceptions of human life now dominate the intellectual scene, the one deriving from classical Hellenism, the other flowing from the melted glaciers of Christian dogma. According to the first view, man is a self-contained spirit, with his happiness depending upon the full realization of all his inherent capacities. His ideal should be the fullness of self-realization. He should aim at the harmonious blending of his diverse interests, recapturing the ancient wisdom of the legendary sages—"nothing in excess" and "know thyself," in the sense of knowing one's limitations. The ideal person is the one whose poise is least disturbed. Protagoras expressed this ideal in the most radical terms when he asserted, "Man is the measure of all things, of things that are that they are, of things that are not that they are not."

This bold "declaration of independence" overlooks an inherent phase of human nature. Man is not content to be self-contained. Put him on a pedestal, balance him in perfect proportions, let him contemplate his own perfection—he will rebel against his own absoluteness, which is also his isolation. The inescapable fact of the human paradox is the human need of serving an ideal, a cause, or some superior being. Great as is man's yearning for mastery and freedom, his passion for the surrender of his self to a nobler, more ultimate self is greater still. If man's active energies are stimulated by success, his sense of purpose is fortified by frustration and failure. The classical ideal is likely to predominate in times when cultivated individuals are enabled to play decisive roles in the transformation of society. The yearning for self-surrender is likely to prevail in times and places when mass-movements reduce the individual to virtual impotence.

In our day, the call to total self-surrender was sounded in the religious domain by Karl Barth and his followers. "God is all. Man is nothing." In the confrontation of man with God, all that is human is turned into nothingness, says Bultmann. On this view, the reality of the infinite vision of God, as portrayed in Scriptures, is all-important, while the tentative moral-rational principles of human conduct are of little or no significance. The preachers of this school adopted the "charismatic" posture; "filled with the Spirit" they announced boldly, "Thus spake the Lord." They disdained the attempt of philosophers to understand the Divine out of the actual complexities of the human situation, the "apologetic" procedure. The humanly reasoned and humanly discovered way does not lead to the vision; ergo, the way is unimportant, close your eyes and leap in faith. It is the vision alone that saves.

That this view of Neo-Orthodoxy does correspond to an aspect of human nature is proven first of all by its popularity in all religious communities. Partially modified and softened, Neo-Orthodoxy is doubtless a potent movement. Its importance derives from the fact that in its conception of human nature it is so utterly consistent with the axioms of the quasi-religions of our day. The Communists, the Nazis, the Fascists—they join in calling for the total self-surrender of the individual to the one all-embracing cause. They are alike in the repudiation of the empirical and the rational, for these standards, they insist, are corrupted by "original sin." While the nature of this "sin" varies for the several proponents of totalitarianism, the conclusion is the same. To find "salvation," the individual must give up his faith in his own powers, his judgment of right and wrong, true and false, and trust the emergent "leviathan," howsoever it is personified.

The fascination of this call to the immolation of the rational self was so great that a nonpolitical version of the philosophy of self-surrender became popular almost as soon as the political totalitarians were largely overcome and defeated. The rise of existentialism may be considered as a philosophical substitute for the poisonous intoxicants of nazism and fascism. This does not constitute a criticism of the existentialist movement, which is right in insisting that there is more to human nature than is revealed in man's intelligence or conscience. The feeling of being properly part of a larger being than is revealed in the rational self is the common postulate of all existentialists. This postulate we accept, but not as an alternative to reason.

As we see it, the classical and the existential view are mutually supplementary in Judaism. The human individual is taken by us to be a "walker," in the language of the Talmud, in contrast to the angels who are described as standing still. Our starting point is not man in himself, but "man facing God." Said the Lord to Abraham, "Walk before me and be complete."[11] Hence, it is necessary for man to worship that which he conceives to be the acme of perfection, the vision representing the articulation of the Divine will here on earth. In the adoration of this vision lies man's freedom, the fulfillment of his deepest self, but he must remember that all religion is man-made. Its genius requires that its myths and rites be treated *as if* they were true. But to imagine that our ideas of the sacred are absolute is to violate the Second Commandment.

God did reveal His will to man, but, that revelation belongs to the human, the historical, the empirical, the moral-rational

521

domain. All that is thus revealed is a way, a point from which to begin and to advance ahead, not a stationary image of perfection.

The Midrash says: "The Torah which is wider and deeper than the ocean, how could God teach it to Moses in forty days? But it is principles (*kelalim*) that God taught Moses."[12]

Thus it is that the vision of Absolute Perfection guards us against absolutizing the methods and procedures leading to it, while the empirical character of the way supplements the emotional appeal of the vision.

An analysis of the contradictions and frustrations of our age will demonstrate the relevance and significance of the Jewish insight that man needs both balance and purpose, a gradualistic way and a vision of the Absolute.

TRADITION
AND CHANGE:
*The Conservative Movement Today**

Tradition and Change[1] is a fine contribution to the mighty task of self-analysis that is now occupying the minds of both our laymen and thinkers. The masses of our followers have not yet reached the point of considering Conservatism as part of the unquestioned heritage of the past. Happily, they are still uneasy and uncertain about the rootedness of the movement in the enduring soil of tradition and about its capacity to produce life-giving fruit for the future; hence, the persistent interest and genuine concern attaching to the question—"What is the Conservative movement?" For the ideologists of the movement, the need of precision in every branch of Jewish theology has long been felt. We are now at the point where the unconscious dynamism of the movement has given way to reflection and self-criticism in preparation for a new burst of creative energy. If all artistic activity must necessarily go through the three phases of vision, work, and reflection—we of the Conservative movement are presently engaged largely in the third phase. The sessions on the philosophy of Jewish Law at our conventions and at special conferences are one manifestation of this phase. The work of the Committee on Jewish Ideology and Program is another expression of the same aspiration. And the appearance of this beautiful volume, under the editorship of Rabbi Mordecai Waxman, is still another effort to clarify our collective goals, methods, aspirations, and achievements.

This volume is a collection of addresses, essays, and excerpts from the writings of the builders of the movement. An extensive

*Reprinted from Conservative Judaism, 1960

and well-written introduction by the editor is followed by articles arranged under three headings: "The Origins of the Conservative Movement," "The Philosophies of Conservative Judaism," and "The Attitudes of the Movement."

It is easy enough to quarrel with the editor in regard to the selection of his materials. Let it be recognized above all that several different principles were utilized in the choice of essays for inclusion in the volume—the fact that a particular essay was not easily available in other publications, the fact that another essay was cast in the form of a summation and proclamation, the fact that still another address mirrored the personality and peculiar approach of one of the architects of the movement. The result is a valuable contribution to the literature of our movement, though it offers neither a representative account of the fullness of its meaning nor an accurate description of the various tensions within it.

The editor is to be heartily commended for his intelligent handling of the delicate assignment that was given to him. He has produced a work that friends and foes of the movement will treasure and utilize for their respective purposes. He has proven that the contending groups within our movement need not neutralize each other, paralyzing the formulation of our thought and the operation of our central institutions. On the assumption that his work will be followed by other anthologies, it is important, first, that we critically examine the material of this volume and, second, that we go on to consider some suggestions for the composition of future and similar anthologies.

Rabbi Waxman's introduction is a balanced and wise survey of the origins of the movement in America. He describes how the movement arose by slow and subtle stages, feeding on its own momentum and attaining self-consciousness virtually in spite of its founders, who believed themselves to be defenders of Orthodoxy. Reluctantly and belatedly, the builders of Conservatism abandoned the word "Orthodoxy," and spoke instead of "normative Judaism," describing Reform and Orthodoxy as "deviationist." To me it is obvious that controversialist

524

terms of this nature belong to the incipient subjective stage of an emergent ideology. A movement that is truly conscious of its own nature does not depend on such self-laudatory epithets. It is easy enough for both Reform and Orthodoxy to reverse this terminology and to describe themselves as being "normative," or in the "vanguard," or in the "mainstream." To be sure, there is a certain measure of plausibility that attaches to a position of centrality, between right and left. But are we willing to state it as an absolute principle that a "middle of the road" position is always to be followed? As a matter of fact, Rabbi Waxman ends this section with the statement that "Conservative Judaism evolved not a doctrine, but a technique."[2] This revealing phrase skirts the issue very neatly. Actually, a "technique," if not employed by opportunists, is always the application of a doctrine. And the use of different "techniques" implies the acceptance of different doctrines.

Thus, as Rabbi Waxman proceeds to spell out the meaning of the Conservative "technique," it becomes painfully clear that the real essence of the movement remains elusive. The emphasis on "Catholic Israel," the high esteem of what is "positive-historical," the principle of "vertical democracy," the value of "modern thought," of "controlled experimentation," of the "theory of leadership"—all these elements have specific and Conservative meanings only in a non-Orthodox realm of discourse. The significance of these terms within Orthodox Judaism would hardly have sanctioned the emergence of Conservatism. It was a changed context of philosophic thought and a revolutionary concept of history which lent new meaning to these and similar ideas, laying the foundation for the several types of Conservative doctrine. And Classical Conservatism, not to speak of Liberal Conservatism and Reconstructionism, is a new doctrine as well as a new technique. But the nature of the context of ideas underlying the Conservative emphasis is completely ignored in Rabbi Waxman's presentation.

As we peruse the volume as a whole, we are struck again and again with the confusion between slogans and principles, tactics and doctrine. Hardly ever is the nerve of essential ideology touched. For instance, in Kohut's essay, we read of a disputation between a Conservative rabbi and a Reform colleague. At the end of the debate, the Conservative spokesman mentions "the limits of revealed law." At this point, the discussion should have begun. Precisely what is meant by "revealed law"? Is it asserted dogmatically that God spoke in so many words? Or is it that the principle of the Law, or its purpose, or its impetus, was Divine? Only in the latter case is there room for debate. In the selection from Solomon Schechter, we read that "real Americanism meant reverence for the Bible as the word of God, obedience to the authority of the Scriptures." Yet, Schechter did not subscribe to a fundamentalist conception of the sanctity of the Bible. The basic question is precisely in what sense is the Bible the word of God? In the context of that particular address, no explanation was possibly called for. But in this anthology, the meaning of this phrase is unclear. Louis Ginzberg's address bristles with ideas, but all the ideas are firmly fixed in an ambiguous context so that they might sound true to both liberals and fundamentalists. Let us look carefully at some of these brilliantly phrased slogans: "That the Torah is law to the Jewish consciousness and Jewish consciousness becomes law to the Torah."[3]

The first part of the sentence is Orthodox, the second is liberal; and the two parts are put together as if the two principles could be synthesized simply by being juxtaposed. Throughout his discourse, Ginzberg appears to assume the rejection of the Orthodox dogma *Torah min hashomaim* ("Torah from heaven"). Yet, he never states this point. Instead, he speaks of "a historic conscience," of "Talmudism" as being different from "Biblical Judaism," of "greater and lesser truths." And when he speaks of the alternative that he rejects, he characterizes it as "vicarious Orthodoxy."[4] Presumably, then, genuine, nonvicarious Orthodoxy, such as the piety of the Hafez Hayyim and the Hazon Ish, is to be commended.

Perhaps the most frequent slogan within our movement and in this volume is the one of "Catholic Israel," or "antisectarianism." The virtue of this term consists in its ambiguity and in its expansive overtones. It meant, firstly, Catholic Judaism in opposition to the German reformers who considered themselves to be the builders of a Jewish Reformation; it meant, secondly, Judaism throughout the world in opposition to Isaac M. Wise's concept of "American Judaism." To Henrietta Szold it meant, thirdly, a form of sanctified ethnicism, which I can best describe as "loyalty in general to the glory of being a Jew in general." She speaks of faith in the individual Jew and of a mysterious quality in the people as a whole, which she describes as "sanity unresolvable by logical analysis."[5] The individual Jew "knows Catholic Israel without a definition," and he is afire with a "whole-souled belief in a mission." Here is another example of the sad datedness of slogans.[6] In the case of the abused slogan "Catholic Israel," too much is made of too little by too many.

The volume reveals not only an extreme dependence on slogans but also a high degree of dissatisfaction with what may properly be designated as the cult of ambiguity. Vigorous dissent is voiced chiefly by men serving in the active rabbinate, such as Rabbi Morris Adler, and by the intellectuals of the school of Professor Mordecai M. Kaplan. On the other hand, the practical uses of ambiguity are demonstrated convincingly by the genial scholar Max Arzt. Here we come to the central problem in the formulation of our ideology.

First, there is need of both principle and slogan, clarity of thought and ambiguity of symbol in any mass-movement.

Second, there must be a clear distinction in the minds of our leaders between principle and slogan, between ideology and propaganda, between symbol and significance.

Third, there must be an inner correspondence and organic relationship between the vital philosophy of the movement and its outer expression in symbols and slogans.

A mass-movement can be held together only by concrete symbols and emotion-stirring slogans. It must be possible for different people to *mean* different things by the same set of rites and dogmas; otherwise the movement is reduced to a school of thought or to an esoteric sect. Thus, in actual practice, symbols stretch like bridges across the chasms yawning between radically different realms of discourse. Maimonides among the Jews in Cairo was like a New York professor cast among the rough cowpunchers of Gopher Prairie; yet he lived with the people, associated with their elders, and prayed as they did. The central formulas of the Jewish faith, from *Shema Yisroel* ("Hear, O Israel") to *Kodosh, Kodosh, Kodosh* ("Holy, Holy, Holy") and *Boruch Kavod Adonai mimekomo* ("Blessed be the glory of the Lord from His place"), were philosophic principles to the learned initiates and emotion-charged slogans of identification to the masses. Symbols and slogans provide a common language more than a common system of ideas, delimiting a definite social reality rather than an intellectual affirmation.

Since the Conservative movement, like the Reform and the Orthodox, comprises a mighty portion of the people as a whole, there is need to resort to symbols and slogans that are sufficiently amorphous to mean many things and to appeal to many tastes; hence, the justification of the preference for ambiguity and expansive phraseology by those who are primarily concerned with the maintenance of the cohesive structure of our central organizations. The advocates of ideological clarification must not overlook the organizational needs of our movement.

At the same time, the converse is also true. If we allow organizational pragmatism to usurp the domain of ideology, then we shall slowly but surely empty our movement of all meaningful content, permitting bluff and propaganda to take the place of genuine thought and conviction. The temptation, or, shall we say, penalty, of those who constantly make use of slogans and symbols is that they eventually lull themselves into the belief that they are thinking logically when they are only engaged in a kind of community-sing. They tend to become oblivious to the demands of precision and logic, mesmerized by their own propaganda.

Yet, it should be possible for us to win the world, at least a modest portion of it, without losing our soul. To this end, an organic relationship between ideology and organizational mythology must be maintained. In the movement as a whole, symbols, rites, and oratorical flourishes must correspond to the thoughts that emerge out of the depths of our being; or else we run the risk of building an empty façade.

Our movement is neither monolithic nor stationary. We run the gamut from liberalism to literalism. An address given by Dr. Louis Finkelstein in 1927 is an excellent statement of what may be considered the position of Liberal Conservatism today. He clearly disavows the literal version of revelation. However, the context of his address implied the important qualification that Halachah is inviolate. The Law is not literally God-given, but it must be treated as if it were. Perhaps the fact that so many of the selections in *Tradition and Change* were addresses rather than essays helps to account for the persistent blurring of all fine distinctions of thought. Undeniably, too, our opinions are subtly modified as we pass through life.

Law in Judaism has always provided the acid test of a philosophy of life. In this collection, the famous Sabbath Responsum together with the minority opinion is reprinted. It is the decision that riding to the synagogue on the Sabbath is permitted. It also allows the utilization of electrical and musical appliances. I believe that the Responsum on the Sabbath is the most significant step ever taken within the Conservative movement in the domain of religious thought and leadership. Both the acceptance of the Responsum by the majority of the committee and the subsequent failure of the movement as a whole to convey its meaning and program to its lay following reflect the inner tensions and paralyzing paradoxes that vitiate so much of our efforts. To be sure, a great deal of our disagreement is verbal and terminological. Working in isolation, we tend to approach problems from different vantage points. The degree of maturation of Conservative thought is evidenced by the fact that three men of diverse backgrounds and experience, such as Adler, Friedman, and I, could jointly write a Responsum, launching a new phase in the thinking of the movement.

A careful reading of Gordis' and Bokser's minority opinions proves that their viewpoint is by no means identical with, or acceptable to, Orthodoxy. Only a theological hairline separates the majority opinion from that of the minority; yet, a hairline makes a tremendous difference. The observance of the Sabbath can hardly be preached in the circumstances of American life if that hairline is not crossed. On the other hand, in New York City and in selected mass-settlement areas throughout the country, the opinions of Bokser and Gordis may be *tactically* preferable.

Essentially, the difference is one of emphasis between the subjective and the objective approaches. The development of Jewish Law was effected subjectively by way of interpretation, objectively by way of *takkanah*-legislation. Surely our sages in every generation believed themselves to be acting in the spirit of the Torah. The acceptance of a new interpretation by the academy and the people was, on the other hand, in effect an act of legislation. In Judaism, the Sanhedrin and its paler representations at various times were both legislative and judicial organs. The two functions were not separated, as in the American government. The continuity of interpretation depends upon a measure of historical naïveté, which we have presumably outgrown. Hence, in sermons, where the subjective side of faith is necessarily stressed, the aspect of continuity will be exhibited, while in scholarly discussions, it is important to see the newness of our viewpoint, our philosophy of revelation, our conception of history, and so on. We may agree that there are occasions when the gulf between the doctrines of literal revelation and prophetic inspiration should be glossed over and occasions when it should

530

be pointed out. At no time, however, should we "who sit in the seat of Moses" presume it to be an act of piety to overlook objective consideration.

As to the practical import of the Sabbath Responsum, I am convinced that it is very considerable. A critic once asked me, "How many Jews, other than rabbis, do you know who will ride on the Sabbath only to the synagogue, or only for a *mizvah?*" This is not the point. The crucial question is whether any Jews do come to the synagogue on the Sabbath because they are told implicitly or explicitly that it is right for them to do so, even if they make use of a motor vehicle to get there. When people come to a synagogue, it is obedience to the promptings of piety—their *yezer tov* ("good desire"), not their *yezer hora* ("evil desire"), that impels them to attend the synagogue. For the implementation of their *yezer tov,* they seek rabbinical guidance; to satisfy their *yezer hora,* they need no guidance from us. As students of the history of religion, we know that equivocation is at times essential, but there are also times and places where it is corrosive of the substance of faith.

The introduction to the United Synagogue Prayer Book, reprinted in *Tradition and Change,* describes the principles underlying the changes made in the Hebrew and English texts. The major innovation was the change of tense from the future to the past in recounting the sacrifices at the Temple. Here not one law but a whole domain of ancient life and hope was declared to be obsolete. The tide of liberalism was running high when Dr. Gordis presided at the editing of the Prayer Book. As a first step, it was a major achievement of epoch-making proportions. Yet, no attempt was made to explore the implications of that step and to consider the meaning of the prayer for the rebuilding of the Temple, especially in the light of the restoration of the State of Israel.

What is it then that we learn concerning the state of our movement as we ponder the contents of this volume?

It is the confusion between the ideological substance of the

531

movement and its organizational structure, sloganry, and façade. Organizations acquire a mythology and a pattern of propaganda that is imposed by the pressures of social life. While we should insist on a measure of correspondence between principle and propaganda, we cannot assume at any one moment that such a correspondence actually exists. Least of all dare we take the straw of sloganry for the seed of genuine thought. Many of the addresses assembled in this volume or contained in the records of the United Synagogue conventions could very easily be given at Reform or Orthodox conventions. Each speaker could, indeed should, appropriate for his organization such fine-sounding terms as "prophetic passion" and "respect for tradition," "dynamic Judaism," and the qualities of "integrity," "authenticity," "loyalty to the mainstream," and *Kelal Yisroel* ("the totality of Israel"), and what have you. There is occasional need and there is an appropriate time for these slogans, but they do not constitute a philosophy of life or of Judaism. There is a time for singing and a time for speaking.

Another aspect of this confusion between façade and substance is reflected in the assumption that the executives of the national institutions may be taken automatically to be the spokesmen of its ideology. This assumption is obviously erroneous. The late Professor Chayyim Tchernowitz in his studies of the evolution of Halachah provided a magnificent scholarly formulation of the Conservative philosophy of law; yet, he was not a member of the Seminary faculty. And the establishment by Rabbi Stephen S. Wise of a Jewish Institute of Religion that would train rabbis for modern Orthodox, Conservative, and Reform pulpits was a practical demonstration of the principle of *Kelal Yisroel*, a demonstration so clear and resonant that hardly a parallel can be found for it. Effective communal leaders cannot be ideologists. We must remember that organizational logic requires the penumbra of ambiguity and equivocation. On the other hand, Maimonides rightly refused to accept the post of *Naggid* ("Prince"), when it was offered to him.

What then is the Conservative movement? Here we need to

return to fundamentals. The movement consists of the people in all the polarity of their motivations, and the intellectuals who express in consistent and fundamental terms the philosophy of life which accords with the aspirations and yearnings of the people. The people of our congregations are motivated in diverse ways by the momentum of habit, by social pressures, above all by a variety of psychic impulsions, powerful even if vague and unconscious. The sociologists who have recently taken up the study of Jewish life have had a field day in ransacking the basement of Jewish loyalty to the synagogue; but the edifice of popular faith has an upper story as well as a basement; *lo alman Yisroel* ("Israel not widowed"). There is an upward surge in all directions of the spirit within our congregations—in the search for truth and the good life, in the yearning for harmony with the all-encompassing mystery of existence, in the quest for the wholeness of our own self, in the longing for a kind of Judaism that will work in the circumstances and ideological climate of our time. Our *Baalai Batim* ("householders") are increasingly men of trained and alert minds, who will not indefinitely be content to chew the straws of self-laudatory slogans. It is for them, the "chosen few," who prepare the road for a growing intellectualized body of men and women, that such volumes as *Tradition and Change* are needed.

We must make clear to ourselves that a philosophy of Judaism is as broad and deep as life itself. It consists firstly of conceptions of God, of human nature, and of the human vocation. Such conceptions need to be elaborated in terms of their philosophical context and their implications. It consists secondly of certain interpretations of the character of Jewish tradition—its law and its legendry, its ethical philosophy and its dogmatic structure, its enduring core and its changing form. Based upon this interpretation, there is need for a continuing evaluation of what is valid and normative, or obsolete and even harmful in the tradition. The technique of "accentuating the positive" has its place, but there is also the need to see the shadows in Jewish lore; otherwise our visions of it will get to look like the nightmarish

533

creations of surrealists. A thorough discrimination between laws and principles and a subsequent examination of the various laws in terms of their inherent principles is the great unfinished task of our generation.

In regard to *Kelal Yisroel* are matters so simple that all we need to do is repeat piously the noble slogans of our founders? The very opposite is the case. In the past sixty years the character of the Jewish people has changed more than in the previous sixteen hundred years. The history of our people reveals to us both a Divine and a demonic impetus. It is a tale of incomparable greatness of soul, but also the record of travail and tragedy. Our task is, therefore, not merely to find and implement a "new Zionism." This very preoccupation is proof of our being enslaved by the magic spell of words and slogans. The problem is not the formulation of a new program for a twentieth-century movement, but an understanding of the diabolic and the Divine in the totality of Jewish experience.

Long ago, Leopold Zunz sought to capture the meaning of Jewish history in the pregnant phrase "monotheism and martyrdom." The demonic, in his view, was the hatred in the hearts of Gentiles, leading to Jewish martyrdom; the Divine was the dedication of Jews to monotheism. We know today that Jewish history was not quite as simple as all this. The essence of secularist Zionism was a courageous "new look" at the totality of Jewish experience, taking account of the realities of Jewish life in all their shadows as well as their lights. Zionism consists in an analysis and an answer. The answer was realized, at least in part, several years ago. What of the analysis demonstrating the inherent danger in Jewish "uniqueness" and "abnormality"? Does it not render absurd all attempts to cling to the pious platitudes of a generation ago? A vigorous confrontation of Jewish history and an interpretation of its meaning is the only way of taking Zionism seriously, though the result of such an exercise is quite likely to be the demand for the dissolution and reconstruction of some Jewish worldwide organizations.

Our time calls for honest analysis, not mystifying symbols. While our Christian brethren face the task of "de-mythologizing" their scheme of salvation, we confront the challenge of "de-mythologizing" the concept of the people Israel.

So long as Israel was only a theological concept, it was right to maintain the ambiguous unity of the empirical people and the vanguard of redeemed humanity. Now that the term is applied to a secular state, we have to distinguish its concrete denotation from the cloudy rhetoric of faith. As a state, Israel stands apart from the eschatological vision, which divides Judaism from Christianity. It is neither subject to moral absolutes, nor immune to criticism. The ideal vision of the "heavenly Jerusalem" belongs to all faiths of the Judeo-Christian tradition.

Once this distinction is made clear, new symbols may emerge out of the contemporary travail. Hopefully, some Israeli citizens will strive to make their state worthy of Isaiah's dream that "out of Zion shall come forth the Law and the Word of God from Jerusalem."[7] This is certainly the devout hope of many Jews in the Diaspora. Christians, too, join in this hope that the earthly Jerusalem, with places holy to three major faiths, will somehow become a unifying shrine and a symbol of the heavenly Jerusalem.

But all such efforts to reconstitute the ancient symbols must first take account of the separation of synagogue from state, the empirical reality from the theological ideal.

THE MEANING OF THE MIZVOTH:

An Analysis of Isaac Heinemann's
Taamai Hamizvoth besafrut Yisroel*

Heinemann's two-volume history of the reasons for the Commandments[1] is a well-written, perceptive study. Beginning with the motivations, stated or implied in the Pentateuch, the author explores the answers found in exegetical and philosophical literature in ancient, medieval, and modern times up to and including the writings of Franz Rosenzweig. The first volume is written in a more popular vein, including a number of selections from Hellenistic and medieval literature, dealing with the underlying motivations of Jewish rites and ceremonies. The second volume, covering the period from Moses Mendelssohn to Franz Rosenzweig, is more discursive and thorough in the treatment of its material.

These two volumes together cover only a fraction of the field blocked out by the title. The author does not take account of the nonspeculative, philosophically naïve stream of Jewish thought, such as is represented in the writings of Rashi, Tosaphists, Rokeach, etc.; nor does he explore the vast reaches of Qabbalah, which is in large measure a grandiose attempt to find a cosmic anchorage for the rites of the faith; nor does he take account of the literature of pietism—Mussar and homiletic literature on the one hand, and Hassidism on the other hand. In the modern period, he ignores the religious nationalists, from Smolenskin to Kuk, as well as the Conservative and Reform spokesmen, though he deals at length with Zecharias Frankel and Franz Rosenzweig.

---

*Printed in Conservative Judaism, 1957

In spite of all these shortcomings, however, these two volumes constitute a precious contribution to the understanding of our faith. No private rabbinical library may be considered complete without them.

Proceeding to a closer examination of this study, we note first the importance of its subject. All who are concerned with the task of guiding the adjustment of the Jewish faith to the exigencies of our rapidly changing world must pay close attention to the study of the "reasons for the Commandments."

While this subject drew only marginal interest from scholars in the generations when the structure of faith appeared to be solid and unshakable, it is now squarely caught in the spotlight of contemporary interest, both in this country and in Israel. In both countries, Judaism is confronted at one and the same time with the necessity of holding on to the Law and the impossibility of applying it.

Page through the four volumes of the *Tur* or the *Shulhan Aruch* and note how little of it is actually practiced among our congregants of the Conservative movement. And, in Israel, does not the Chief Rabbinate maintain that even if it had the power, it would not enforce the penalties for Sabbath desecration, and even if it obtained possession of the old city of Jerusalem, it would not reinstitute the Holy Temple, the sacrificial system, and a fully authoritative Sanhedrin? The Law, as an organic unit, complete and self-regulating, functions only in the life of a marginal self-isolating group, and there only in moribund fashion. For religious Jews, whether they call themselves Orthodox, Conservative, or Reform, it is not the Law as a unit but certain *mizvoth* that serve as the concrete embodiments of their faith, more and different *mizvoth* in the case of one group than in another.

We have arrived, therefore, at a strange inversion of values within the structure of Judaism: *The grand edifice of Halachah is now Aggadah, and the vast domain of Aggadah is now Halachah.*

Halachah, the stupendous body of legalistic reasoning, is no longer regulative in the actual daily life of our people. Its strength lay in the circumstance of its inseparability from the life of the people. Halachah was not an unworldly, transcendental cluster of ideals, a utopia for the future, nor a body of learning for scholars, nor a manual of discipline for saints. It was meant to be a rigid, detailed code for daily living, the actual blueprint of Jewish society, except for the sections that described the sacrificial system in the Holy Temple. Today, all of Halachic literature, not merely stray portions that were already obsolete when the Talmud was composed, falls in the category of edifying and sacred literature—*Derosh vekabel sechar* ("Study and receive reward for studying"). Thus, Halachah has now fallen into the former place of the Aggadah. Rabbi Soloveitchik's attempts to derive a philosophy out of the categories of Halachah are altogether in keeping with this changed status of the Law.

On the other hand, Aggadah, growing luxuriously through the centuries in the relative freedom of nonstandardization, is now become Halachah. The richness and many-sidedness of the Aggadah was due, in large measure, to the nonauthoritative character of its teachings. The Gaonim declared that the Aggadic portions of the Talmud were only speculations, which a pious Jew might accept or reject as he pleases. This position was restated by Nahmanides and other Jewish disputants. Maimonides did not scruple to condemn some Aggadic sayings, explicitly and by indirection. *Ain meshivin al Ho Aggadah* ("One does not dispute Aggadic sayings") was long an accepted principle in Jewish life.[2] Not the peculiar quality of "organic thinking," but the fact that the element of inflexible firmness was reserved for the domain of law, accounts for the variety and multiplicity of views in Aggadah. The same Rabbi Akiba can suggest in one passage that the Messiah will sit on a chair next to the throne of God in order to judge the nations in the Day of Judgment and on another occasion apply to Bar Kochba the Messianic verse *Dorach Kochav miyaakov* ("A star has arisen out of Jacob").[3]

Today, however, Aggadah becomes the sole content of the

heritage we seek to preserve and to advance—ideas concerning God, man's destiny, the nature of the good life, the relationship between the people of Israel and the Torah, the conception of mankind, and the doctrine of immortality. These ideas, comprised in the general term "ethical monotheism" are our stock in trade. It is for their sake that all else in Judaism is in theory justified. Hence, we must bend every effort to make certain that the coinage of thought in our tradition is not debased. As the quality of firmness and exactitude is lost by Jewish law, theological thinking must become more vigorous and precise. We must not allow marginal or peripheral trends to be represented as the whole of Judaism. A synoptic vision of the totality of our Aggadah is needed now more than ever before, for to us, Aggadoth are not legends; they are shafts of light cast into the mystery of existence by saints and sages—and this, the totality of Jewish insight, is the living treasure, the regulating philosophy of our life as a people.

The study of *taamdi hamizvoth* ("reasons for the Commandments") is a critical portion of the Aggadah, for it explores the shifting area where Halachah, philosophy, and the spirit of the age coincide. It is also a domain of thought and feeling that can be explored only with great difficulty, since the meaning of every statement can be assayed only in the light of its context. Heinemann, a methodical and profound scholar, combining the precision of German erudition with the "atmosphere of the land of Israel," is excellently equipped to carry out this undertaking.

What is the predominant feature of the panorama that the author unfolds? I believe it is the amazing unity of thought and feeling that prevails in spite of the continuously changing idiom of expression and an immense variety of intellectual climates. It is the unity of substance and impetus in a moving stream, not the uniformity of color in a painted wall. In every age, the varied trends within the stream of Judaism were represented in different proportions of volume and power, some rising to the surface or moving to the center, while others that were formerly central and predominant moved to the bottom or to the marshy banks. But nearly every trend can be traced to its Biblical wellspring, and the mighty stream still rushes on.

The overall pattern for the reasons of the Commandments is provided for us in a saying of Hasdai Crescas: "Rational from the position of the Commander, irrational from the position of those commanded." In all ages, Judaism maintained that God was no self-willed tyrant, capable of acting capriciously or unworthily. Hence, the *mizvoth* of Judaism may be assumed to be expressions of His wisdom and His goodness as well as His will. Now, our knowledge of right and wrong and our intellect are reflections of the Divine will and reason, but no more than reflections, apprehending only a finite portion of the infinite whole. Hence, we may understand *some* of the reasons for the Commandments and we ought to strive to discover as much of His wisdom as is humanly possible, but we cannot ever hope to know *all* of God's reasons for His laws; hence, the invariable formula—rational for the Commander, irrational for those commanded.

This formula holds true for the entire range of Jewish thought, from the Biblical period down to the modern movements of Conservatism and Reform. In Holy Scriptures, God is represented as good, wise, and just, and His laws as models of righteousness.[3a] Mankind generally is punished only for infractions of the law of kindness that God placed within their hearts, as in the tales of the Deluge, Cain, Ham, Sodom, the city of Nineveh, and the unforgivable sins mentioned by Amos. The Torah also assumes a natural feeling for holiness (*kedushah*), and a natural revulsion against abominations (*tumeah*). But the Jewish people are commanded to observe many and diverse precepts for which there are no apparent justifications. In the Talmud, these irrational observances are categorized as "things which are disputed by the evil desire and the heathen," or in other versions by Satan, and concerning which the Lord asserts, "I, the Lord have legislated, you have no right to question them."[4] This irrationality is occasionally carried to the point where it is forbidden to seek any rational explanations of the Commandments.[5] Only occasionally, however, is the efficacy of *mizvoth* assumed to be automatic and quasi-magical. By and large, the *mizvoth* are placed within a field of force, more or less midway between the Divine, superrational pole, and the human pole of thought and conscience.

In modern Judaism, this polarity still obtains. Even when we do not assume that the *mizvoth* were literally spoken by God, we accept them as "given" for us by the processes of history, and we believe that God calls unto us out of the pulls and pressures of our contemporary situation. Hence, as long as we do not become Ethical Culturists, we operate with the basic polarity—rational for the Commander, irrational for those commanded. Furthermore, on the basis of our knowledge of depth-psychology, we admit the need of an irrational element in our worship that points to and establishes symbolic contact with the irrational substratum of our personalities.

A grave question confronts us at this point. Why did the literalists not rest content with the dogmatic belief that God commanded all the *mizvoth?* Why did they strive for reasons, explanations, and motivations? Down to the opening of the modern period, the dogma of a literal revelation of specific *mizvoth* at Sinai was not questioned. While Maimonides limited the extent of revelation to the Pentateuch and to the several Halachoth that are specifically attributed to Moses at Sinai in the Talmud, Halevi assumed the help of God for the sages of the Mishnah and the builders of the entire Halachah. If then God demanded that all the *mizvoth* be observed, why speculate concerning the efficacy and merit of this or that *mizvah?*

Halevi does indeed maintain that the naïve believer, who neither questions nor speculates, is to be preferred over the believer who comes armed with philosophical weapons against an assortment of doubts. Some modern scholars, like S. D. Luzzatto, concur in this judgment, maintaining that it was the infection

541

of Hellenism or "Atticism" that led Jewish thinkers to concern themselves with *taamai hamizvoth*. Heinemann disputes this thesis, pointing out that the tendency to look for reasons of the Commandments is already found in the Bible as well as in the Talmud and the Midrashim.

The answer to our query, I believe, is to be found in the craving of the human personality for *wholeness*.

The urge to reflect on one's beliefs and to probe ideas with the scalpel of criticism is as native to the human soul as the yearning for anchorage in reality and the feeling of dependence on the Creator.

The ideal of precision in thought and exactitude in analysis comes to us from Hellenic sources, but the organon of logic is universal and natural. Thus, even the ultrapious find themselves driven by an inner necessity to seek reasons for His commands and to conceive of their faith as a rational system. It is simply impossible for the soul to rest forever in the dark privacy of subjective belief and feeling. From the domain of subjectivity, wherein the feeling, the dogma, the people, the tradition, and all that is of one's own are extolled, a great soul must go on to take account of the human, the rational, and the universal. God designed us to be *whole*—living both in subjective feeling and objective thought. True, a pietist might venture into the realm of reason, with the sole object in view of confounding reason by the weapons of reason, deriving from this dubious shadow-boxing the illusion of objectivity. The history of theological thought is full of such exercises in futility. But then, even in its confusion, the indomitable urge toward objectivity is acknowledged.

By the same token, this recognition of the wholeness of personality poses a constant warning to rationalists. In their eagerness to reduce the entire life of faith to the principles of rationality, they must learn to take account of the irreducible domain of subjective feeling and judgment. In part, this dominion is determined by the exigencies of history, whereby a people comes to accept a certain pattern of beliefs and practices as the text and context of its hymn to the supreme mysterious source of existence. In part, this realm is preempted by the yearning for spiritual aloneness, the assertion of individuality, and even irrationality, as a means of reflecting the essential irrationality of our unconscious self. Wholeness is the key to the life of the spirit, but this wholeness is dynamic in character, never resting in the perfection of its balance, but always moving in restless alternation, from the pole of subjectivity to the pole of objectivity, and back again.

In the evolution of Judaism, Hellenic culture provided the first great impetus toward objective rationality; hence, the contrast between Palestinian Judaism, as reflected in Talmud and Midrash, and Hellenistic Judaism, as embodied in the writings of Philo. The author points out that the Hellenistic writers referred to revelation at Sinai only sparingly, hardly daring to base the entire weight of faith on this one dogma. Nor did they stress the virtue of obedience. But they concentrated all their acumen on the task of allegorization, whereby the classic heroes of Scripture were converted into symbols of various kinds of virtue. In this manner, their national tradition was transformed into a universal essay on the steps leading to the perfection of man's virtue and the nearness of God.

The allegories of Hellenistic Judaism appear grotesquely artificial to us, but then, as we learn from Gilbert Murray, vast and intricate allegorical systems were actually employed in the ancient Greek world by such men as Heraclitus and Pythagoras. It was through allegorizations that the pagan world achieved an uneasy peace between their myths and their philosophies. In the deepest sense, we know now the movement from subjective piety to objective rationality cannot but convert the beliefs and practices of religion into allegories. Even our most abstract formulas are seen to be signposts, pointing toward the Divine mystery, not molds embracing and containing it. True, the Hellenists and medieval philosophers thought they could express the truth to the chosen few without allegories. But we know better.

In a general way, Philo laid the basis for philosophical religion, as Professor Wolfson proves. Philo stressed autonomous motivation; that is, the communicant finds reasons in his own conscience for living in accordance with the Law. He introduced the Greek conception of the "natural," or "unwritten," law as the test of all positive legislation. He overlooked national-historical considerations and based his argument on general human experience. Because of his unwillingness to posit a specifically Jewish realm of discourse, Philo leaves out of his system the ideal of holiness and the love of God.

Fascinating panoramas are unveiled before us as we follow Heinemann in the study of medieval philosophy. Saadia operates with the basic analogy of master and slaves. *Mizvoth* are so many opportunities for the earning of merit by the slaves so that they need not be undeserving recipients of His free grace. On the other hand, Bahya regards God as the One, through whose free gift of grace we are enabled to pray in purity of soul. For Halevi, human perfection is not enough. The goal of the *mizvoth* is to enable us to fulfill our Jewish quality. His piety borders on the magical. The author's avoidance of Qabbalah and Mussar blinds him to the realization that Halevi's thought is proto-Qabbalistic and theosophic. Abraham Ibn Ezra contributes the dubious support of astrology to the understanding of the Sabbath. Ibn Daud ranges the *mizvoth* in the order of their importance, assigning the least value to the "irrational" observances, such as the laws of *kashruth*. The author, in his bias against Conservatism and Reform, strives in vain to show that Ibn Daud's perception of differences in the value of *mizvoth* was not an anticipation of the spirit of Reform. To Ibn Daud, the essence of Torah was not the Golden Rule of ethics, but faith, in which judgment he reflected the spirit of medieval life.

In his treatment of Maimonides, the author fails to maintain his usually keen perceptiveness. He notes the complexity of the greater master's approach, as evidenced in the contrast between the views expressed in the *Mishneh Torah* and the philosophy described in the *Moreh*. He should have taken account of the hints Maimonides himself has thrown out for the understanding of this contrast, namely, the distinction between "true" and "necessary" ideas.[6] This distinction was widely accepted in both Christian and Moslem theological circles, especially in the schools of Paris and Cairo.

In his eagerness to sustain a mild polemic against Reform tendencies, Heinemann fails to account for Maimonides' insistence that details of *mizvoth* can have no rational explanation, just as he fails to comprehend why Gersonides, who carried the logic of rationalism further than any of his predecessors, should have felt bound to offer reasons for every detail of the Law. In general, the author deals with stray comments of Maimonides, rather than with the central implications of his essential thought. Thus, he stresses Maimonides' failure to mention the doctrine, *Mizvoth betailot leatid lavo* ("The Commandments will be abolished in the time to come"), on the one hand, and his copious treatment of the section on *kodoshim* ("sacrifices"), on the other hand. But the relative value of *mizvoth* is stated clearly throughout the *Guide* (especially in *Guide* III, 51), and the restoration of the sacrificial system was to his contemporaries a symbolic affirmation of the belief in Messianic redemption.

The author takes note of the salient features in Gersonides' explanation of *taamai hamizvoth*, but he fails to glimpse the tortured soul of that philosophical genius, who knew both the logic and the danger of rationalism only too well. Emphasis on the essential goal of religion, with the consequent imputation of only relative value to *mizvoth*, was a dangerous doctrine in an age when the instinctive impulse of survival needed the hypnotic zeal of martyrdom. Also, rationalism had ceased to be a method and had become an institution, with rigidities all its own. Thus, Gersonides reintroduced astrological considerations in his attempt to account for the details of *mizvoth*. He declared that while the Sabbath was designed to give us time to reflect on the mysteries of the universe, the seventh day of the week was chosen that the Jews might be protected from the evil influences emanating from the stars on that day. A similar reason was given by him for the choice of Yom Kippur.[7]

In dealing with Hasdai Crescas, the author extols him as the most original of all medieval philosophers, failing to realize that this tragic philosopher virtually substituted the *élan* of Christianity for the vital essence of Judaism. To Crescas, Torah is the religion of redemption from original sin and from the influence of the stars; Torah is the discipline that leads us to the love of God; the sacrifice of Isaac was an all-inclusive sacrifice for the redemption of the entire Jewish people; the rite of circumcision had a mystical and sacramental effect.

Here again, Heinemann's abstraction of the opinions of philosophers from those of Qabbalists gives his treatment an aspect of unreality, for Crescas accepted in part and rejected in part the ideas of the Qabbalists, many of whom were his friends and acquaintances. For example, when Crescas states that the reason for the rite of *Sair la Azazel* ("the goat offered to Azazel") was the symbolic indication that Israel worshiped only one God, he certainly knew and intentionally opposed the explanation of the Qabbalists.[8]

In Albo's world-view, Qabbalistic motives loom large. The sacrifice of Isaac is compared with the death of Jesus and declared to be more efficacious for salvation than the involuntary death of the Christian Savior. The author overlooks Albo's insistence that even one *mizvah* can lead to "human perfection," an argument that needed to be asserted against the Christian claim that the Law is powerless to effect salvation.[9] Nor does he take account of the reasons that led Albo to declare that *mizvoth* may be modified in keeping with the needs of different peoples and the exigencies of climate.[10]

The author concludes the first volume without taking due account of the tension between ethnocentrism and humanism in the explanation of *mizvoth*. The variation in intensity of ethnocentric feelings was nearly always proportionate to the ebb and flow of the tide of persecution. In a cruel era, a philosophical preacher like Jacob Anatoli could easily account for the dietary laws by assuming that God loves the Jews, guarding them from foods that are harmful to the soul, while He hates the non-Jews. One wishes[11] too that the author had included Isaac Arama in his study, whose doctrine of a predestined "harmony" between Torah and nature was immensely popular in later Jewish thought.

In the second volume, the author renders an invaluable service to students by collating material from diverse sources, many of which are inaccessible even to scholars. He begins his survey with the interesting personality of Moses Mendelssohn, who may be claimed, strangely enough, by the Neo-Orthodox, the Conservative, and the Reform. This "Jewish Socrates" was personally so observant that he even insisted on retaining the prohibition of non-Jewish wine, though the sixteenth-century historian Solomon Ibn Verga already presented ample proof of its pernicious effect on Gentile-Jewish relations.[12] He rejected the slightest attempt at Biblical criticism on the ground that "we Jews have the tradition of our fathers." Though he maintained that Judaism had no dogmas, he regarded belief in the Divine authorship of the oral Law as one of the "roots" of the faith. On the other hand, he allowed that the Jewish ritual is good only for Jews and that other nations may have received other rituals for their peoples,[13] thus disregarding the *mizvah* of "bringing people under the wings of the *Shechinah*" and all that the concept of *Shechinah* in relation to Israel implied.[14]

He ventured to set up as the acid test of a true religion whether or not it affirms the principle of exclusive salvation: "No religion can be true which excludes those who do not adhere to it from the bliss of eternal happiness, which the Creator designed for all His creatures. This rule I dare to set up as the acid test of religion." [15] By means of this standard, not only the faith of Rashi but also that of Maimonides would fail to pass muster, for both authorities claim that the "seven *mizvoth* of the sons of Noah" must be performed on the ground of their being

547

ordained by Moses; although Rashi and his followers exempted their Christian contemporaries from the category of idolaters, they did not include them in the category of *ger toshav* ("a semi-proselyte"); the Talmud takes it for granted that the "nations of the world" did not observe the *sheva mizvoth* ("seven commandments"); Maimonides includes the Christians in the category of idolaters; and only Rabbi Menahem Hameiri, of all the great codifiers, specifically declared his Christian contemporaries to be in the category of "the pious among the nations."[16]

Wherein, to be exact, did Moses Mendelssohn depart from the path of tradition? That his life represented a departure, to some extent, there can be no question. Heinemann refuses to accept the thesis of nationalist historians, like Smolenskin, that Mendelssohn was an assimilationist. And I concur with the author in this judgment. But I believe that Mendelssohn reduced the *mizvoth* to a position of relative unimportance. We are obligated to observe them not because they are intrinsically good and useful, either in this life or in the hereafter, but because God commanded them at Sinai. But if this belief, in its stark literalness, is once cast in doubt, the whole edifice topples into a shambles. To be sure, Mendelssohn also discovered in the "progressive educational theories" of his day the rationalization of *mizvoth* as a form of action-writing — i.e. education in right thinking through action-symbols. But then he had to concede that the educational system of modern Europe frequently led to good and true philosophical ideas, while the rigid structure of *mizvoth*, as practiced by the masses, failed to lead to this result.

In the inexorable march of history, Mendelssohn's views were negated by the course of events. The laws could not be maintained in their totality in an emancipated society. Therefore, Judaism had to depend on the merits of its ideas, not on the validity of its regimen of conduct. The ideology of classical Reform grew out of the compulsions of reality, which breached the walls of the Law and presented a mortal challenge to the Jewish faith.

The author's discussion of Frankel's philosophy of Judaism is particularly noteworthy. Frankel believed that the consensus of the community represented a kind of "indirect revelation." "There is a kind of revelation, too, in the general consensus of a community. As long as that invisible revelation keeps pace with the vitality of the religious life of that community and its unity, it is deserving of recognition no less than the direct form of revelation."[17]

This principle, occurring in Islam and Christianity as well as in Judaism, was given special prominence in the Conservative movement for two reasons. First, its principal use in modern times was to sanction the obsolescence of old laws rather than the creation of new *minhagim* ("customs"). Second, it coincided with the growing shift of the flow of Jewish loyalty from the channel of religion to that of nationalism. Frankel was one of the builders of a nationalistic ideology. "The Torah, the people of Israel, and the Holy Land— there is among them a magical unity; they are bound together by unbreakable and invisible bonds."[18]

Frankel was possibly the originator of that peculiar paradox in the soul of Conservative leadership—their distrust of their own judgment and their lack of faith in their own decisions. Thus, Frankel believed that the attempt of Alexandrian Jewry to be at home in both Hellenistic culture and Jewish faith was an abject failure. Yet, he knew that he and his colleagues were more akin in spirit to the Jewish philosophers of Alexandria than to the Pharisaic sages in Palestine; hence, the split personality of some Conservative leaders.

The great scholar Samuel David Luzzatto represented a form of Jewish theology that might be described as a romantic brand of desperate piety. Romantic it was, because its pattern of piety was completely emotional. "What philosophy seeks is the truth; what religion seeks is goodness and righteousness. Man is not altogether Reason, but he is also poetry, and religion was given in order to lead his poetry toward the good and the just."[19] God even employed superstition and falsehood as part of the faith He has given.[20] "Desperate piety" is an apt name for

Luzzatto's theology, for it rested on the psychological reaction of defiance. After ridiculing the "mission-theory" of Reform, he asserted his own faith as follows: "I shall be a Jew that my son shall be a Jew; as my father gave me faith, I shall give faith to my children." Luzzatto's protest against Atticism entered into the stream of Jewish thought. He viewed Judaism as a kind of Jesuit Catholicism, save that it fostered the spirit of nationalism. The dietary laws were a mark of superior dignity, encouraging ethnic pride. The sacrifices were good for the piety of the "masses." Luzzatto reasserted the philosophy of Halevi, but whereas Halevi serenely believed his ideas, Luzzatto shouted them—to silence his own doubts as well as the doubts of his contemporaries.

In every generation, there are strong personalities, favored by narrow loyalties and curious intellectual blind spots, for whom the challenge of religion is presented in the dogmatic form of "all or nothing." For such Jews, the writings of Samson Raphael Hirsch constitute an inexhaustible mine of inspiration. In contrast to Frankel, Hirsch was an individualist, making light of the ideal of community or the "peoplehood" of Israel. Disavowing Jewish nationalism in any modern or secular sense, he described the land of Israel as "a land that consumes its inhabitants," in which it is extremely difficult to live a good or holy life.[21] He, too, accepted a form of revelation, other than the Torah, but for him that Divine teaching was contained in the "inner revelation" of conscience and in the spirit of the age. The Declaration of the Rights of Man during the French Revolution was "one of the hours when God entered into history."[22]

The attitude to *minhagim* of the founder of *Trennungs-Orthodoxie* is most interesting, for he was ready at one time to abolish *Kol Nidre* ("all vows"). Torah, for Hirsch, was not intended to "express religious feeling," but to oppose human feeling. Yet he thought of himself, and with a small measure of justice, as a "Jewish humanist." He pleaded for the full development of the "*Yisroel*-man." God created all things in accordance with their kind, and Torah is the ideal pattern for the Jewish man. The word "Torah" means impregnation, i.e. impregnation with seeds of growth into the fullness of Jewish manhood, "fostering within us the seeds of truth and goodness." Thus, he reintroduced the esthetic element into Judaism, as well as an appreciation of the joy of life. "Our sorry fate overtook us, not because we laughed too much and cried too little in our good days, but because we cried too much and laughed too little.[23] Most interesting is Hirsch's explanation of the prohibition of usury. It was a ritual ceremony, he claimed, intended to remind us of God's sovereignty. Therefore, its limitation to Jews is understandable.

Of all twentieth-century thinkers, Heinemann includes only Franz Rosenzweig in his study. The gulf between Rosenzweig and his predecessors is not made clear by the author. But while all the other Jewish theologians operated with the dogmatic assertion of the Divine dictation of the words of the Torah, Rosenzweig knew and accepted the results of historical criticism. For him, the Torah was Divine in two senses: first, in the sense of being produced by several writers, legislators, and editors in the spirit of Divine love; and second, indeed, pre-eminently, because it proved historically to be an excellent vehicle for the two-way passage of love, from God to man and from man to God. It is in the second sense of revelation that the Holy Scriptures are most effective, and in this sense, it is more true and more relevant to note that the Torah *becomes* God's word, rather than to say that it *is* so automatically. The word of God is not like a ray of light, which impinges upon all surfaces, penetrating only those that are translucent; rather, it is like the flame of an electric arc which comes into being only when both the cathode and the anode are ready. The same verse may be objectively known as the fragment of an ancient myth and subjectively experienced as an instrument of Divine love.

For Rosenzweig, it is not the Law as a whole but so many *mizvoth* that constitute the bridge between man and God. A *mizvah* that no longer functions as a conductor of the Divine may be treated reverently, but it need no longer be observed. It is the positive commands of the Torah that stand out as possible conductors, whereas the negative commands are of value only insofar as they help set the mood for the observance of a positive commandment.

The full meaning of Rosenzweig's thought can be appreciated only in the light of his total philosophy. His comments on detailed observances, especially in *The Star of Redemption,* are of minor significance, since he was then quite unfamiliar with the historic foundation and true impact of Halachah.

The two volumes of Heinemann's *Taamai Hamizvoth* are enriched by copious notes which reflect a vast range of deep and rare scholarship. His work is a magnificent gift on the altar of Jewish learning. *Taro olov berocho*—May he be blessed!

THE NATURE
AND TASK
OF LIBERAL JUDAISM

Pragmatic, all too pragmatic, were the issues and considerations that produced the concatenation of organizations in American Jewish life. In the domain of religion, as in the issues of public relations, the ideologists limped lamely after the managers, producing "philosophies" to order and justifying the ways of politicians to the community.

In view of the rapid growth of American Jewry in the past years, this situation was probably inevitable. But must it be permanent? Must American Jewry in all future generations be confined to the grooves that were cut in the age of transition and confusion? We believe that it is high time for the logic of ideological integrity and inner consistency to assert itself in Jewish life, lest we court the multiple dangers of communal vulgarity and intellectual bankruptcy. Already the sinister symptoms of degeneracy can be seen on all sides. The "managers" are steadily taking over our religious, as well as our philanthropic and communal, institutions. For them, the "success" of whatever organization or campaign they happen to serve ranks as an end in itself. Bluff and propaganda come to take the place of idealism and education. The public is not to be edified but persuaded, intellectuals and ideologists are not to be consulted but manipulated, ideas and ideals are not to be explored and served but exploited and sold by a new class of "spiritual salesmen."

It is idle to blame any one individual or organization for the misuse of power. The whole of Jewish life is today caught in a mad competitive struggle for public support. The "managers" know their trade. It is their business to debase the coinage of thought in order to facilitate the uncritical acceptance of campaigns, but they move to the center of the stage only when the intellectuals have neutralized each other.

This essay is an attempt to reveal and clarify the true lines of division in Jewish ideology, to indicate the organizational consequences of this division, and to call for a course of action that would reinstate the logic of value and purpose in the Jewish community.

Whether we apply the methods of philosophical or psychological analysis to the understanding of the Jewish faith, we arrive at the same basic distinction between fundamentalism and liberalism.

Psychologically, faith is either projection or rejection, a movement toward the infinite or a drawing away from its terrors. It is either man's perpetual submission to the glory of God in openness of soul, or it is man's attempt to shield his soul against the Divine challenge by surrounding himself with the safe walls of dogma and ritual. In its first form, faith is liberal, deriving from the inner life of the soul in its growth; it is an expression of love, courage, and integrity. It is always short of fulfillment, looking into open horizons; it is always a becoming, never a possession. In the second form, faith is a reaction against the fear of the mystery beyond and the depths of one's own being. It is the religion of the "authoritarian" personality, who fears doubt and the dark unknown as the fiendish instruments of the Devil, preferring comfortable and flattering dogmas to the uncertainties and anxieties of real life. It is the attempt to reduce the Divine to possessible dimensions so that it can be signed, sealed, and delivered in perpetuity.

Philosophically, liberalism examines all truth by reference to the living values of man's intelligence and conscience, while fundamentalism relies on an extrahuman source of truth, a book or set of books, an institution or a quasi-magical person.

Liberalism may or may not reject *ethnicism,* but it always

subjects ethnic feelings and aims to moral-rational scrutiny. It clings neither to an ideal past nor to a fancied picture of the ideal future, since its yardstick is the living word of God in the heart of man. Hence, it is neither archaistic nor futuristic in culture and religion, as it is neither reactionary nor revolutionary in social life and politics. The liberal works within history, but he examines all things in the light of suprahistorical principles.

Seeds of both liberalism and fundamentalism are scattered abundantly in our great tradition, so that partisans of both viewpoints may cogently claim to uphold "genuine," or "authentic," or "normative" Judaism. The rich and variegated dialectic of historic Judaism was not forced into rigid molds by the ruthless power of a central authority. Warrant may accordingly be found in it for inclining the balance in one direction or the other.

From the standpoint of inner consistency, Judaism depends ultimately upon one dogma—the assertion of Divine revelation at Sinai, *Torah Mi Sinai*. The medieval theologians may have argued about the number of *Ikkarim* ("Essential Beliefs") and a Moses Mendelssohn, eager to exhibit his faith at its best to his rationalistic friends, may have maintained that Judaism possessed no "dogmas." The fact remains that the entire literature of Torah and the inner logic of the Jewish faith go back ultimately to the one doctrine of Divine Revelation at Sinai.

Divine revelation may be understood either in a fundamentalist or in a nonfundamentalist, universal sense. The logic of fundamentalism is as simple as it is naïve. God dictated the Torah to Moses, who wrote it down like a secretary word for word, except that he used tears instead of ink for the last eight verses. In addition, the Lord taught the entire oral Law to Moses.

This is the essence of fundamentalism; everything else is commentary. In Talmud and Midrash, as well as in Jewish medieval philosophy, there are numerous hints and arguments blurring the sharp outlines of this position and reflecting the genius of a budding rationalism. One rabbi may insist that Moses was given only general rules (*Kelalim*), whereas the oral Law was developed by scribes and sages who applied those rules. Another rabbi may point out that diverse, and even contrary, opinions may be derived "from one shepherd." Still another rabbi won a debate in an academy on the principle that "Torah is not in heaven." Its words may be sacred, but the meaning of these words is for man to expound.

Such attempts to soften the logic of fundamentalism are paralleled in our day by the hesitation of certain scholars to apply the critical-historical methods of research beyond an arbitrary date. Some would begin their historical research with the Mishnah or *Tosefta*. All that occurred before that date was immune to criticism. Others dared to go beyond Rabbi Akiba, but they stopped short at the time of Ezra. In our own day, one may still encounter highly placed "theologians" who prize the historical approach very highly and apply it meticulously to the writings and the prophets, but not to the Pentateuch.

These degrees of consistency are interesting from the psychological viewpoint, but they are logically of no consequence. To the liberal, beliefs must be rooted in the laws of truth implicit in the structure of nature and human nature. When history is studied objectively, there is no more reason to assume that Moses was commanded to exterminate the Canaanites than that Attila was given a Divine mandate to massacre his millions of victims.

A contemporary theologian, who views all things through the rosy haze of romanticism, inquires why it is difficult for moderns to believe that God commanded the laws of *Kashruth,* if they find it easy to assume that the Divine will is reflected in the "still, small voice" of conscience. The answer is that the quest of inner truthfulness is of a human and universal nature. All that is true and good is so for all men. It is in our common humanity that the "image of God" is contained; to listen to His word is not to "hear voices" or to "speak in tongues" but to follow faithfully the inner logic of spiritual growth. It is this yearning for the "purity" of logical thought, to use a term of Hermann Cohen's, that we express in the refusal to set artificial barriers against the outreaching of our mind and heart for the fullness of truth. "The seal of the Holy One, Blessed be He, is truth," or, to put it differently, the Divine word is immanent in the laws of truthfulness. Hence, in examining the claim of the Divine word for *Kashruth*, we recognize, firstly, that it is not valid by any human or universal standards; secondly, we take into consideration all that we know about the food tabus of the ancient world. Our conclusion is inescapable: whatever validity *Kashruth* may have is of a private or subjective nature, as will soon be explained.

Fundamentalists regard belief as an expression of virtue. Dogmas constitute their protection against the inner unconscious world, which they distrust, and the outer world, which they fear. The more difficult it is to believe this or that dogma, the more meritorious it is to assert its truth. One recalls the adventures of Alice, in *Alice in Wonderland,* who found it "difficult to believe" the age of the queen. Alice was shown how to overcome her scruples. She was to close her eyes, bow her head, "take a deep breath and believe." That method works wonders.

Liberalism reflects the "sparks of holiness" inherent in life itself. It begins with the promptings of one's own heart and mind, not with a book or set of books. And it challenges each person to discover the meaning of the Divine image in his own soul. Since human nature is one, both at its highest and at its lowest reaches, we discover within ourselves a threefold yearning —the quest for truth, even if it hurts; the aspiration to make the fullness of our being count for good in the manifold pathways of life; the longing for self-inclusion within the resonance of Divine harmony.

It is the third aspect of man's spiritual life that is most complex and elusive. It has been described in many ways, each "true" to one or more of its shimmering surfaces. Thus, philosophers spoke of the apprehension of the beautiful, of the feeling of dependence, of the experience of holiness, of the sense of a *mysterium tremendum,* compounded of awe and sublimity and a whole-souled listening, of a personalized "I-thou" relation between man

557

and God. The latest vocabulary of this genre contains such phrases as cosmic anxiety, the category of paradox, the predicament of man, and the so-called dimension of depth.

These poetical rhapsodies may be overextended in either of two directions. If the individualistic strain is continued, the exotic domain of mysticism is reached, with its deep valleys of "the dark night of the soul" and its lofty peaks of "ineffable" ecstasies. If the social phase of the search for harmony is developed, its implications for man's "rootedness" and "sense of belonging" in society are uncovered. It then becomes easy enough to draw the veil of romantic haze over all that belongs to one's ethnic or cultural group and to wrap a mantle of holiness over all that is characteristic of the group. In primitive religion, as Lévy-Bruhl and Durkheim have shown, ethnicism, ritualism, and faith are virtually identical. And the primitive mentality is ever ready to reassert itself.

There is one essential difference between the yearning of the soul for harmony and the quest for truth and goodness. In seeking truth, we eliminate ourselves altogether from the equations of experience, adopting a perfectly objective attitude. Any deviation from the claims of objectivity is a source of error. In reaching for goodness, we place our subjective being within the overarching dome of objectivity, but we do not eliminate our self from the formulas of ethics. On the contrary, to make the most of our lives for the good of society is the central purpose of ethics. Thus, our subjective interests and concerns are embraced and transformed, but not negated, in the majestic domain of ethical laws.

The quest for harmony appears to be totally subjective. In it, the yearning of the individual for the fullness of meaning, value, and purpose is the core of experience. The quality of objectivity is by no means lacking. In the appreciation of the beautiful, personal interests are entirely irrelevant, as Kant pointed out. Yet, the esthetic element is only the outer radiance of the quest of the soul to be taken up and carried in the universal harmony of creation. The essence of the experience is so deeply personal that one finds it necessary to shut out the outside world in order

558

to heed the promptings of the soul. The individual, in his "loneliness," in his "anxiety," in his awareness of his "sinfulness," in his consciousness of being stripped of all "protective measures" built up by society against the vastness of the enveloping darkness, discovers that "call" which is the nuclear experience of personal religion.

Thus, a liberal faith is sorely incomplete if it fails to allow for the role of subjectivity in human life. Liberal Judaism differs from unattached and uncommitted liberalism in that it embraces the subjective life and tradition of the Jewish community. Recognizing the double phase of human life, we know that we are not true to the fullness of our being unless we learn to live in both the objective and subjective worlds. The life of spirit is not a static relationship, but perpetual movement, in which attention moves from the universal to the particular and back again, from the objective to the subjective and back again. To live meaningfully is to live in this state of alternation, whereby the subjective sense of worth is examined objectively and the principles of the objective world are bathed in the glow of intense subjective experience.

The subjective-objective paradox is man's opportunity for greatness and also the bane of his attempt to scale the ladder of culture and religion. The opportunity for spiritual growth arises out of the constant tension and alternation of viewpoint, while the danger of stagnation and frustration consists in the temptation to identify oneself completely with either one or the other phase of spiritual life.

The devotees of reason, who ruthlessly scorn all that is private, mystery-laden, and holy, are the Jacobins of history. And the victims of their zeal were manifold. Since the subjective world cannot be eliminated from human experience, any pretense to do so ends in the representation of purely subjective drives as the flawless principles of the goddess reason.

On the other hand, the more usual tendency is to seek the comforting shadows of subjectivity and to render only lip service to objective considerations. Most people even today are still dwellers in ancestral caves, hanging out the banners of objective idealism at the entrance for the benefit of others. It is difficult to live in the two worlds of objective criticism and subjective patterns of life. Yet, this is our human destiny.

The mind of man is like the restless surface of the mighty deep. It might seek for truth by calming the waves, stilling even the laughing ripples in the dawn, in order to reflect more truly the blue of the heavens. Or it can turn inward, seeking full identification with the core of being by descending to the dark depths of its own self. Both ways are phases of the total truth. The two procedures are opposites, but not contradictory, for the fullness of truth is many-sided.

In liberal Judaism, we are bidden to maintain taut and vibrant the strings of the spiritual life, the one end of which is derived from our total commitment to our sacred tradition and the other end of which is directed toward the universal ideals of mankind. But the two directions of our spiritual life are not to be kept apart, for the human mind is one. Each way of seeing truth must be balanced, corrected, and supplemented by the other way.

Liberal Judaism may come in diverse forms. If it be granted that the life of the spirit requires the tension between subjective and objective attitudes, there are several ways in which this synthesis may be achieved.

We may accept the entire Halachah, as it has come down to us from the past, *as if* it were literally valid and Divinely revealed. This acceptance of the total pattern of religious life as the subjective home of one's spiritual existence by no means precludes the truths of objectivity. The sacred tradition is employed as the *collective text* of Jewish spiritual life. The same text may inspire an infinity of sermons. We set ourselves consciously to utilize our tradition as the vantage point for the comprehension of life, knowing full well that an element of arbitrariness enters into our resolve. Once the choice is made on behalf of identification with the Jewish tradition, we may assert that the inner logic of that tradition must be allowed to hold sway; hence, the observance of the Halachah, in its totality and in keeping with its own inherent genius. Such is the possible theology of a liberal Orthodoxy, or better, to avoid confusion, liberal Traditionalism. The absolute openness of mind and heart that is liberalism is in this movement supplemented by subjective adherence to the firm and unchanging canons of the Law.

Another synthesis of the two directions of the spiritual life is liberal Conservatism. Like Traditionalism, it accepts the binding character of Halachah, but it insists on continuing the process of Halachah legislation so that the standards and practices of modern Judaism might correspond to the ideals and needs of our contemporary world. Liberal Conservatism, like Traditionalism, accepts Halachah on the basis of *as if*, but it draws practical inferences from this conditional status of the Law. Within Halachah, it recognizes the stream of ideals and motivations which may be designated as *taamai hamizvoth* ("reasons for the Commandments"), and it maintains that the ideals behind the Law are subject to revision in the light of the universal principles of the objective world; hence, a liberal Conservatism, liberal in thought, conservative, not orthodox, in ritual practice.

Reform constitutes yet another synthesis of objective truth and subjective collective tradition. The element of subjective submission to the guidance of our historic tradition is not lacking in Reform, as the universalist spirit is not lacking in Conservatism.

But Reform denies the worth of *laws* governing the domain of religious life. It accentuates the value of "customs and ceremonies," and in all likelihood, it will in the future be positively disposed toward the formulation and acceptance of *standards* of Jewish observance. Reform, too, accepts the *as if* of the religious tradition of Judaism, though in its own selective way; otherwise it would be universalism.

Not all who are Reform presumably share in the liberal spirit, even as only a goodly fraction of the Conservative and modern Orthodox rabbinates subscribes to the liberal approach. While the impetus of religious dogma counteracts liberalism in the latter groups, resurgent ethnicism and fear of offending popular prejudice keep the genius of liberalism enchained within the camp of Reform. In modern history, the subjective perversions of ethnicism proved far more potent obstacles to overcome than the patterns of religious belief and practice.

In any case, Jewish liberalism presents an inner unity of thought and purpose within a threefold pattern of religious practice and ritual. While the maintenance of national organizations for the promotion of these diverse expressions of liberal Judaism is important, *there is need of an all-embracing Conference of Rabbis and Scholars for the cultivation of the core of liberal thought.* In relation to many significant issues in Jewish life, this awareness of unity on the part of all liberals could prove to be the decisive factor.

In terms of external rites and observances, the façade of unity among Reform, Conservative, and Traditionalist congregations is becoming steadily more apparent. But this creeping process of equalization is frequently the result of the progressive erosion of all convictions and is devoid of the fervor and nobility of ideology. We argue here for the continuance of diversity in ritual and for the emergence of a *common ideological platform of liberal Judaism,* which would deal with the major issues of the Jewish world—the status of the community itself, the task of winning the battle for Judaism on the fringes of the community, the promulgation of a liberal faith in Israel and throughout the world.

What are the Jews of America to think of themselves? Are they a national or ethnic minority, on the one hand, like the Negroes and the slowly disintegrating colonies of European immigrants, or are they a religious community? This question has been virtually settled by the progressive crystallization of sentiment in recent years. It can hardly be challenged that American Jews have come to regard themselves as a religious community, belonging to the warp and woof of the American nation.

Yet this emerging consciousness of American Jewry is even now counteracted by several forces. We can afford to ignore such quaint rationalizations of vestigial Zionist sentiments as those of Ben Halpern, who substitutes ethnic zealotry for the Jewish faith and the commandment to cultivate "a sense of alienism" in American Jews for all the commandments of our sacred tradition. The bankruptcy of intellectualized ethnicism is now virtually complete.

The menace to Jewish status derives today from the non-intellectual dead weight of organizational vested interests.

Organizations are to ideologies as bodies are to souls. Their very structure and day-by-day functioning represents a concrete philosophy, which speaks louder than the propaganda of the "managers" or the "ghostwritten" addresses of the figureheads.

The Jewish federations and welfare funds do not as a rule act as if they represented the interests and concerns of a religious community. Not because they represent a contrary or opposing philosophy—they do not. But the paralysis of the religious leadership in America has been such as to leave an empty field for faceless, purposeless, managerial activity. Failure to express in organizational terms a valid philosophy of Jewish life means in practice the acceptance of a nonideological separatist mentality—the mentality of a "self-segregating minority." While minorities generally may not be liked, a self-segregating minority is positively hated.

Compare the budget and structure of the Jewish philanthropic organization with those of any other religious community in the United States, and the difference will strike you between the eyes! It is not a difference that anyone willed—all pilpulistic casuistry about "Jewish uniqueness" notwithstanding. Our budgets are pitifully short on matters that are supposed to represent our *raison d'être*, and they are immensely weighted in favor of the elements that we are supposed to share with our non-Jewish neighbors. Our communal structure, such as it is, is in fact that of a self-segregating racial minority, though the leaders of nearly all communities sincerely disavow any such status. A Jewish community, empty of purpose and devoid of a philosophy of life, is in fact defined by its own least common denominator—namely, its ethnic heritage. This heritage is not, among Jewish people, a natural burden; it is willfully re-created in every generation. If the wine has evaporated from the barrel, the yeast remains.

The American Jewish community would never have assumed its faceless posture if our religious leadership had not become hopelessly fragmentized. The organization of the Jewish community will acquire meaning and purpose only if a realignment should take place, bringing all liberal forces together. When the lines are drawn between fundamentalism, on the one hand, and liberalism, in its diverse forms, on the other hand, the preponderance of the progressive elements will become obvious. Inevitably and by degrees, the organization of the Jewish community will be transformed in keeping with the philosophy of liberalism. The same individuals now control the federations and the congregations; yet, these same people present on one board the facelessness of a vestigial "minority," on the other, the ideology of a religious community. As long as the community is hopelessly fragmentized into groups, which cannot speak for the majority, this result is inevitable. A realignment on the basis of liberalism would lead to the emergence of either one community endowed with purpose and worth or, at worst, two communities, each cognizant of its philosophy and program.

The crucial fact is the absence of any secularist ideology in American Jewish life, and the paradoxical circumstance that in its central organizations, the Jewish community is secularist by default in spite of occasional anguished and sincere protestations.

As to the intellectual spokesmen of liberal Judaism, we witness today a "failure of nerve," a fear of resisting popular prejudice, and an eagerness to mouth the platitudes of the age—a state of affairs that was almost unthinkable a generation ago. The liberal faith is on the decline because of disorganization and disunity. Even prophets can make themselves heard only in a society of "sons of prophets."

From the standpoint of liberal Judaism, the many Jewish liberals, who are identified neither in theory nor in practice with the religious tradition of Judaism, constitute a major challenge. There is nothing to be gained by the setting up of a category of "secularists" within the religious community of Judaism, save the compounding of confusion. Those who are Jews by birth and religiously uncommitted belong to the vast marginal domain of the Jewish community. While fundamentalist Judaism may appeal to them, in whole or in part, liberal Judaism in its diverse manifestations is primarily challenged to win them over. But until they are won over to one or another form of the Jewish faith, they form one of the many marginal bands that are so characteristic of every free society.

No statistics are presently available as to the number of "lax" and "lapsed" Jews. In a recent survey concluded by the Catholic Church in several metropolitan centers, it was found that the number of "lapsed" Catholics, i.e. those who ignore altogether the services of the Church, reached the amazing proportion of 30 per cent of the registered Catholics. If the percentage of "lapsed" Jews is equally high, we can recognize the immensity of the challenge that liberal Judaism faces. Our first task, it would seem, is to dig up the relevant facts in every community and to devise a program to meet it. This task is properly the responsibility of liberal Judaism as a whole, not of any one of its three denominational organizations.

A vast marginal group of the Jewish community has come to public notice only recently. I refer to the intermarried couples that live in semi-anonymity in every great metropolitan center. In a survey of the Jewish community of Washington, D.C., the number of homes in which an unconverted Christian formed part of the family was found to be between thirty-three hundred and four thousand. In the case of roughly one-third of this number, the wife was Jewish and the husband Christian. In nearly every case, the provision made by the family for the religious education of their children was pitiful.

These couples constitute the peculiar responsibility of liberal Judaism, since the fundamentalists have no message for these people. They can cite the Law and list the dire punishments therein enumerated; but they cannot bring a sense of mutual respect, a glow of dignity and rightness, a feeling of belonging to the advancing current of humanity, a way of seeing their family life against the background of the past and the perspectives of the future.

Jewish fundamentalists and rabid ethnicists can bring to an

intermarried couple only bitterness and resentment. To a funda-mentalist, another faith is an abomination (*avodah zarah*); to a zealous racialist, intermarriage is the ultimate crime. Only liberal Jews can bring to an intermarried couple a message of self-acceptance based on genuine feelings of mutual reverence. From the liberal standpoint, the core of faith is the same in all forms of enlightened religion. Hence, devotees of different religions need not confront each other with the implacable choice of *either* one religion or the other. They can view their own faith and that of their marriage partner in the spirit of "mine *and* thine."

To the Jewish member of the marriage, liberal Judaism can bring an interpretation that represents the Jew as an integral member of Western society and Judaism as a creative element in Western civilization. The Jew could learn to accept his heri-tage as one of the most important sources of enlightened religion and modern culture. The non-Jewish partner could simulta-neously learn to accept the Jewish memories and loyalties of the Jewish partner as positive aids to the creation of an atmo-sphere of religious dedication in their home. Similarly, the Jewish partner could learn to recognize the essence of his liberal faith in the religious heritage of his non-Jewish partner. The children could learn to acquire a *positive* attitude to *both* religious tradi-tions of their parents. When they reach adulthood, they will choose to identify themselves with one or the other religious community. Whatever their choice, they will possess a warm appreciation of the Jewish faith. On their pilgrimage through life, they will be sustained by a sense of wholehearted identi-fication with *both* religious traditions of their parents. Perhaps, too, they will recognize themselves to be peculiarly suited for the role of overcoming the multiple barriers of hate and prejudice that still plague our society.

At the present time, this vast marginal group of possibly half a million people is totally neglected by the Jewish commu-nity. Here is a task of vast proportions for liberal Judaism to undertake.

Several spokesmen of Conservatism and Reform have expressed the opinion that there was no room in Israel for their brand of Judaism. On the other hand, both the Rabbinical Assembly and the Central Conference of American Rabbis are eager to establish branches of their respective movements in Israel. The Central Conference invited the Rabbinical Assembly to join it in the sponsorship of a non-Orthodox religious movement in Israel.

Here, at long last, is a healthy approach. Both Reform and Conservatism arose in response to two challenges—the challenge of reinterpretation and reconstruction made necessary by the genius of liberalism and the challenge of adaptation to the peculiar strains and stresses of American life. Insofar as either the Reform or the Conservative pattern represents the *tactics of adaptation,* Israeli society can hardly benefit from its examples. Insofar as these movements represent *a synthesis of the liberal philosophy and the tradition of Judaism,* they constitute a peculiar challenge to the liberal-minded people of Israel.

It follows that not only in the State of Israel but throughout the Jewish Diaspora, the Reform and Conservative movements should work together as bearers of Jewish liberalism. The need of winning Israeli youth away from nihilism and materialism is now generally recognized, but this need can be met only if Reform, Conservative, and Traditionalist leaders can bring themselves to shift emphasis away from *adaptationist tactics* and toward the core of *religious liberalism* in their respective movements.

Outside of the State of Israel, the countries of Latin America and Western Europe constitute a vast challenge for liberal Judaism. The fundamentalists in all these countries have won the allegiance of only a tiny fraction of the Jewish people. Throughout the Western world, there is a hunger for a rational faith. Thus far only crumbs have been supplied to them from the table of American Jewry.

Even in Soviet Russia, liberal Judaism may yet strike firm roots. The hopes of humanity today rest on a progressive diminution of the gulf between the Soviet people and the Western world. If such a process of mutual tolerance should one day be started and the iron curtain be lifted, then liberal Judaism will face an immense opportunity in the Soviet world. The remnants of Orthodoxy in Russia today have high visibility, especially for tourists, but they consist only of aged "fossils," dating from prerevolutionary days. Neither Orthodoxy nor Zionism has a message of worth and dignity for the two generations of Soviet Jews that desire to remain in their native country. On the other hand, liberal Judaism is an authentic product of the Western world, thoroughly attuned to the genius of science and fully in accord with the noblest reaches of the modern spirit. To the extent to which Soviet Russia returns to the West, liberal Judaism will face the opportunity of regaining the allegiance of its Russian brethren.

In sum, the great need in Jewish life today is the consolidation of all liberal forces. The core of our liberal faith, a synthesis of objective truth with the subjective loyalties and symbols of our sacred tradition, is the same within the Reform, the Conservative, and the Traditionalist groups. However, within each group, as presently constituted, the liberal elements are frustrated and frequently confused by the momentum of the past, the "pragmatic" considerations of short-sighted leaders, and the willful maneuvers of the managers of organizational vested interests.

Great are the tasks of a resurgent Jewish liberalism in awakening the spirit of prophetic fervor, in lending status and dignity to the Jewish community, in winning over marginal elements, in undertaking a nationwide and worldwide movement for liberal Judaism.

To this end, a way must be found for the formation of a Conference of Liberal Rabbis and Scholars, which would include all spokesmen for nonfundamentalist Judaism.

ASSIMILATION, INTEGRATION, SEGREGATION:
*The Road to the Future**

In our fast-moving world one must be inordinately clairvoyant or narrowly fanatical to risk any predictions concerning the future. The Jewish situation anywhere in the world is always sensitive to a variety of social pressures and to the shifting winds of the spiritual climate. There is scarcely a social phenomenon on the international scene that does not in some way affect the balance of forces determining the status and hopes of world Jewry. On any rational basis, it is possible for us to take account of presently visible factors only and to admit that all our conclusions are tentative, for if the past is any indication of the future, the even course of human events is likely to be interrupted by treacherous curves and hairpin turns.

If there is one prediction that we may hazard concerning the future of American Jewry, it is negative in character. We may assume with little fear of contradiction that the American Jewish community will not be monolithic, culturally or religiously, or even of relatively uniform texture. The free atmosphere of America makes it possible for any group of Jewish people, however small, to cultivate its own ideology and to build up institutions devoted to its perpetuation. Nor must we forget that ideologies are in the final analysis reflections of certain temperaments or character configurations, so that any way of thinking or living that is socially effective is probably embraced in response to certain psychic needs. The three major interpretations of the Jewish faith—Orthodoxy, Conservatism, and Reform—have endured long enough for us to recognize that they correspond in

*Reprinted from Judaism, 1959

many instances to specific character types. It is not difficult to discover the springs of character and blocks of experience that make for a militant Jewish nationalism, on the one hand, or a hysterically precipitous assimilationism, on the other hand.

But while American society allows for the profusion of variety in marginal areas and fringe situations, it also favors the emergence and dominance of certain standard types. A massive mainstream flows mightily in the center, while many interesting eddies form along the uneven banks. All students of American society, from Tocqueville to Commager, concur in the recognition of a distinctively American character and of a widely pervasive pressure to conform to that type. Assuming a similar development in the case of the Jewish community, we can foresee the eventual dominance of certain Jewish types and attitudes. While all kinds of exotic combinations may continue to flourish on the sidelines, the standard Jewish personality of the future is even now being fashioned by the intangible realities of American society.

By the standard Jew we mean not the typical Jew, who represents the statistical average of all measurable qualities, but the personality pattern that the typical Jew seeks to approximate. The community, in all its institutions and in its multifarious dynamism, is nothing but the shadow of the standard Jew, reflecting the contours of his values and the play of loyalties within his personality.

In this essay, I propose to show, first, that the dominant Jewish personality of the future will identify himself more intimately with the American people than Jews have ever before succeeded in doing; second, that this development is likely to eventuate in the paradoxical situation where both the currents away from and toward Judaism will be immensely accelerated; third, that in the foreseeable future Jewish faith and culture will attain unprecedented heights of achievement even as the floodwaters of assimilation rise menacingly.

To appreciate the play of forces within the Jewish community, we have to accord due weight to its comparative youthfulness.

While twenty-three Jews landed in New Amsterdam three hundred years ago, the vast majority of American Jews are sons and daughters of recent immigrants. With a total population of only a quarter million in 1880, when the mass migration of Russian Jews was begun, we may readily calculate that only 10 per cent of our community can claim a residence of more than two generations. To be sure, the minority of early settlers did enjoy the hegemony of leadership down to the first half of the twentieth century by reason of its superior wealth and culture. But only the lingering remnants of this predominance are in evidence today, with the policies of the Jewish community reflecting ever more clearly the sentiments and convictions of the descendants of the East European immigrants. Here and there, especially in philanthropic circles, the impetus of the older type of leadership is still felt, but in the community as a whole, the prevailing spirit is that of a human mass that has but recently come into its own.

In every domain of activity within the Jewish community, traditions are still fluid and uncertain. In the sphere of religion, the Orthodox leaders are most painfully aware that their adherents have not yet fully absorbed the total impact of the American environment. Their greatest authorities are men who think and speak in Yiddish; their typical institutions are conceived in the ambition to slow down the ponderous processes of acculturation; their typical followers are still the men and women of the "old country" or their immediate descendants. The Conservative movement owes its very existence to the conviction that American Judaism is only now beginning to emerge; hence, its avid search for new patterns, its bold experimentalism, and its faith in the creative genius of the people. The Reform movement of today turns its back upon its own classical traditions in its eagerness to keep abreast of the surging currents in Jewish life.

In the community generally, there is hardly any activity that is not secretly questioned even by its most ardent supporters. The rising generation of community leaders is beginning to rethink first principles. Does the settlement-house kind of activity still make sense? Is a community center dedicated to the cultivation of "Jewish culture," apart from religion, either necessary or desirable in the ideal American community? What are the reasons for the investment of huge sums in "Jewish hospitals"? Would not the Jewish medical practitioner be better served if Jewish wealth were given in equally generous measure to the great general and university hospitals in every large city?

These and similar questions being raised ever more insistently in community forums throughout the nation are indicative of a soul-searching that is long overdue. In the past quarter century, the needs of Jews abroad were so overwhelming in scope and urgency that little attention and energy were left for the consideration of basic issues at home. Federations and welfare funds are scarcely one generation old, and they are still largely non-ideological mechanical fund-raising devices, held in line by the pull of the purse strings, the deft manipulation of professional managers, and the avidity of the *nouveaux riche* for the approval of the older financial aristocracy. Any way you look at it, the American Jewish community is still young, and its future shape undetermined.

Two approaches are available to us as we seek to comprehend the inner dynamism of the emergent Jewish community. We may begin with a definition of the Jewish people and descend to an understanding of the situation of its American portion, arriving ultimately at a representation of the individuals making up the chain of Jewish communities. In this path, we shall be dealing with controversial abstractions, long before we come to grips with reality, and face the danger of losing our way in such endless disputes as those raging round the following questions: What are we—a race, a nation, a religion, a "*kith*," a "unique" blend of many elements, a "freak of history," a "civilizational fossil"? And what is the legitimate goal of our group *vis-à-vis* the general community? Is it integration or assimilation? Or is it, perchance, a synthesis of cultural pluralism and global ethnicism?

The second approach is simpler by far and, in keeping with

the inductive method of science, proceeds from the particular to the universal. We begin with the Jewish individual and then proceed to determine which loyalties and ideals, institutions and practices are likely to serve the growth of his personality, and which entanglements cannot but enchain him in a maze of contradictions and confusions. This approach is, moreover, in consonance with the emphasis on the worth of the individual, which was first projected into world affairs during the Renaissance, and which achieved its greatest triumphs here in the United States. If there is one quality of thought or sentiment that is "characteristically American," it is precisely this insistence on seeing all things from the standpoint of the individual. As Professor Ralph Perry put it in his brilliant study of the American mind:

"At the same time there has emerged from all this variety of impacts a characteristic American response—a selective response which tries all things but assimilates or rejects; a resultant of many causes, which itself acts as a cause.

"The latest misleading name for this selective response, this American bias, is "collective individualism"! The term individualism signifies the irreducible reality, the genuine causal efficacy and the ultimate worth of the individual. . . . Collective individualism is the conscious philosophy, or fundamental belief, or unconscious presupposition, which credits such individuals, whether in competition or in concert, with a power to modify their environment and subject it to their ends; which endorses their claim to be masters and beneficiaries of social institutions; and which credits them with a hand in the making of history."[1]

We may expect, therefore, that the continuous pressure of American civilization will result in an increasing emphasis on the values of the Jewish individual. Indeed, this impact of the American vision happens to coincide in direction, if not in content, with the two most important movements in the history of modern Jewry—the emancipation and Herzlian Zionism. It was the chief ambition of the architects of Jewish emancipation to break down the isolation of the Jewish groups and to project the individual as the agent responsible both for the Jewish destiny and the Jewish faith. This ambition was perhaps best phrased in the famous slogan of Clermont-Tonnerre, "To the Jews as individuals, everything; to the Jews as a nation, nothing." Whereas during the Middle Ages the Jews constituted a community, dealing with the powers that were on a group basis, the emancipation aimed at the abolition of any lingering traces of a Jewish "nation within a nation" so that the individual could stand or fall on his own merits. The inner acceptance of this philosophy was embraced in the ideology of classical Reform.

Herzlian Zionism, too, was a rebellion against the "uniqueness" of the Jewish status, resulting from the presumed failure of the emancipation. Only in a land of their own would Jews be completely free to be simply individuals, picking and choosing out of their heritage, and out of European culture generally, whatsoever might appeal to them, without feeling themselves any longer dogged by the pursuing shadow of the collective fate. Furthermore, Herzl and several of his associates argued that if Zionism draws away from European lands those who desire to preserve their Jewish national identity, the path of perfect assimilation will be made smoother for those who choose to stay in the Diaspora. Thus, the "uniqueness" of the Jewish collective identity will be dissipated. Some Jews will become members of a "nation like other nations"; the rest of Jewry will no longer feel restrained from becoming in good conscience nationals of the land of their birth, Jewish Germans, Jewish Frenchmen, and so on. In either case they will be free men and women. It was Herzl's ardent ambition to liberate the Jewish individual in Palestine, as well as in the Diaspora, from the crushing shadow of a "unique" form of group existence. In his vision of the "Old-New Land," there was to be no unitary Jewish culture, not even one prevailing language, but a heterogenous mass of many different individuals using a variety of languages and representing diverse national cultures, each finding a hospitable haven for the fullest assertion of his individuality.

Ahad Ha'am, living in the midst of a community that had not yet tasted the sweetness of the dream of assimilation and had not felt the subsequent bitterness, could only note the negative aspects of Herzl's vision; hence, his scathing critique of Herzl's book. The Russian Jews of Ahad Ha'am's generation could hardly have been expected to appreciate the poignant pathos of Herzl's yearning for the consumation of the individual's freedom. There can be no doubt, however, that Herzl's, not Ahad Ha'am's, milieu and experience correspond more closely to the mental and social atmosphere of the American Jew.

Here, the emancipation is a far more potent reality than anywhere in Herzl's Europe. Here, even the occasional failures of the promise of emancipation can not negate the dream itself, for the emancipation is to us not a revolution but an axiom of American civilization. Thus, the impetus of Jewish life and American culture combine to put the Jewish individual in the forefront, rather than the status of the group. There does not exist one basic instrument for identification with the Jewish group, though the synagogue is rapidly becoming such a unit, especially in the smaller communities and in Jewish suburbia. Every synagogue is free to reflect the ideas and sentiments of its members. The individual is the focus of all values; affiliation with Judaism is entirely voluntary and undetermined both in degree and in kind.

Self-evident as this approach may seem, we must linger a little at this point in order to deal with the objection that the group and not the individual is primary in matters of culture. The implications of an individualistic approach are indeed revolutionary, and it may well be urged that by beginning with the individual, we do not take account of the "uniqueness" of the group, in all its mystical depth, and thereby do violence to its nature.

Let us concede then at the outset that all forms of culture are group phenomena. But let us also bear in mind that all advances in culture or religion were occasioned by individuals

575

who successfully resisted the spell of group culture. For our purposes, we may define culture as the way people live, feel, and think, aspire and dream, and the way in which they articulate their inner life. In history, culture comes in plural and particularistic forms, as the cultures or subcultures of certain tribes, ethnic groups, nations, and races at different epochs in their development. Every individual is born and raised in a specific culture and even subculture, his personality being molded by the ideas and practices prevailing within the "closed society" of which he is part. But the growth of the individual and of the culture itself is achieved necessarily by resistance to the pressure of the "closed society," whether this advance consists in the promulgation of more universal values than those of the limited group, or whether it consists of the deepening of the inherent values of the "closed society." Invariably the exponents of each culture at its best constitute a small "creative minority" within it, to use a phrase of Toynbee's, or "the remnant that returns," to use an expression of Isaiah's. Only when a group is devoid of power to control its own destiny does it sometimes appear that the "creative minority" represents the entire group, since in that case the artistic and literary production of the elite constitute the only expressions of the life of the collective body. In brief, culture is of the group, but creativity in culture is of the individual.

Since we are concerned with the emergence of the standard American Jewish personality, we deal not with a static cultural situation but with the dynamic play of forces at the intersection of diverse cultures and ethnic loyalties. To appraise affairs fundamentally, we have to begin with rock-bottom reality, the mass of Jewish individuals seeking happiness and fulfillment. For us, the spiritual growth of the Jewish individual and his well-being constitute together the measure of all things. Everything else is superstructure that is all too often compounded of the debris of hollow clichés and outdated slogans. The individual is the one firm focus by reference to which all claims of a material or spiritual nature are to be judged. "The Sabbath is given over to you, not you to the Sabbath."[2]

To allow for the progressive emergence of the empirical individual is to envision the future Jewish community as consisting of Jewish Americans, not American Jews. Abstract and subtle as this distinction may appear to be, the fundamental issues of Jewish life hinge upon it. Although it has become fashionable in our day to ignore the subtleties of classical logic, it is nevertheless true that people assume the genus and differentia of definitions in all their thinking and even in their everyday speech. Talk to any thoughtful Jew regarding the shape of the future, and back of his earnest soul-searching you will encounter the question, What am I essentially—a Jew or an American? He knows that both designations apply to him, but he desires to know whether in the domain of civil and public affairs he *is* the one or the other, automatically, as it were, apart from any volition or action on his part. Compliance with the law of the land is never in question among our people, but there is considerable confusion regarding the ultimate source out of which our loyalties, sentiments, and judgments spring into being. All American Zionists agree that our people owe "political loyalty" to America alone, but some of our people sometimes stress the adjective "political" as if it bore the connotations ephemeral and superficial. Still unresolved for many people is the feeling of fraternal unity, the sense of mine and thine, the awareness of one's identity. It is this core of identity, underlying all loyalties, that is basically in question whenever we discuss the shape of the future.

Generally, it is the realm of discourse that determines when any particular quality becomes substantive or adjectival. Thus, when the affairs of this world are in question, we speak of Methodist or Episcopalian or agnostic or fundamentalist Americans. If we move in the theological realm of dogmas, beliefs, and practices, then we may contrast American Protestants with British Protestants. The separation of Church and State became possible when religious differences were recognized to be matters of private conscience, relatively unimportant to the actual struggle of national or territorial groups for "a place in the sun." Thus, in the modern world, geographical and national bonds become substantive, with religious affiliations being recognized as adjectival in character. If the same situation is presumed to apply to Jews, then we may conclude that in all matters relating to the struggle of nations, we are on the way to becoming Jewish Americans.

Our point may be clarified by the following analogy. We may think of people as being subject to both horizontal loyalties, relating them to their fellow men, and vertical loyalties, relating them to universal human ideals. There is always tension and sometimes conflict between different horizontal loyalties, but none between horizontal and vertical loyalties. Of course, vertical ideals may lead indirectly to horizontal loyalties, but then they are subject to many qualifications, varying in accord with the intellectual climate prevailing in different parts of the world. Thus, Christians of one or another denomination, because of their loyalty to their faith, may establish a "mission" in a specific portion of the globe, acquiring, in a remote people, horizontal friendly interests that derive ultimately from a vertical, heaven-directed loyalty.

If now we allow for the increasing emphasis on individualism to run its course, we cannot see any reason for believing that the Jew will hold on to those horizontal loyalties that the rest of the American people have discarded. His vertical loyalties to Judaism will cause him to entertain horizontal loyalties to the bearers of Judaism wherever they may be, but such loyalties will be variable quantities, dependent upon many factors. There are probably three million Jews in Soviet Russia and in its satellites, men and women who are closer to us, in point of ethnic kinship and cultural background, than any other branch of world Jewry. But in terms of faith and political realities, the bonds between them and us are becoming ever more tenuous. Hence, looking into the future, we cannot but envisage the virtually complete severance of these bonds. On the other hand, the brown Jews of North Africa and the black Jews of Africa and Asia, much as they differ from us in race, are likely to be the objects of our enduring concern. If our hopes for the revival of Judaism in Israel are fulfilled, American Jews of the future will look to Israel as their spiritual center. If, on the other hand, the "Canaanite" mentality should gain ascendancy in the land of Israel, the bonds of loyalty between them and our children will become vestigial and minimal.

Basically, we assume that in the future American Jews will come to enjoy in their own mind and heart that status which the nineteenth-century Jews of Germany and France strove to achieve with might and main. It was a pathetic and stultifying experience for our people to imagine that they could become overnight Germans or Frenchmen "of the Mosaic faith." The term "German" or "French" included a profound strand of meaning which Jews could never make their own. They could become the best of all possible citizens, but they could not become part of those mystical biological entities that the European nations thought they were.

Between the state, as a political entity, and the nation, as a biological phenomenon, there flows unevenly the stream of cultural tradition, now swelling into a mighty tide, now ebbing into a shallow mud flat. But identifying themselves wholeheartedly with this cultural stream, the European Jews believed that they could ignore the bedrock of popular biology. However, the course of events in certain countries, though not in all the lands of Europe, proved them to be wrong. Modern nationalism became infected with the virus of biological romanticism ever more deeply, with catastrophic results for Jewish hopes on the European continent, save in England, France, the Low Countries, the Scandinavian countries, and Italy.

In contrast to the European situation, the term "American" does not contain any specific biological connotations, nor is it likely to acquire them in the foreseeable future. It is in the full light of history that the American people is emerging, and Jews have always been part of it. Hence, the ideal of Americanism cannot be so defined as to exclude Jewish Americans, and it is this ideal that carries potentially the greatest momentum. Of course, there is the term "Gentile," the last holdout of the under world of prejudice, but it is so vacuous and all-inclusive a word as to be devoid of any serious possibilities for romantic aggrandizement. Only the imagination of a maniac could concoct out of the qualities of all nations on earth a unique Aryan essence that is presumably lacking among Jews. The "national origin" immigration laws were not ethnically exclusive in nature. Their aim was not the attainment of racial purity but rather the maintenance of racial balance. Although they were until recently discriminatory, these laws reflect the implicit recognition of the rights of all groups, albeit in the heavy-handed, rough-and-ready way of demagogues and of the untutored masses that follow them. Of decisive importance is the fact that the term "American" cannot serve the foul purposes of ethnic anti-Semitism.

Hence, it is altogether possible for the American Jew to achieve that fullness of integration with "the people of the land" that was denied to the Jews of Central Europe. Here the Jewish immigrant may well strive to become part not only of the "political" state that is America, but of that popular matrix of sentiments, ideals, memories and dreams, traditions, and even prejudices that constitute the American nation. If to be at home is not only to be in the possession of "rights" but also to be part of the people to whose service the political machinery of the state is dedicated, then the Jew can be here utterly at home, thinking of himself as an American of the Jewish faith, as "normal" in the civil sense of the term as any other citizen of the great country. This consummation, so ardently desired by the Jews of Western Europe for a century and a half, is here embraced in the cherished tradition of the country and in its basic social structure.

Ever since the brilliant essay of Ahad Ha'am on this theme was published, Jewish thinkers were familiar with the distinction between two kinds of assimilation—the healthy kind, in which a people digests and absorbs into itself whatever in the culture of the environment is suited to its nature, and the unhealthy kind,

580

in which a people loses its own identity, dissolving completely within the "melting pot." This analysis is indeed extremely cogent in the consideration of certain cultural issues, but it is not relevant to the basic question of identification. Basically, the Jewish individual, not the group, is the subject of the integrating, or the assimilating, process. When he asks, "What should I know myself to be?" the healthy answer is the one that takes account of his particular position on the historical scene, his spiritual welfare, and his happiness. The historical position of the American Jew is the same as that of other descendants of immigrants; his spiritual welfare and his happiness both dictate a conception of Jewish loyalties that assigns them to the domain of vertical values where they supplement his American horizontal loyalties. For a century and a half, Jewish people in the Western world have been yearning and battling for "normality." This goal is now definitely on the horizon.

But so new is this possibility to the historical experience of our people that it appears to carry the overtones of treachery or desertion. Is there any moral backsliding in the notion of Jews considering themselves part of the American nation, with their Jewish loyalties falling in the adjectival category of faith and tradition? Let us hold up to analysis the varied meanings of the term "Jewish" in order that we might see exactly what is involved in the emergence of the Jewish American. Insofar as the term "Jewish" denotes our religious heritage, there is manifestly nothing narrowing or cramping in our conception, providing this heritage is taken seriously. In the mouth of marginal Jews this conception is tantamount to the avowal of total assimilation. What is at fault, however, is not their conception, but the virtual nonexistence in the Jewish consciousness of those people of any vertical loyalties. Loyalty to the Jews of Israel and other lands will depend upon the strength of the shared vertical Jewish loyalties both here and there. If then any objection is raised to this concept, it can only be on the ground of elements in our heritage that are neither national nor religious, but ethnic and quasi-metaphysical.

581

Indeed, there flows in the heritage of both Jews and Christians a current of thought and sentiment that would set the Jew apart from the rest of mankind by a mystical, metaphysical "iron curtain." In a previous chapter, I referred to this dark protean residue of feeling and phantasy as the "meta-myth." On the Christian side of the curtain, this semiconscious penumbra accounts for the deeper layers of the miasma of anti-Semitism, out of which there issues the ghostly stereotypes of the Jew as nonhuman, hence, a subhuman creature. These layers have been subjected to careful scrutiny in our own day. On the Jewish side, the notions deriving from the powerful undertow are difficult to identify. Yet, they are by no means unimportant in a study of the integration of the American Jew. Let us recall that the import of Napoleon's questions to the Assembly of the Elders was not whether Jews were willing to be "politically loyal" to the new state, but whether they were willing to consider Frenchmen as their "brothers." In his own rough dictatorial way, he sought to probe the scope and depth of the "ethnic exclusiveness" of Jewish people, which the reactionaries of his day did their best to exaggerate.

It would be idle to deny the occasional occurrence in Jewish writings of statements reflecting an isolationist ethnicism that is truly incompatible with the concept of an emergent American nation. But we maintain that Judaism also contains a stream of thought and feeling disavowing any such attitudes. In the tension between ethnicism and religion in Judaism, the healthy equilibrium was disturbed not infrequently by one tendency or the other. Because of the balance of contending forces within it, Judaism was able to assume in every age a form suitable to the noblest challenges of that age and its social realities. But such a synthesis cannot be achieved without a clear understanding of the elements that are rejected, as well as those that are embraced, in our interpretation of Judaism.

The mystical and extremely powerful feeling of "difference" between Jew and Gentile is an inescapable factor that cannot be ignored in any discussion of the future of the American

582

Jewish community. The nature of this feeling on the part of Gentiles has been examined by psychologists and sociologists. There is unanimous agreement that this feeling is not due to any instinctive reaction against the Jewish "race." We must now inquire whether on the Jewish side this feeling is a psychosomatic reaction or an intuitive perception of the "peculiar" nature of our being, the fact that we are indeed "different."

At the outset, we must learn to distinguish between the sense of difference that is derived from vertical loyalties and the feelings of difference that are postulated on the horizontal plane. Vertical loyalties are altogether natural, healthy, and nonaggressive. In a sense, every culture and national tradition is a unique phenomenon, and there are several respects in which the vertical values of Judaism may be legitimately contrasted with the values of all other European groups, taken as a unit. On the vertical plane, there is no antagonism between the unique values of different groups. On the contrary, all cultured people feel enriched by whatever wealth may be produced by any national group. We Jews, victims though we were only recently of German hysteria and fury, nevertheless feel enriched by the music of a Beethoven, the philosophy of a Kant, the poetic maturity of a Goethe. On the other hand, any claims of difference on the horizontal plane cannot but result in hatred and arrogance, antagonism and aggression.

In normative Judaism, the claim of Israel to be an *Am Segulah* was always conceived in terms of vertical values. Thus, the *berakhah* over the Torah asserts that we are "chosen" because we are the bearers of Torah. The prophets were especially determined to elevate the Jewish sense of difference into the realm of spiritual loyalties. But if the psychology of Jewish people in all its facets is to be understood, we must bring up from the shadowy limbo the feelings of racial pride and arrogance that were associated at various times with the conception of a "treasured people." Slumbering in the collective subconscious of our people and recorded in a multitude of dusty tomes, this assertion of the superiority of the Jewish race would long ago have disappeared from the realm of practical affairs were it not for the new lease on life bestowed upon it by the Hitlerite madness. If Jewish people are attacked persistently as a "race," set apart by a mythical chasm from the rest of humanity, then it is natural for Jews to react in the same terms. We are still suffering from the aftereffects of the Hitlerite "shocks," which in many cases have brought the negative phases of ethnicism to dominance. In the psychoanalysis of an individual, forgotten memories have to be exposed to view if the patient is to be cured. Similarly, if we are to distinguish between healthy and sickly forms in which our "uniqueness" and "difference" are asserted, we must recall that the sickly forms always hovered on the fringe of normative Judaism, becoming predominant in the minds of Jewish people from time to time.

No widely held idea can be entertained by any group over a long period of time in absolute sameness and with perfect equilibrium among its varying facets and emphases. How then can we expect the notion of a "treasured people" to have been held at all times in the stillness of its prophetic perfection? Thus, Ezra's banishment of the Gentile wives and their children could not have been justified by the standards of a man like Rabbi Joshua ben Hananiah. We read in the Talmud that Rabbi Joshua insisted on the right of an Ammonite to marry a Jewess on the ground that "Sennacherib came and mixed up the nations."[3] The decrees concerning the "uncleanliness" of Gentiles and the interdiction of their oil, milk, and bread were similarly motivated by the excessive growth of ethnic zealotry.[4] Rabbi Eliezer's insistence that the "pious of the nations do not share in the World to Come" was certainly due to his nationalistic bias, as the contrary view of Rabbi Joshua ben Hananiah was a reflection of his consistent liberalism. Let us savor the taste of such passages as the following, without succumbing to the fascination of an all-reconciling and all-misunderstanding *pilpulistic* mentality: "For a holy people art thou to the Lord, Thy God . . . Hence we learn that *everyone* in Israel is accounted by the

584

Holy One, Blessed be He, to be like all the nations of the world."[5]

"You are called 'man,' but the nations of the world are not called 'man.' "[5a]

"All Israelites are sons of kings."[6]

"When the serpent cohabited with Eve, he threw corruption into her. Israel, having been at Sinai, its flow of corruption was stopped. The nations, not having stood at Sinai, their corruption did not cease."[7]

"When the Messiah comes, all people will be servants unto Israel."[8]

A highly esteemed author of a very popular pietistic work even dealt seriously with the question of why the nations have the same appearance as Jews, though the souls of the Israelites derive from the spirit of holiness, while the souls of the nations issue out of the spirit of uncleanliness.[9]

We need hardly explore this shadowy underworld of Judaism any further in order to realize that the seeming axioms of Jewish ethnic "uniqueness" were based upon ideas that our people today reject with the utmost vehemence. As the full depth of anti-Semitism cannot be understood apart from the myths of the ancient and medieval world, the pathos of racial "uniqueness" cannot be seen in its true nature apart from the acrimonious context in which it was conceived and nurtured. It is the same tradition that contains those noble teachings which have always counterbalanced the impact of glorified ethnicism.

Thus, many authors of the Talmud loved to imagine that some of the greatest rabbis were descended from Gentiles. One rabbi declared that a "Gentile who studies the Torah is like unto a high priest."[10] Another insisted that the special status of Jews as "sons" of the Lord is dependent upon their good conduct. One sage was so all-embracing in his breadth of view as to confer the name Jew on all who deny the validity of idolatry.[11] While the discriminations in Jewish Law against pagans are well-known, few are aware that the Talmud teaches the principle of universal philanthropy—"We are in duty bound to feed the poor of the nations together with the Jewish poor."[12] By the same token, the ambiguous attitude of Jewish Law toward Christians furnished inexhaustible material for renegades and hate merchants, but the views of a philosophic codifier like Rabbi Menahem Meiri, who specifically and systematically reinstated the category of monotheists in Jewish Law, did not become known until our own day.[13]

Indeed, our tradition is just as capable of furnishing aid and comfort to a humane liberalism as to a zealous ethnicism. Since the fury of ethnic zeal is sustained by the twin-headed Hydra of dogmatism and bitterness, we may look forward to the steady decline of the isolationist component of ethnicism within the pattern of contemporary Judaism. Thus, the aura of plausibility that clung to the dogma of racial "uniqueness" for so many decades is due to fade away along with the associated ideas and exotic phantasies of the twilight realm of Qabbalah.

The enduring interest of American Jewry in Jews of all lands, especially of Israel, is likely to accelerate this development, rather than to retard it. As time goes on, Israel will come to occupy in the consciousness of American Jews the same place as do the other lands in the hearts of the immigrants to these shores. Before the rise of the State of Israel, Jewish immigrants differed from all others in that there was no specific geographical focus for their sentiments. Jews were loyal to the world fellowship of Israel and its tradition, rather than to any specific country. Insofar as this universal fellowship is progressively being narrowed to one place on the map, Jewish people too will have a place "whence" in spirit they had come. Their national feelings will thus tend to follow the pattern of the steadily weakening national sentiments of other immigrant groups. The progressive preponderance of Oriental and African elements within the population of Israel might also serve as an additional demonstration that world Jewry is a fellowship of the spirit, not of blood or civilization.

Does the transformation of the genus "Jew living in America" to the genus "Jewish American" involve the progressive lessening of Jewish religious-cultural loyalties? The answer to this question is both Yes and No. On the one hand, the consciousness of "normality" will encourage those who have no feeling for the values of our tradition to drift into the anonymity of the general community. The Jewishly ignorant and the embittered, the eager opportunists and the dust-dry rationalists, the rootless intellectuals and the witless hangers-on will be likely to desert our ranks in a steady procession. On the other hand, the contrary tendency will also be intensified. Since the Jewish quality of one's being can no longer be regarded as an automatic category into which people fall with or without their will, it must necessarily find expression in positive acts of identification. Precisely because it fits into the American pattern of a unitary nation with multiple faiths, Jewish loyalty will derive accessions of strength from both the pervasive atmosphere of American culture and the momentum of Jewish tradition.

Political loyalties, social ties, and cultural-religious ideals constitute, respectively, the three dimensions of social life. If Jewishness is regarded as falling into the fundamental dimensions of our nature, like length and breadth, then it need not find expression in the cultural-religious dimension of height at all. Thus, in Israel, Jewish loyalty is preempted by all the ordinary tasks and concerns of citizenship and is not impelled to flow in religious channels, while, in the Diaspora, it tends even now to be felt in the dimension of height and asserted in humanitarian cultural and religious terms. This instructive contrast will become ever more apparent as Jews in America liberate themselves from the lingering social pressures that hemmed in the Jewish community of the past like an iron ring. Already, American Jews are beginning to act on an instinctive assumption of their status as Jewish Americans. The Central Conference of American Rabbis has adopted a program of proselytization among Gentiles, demonstrating by an action-symbol that Judaism is essentially a faith. Could it have launched this program earlier without provoking a storm of protests?

Already it is clear that Judaism in America, revolving around a typical modern congregation, is more likely to endure than Orthodoxy in Israel. In spite of its virtual state monopoly, Orthodoxy in Israel is gradually withdrawing into a ghetto of its own making, becoming desiccated and fossilized. In contrast, Judaism in America is constantly challenged to prove its worth, hence, its vitality and vibrancy. Whatever is lost through the defection of Jews whose sole claim to the name is that of ethnic descent is likely to be more than made up by the enhanced determination of the three-dimensional Jews to respond affirmatively to the inescapable challenge of the American environment.

In sum, the complex strands of Jewish loyalty were always woven out of the rugged and earthy feelings of blood-kinship, as well as out of the fine and ethereal ideals of faith. The proportion and relative potency of these elements varied in accord with the liberalism and breadth of view of individual Jews and the fluctuation of fortune in our long history. During the past century, two causes combined to reduce the potency and relevance of faith—the growing secularization of life and the tightening of the vise of hatred directed against all Jews. Thus, the bonds of Jewish loyalty consisted, for many of our contemporaries, of the dark and mystical threads of "blood and soil," reinforced by the feelings of resentment against the outside world and enveloped in the fluffy clouds of nostalgic affection for ancient "ways of life." The resulting complex of emotions was unsatisfactory and, hence, dynamic in character, issuing in a longing for the "normalization" of feeling, either in the attainment of the fullness of emancipation or in the radical solution of the "ingathering of the exiles." The glowing promise of emancipation could not be realized in those lands where the national loyalty of Gentiles was conceived predominantly in ethnic and mystical terms. Standing at the threshold of the fourth century of Jewish life in America, we can foresee the progressive "normalization" of Jewish feeling; hence, the shrinking of the ethnic strands of loyalty, the forging of ever stronger bonds of fraternity with the American people, and the steady growth of the ideal and religious components of Judaism.

This essay was written more than fifteen years ago. Its central thesis of the increasing acculturation of American Jews has become clearer in the past decade and a half. The great outpouring of Jewish sentiment and commitment in May and June of 1967 was not proof of the reversal of this process; on the contrary, it revealed the calm confidence of American Jews in the conscience of their countrymen. The very life of two and a half million Jews was threatened with annihilation. Here and in all Western countries, Jews could count on the sympathy and help of their Christian neighbors. Even in France, De Gaulle's policy was contrary to the feelings of the masses. Having come to take their Americanism for granted, Jews could afford to react more generously to the needs of a besieged Israel.

NOTES

PART ONE

The Jewish-Christian Dialogue

The Case for the Dialogue
1. "Anti-Semitism in the New Testament," *Theological Studies,* Woodstock, Md., 1964.
2. Hosea 13:2.
3. Katharine T. Hargrove, ed., *The Star and the Cross,* Milwaukee, Bruce, 1966, p. 313.
4. Hagigah 13a. Sanhedrin 59a.
5. Abodah Zara, Tossefot 2a. Jacob Katz, *Exclusiveness and Tolerance,* New York, Oxford University Press, 1961, p. 34.
6. Baba Kama 38a.
7. I Corinthians 12:3. See Augustin Cardinal Bea, *The Church and the Jewish People,* New York, Harper & Row, 1966, p. 19.
8. *Kether Shem* Tov.

Mutually Challenging, Not Mutually Contradictory
1. "Anti-Semitism in the New Testament," *op. cit.*
2. Philo, *De Cherubim,* Loeb, ed., pp. 29, 99-100. Exodus Rabba 25:8.
3. Judah Halevi, *The Kusari,* IV, 16.
4. Israel I. Efros, *Ancient Jewish Philosophy,* Detroit, Wayne State University Press, 1964.
5. Leviticus 16:16. Yoma 56b.
6. Megillah 29a.
7. Genesis Rabba 47.
8. Tana dibai Eliyahu 9.
9. Harry A. Wolfson, *The Philosophy of the Church Fathers,* Cambridge, Mass., Harvard University Press, 1964, pp. 141-287. See also W. D. Davies, *Paul and Rabbinic Judaism* S.P.C.K., London, 1958.
10. Sotah 14a.

11. Sanhedrin 90a. Rashi, *ad loc.* James 2:14-26.
12. Strack-Billerbeck, *Kommentar zum Neuen Testament*, 110, 479.
13. Aboth 1:2.
14. Megillah 26a.
15. Aboth 2:5.
16. Aboth 1:13.
17. Taanith 2a.
18. Kiddushin 49b.
19. Abodah Zara 10b.
20. Aboth 4:2.
21. Saadia, *Emunot Vedeot*, V, 1.
22. Yebamot 121b.
23. Mechilta, Bo 9.
24. Aboth di R. Nathan 38.
25. Romans 8:1-2.
26. James 2:19-20.
27. From *Passage to India*.
28. Sanhedrin 11:1.
29. Strack-Billerbeck, IV, 4.
30. Baba Mezia 84a.
31. Gittin 56a. Yoma 86b.
32. High Holiday Prayer Book, Mussaf for Yom Kippur.
33. Hagigah 12b. Menahot 110a.
34. Genesis Rabba 30:10.
35. Micah 6:8.
36. Mechilta, Yithro 6.
37. Romans 1.
38. Shabbat 104a. Yoma 38b.
39. Psalms 145:18.
40. J. Taanith 4. B.T. Gittin 58b.
41. Baba Bathra 16a.
42. Kiddushin 30b.
43. Sukkah 52b.
44. Shabbat 146a.
45. Sotah 3a.
46. Sukkah 52b.
47. Kethuboth 103b.
48. Deuteronomy Rabba 2:1.
49. Deuteronomy 6:5-9.
50. Pesahim 50b.
51. Aboth 6.
52. Baba Mezia 30b.
53. Baba Mezia 8a.
54. Kethuboth 8a.

55. Hagigah 10a.
56. Sotah 47a.
57. Berochot 17a.
58. I Corinthians 15:51-52.
59. I Thessalonians 4:15-17.
60. J. Taanith 1:2. Pirke di R. Eliezer 46. B.T. Nidah 61b. Bereshit Rabba 98:9. Qohelet Rabba 11:8. Yalkut Shimoni, Tehillim 621. Vayikra Rabba 13:3.
61. J. Berochot 9.
62. Yoma 73b.
63. Sotah 37a. Shabbat 55a. Tanhuma, Numbers 14. Leviticus Rabba 6:36.
64. Proverbs 3:6.
65. Berochot 63a.
66. Leo Baeck, *Judaism and Christianity*, Philadelphia, Jewish Publication Society, 1958, p. 196.
67. *Ibid.*, p. 190.
68. *Ibid.*, p. 197.
69. *Ibid.*, p. 198.
70. *Ibid.*, p. 215.
71. *Ibid.*
72. Taanith 8a, 16a. Tana dibai Eliyahu Zuta, 11. Midrash Isaiah 445, 449. Pesikta Rabbati 1, 37, 2. Sanhedrin 46a.
73. Torat Kohanim, Kedoshim 19.
74. Acts 4:32-5:11.
75. J. Berochot 9:5.
76. Mesilat Yesharim 19.
77. Kiddushin 31a.
78. Deuteronomy 18:13.
79. Isaiah 66:2.

New Grounds for a Jewish-Christian Symbiosis
1. Aboth 4:1. Baba Bathra 21a.
2. Hannah Arendt, *Eichmann in Jerusalem*, rev. ed., New York, Viking, 1965, p. 141.
3. Micah 4:5.
4. Psalms 118:24.

Perspectives for the Study of the New Testament and Rabbinic Literature
1. Psalms 130:1.
1a. *Tanya*, or *Likkutai Amorim*, ch. 8.
1b. I Corinthians 12:3.
2. Isaiah 29:13.

3. Airubin 13b.
4. Jeremiah 12:1.
5. Franz Rosenzweig, *Briefe*, Schocken, Berlin, 1935, p. 518.
6. Acts 22:3.
7. Acts 24:5.
8. Acts 24:14.
9. John 8:44.
10. Sanhedrin 37a.
11. Josephus, *Antiquities*, XX, 9, 1.
12. Aidoyot 1:5. Baba Kama 117a. Airubin 13b.
12a. Halevi, *The Kusari*, IV, 23. Maimonides' Code, *Hilchot Melochim*, X, 14 (left out some printed editions).
13. Shabbat 133b. Baba Mezia 30b.
13a. Acts 15:29.
14. Jeremiah 18:18.

Response to Father Daniélou's Dialogue with Israel *and Cardinal Bea's* The Church and the Jewish People

1. Jean Daniélou, *Dialogue with Israel*, Baltimore, Helicon Press, 1967.
2. Habakkuk 2:4. Makkot 24a.
3. Amos 5:4.
4. Daniélou, p. 14.
5. Genesis Rabba 2:4.
6. *The Torah*, Philadelphia, Jewish Publication Society, 1962, p. 3.
7. Deuteronomy 6:4.
8. I Corinthians 1:23.
9. Genesis 22.
10. Amos 5:15.
10a. J. B. Agus, *The Vision and the Way*, New York, Ungar, 1966, pp. 77-92.
11. Such passages are: Galatians 3:13. I Thessalonians 2:15-16. John 8:44.
12. John 2:13-22.
12a. I Corinthians 12:3.
13. Mishna, Sanhedrin 7:5. S. Zeitlin, *The Rise and Fall of the Judian State*, Philadelphia, Jewish Publication Society, 1967, p. 167. Julius Wellhausen, *Das Evangelium Marci*, Berlin, 1961, pp. 23, 162.
13a. Maimonides' Code, *Hilchot Melochim*, XI, 4.
14. Baba Kama, 38a.
15. Sanhedrin, 59a.
16. Tana dibai Eliyahu, 9.
16a. I Samuel 16:7.

17. ". . . the letter denotes any writing that is external to man, even that of the moral precepts such as are contained in the Gospels. Therefore, the letter even of the Gospel would kill, unless there were the inward presence of the healing grace of faith." Aquinas, *Summa Theologica*, I-II, 106a, 2.
18. Deuteronomy 29:29.
18a. Tosefta, Sanhedrin 13.
18b. Halevi, *The Kusari*, IV, 23.
19. Micah 4:5.
20. Augustin Cardinal Bea, *op. cit.*
21. *Ibid.*, p. 28.
22. *Ibid.*, p. 39.
23. *Ibid.*, p. 68.
24. *Ibid.*, p. 70.
25. *Ibid.*, p. 78.
26. *Ibid.*, p. 85.
27. *Ibid.*, p. 94.
28. *Ibid.*, p. 122.

PART TWO
Dialogue with Historians

Toynbee and Judaism
1. Arnold J. Toynbee, *A Study of History*, New York, Oxford University Press, 1935-1961.
2. Yizhak Ben-Zvi and David Ben-Gurion, *Eretz Yisroel*, New York, Poalei Zion Party, 1918.
3. *Ibid.*, p. 326.
4. Tanhuma, Tzav.
5. Numbers 23:9.
6. Amos 9:7.
7. Isaiah 56:6.
8. Ezekiel 16:6.
9. Ezekiel 20:33.
10. Toynbee, VIII, 296.
11. Shabbat 146a. Zohar, Bereshit 57b.
12. Pesahim 118a.
13. Berochot 5a. See also Max Brod, *Heidentum, Christentum, Judentum*.
14. Berochot 5a.
15. Halevi, *The Kusari*, II, 34, 44.
16. Shir Hashirim Rabba 1.
17. Shir Hashirim Rabba 4.

18. Shemot Rabba, Tezaveh.
19. Jeremiah 30:7.
20. Sanhedrin 98b. Yalkut, Isaiah, 445, 469, 476, 499. Pesikta Rabbati 35. 2.

Toynbee's Letter to the Hebrews
1. We did not deal with the judgments concerning contemporary problems that Toynbee offered from time to time—especially in response to the prodding of Jewish individuals or groups—such as his assertions concerning the Arab refugees and the guilt of the Israeli government. Israel is quite capable of defending its interests. My concern was to clarify misunderstandings so that Judaism might be properly presented in Toynbee's writings to the intellectual world generally and to the hundreds of thousands of Jewish collegiates in particular.
2. Toynbee, XII, 514.
2a. J. B. Agus, *The Meaning of Jewish History*, 2 volumes, New York, Abelard-Schuman, 1963.
3. Toynbee, XII, 279.
4. Genesis 29:4. Deuteronomy 26:5.
5. Toynbee, XII, 435.
6. Shabbat 12b. Halevi, *The Kusari*, II, 68.
7. Samson Raphael Hirsch, "Jüdische Welt und Lebensanschauungen," *Gesammelte Schriften*, Frankfurt a. M., 1910, V, 145.
8. Maimonides, *Guide for the Perplexed*, III, 47.
9. Toynbee, XII, 299.
10. *Ibid.*, p. 515.

Toward a Philosophy of Jewish History
1. Philo, *De Specialibus Legibus*, IV, 39, 79.
2. Harry A. Wolfson, *Philo*, Cambridge, Mass., Harvard University Press, 1947, II, 408-409.
3. Pesahim 87b.
4. J. B. Agus, *Modern Philosophies of Judaism*, New York, Behrman, 1940, p. 364.
4a. Isaiah 40:8.
5. N. Krochmal, *Moreh Nevuhai Hazeman*, ch. 7-10.
6. *Ibid.*, ch. 7.
7. Simon Dubnow, *Divrai Y'mai Am Olam*, I, 5, Devir, Tel Aviv, 1934.
8. J. Klausner, *Historia Shel Habayit Hasheni*, V, 9. Ahiasaf, Jerusalem, 1951.
8a. Gittin 55b-57a
9. E. Silberner, *Hasozializm Hamaaravi Ushealat Hayehudim*, Mossad Bialick, Jerusalem, 1955.

10. Dubnow, I, 222.
11. *Ibid.*, p. 6.
11a. I Maccabees 7:13.
11b. Josephus, *Antiquities*, XIV, 3, *Wars*, II, 6.
12. Klausner, IV, 261.
13. Galatians 3:28.
14. Klausner, V, 129.
15. *Ibid.*, p. 130.
16. Dubnow, II, 322.
17. *Ibid.*, p. 323.
18. *Ibid.*, p. 334.
19. Matthew 15:21-28.
19a. Gittin 56a, 57b. Yoma 71a. Berochot 27b. Commentary of R. Nissin.
20. Yebamot 46a.
21. Yehezkel Kaufmann, *Golah V'naichar*, III, 70.
22. Dubnow, VIII, 93. Y. Rosenthal, *Talpioth*, 1950, p. 565.
23. Dubnow, VIII, 196.
24. *Ibid.*, IX, 23.
25. *Ibid.*, p. 26.
26. *Ibid.*, p. 27.
27. *Ibid.*, p. 88.
28. E. Silberner, *Hasozialism Hamaarovi*, Jerusalem, 1955, p. 14.
29. Dubnow, X, 10.
30. *Ibid.*, p. 15.
31. Karl Marx, *Zur Judenfrage*.
32. J. S. Bloch, *My Reminiscences*, New York, p. 152. I. Elbogen, *A Century of Jewish Life*, Philadelphia, Jewish Publication Society, 1944, p. 707.
33. Silberner, p. 85.
33a. Werner Sombart, *Die Zukunft der Juden*, 1912.
34. Silberner, p. 52.
35. N. Berdyaev as quoted in Patkin's *The Origins of the Russian Jewish Labor Movement*, F. W. Cheshire Publishing Ltd., Melbourne, 1947.
36. All quotations from the collected Hebrew writings of J. H. Brenner, VI. See Kaufman, IV, 405.
37. S. W. Baron, *A Social and Religious History of the Jews*, New York, Columbia University Press, 1952-1960, I, 5.
38. *Ibid.*, p. 7.
39. *Ibid.*, p. 11.
40. *Ibid.*, p. 10.
41. *Ibid.*, p. 13.
42. *Ibid.*, p. 15.

43. *Ibid.*, p. 17.
44. *Ibid.*, p. 164.
45. *Ibid.*, II, p. 69.
46. Kaufmann, II, 81.
47. Baron, II, 81.
48. Fritz Baer, *Yisroel Baamim*, p. 37.
49. I Kings 11:41.
49a. Baba Kama 82b, 83a. Sotah 49a. Menahot 99b. Saul Lieberman, *Hellenism in Jewish Palestine*, New York, J.T.S., 1950, pp. 100-114.
50. Deuteronomy 7:8.
51. Isaiah 53.
52. Kiddushin 36a.
53. See Gedalia Alon, *Toldoth Hayehudim B'eretz, Yisroel Bitkufath, Hamishnah Vehatalmud*, I, 231-232. Y. F. Baer, *Toldoth Hayehudim Bisfarad Hanotzrith*, II, 445, 449, 459.
54. See the *Studies in Prejudice* series, published by the American Jewish Committee.
55. I. Elbogen, p. 165.
56. Toynbee, VIII, 10.
57. Kaufmann, II, 188.
58. H. v. Treitschke, *Ein Wort über das Judentum.*
59. On the ambiguous attitude of H. Graetz, see Kaufmann, II, 190.
60. Elbogen, p. 902.
61. Will Herberg, *Protestant, Catholic, Jew*, New York, Doubleday, 1955, p. 49.

PART THREE
Dialogue with the New Atheists

Response to the "God Is Dead" Movement

1. Oswald Spengler, *Decline of the West*, New York, Knopf, 1928, II, 265.
1a. 1 Corinthians 15:55.
2. Thomas Altizer, *Oriental Mysticism and Biblical Eschatology*, Philadelphia, Westminster Press, 1961, p. 180.
2a. Aboth 5:6.
2b. Proverbs 20:27.
3. Altizer, p. 156.

PART FOUR
Dialogue with Secular Ideologies

Mass-Crime and the Judeo-Christian Tradition

1. Summarizing the research of Bettelheim and Janowitz, Gordon

Allport writes in *The Nature of Prejudice*: "What sins do we find in our nature? On the one hand, sins of the flesh. We have to fight against lechery, laziness, aggression, and slovenliness. Hence, we personify these evils in the *Negro*. On the other hand, we have to fight against the sins of pride, deceit, unsocialized egotism, and grasping ambition. We personify these evils in the Jew. The Negro reflects our own 'id' impulses; the Jew reflects our own violations of our 'superego' (conscience)."

2. William L. Shirer, *The Rise and Fall of the Third Reich*, New York, Simon and Schuster, 1960, p. 235.
3. Heinrich Hermelink, *Kirche im Kampf*, 1950, pp. 31-32.
4. Quoted by Shirer, p. 239.
5. *Ibid.*
6. Hermelink, p. 476.
7. Michael von Faulhaber, *Judentum, Christentum, Germanentum*, containing his sermons at Munich in 1933.
8. Count Carlo Sforza, "The Vatican and the War," *Free World*, October 1941, pp. 53-54.
9. Shirer, p. 234.
10. To be sure, hundreds and even thousands of ministers and priests paid the supreme penalty for their opposition to the Nazi juggernaut. For the most part, their resistance was due to the Nazi policy of keeping the Slavs as a race of slaves by cutting off their intelligentsia. Thus, 2,000 Polish priests were executed within a few weeks of the conquest. From April 1940 to 1945, 2,800 Polish clerics were imprisoned in Dachau. Yet few Catholics and Protestants combatted Nazism as a matter of principle as long as they themselves were not the targets of Teutonic fury. With less education and more inspiration, the Yugoslav Orthodox priests bravely protested against anti-Jewish atrocities. In May 1943 alone, 600 Greek Orthodox priests were arrested because they refused to preach anti-Jewish sermons.

Freedom and the Judeo-Christian Tradition
1. Genesis 1:27.
2. Arthur O. Lovejoy, *Reflections on Human Nature*, Baltimore, Johns Hopkins, 1961, p. 37.

Jewish Philosophy and World Tensions
1. Genesis Rabba 1:10.
2. Sukkah 5a.
3. Horayoth 8a. Makkoth 24a.
4. Isaiah 51:16.
5. Hullin 139b.

6. Deuteronomy 13:3.
7. Jeremiah 12:1.
8. Jeremiah 9:5, 23-24.
9. Berochot 33a.
10. Maimonides, III, 51.
11. Shabbat 88a.
12. Zechariah 14:9.
13. Genesis 18:19.
14. Yoma 67b.
15. Berochot 52a.
16. Sifri 49.
17. Taanith 5a.
18. Yoma 86a.
19. Berochot 34a.
20. Martin Buber, *Tales of Hassidim*, Later Masters, New York, Schocken, 1964, p. 192.
21. This interpretation of the dynamic impetus of Jewish thought casts some light on the evolution of the Christian faith. Beginning as a pseudo-Messianic movement within Judaism, it first criticized the Law and then repudiated its validity altogether. The "World to Come" was virtually here, the early Christians believed, hence, their impatience with the Law and its guardians, the Pharisees. But as the Christian community grew and expanded, its pseudo-Messianic character was outgrown. Only sectarian groups, the Montanists, and medieval millenarians manifested the Messianic mentality. On the whole, the Church re-created the creative tension of Judaism in two ways—by the formulation of its own canons, which were every bit as casuistic as the laws of the Talmud, and by the reintroduction of Greek philosophy. A history of Western Christianity could be written in terms of this polarity and its occasional distortions.
22. Genesis 17:1.
23. I Corinthians 12:3.

Toward a Philosophy of Hope
1. Jeremiah 18:18.
2. Jeremiah 12:1.
3. Micah 6:8.
4. Isaiah 51:2.

PART FIVE
Dialogue Within Judaism

The Prophet in Modern Hebrew Literature
1. In *Emunot Vedeot*, VIII, 6, Saadia describes the Messianic age

as follows: "Then prophecy will reappear in the midst of our people so that even our sons and slaves will prophesy. Thus, Joel declared: 'And it shall come to pass afterward, that I will pour out my Spirit upon all flesh. And your sons and your daughters shall prophesy. Your old men shall dream dreams, your young men shall see visions. And also upon the servants and upon the hand-maids in those days will I pour out my Spirit' (Joel 2:28-29).

"It follows that when one of the children of Israel will go to a distant land and say, 'I am of Israel,' people will say to him, 'Tell us what the morrow will bring!'"

2. Yeshurun Kesheth expatiates on the modern significance of the prophetic heritage in his brilliant essay "Shirath Hamikra" (*Devir*, Tel Aviv, 1955). He maintains that only a return to the prophetic pattern of spirituality can save mankind, for in prophecy "the love of truth is blended with the love of the good" (p. 90). Though his analytical procedure is different from the one followed in this essay, he too recognizes the phenomenon of prophecy as the epitome of Hebraic cultural creativity.

3. The hero-image of medieval knighthood is a composite creation, containing two antithetical facets, one deriving from Christianity, the other from primitive paganism; the one appealing to Christian culture, the other to the aggressive instincts of preculture man.

4. Instructive is the observation of the Midrash concerning the difference between Abraham and Noah, Jewish prophet and non-Jewish saint. While Abraham attained perfection of piety by his own powers, Noah needed the constant aid and support of God (Genesis Rabba 30:10).

5. Evelyn Underhill devotes a chapter to this stage in the life of the mystic in her book *Mysticism*, 1911.

6. In Qabbalah, where vestiges of the prophetic tradition are contained, Din, or the incomprehensible Divine decree, is in the highest spheres, completely absorbed in Rahamim, which is the humanly experienced quality of mercy.

7. Mechilta, Bo.

8. Isaiah 8:17.

9. R. Hasdai Crescas offers a somewhat similar explanation of the failure of the prophets to organize preaching missions to the Gentiles. They preach *about* other nations, not *to* them (*Or Adonai*, II, 4, 3).

10. Abodah Zara 20b. Maimonides, II, 45.

11. Isaiah 13:12-13. The translation should be in the present, not past, or future tense.

12. Sanhedrin 21b.

12a. Baba Bathra 12a.

13. A. Jellinek, *Midrash Eleh Ezkerah*, pp. 64-72.
14. Taanith 24a.
15. Y. Zinberg, *Di Geshikhte fun der Literatur bei Yidn*, V, 221.
16. Z. H. Kaidanover, *Kav Hayashar*, Vilna, 1875, ch. 1.
17. Elijah di Vidas, *Reshith Hochmah*, First Gate, Tractate *Gehinnom*.
18. Moses Luzzatto, *Mesillath Yesharim*, ch. 1.
19. *Ibid.*, ch. 26.
20. *Ibid.*, ch. 11.
21. *Ibid.*, ch. 20.
22. *Ibid.*
23. Menahot 99b.
24. See description of five states of ecstasy in *Kuntros Hahithpaaluth* by Der Miteler Rav, printed by Kehot, Brooklyn.
25. Nahman, *Likkutei Moharan* 1:9, 118.
26. Shneur Zalman, *Tanya*, ch. 2.
27. Elimelech, *No'am Elimelech*, lech lecha.
28. *Ibid.*, Miketz.
29. *Ibid.*, Shemoth.
30. Zephaniah 3:9.
31. *Zohar*, Bereshit, 47a. *Zohar Hodosh*, Bereshit, 10:3.
32. Shneur Zalman, *Likkutei Amorim*, ch. 1, 6.
33. Shivhei HaBesht, 34, Talpiot, ed.
34. L. J. Perez, story of *If Not Higher*.
35. See Alfasi's *Ger*, a history of the "Gerer" dynasty.
36. See S. Ginsburg's *Historishe Verk*, I, 63.
37. Aryeh Simon and Yoseph Eliyah Heller, *Ahad Ha'am*, Philadelphia, Jewish Publication Society, 1960, p. 97.
38. Ahad Ha'am, *Navi Vekohen*.
39. Ahad Ha'am, *Tehiyah* and *Beri'ah*.
40. Ahad Ha'am, *Al Parashath Derachim*, introduction to I. See Kaufmann, IV, 370.
41. Thus, S. D. Luzzatto regards the quality of pity as the essentially Jewish contribution to ethics, while Kant is the great expounder of ethics as absolute justice.
42. Simon and Heller, p. 189.
43. *Ibid.*, p. 15.
44. For Magnes' leadership and prophetic character, see Norman Bentwich's *For Zion's Sake*, ch. 12, 13.
45. See S. Niger's introduction to the collection of Bialiks Yiddish poems.
46. Jeremiah 12:1.
47. J. H. Brenner, *Bahayim Uvasafruth*, VI, 325.
48. Kaufmann, IV, 408.

49. Quoted from Brenner in Fichman's *Lashon Vasefer*, V, 69.
50. Uri Zevi Greenberg, *Rehovoth HaNahar*, pp. 169, 291.
51. *Ibid.*, p. 165.
52. S. Halkin, *Modern Hebrew Literature*, New York, Schocken, 1950, p. 135.
53. Deuteronomy 6:4.
54. For examples, see Agus' *Banner of Jerusalem*, New York, Bloch, 1946.
55. Halkin, p. 205.
56. *Ibid.*
57. M. Shoham, *Zor and Yerusholaim*.
58. However, the prophetic spirit is here held down chiefly by the dead weight of "crowd psychology," which crushes all idealistic efforts. When the several hero-images fail to inspire and to evoke emulation, the fickle mob with its tinsel idols achieves predominance, so that popularity takes the place of moral authority, conformity the place of rightness, the statistical Mr. Average the place of the ideal hero.
59. Psalms 34:10.

Faith and Law
 1. Numbers 23:19.
 2. Deuteronomy 32:4.
 3. Genesis Rabba 39.
 4. Isaiah 51:2.
 5. Genesis 17:1.
 6. Zechariah 14:9.
 7. Deuteronomy 33:27.
 8. Psalms 36:9.
 9. Isaiah 55:9.
10. Makkoth 24n.
11. Berochot 64a.
12. Genesis 12:3.
13. Genesis 18:19.
14. Isaiah 43:10.
15. Isaiah 1:9.
16. Isaiah 29:13.
17. Deuteronomy 18:18.
18. Deuteronomy 17:11. J. Horayot 1:1.
19. Nahmanides' introduction to his commentary on the Torah.
20. Maimonides, *Guide* III, 28 and 36.
21. Jeremiah 33:25.
22. Baba Mezia 56a.

Jewish Ethics
1. Leviticus 19:2.
2. Genesis Rabba 9:7.
3. Yebamot 20a.
4. Genesis 2:20.
5. Deuteronomy 18:13.
6. Kiddushin 42b.
7. Genesis 17:5.
8. Genesis 18:25.
9. Genesis 15:13.
10. Leviticus 18:5. Deuteronomy 4:6.
11. Genesis 18:19.
12. Baeck, *op. cit.*
13. Jeremiah 18:18.
14. Proverbs 8:22.
15. Micah 6:8.
16. Matthew 5:17, 7:12.
17. Berochot 7a.
18. Tana dibai Eliyahu Rabba 10.
19. Nedarim 37a.
20. Aboth 6:6. J. Shabbat 1:3.
21. Aboth 3:22.
22. Berochot 64a.
23. Abodah Zara 10b.
24. Saadia, X, 15.
25. Bahya Ibn Pakuda, *Duties of the Heart*, IX, 2.
26. Maimonides, III, 51.
27. Psalms 100:2.
28. Agus, *Guideposts in Modern Judaism*, New York, Bloch, 1954, p. 20.
29. Agus, *The Vision and the Way*, p. 20.

The Concept of Israel
1. Genesis 32:28.
2. *De Congressu Eruditorum Causa*, 10.
3. The school of Shammai maintained that divorce was permissible only in the event of the woman's adultery. Their attitude was similar to that of Jesus (Sanhedrin 90a).
4. Hosea 2:1. Exodus 4:22, 19:5.
5. Ezekiel 20:32.
6. II Kings 19:15-31, 23:25-27.
7. Jeremiah 10:11.

8. The notion of "correspondence," which was developed extensively in Qabbalah and in the medieval commentaries, was probably contained in the Torah. The vessels of the Sanctuary were modeled after heavenly patterns (Exodus 25:9). In the higher reaches of pagan thought, the same assumption was axiomatic—the ritual on earth affected a corresponding reality in the invisible world.

Abraham Ibn Ezra (Exodus 25:40, *Commentary*) lays down a general principle: "We know that His Glory fills the world; still, there are places where His Power is more manifest than in others, either because the recipient is more adapted, or because of the higher Power supervening above a certain area. Therefore, the place of the Holy Temple was chosen. And if the Lord put wisdom in your heart, you will understand the Ark, the Cover, the Cherubim that spread out their wings . . . These are the Glory of the Lord."

9. Isaiah 56:3. Esther 9:27. Zechariah 2:15. Daniel 11:34.

10. Thus the Hellenizers are described as eager "to conclude a *covenant* with the nations around us." The Covenant of Israel with God interposed an obstacle to their fraternity with their neighbors (I Maccabees 1:11).

11. On the other hand, in times of peace, the concept of Israel was expanded generously to include "those who seek the Lord," or "those who fear the Lord" (Psalms 34:11, 69:33, 118:4, 135:20).

12. This much-quoted passage occurs in various forms. A more careful formulation is this: "Three series of levels are bound together: the Holy One, blessed be He, Torah, and Israel" (*Zohar*, Vayikro, 73; also *Zohar*, Vayikro, 93).

13. *Zohar*, Beshalah, II, 64b. Rabbi Shimeon asks how the generation of the desert could doubt if the Lord was among them, seeing that the clouds of Glory were around them. He answers that they sought to know the relation between "the Ancient One, the Hidden of Hidden," and the "Miniature Face *(Zeir Anpin)* that is called YHVH."

14. "The Commandments of the Torah are all limbs and fragments that add up to one mystery. . . . He who removes even one of the Commandments, it is as if he diminished the image of the faith . . . for they all add up to the pattern of Man. . . . For this reason, Israel is called one people . . ." (*Zohar*, Teruma, 162b). Nahmanides in the introduction to his commentary on the Pentateuch: "We have a true tradition that the entire Torah consists of the Names of the Holy One, blessed be He . . . that the Torah

written with black fire on white fire was to be so construed . . ."

15. "And when the Holy One, blessed be He, decided to destroy His House below and the Holy Land below, He first removed the Holy Land above *(Shechinah)* and lowered it from the level where it drew from the Holy heavens *(Tiferet)*, and only then did He destroy the earth below" *(Zohar* II, 175a). This action was in keeping with the general principle, "The Lord does not cause a nation to fall, before He casts down its prince above" (Shemot, Rabba 21a).

16. Hullin 91b. Bereshit Rabba 82.

17. Rashi, in Hullin 91b: the image of Jacob was that of the man in the Divine Chariot.

18. Rashi, Genesis 1:2.

19. Shabbat 152b.

20. Bereshit Rabba 47.

21. Baba Mezia 85b.

22. Bereshit Rabba 51.

23. Sotah 17a.

24. Aboth 3:7.

25. Megillah 29a. The commentary of the *Mahavsha* distinguishes between the *Shechinah,* as such, and *giluy shechinah,* the revelation of the Divine Presence.

26. Rosh Hashono 31a. Shemot Rabba 2:2.

27. Menahot 110a. In time to come, the altar that is above will descend to earth (*Midrash Aseret Hadibrot,* 1).

28. Megillah 29a.

29. Berochot, 7a.

30. Halevi, *The Kusari,* V, 23.

31. Shabbat 31a. Sanhedrin 96a.

32. Baba Bathra 15b.

33. Baba Bathra 9.

34. Berochot 43a. Kiddushin 31a.

35. Hagigah 16a.

36. Shabbat 12b.

37. Hagigah 15b.

38. R. Hayim Volozhin, *Nefesh Hahayim,* II, 11.

39. Berochot 35b.

40. Menahot 53a.

41. Pesahim 87a.

42. Jeremiah 15:17.

43. Lamentations, Rabba.

44. "Woe is to the wicked who say that the Torah is only the narra-

tive, for they look at the garment only. . . . The narratives are the garment of Torah . . ." (*Zohar*, Bamidbar 152).

45. *Zohar*, Vayikro 73.
46. *Zohar*, Vayikro 93.
47. *Tikkunai Zohar*, 21.
48. Bereshit Rabba, 1.
49. *Ibid.*
50. Tanhuma, Behukotai 2.
51. Yebamot 63a.
52. *Ibid.*
53. Shabbat 156a.
54. Hullin 91a.
55. Sanhedrin 90a.
56. *Zohar*, Bamidbar 244.
57. *Zohar*, Bamidbar 147.
58. Yomah 38b.
59. Sukkah 45b.
60. Raya Mehemna, Deuteronomy, Tetse.
61. *Tikkunai Zohar*, 32, p. 72b. R. Margolis, *Shaarai Zohar*, Jerusalem, 1956. Berochot 15b.
62. R. Elimelech, *No'am Elimelech*, Vayehi.
63. Shabbat 146a.
64. *Ibid.*
65. See R. Margolis, *Shaarai Zohar*, in reference to Yebamot 49a and Shabbat 146a.
66. Halevi, *The Kusari*, I, 115.
67. Kiddushin, 70b.
68. Halevi, *The Kusari*, I, 109.
69. *Kitvai Maharal MiPrag*, I, 127.
70. *Tanya*, ch. 1, 2.
71. R. Zadok HaKohen, *Zidkat HaZadik*, 256, 257.
72. Megillah, 13a.
73. Hosea 2:23.
74. Pesahim, 87a.
75. Vayikra Rabba 6:8.
76. Tanhuma, Deuteronomy 52.
77. Yalkut, II Kings 296.
78. Nedarim, 32a.
79. Proverbs 14, 34.
80. Yebamot, 48b.
81. Baba Bathra, 10b.
82. See note by W. Bacher, *Agadot Tanaim Veamoraim*, I, 26.
83. J. Berochot 2:1, *Standard Prayer Book for Rosh Hashono and*

Yom Kippur: "Repentance, prayer, and charity avert the severe decree." Also, Berochot 17a and 26a.

84. Yoma 87a.
85. Yebamot, 57a.
86. Yadaim 4, 4.
87. Abodah Zara 64b.
88. Tosefto, Sanhedrin 13.
89. Ish Sholom, ed., *Tana dibai Eliyahu*, ch. 45.
90. *Ibid.*, ch. 135.
91. Seder Eliyahu Raba, 2.
92. *Ibid.*, p. 121.
93. *Ibid.*, p. 14.
94. *Shulhan Aruch*, Yore Dea, 268.
95. Horayot 13a.
96. Shebuot 39a.
97. Yebamot 109b.
98. Abodah Zara 3b.
99. Yebamot 102a.
100. J. Bikkurim 1:4.
101. *De Confusione Linguarum*, M. I. 426. Genesis 17:5.
102. *De Congressu Eruditionis Gratia*.
103. *De Virtutibus*.
104. *De Abrahamo*, M., 1, 15.
105. Wolfson, *Philo*, II, p. 401, Note 25.
106. Praem 26, 152.
107. *Moses* II, 7, 44. Wolfson, in Note 100 of *Philo* (II, p. 417), equates the opinion of Philo with that of the Talmud, citing as reference, Abodah Zara 24a. But the term *gerim gerurim* connotes contempt and a lower status than that of righteous proselytes, let alone Israelites. That term is still compatible with another reference in the Talmud that in the Messianic age all Gentiles will become "slaves of Israel." Airubin 43b.
Rashi explains the term *gerim gerurim* ("dragged converts,") as meaning that "they will convert of their own accord, but we shall not receive them, because their motivation is the triumph of Israel." This interpretation is in accord with the oft-quoted principle: "We do not receive converts in the days of the Messiah. So too, converts were not accepted in the days of Kings David and Solomon." See Yebamot 24a. In the Talmudic text, the implication is that the Lord will delight in humiliating them. See Abodah Zara 3b.
108. See Tossafot on Abodah Zara 2a.
109. Maimonides, *Yad*, Hilchot Issurai Bia, 14:7.

110. The distinction between Maimonides' legalistic and philosophic works has been the subject of heated debates. Philosophy deals with principles, not laws. In the long night of exile and dispersion, the medieval rabbis felt powerless to amend the law and to bring it into conformity with their principles. See Maimonides, *Yad*, Hilchot Issurai Bia, 14:7.

111. I. Arame, *Akedat Yizhak*, 60.

112. Maimonides, *Guide*, III, 51.

113. Shem Tov ben Joseph, ad hoc.

114. Teshuvot HoRambam.

115. Maimonides, III, 28 and 36.

116. *Akedat Yizhak*, Gates 15, 31, 38, 56.

117. J. Albo, *Sefer HaIkkarim*, I, 25.

118. *Ibid.*, 23.

119. Seforno, *Commentary on the Pentateuch*. Exodus 19:6.

120. I. Abravanel, *Mashmia Yeshuah*, Saloniki, 1526, Amsterdam, 1644.

121. I. Baer, *A History of the Jews in Spain*, Philadelphia, Jewish Publication Society, 1961, p. 335, Note, p. 446.

122. *Tractatus Theologica Politicus*, R. H. M. Elwes, transl., London, 1909, ch. 5.

123. *Jerusalem*, Part II.

124. Rabbi Ishmael of Modena (1723-1811), a leading Halachic authority, wrote as follows in answer to Napoleon's inquiry about "fraternity": "Though the term brotherhood implies natural kinship, there is a unity of faith between the Frenchmen, or the other peoples of Europe, and the Jews. Since these nations serve the One God, each in their own way, they are now accounted in the eyes of the children of Israel as brothers, for we are obligated to deal with them in fraternity and love, in friendship and peace, and the Holy Torah commands us to help their needy." See J. B. Agus, *The Meaning of Jewish History*, II, 330.

125. Agus II, 338.

126. About Fichte's opposition to Jewish emancipation and his concept of the eternal struggle between the people of *Vernunft* and the people of *Vers.and*, see Agus, *op. cit.*, pp. 333-342.

127. Toussenel, a notorious socialist, in *Jews, the Kings of the Epoch*, wrote: "Like the masses of the people, I apply the odious name of Jew to all the people who lived by the manipulation of money, to all the exploiting parasites who live by the sweat of others."

128. The pre-Marxist socialists of France were generally anti-Semitic. So were Fourier, Toussenel, and Leroux. Even Karl Marx, in his

youthful articles on the question of Jewish emancipation, maintained that the real problem was emancipation from Jewry. He identified Jewry with the capitalists. It is only in the latter two decades of the nineteenth century that the socialists of Europe realized that anti-Semitism, as the "socialism of fools," was a tool of the reactionary forces. See Agus, *op. cit.*, pp. 334-344.

129. "But every true Jew, be he orthodox or liberal, feels in the depths of his being that there is something in the spirit of our people—though we do not know what it is—which has prevented us from following the rest of the world along the beaten path, has led to our producing this Judaism of ours, and has kept us and our Judaism 'in a corner' to this day, because we cannot abandon the distinctive outlook on which Judaism is based. Let those who still have this feeling remain within the fold; let those who have lost it go elsewhere. There is no room for compromise."

This excerpt from Ahad Ha'am's reply to Montefiore reveals the pathetic contradiction between his "sovereignty of reason" in matters of faith and his surrender to what may be called the "sovereignty of feeling" in urging the authority of a sense of radical difference. See Leon Simon, *Ahad Ha'am*, p. 127.

130. See B. Disraeli, *Coningsby*: "The Jews, independently of the capital qualities for citizenship which they possess, are a race essentially monarchical, deeply religious and essentially Tories. The fact is, you cannot crush a pure race of Caucasian organization."

131. See Louise Elliott Dalby, *Léon Blum, The Evolution of a Socialist*, New York, 1963. Blum is quoted as believing that the Jew would take an active part in the building of a socialist state because of the "national law of their race." For Blum, the Jewish religion was only a tissue of ceremonies, but the real faith of the Jew was justice. "If Christ preached charity, Jehovah wanted justice," or "it is not an oversight of Providence that Marx and Lassalle were Jews." Blum felt that the "essence of Jewish thought is, perhaps, the gift for ideal reconstruction of the world."

132. By the term "ultra-Orthodox," I refer here to the members of the *Agudat Yisroel*, not to the still more zealous pietists such as the Grand Rabbi of Satmar (Rabbi Joel Taitelbaum). This group holds that it is a sin to participate in the government of Israel to the extent of voting in the elections to the *Keneset*. Their main reason is the statement in the Talmud that the Israelites took an oath not to come out from exile by collective effort and "not to force the End" (see Kethubot 111a).

Referring to the decimation of world Jewry in our day, this rabbi

610

writes: "Now in our generation it is not necessary to go searching for hidden reasons, since the sin which brought this catastrophe upon us is clearly stated in the words of our Sages who, in turn, learned it from the Holy Writ—not to end the exile by a united effort and not to force the End, 'lest I make your flesh free for all like that of the deer and the antelope'" (*Vayoel Moshe*, Brooklyn, 1959, p. 5).

And he thinks of redemption as occurring through repentance and the works of piety: "For the Holy Temple above is constructed through the labors of the saints and their good deeds. And when it is completed, our righteous Messiah will come, but the wicked cause the destruction of that which the saints build up" (*ibid.*, p. 11).

The first task of the Messiah, who will bring back the *Urim Vethumim*, is to compel Israel to return to the ways of Torah (*ibid.*, p. 134). The first group of those resurrected from the dead will precede the Messiah or accompany Him when He is revealed (*ibid.*, p. 135).

133. The Maharal of Prague, favorite author of Chief Rabbi A. I. Kuk: "It is impossible for redemption, that is, an exalted form of existence, to come all at once." See *Kol Kitvai Maharal*, II, p. 347.
134. Agus, *Banner of Jerusalem*, p. 61.
135. A. J. Kuk, *Azkarah*, II, p. 364.
136. *Shabbat Haaretz*, Introduction, sec. ed., p. 7.
137. Kuk, *Orot Hakodesh*, pp. 133, 134.
138. Agus, *op. cit.*, p. 215.
139. *Loc. cit.*
140. Martin Buber, *Israel and Palestine*, London, 1952, Introduction.
141. *Ibid.*, p. 49.
142. *Ibid.*, p. 147.
143. *Ibid.*, pp. 160-161.
144. Sidney and Beatrice Rome, eds., *Philosophic Interrogations*, New York, 1964. Buber replies to my question on pp. 77, 78.
145. The elaboration of the infinite pathway of the "duties of the heart" was the meeting ground of the philosophical and Qabbalist schools, as well as the preoccupation of the popular preachers. See Bahya Ibn Pakuda, *Duties of the Heart*, Introduction.
146. Mordecai M. Kaplan, *Judaism as a Civilization*, New York, Macmillan, 1935.
147. Agus, *Modern Philosophies of Judaism*, New York, Behrman, 1941.
148. Rosenzweig, *op. cit.*, p. 670.
149. *Ibid.*, p. 580.

Faith and Interfaith
1. Psalms 36:9.
2. Micah 6:8.
3. I Corinthians 13:1-7.
4. Micah 4:5.

The Enduring Tensions in Judaism
1. Isaiah 44:6.
2. Bereshit Rabba 68:10.
3. Isaiah 6:3.
4. Psalms 34:8.
5. Proverbs 3:17, 29:18.
6. Jeremiah 18:18.
7. Aboth 2:11, 12.
8. Wolfson, *Philo,* II, 99.
9. *Ibid.,* I, 201.
10. Genesis 3:5.
10a. Makkoth 23a.
11. Genesis 17:1.
12. Shemot Rabba 41:6. Tanhuma, Tisa, 16. Ish Sholom, ed., *Seder Eliyahu Zutta*, ch. 2.

Tradition and Change
1. Mordecai Waxman, ed., *Tradition and Change, The Development of the Conservative Movement,* New York, Burning Bush Press, 1958.
2. *Ibid.,* p. 14.
3. *Ibid.,* p. 132.
4. *Ibid.,* p. 136.
5. *Ibid.,* p. 125.
6. *Ibid.,* p. 113.
7. Isaiah 2:3.

The Meaning of the Mizvoth
1. Isaac Heinemann, *Taamai Hamizvoth besafrut Yisroel,* Jerusalem, 2 volumes.
2. Tikkunai Zohar Hadosh 16.
3. Hagigah 14a. J. Taanith 8:4.
3a. Deuteronomy 4:8.
4. Yoma 67b.
5. Berochot 33b.
6. Maimonides, II, 28-29.
7. Heinemann, I, 99.

8. Gersonides, Commentary on Pentateuch, I, 99.
9. Nahmanides, Commentary on Pentateuch, Leviticus, Ahre Mot, 16:8. Zohar on same verse.
10. I, Albo, Sefer Haikkarim, I, 23.
11. *Ibid.*, III, 16.
12. Solomon Ibn Verga, *Shebet Yehuda*, Behr, ed., Jerusalem, 1947, p. 31.
13. Heinemann, II, 38.
14. Nedarim 32a. Berochot 7a.
15. Moses Mendelssohn, *Kithvai Mendelssohn*, VII, 218.
16. See *Zion*, 5713, pp. 15-30.
17. Z. Frankel, *Zeitschrift für die religiösen Interessen des Judentums*, II, 15.
18. Heinemann, II, 178.
19. *Ibid.*, p. 64.
20. This is how Luzzatto interpreted Exodus 30:11-16 and II Samuel 24:1-25.
21. Heinemann, II, 158.
22. S. R. Hirsch, *Kithvai*, V, p. 546.
23. *Ibid.*, VI, 43.

Assimilation, Integration, Segregation
1. Ralph Barton Perry, *Characteristically American*, New York, Knopf, 1949, pp. 36-37.
2. Mechilta, Yithro.
3. Berochot 28a.
4. Shabbat 17a and 153.
5. Ish Sholom, ed., *Sifra D'be Rab*, 97.
5a. Yebamoth 61a.
6. Shabbat 128a.
7. Shabbat 146a.
8. Erubin 43b.
9. Isaiah Halevi Hurwitz, *Shnai Luhot Haberit*, p. 15.
10. Baba Kama 38a.
11. Megillah 13a.
12. Gittin 61a.
13. Beth Habehirah on Abodah Zara, by M. Meiri, ed., A. Schreiber, New York, 1944, pp. 46, 591. See Jacob Katz's *Exclusiveness and Tolerance*, New York, 1962, pp. 119-128.

INDEX

Abner of Burgos, 475
Abraham Ibn Daud, 544
Abraham Ibn Ezra, 463, 544
Absolutism, xii, 14, 30, 31, 35, 74, 81, 84, 87
  truths, 311, 411
Abulafia, 395
Adler, M., 527, 530
Aggioramento, 5, 97, 98
A'had Ha'am, 79, 90, 189, 195, 197, 205, 235, 320, 321, 409, 413, 416, 423, 481, 486, 488, 490, 575, 580
Akiba, Rabbi, 203, 538, 556
Albo, J., 472, 546
Altizer, I., 245, 255
Amos, 25, 32, 393, 540
Anatoli, J., 547
Anti-Semitism, 4, 5, 6, 17, 18, 20, 22, 24, 38, 66, 74, 77, 103, 125, 148, 184, 185, 195, 196, 197, 204, 228, 233 (cultural), 247, 176, 179, 259-282, 285, 302, 452, 479, 483, 493, 495, 580, 582
Aquinas, Th., 83
Arabs, 158, 239, 412, 486
Arab refugees, 138
Arame, I., 313, 469, 472, 547
Arendt, H., 74
Aristobulus, 12
Aristotle, 83
Aryan, xiv, 74, 79, 230, 304, 580
Arzt, M., 527
Assimilation, 217
Augustine, 83

Baeck, L., 58, 178, 209, 295
Baer, F., 214
Baer-Hoffman, R., 421
Bahya Ibn Pakuda, 544
Baron, S., 157, 212, 213, 215, 226
Barth, K., 520
Bea, Cardinal, 27, 38, 114, 127
Ben Gurion, 140
Ben Zoma, 91
Ben Zvi, 140
Benjamin of Tiberius, 7
Berdayaev, N., 360
Berdichevski, M., 416
Bergson, H., 388
Besht (Israel Baal Shem Tov), 16, 223, 399, 402, 408
Bialik, H., 409, 414-416
Bloch, J., 207
Blum, L., 481
Bokser, B., 530
Börne, L., 401
Brenner, J. H., 417
Brown, Robert, 14
Buber, M., xi, 92, 98, 221, 318, 428, 440, 487-489
Buddhism, 49
Bultman, R., 70
Bund, 208, 491

Calvinism, 71
Catholicism, 5, 6, 9, 14, 17, 18, 21, 26, 47, 71, 73, 81, 83, 97, 137, 291, 300, 308, 386
Chonobaskion, 7
Chosen people, chosenness, 71, 77, 82, 89, 118, 139, 181,

618

Murray, G., 543
Mussar movement, 449, 518, 536, 544
Mysticism, 319, 389, 395, 397, 400, 404, 420, 490, 558
Mythology, myths, 11, 24, 70, 75, 83, 86, 98, 101, 103, 244, 245, 262, 276, 292, 373, 375

Nahman of Bratslav, 400
Nahmanides, M., 538
Napoleon, 203
Nationalism, 336, 407-409, 410-425
Nazism, xv, 4, 18, 29, 66, 70, 73, 76, 233, 259-267, 275, 285, 287, 304, 373, 481
New Testament, 5, 6, 8, 34, 37, 102
Nicholas de Lyra, 13
Niebuhr, R., 91, 359
Niemoller, M., 291, 304, 494
Nietzsche, F., 303
Nihilism, 86, 89
Nordau, M., 235

Orthodoxy, 5, 13, 18, 48, 101, 177, 481, 482, 495, (Neo-), 520, 537, 547, 550
Otto, R., 95

Pascal, B., 95
Paul, 15, 49, 55, 60, 96, 110, 116, 181, 201
Perry, R., 573
Pharisees, 8, 39, 100, 108, 201, 302
Philo, 12, 83, 181, 326, 394, 450, 466, 515, 543, 544
Philosophy, Jewish, 12, 317, 318, 319
Pinhas ben Yair, 390

Pinsker, L., 196, 488
Pius XI, 292
Pius XII, 76, 292
Plato, 295, 308, 466
Polish, D., 81
Populists, 24
Prophetic, Prophecy, xv, 12, 28, 84, 91, 97, 112, 182, 190, 278, 293, 294, 438, 446, 460, 505, 508
Protestant, 18, 19, 26, 29, 76, 304, 312
Pseudo-Messianism, 92, 232, 334, 337, 389, 417, 497, 498, 517
Pythagoras, 543

Qabbalah, 15, 93, 329, 394, 395, 398, 402, 418, 430, 484 (new Q.), 458, 459, 460, 477, 536, 544, 546, 586

Rabban Gamliel, 108
Rabbinic Judaism, 110, 257
Rabbis, 4, 44, 54, 71, 95, 318
Racism, 205, 304, 459, 489
Raphael of Barshad, 99
Rashi, 13, 547
Reconstructionism, 491
Reform, 5, 81, 98, 178, 174, 190, 192, 405, 484, 492, 494, 537, 540, 544, 547, 548, 561, 571, 574, 589, 587
Reformation, 305, 507
Religion, 342, 347, 348, 349, 354-361
Religious Consciousness, 266, 267
Renaissance, xv, 305, 397, 573
Resurrection, 83, 191
Revelation, 6, 521
Riesser, G., 203, 205
Ritualism, 366, 370
Robespierre, 308
Romantic nationalism, 407-409, 410-425